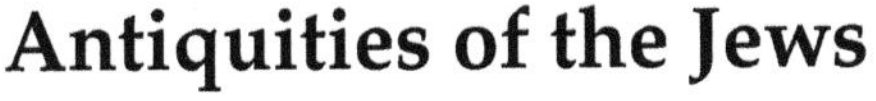

Antiquities of the Jews

Antiquities of the Jews

Volume 2

Flavius Josephus

Waking Lion Press

ISBN 978-1-4341-1507-2

Published by Waking Lion Press, an imprint of The Editorium

The Editorium, LLC
West Valley City, UT 84128-3917
wakinglionpress.com
wakinglion@editorium.com

Contents

Book 11

Containing the Interval of Two Hundred and Fifty-Three Years and Five Months, from the First of Cyrus to the Death of Alexander the Great

1 *How Cyrus, King of the Persians, Delivered the Jews Out of Babylon and Suffered Them to Return to Their Own Country and to Build Their Temple, for Which Work He Gave Them Money*

1. IN the first year of the reign of Cyrus[1] which was the seventieth from the day that our people were removed out of their own land into Babylon, God commiserated the captivity and calamity of these poor people, according as he had foretold to them by Jeremiah the prophet, before the destruction of the city, that after they had served Nebuchadnezzar and his posterity, and after they had undergone that servitude seventy years, he would restore them again to the land of their fathers, and they should build their temple, and enjoy their ancient prosperity. And these things God did afford them; for he stirred up the mind of Cyrus, and made him write this throughout all Asia: "Thus saith Cyrus the king: Since God Almighty hath appointed me to be king of the habitable earth, I believe that he is that God which

---

1. This Cyrus is called God's shepherd by Xenophon, as well as by Isaiah, Isaiah 44:28; as also it is said of him by the same prophet, that "I will make a man more precious than fine gold, even a man than the golden wedge of Ophir," Isaiah 13:12, which character makes Xenophon's most excellent history of him very credible.

the nation of the Israelites worship; for indeed he foretold my name by the prophets, and that I should build him a house at Jerusalem, in the country of Judea."

2. This was known to Cyrus by his reading the book which Isaiah left behind him of his prophecies; for this prophet said that God had spoken thus to him in a secret vision: "My will is, that Cyrus, whom I have appointed to be king over many and great nations, send back my people to their own land, and build my temple." This was foretold by Isaiah one hundred and forty years before the temple was demolished. Accordingly, when Cyrus read this, and admired the Divine power, an earnest desire and ambition seized upon him to fulfill what was so written; so he called for the most eminent Jews that were in Babylon, and said to them, that he gave them leave to go back to their own country, and to rebuild their city Jerusalem,[2] and the temple of God, for that he would be their assistant, and that he would write to the rulers and governors that were in the neighborhood of their country of Judea, that they should contribute to them gold and silver for the building of the temple, and besides that, beasts for their sacrifices.

3. When Cyrus had said this to the Israelites, the rulers of the two tribes of Judah and Benjamin, with the Levites and priests, went in haste to Jerusalem; yet did many of them stay at Babylon, as not willing to leave their possessions; and when they were come thither, all the king's friends assisted them, and brought in, for the building of the temple, some gold, and some silver, and some a great many cattle and horses. So they performed their vows to God, and offered the sacrifices that had been accustomed of old time; I mean this upon the rebuilding of their city, and the revival of the ancient practices relating to their worship. Cyrus also sent back to them the vessels of God which king

---

2. This leave to build Jerusalem, sect. 3, and this epistle of Cyrus to Sisinnes and Sathrabuzanes, to the same purpose, are most unfortunately omitted in all our copies but this best and completest copy of Josephus; and by such omission the famous prophecy of Isaiah, Isaiah 44:28, where we are informed that God said of or to Cyrus, "He is my shepherd, and shall perform all my pleasure; even saying to Jerusalem, Thou shalt be built, and to the temple, Thy foundation shall be laid," could not hitherto be demonstrated from the sacred history to have been completely fulfilled, I mean as to that part of it which concerned his giving leave or commission for rebuilding the city Jerusalem as distinct from the temple, whose rebuilding is alone permitted or directed in the decree of Cyrus in all our copies.

Nebuchadnezzar had pillaged out of the temple, and had carried to Babylon. So he committed these things to Mithridates, the treasurer, to be sent away, with an order to give them to Sanabassar, that he might keep them till the temple was built; and when it was finished, he might deliver them to the priests and rulers of the multitude, in order to their being restored to the temple. Cyrus also sent an epistle to the governors that were in Syria, the contents whereof here follow:

"King Cyrus to Sisinnes and Sathrabuzanes Sendeth Greeting

"I have given leave to as many of the Jews that dwell in my country as please to return to their own country, and to rebuild their city, and to build the temple of God at Jerusalem on the same place where it was before. I have also sent my treasurer Mithridates, and Zorobabel, the governor of the Jews, that they may lay the foundations of the temple, and may build it sixty cubits high, and of the same latitude, making three edifices of polished stones, and one of the wood of the country, and the same order extends to the altar whereon they offer sacrifices to God. I require also that the expenses for these things may be given out of my revenues. Moreover, I have also sent the vessels which king Nebuchadnezzar pillaged out of the temple, and have given them to Mithridates the treasurer, and to Zorobabel the governor of the Jews, that they may have them carried to Jerusalem, and may restore them to the temple of God. Now their number is as follows: Fifty chargers of gold, and five hundred of silver; forty Thericlean cups of gold, and five hundred of silver; fifty basons of gold, and five hundred of silver; thirty vessels for pouring [the drink-offerings], and three hundred of silver; thirty vials of gold, and two thousand four hundred of silver; with a thousand other large vessels.[3] I permit them to have the same honor which they were used to have from their forefathers, as also for their small cattle, and for wine and oil, two hundred and five thousand and five hundred drachme; and for wheat flour, twenty thousand and five hundred artabae; and I give order that these expenses shall be given them out of the tributes due from Samaria. The priests shall also offer these sacrifices according to the laws of Moses in Jerusalem; and

3. Of the true number of golden and silver vessels here and elsewhere belonging to the temple of Solomon, see the description of the temples, chap. 13.

when they offer them, they shall pray to God for the preservation of the king and of his family, that the kingdom of Persia may continue. But my will is, that those who disobey these injunctions, and make them void, shall be hung upon a cross, and their substance brought into the king's treasury." And such was the import of this epistle. Now the number of those that came out of captivity to Jerusalem, were forty-two thousand four hundred and sixty-two.

2 *How Upon the Death of Cyrus the Jews Were Hindered in Building of the Temple by the Cutheans, and the Neighboring Governors; and How Cambyses Entirely Forbade the Jews to Do Any Such Thing*

1. WHEN the foundations of the temple were laying, and when the Jews were very zealous about building it, the neighboring nations, and especially the Cutheans, whom Shalmanezer, king of Assyria, had brought out of Persia and Media, and had planted in Samaria, when he carried the people of Israel captives, besought the governors, and those that had the care of such affairs, that they would interrupt the Jews, both in the rebuilding of their city, and in the building of their temple. Now as these men were corrupted by them with money, they sold the Cutheans their interest for rendering this building a slow and a careless work, for Cyrus, who was busy about other wars, knew nothing of all this; and it so happened, that when he had led his army against the Massagetae, he ended his life.[4] But when Cambyses, the

4. Josephus here follows Herodotus, and those that related how Cyrus made war with the Scythians and Massagets, near the Caspian Sea, and perished in it; while Xenophon's account, which appears never to have been seen by Josephus, that Cyrus died in peace in his own country of Persia, is attested to by the writers of the affairs of Alexander the Great, when they agree that he found Cyrus's sepulcher at Pasargadae, near Persepolis. This account of Xenophon is also confirmed by the circumstances of Cambyses, upon his succession to Cyrus, who, instead of a war to avenge his father's death upon the Scythians and Massagets, and to prevent those nations from overrunning his northern provinces, which would have been the natural consequence of his father's ill success and death there, went immediately to an Egyptian war, long ago begun by Cyrus, according to Xenophon, p. 644, and conquered that kingdom; nor is there, that I ever heard of, the least mention in the reign of Cambyses of any war against the Scythians and Massagets that he was ever engaged in all his life.

son of Cyrus, had taken the kingdom, the governors in Syria, and Phoenicia, and in the countries of Amlnon, and Moab, and Samaria, wrote an epistle to Calnbyses; whose contents were as follow: "To our lord Cambyses. We thy servants, Rathumus the historiographer, and Semellius the scribe, and the rest that are thy judges in Syria and Phoenicia, send greeting. It is fit, O king, that thou shouldst know that those Jews which were carried to Babylon are come into our country, and are building that rebellious and wicked city, and its market-places, and setting up its walls, and raising up the temple; know therefore, that when these things are finished, they will not be willing to pay tribute, nor will they submit to thy commands, but will resist kings, and will choose rather to rule over others than be ruled over themselves. We therefore thought it proper to write to thee, O king, while the works about the temple are going on so fast, and not to overlook this matter, that thou mayst search into the books of thy fathers, for thou wilt find in them that the Jews have been rebels, and enemies to kings, as hath their city been also, which, for that reason, hath been till now laid waste. We thought proper also to inform thee of this matter, because thou mayst otherwise perhaps be ignorant of it, that if this city be once inhabited and be entirely encompassed with walls, thou wilt be excluded from thy passage to Celesyria and Phoenicia."

2. When Cambyses had read the epistle, being naturally wicked, he was irritated at what they told him, and wrote back to them as follows: "Cambyses the king, to Rathumus the historiographer, to Beeltethmus, to Semellius the scribe, and the rest that are in commission, and dwelling in Samaria and Phoenicia, after this manner: I have read the epistle that was sent from you; and I gave order that the books of my forefathers should be searched into, and it is there found that this city hath always been an enemy to kings, and its inhabitants have raised seditions and wars. We also are sensible that their kings have been powerful and tyrannical, and have exacted tribute of Celesyria and Phoenicia. Wherefore I gave order, that the Jews shall not be permitted to build that city, lest such mischief as they used to bring upon kings be greatly augmented." When this epistle was read, Rathumus, and Semellius the scribe, and their associates, got suddenly on horseback, and made haste to Jerusalem; they also brought a great company with them, and forbade the Jews to build the city and the temple.

Accordingly, these works were hindered from going on till the second year of the reign of Darius, for nine years more; for Cambyses reigned six years, and within that time overthrew Egypt, and when he was come back, he died at Damascus.

3 *How After the Death of Cambyses and the Slaughter of the Magi but under the Reign of Darius, Zorobabel Was Superior to the Rest 1n the Solution of Problems and Thereby Obtained This Favor of the King, That the Temple Should Be Built*

1. AFTER the slaughter of file Magi, who, upon the death of Cambyses, attained the government of the Persians for a year, those families which were called the seven families of the Persians appointed Darius, the son of Hystaspes, to be their king. Now he, while he was a private man, had made a vow to God, that if he came to be king, he would send all the vessels of God that were in Babylon to the temple at Jerusalem. Now it so fell out, that about this time Zorobabel, who had been made governor of the Jews that had been in captivity, came to Darius, from Jerusalem; for there had been an old friendship between him and the king. He was also, with two others, thought worthy to be guard of the king's body; and obtained that honor which he hoped for.

2. Now, in the first year of the king's reign, Darius feasted those that were about him, and those born in his house, with the rulers of the Medes, and princes of the Persians, and the toparchs of India and Ethiopia, and the generals of the armies of his hundred and twenty-seven provinces. But when they had eaten and drunk to satiety, and abundantly, they every one departed to go to bed at their own houses, and Darius the king went to bed; but after he had rested a little part of the night, he awaked, and not being able to sleep any more, he fell into conversation with the three guards of his body, and promised, that to him who should make an oration about points that he should inquire of, such as should be most agreeable to truth, and to the dictates of wisdom, he would grant it as a reward of his victory, to put on a purple garment, and to drink in cups of gold, and to sleep upon gold, and to have a chariot with bridles of gold, and a head tire of fine linen, and a chain of gold about his neck, and to sit next to himself, on account of his wisdom; "and," says he, "he shall be called my cousin." Now when

he had promised to give them these gifts, he asked the first of them, "Whether wine was not the strongest?"—the second, "Whether kings were not such?"—and the third, "Whether women were not such? or whether truth was not the strongest of all?" When he had proposed that they should make their inquiries about these problems, he went to rest; but in the morning he sent for his great men, his princes, and toparchs of Persia and Media, and set himself down in the place where he used to give audience, and bid each of the guards of his body to declare what they thought proper concerning the proposed questions, in the hearing of them all.

3. Accordingly, the first of them began to speak of the strength of wine, and demonstrated it thus: "When," said he," I am to give my opinion of wine, O you men, I find that it exceeds every thing, by the following indications: It deceives the mind of those that drink it, and reduces that of the king to the same state with that of the orphan, and he who stands in need of a tutor; and erects that of the slave to the boldness of him that is free; and that of the needy becomes like that of the rich man, for it changes and renews the souls of men when it gets into them; and it quenches the sorrow of those that are under calamities, and makes men forget the debts they owe to others, and makes them think themselves to be of all men the richest; it makes them talk of no small things, but of talents, and such other names as become wealthy men only; nay more, it makes them insensible of their commanders, and of their kings, and takes away the remembrance of their friends and companions, for it arms men even against those that are dearest to them, and makes them appear the greatest strangers to them; and when they are become sober, and they have slept out their wine in the night, they arise without knowing any thing they have done in their cups. I take these for signs of power, and by them discover that wine is the strongest and most insuperable of all things."

4. As soon as the first had given the forementioned demonstrations of the strength of wine, he left off; and the next to him began to speak about the strength of a king, and demonstrated that it was the strongest of all, and more powerful than any thing else that appears to have any force or wisdom. He began his demonstration after the following manner; and said," They are men who govern all things; they force the earth and the sea to become profitable to them in what they desire, and over these men do kings rule, and over them

they have authority. Now those who rule over that animal which is of all the strongest and most powerful, must needs deserve to be esteemed insuperable in power and force. For example, when these kings command their subjects to make wars, and undergo dangers, they are hearkened to; and when they send them against their enemies, their power is so great that they are obeyed. They command men to level mountains, and to pull down walls and towers; nay, when they are commanded to be killed and to kill, they submit to it, that they may not appear to transgress the king's commands; and when they have conquered, they bring what they have gained in the war to the king. Those also who are not soldiers, but cultivate the ground, and plough it, and when, after they have endured the labor and all the inconveniences of such works of husbandry, they have reaped and gathered in their fruits, they bring tributes to the king; and whatsoever it is which the king says or commands, it is done of necessity, and that without any delay, while he in the mean time is satiated with all sorts of food and pleasures, and sleeps in quiet. He is guarded by such as watch, and such as are, as it were, fixed down to the place through fear; for no one dares leave him, even when he is asleep, nor does any one go away and take care of his own affairs; but he esteems this one thing the only work of necessity, to guard the king, and accordingly to this he wholly addicts himself. How then can it be otherwise, but that it must appear that the king exceeds all in strength, while so great a multitude obeys his injunctions?"

5. Now when this man had held his peace, the third of them, who was Zorobabel, began to instruct them about women, and about truth, who said thus: "Wine is strong, as is the king also, whom all men obey, but women are superior to them in power; for it was a woman that brought the king into the world; and for those that plant the vines and make the wine, they are women who bear them, and bring them up: nor indeed is there any thing which we do not receive from them; for these women weave garments for us, and our household affairs are by their means taken care of, and preserved in safety; nor can we live separate from women. And when we have gotten a great deal of gold and silver, and any other thing that is of great value, and deserving regard, and see a beautiful woman, we leave all these things, and with open mouth fix our eyes upon her countenance, and are willing to forsake what we have, that we may enjoy her beauty, and procure

it to ourselves. We also leave father, and mother, and the earth that nourishes us, and frequently forget our dearest friends, for the sake of women; nay, we are so hardy as to lay down our lives for them. But what will chiefly make you take notice of the strength of women is this that follows: Do not we take pains, and endure a great deal of trouble, and that both by land and sea, and when we have procured somewhat as the fruit of our labors, do not we bring them to the women, as to our mistresses, and bestow them upon them? Nay, I once saw the king, who is lord of so many people, smitten on the face by Apame, the daughter of Rabsases Themasius, his concubine, and his diadem taken away from him, and put upon her own head, while he bore it patiently; and when she smiled he smiled, and when she was angry he was sad; and according to the change of her passions, he flattered his wife, and drew her to reconciliation by the great humiliation of himself to her, if at my time he saw her displeased at him."

6. And when the princes and rulers looked one upon another, he began to speak about truth; and he said, "I have already demonstrated how powerful women are; but both these women themselves, and the king himself, are weaker than truth; for although the earth be large, and the heaven high, and the course of the sun swift, yet are all these moved according to the will of God, who is true and righteous, for which cause we also ought to esteem truth to be the strongest of all things, and that what is unrighteous is of no force against it. Moreover, all things else that have any strength are mortal and short-lived, but truth is a thing that is immortal and eternal. It affords us not indeed such a beauty as will wither away by time, nor such riches as may be taken away by fortune, but righteous rules and laws. It distinguishes them from injustice, and puts what is unrighteous to rebuke."[5]

---

5. The reader is to note, that although the speeches or papers of these three of the king's guard are much the same, in our Third Book of Esdras, ch. 3. and 4., as they are here in Josephus, yet that the introduction of them is entirely different, while in our Esdras the whole is related as the contrivance of the three of the king's guards themselves; and even the mighty rewards are spoken of as proposed by themselves, and the speeches are related to have been delivered by themselves to the king in writing, while all is contrary in Josephus. I need not say whose account is the most probable, the matters speak for themselves; and there can be no doubt but Josephus's history is here to be very much preferred before the other. Nor indeed does it seem to me at all unlikely that the whole was a contrivance of king Darius's own, in order

7. So when Zorobabel had left off his discourse about truth, and the multitude had cried out aloud that he had spoken the most wisely, and that it was truth alone that had immutable strength, and such as never would wax old, the king commanded that he should ask for somewhat over and above what he had promised, for that he would give it him because of his wisdom, and that prudence wherein he exceeded the rest; "and thou shalt sit with me," said the king, "and shalt be called my cousin." When he had said this, Zorobabel put him in mind of the vow he had made in case he should ever have the kingdom. Now this vow was, "to rebuild Jerusalem, and to build therein the temple of God; as also to restore the vessels which Nebuchadnezzar had pillaged, and carried to Babylon. And this," said he, "is that request which thou now permittest me to make, on account that I have been judged to be wise and understanding."

8. So the king was pleased with what he had said, and arose and kissed him; and wrote to the toparchs and governors, and enjoined them to conduct Zorobabel and those that were going with him to build the temple. He also sent letters to those rulers that were in Syria and Phoenicia to cut down and carry cedar trees from Lebanon to Jerusalem, and to assist him in building the city. He also wrote to them, that all the captives who should go to Judea should be free; and he prohibited his deputies and governors to lay any king's taxes upon the Jews; he also permitted that they should have all that land which they could possess themselves of without tributes. He also enjoined the Idumeans and Samaritans, and the inhabitants of Celesyria, to restore those villages which they had taken from the Jews; and that, besides all this, fifty talents should be given them for the building of the temple. He also permitted them to offer their appointed sacrifices, and that whatsoever the high priest and the priests wanted, and those

---

to be decently and inoffensively put in mind by Zorobabel of fulfilling his old vow for the rebuilding of Jerusalem and the temple, and the restoration of the worship of the "one true God" there. Nor does the full meaning of Zorobabel, when he cries out, 3 Esd. 4. 41), "Blessed be the God of truth;" and here, "God is true and righteous;" or even of all the people, 3 Esd. 4. 41, "Great is truth, and mighty above all things;" seem to me much different from this, "There is but one true God, the God of Israel." To which doctrine, such as Cyrus and Darius; etc., the Jews' great patrons, seem not to have been very averse, though the entire idolatry of their kingdoms made them generally conceal it.

sacred garments wherein they used to worship God, should be made at his own charges; and that the musical instruments which the Levites used in singing hymns to God should be given them. Moreover, he charged them, that portions of land should be given to those that guarded the city and the temple, as also a determinate sum of money every year for their maintenance; and withal he sent the vessels. And all that Cyrus intended to do before him relating to the restoration of Jerusalem, Darius also ordained should be done accordingly.

9. Now when Zorobabel had obtained these grants from the king, he went out of the palace, and looking up to heaven, he began to return thanks to God for the wisdom he had given him, and the victory he had gained thereby, even in the presence of Darius himself; for, said he, "I had not been thought worthy of these advantages, O Lord, unless thou hadst been favorable to me." When therefore he had returned these thanks to God for the present circumstances he was in, and had prayed to him to afford him the like favor for the time to come, he came to Babylon, and brought the good news to his countrymen of what grants he had procured for them from the king; who, when they heard the same, gave thanks also to God that he restored the land of their forefathers to them again. So they betook themselves to drinking and eating, and for seven days they continued feasting, and kept a festival, for the rebuilding and restoration of their country: after this they chose themselves rulers, who should go up to Jerusalem, out of the tribes of their forefathers, with their wives, and children, and cattle, who traveled to Jerusalem with joy and pleasure, under the conduct of those whom Darius sent along with them, and making a noise with songs, and pipes, and cymbals. The rest of the Jewish multitude also besides accompanied them with rejoicing.

10. And thus did these men go, a certain and determinate number out of every family, though I do not think it proper to recite particularly the names of those families, that I may not take off the mind of my readers from the connexion of the historical facts, and make it hard for them to follow the coherence of my narrations; but the sum of those that went up, above the age of twelve years, of the tribes of Judah and Benjamin, was four hundred and sixty-two myriads

and eight thousand[6] the Levites were seventy-four; the number of the women and children mixed together was forty thousand seven hundred and forty-two; and besides these, there were singers of the Levites one hundred and twenty-eight, and porters one hundred and ten, and of the sacred ministers three hundred and ninety-two; there were also others besides these, who said they were of the Israelites, but were not able to show their genealogies, six hundred and sixty-two: some there were also who were expelled out of the number and honor of the priests, as having married wives whose genealogies they could not produce, nor were they found in the genealogies of the Levites and priests; they were about five hundred and twenty-five: the multitude also of servants that followed those that went up to Jerusalem were seven thousand three hundred and thirty-seven; the singing men and singing women were two hundred and forty-five; the camels were four hundred and thirty-five; the beasts used to the yoke were five thousand five hundred and twenty-five; and the governors of all this multitude thus numbered were Zorobabel, the son of Salathiel, of the posterity of David, and of the tribe of Judah; and Jeshua, the son of Josedek the high priest; and besides these there were Mordecai and Serebeus, who were distinguished from the multitude, and were rulers, who also contributed a hundred pounds of gold, and five thousand of silver. By this means therefore the priests and the Levites, and a certain part of the entire people of the Jews that were in Babylon, came and dwelt in Jerusalem; but the rest of the multitude returned every one to their own countries.

---

6. This strange reading in Josephus's present copies of four millions instead of forty thousand, is one of the grossest errors that is in them, and ought to be corrected from Ezra 2:61; 1 Esd. 5:40; and Nehemiah 7:66, who all agree the general sum was but about forty-two thousand three hundred and sixty. It is also very plain that Josephus thought, that when Esdras afterwards brought up another company out of Babylon and Persia, in the days of Xerxes, they were also, as well as these, out of the two tribes, and out of them only, and were in all no more than "a seed" and "a remnant," while an "immense number" of the ten tribes never returned, but, as he believed, continued then beyond Euphrates, ch. 5. sect. 2, 3; of which multitude, the Jews beyond Euphrates, he speaks frequently elsewhere, though, by the way, he never takes them to be idolaters, but looks on them still as observers of the laws of Moses. The "certain part" of the people that now came up from Babylon, at the end of this chapter, imply the same smaller number of Jews that now came up, and will no way agree with the four millions.

Chapter 4

4 *How the Temple Was Built While the Cutheans Endeavored in Vain to Obstruct the Work*

1. NOW in the seventh month after they were departed out of Babylon, both Jeshua the high priest, and Zorobabel the governor, sent messengers every way round about, and gathered those that were in the country together to Jerusalem universally, who came very gladly thither. He then built the altar on the same place it had formerly been built, that they might offer the appointed sacrifices upon it to God, according to the laws of Moses. But while they did this, they did not please the neighboring nations, who all of them bare an ill-will to them. They also celebrated the feast of tabernacles at that time, as the legislator had ordained concerning it; and after they offered sacrifices, and what were called the daily sacrifices, and the oblations proper for the Sabbaths, and for all the holy festivals. Those also that had made vows performed them, and offered their sacrifices from the first day of the seventh month. They also began to build the temple, and gave a great deal of money to the masons and to the carpenters, and what was necessary for the maintenance of the workmen. The Sidonians also were very willing and ready to bring the cedar trees from Libanus, to bind them together, and to make a united float of them, and to bring them to the port of Joppa, for that was what Cyrus had commanded at first, and what was now done at the command of Darius.

2. In the second year of their coming to Jerusalem, as the Jews were there in the second month, the building of the temple went on apace; and when they had laid its foundations on the first day of the second month of that second year, they set, as overseers of the work, such Levites as were full twenty years old; and Jeshua and his sons and brethren, and Codmiel the brother of Judas, the son of Aminadab, with his sons; and the temple, by the great diligence of those that had the care of it, was finished sooner than any one would have expected. And when the temple was finished, the priests, adorned with their accustomed garments, stood with their trumpets, while the Levites, and the sons of Asaph, stood and sung hymns to God, according as David first of all appointed them to bless God. Now the priests and Levites, and the elder part of the families, recollecting with themselves how much greater and more sumptuous the old temple had been, seeing that now made how much inferior it was, on account

of their poverty, to that which had been built of old, considered with themselves how much their happy state was sunk below what it had been of old, as well as their temple. Hereupon they were disconsolate, and not able to contain their grief, and proceeded so far as to lament and shed tears on those accounts; but the people in general were contented with their present condition; and because they were allowed to build them a temple, they desired no more, and neither regarded nor remembered, nor indeed at all tormented themselves with the comparison of that and the former temple, as if this were below their expectations; but the wailing of the old men and of the priests, on account of the deficiency of this temple, in their opinion, if compared with that which had been demolished, overcame the sounds of the trumpets and the rejoicing of the people.

3. But when the Samaritans, who were still enemies to the tribes of Judah and Benjamin, heard the sound of the trumpets, they came running together, and desired to know what was the occasion of this tumult; and when they perceived that it was from the Jews, who had been carried captive to Babylon, and were rebuilding their temple, they came to Zorobabel and to Jeshua, and to the heads of the families, and desired that they would give them leave to build the temple with them, and to be partners with them in building it; for they said, "We worship their God, and especially pray to him, and are desirous of their religious settlement, and this ever since Shalmanezer, the king of Assyria, transplanted us out of Cuthah and Media to this place." When they said thus, Zorobabel and Jeshua the high priest, and the heads of the families of the Israelites, replied to them, that it was impossible for them to permit them to be their partners, whilst they [only] had been appointed to build that temple at first by Cyrus, and now by Darius, although it was indeed lawful for them to come and worship there if they pleased, and that they could allow them nothing but that in common with them, which was common to them with all other men, to come to their temple and worship God there.

4. When the Cuthearts heard this, for the Samaritans have that appellation, they had indignation at it, and persuaded the nations of Syria to desire of the governors, in the same manner as they had done formerly in the days of Cyrus, and again in the days of Cambyses afterwards, to put a stop to the building of the temple, and to endeavor to delay and protract the Jews in their zeal about it. Now at this

time Sisinnes, the governor of Syria and Phoenicia, and Sathrabuzanes, with certain others, came up to Jerusalem, and asked the rulers of the Jews, by. whose grant it was that they built the temple in this manner, since it was more like to a citadel than a temple? and for what reason it was that they built cloisters and walls, and those strong ones too, about the city? To which Zorobabel and Jeshua the high priest replied, that they were the servants of God Almighty; that this temple was built for him by a king of theirs, that lived in great prosperity, and one that exceeded all men in virtue; and that it continued a long time, but that because of their fathers' impiety towards God, Nebuchadnezzar, king of the Babylonians and of the Chaldeans, took their city by force, and destroyed it, and pillaged the temple, and burnt it down, and transplanted the people whom he had made captives, and removed them to Babylon; that Cyrus, who, after him, was king of Babylonia and Persia, wrote to them to build the temple, and committed the gifts and vessels, and whatsoever Nebuchadnezzar had carried out of it, to Zorobabel, and Mithridates the treasurer; and gave order to have them carried to Jerusalem, and to have them restored to their own temple, when it was built; for he had sent to them to have that done speedily, and commanded Sanabassar to go up to Jerusalem, and to take care of the building of the temple; who, upon receiving that epistle from Cyrus, came, and immediately laid its foundations; "and although it hath been in building from that time to this, it hath not yet been finished, by reason of the malignity of our enemies. If therefore you have a mind, and think it proper, write this account to Darius, that when he hath consulted the records of the kings, he may find that we have told you nothing that is false about this matter."

5. When Zorobabel and the high priest had made this answer, Sisinnes, and those that were with him, did not resolve to hinder the building, until they had informed king Darius of all this. So they immediately wrote to him about these affairs; but as the Jews were now under terror, and afraid lest the king should change his resolutions as to the building of Jerusalem and of the temple, there were two prophets at that time among them, Haggai and Zechariah, who encouraged them, and bid them be of good cheer, and to suspect no discouragement from the Persians, for that God foretold this to them. So, in dependence on those prophets, they applied themselves earnestly to building, and did not intermit one day.

6. Now Darius, when the Samaritans had written to him, and in their epistle had accused the Jews, how they fortified the city, and built the temple more like to a citadel than to a temple; and said, that their doings were not expedient for the king's affairs; and besides, they showed the epistle of Cambyses, wherein he forbade them to build the temple: and when Darius thereby understood that the restoration of Jerusalem was not expedient for his affairs, and when he had read the epistle that was brought him from Sisinnes, and those that were with him, he gave order that what concerned these matters should be sought for among the royal records. Whereupon a book was found at Ecbatana, in the tower that was in Media, wherein was written as follows: "Cyrus the king, in the first year of his reign, commanded that the temple should be built in Jerusalem; and the altar in height threescore cubits, and its breadth of the same, with three edifices of polished stone, and one edifice of stone of their own country; and he ordained that the expenses of it should be paid out of the king's revenue. He also commanded that the vessels which Nebuchadnezzar had pillaged [out of the temple], and had carried to Babylon, should be restored to the people of Jerusalem; and that the care of these things should belong to Sanabassar, the governor and president of Syria and Phoenicia, and his associates, that they may not meddle with that place, but may permit the servants of God, the Jews and their rulers, to build the temple. He also ordained that they should assist them in the work; and that they should pay to the Jews, out of the tribute of the country where they were governors, on account of the sacrifices, bulls, and rams, and lambs, and kids of the goats, and fine flour, and oil, and wine, and all other things that the priests should suggest to them; and that they should pray for the preservation of the king, and of the Persians; and that for such as transgressed any of these orders thus sent to them, he commanded that they should be caught, and hung upon a cross, and their substance confiscated to the king's use. He also prayed to God against them, that if any one attempted to hinder the building of the temple, God would strike him dead, and thereby restrain his wickedness."

7. When Darius had found this book among the records of Cyrus, he wrote an answer to Sisinnes and his associates, whose contents were these: "King Darius to Sisinnes the governor, and to Sathrabuzanes, sendeth greeting. Having found a copy of this epistle among the

records of Cyrus, I have sent it you; and I will that all things be done as is therein written. Fare ye well." So when Sisinnes, and those that were with him, understood the intention of the king, they resolved to follow his directions entirely for the time to come. So they forwarded the sacred works, and assisted the elders of the Jews, and the princes of the Sanhedrim; and the structure of the temple was with great diligence brought to a conclusion, by the prophecies of Haggai and Zechariah, according to God's commands, and by the injunctions of Cyrus and Darius the kings. Now the temple was built in seven years' time. And in the ninth year of the reign of Darius, on the twenty-third day of the twelfth month, which is by us called Adar, but by the Macedonians Dystrus, the priests, and Levites, and the other multitude of the Israelites, offered sacrifices, as the renovation of their former prosperity after their captivity, and because they had now the temple rebuilt, a hundred bulls, two hundred rains, four hundred lambs, and twelve kids of the goats, according to the number of their tribes, (for so many are the tribes of the Israelites,) and this last for the sins of every tribe. The priests also and the Levites set the porters at every gate, according to the laws of Moses. The Jews also built the cloisters of the inner temple that were round about the temple itself.

8. And as the feast of unleavened bread was at hand, in the first month, which, according to the Macedonians, is called Xanthicus, but according to us Nisan, all the people ran together out of the villages to the city, and celebrated the festival, having purified themselves, with their wives and children, according to the law of their country; and they offered the sacrifice which was called the Passover, on the fourteenth day of the same month, and feasted seven days, and spared for no cost, but offered whole burnt-offerings to God, and performed sacrifices of thanksgiving, because God had led them again to the land of their fathers, and to the laws thereto belonging, and had rendered the mind of the king of Persia favorable to them. So these men offered the largest sacrifices on these accounts, and used great magnificence in the worship of God, and dwelt in Jerusalem, and made use of a form of government that was aristocratical, but mixed with an oligarchy, for the high priests were at the head of their affairs, until the posterity of the Asamoneans set up kingly government; for before their captivity, and the dissolution of their polity, they at first had kingly government from Saul and David for five hundred and

thirty-two years, six months, and ten days; but before those kings, such rulers governed them as were called judges and monarchs. Under this form of government they continued for more than five hundred years after the death of Moses, and of Joshua their commander. And this is the account I had to give of the Jews who had been carried into captivity, but were delivered from it in the times of Cyrus and Darius.

9.[7] But the Samaritans, being evil and enviously disposed to the Jews, wrought them many mischiefs, by reliance on their riches, and by their pretense that they were allied to the Persians, on account that thence they came; and whatsoever it was that they were enjoined to pay the Jews by the king's order out of their tributes for the sacrifices, they would not pay it. They had also the governors favorable to them, and assisting them for that purpose; nor did they spare to hurt them, either by themselves or by others, as far as they were able. So the Jews determined to send an embassage to king Darius, in favor of the people of Jerusalem, and in order to accuse the Samaritans. The ambassadors were Zorobabel, and four others of the rulers; and as soon as the king knew from the ambassadors the accusations and complaints they brought against the Samaritans, he gave them an epistle to be carried to the governors and council of Samaria; the contents of which epistle were these: "King Darius to Tanganas and Sambabas, the governors of the Sainaritans, to Sadraces and Bobelo, and the rest of their fellow servants that are in Samaria: Zorobabel, Ananias, and Mordecai, the ambassadors of the Jews, complain of you, that you obstruct them in the building of the temple, and do not supply them with the expenses which I commanded you to do for the offering their sacrifices. My will therefore is this, That upon the reading of this epistle, you supply them with whatsoever they want for their sacrifices, and that out of the royal treasury, of the tributes of Samaria, as the priest shall desire, that they may not leave off offering their daily sacrifices, nor praying to God for me and the Persians." And these were the contents of that epistle.

---

7. The history contained in this section is entirely wanting in all our other copies, both of Ezra and Esdras.

Chapter 5

5 *How Xerxes the Son of Darius Was Well Disposed to the Jews; as Also Concerning Esdras and Nehemiah,*

1. UPON the death of Darius, Xerxes his son took the kingdom, who, as he inherited his father's kingdom, so did he inherit his piety towards God, and honor of him; for he did all things suitably to his father relating to Divine worship, and he was exceeding friendly to the Jews. Now about this time a son of Jeshua, whose name was Joacim, was the high priest. Moreover, there was now in Babylon a righteous man, and one that enjoyed a great reputation among the multitude. He was the principal priest of the people, and his name was Esdras. He was very skillful in the laws of Moses, and was well acquainted with king Xerxes. He had determined to go up to Jerusalem, and to take with him some of those Jews that were in Babylon; and he desired that the king would give him an epistle to the governors of Syria, by which they might know who he was. Accordingly, the king wrote the following epistle to those governors: "Xerxes, king of kings, to Esdras the priest, and reader of the Divine law, greeting. I think it agreeable to that love which I bear to mankind, to permit those of the Jewish nation that are so disposed, as well as those of the priests and Levites that are in our kingdom, to go together to Jerusalem. Accordingly, I have given command for that purpose; and let every one that hath a mind go, according as it hath seemed good to me, and to my seven counselors, and this in order to their review of the affairs of Judea, to see whether they be agreeable to the law of God. Let them also take with them those presents which I and my friends have vowed, with all that silver and gold that is found in the country of the Babylonians, as dedicated to God, and let all this be carried to Jerusalem to God for sacrifices. Let it also be lawful for thee and thy brethren to make as many vessels of silver and gold as thou pleasest. Thou shalt also dedicate those holy vessels which have been given thee, and as many more as thou hast a mind to make, and shall take the expenses out of the king's treasury. I have, moreover, written to the treasurers of Syria and Phoenicia, that they take care of those affairs that Esdras the priest, and reader of the laws of God, is sent about. And that God may not be at all angry with me, or with my children, I grant all that is necessary for sacrifices to God, according to the law, as far as a hundred cori of wheat. And I enjoin you not to lay any treacherous imposition, or any tributes,

upon their priests or Levites, or. sacred singers, or porters, or sacred servants, or scribes of the temple. And do thou, O Esdras, appoint judges according to the wisdom [given thee] of God, and those such as understand the law, that they may judge in all Syria and Phoenicia; and do thou instruct those also which are ignorant of it, that if any one of thy countrymen transgress the law of God, or that of the king, he may be punished, as not transgressing it out of ignorance, but as one that knows it indeed, but boldly despises and contemns it; and such may be punished by death, or by paying fines. Farewell."

2. When Esdras had received this epistle, he was very joyful, and began to worship God, and confessed that he had been the cause of the king's great favor to him, and that for the same reason he gave all the thanks to God. So he read the epistle at Babylon to those Jews that were there; but he kept the epistle itself, and sent a copy of it to all those of his own nation that were in Media. And when these Jews had understood what piety the king had towards God, and what kindness he had for Esdras, they were all greatly pleased; nay, many of them took their effects with them, and came to Babylon, as very desirous of going down to Jerusalem; but then the entire body of the people of Israel remained in that country; wherefore there are but two tribes in Asia and Europe subject to the Iomans, while the ten tribes are beyond Euphrates till now, and are an immense multitude, and not to be estimated by numbers. Now there came a great number of priests, and Levites, and porters, and sacred singers, and sacred servants to Esdras. So he gathered those that were in the captivity together beyond Euphrates, and staid there three days, and ordained a fast for them, that they might make their prayers to God for their preservation, that they might suffer no misfortunes by the way, either from their enemies, or from any other ill accident; for Esdras had said beforehand that he had told the king how God would preserve them, and so he had not thought fit to request that he would send horsemen to conduct them. So when they had finished their prayers, they removed from Euphrates on the twelfth day of the first month of the seventh year of the reign of Xerxes, and they came to Jerusalem on the fifth month of the same year. Now Esdras presented the sacred money to the treasurers, who were of the family of the priests, of silver six hundred and fifty talents, vessels of silver one hundred talents, vessels of gold twenty talents, vessels of brass, that was more

precious than gold,[8] twelve talents by weight; for these Presents had been made by the king and his counselors, and by all the Israelites that staid at Babylon. So when Esdras had delivered these things to the priests, he gave to God, as the appointed sacrifices of whole burnt-offerings, twelve bulls on account of the common preservation of the people, ninety rams, seventy-two lambs, and twelve kids of the goats, for the remission of sins. He also delivered the king's epistle to the king's officers, and to the governors of Celesyria and Phoenicia; and as they were under a necessity of doing what was enjoined by him, they honored our nation, and were assistant to them in all their necessities.

3. Now these things were truly done under the conduct of Esdras; and he succeeded in them, because God esteemed him worthy of the success of his conduct, on account of his goodness and righteousness. But some time afterward there came some persons to him, and brought an accusation against certain of the multitude, and of the priests and Levites, who had transgressed their settlement, and dissolved the laws of their country, by marrying strange wives, and had brought the family of the priests into confusion. These persons desired him to support the laws, lest God should take up a general anger against them all, and reduce them to a calamitous condition again. Hereupon he rent his garment immediately, out of grief, and pulled off the hair of his head and beard, and cast himself upon the ground, because this crime had reached the principal men among the people; and considering that if he should enjoin them to cast out their wives, and the children they had by them, he should not be hearkener to, he continued lying upon the ground. However, all the better sort came running to him, who also themselves wept, and partook of the grief he was under for what had been done. So Esdras rose up from the ground, and stretched out his hands towards heaven, and said that he was ashamed to look towards it, because of the sins which the people had committed, while they had cast out of their memories what their fathers had undergone on account of their wickedness; and he besought God, who had saved a seed and a remnant out of the calamity and captivity they had been in, and had restored them again to Jerusalem, and to their own land, and

8. Dr. Hudson takes notice here, that this kind of brass or copper, or rather mixture of gold and brass or copper, was called aurichalcum, and that this was of old esteemed the most precious of all metals.

had obliged the kings of Persia to have compassion on them, that he would also forgive them their sins they had now committed, which, though they deserved death, yet, was it agreeable to the mercy of God, to remit even to these the punishment due to them.

4. After Esdras had said this, he left off praying; and when all those that came to him with their wives and children were under lamentation, one whose name was Jechonias, a principal man in Jerusalem, came to him, and said that they had sinned in marrying strange wives; and he persuaded him to adjure them all to cast those wives out, and the children born of them, and that those should be punished who would not obey the law. So Esdras hearkened to this advice, and made the heads of the priests, and of the Levites, and of the Israelites, swear that they would put away those wives and children, according to the advice of Jechonias. And when he had received their oaths, he went in haste out of the temple into the chamber of Johanan, the son of Eliasib, and as he had hitherto tasted nothing at all for grief, so he abode there that day. And when proclamation was made, that all those of the captivity should gather themselves together to Jerusalem, and those that did not meet there in two or three days should be banished from the multitude, and that their substance should b appropriated to the uses of the temple, according to the sentence of the elders, those that were of the tribes of Judah and Benjamin came together in three days, viz. on the twentieth day of the ninth month, which, according to the Hebrews, is called Tebeth, and according to the Macedonians, Apelleius. Now as they were sitting in the upper room of the temple, where the elders also were present, but were uneasy because of the cold, Esdras stood up and accused them, and told them that they had sinned in marrying wives that were not of their own nation; but that now they would do a thing both pleasing to God, and advantageous to themselves, if they would put those wives away. Accordingly, they all cried out that they would do so. That, however, the multitude was great, and that the season of the year was winter, and that this work would require more than one or two days. "Let their rulers, therefore, [said they,] and those that have married strange wives, come hither at a proper time, while the elders of every place, that are in common to estimate the number of those that have thus married, are to be there also." Accordingly, this was resolved on by them, and they began the inquiry after those that had married strange wives on the first day of

the tenth month, and continued the inquiry to the first day of the next month, and found a great many of the posterity of Jeshua the high priest, and of the priests and Levites, and Israelites, who had a greater regard to the observation of the law than to their natural affection,[9] and immediately cast out their wives, and the children which were born of them. And in order to appease God, they offered sacrifices, and slew rams, as oblations to him; but it does not seem to me to be necessary to set down the names of these men. So when Esdras had reformed this sin about the marriages of the forementioned persons, he reduced that practice to purity, so that it continued in that state for the time to come.

5. Now when they kept the feast of tabernacles in the seventh month[10] and almost all the people were come together to it, they went up to the open part of the temple, to the gate which looked eastward, and desired of Esdras that the laws of Moses might be read to them. Accordingly, he stood in the midst of the multitude and read them; and this he did from morning to noon. Now, by hearing the laws read to them, they were instructed to be righteous men for the present and for the future; but as for their past offenses, they were displeased at themselves, and proceeded to shed tears on their account, as considering with themselves that if they had kept the law, they had endured none of these miseries which they had experienced. But when Esdras saw them in that disposition, he bade them go home, and not weep, for that it was a festival, and that they ought not to weep

---

9. This procedure of Esdras, and of the best part of the Jewish nation, after their return from the Babylonish captivity, of reducing the Jewish marriages, once for all, to the strictness of the law of Moses, without any regard to the greatness of those who had broken it, and without regard to that natural affection or compassion for their heathen wives, and their children by them, which made it so hard for Esdras to correct it, deserves greatly to be observed and imitated in all attempts for reformation among Christians, the contrary conduct having ever been the bane of true religion, both among Jews and Christians, while political views, or human passions, or prudential motives, are suffered to take place instead of the Divine laws, and so the blessing of God is forfeited, and the church still suffered to continue corrupt from one generation to another. See ch. 8. sect. 2.

10. This Jewish feast of tabernacles was imitated in several heathen solemnities, as Spanheim here observes and proves. He also further observes presently, what great regard many heathens had to the monuments of their forefathers, as Nehemiah had here, sect. 6.

thereon, for that it was not lawful so to do.[11] He exhorted them rather to proceed immediately to feasting, and to do what was suitable to a feast, and what was agreeable to a day of joy; but to let their repentance and sorrow for their former sins be a security and a guard to them, that they fell no more into the like offenses. So upon Esdras's exhortation they began to feast; and when they had so done for eight days, in their tabernacles, they departed to their own homes, singing hymns to God, and returning thanks to Esdras for his reformation of what corruptions had been introduced into their settlement. So it came to pass, that after he had obtained this reputation among the people, he died an old man, and was buried in a magnificent manner at Jerusalem. About the same time it happened also that Joacim, the high priest, died; and his son Eliasib succeeded in the high priesthood.

6. Now there was one of those Jews that had been carried captive who was cup-bearer to king Xerxes; his name was Nehemiah. As this man was walking before Susa, the metropolis of the Persians, he heard some strangers that were entering the city, after a long journey, speaking to one another in the Hebrew tongue; so he went to them, and asked them whence they came. And when their answer was, that they came from Judea, he began to inquire of them again in what state the multitude was, and in what condition Jerusalem was; and when they replied that they were in a bad state[12] for that their walls were thrown down to the ground, and that the neighboring nations did a great deal of mischief to the Jews, while in the day time they overran the country, and pillaged it, and in the night did them mischief, insomuch that not a few were led away captive out of the country, and out of Jerusalem itself, and that the roads were in the day time found full of dead men. Hereupon Nehemiah shed tears, out of commiseration of the calamities of his countrymen; and, looking up to heaven, he said, "How long, O Lord, wilt thou overlook our nation, while it suffers so great miseries, and while we are made the prey

---

11. This rule of Esdras, not to fast on a festival day, is quoted in the Apostolical Constitutions, B. V., as obtaining among Christians also.

12. This miserable condition of the Jews, and their capital, must have been after the death of Esdras, their former governor, and before Nehemiah came with his commission to build the walls of Jerusalem. Nor is that at all disagreeable to these histories in Josephus, since Esdras came on the seventh, and Nehemiah not till the twenty-fifth of Xerxes, at the interval of eighteen years.

and spoil of all men?" And while he staid at the gate, and lamented thus, one told him that the king was going to sit down to supper; so he made haste, and went as he was, without wishing himself, to minister to the king in his office of cup-bearer. But as the king was very pleasant after supper, and more cheerful than usual, he cast his eyes on Nehemiah, and seeing him look sad, he asked him why he was sad. Whereupon he prayed to God to give him favor, and afford him the power of persuading by his words, and said, "How can I, O king, appear otherwise than thus, and not be in trouble, while I hear that the walls of Jerusalem, the city where are the sepulchers of my fathers, are thrown down to the ground, and that its gates are consumed by fire? But do thou grant me the favor to go and build its wall, and to finish the building of the temple." Accordingly, the king gave him a signal that he freely granted him what he asked; and told him that he should carry an epistle to the governors, that they might pay him due honor, and afford him whatsoever assistance he wanted, and as he pleased. "Leave off thy sorrow then," said the king, "and be cheerful in the performance of thy office hereafter." So Nehemiah worshipped God, and gave the king thanks for his promise, and cleared up his sad and cloudy countenance, by the pleasure he had from the king's promises. Accordingly, the king called for him the next day, and gave him an epistle to be carried to Adeus, the governor of Syria, and Phoenicia, and Samaria; wherein he sent to him to pay due honor to Nehemiah, and to supply him with what he wanted for his building.

7. Now when he was come to Babylon, and had taken with him many of his countrymen, who voluntarily followed him, he came to Jerusalem in the twenty and fifth year of the reign of Xerxes. And when he had shown the epistles to God[13] he gave them to Adeus, and to the other governors. He also called together all the people to Jerusalem, and stood in the midst of the temple, and made the following speech to them: "You know, O Jews, that God hath kept our fathers, Abraham,

13. This showing king Xerxes's epistles to God, or laying them open before God in the temple, is very like the laying open the epistles of Sennacherib before him also by Hezekiah, 2 Kings 19:14; Isaiah 37:14, although this last was for a memorial, to put him in mind of the enemies, in order to move the Divine compassion, and the present as a token of gratitude for mercies already received, as Hayercamp well observes on this place.

and Isaac, and Jacob, in mind continually, and for the sake of their righteousness hath not left off the care of you. Indeed he hath assisted me in gaining this authority of the king to raise up our wall, and finish what is wanting of the temple. I desire you, therefore who well know the ill-will our neighboring nations bear to us, and that when once they are made sensible that we are in earnest about building, they will come upon us, and contrive many ways of obstructing our works, that you will, in the first place, put your trust in God, as in him that will assist us against their hatred, and to intermit building neither night nor day, but to use all diligence, and to hasten on the work, now we have this especial opportunity for it." When he had said this, he gave order that the rulers should measure the wall, and part the work of it among the people, according to their villages and cities, as every one's ability should require. And when he had added this promise, that he himself, with his servants, would assist them, he dissolved the assembly. So the Jews prepared for the work: that is the name they are called by from the day that they came up from Babylon, which is taken from the tribe of Judah,. which came first to these places, and thence both they and the country gained that appellation.

8. But now when the Ammonites, and Moabites, and Samaritans, and all that inhabited Celesyria, heard that the building went on apace, they took it heinously, and proceeded to lay snares for them, and to hinder their intentions. They also slew many of the Jews, and sought how they might destroy Nehemiah himself, by hiring some of the foreigners to kill him. They also put the Jews in fear, and disturbed them, and spread abroad rumors, as if many nations were ready to make an expedition against them, by which means they were harassed, and had almost left off the building. But none of these things could deter Nehemiah from being diligent about the work; he only set a number of men about him as a guard to his body, and so unweariedly persevered therein, and was insensible of any trouble, out of his desire to perfect this work. And thus did he attentively, and with great forecast, take care of his own safety; not that he feared death, but of this persuasion, that if he were dead, the walls for his citizens would never be raised. He also gave orders that the builders should keep their ranks, and have their armor on while they were building. Accordingly, the mason had his sword on, as well as he that brought the materials for building. He also appointed that their shields should

lie very near them; and he placed trumpeters at every five hundred feet, and charged them, that if their enemies appeared, they should give notice of it to the people, that they might fight in their armor, and their enemies might not fall upon them naked. He also went about the compass of the city by night, being never discouraged, neither about the work itself, nor about his own diet and sleep, for he made no use of those things for his pleasure, but out of necessity. And this trouble he underwent for two years and four months;[14] for in so long a time was the wall built, in the twenty-eighth year of the reign of Xerxes, in the ninth month. Now when the walls were finished, Nehemiah and the multitude offered sacrifices to God for the building of them, and they continued in feasting eight days. However, when the nations which dwelt in Syria heard that the building of the wall was finished, they had indignation at it. But when Nehemiah saw that the city was thin of people, he exhorted the priests and the Levites that they would leave the country, and remove themselves to the city, and there continue; and he built them houses at his own expenses; and he commanded that part of the people which were employed in cultivating the land to bring the tithes of their fruits to Jerusalem, that the priests and Levites having whereof they might live perpetually, might not leave the Divine worship; who willingly hearkened to the constitutions of Nehemiah, by which means the city Jerusalem came to be fuller of people than it was before. So when Nehemiah had done many other excellent things, and things worthy of commendation, in a glorious manner, he came to a great age, and then died. He was a man of a good and righteous disposition, and very ambitious to make his own

---

14. It may not be very improper to remark here, with what an unusual accuracy Josephus determines these years of Xerxes, in which the walls of Jerusalem were built, viz. that Nehemiah came with his commission in the twenty-fifth of Xerxes, that the walls were two years and four months in building, and that they were finished on the twenty-eighth of Xerxes, sect. 7, 8. It may also be remarked further, that Josephus hardly ever mentions more than one infallible astronomical character, I mean an eclipse of the moon, and this a little before the death of Herod the Great, Antiq. B. XVII. ch. 6. sect. 4. Now on these two chronological characters in great measure depend some of the most important points belonging to Christianity, viz. the explication of Daniel's seventy weeks, and the duration of our Savior's ministry, and the time of his death, in correspondence to those seventy weeks. See the Supplement to the Lit. Accorap. of Proph. p. 72.

nation happy; and he hath left the walls of Jerusalem as an eternal monument for himself. Now this was done in the days of Xerxes.

6 *Concerning Esther and Mordecai and Haman; and How in the Reign of Artaxerxes the Whole Nation of the Jews Was in Danger of Perishing*

1. AFTER the death of Xerxes, the kingdom came to be transferred to his son Cyrus, whom the Greeks called Artaxerxes. When this man had obtained the government over the Persians, the whole nation of the Jews,[15] with their wives and children, were in danger of perishing; the occasion whereof we shall declare in a little time; for it is proper, in the first place, to explain somewhat relating to this king, and how he came to marry a Jewish wife, who was herself of the royal family also, and who is related to have saved our nation; for when Artaxerxes had taken the kingdom, and had set governors over the hundred twenty and seven provinces, from India even unto Ethiopia, in the third year of his reign, he made a costly feast for his friends, and for the nations of Persia, and for their governors, such a one as was proper for a king

15. Since some skeptical persons are willing to discard this Book of Esther as no true history; and even our learned and judicious Dr. Wall, in his late posthumous Critical Notes upon all the other Hebrew books of the Old Testament, gives none upon the Canticles, or upon Esther, and seems thereby to give up this book, as well as he gives up the Canticles, as indefensible; I shall venture to say, that almost all the objections against this Book of Esther are gone at once, if, as we certainly ought to do, and as Dean Prideaux has justly done, we place this history under Artsxerxes Longimanus, as do both the Septuagint interpretation and Josephus. The learned Dr. Lee, in his posthumous Dissertation on the Second Book of Esdras, p. 25, also says, that "the truth of this history is demonstrated by the feast of Purlin, kept up from that time to this very day. And this surprising providential revolution in favor of a captive people, thereby constantly commemorated, standeth even upon a firmer basis than that there ever was such a man as king Alexander [the Great] in the world, of whose reign there is no such abiding monument at this day to be found any where. Nor will they, I dare say, who quarrel at this or any other of the sacred histories, find it a very easy matter to reconcile the different accounts which were given by historians of the affairs of this king, or to confirm any one fact of his whatever with the same evidence which is here given for the principal fact in this sacred book, or even so much as to prove the existence of such a person, of whom so great things are related, but. upon granting this Book of Esther, or sixth of Esdras, (as it is placed in some of the most ancient copies of the Vulgate,) to be a most true and certain history," etc.

to make, when he had a mind to make a public demonstration of his riches, and this for a hundred and fourscore days; after which he made a feast for other nations, and for their ambassadors, at Shushan, for seven days. Now this feast was ordered after the manner following: He caused a tent to be pitched, which was supported by pillars of gold and silver, with curtains of linen and purple spread over them, that it might afford room for many ten thousands to sit down. The cups with which the waiters ministered were of gold, and adorned with precious stones, for pleasure and for sight. He also gave order to the servants that they should not force them to drink, by bringing them wine continually, as is the practice of the Persians, but to permit every one of the guests to enjoy himself according to his own inclination. Moreover, he sent messengers through the country, and gave order that they should have a remission of their labors, and should keep a festival many days, on account of his kingdom. In like manner did Vashti the queen gather her guests together, and made them a feast in the palace. Now the king was desirous to show her, who exceeded all other women in beauty, to those that feasted with him, and he sent some to command her to come to his feast. But she, out of regard to the laws of the Persians, which forbid the wives to be seen by strangers, did not go to the king[16] and though he oftentimes sent the eunuchs to her, she did nevertheless stay away, and refused to come, till the king was so much irritated, that he brake up the entertainment, and rose up, and called for those seven who had the interpretation of the laws committed to them, and accused his wife, and said that he had been affronted by her, because that when she was frequently called by him to his feast, she did not obey him once. He therefore gave

16. If the Chaldee paraphrast be in the right, that Artaxerxes intended to show Vashti to his guests naked, it is no wonder at all that she would not submit to such an indignity; but still if it were not so gross as that, yet it might, in the king's cups, be done in a way so indecent, as the Persian laws would not then bear, no more than the common laws of modesty. And that the king had some such design seems not improbable, for otherwise the principal of these royal guests could be no strangers to the queen, nor unapprized of her beauty, so far as decency admitted. However, since Providence was now paving the way for the introduction of a Jewess into the king's affections, in order to bring about one of the most wonderful deliverances which the Jewish or any other nation ever had, we need not be further solicitous about the motives by which the king was induced to divorce Vashti, and marry Esther.

order that they should inform him what could be done by the law against her. So one of them, whose name was Memucan, said that this affront was offered not to him alone, but to all the Persians, who were in danger of leading their lives very ill with their wives, if they must be thus despised by them; for that none of their wives would have any reverence for their husbands, if they had" such an example of arrogance in the queen towards thee, who rulest over all." Accordingly, he exhorted him to punish her, who had been guilty of so great an affront to him, after a severe manner; and when he had so done, to publish to the nations what had been decreed about the queen. So the resolution was to put Vashti away, and to give her dignity to another woman.

2. But the king having been fond of her, did not well bear a separation, and yet by the law he could not admit of a reconciliation; so he was under trouble, as not having it in his power to do what he desired to do. But when his friends saw him so uneasy, they advised him to cast the memory of his wife, and his love for her, out of his mind, but to send abroad over all the habitable earth, and to search out for comely virgins, and to take her whom he should best like for his wife, because his passion for his former wife would be quenched by the introduction of another, and the kindness he had for Vashti would be withdrawn from her, and be placed on her that was with him. Accordingly, he was persuaded to follow this advice, and gave order to certain persons to choose out of the virgins that were in his kingdom those that were esteemed the most comely. So when a great number of these virgins were gathered together, there was found a damsel in Babylon, whose parents were both dead, and she was brought up with her uncle Mordecai, for that was her uncle's name. This uncle was of the tribe of Benjamin, and was one of the principal persons among the Jews. Now it proved that this damsel, whose name was Esther, was the most beautiful of all the rest, and that the grace of her countenance drew the eyes of the spectators principally upon her. So she was committed to one of the eunuchs to take the care of her; and she was very exactly provided with sweet odors, in great plenty, and with costly ointments, such as her body required to be anointed withal; and this was used for six months by the virgins, who were in number four hundred. And when the eunuch thought the virgins had been sufficiently purified, in the fore-mentioned time, and were now

fit to go to the king's bed, he sent one to be with the king ever day. So when he had accompanied with her, he sent her back to the eunuch; and when Esther had come to him, he was pleased with her, and fell in love with the damsel, and married her, and made her his lawful wife, and kept a wedding feast for her on the twelfth month of the seventh year of his reign, which was called Adar. He also sent angari, as they are called, or messengers, unto every nation, and gave orders that they should keep a feast for his marriage, while he himself treated the Persians and the Medes, and the principal men of the nations, for a whole month, on account of this his marriage. Accordingly, Esther came to his royal palace, and he set a diadem on her head. And thus was Esther married, without making known to the king what nation she was derived from. Her uncle also removed from Babylon to Shushan, and dwelt there, being every day about the palace, and inquiring how the damsel did, for he loved her as though she had been his own daughter.

3. Now the king had made a law,[17] that none of his own people should approach him unless he were called, when he sat upon his throne and men, with axes in their hands, stood round about his throne, in order to punish such as approached to him without being called. However, the king sat with a golden scepter in his hand, which he held out when he had a mind to save any one of those that approached to him without being called, and he who touched it was free from danger. But of this matter we have discoursed sufficiently.

4. Some time after this [two eunuchs], Bigthan and Teresh, plotted against the king; and Barnabazus, the servant of one of the eunuchs, being by birth a Jew, was acquainted with their conspiracy, and discovered it to the queen's uncle; and Mordecai, by the means of Esther, made the conspirators known to the king. This troubled the king; but he discovered the truth, and hanged the eunuchs upon a cross, while at that time he gave no reward]: to Mordecai, who had

17. Herodotus says that this law [against any one's coming uncalled to the kings of Persia when they were sitting on their thrones] was first enacted by Deioces [i.e. by him who first withdrew the Medes from the dominion of the Assyrians, and himself first reigned over them]. Thus also, lays Spanheim, stood guards, with their axes, about the throne of Tenus, or Tenudus, that the offender might by them be punished immediately.

been the occasion of his preservation. He only bid the scribes to set down his name in the records, and bid him stay in the palace, as an intimate friend of the king.

5. Now there was one Haman, the son of Amedatha, by birth an Amalekite, that used to go in to the king; and the foreigners and Persians worshipped him, as Artaxerxes had commanded that such honor should be paid to him; but Mordecai was so wise, and so observant of his own country's laws, that he would not worship the man[18] When Haman observed this, he inquired whence he came; and when he understood that he was a Jew, he had indignation at him, and said within himself, that whereas the Persians, who were free men, worshipped him, this man, who was no better than a slave, does not vouchsafe to do so. And when he desired to punish Mordecai, he thought it too small a thing to request of the king that he alone might be punished; he rather determined to abolish the whole nation, for he was naturally an enemy to the Jews, because the nation of the Amalekites, of which he was; had been destroyed by them. Accordingly he came to the king, and accused them, saying, "There is a certain wicked nation, and it is dispersed over all the habitable earth the was under his dominion; a nation separate from others, unsociable, neither admitting the same sort of Divine worship that others do, nor using laws like to the laws of others, at enmity with thy people, and with all men, both in their manners and practices. Now, if thou wilt be a benefactor to thy subjects, thou wilt give order to destroy them utterly, and not leave the least remains of them, nor preserve any of them, either for slaves or for captives." But that the king might not be damnified by the loss of the tributes which the Jews paid him, Haman promised to give him out of his own estate forty thousand talents whensoever he pleased; and he said he would pay this money very willingly, that the kingdom might. be freed from such a misfortune.

---

18. Whether this adoration required of Mordecai to Haman were by him deemed too like the adoration due only to God, as Josephus seems here to think, as well as the Septuagint interpreters also, by their translation of Esther 13:12–14, or whether he thought he ought to pay no sort of adoration to an Amalekite, which nation had been such great sinners as to have been universally devoted to destruction by God himself, Exodus 17:14–16; 1 Samuel 15:18, or whether both causes concurred, cannot now, I doubt, be certainly determined.

6. When Haman had made this petition, the king both forgave him the money, and granted him the men, to do what he would with them. So Haman, having gained what he desired, sent out immediately a decree, as from the king, to all nations, the contents whereof were these: "Artaxerxes, the great king, to the rulers of the hundred twenty and seven provinces, from India to Ethiopia, sends this writing. Whereas I have governed many nations, and obtained the dominions of all the habitable earth, according to my desire, and have not been obliged to do any thing that is insolent or cruel to my subjects by such my power, but have showed myself mild and gentle, by taking care of their peace and good order, and have sought how they might enjoy those blessings for all time to come. And whereas I have been kindly informed by Haman, who, on account of his prudence and justice, is the first in my esteem, and in dignity, and only second to myself, for his fidelity and constant good-will to me, that there is an ill-natured nation intermixed with all mankind, that is averse to our laws, and not subject to kings, and of a different conduct of life from others, that hateth monarchy, and of a disposition that is pernicious to our affairs, I give order that all these men, of whom Haman our second father hath informed us, be destroyed, with their wives and children, and that none of them be spared, and that none prefer pity to them before obedience to this decree. And this I will to be executed on the fourteenth day of the twelfth month of this present year, that so when all that have enmity to us are destroyed, and this in one day, we may be allowed to lead the rest of our lives in peace hereafter." Now when this decree was brought to the cities, and to the country, all were ready for the destruction and entire abolishment of the Jews, against the day before mentioned; and they were very hasty about it at Shushan, in particular. Accordingly, the king and Haman spent their time in feasting together with good cheer and wine, but the city was in disorder.

7. Now when Mordecai was informed of what was done, he rent his clothes, and put on sackcloth, and sprinkled ashes upon his head, and went about the city, crying out, that "a nation that had been injurious to no man was to be destroyed." And he went on saying thus as far as to the king's palace, and there he stood, for it was not lawful for him to go into it in that habit. The same thing was done by all the Jews that were in the several cities wherein this decree

was published, with lamentation and mourning, on account of the calamities denounced against them. But as soon as certain persons had told the queen that Mordecai stood before the court in a mourning habit, she was disturbed at this report, and sent out such as should change his garments; but when he could not be induced to put off his sackcloth, because the sad occasion that forced him to put it on was not yet ceased, she called the eunuch Acratheus, for he was then present, and sent him to Mordecai, in order to know of him what sad accident had befallen him, for which he was in mourning, and would not put off the habit he had put on at her desire. Then did Mordecai inform the eunuch of the occasion of his mourning, and of the decree which was sent by the king into all the country, and of the promise of money whereby Haman brought the destruction of their nation. He also gave him a copy of what was proclaimed at Shushan, to be carried to Esther; and he charged her to petition the king about this matter, and not to think it a dishonorable thing in her to put on a humble habit, for the safety of her nation, wherein she might deprecate the ruin of the Jews, who were in danger of it; for that Haman, whose dignity was only inferior to that of the king, had accused the Jews, and had irritated the king against them. When she was informed of this, she sent to Mordecai again, and told him that she was not called by the king, and that he who goes in to him without being called, is to be slain, unless when he is willing to save any one, he holds out his golden scepter to him; but that to whomsoever he does so, although he go in without being called, that person is so far from being slain, that he obtains pardon, and is entirely preserved. Now when the eunuch carried this message from Esther to Mordecai, he bade him also tell her that she must not only provide for her own preservation, but for the common preservation of her nation, for that if she now neglected this opportunity, there would certainly arise help to them from God some other way, but she and her father's house would be destroyed by those whom she now despised. But Esther sent the very same eunuch back to Mordecai [to desire him] to go to Shushan, and to gather the Jews that were there together to a congregation, and to fast and abstain from all sorts of food, on her account, and [to let him know that] she with her maidens would do the same: and then she promised that she would go to the king, though it were against the law, and that if she must die for it, she would not refuse it.

8. Accordingly, Mordecai did as Esther had enjoined him, and made the people fast; and he besought God, together with them, not to overlook his nation, particularly at this time, when it was going to be destroyed; but that, as he had often before provided for them, and forgiven, when they had sinned, so he would now deliver them from that destruction which was denounced against them; for although it was not all the nation that had offended, yet must they so ingloriously be slain, and that he was himself the occasion of the wrath of Haman, "Because," said he, "I did not worship him, nor could I endure to pay that honor to him which I used to pay to thee, O Lord; for upon that his anger hath he contrived this present mischief against those that have not transgressed thy laws." The same supplications did the multitude put up, and entreated that God would provide for their deliverance, and free the Israelites that were in all the earth from this calamity which was now coming upon them, for they had it before their eyes, and expected its coming. Accordingly, Esther made supplication to God after the manner of her country, by casting herself down upon the earth, and putting on her mourning garments, and bidding farewell to meat and drink, and all delicacies, for three days' time; and she entreated God to have mercy upon her, and make her words appear persuasive to the king, and render her countenance more beautiful than it was before, that both by her words and beauty she might succeed, for the averting of the king's anger, in case he were at all irritated against her, and for the consolation of those of her own country, now they were in the utmost danger of perishing; as also that he would excite a hatred in the king against the enemies of the Jews, and those that had contrived their future destruction, if they proved to be contemned by him.

9. When Esther had used this supplication for three days, she put off those garments, and changed her habit, and adorned herself as became a queen, and took two of her handmaids with her, the one of which supported her, as she gently leaned upon her, and the other followed after, and lifted up her large train (which swept along the ground) with the extremities of her fingers. And thus she came to the king, having a blushing redness in her countenance, with a pleasant agreeableness in her behavior; yet did she go in to him with fear; and as soon as she was come over against him, as he was sitting on his throne, in his royal apparel, which was a garment interwoven with gold and

precious stones, which made him seem to her more terrible, especially when he looked at her somewhat severely, and with a countenance on fire with anger, her joints failed her immediately, out of the dread she was in, and she fell down sideways in a swoon: but the king changed his mind, which happened, as I suppose, by the will of God, and was concerned for his wife, lest her fear should bring some very ill thing upon her, and he leaped from his throne, and took her in his arms, and recovered her, by embracing her, and speaking comfortably to her, and exhorting her to be of good cheer, and not to suspect any thing that was sad on account of her coming to him without being called, because that law was made for subjects, but that she, who was a queen, as well as he a king, might be entirely secure; and as he said this, he put the scepter into her hand, and laid his rod upon her neck, on account of the law; and so freed her from her fear. And after she had recovered herself by these encouragements, she said, "My lord, it is not easy for me, on the sudden, to say what hath happened, for as soon as I saw thee to be great, and comely, and terrible, my spirit departed from me, and I had no soul left in me." And while it was with difficulty, and in a low voice, that she could say thus much, the king was in a great agony and disorder, and encouraged Esther to be of good cheer, and to expect better fortune, since he was ready, if occasion should require it, to grant her the half of his kingdom. Accordingly, Esther desired that he and his friend Haman would come to her to a banquet, for she said she had prepared a supper for him. He consented to it; and when they were there, as they were drinking, he bid Esther to let him know what she desired; for that she should not be disappointed though she should desire the half of his kingdom. But she put off the discovery of her petition till the next day, if he would come again, together with Haman, to her banquet.

10. Now when the king had promised so to do, Haman went away very glad, because he alone had the honor of supping with the king at Esther's banquet, and because no one else partook of the same honor with kings but himself; yet when he saw Mordecai in the court, he was very much displeased, for he paid him no manner of respect when he saw him. So he went home and called for his wife Zeresh, and his friends, and when they were come, he showed them what honor he enjoyed not only from the king, but from the queen also, for as he alone had that day supped with her, together with the king, so was he

also invited again for the next day; yet," said he, "am I not pleased to see Mordecai the Jew in the court." Hereupon his wife Zeresh advised him to give order that a gallows should be made fifty cubits high, and that in the morning he should ask it of the king that Mordecai might be hanged thereon. So he commended her advice, and gave order to his servants to prepare the gallows, and to place it in the court, for the punishment of Mordecai thereon, which was accordingly prepared. But God laughed to scorn the wicked expectations of Haman; and as he knew what the event would be, he was delighted at it, for that night he took away the king's sleep; and as the king was not willing to lose the time of his lying awake, but to spend it in something that might be of advantage to his kingdom, he commanded the scribe to bring him the chronicles of the former kings, and the records of his own actions; and when he had brought them, and was reading them, one was found to have received a country on account of his excellent management on a certain occasion, and the name of the country was set down; another was found to have had a present made him on account of his fidelity: then the scribe came to Bigthan and Teresh, the eunuchs that had made a conspiracy against the king, which Mordecai had discovered; and when the scribe said no more but that, and was going on to another history, the king stopped him, and inquired "whether it was not added that Mordecai had a reward given him?" and when he said there was no such addition, he bade him leave off; and he inquired of those that were appointed for that purpose, what hour of the night it was; and when he was informed that it was already day, he gave order, that if they found any one of his friends already come, and standing before the court, they should tell him. Now it happened that Haman was found there, for he was come sooner than ordinary to petition the king to have Mordecai put to death; and when the servants said that Haman was before the court, he bid them call him in; and when he was come in, he said, "Because I know that thou art my only fast friend, I desire thee to give me advice how I may honor one that I greatly love, and that after a manner suitable to my magnificence." Now Haman reasoned with himself, that what opinion he should give it would be for himself, since it was he alone who was beloved by the king: so he gave that advice which he thought of all other the best; for he said, "If thou wouldst truly honor a man whom thou sayest thou dost love, give order that he may ride on horseback, with the same garment on which thou wearest, and with a gold chain about his neck, and let one of thy intimate friends go before him, and proclaim through the whole city, that whosoever the king honoreth obtaineth this mark of his honor." This was the advice which Haman gave, out of a supposal that such a reward would come to himself. Hereupon the king was pleased with the advice, and said, "Go thou therefore, for thou hast the horse, the garment, and the chain, ask for Mordecai the Jew, and give him those things, and go before his horse and proclaim accordingly; for thou art," said he, "my intimate friend, and hast given me good advice; be thou then the minister of what thou hast advised me to. This shall be his reward from us, for preserving my life." When he heard this order, which was entirely unexpected, he was confounded in his mind, and knew not what to do. However, he went out and led the horse, and took the purple garment, and the golden chain for the neck, and finding Mordecai before the court, clothed in sackcloth, he bid him put that garment off, and put the purple garment on. But Mordecai, not knowing the truth of the matter, but thinking that it was done in mockery, said, "O thou wretch, the vilest of all mankind, dost thou thus laugh at our calamities?" But when he was satisfied that the king bestowed this honor upon him, for the deliverance he had procured him when he convicted the eunuchs who had conspired against him, he put on that purple garment which the king always wore, and put the chain about his neck, and got on horseback, and went round the city, while Haman went before and proclaimed, "This shall be the reward which the king will bestow on every one whom he loves, and esteems worthy of honor." And when they had gone round the city, Mordecai went in to the king; but Haman went home, out of shame, and informed his wife and friends of what had happened, and this with tears; who said, that he would never be able to be revenged of Mordecai, for that God was with him.

11. Now while these men were thus talking one to another, Esther's eunuchs hastened Haman away to come to supper; but one of the eunuchs, named Sabuchadas, saw the gallows that was fixed in Haman's house, and inquired of one of his servants for what purpose they had prepared it. So he knew that it was for the queen's uncle, because Haman was about to petition the king that he might be punished; but at present he held his peace. Now when the king, with Haman, were at the banquet, he desired the queen to tell him what gifts she

desired to obtain, and assured her that she should have whatsoever she had a mind to. She then lamented the danger her people were in; and said that "she and her nation were given up to be destroyed, and that she, on that account, made this her petition; that she would not have troubled him if he had only given order that they should be sold into bitter servitude, for such a misfortune would not have been intolerable; but she desired that they might be delivered from such destruction." And when the king inquired of her whom was the author of this misery to them, she then openly accused Haman, and convicted him, that he had been the wicked instrument of this, and had formed this plot against them. When the king was hereupon in disorder, and was gone hastily out of the banquet into the gardens, Haman began to intercede with Esther, and to beseech her to forgive him, as to what he had offended, for he perceived that he was in a very bad case. And as he had fallen upon the queen's bed, and was making supplication to her, the king came in, and being still more provoked at what he saw, "O thou wretch," said he, "thou vilest of mankind, dost thou aim to force in wife?" And when Haman was astonished at this, and not able to speak one word more, Sabuchadas the eunuch came in and accused Haman, and said," He found a gallows at his house, prepared for Mordecai; for that the servant told him so much upon his inquiry, when he was sent to him to call him to supper." He said further, that the gallows was fifty cubits high: which, when the king heard, he determined that Haman should be punished after no other manner than that which had been devised by him against Mordecai; so he gave order immediately that he should be hung upon those gallows, and be put to death after that manner. And from hence I cannot forbear to admire God, and to learn hence his wisdom and his justice, not only in punishing the wickedness of Haman, but in so disposing it, that he should undergo the very same punishment which he had contrived for another; as also because thereby he teaches others this lesson, that what mischiefs any one prepares against another, he, without knowing of it, first contrives it against himself.

12. Wherefore Haman, who had immoderately abused the honor he had from the king, was destroyed after this manner, and the king granted his estate to the queen. He also called for Mordecai, (for Esther had informed him that she was akin to him,) and gave that ring to Mordecai which he had before given to Haman. The queen also gave

Haman's estate to Mordecai; and prayed the king to deliver the nation of the Jews from the fear of death, and showed him what had been written over all the country by Haman the son of Ammedatha; for that if her country were destroyed, and her countrymen were to perish, she could not bear to live herself any longer. So the king promised her that he would not do any thing that should be disagreeable to her, nor contradict what she desired; but he bid her write what she pleased about the Jews, in the king's name, and seal it with his seal, and send it to all his kingdom, for that those who read epistles whose authority is secured by having the king's seal to them, would no way contradict what was written therein. So he commanded the king's scribes to be sent for, and to write to the nations, on the Jews' behalf, and to his lieutenants and governors, that were over his hundred twenty and seven provinces, from India to Ethiopia. Now the contents of this epistle were these: "The great king Artaxerxes to our rulers, and those that are our faithful subjects, sendeth greeting.[19] Many men there are who, on account of the greatness of the benefits bestowed on them, and because of the honor which they have obtained from the wonderful kind treatment of those that bestowed it, are not only injurious to their inferiors, but do not scruple to do evil to those that have been their benefactors, as if they would take away gratitude from among men, and by their insolent abuse of such benefits as they never expected, they turn the abundance they have against those that are the authors of it, and suppose they shall lie concealed from God in that case, and avoid that vengeance which comes from him. Some of these men, when they have had the management of affairs committed to them by their friends, and bearing private malice of their own against some others, by deceiving those that have the power, persuade them to be angry at such as have done them no harm, till they are in danger

19. The true reason why king Artaxerxes did not here properly revoke his former barbarous decree for the universal slaughter of the Jews, but only empowered and encouraged the Jews to fight for their lives, and to kill their enemies, if they attempted their destruction, seems to have been that old law of the Medes and Persians, not yet laid aside, that whatever decree was signed both by the king and his lords could not be changed, but remained unalterable, Daniel 6:7–9, 12, 15, 17; Esther 1:19; 8:8. And Haman having engrossed the royal favor might perhaps have himself signed this decree for the Jews' slaughter instead of the ancient lords, and so might have rendered it by their rules irrevocable.

of perishing, and this by laying accusations and calumnies: nor is this state of things to be discovered by ancient examples, or such as we have learned by report only, but by some examples of such impudent attempts under our own eyes; so that it is not fit to attend any longer to calumnies and accusations, nor to the persuasions of others, but to determine what any one knows of himself to have been really done, and to punish what justly deserves it, and to grant favors to such as are innocent. This hath been the case of Haman, the son of Ammedatha, by birth an Amalekite, and alien from the blood of the Persians, who, when he was hospitably entertained by us, and partook of that kindness which we bear to all men to so great a degree, as to be called my father, and to be all along worshipped, and to have honor paid him by all in the second rank after the royal honor due to ourselves, he could not bear his good fortune, nor govern the magnitude of his prosperity with sound reason; nay, he made a conspiracy against me and my life, who gave him his authority, by endeavoring to take away Mordecai, my benefactor, and my savior, and by basely and treacherously requiring to have Esther, the partner of my life, and of my dominion, brought to destruction; for he contrived by this means to deprive me of my faithful friends, and transfer the government to others:[20] but since I perceived that these Jews, that were by this pernicious fellow devoted to destruction, were not wicked men, but conducted their lives after the best manner, and were men dedicated to the worship of that God who hath preserved the kingdom to me and to my ancestors, I do not only free them from the punishment which the former epistle, which was sent by Haman, ordered to be inflicted on them, to which if you refuse obedience, you shall do well;

---

20. These words give an intimation as if Artaxerxes suspected a deeper design in Haman than openly appeared, viz. that knowing the Jews would be faithful to him, and that he could never transfer the crown to his own family, who was an Agagite, Esther 3:1, 10, or of the posterity of Agag, the old king of the Amalekites, 1 Samuel 15:8, 32, 33, while they were alive, and spread over all his dominions, he therefore endeavored to destroy them. Nor is it to me improbable that those seventy-five thousand eight hundred of the Jews' enemies which were soon destroyed by the Jews, on the permission of the king, which must be on some great occasion, were Amalekites, their old and hereditary enemies, Exodus 17:14, 15; and that thereby was fulfilled Balaam's prophecy, "Amalek was the first of the nations, but his latter end shall be, that he perish for ever" Numbers 24:20.

but I will that they have all honor paid to them. Accordingly, I have hanged up the man that contrived such things against them, with his family, before the gates of Shushan; that punishment being sent upon him by God, who seeth all things. And I give you in charge, that you publicly propose a copy of this epistle through all my kingdom, that the Jews may be permitted peaceably to use their own laws, and that you assist them, that at the same season whereto their miserable estate did belong, they may defend themselves the very same day from unjust violence, the thirteenth day of the twelfth month, which is Adar; for God hath made that day a day of salvation instead of a day of destruction to them; and may it be a good day to those that wish us well, and a memorial of the punishment of the conspirators against us: and I will that you take notice, that every city, and every nation, that shall disobey any thing that is contained in this epistle, shall be destroyed by fire and sword. However, let this epistle be published through all the country that is under our obedience, and let all the Jews, by all means, be ready against the day before mentioned, that they may avenge themselves upon their enemies."

13. Accordingly, the horsemen who carried the epistles proceeded on the ways which they were to go with speed: but as for Mordecai, as soon as he had assumed the royal garment, and the crown of gold, and had put the chain about his neck, he went forth in a public procession; and when the Jews who were at Shushan saw him in so great honor with the king, they thought his good fortune was common to themselves also, and joy and a beam of salvation encompassed the Jews, both those that were in the cities, and those that were in the countries, upon the publication of the king's letters, insomuch that many even of other nations circumcised their foreskin for fear of the Jews, that they might procure safety to themselves thereby; for on the thirteenth day of the twelfth month, which according to the Hebrews is called Adar, but according to the Macedonians, Dystrus, those that carried the king's epistle gave them notice, that the same day wherein their danger was to have been, on that very day should they destroy their enemies. But now the rulers of the provinces, and the tyrants, and the kings, and the scribes, had the Jews in esteem; for the fear they were in of Mordecai forced them to act with discretion. Now when the royal decree was come to all the country that was subject to the king, it fell out that the Jews at Shushan slew five hundred

of their enemies; and when the king had told Esther the number of those that were slain in that city, but did not well know what had been done in the provinces, he asked her whether she would have any thing further done against them, for that it should be done accordingly: upon which she desired that the Jews might be permitted to treat their remaining enemies in the same manner the next day; as also that they might hang the ten sons of Haman upon the gallows. So the king permitted the Jews so to do, as desirous not to contradict Esther. So they gathered themselves together again on the fourteenth day of the month Dystrus, and slew about three hundred of their enemies, but touched nothing of what riches they had. Now there were slain by the Jews that were in the country, and in the other cities, seventy-five thousand of their enemies, and these were slain on the thirteenth day of the month, and the next day they kept as a festival. In like manner the Jews that were in Shushan gathered themselves together, and feasted on the fourteenth day, and that which followed it; whence it is that even now all the Jews that are in the habitable earth keep these days festival, and send portions to one another. Mordecai also wrote to the Jews that lived in the kingdom of Artaxerxes to observe these days, and celebrate them as festivals, and to deliver them down to posterity, that this festival might continue for all time to come, and that it might never be buried in oblivion; for since they were about to be destroyed on these days by Haman, they would do a right thing, upon escaping the danger in them, and on them inflicting punishment on their enemies, to observe those days, and give thanks to God on them; for which cause the Jews still keep the forementioned days, and call them days of Phurim [or Purim.][21] And Mordecai became a great and

---

21. Take here part of Reland's note on this disputed passage: "In Josephus's copies these Hebrew words, 'days of Purim,' or ' lots,' as in the Greek copies of Esther, ch. 9:26, 28–32, is read 'days of Phurim,' or 'days of protection,' but ought to be read' days of Parira,' as in the Hebrew; than which creation," says he, "nothing is more certain." And had we any assurance that Josephus's copy mentioned the "casting of lots," as our other copies do, Esther 3:7, I should fully agree with Reland; but, as it now stands, it seems to me by no means certain. As to this whole Book of Esther in the present Hebrew copy, it is so very imperfect, in a case where the providence of God was so very remarkable, and the Septuagint and Josephus have so much of religion, that it has not so much as the name of God once in it; and it is hard to say who made that epitome which the Masorites have given us for the genuine book

illustrious person with the king, and assisted him in the government of the people. He also lived with the queen; so that the affairs of the Jews were, by their means, better than they could ever have hoped for. And this was the state of the Jews under the reign of Artaxerxes.

7 *How John Slew His Brother Jesus in the Temple; and How Bagoses Offered Many Injuries to the Jews; and What Sanballat Did*

1. WHEN Eliashib the high priest was dead, his son Judas succeeded in the high priesthood; and when he was dead, his son John took that dignity; on whose account it was also that Bagoses, the general of another Artaxerxes's army,[22] polluted the temple, and imposed tributes on the Jews, that out of the public stock, before they offered the daily sacrifices, they should pay for every lamb fifty shekels. Now Jesus was the brother of John, and was a friend of Bagoses, who had promised to procure him the high priesthood. In confidence of whose support, Jesus quarreled with John in the temple, and so provoked his brother, that in his anger his brother slew him. Now it was a horrible thing for John, when he was high priest, to perpetrate so great a crime, and so much the more horrible, that there never was so cruel and impious a thing done, neither by the Greeks nor Barbarians. However,

---

itself; no religious Jews could well be the authors of it, whose education obliged them to have a constant regard to God, and whatsoever related to his worship; nor do we know that there ever was so imperfect a copy of it in the world till after the days of Barchochab, in the second century.

22. Concerning this other Artaxerxes, called Muemon, and the Persian affliction and captivity of the Jews under him, occasioned by the murder of the high priest's brother in the holy house itself, see Authent. Rec. at large, p. 49. And if any wonder why Josephus wholly omits the rest of the kings of Persia after Artaxerxes Mnemon, till he came to their last king Darius, who was conquered by Alexander the Great, I shall give them Vossius's and Dr. Hudson's answer, though in my own words, viz. that Josephus did not do ill in admitting those kings of Persia with whom the Jews had no concern, because he was giving the history of the Jews, and not of the Persians [which is a sufficient reason also why he entirely omits the history and the Book of Job, as not particularly relating to that nation]. He justly therefore returns to the Jewish affairs after the death of Longimanus, without any intention of Darius II. before Artaxerxes Mnemon, or of Ochus or Arogus, as the Canon of Ptolemy names them, after him. Nor had he probably mentioned this other Artaxerxes, unless Bagoses, one of the governors and commanders under him, had occasioned the pollution of the Jewish temple, and had greatly distressed the Jews upon that pollution.

God did not neglect its punishment, but the people were on that very account enslaved, and the temple was polluted by the Persians. Now when Bagoses, the general of Artaxerxes's army, knew that John, the high priest of the Jews, had slain his own brother Jesus in the temple, he came upon the Jews immediately, and began in anger to say to them," Have you had the impudence to perpetrate a murder in your temple?" And as he was aiming to go into the temple, they forbade him so to do; but he said to them," Am not I purer than he that was slain in the temple?" And when he had said these words, he went into the temple. Accordingly, Bagoses made use of this pretense, and punished the Jews seven years for the murder of Jesus.

2. Now when John had departed this life, his son Jaddua succeeded in the high priesthood. He had a brother, whose name was Manasseh. Now there was one Sanballat, who was sent by Darius, the last king [of Persia], into Samaria. He was a Cutheam by birth; of which stock were the Samaritans also. This man knew that the city Jerusalem was a famous city, and that their kings had given a great deal of trouble to the Assyrians, and the people of Celesyria; so that he willingly gave his daughter, whose name was Nicaso, in marriage to Manasseh, as thinking this alliance by marriage would be a pledge and security that the nation of the Jews should continue their good-will to him.

8 *Concerning Sanballat and Manasseh, and the Temple Which They Built on Mount Gerizzim; as Also How Alexander Made His Entry into the City Jerusalem, and What Benefits He Bestowed on the Jews*

1. ABOUT this time it was that Philip, king of Macedon, was treacherously assaulted and slain at Egae by Pausanias, the son of Cerastes, who was derived from the family of Oreste, and his son Alexander succeeded him in the kingdom; who, passing over the Hellespont, overcame the generals of Darius's army in a battle fought at Granicum. So he marched over Lydia, and subdued Ionia, and overran Caria, and fell upon the places of Pamphylia, as has been related elsewhere.

2. But the elders of Jerusalem being very uneasy that the brother of Jaddua the high priest, though married to a foreigner, should be a partner with him in the high priesthood, quarreled with him; for they

esteemed this man's marriage a step to such as should be desirous of transgressing about the marriage of [strange] wives, and that this would be the beginning of a mutual society with foreigners, although the offense of some about marriages, and their having married wives that were not of their own country, had been an occasion of their former captivity, and of the miseries they then underwent; so they commanded Manasseh to divorce his wife, or not to approach the altar, the high priest himself joining with the people in their indignation against his brother, and driving him away from the altar. Whereupon Manasseh came to his father-in-law, Sanballat, and told him, that although he loved his daughter Nicaso, yet was he not willing to be deprived of his sacerdotal dignity on her account, which was the principal dignity in their nation, and always continued in the same family. And then Sanballat promised him not only to preserve to him the honor of his priesthood, but to procure for him the power and dignity of a high priest, and would make him governor of all the places he himself now ruled, if he would keep his daughter for his wife. He also told him further, that he would build him a temple like that at Jerusalem, upon Mount Gerizzini, which is the highest of all the mountains that are in Samaria; and he promised that he would do this with the approbation of Darius the king. Manasseh was elevated with these promises, and staid with Sanballat, upon a supposal that he should gain a high priesthood, as bestowed on him by Darius, for it happened that Sanballat was then in years. But there was now a great disturbance among the people of Jerusalem, because many of those priests and Levites were entangled in such matches; for they all revolted to Manasseh, and Sanballat afforded them money, and divided among them land for tillage, and habitations also, and all this in order every way to gratify his son-in-law.

3. About this time it was that Darius heard how Alexander had passed over the Hellespont, and had beaten his lieutenants in the battle at Granicum, and was proceeding further; whereupon he gathered together an army of horse and foot, and determined that he would meet the Macedonians before they should assault and conquer all Asia. So he passed over the river Euphrates, and came over Taurus, the Cilician mountain, and at Issus of Cilicia he waited for the enemy, as ready there to give him battle. Upon which Sanballat was glad that Darius was come down; and told Manasseh that he would suddenly

perform his promises to him, and this as soon as ever Darius should come back, after he had beaten his enemies; for not he only, but all those that were in Asia also, were persuaded that the Macedonians would not so much as come to a battle with the Persians, on account of their multitude. But the event proved otherwise than they expected; for the king joined battle with the Macedonians, and was beaten, and lost a great part of his army. His mother also, and his wife and children, were taken captives, and he fled into Persia. So Alexander came into Syria, and took Damascus; and when he had obtained Sidon, he besieged Tyre, when he sent all epistle to the Jewish high priest, to send him some auxiliaries, and to supply his army with provisions; and that what presents he formerly sent to Darius, he would now send to him, and choose the friendship of the Macedonians, and that he should never repent of so doing. But the high priest answered the messengers, that he had given his oath to Darius not to bear arms against him; and he said that he would not transgress this while Darius was in the land of the living. Upon hearing this answer, Alexander was very angry; and though he determined not to leave Tyre, which was just ready to be taken, yet as soon as he had taken it, he threatened that he would make an expedition against the Jewish high priest, and through him teach all men to whom they must keep their oaths. So when he had, with a good deal of pains during the siege, taken Tyre, and had settled its affairs, he came to the city of Gaza, and besieged both the city and him that was governor of the garrison, whose name was Babemeses.

4. But Sanballat thought he had now gotten a proper opportunity to make his attempt, so he renounced Darius, and taking with him seven thousand of his own subjects, he came to Alexander; and finding him beginning the siege of Tyre, he said to him, that he delivered up to him these men, who came out of places under his dominion, and did gladly accept of him for his lord instead of Darius. So when Alexander had received him kindly, Sanballat thereupon took courage, and spake to him about his present affair. He told him that he had a son-in-law, Manasseh, who was brother to the high priest Jaddua; and that there were many others of his own nation, now with him, that were desirous to have a temple in the places subject to him; that it would be for the king's advantage to have the strength of the Jews divided into two parts, lest when the nation is of one mind, and united, upon

any attempt for innovation, it prove troublesome to kings, as it had formerly proved to the kings of Assyria. Whereupon Alexander gave Sanballat leave so to do, who used the utmost diligence, and built the temple, and made Manasseh the priest, and deemed it a great reward that his daughter's children should have that dignity; but when the seven months of the siege of Tyre were over, and the two months of the siege of Gaza, Sanballat died. Now Alexander, when he had taken Gaza, made haste to go up to Jerusalem; and Jaddua the high priest, when he heard that, was in an agony, and under terror, as not knowing how he should meet the Macedonians, since the king was displeased at his foregoing disobedience. He therefore ordained that the people should make supplications, and should join with him in offering sacrifice to God, whom he besought to protect that nation, and to deliver them from the perils that were coming upon them; whereupon God warned him in a dream, which came upon him after he had offered sacrifice, that he should take courage, and adorn the city, and open the gates; that the rest should appear in white garments, but that he and the priests should meet the king in the habits proper to their order, without the dread of any ill consequences, which the providence of God would prevent. Upon which, when he rose from his sleep, he greatly rejoiced, and declared to all the warning he had received from God. According to which dream he acted entirely, and so waited for the coming of the king.

5. And when he understood that he was not far from the city, he went out in procession, with the priests and the multitude of the citizens. The procession was venerable, and the manner of it different from that of other nations. It reached to a place called Sapha, which name, translated into Greek, signifies a prospect, for you have thence a prospect both of Jerusalem and of the temple. And when the Phoenicians and the Chaldeans that followed him thought they should have liberty to plunder the city, and torment the high priest to death, which the king's displeasure fairly promised them, the very reverse of it happened; for Alexander, when he saw the multitude at a distance, in white garments, while the priests stood clothed with fine linen, and the high priest in purple and scarlet clothing, with his mitre on his head, having the golden plate whereon the name of God was engraved, he approached by himself, and adored that name, and first saluted the high priest. The Jews also did all together, with

one voice, salute Alexander, and encompass him about; whereupon the kings of Syria and the rest were surprised at what Alexander had done, and supposed him disordered in his mind. However, Parmenio alone went up to him, and asked him how it came to pass that, when all others adored him, he should adore the high priest of the Jews? To whom he replied, "I did not adore him, but that God who hath honored him with his high priesthood; for I saw this very person in a dream, in this very habit, when I was at Dios in Macedonia, who, when I was considering with myself how I might obtain the dominion of Asia, exhorted me to make no delay, but boldly to pass over the sea thither, for that he would conduct my army, and would give me the dominion over the Persians; whence it is that, having seen no other in that habit, and now seeing this person in it, and remembering that vision, and the exhortation which I had in my dream, I believe that I bring this army under the Divine conduct, and shall therewith conquer Darius, and destroy the power of the Persians, and that all things will succeed according to what is in my own mind." And when he had said this to Parmenio, and had given the high priest his right hand, the priests ran along by him, and he came into the city. And when he went up into the temple, he offered sacrifice to God, according to the high priest's direction, and magnificently treated both the high priest and the priests. And when the Book of Daniel was showed him[23] wherein Daniel declared that one of the Greeks should destroy the empire of the Persians, he supposed that himself was the person intended. And as he was then glad, he dismissed the multitude for the present; but the next day he called them to him, and bid them ask what favors they pleased of him; whereupon the high priest desired that they might enjoy the laws of their forefathers, and might pay no tribute on the seventh year. He granted all they desired. And when they entreared him that he would permit the Jews in Babylon and Media to enjoy their own laws also, he willingly promised to do hereafter what they desired. And when he said to the multitude, that if any of them would enlist themselves in his army, on this condition, that they should continue under the laws of their forefathers, and live according

23. The place showed Alexander might be Daniel 7:6; 8:3–8, 20—22; 11:3; some or all of them very plain predictions of Alexander's conquests and successors.

to them, he was willing to take them with him, many were ready to accompany him in his wars.

6. So when Alexander had thus settled matters at Jerusalem, he led his army into the neighboring cities; and when all the inhabitants to whom he came received him with great kindness, the Samaritans, who had then Shechem for their metropolis, (a city situate at Mount Gerizzim, and inhabited by apostates of the Jewish nation,) seeing that Alexander had so greatly honored the Jews, determined to profess themselves Jews; for such is the disposition of the Samaritans, as we have already elsewhere declared, that when the Jews are in adversity, they deny that they are of kin to them, and then they confess the truth; but when they perceive that some good fortune hath befallen them, they immediately pretend to have communion with them, saying that they belong to them, and derive their genealogy from the posterity of Joseph, Ephraim, and Manasseh. Accordingly, they made their address to the king with splendor, and showed great alacrity in meeting him at a little distance from Jerusalem. And when Alexander had commended them, the Shechemites approached to him, taking with them the troops that Sanballat had sent him, and they desired that he would come to their city, and do honor to their temple also; to whom he promised, that when he returned he would come to them. And when they petitioned that he would remit the tribute of the seventh year to them, because they did but sow thereon, he asked who they were that made such a petition; and when they said that they were Hebrews, but had the name of Sidonians, living at Shechem, he asked them again whether they were Jews; and when they said they were not Jews, "It was to the Jews," said he, "that I granted that privilege; however, when I return, and am thoroughly informed by you of this matter, I will do what I shall think proper." And in this manner he took leave of the Shechenlites; but ordered that the troops of Sanballat should follow him into Egypt, because there he designed to give them lands, which he did a little after in Thebais, when he ordered them to guard that country.

7. Now when Alexander was dead, the government was parted among his successors, but the temple upon Mount Gerizzim remained. And if any one were accused by those of Jerusalem of having eaten

things common[24] or of having broken the sabbath, or of any other crime of the like nature, he fled away to the Shechemites, and said that he was accused unjustly. About this time it was that Jaddua the high priest died, and Onias his son took the high priesthood. This was the state of the affairs of the people of Jerusalem at this time.

---

24. Here Josephus uses the very word *koinophagia* "eating things common," for "eating things unclean;" as does our New Testament, Acts x. 14,15, 28; xi. 8, 9; Rom. xiv. 14.

Book 12

Containing the Interval of a Hundred and Seventy Years, from the Death of Alexander the Great to the Death of Judas Maccabeus

1 *How Ptolemy the Son of Lagus Took Jerusalem and Judea by Deceit and Treachery, and Carried Many Thence, and Planted Them in Egypt*

1. NOW when Alexander, king of Macedon, had put an end to the dominion of the Persians, and had settled the affairs in Judea after the forementioned manner, he ended his life. And as his government fell among many, Antigonus obtained Asia, Seleucus Babylon; and of the other nations which were there, Lysimachus governed the Hellespont, and Cassander possessed Macedonia; as did Ptolemy the son of Lagus seize upon Egypt. And while these princes ambitiously strove one against another, every one for his own principality, it came to pass that there were continual wars, and those lasting wars too; and the cities were sufferers, and lost a great many of their inhabitants in these times of distress, insomuch that all Syria, by the means of Ptolemy the son of Lagus, underwent the reverse of that denomination of Savior, which he then had. He also seized upon Jerusalem, and for that end made use of deceit and treachery; for as he came into the city on a sabbath day, as if he would offer sacrifices[1] he, without any trouble,

1. Here Josephus uses the very word koinopltagia, "eating things common," for "eating things unclean;" as does our New Testament, Acts 10:14, 15, 28; 11:8, 9; Romans 14:14,

gained the city, while the Jews did not oppose him, for they did not suspect him to be their enemy; and he gained it thus, because they were free from suspicion of him, and because on that day they were at rest and quietness; and when he had gained it, he ruled over it in a cruel manner. Nay, Agatharchides of Cnidus, who wrote the acts of Alexander's successors, reproaches us with superstition, as if we, by it, had lost our liberty; where he says thus: "There is a nation called the nation of the Jews, who inhabit a city strong and great, named Jerusalem. These men took no care, but let it come into the hands of Ptolemy, as not willing to take arms, and thereby they submitted to be under a hard master, by reason of their unseasonable superstition." This is what Agatharchides relates of our nation. But when Ptolemy had taken a great many captives, both from the mountainous parts of Judea, and from the places about Jerusalem and Samaria, and the places near Mount Gerizzim, he led them all into Egypt,[2] and settled them there. And as he knew that the people of Jerusalem were most faithful in the observation of oaths and covenants; and this from the answer they made to Alexander, when he sent an embassage to them, after he had beaten Darius in battle; so he distributed many of them into garrisons, and at Alexandria gave them equal privileges of citizens with the Macedonians themselves; and required of them to take their oaths, that they would keep their fidelity to the posterity of those who committed these places to their care. Nay, there were not a few other Jews who, of their own accord, went into Egypt, as invited by the goodness of the soil, and by the liberality of Ptolemy. However, there were disoders among their posterity, with relation to

---

2. The great number of these Jews and Samaritans that were formerly carried into Egypt by Alexander, and now by Ptolemy the son of Lagus, appear afterwards in the vast multitude who as we shall see presently, were soon ransomed by Philadelphus, and by him made free, before he sent for the seventy-two interpreters; in the many garrisons and other soldiers of that nation in Egypt; in the famous settlement of Jews, and the number of their synagogues at Alexandria, long afterward; and in the vehement contention between the Jews and Samatitans under Philometer, about the place appointed for public worship in the law of Moses, whether at the Jewish temple of Jerusalem, or at the Samaritan temple of Gerizzim; of all which our author treats hereafter. And as to the Samaritans carried into Egypt under the same princes, Scaliger supposes that those who have a great synagogue at Cairo, as also those whom the Arabic geographer speaks of as having seized on an island in the Red Sea, are remains of them at this very day, as the notes here inform us.

the Samaritans, on account of their resolution to preserve that conduct of life which was delivered to them by their forefathers, and they thereupon contended one with another, while those of Jerusalem said that their temple was holy, and resolved to send their sacrifices thither; but the Samaritans were resolved that they should be sent to Mount Gerizzim.

2 *How Ptolemy Philadelphus Procured the Laws of the Jews to Be Translated into the Greek Tongue and Set Many Captives Free, and Dedicated Many Gifts to God*

1. WHEN Alexander had reigned twelve years, and after him Ptolemy Soter forty years, Philadelphus then took the kingdom of Egypt, and held it forty years within one. He procured the law to be interpreted, and set free those that were come from Jerusalem into Egypt, and were in slavery there, who were a hundred and twenty thousand. The occasion was this: Demetrius Phalerius, who was library keeper to the king, was now endeavoring, if it were possible, to gather together all the books that were in the habitable earth, and buying whatsoever was any where valuable, or agreeable to the king's inclination, (who was very earnestly set upon collecting of books,) to which inclination of his Demetrius was zealously subservient. And when once Ptolemy asked him how many ten thousands of books he had collected, he replied, that he had already about twenty times ten thousand; but that, in a little time, he should have fifty times ten thousand. But be said he had been informed that there were many books of laws among the Jews worthy of inquiring after, and worthy of the king's library, but which, being written in characters and in a dialect of their own, will cause no small pains in getting them translated into the Greek tongue;[3] that the character in which they are written seems to be like to that which is the proper character of the Syrians, and that its sound,

---

3. Of the translation of the other parts of the Old Testament by seventy Egyptian Jews, in the reigns of Ptolemy the son of Lagus, and Philadelphus; as also of the translation of the Pentateuch by seventy-two Jerusalem Jews, in the seventh year of Philadelphus at Alexandria, as given us an account of by Aristeus, and thence by Philo and Josephus, with a vindication of Aristeus's history; see the Appendix to Lit. Accorap. of Proph. at large, p. 117—152.

when pronounced, is like theirs also; and that this sound appears to be peculiar to themselves. Wherefore he said that nothing hindered why they might not get those books to be translated also; for while nothing is wanting that is necessary for that purpose, we may have their books also in this library. So the king thought that Demetrius was very zealous to procure him abundance of books, and that he suggested what was exceeding proper for him to do; and therefore he wrote to the Jewish high priest, that he should act accordingly.

2. Now there was one Aristeus, who was among the king's most intimate friends, and on account of his modesty very acceptable to him. This Aristeus resolved frequently, and that before now, to petition the king that he would set all the captive Jews in his kingdom free; and he thought this to be a convenient opportunity for the making that petition. So he discoursed, in the first place, with the captains of the king's guards, Sosibius of Tarentum, and Andreas, and persuaded them to assist him in what he was going to intercede with the king for. Accordingly Aristeus embraced the same opinion with those that have been before mentioned, and went to the king, and made the following speech to him: "It is not fit for us, O king, to overlook things hastily, or to deceive ourselves, but to lay the truth open. For since we have determined not only to get the laws of the Jews transcribed, but interpreted also, for thy satisfaction, by what means can we do this, while so many of the Jews are now slaves in thy kingdom? Do thou then what will be agreeable to thy magnanimity, and to thy good nature: free them from the miserable condition they are in, because that God, who supporteth thy kingdom, was the author of their laws as I have learned by particular inquiry; for both these people, and we also, worship the same God the framer of all things. We call him, and that truly, by the name of life, or Jupiter, because he breathes life into all men. Wherefore do thou restore these men to their own country, and this do to the honor of God, because these men pay a peculiarly excellent worship to him. And know this further, that though I be not of kin to them by birth, nor one of the same country with them, yet do I desire these favors to be done them, since all men are the workmanship of God; and I am sensible that he is well-pleased with those that do good. I do therefore put up this petition to thee, to do good to them."

3. When Aristeus was saying thus, the king looked upon him with a cheerful and joyful countenance, and said, "How many ten thousands dost thou suppose there are of such as want to be made free?" To which Andreas replied, as he stood by, and said," A few more than ten times ten thousand." The king made answer, "And is this a small gift that thou askest, Aristeus?" But Sosibius, and the rest that stood by, said that he ought to offer such a thank-offering as was worthy of his greatness of soul, to that God who had given him his kingdom. With this answer he was much pleased; and gave order, that when they paid the soldiers their wages, they should lay down [a hundred and] twenty drachmas[4] for every one of the slaves? And he promised to publish a magnificent decree, about what they requested, which should confirm what Aristeus had proposed, and especially what God willed should be done; whereby he said he would not only set those free who had been led away captive by his father and his army, but those who were in this kingdom before, and those also, if any such there were, who had been brought away since. And when they said that their redemption money would amount to above four hundred talents, he granted it. A copy of which decree I have determined to preserve, that the magnanimity of this king may be made known. Its contents were as follows: "Let ail those who were soldiers under our father, and who, when they overran Syria and Phoenicia, and laid waste Judea, took the Jews captives, and made them slaves, and brought them into our cities, and into this country, and then sold them; as also all those that were in my kingdom before them, and if there be any that have been lately brought thither,—be made free by those that possess them; and let them accept of [a hundred and] twenty drachmas for every slave.

4. Although this number one hundred and twenty drachmee [of Alexandria, or sixty Jewish shekels] be here three times repeated, and that in all Josephus's copies, Greek and Latin; yet since all the copies of Aristeus, whence Josephus took his relation, have this sum several times, and still as no more than twenty drachmae, or ten Jewish shekels; and since the sum of the talents, to be set down presently, which is little above four hundred and sixty, for somewhat more than one hundred thousand slaves, and is nearly the same in Josephus and Aristeus, does better agree to twenty than to one hundred and twenty drachmae; and since the value of a slave of old was at the utmost but thirty shekels, or sixty drachmae; see Exodus 21:32; while in the present circumstances of these Jewish slaves, and those so very numerous, Philadelphus would rather redeem them at a cheaper than at a dearer rate;—there is great reason to prefer here Aristeus's copies before Josephus's.

And let the soldiers receive this redemption money with their pay, but the rest out of the king's treasury: for I suppose that they were made captives without our father's consent, and against equity; and that their country was harassed by the insolence of the soldiers, and that, by removing them into Egypt, the soldiers have made a great profit by them. Out of regard therefore to justice, and out of pity to those that have been tyrannized over, contrary to equity, I enjoin those that have such Jews in their service to set them at liberty, upon the receipt of the before-mentioned sum; and that no one use any deceit about them, but obey what is here commanded. And I will that they give in their names within three days after the publication of this edict, to such as are appointed to execute the same, and to produce the slaves before them also, for I think it will be for the advantage of my affairs. And let every one that will inform against those that do not obey this decree, and I will that their estates be confiscated into the king's treasury." When this decree was read to the king, it at first contained the rest that is here inserted, and omitted only those Jews that had formerly been brought, and those brought afterwards, which had not been distinctly mentioned; so he added these clauses out of his humanity, and with great generosity. He also gave order that the payment, which was likely to be done in a hurry, should be divided among the king's ministers, and among the officers of his treasury. When this was over, what the king had decreed was quickly brought to a conclusion; and this in no more than seven days' time, the number of the talents paid for the captives being above four hundred and sixty, and this, because their masters required the [hundred and] twenty drachmas for the children also, the king having, in effect, commanded that these should be paid for, when he said in his decree, that they should receive the forementioned sum for every slave.

4. Now when this had been done after so magnificent a manner, according to the king's inclinations, he gave order to Demetrius to give him in writing his sentiments concerning the transcribing of the Jewish books; for no part of the administration is done rashly by these kings, but all things are managed with great circumspection. On which account I have subjoined a copy of these epistles, and set down the multitude of the vessels sent as gifts [to Jerusalem], and the construction of every one, that the exactness of the artificers' workmanship, as it appeared to those that saw them, and which

workman made every vessel, may be made manifest, and. this on account of the excellency of the vessels themselves. Now the copy of the epistle was to this purpose: "Demetrius to the great king. When thou, O king, gavest me a charge concerning the collection of books that were wanting to fill your library, and concerning the care that ought to be taken about such as are imperfect, I have used the utmost diligence about those matters. And I let you know, that we want the books of the Jewish legislation, with some others; for they are written in the Hebrew characters, and being in the language of that nation, are to us unknown. It hath also happened to them, that they have been transcribed more carelessly than they ought to have been, because they have not had hitherto royal care taken about them. Now it is necessary that thou shouldst have accurate copies of them. And indeed this legislation is full of hidden wisdom, and entirely blameless, as being the legislation of God; for which cause it is, as Hecateus of Abdera says, that the poets and historians make no mention of it, nor of those men who lead their lives according to it, since it is a holy law, and ought not to be published by profane mouths. If then it please thee, O king, thou mayst write to the high priest of the Jews, to send six of the elders out of every tribe, and those such as are most skillful of the laws, that by their means we may learn the clear and agreeing sense of these books, and may obtain an accurate interpretation of their contents, and so may have such a collection of these as may be suitable to thy desire."

5. When this epistle was sent to the king, he commanded that an epistle should be drawn up for Eleazar, the Jewish high priest, concerning these matters; and that they should inform him of the release of the Jews that had been in slavery among them. He also sent fifty talents of gold for the making of large basons, and vials, and cups, and an immense quantity of precious stones. He also gave order to those who had the custody of the chest that contained those stones, to give the artificers leave to choose out what sorts of them they pleased. He withal appointed, that a hundred talents in money should be sent to the temple for sacrifices, and for other uses. Now I will give a description of these vessels, and the manner of their construction, but not till after I have set down a copy of the epistle which was written to Eleazar the high priest, who had obtained that dignity on the occasion following: When Onias the high priest was dead, his son Simon became his successor. He was called Simon the

Just[5] because of both his piety towards God, and his kind disposition to those of his own nation. When he was dead, and had left a young son, who was called Onias, Simon's brother Eleazar, of whom we are speaking, took the high priesthood; and he it was to whom Ptolemy wrote, and that in the manner following: "King Ptolemy to Eleazar the high priest, sendeth greeting. There are many Jews who now dwell in my kingdom, whom the Persians, when they were in power, carried captives. These were honored by my father; some of them he placed in the army, and gave them greater pay than ordinary; to others of them, when they came with him into Egypt, he committed his garrisons, and the guarding of them, that they might be a terror to the Egyptians. And when I had taken the government, I treated all men with humanity, and especially those that are thy fellow citizens, of whom I have set free above a hundred thousand that were slaves, and paid the price of their redemption to their masters out of my own revenues; and those that are of a fit age, I have admitted into them number of my soldiers. And for such as are capable of being faithful to me, and proper for my court, I have put them in such a post, as thinking this [kindness done to them] to be a very great and an acceptable gift, which I devote to God for his providence over me. And as I am desirous to do what will be grateful to these, and to all the other Jews in the habitable earth, I have determined to procure an interpretation of your law, and to have it translated out of Hebrew into Greek, and to be deposited in my library. Thou wilt therefore do well to choose out and send to me men of a good character, who are now elders in age, and six in number out of every tribe. These, by their age, must be skillful in the laws, and of abilities to make an accurate interpretation of them; and when this shall be finished, I shall think that I have done a work glorious to myself. And I have sent to thee Andreas, the captain of my guard, and Aristeus, men whom I have in very great esteem; by whom I have sent those first-fruits which I have dedicated to the temple, and to the sacrifices, and to other uses, to the value of a hundred talents. And if thou wilt send to us, to let us know what thou wouldst have further, thou wilt do a thing acceptable to me."

---

5. We have a very great encomium of this Simon the Just, the son of Onias, in the fiftieth chapter of the Ecclesiasticus, through the whole chapter. Nor is it improper to consult that chapter itself upon this occasion.

6. When this epistle of the king was brought to Eleazar, he wrote an answer to it with all the respect possible: "Eleazar the high priest to king Ptolemy, sendeth greeting. If thou and thy queen Arsinoe,[6] and thy children, be well, we are entirely satisfied. When we received thy epistle, we greatly rejoiced at thy intentions; and when the multitude were gathered together, we read it to them, and thereby made them sensible of the piety thou hast towards God. We also showed them the twenty vials of gold, and thirty of silver, and the five large basons, and the table for the shew-bread; as also the hundred talents for the sacrifices, and for the making what shall be needful at the temple; which things Andreas and Aristeus, those most honored friends of thine, have brought us; and truly they are persons of an excellent character, and of great learning, and worthy of thy virtue. Know then that we will gratify thee in what is for thy advantage, though we do what we used not to do before; for we ought to make a return for the numerous acts of kindness which thou hast done to our countrymen. We immediately, therefore, offered sacrifices for thee and thy sister, with thy children and friends; and the multitude made prayers, that thy affairs may be to thy mind, and that thy kingdom may be preserved in peace, and that the translation of our law may come to the conclusion thou desirest, and be for thy advantage. We have also chosen six elders out of every tribe, whom we have sent, and the law with them. It will be thy part, out of thy piety and justice, to send back the law, when it hath been translated, and to return those to us that bring it in safety. Farewell."

7. This was the reply which the high priest made. But it does not seem to me to be necessary to set down the names of the seventy [two] elders who were sent by Eleazar, and carried the law, which yet were subjoined at the end of the epistle. However, I thought it not improper to give an account of those very valuable and artificially contrived vessels which the king sent to God, that all may see how great a regard

---

6. When we have here and presently mention made of Philadelphus's queen and sister Arsinoe, we are to remember, with Spanheim, that Arsinoe was both his sister and his wife, according to the old custom of Persia, and of Egypt at this very time; nay, of the Assyrians long afterwards. See Antiq. B. XX. ch. 2. sect. 1. Whence we have, upon the coins of Philadelphus, this known inscription, "The divine brother and sister."

the king had for God; for the king allowed a vast deal of expenses for these vessels, and came often to the workmen, and viewed their works, and suffered nothing of carelessness or negligence to be any damage to their operations. And I will relate how rich they were as well as I am able, although perhaps the nature of this history may not require such a description; but I imagine I shall thereby recommend the elegant taste and magnanimity of this king to those that read this history.

8. And first I will describe what belongs to the table. It was indeed in the king's mind to make this table vastly large in its dimensions; but then he gave orders that they should learn what was the magnitude of the table which was already at Jerusalem, and how large it was, and whether there was a possibility of making one larger than it. And when he was informed how large that was which was already there, and that nothing hindered but a larger might be made, he said that he was willing to have one made that should be five times as large as the present table; but his fear was, that it might be then useless in their sacred ministrations by its too great largeness; for he desired that the gifts he presented them should not only be there for show, but should be useful also in their sacred ministrations. According to which reasoning, that the former table was made of so moderate a size for use, and not for want of gold, he resolved that he would not exceed the former table in largeness; but would make it exceed it in the variety and elegancy of its materials. And as he was sagacious in observing the nature of all things, and in having a just notion of what was new and surprising, and where there was no sculptures, he would invent such as were proper by his own skill, and would show them to the workmen, he commanded that such sculptures should now be made, and that those which were delineated should be most accurately formed by a constant regard to their delineation.

9. When therefore the workmen had undertaken to make the table, they framed it in length two cubits [and a half], in breadth one cubit, and in height one cubit and a half; and the entire structure of the work was of gold. They withal made a crown of a hand-breadth round it, with wave-work wreathed about it, and with an engraving which imitated a cord, and was admirably turned on its three parts; for as they were of a triangular figure, every angle had the same disposition of its sculptures, that when you turned them about, the very same form of them was turned about without any variation. Now that part

of the crown-work that was enclosed under the table had its sculptures very beautiful; but that part which went round on the outside was more elaborately adorned with most beautiful ornaments, because it was exposed to sight, and to the view of the spectators; for which reason it was that both those sides which were extant above the rest were acute, and none of the angles, which we before told you were three, appeared less than another, when the table was turned about. Now into the cordwork thus turned were precious stones inserted, in rows parallel one to the other, enclosed in golden buttons, which had ouches in them; but the parts which were on the side of the crown, and were exposed to the sight, were adorned with a row of oval figures obliquely placed, of the most excellent sort of precious stones, which imitated rods laid close, and encompassed the table round about. But under these oval figures, thus engraven, the workmen had put a crown all round it, where the nature of all sorts of fruit was represented, insomuch that the bunches of grapes hung up. And when they had made the stones to represent all the kinds of fruit before mentioned, and that each in its proper color, they made them fast with gold round the whole table. The like disposition of the oval figures, and of the engraved rods, was framed under the crown, that the table might on each side show the same appearance of variety and elegancy of its ornaments; so that neither the position of the wave-work nor of the crown might be different, although the table were turned on the other side, but that the prospect of the same artificial contrivances might be extended as far as the feet; for there was made a plate of gold four fingers broad, through the entire breadth of the table, into which they inserted the feet, and then fastened them to the table by buttons and button-holes, at the place where the crown was situate, that so on what side soever of the table one should stand, it might exhibit the very same view of the exquisite workmanship, and of the vast expeses bestowed upon it: but upon the table itself they engraved a meander, inserting into it very valuable stones in the middle like stars, of various colors; the carbuncle and the emerald, each of which sent out agreeable rays of light to the spectators; with such stones of other sorts also as were most curious and best esteemed, as being most precious in their kind. Hard by this meander a texture of net-work ran round it, the middle of which appeared like a rhombus, into which were inserted rock-crystal and amber, which, by the great resemblance of the appearance they made, gave wonderful delight to those that saw them. The chapiters of the feet imitated the first buddings of lilies, while their leaves were bent and laid under the table, but so that the chives were seen standing upright within them. Their bases were made of a carbuncle; and the place at the bottom, which rested on that carbuncle, was one palm deep, and eight fingers in breadth. Now they had engraven upon it with a very fine tool, and with a great deal of pains, a branch of ivy and tendrils of the vine, sending forth clusters of grapes, that you would guess they were nowise different from real tendrils; for they were so very thin, and so very far extended at their extremities, that they were moved with the wind, and made one believe that they were the product of nature, and not the representation of art. They also made the entire workmanship of the table appear to be threefold, while the joints of the several parts were so united together as to be invisible, and the places where they joined could not be distinguished. Now the thickness of the table was not less than half a cubit. So that this gift, by the king's great generosity, by the great value of the materials, and the variety of its exquisite structure, and the artificer's skill in imitating nature with graying tools, was at length brought to perfection, while the king was very desirous, that though in largeness it were not to be different from that which was already dedicated to God, yet that in exquisite workmanship, and the novelty of the contrivances, and in the splendor of its construction, it should far exceed it, and be more illustrious than that was.

10. Now of the cisterns of gold there were two, whose sculpture was of scale-work, from its basis to its belt-like circle, with various sorts of stones enchased in the spiral circles. Next to which there was upon it a meander of a cubit in height; it was composed of stones of all sorts of colors. And next to this was the rod-work engraven; and next to that was a rhombus in a texture of net-work, drawn out to the brim of the basin, while small shields, made of stones, beautiful in their kind, and of four fingers' depth, filled up the middle parts. About the top of the basin were wreathed the leaves of lilies, and of the convolvulus, and the tendrils of vines in a circular manner. And this was the construction of the two cisterns of gold, each containing two firkins. But those which were of silver were much more bright and splendid than looking-glasses, and you might in them see the images that fell upon them more plainly than in the other. The king also

ordered thirty vials; those of which the parts that were of gold, and filled up with precious stones, were shadowed over with the leaves of ivy and of vines, artificially engraven. And these were the vessels that were after an extraordinary manner brought to this perfection, partly by the skill of the workmen, who were admirable in such fine work, but much more by the diligence and generosity of the king, who not only supplied the artificers abundantly, and with great generosity, with what they wanted, but he forbade public audiences for the time, and came and stood by the workmen, and saw the whole operation. And this was the cause why the workmen were so accurate in their performance, because they had regard to the king, and to his great concern about the vessels, and so the more indefatigably kept close to the work.

11. And these were what gifts were sent by Ptolemy to Jerusalem, and dedicated to God there. But when Eleazar the high priest had devoted them to God, and had paid due respect to those that brought them, and had given them presents to be carried to the king, he dismissed them. And when they were come to Alexandria, and Ptolemy heard that they were come,and that the seventy elders were come also, he presently sent for Andreas and Aristens, his ambassadors, who came to him, and delivered him the epistle which they brought him from the high priest, and made answer to all the questions he put to them by word of mouth. He then made haste to meet the elders that came from Jerusalem for the interpretation of the laws; and he gave command, that every body who came on other occasions should be sent away, which was a thing surprising, and what he did not use to do; for those that were drawn thither upon such occasions used to come to him on the fifth day, but ambassadors at the month's end. But when he had sent those away, he waited for these that were sent by Eleazar; but as the old men came in with the presents, which the high priest had given them to bring to the king, and with the membranes, upon which they had their laws written in golden letters[7] he put questions to them concerning those books; and when they had taken off the covers wherein they were wrapt up, they showed him

7. The Talmudists say, that it is not lawful to write the law in letters of gold, contrary to this certain and very ancient example. See Hudson's and Reland's notes here.

the membranes. So the king stood admiring the thinness of those membranes, and the exactness of the junctures, which could not be perceived; (so exactly were they connected one with another;) and this he did for a considerable time. He then said that he returned them thanks for coming to him, and still greater thanks to him that sent them; and, above all, to that God whose laws they appeared to be. Then did the elders, and those that were present with them, cry out with one voice, and wished all happiness to the king. Upon which he fell into tears by the violence of the pleasure he had, it being natural to men to afford the same indications in great joy that they do under sorrows. And when he had bid them deliver the books to those that were appointed to receive them, he saluted the men, and said that it was but just to discourse, in the first place, of the errand they were sent about, and then to address himself to themselves. He promised, however, that he would make this day on which they came to him remarkable and eminent every year through the whole course of his life; for their coming to him, and the victory which he gained over Antigonus by sea, proved to be on the very same day. He also gave orders that they should sup with him; and gave it in charge that they should have excellent lodgings provided for them in the upper part of the city.

12. Now he that was appointed to take care of the reception of strangers, Nicanor by name, called for Dorotheus, whose duty it was to make provision for them, and bid him prepare for every one of them what should be requisite for their diet and way of living; which thing was ordered by the king after this manner: he took care that those that belonged to every city, which did not use the same way of living, that all things should be prepared for them according to the custom of those that came to him, that, being feasted according to the usual method of their own way of living, they might be the better pleased, and might not be uneasy at any thing done to them from which they were naturally averse. And this was now done in the case of these men by Dorotheus, who was put into this office because of his great skill in such matters belonging to common life; for he took care of all such matters as concerned the reception of strangers, and appointed them double seats for them to sit on, according as the king had commanded him to do; for he had commanded that half of their seats should be set at his right hand, and the other half behind his

table, and took care that no respect should be omitted that could be shown them. And when they were thus set down, he bid Dorotheus to minister to all those that were come to him from Judea, after the manner they used to be ministered to; for which cause he sent away their sacred heralds, and those that slew the sacrifices, and the rest that used to say grace; but called to one of those that were come to him, whose name was Eleazar, who w a priest, and desired him to say grace;[8] who then stood in the midst of them, and prayed, that all prosperity might attend the king, and those that were his subjects. Upon which an acclamation was made by the whole company, with joy and a great noise; and when that. was over, they fell to eating their supper, and to the enjoyment of what was set before them. And at a little interval afterward, when the king thought a sufficient time had been interposed, he began to talk philosophically to them, and he asked every one of them a philosophical question[9] and such a one as might give light in those inquiries; and when they had explained all the problems that had been proposed by the king about every point, he was well-pleased with their answers. This took up the twelve days in which they were treated; and he that pleases may learn the particular questions in that book of Aristeus, which he wrote on this very occasion.

13. And while not the king only, but the philosopher Menedemus also, admired them, and said that all things were governed by Providence, and that it was probable that thence it was that such force or beauty was discovered in these men's words, they then left off asking any more such questions. But the king said that he had gained very great advantages by their coming, for that he had received this profit from them, that he had learned how he ought to rule his subjects. And

---

8. This is the most ancient example I have met with of a grace, or short prayer, or thanksgiving before meat; which, as it is used to be said by a heathen priest, was now said by Eleazar, a Jewish priest, who was one of these seventy-two interpreters. The next example I have met with, is that of the Essenes, (Of the War, B. II. ch. 8. sect. 5,) both before and after it; those of our Savior before it, Mark 8:6; John 6:11, 23; and St. Paul, Acts 27:35; and a form of such a grace or prayer for Christians, at the end of the fifth book of the Apostolical Constitutions, which seems to have been intended for both times, both before and after meat.

9. They were rather political questions and answers, tending to the good and religious government of mankind.

he gave order that they should have every one three talents given them, and that those that were to conduct them to their lodging should do it. Accordingly, when three days were over, Demetrius took them, and went over the causeway seven furlongs long: it was a bank in the sea to an island. And when they had gone over the bridge, he proceeded to the northern parts, and showed them where they should meet, which was in a house that was built near the shore, and was a quiet place, and fit for their discoursing together about their work. When he had brought them thither, he entreated them (now they had all things about them which they wanted for the interpretation of their law) that they would suffer nothing to interrupt them in their work. Accordingly, they made an accurate interpretation, with great zeal and great pains, and this they continued to do till the ninth hour of the day; after which time they relaxed, and took care of their body, while their food was provided for them in great plenty: besides, Dorotheus, at the king's command, brought them a great deal of what was provided for the king himself. But in the morning they came to the court and saluted Ptolemy, and then went away to their former place, where, when they had washed their hands,[10] and purified themselves, they betook themselves to the interpretation of the laws. Now when the law was transcribed, and the labor of interpretation was over, which came to its conclusion in seventy-two days, Demetrius gathered all the Jews together to the place where the laws were translated, and where the interpreters were, and read them over. The multitude did also approve of those elders that were the interpreters of the law. They withal commended Demetrius for his proposal, as the inventor of what was greatly for their happiness; and they desired that he would give leave to their rulers also to read the law. Moreover, they all, both the priest and the ancientest of the elders, and the principal men of their commonwealth, made it their request, that since the interpretation was happily finished, it might continue in the state it now was, and might

---

10. This purification of the interpreters, by washing in the sea, before they prayed to God every morning, and before they set about translating, may be compared with the like practice of Peter the apostle, in the Recognitions of Clement, B. IV. ch. 3., and B. V. ch. 36., and with the places of the Proseuchre, or of prayer, which were sometimes built near the sea or rivers also; of which matter see Antiq. B. XIV. ch. 10. sect. 9,3; Acts 16:13. 16.

not be altered. And when they all commended that determination of theirs, they enjoined, that if any one observed either any thing superfluous, or any thing omitted, that he would take a view of it again, and have it laid before them, and corrected; which was a wise action of theirs, that when the thing was judged to have been well done, it might continue for ever.

14. So the king rejoiced when he saw that his design of this nature was brought to perfection, to so great advantage; and he was chiefly delighted with hearing the Laws read to him; and was astonished at the deep meaning and wisdom of the legislator. And he began to discourse with Demetrius, "How it came to pass, that when this legislation was so wonderful, no one, either of the poets or of the historians, had made mention of it." Demetrius made answer, "that no one durst be so bold as to touch upon the description of these laws, because they were Divine and venerable, and because some that had attempted it were afflicted by God." He also told him, that "Theopompus was desirous of writing somewhat about them, but was thereupon disturbed in his mind for above thirty days' time; and upon some intermission of his distemper, he appeased God [by prayer], as suspecting that his madness proceeded from that cause." Nay, indeed, he further saw in a dream, that his distemper befell him while he indulged too great a curiosity about Divine matters, and was desirous of publishing them among common men; but when he left off that attempt, he recovered his understanding again. Moreover, he informed him of Theodectes, the tragic poet, concerning whom it was reported, that when in a certain dramatic representation he was desirous to make mention of things that were contained in the sacred books, he was afflicted with a darkness in his eyes; and that upon his being conscious of the occasion of his distemper, and appeasing God [by prayer], he was freed from that affliction.

15. And when the king had received these books from Demetrius, as we have said already, he adored them, and gave order that great care should be taken of them, that they might remain uncorrupted. He also desired that the interpreters would come often to him out of Judea, and that both on account of the respects that he would pay them, and on account of the presents he would make them; for he said it was now but just to send them away, although if, of their own accord, they would come to him hereafter, they should obtain all that their

own wisdom might justly require, and what his generosity was able to give them. So he then sent them away, and gave to every one of them three garments of the best sort, and two talents of gold, and a cup of the value of one talent, and the furniture of the room wherein they were feasted. And these were the things he presented to them. But by them he sent to Eleazar the high priest ten beds, with feet of silver, and the furniture to them belonging, and a cup of the value of thirty talents; and besides these, ten garments, and purple, and a very beautiful crown, and a hundred pieces of the finest woven linen; as also vials and dishes, and vessels for pouring, and two golden cisterns to be dedicated to God. He also desired him, by an epistle, that he would give these interpreters leave, if any of them were desirous of coming to him, because he highly valued a conversation with men of such learning, and should be very willing to lay out his wealth upon such men. And this was what came to the Jews, and was much to their glory and honor, from Ptolemy Philadelphus.

3 *How the Kings of Asia Honored the Nation of the Jews and Made Them Citizens of Those Cities Which They Built*

1. THE Jews also obtained honors from the kings of Asia when they became their auxiliaries; for Seleucus Nicator made them citizens in those cities which he built in Asia, and in the lower Syria, and in the metropolis itself, Antioch; and gave them privileges equal to those of the Macedonians and Greeks, who were the inhabitants, insomuch that these privileges continue to this very day: an argument for which you have in this, that whereas the Jews do not make use of oil prepared by foreigners,[11] they receive a certain sum of money from the proper officers belonging to their exercises as the value of that oil; which money, when the people of Antioch would have deprived them of,

11. The use of oil was much greater, and the donatives of it much more valuable, in Judea, and the neighboring countries, than it is amongst us. It was also, in the days of Josephus, thought unlawful for Jews to make use of any oil that was prepared by heathens, perhaps on account of some superstitions intermixed with its preparation by those heathens. When therefore the heathens were to make them a donative of oil,: they paid them money instead of it. See Of the War, B. II. ch. 21. sect. 2; the Life of Josephus, sect. 13; and Hudson's note on the place before us.

in the last war, Mucianus, who was then president of Syria, preserved it to them. And when the people of Alexandria and of Antioch did after that, at the time that Vespasian and Titus his son governed the habitable earth, pray that these privileges of citizens might be taken away, they did not obtain their request. in which behavior any one may discern the equity and generosity of the Romans,[12] especially of Vespasian and Titus, who, although they had been at a great deal of pains in the war against the Jews, and were exasperated against them, because they did not deliver up their weapons to them, but continued the war to the very last, yet did not they take away any of their forementioned privileges belonging to them as citizens, but restrained their anger, and overcame the prayers of the Alexandrians and Antiochians, who were a very powerful people, insomuch that they did not yield to them, neither out of their favor to these people, nor out of their old grudge at those whose wicked opposition they had subdued in the war; nor would they alter any of the ancient favors granted to the Jews, but said, that those who had borne arms against them, and fought them, had suffered punishment already, and that it was not just to deprive those that had not offended of the privileges they enjoyed.

2. We also know that Marcus Agrippa was of the like disposition towards the Jews: for when the people of Ionia were very angry at them, and besought Agrippa that they, and they only, might have those privileges of citizens which Antiochus, the grandson of Seleucus, (who by the Greeks was called *The God,*) had bestowed on them, and desired that, if the Jews were to be joint-partakers with them, they might be obliged to worship the gods they themselves worshipped: but when these matters were brought to the trial, the Jews prevailed, and obtained leave to make use of their own customs, and this under the patronage of Nicolaus of Damascus; for Agrippa gave sentence that he could not innovate. And if any one hath a mind to know this

12. This, and the like great and just characters, of the justice, and equity. and generosity of the old Romans, both to the Jews and other conquered nations, affords us a very good reason why Almighty God, upon the rejection of the Jews for their wickedness, chose them for his people, and first established Christianity in that empire; of which matter see Josephus here, sect. 2; as also Antiq. B. XIV. ch. 10. sect. 22, 23; B. XVI. ch. 2. sect. 4.

matter accurately, let him peruse the hundred and twenty-third and hundred and twenty-fourth books of the history of this Nicolaus. Now as to this determination of Agrippa, it is not so much to be admired, for at that time our nation had not made war against the Romans. But one may well be astonished at the generosity of Vespasian and Titus, that after so great wars and contests which they had from us, they should use such moderation. But I will now return to that part of my history whence I made the present digression.

3. Now it happened that in the reign of Antiochus the Great, who ruled over all Asia, that the Jews, as well as the inhabitants of Celesyria, suffered greatly, and their land was sorely harassed; for while he was at war with Ptolemy Philopater, and with his son, who was called Epiphanes, it fell out that these nations were equally sufferers, both when he was beaten, and when he beat the others: so that they were very like to a ship in a storm, which is tossed by the waves on both sides; and just thus were they in their situation in the middle between Antiochus's prosperity and its change to adversity. But at length, when Antiochus had beaten Ptolemy, he seized upon Judea; and when Philopater was dead, his son sent out a great army under Scopas, the general of his forces, against the inhabitants of Celesyria, who took many of their cities, and in particular our nation; which when he fell upon them, went over to him. Yet was it not long afterward when Antiochus overcame Scopas, in a battle fought at the fountains of Jordan, and destroyed a great part of his army. But afterward, when Antiochus subdued those cities of Celesyria which Scopas had gotten into his possession, and Samaria with them, the Jews, of their own accord, went over to him, and received him into the city [Jerusalem], and gave plentiful provision to all his army, and to his elephants, and readily assisted him when he besieged the garrison which was in the citadel of Jerusalem. Wherefore Antiochus thought it but just to requite the Jews' diligence and zeal in his service. So he wrote to the generals of his armies, and to his friends, and gave testimony to the good behavior of the Jews towards him, and informed them what rewards he had resolved to bestow on them for that their behavior. I will set down presently the epistles themselves which he wrote to the generals concerning them, but will first produce the testimony of Polybius of Megalopolis; for thus does he speak, in the sixteenth book of his history: "Now Scopas, the general of

Ptolemy's army, went in haste to the superior parts of the country, and in the winter time overthrew the nation of the Jews?' He also saith, in the same book, that "when Seopas was conquered by Antiochus, Antiochus received Batanea, and Samaria, and Abila, and Gadara; and that, a while afterwards, there came in to him those Jews that inhabited near that temple which was called Jerusalem; concerning which, although I have more to say, and particularly concerning the presence of God about that temple, yet do I put off that history till another opportunity." This it is which Polybius relates. But we will return to the series of the history, when we have first produced the epistles of king Antiochus.

King Antiochus to Ptolemy, Sendeth Greeting

"Since the Jews, upon our first entrance on their country, demonstrated their friendship towards us, and when we came to their city [Jerusalem], received us in a splendid manner, and came to meet us with their senate, and gave abundance of provisions to our soldiers, and to the elephants, and joined with us in ejecting the garrison of the Egyptians that were in the citadel, we have thought fit to reward them, and to retrieve the condition of their city, which hath been greatly depopulated by such accidents as have befallen its inhabitants, and to bring those that have been scattered abroad back to the city. And, in the first place, we have determined, on account of their piety towards God, to bestow on them, as a pension, for their sacrifices of animals that are fit for sacrifice, for wine, and oil, and frankincense, the value of twenty thousand pieces of silver, and [six] sacred artabrae of fine flour, with one thousand four hundred and sixty medimni of wheat, and three hundred and seventy-five medimni of salt. And these payments I would have fully paid them, as I have sent orders to you. I would also have the work about the temple finished, and the cloisters, and if there be any thing else that ought to be rebuilt. And for the materials of wood, let it be brought them out of Judea itself and out of the other countries, and out of Libanus tax free; and the same I would have observed as to those other materials which will be necessary, in order to render the temple more glorious; and let all of that nation live according to the laws of their own country; and let the senate, and the priests, and the scribes of the temple, and the sacred singers, be discharged from poll-money and the crown tax and other taxes also. And that the city may the sooner recover its inhabitants, I grant a discharge from taxes for three years to its present inhabitants, and to such as shall come to it, until the month Hyperheretus. We also discharge them for the future from a third part of their taxes, that the losses they have sustained may be repaired. And all those citizens that have been carried away, and are become slaves, we grant them and their children their freedom, and give order that their substance be restored to them."

4. And these were the contents of this epistle. He also published a decree through all his kingdom in honor of the temple, which contained what follows: "It shall be lawful for no foreigner to come within the limits of the temple round about; which thing is forbidden also to the Jews, unless to those who, according to their own custom, have purified themselves. Nor let any flesh of horses, or of mules, or of asses, he brought into the city, whether they be wild or tame; nor that of leopards, or foxes, or hares; and, in general, that of any animal which is forbidden for the Jews to eat. Nor let their skins be brought into it; nor let any such animal be bred up in the city. Let them only be permitted to use the sacrifices derived from their forefathers, with which they have been obliged to make acceptable atonements to God. And he that transgresseth any of these orders, let him pay to the priests three thousand drachmae of silver." Moreover, this Antiochus bare testimony to our piety and fidelity, in an epistle of his, written when he was informed of a sedition in Phrygia and Lydia, at which time he was in the superior provinces, wherein he commanded Zenxis, the general of his forces, and his most intimate friend, to send some of our nation out of Babylon into Phrygia. The epistle was this:

King Antiochus to Zeuxis His Father, Sendeth Greeting

"If you are in health, it is well. I also am in health. Having been informed that a sedition is arisen in Lydia and Phrygia, I thought that matter required great care; and upon advising with my friends what was fit to be done, it hath been thought proper to remove two thousand families of Jews, with their effects, out of Mesopotamia and Babylon, unto the castles and places that lie most convenient; for I am persuaded that they will be well-disposed guardians of our possessions, because of their piety towards God, and because I know that my predecessors have borne witness to them, that they are faithful, and with alacrity do what they are desired to do. I will, therefore, though it be a laborious work, that thou remove these Jews, under a promise, that they shall be permitted to use their own laws. And when thou shalt have brought them to the places forementioned, thou shalt give everyone of their families a place for building their houses, and a portion of the land for their husbandry, and for the plantation of their vines; and thou shalt discharge them from paying taxes of the fruits of the earth for ten years; and let them have a proper quantity of wheat for the maintenance of their servants, until they receive bread corn out of the earth; also let a sufficient share be given to such as minister to them in the necessaries of life, that by enjoying the effects of our humanity, they may show themselves the more willing and ready about our affairs. Take care likewise of that nation, as far as thou art able, that they may not have any disturbance given them by any one." Now these testimonials which I have produced are sufficient to declare the friendship that Antiochus the Great bare to the Jews.

4 *How Antiochus Made a League with Ptolemy and How Onias Provoked Ptolemy Euergetes to Anger; and How Joseph Brought All Things Right Again, and Entered into Friendship with Him; and What Other Things Were Done by Joseph, and His Son Hyrcanus*

1. AFTER this Antiochus made a friendship and league with Ptolemy, and gave him his daughter Cleopatra to wife, and yielded up to him Celesyria, and Samaria, and Judea, and Phoenicia, by way of dowry. And upon the division of the taxes between the two kings, all the principal men framed the taxes of their several countries, and collecting the sum that was settled for them, paid the same to the [two] kings. Now at this time the Samaritans were in a flourishing condition, and much distressed the Jews, cutting off parts of their land, and carrying off slaves. This happened when Onias was high priest; for after Eleazar's death, his uncle Manasseh took the priesthood, and after he had ended his life, Onias received that dignity. He was the son of Simon, who was called *The Just:* which Simon was the brother

of Eleazar, as I said before. This Onias was one of a little soul, and a great lover of money; and for that reason, because he did not pay that tax of twenty talents of silver, which his forefathers paid to these things out of their own estates, he provoked king Ptolemy Euergetes to anger, who was the father of Philopater. Euergetes sent an ambassador to Jerusalem, and complained that Onias did not pay his taxes, and threatened, that if he did not receive them, he would seize upon their land, and send soldiers to live upon it. When the Jews heard this message of the king, they were confounded; but so sordidly covetous was Onias, that nothing of things nature made him ashamed.

2. There was now one Joseph, young in age, but of great reputation among the people of Jerusalem, for gravity, prudence, and justice. His father's name was Tobias; and his mother was the sister of Onias the high priest, who informed him of the coming of the ambassador; for he was then sojourning at a village named Phicol,[13] where he was born. Hereupon he came to the city [Jerusalem], and reproved Onias for not taking care of the preservation of his countrymen, but bringing the nation into dangers, by not paying this money. For which preservation of them, he told him he had received the authority over them, and had been made high priest; but that, in case he was so great a lover of money, as to endure to see his country in danger on that account, and his countrymen suffer the greatest damages, he advised him to go to the king, and petition him to remit either the whole or a part of the sum demanded. Onias's answer was this: That he did not care for his authority, and that he was ready, if the thing were practicable, to lay down his high priesthood; and that he would not go to the king, because he troubled not himself at all about such matters. Joseph then asked him if he would not give him leave to go ambassador on behalf of the nation. He replied, that he would give him leave. Upon which Joseph went up into the temple, and called the multitude together to a congregation, and exhorted them not to be disturbed nor aftrighted, because of his uncle Onias's carelessness, but desired them to be at rest, and not terrify themselves with fear about it; for he promised them

---

13. The name of this place, Phicol, is the very same with that of the chief captain of Abimelech's host, in the days of Abraham, Genesis 21:22, and might possibly be the place of that Phicol's nativity or abode, for it seems to have been in the south part of Palestine, as that was.

that he would be their ambassador to the king, and persuade him that they had done him no wrong. And when the multitude heard this, they returned thanks to Joseph. So he went down from the temple, and treated Ptolemy's ambassador in a hospitable manner. He also presented him with rich gifts, and feasted him magnificently for many days, and then sent him to the king before him, and told him that he would soon follow him; for he was now more willing to go to the king, by the encouragement of the ambassador, who earnestly persuaded him to come into Egypt, and promised him that he would take care that he should obtain every thing that he desired of Ptolemy; for he was highly pleased with his frank and liberal temper, and with the gravity of his deportment.

3. When Ptolemy's ambassador was come into Egypt, he told the king of the thoughtless temper of Onias; and informed him of the goodness of the disposition of Joseph; and that he was coming to him to excuse the multitude, as not having done him any harm, for that he was their patron. In short, he was so very large in his encomiums upon the young man, that he disposed both the king and his wife Cleopatra to have a kindness for him before he came. So Joseph sent to his friends at Samaria, and borrowed money of them, and got ready what was necessary for his journey, garments and cups, and beasts for burden, which amounted to about twenty thousand drachmae, and went to Alexandria. Now it happened that at this time all the principal men and rulers went up out of the cities of Syria and Phoenicia, to bid for their taxes; for every year the king sold them to the men of the greatest power in every city. So these men saw Joseph journeying on the way, and laughed at him for his poverty and meanness. But when he came to Alexandria, and heard that king Ptolemy was at Memphis, be went up thither to meet with him; which happened as the king was sitting in his chariot, with his wife, and with his friend Athenion, who was the very person who had been ambassador at Jerusalem, and had been entertained by Joseph. As soon therefore as Athenion saw him, he presently made him known to the king, how good and generous a young man he was. So Ptolemy saluted him first, and desired him to come up into his chariot; and as Joseph sat there, he began to complain of the management of Onias: to which he answered, "Forgive him, on account of his age; for thou canst not certainly be unacquainted with this, that old men and infants have their minds exactly alike; but thou

shalt have from us, who are young men, every thing thou desirest, and shalt have no cause to complain." With this good humor and pleasantry of the young man, the king was so delighted, that he began already, as though he had had long experience of him, to have a still greater affection for him, insomuch that he bade him take his diet in the king's palace, and be a guest at his own table every day. But when the king was come to Alexandria, the principal men of Syria saw him sitting with the king, and were much offended at it.

4. And when the day came on which the king was to let the taxes of the cities to farm, and those that were the principal men of dignity in their several countries were to bid for them, the sum of the taxes together, of Celesyria, and Phoenicia, and Judea, with Samaria, [as they were bidden for,] came to eight thousand talents. Hereupon Joseph accused the bidders, as having agreed together to estimate the value of the taxes at too low a rate; and he promised that he would himself give twice as much for them: but for those who did not pay, he would send the king home their whole substance; for this privilege was sold together with the taxes themselves. The king was pleased to hear that offer; and because it augmented his revenues, he said he would confirm the sale of the taxes to him. But when he asked him this question, Whether he had any sureties that would be bound for the payment of the money? he answered very pleasantly, "I will give such security, and those of persons good and responsible, and which you shall have no reason to distrust." And when he bid him name them who they were, he replied, "I give thee no other persons, O king, for my sureties, than thyself, and this thy wife; and you shall be security for both parties." So Ptolemy laughed at the proposal, and granted him the farming of the taxes without any sureties. This procedure was a sore grief to those that came from the cities into Egypt, who were utterly disappointed; and they returned every one to their own country with shame.

5. But Joseph took with him two thousand foot soldiers from the king, for he desired he might have some assistance, in order to force such as were refractory in the cities to pay. And borrowing of the king's friends at Alexandria five hundred talents, he made haste back into Syria. And when he was at Askelon, and demanded the taxes of the people of Askelon, they refused to pay any thing, and affronted him also; upon which he seized upon about twenty of the principal men,

and slew them, and gathered what they had together, and sent it all to the king, and informed him what he had done. Ptolemy admired the prudent conduct of the man, and commended him for what he had done, and gave him leave to do as he pleased. When the Syrians heard of this, they were astonished; and having before them a sad example in the men of Askelon that were slain, they opened their gates, and willingly admitted Joseph, and paid their taxes. And when the inhabitants of Scythopolis attempted to affront him, and would not pay him those taxes which they formerly used to pay, without disputing about them, he slew also the principal men of that city, and sent their effects to the king. By this means he gathered great wealth together, and made vast gains by this farming of the taxes; and he made use of what estate he had thus gotten, in order to support his authority, as thinking it a piece of prudence to keep what had been the occasion and foundation of his present good fortune; and this he did by the assistance of what he was already possessed of, for he privately sent many presents to the king, and to Cleopatra, and to their friends, and to all that were powerful about the court, and thereby purchased their good-will to himself.

6. This good fortune he enjoyed for twenty-two years, and was become the father of seven sons by one wife; he had also another son, whose name was Hyrcanus, by his brother Solymius's daughter, whom he married on the following occasion. He once came to Alexandria with his brother, who had along with him a daughter already marriageable, in order to give her in wedlock to some of the Jews of chief dignity there. He then supped with the king, and falling in love with an actress that was of great beauty, and came into the room where they feasted, he told his brother of it, and entreated him, because a Jew is forbidden by their law to come near to a foreigner, to conceal his offense; and to be kind and subservient to him, and to give him an opportunity of fulfilling his desires. Upon which his brother willingly entertained the proposal of serving him, and adorned his own daughter, and brought her to him by night, and put her into his bed. And Joseph, being disordered with drink, knew not who she was, and so lay with his brother's daughter; and this did he many times, and loved her exceedingly; and said to his brother, that he loved this actress so well, that he should run the hazard of his life [if he must part with her], and yet probably the king would not give him leave [to

take her with him]. But his brother bid him be in no concern about that matter, and told him he might enjoy her whom he loved without any danger, and might have her for his wife; and opened the truth of the matter to him, and assured him that he chose rather to have his own daughter abused, than to overlook him, and se him come to [public] disgrace. So Joseph commended him for this his brotherly love, and married his daughter; and by her begat a son, whose name was Hyrcanus, as we said before. And when this his youngest son showed, at thirteen years old, a mind that was both courageous and wise, and was greatly envied by his brethren, as being of a genius much above them, and such a one as they might well envy, Joseph had once a mind to know which of his sons had the best disposition to virtue; and when he sent them severally to those that had then the best reputation for instructing youth, the rest of his children, by reason of their sloth and unwillingness to take pains, returned to him foolish and unlearned. After them he sent out the youngest, Hyrcanus, and gave him three hundred yoke of oxen, and bid him go two days' journey into the wilderness, and sow the land there, and yet kept back privately the yokes of the oxen that coupled them together. When Hyrcanus came to the place, and found he had no yokes with him, he contenmed the drivers of the oxen, who advised him to send some to his father, to bring them some yokes; but he thinking that he ought not to lose his time while they should be sent to bring him the yokes, he invented a kind of stratagem, and what suited an age older than his own; for he slew ten yoke of the oxen, and distributed their flesh among the laborers, and cut their hides into several pieces, and made him yokes, and yoked the oxen together with them; by which means he sowed as much land as his father had appointed him to sow, and returned to him. And when he was come back, his father was mightily pleased with his sagacity, and commended the sharpness of his understanding, and his boldness in what he did. And he still loved him the more, as if he were his only genuine son, while his brethren were much troubled at it.

7. But when one told him that Ptolemy had a son just born, and that all the principal men of Syria, and the other countries subject to him, were to keep a festival, on account of the child's birthday, and went away in haste with great retinues to Alexandria, he was himself indeed hindered from going by old age; but he made trial of his sons,

whether any of them would be willing to go to the king. And when the elder sons excused themselves from going, and said they were not courtiers good enough for such conversation, and advised him to send their brother Hyrcanus, he gladly hearkened to that advice, and called Hyrcanus, and asked him whether he would go to the king, and whether it was agreeable to him to go or not. And upon his promise that he would go, and his saying that he should not want much money for his journey, because he would live moderately, and that ten thousand drachmas would be sufficient, he was pleased with his son's prudence. After a little while, the son advised his father not to send his presents to the king from thence, but to give him a letter to his steward at Alexandria, that he might furnish him with money, for purchasing what should be most excellent and most precious. So he thinking that the expense of ten talents would be enough for presents to be made the king, and commending his son, as giving him good advice, wrote to Arion his steward, that managed all his money matters at Alexandria; which money was not less than three thousand talents on his account, for Joseph sent the money he received in Syria to Alexandria. And when the day appointed for the payment of the taxes to the king came, he wrote to Arion to pay them. So when the son had asked his father for a letter to the steward, and had received it, he made haste to Alexandria. And when he was gone, his brethren wrote to all the king's friends, that they should destroy him.

8. But when he was come to Alexaudria, he delivered his letter to Arion, who asked him how many talents he would have (hoping he would ask for no more than ten, or a little more); he said he wanted a thousand talents. At which the steward was angry, and rebuked him, as one that intended to live extravagantly; and he let him know how his father had gathered together his estate by painstaking, and resisting his inclinations, and wished him to imitate the example of his father: he assured him withal, that he would give him but ten talents, and that for a present to the king also. The son was irritated at this, and threw Arion into prison. But when Arion's wife had informed Cleopatra of this, with her entreaty, that she would rebuke the child for what he had done, (for Arion was in great esteem with her,) Cleopatra informed the king of it. And Ptolemy sent for Hyrcanus, and told him that he wondered, when he was sent to him by his father, that he had not yet come into his presence, but had laid the steward in prison.

And he gave order, therefore, that he should come to him, and give an account of the reason of what he had done. And they report that the answer he made to the king's messenger was this: That "there was a law of his that forbade a child that was born to taste of the sacrifice, before he had been at the temple and sacrificed to God. According to which way of reasoning he did not himself come to him in expectation of the present he was to make to him, as to one who had been his father's benefactor; and that he had punished the slave for disobeying his commands, for that it mattered not Whether a master was little or great: so that unless we punish such as these, thou thyself mayst also expect to be despised by thy subjects." Upon hearing this his answer he fell a laughing, and wondered at the great soul of the child.

9. When Arion was apprized that this was the king's disposition, and that he had no way to help himself, he gave the child a thousand talents, and was let out of prison. So after three days were over, Hyrcanus came and saluted the king and queen. They saw him with pleasure, and feasted him in an obliging manner, out of the respect they bare to his father. So he came to the merchants privately, and bought a hundred boys, that had learning, and were in the flower of their ages, each at a talent apiece; as also he bought a hundred maidens, each at the same price as the other. And when he was invited to feast with the king among the principal men in the country, he sat down the lowest of them all, because he was little regarded, as a child in age still; and this by those who placed every one according to their dignity. Now when all those that sat with him had laid the bones Of the several parts on a heap before Hyrcanus, (for they had themselves taken away the flesh belonging to them,) till the table where he sat was filled full with them, Trypho, who was the king's jester, and was appointed for jokes and laughter at festivals, was now asked by the guests that sat at the table [to expose him to laughter]. So he stood by the king, and said, "Dost thou not see, my lord, the bones that lie by Hyrcanus? by this similitude thou mayst conjecture that his father made all Syria as bare as he hath made these bones." And the king laughing at what Trypho said, and asking of Hyrcanus, How he came to have so many bones before him? he replied," Very rightfully, my lord; for they are dogs that eat the flesh and the bones together, as these thy guests have done, (looking in the mean time at those guests,) for there is nothing before them; but they are men that eat

the flesh, and cast away the hones, as I, who am also a man, have now done." Upon which the king admired at his answer, which was so wisely made; and bid them all make an acclamation, as a mark of their approbation of his jest, which was truly a facetious one. On the next day Hyrcanus went to every one of the king's friends, and of the men powerful at court, and saluted them; but still inquired of the servants what present they would make the king on his son's birthday; and when some said that they would give twelve talents, and that others of greater dignity would every one give according to the quantity of their riches, he pretended to every one of them to be grieved that he was not able to bring so large a present; for that he had no more than five talents. And when the servants heard what he said, they told their masters; and they rejoiced in the prospect that Joseph would be disapproved, and would make the king angry, by the smallness of his present. When the day came, the others, even those that brought the most, offered the king not above twenty talents; but Hyrcanus gave to every one of the hundred boys and hundred maidens that he had bought a talent apiece, for them to carry, and introduced them, the boys to the king, and the maidens to Cleopatra; every body wondering at the unexpected richness of the presents, even the king and queen themselves. He also presented those that attended about the king with gifts to the value of a great number of talents, that he might escape the danger he was in from them; for to these it was that Hyrcanus's brethren had written to destroy him. Now Ptolemy admired at the young man's magnanimity, and commanded him to ask what gift he pleased. But he desired nothing else to be done for him by the king than to write to his father and brethren about him. So when the king had paid him very great respects, and had given him very large gifts, and had written to his father and his brethren, and all his commanders and officers, about him, he sent him away. But when his brethren heard that Hyrcanus had received such favors from the king, and was returning home with great honor, they went out to meet him, and to destroy him, and that with the privity of their father; for he was angry at him for the [large] sum of money that he bestowed for presents, and so had no concern for his preservation. However, Joseph concealed the anger he had at his son, out of fear of the king. And when Hyrcanus's brethren came to fight him, he slew many others of those that were with them, as also two of his brethren themselves; but the rest of them escaped to Jerusalem to their father. But when Hyrcanus came to the city, where nobody would receive him, he was afraid for himself, and retired beyond the river Jordan, and there abode, but obliging the barbarians to pay their taxes.

10. At this time Seleucus, who was called Soter, reigned over Asia, being the son of Antiochus the Great. And [now] Hyrcanus's father, Joseph, died. He was a good man, and of great magnanimity; and brought the Jews out of a state of poverty and meanness, to one that was more splendid. He retained the farm of the taxes of Syria, and Phoenicia, and Samaria twenty-two years. His uncle also, Onias, died [about this time], and left the high priesthood to his son Simeon. And when he was dead, Onias his son succeeded him in that dignity. To him it was that Areus, king of the Lacedemonians, sent an embassage, with an epistle; the copy whereof here follows:

"Areus, King of the Lacedemonians, to Onias, Sendeth Greeting

"We have met with a certain writing, whereby we have discovered that both the Jews and the Lacedemonians are of one stock, and are derived from the kindred of Abraham[14] It is but just therefore that you, who are our brethren, should send to us about any of your concerns as you please. We will also do the same thing, and esteem your concerns as our own, and will look upon our concerns as in common with yours. Demoteles, who brings you this letter, will bring your answer back to

14. Whence it comes that these Lacedemonians declare themselves here to be of kin to the Jews, as derived from the same ancestor, Abraham, I cannot tell, unless, as Grotius supposes, they were derived from Dores, that came of the Pelasgi. These are by Herodotus called Barbarians, and perhaps were derived from the Syrians and Arabians, the posterity of Abraham by Keturah. See Antiq. B. XIV. ch. 10. sect. 22; and Of the War, B. I. ch. 26. sect. l; and Grot. on 1 Macc. 12:7. We may further observe from the Recognitions of Clement, that Eliezer, of Damascus, the servant of Abraham, Genesis 15:2; 24., was of old by some taken for his son. So that if the Lacedemonians were sprung from him, they might think themselves to be of the posterity of Abraham, as well as the Jews, who were sprung from Isaac. And perhaps this Eliezer of Damascus is that very Damascus whom Trogus Pompeius, as abridged by Justin, makes the founder of the Jewish nation itself, though he afterwards blunders, and makes Azelus, Adores, Abraham, and Israel kings of Judea, and successors to this Damascus. It may not be improper to observe further, that Moses Chorenensis, in his history of the Armenians, informs us, that the nation of the Parthians was also derived from Abraham by Keturah and her children.

us. This letter is four-square; and the seal is an eagle, with a dragon in his claws."

11. And these were the contents of the epistle which was sent from the king of the Lacedemonians. But, upon the death of Joseph, the people grew seditious, on account of his sons. For whereas the elders made war against Hyrcanus, who was the youngest of Joseph's sons, the multitude was divided, but the greater part joined with the elders in this war; as did Simon the high priest, by reason he was of kin to them. However, Hyrcanus determined not to return to Jerusalem any more, but seated himself beyond Jordan, and was at perpetual war with the Arabians, and slew many of them, and took many of them captives. He also erected a strong castle, and built it entirely of white stone to the very roof, and had animals of a prodigious magnitude engraven upon it. He also drew round it a great and deep canal of water. He also made caves of many furlongs in length, by hollowing a rock that was over against him; and then he made large rooms in it, some for feasting, and some for sleeping and living in. He introduced also a vast quantity of waters which ran along it, and which were very delightful and ornamental in the court. But still he made the entrances at the mouth of the caves so narrow, that no more than one person could enter by them at once. And the reason why he built them after that manner was a good one; it was for his own preservation, lest he should be besieged by his brethren, and run the hazard of being caught by them. Moreover, he built courts of greater magnitude than ordinary, which he adorned with vastly large gardens. And when he had brought the place to this state, he named it Tyre. This place is between Arabia and Judea, beyond Jordan, not far from the country of Heshbon. And he ruled over those parts for seven years, even all the time that Seleucus was king of Syria. But when he was dead, his brother Antiochus, who was called Epiphanes, took the kingdom. Ptolemy also, the king of Egypt, died, who was besides called Epiphanes. He left two sons, and both young in age; the elder of which was called Philometer, and the youngest Physcon. As for Hyrcanus, when he saw that Antiochus had a great army, and feared lest he should be caught by him, and brought to punishment for what he had done to the Arabians, he ended his life, and slew himself with his own hand; while Antiochus seized upon all his substance.

5 *How, Upon the Quarrels One Against Another About the High Priesthood Antiochus Made an Expedition Against Jerusalem, Took the City and Pillaged the Temples. and Distressed the Jews' as Also How Many of the Jews Forsook the Laws of Their Country; and How the Samaritans Followed the Customs of the Greeks and Named Their Temple at Mount Gerizzim the Temple of Jupiter Hellenius*

1. ABOUT this time, upon the death of Onias the high priest, they gave the high priesthood to Jesus his brother; for that son which Onias left [or Onias IV.] was yet but an infant; and, in its proper place, we will inform the reader of all the circumstances that befell this child. But this Jesus, who was the brother of Onias, was deprived of the high priesthood by the king, who was angry with him, and gave it to his younger brother, whose name also was Onias; for Simon had these three sons, to each of which the priesthood came, as we have already informed the reader. This Jesus changed his name to Jason, but Onias was called Menelaus. Now as the former high priest, Jesus, raised a sedition against Menelaus, who was ordained after him, the multitude were divided between them both. And the sons of Tobias took the part of Menelaus, but the greater part of the people assisted Jason; and by that means Menelaus and the sons of Tobias were distressed, and retired to Antiochus, and informed him that they were desirous to leave the laws of their country, and the Jewish way of living according to them, and to follow the king's laws, and the Grecian way of living. Wherefore they desired his permission to build them a Gymnasium at Jerusalem.[15] And when he had given them leave, they also hid the circumcision of their genitals, that even when they were naked they might appear to be Greeks. Accordingly, they left off all the customs that belonged to their own country, and imitated the practices of the other nations.

---

15. This word" Gymnasium" properly denotes a place where the exercises were performed naked, which because it would naturally distinguish circumcised Jews from uncircumcised Gentiles, these Jewish apostates endeavored to appear uncircumcised, by means of a surgical operation, hinted at by St. Paul, 1 Corinthians 7:18, and described by Celsus, B. VII. ch. 25., as Dr. Hudson here informs us.

2. Now Antiochus, upon the agreeable situation of the affairs of his kingdom, resolved to make an expedition against Egypt, both because he had a desire to gain it, and because he contemned the son of Ptolemy, as now weak, and not yet of abilities to manage affairs of such consequence; so he came with great forces to Pelusium, and circumvented Ptolemy Philometor by treachery, and seized upon Egypt. He then came to the places about Memphis; and when he had taken them, he made haste to Alexandria, in hopes of taking it by siege, and of subduing Ptolemy, who reigned there. But he was driven not only from Alexandria, but out of all Egypt, by the declaration of the Romans, who charged him to let that country alone; according as I have elsewhere formerly declared. I will now give a particular account of what concerns this king, how he subdued Judea and the temple; for in my former work I mentioned those things very briefly, and have therefore now thought it necessary to go over that history again, and that with great accuracy.

3. King Antiochus returning out of Egypt[16] for fear of the Romans, made an expedition against the city Jerusalem; and when he was there, in the hundred and forty-third year of the kingdom of the Seleucidse, he took the city without fighting, those of his own party opening the gates to him. And when he had gotten possession of Jerusalem, he slew many of the opposite party; and when he had plundered it of a great deal of money, he returned to Antioch.

4. Now it came to pass, after two years, in the hundred forty and fifth year, on the twenty-fifth day of that month which is by us called Chasleu, and by the Macedonians Apelleus, in the hundred and fifty-third olympiad, that the king came up to Jerusalem, and, pretending peace, he got possession of the city by treachery; at which time he spared not so much as those that admitted him into it, on account of the riches that lay in the temple; but, led by his covetous inclination, (for he saw there was in it a great deal of gold, and many ornaments

---

16. Hereabout Josephus begins to follow the First Book of the Maccabees, a most excellent and most authentic history; and accordingly it is here, with great fidelity and exactness, abridged by him; between whose present copies there seem to be fewer variations than in any other sacred Hebrew book of the Old Testament whatsoever, (for this book also was originally written in Hebrew,) which is very natural, because it was written so much nearer to the times of Josephus than the rest were.

that had been dedicated to it of very great value,) and in order to plunder its wealth, he ventured to break the league he had made. So he left the temple bare, and took away the golden candlesticks, and the golden altar [of incense], and table [of shew-bread], and the altar [of burnt-offering]; and did not abstain from even the veils, which were made of fine linen and scarlet. He also emptied it of its secret treasures, and left nothing at all remaining; and by this means cast the Jews into great lamentation, for he forbade them to offer those daily sacrifices which they used to offer to God, according to the law. And when he had pillaged the whole city, some of the inhabitants he slew, and some he carried captive, together with their wives and children, so that the multitude of those captives that were taken alive amounted to about ten thousand. He also burnt down the finest buildings; and when he had overthrown the city walls, he built a citadel in the lower part of the city,[17] for the place was high, and overlooked the temple; on which account he fortified it with high walls and towers, and put into it a garrison of Macedonians. However, in that citadel dwelt the impious and wicked part of the [Jewish] multitude, from whom it proved that the citizens suffered many and sore calamities. And when the king had built an idol altar upon God's altar, he slew swine upon it, and so offered a sacrifice neither according to the law, nor the Jewish religious worship in that country. He also compelled them to forsake the worship which they paid their own God, and to adore those whom he took to be gods; and made them build temples, and raise idol altars in every city and village, and offer swine upon them every day. He also commanded them not to circumcise their sons, and threatened to punish any that should be found to have transgressed his injunction. He also appointed overseers, who should compel them to do what he commanded. And indeed many Jews there were who complied with the king's commands, either voluntarily, or out of fear of the penalty

17. This citadel, of which we have such frequent mention in the following history, both in the Maccabees and Josephus, seems to have been a castle built on a hill, lower than Mount Zion, though upon its skirts, and higher than Mount Moriah, but between them both; which hill the enemies of the Jews now got possession of, and built on it this citadel, and fortified it, till a good while afterwards the Jews regained it, demolished it, and leveled the hill itself with the common ground, that their enemies might no more recover it, and might thence overlook the temple itself, and do them such mischief as they had long undergone from it, Antiq. B. XIII. ch. 6. sect. 6.

that was denounced. But the best men, and those of the noblest souls, did not regard him, but did pay a greater respect to the customs of their country than concern as to the punishment which he threatened to the disobedient; on which account they every day underwent great miseries and bitter torments; for they were whipped with rods, and their bodies were torn to pieces, and were crucified, while they were still alive, and breathed. They also strangled those women and their sons whom they had circumcised, as the king had appointed, hanging their sons about their necks as they were upon the crosses. And if there were any sacred book of the law found, it was destroyed, and those with whom they were found miserably perished also.

5. When the Samaritans saw the Jews under these sufferings, they no longer confessed that they were of their kindred, nor that the temple on Mount Gerizzim belonged to Almighty God. This was according to their nature, as we have already shown. And they now said that they were a colony of Medes and Persians; and indeed they were a colony of theirs. So they sent ambassadors to Antiochus, and an epistle, whose contents are these: "To king Antiochus the god, Epiphanes, a memorial from the Sidonians, who live at Shechem. Our forefathers, upon certain frequent plagues, and as following a certain ancient superstition, had a custom of observing that day which by the Jews is called the Sabbath.[18] And when they had erected a temple at the mountain called Gerrizzim, though without a name, they offered upon it the proper sacrifices. Now, upon the just treatment of these wicked Jews, those that manage their affairs, supposing that we were of kin to them, and practiced as they do, make us liable to the same accusations, although we be originally Sidonians, as is evident from the public records. We therefore beseech thee, our benefactor and Savior, to give order to Apollonius, the governor of this part of the country, and to Nicanor, the procurator of thy affairs, to give us no disturbance, nor to lay to our charge what the Jews are accused for, since we are aliens from their nation, and from their customs; but let our temple, which at present hath no name at all be named the Temple of Jupiter Hellenius. If this were once done, we should be no longer disturbed, but should

---

18. This allegation of the Samaritans is remarkable, that though they were not Jews, yet did they, from ancient times, observe the Sabbath day, and, as they elsewhere pretend, the Sabbatic year also, Antiq. B. XI. ch. 8. sect. 6.

be more intent on our own occupation with quietness, and so bring in a greater revenue to thee." When the Samaritans had petitioned for this, the king sent them back the following answer, in an epistle: "King Antiochus to Nicanor. The Sidonians, who live at Shechem, have sent me the memorial enclosed. When therefore we were advising with our friends about it, the messengers sent by them represented to us that they are no way concerned with accusations which belong to the Jews, but choose to live after the customs of the Greeks. Accordingly, we declare them free from such accusations, and order that, agreeable to their petition, their temple be named the Temple of Jupiter Hellenius." He also sent the like epistle to Apollonius, the governor of that part of the country, in the forty-sixth year, and the eighteenth day of the month Hecatorabeom

6 *How, Upon Antiochus's Prohibition to the Jews to Make Use of the Laws of Their Country Mattathias, the Son of Asamoneus, Alone Despised the King, and Overcame the Generals of Antiochus's Army; as Also Concerning the Death of Mattathias, and the Succession of Judas*

1. NOW at this time there was one whose name was Mattathias, who dwelt at Modin, the son of John, the son of Simeon, the son of Asamoneus, a priest of the order of Joarib, and a citizen of Jerusalem. He had five sons; John, who was called Gaddis, and Simon, who was called Matthes, and Judas, who was called Maccabeus,[19] and Eleazar, who was called Auran, and Jonathan, who was called Apphus. Now this Mattathias lamented to his children the sad state of their affairs, and the ravage made in the city, and the plundering of the temple, and the calamities the multitude were under; and he told them that it was better for them to die for the laws of their country, than to live so ingloriously as they then did.

---

19. That this appellation of Maccabee was not first of all given to Judas Maccabeus, nor was derived from any initial letters of the Hebrew words on his banner, "Mi Kamoka Be Elire, Jehovah?" ("Who is like unto thee among the gods, O Jehovah?") Exodus 15:11 as the modern Rabbins vainly pretend, see Authent. Rec. Part I. p. 205, 206. Only we may note, by the way, that the original name of these Maccabees, and their posterity, was Asamoneans; which was derived from Asamoneus, the great-grandfather of Mattathias, as Josephus here informs us.

2. But when those that were appointed by the king were come to Modin, that they might compel the Jews to do what they were commanded, and to enjoin those that were there to offer sacrifice, as the king had commanded, they desired that Mattathias, a person of the greatest character among them, both on other accounts, and particularly on account of such a numerous and so deserving a family of children, would begin the sacrifice, because his fellow citizens would follow his example, and because such a procedure would make him honored by the king. But Mattathias said he would not do it; and that if all the other nations would obey the commands of Antiochus, either out of fear, or to please him, yet would not he nor his sons leave the religious worship of their country. But as soon as he had ended his speech, there came one of the Jews into the midst of them, and sacrificed, as Antiochus had commanded. At which Mattathias had great indignation, and ran upon him violently, with his sons, who had swords with them, and slew both the man himself that sacrificed, and Apelles the king's general, who compelled them to sacrifice, with a few of his soldiers. He also overthrew the idol altar, and cried out, "If," said he," any one be zealous for the laws of his country, and for the worship of God, let him follow me." And when he had said this, he made haste into the desert with his sons, and left all his substance in the village. Many others did the same also, and fled with their children and wives into the desert, and dwelt in caves. But when the king's generals heard this, they took all the forces they then had in the citadel at Jerusalem, and pursued the Jews into the desert; and when they had overtaken them, they in the first place endeavored to persuade them to repent, and to choose what was most for their advantage, and not put them to the necessity of using them according to the law of war. But when they would not comply with their persuasions, but continued to be of a different mind, they fought against them on the sabbath day, and they burnt them as they were in the caves, without resistance, and without so much as stopping up the entrances of the caves. And they avoided to defend themselves on that day, because they were not willing to break in upon the honor they owed the sabbath, even in such distresses; for our law requires that we rest upon that day. There were about a thousand, with their wives and children, who were smothered and died in these caves; but many of those that escaped joined themselves to Mattathias, and appointed him to be their ruler,

who taught them to fight, even on the sabbath day; and told them that unless they would do so, they would become their own enemies, by observing the law [so rigorously], while their adversaries would still assault them on this day, and they would not then defend themselves, and that nothing could then hinder but they must all perish without fighting. This speech persuaded them. And this rule continues among us to this day, that if there be a necessity, we may fight on sabbath days. So Mattathias got a great army about him, and overthrew their idol altars, and slew those that broke the laws, even all that he could get under his power; for many of them were dispersed among the nations round about them for fear of him. He also commanded that those boys which were not yet circumcised should be circumcised now; and he drove those away that were appointed to hinder such their circumcision.

3. But when he had ruled one year, and was fallen into a distemper, he called for his sons, and set them round about him, and said, "O my sons, I am going the way of all the earth; and I recommend to you my resolution, and beseech you not to be negligent in keeping it, but to be mindful of the desires of him who begat you, and brought you up, and to preserve the customs of your country, and to recover your ancient form of government, which is in danger of being overturned, and not to be carried away with those that, either by their own inclination, or out of necessity, betray it, but to become such sons as are worthy of me; to be above all force and necessity, and so to dispose your souls, as to be ready, when it shall be necessary, to die for your laws; as sensible of this, by just reasoning, that if God see that you are so disposed he will not overlook you, but will have a great value for your virtue, and will restore to you again what you have lost, and will return to you that freedom in which you shall live quietly, and enjoy your own customs. Your bodies are mortal, and subject to fate; but they receive a sort of immortality, by the remembrance of what actions they have done. And I would have you so in love with this immortality, that you may pursue after glory, and that, when you have undergone the greatest difficulties, you may not scruple, for such things, to lose your lives. I exhort you, especially, to agree one with another; and in what excellency any one of you exceeds another, to yield to him so far, and by that means to reap the advantage of every one's own virtues. Do you then esteem Simon as your father, because he is a man

of extraordinary prudence, and be governed by him in what counsels be gives you. Take Maccabeus for the general of your army, because of his courage and strength, for he will avenge your nation, and will bring vengeance on your enemies. Admit among you the righteous and religious, and augment their power."

4. When Mattathias had thus discoursed to his sons, and had prayed to God to be their assistant, and to recover to the people their former constitution, he died a little afterward, and was buried at Modin; all the people making great lamentation for him. Whereupon his son Judas took upon him the administration of public affairs, in the hundred fbrty and sixth year; and thus, by the ready assistance of his brethren, and of others, Judas cast their enemies out of the country, and put those of their own country to death who had transgressed its laws, and purified the land of all the pollutions that were in it.

7 *How Judas Overthrew the Forces of Apollonius and Seron and Killed the Generals of Their Armies Themselves; and How When, a Little While Afterwards Lysias and Gorgias Were Beaten He Went Up to Jerusalem and Purified the Temple*

1. WHEN Apollonius, the general of the Samaritan forces, heard this, he took his army, and made haste to go against Judas, who met him, and joined battle with him, and beat him, and slew many of his men, and among them Apollonius himself, their general, whose sword being that which he happened then to wear, he seized upon, and kept for himself; but he wounded more than he slew, and took a great deal of prey from the enemy's camp, and went his way. But when Seron, who was general of the army of Celesyria, heard that many had joined themselves to Judas, and that he had about him an army sufficient for fighting, and for making war, he determined to make an expedition against him, as thinking it became him to endeavor to punish those that transgressed the king's injunctions. He then got together an army, as large as he was able, and joined to it the runagate and wicked Jews, and came against Judas. He came as far as Bethhoron, a village of Judea, and there pitched his camp; upon which Judas met him; and when he intended to give him battle, he saw that his soldiers were backward to fight, because their number was small, and because they

wanted food, for they were fasting, he encouraged them, and said to them, that victory and conquest of enemies are not derived from the multitude in armies, but in the exercise of piety towards God; and that they had the plainest instances in their forefathers, who, by their righteousness, exerting themselves on behalf of their own laws, and their own children, had frequently conquered many ten thousands,—for innocence is the strongest army. By this speech he induced his men to contenm the multitude of the enemy, and to fall upon Seron. And upon joining battle with him, he beat the Syrians; and when their general fell among the rest, they all ran away with speed, as thinking that to be their best way of escaping. So he pursued them unto the plain, and slew about eight hundred of the enemy; but the rest escaped to the region which lay near to the sea.

2. When king Antiochus heard of these things, he was very angry at what had happened; so he got together all his own army, with many mercenaries, whom he had hired from the islands, and took them with him, and prepared to break into Judea about the beginning of the spring. But when, upon his mustering his soldiers, he perceived that his treasures were deficient, and there was a want of money in them, for all the taxes were not paid, by reason of the seditions there had been among the nations he having been so magnanimous and so liberal, that what he had was not sufficient for him, he therefore resolved first to go into Persia, and collect the taxes of that country. Hereupon he left one whose name was Lysias, who was in great repute with him governor of the kingdom, as far as the bounds of Egypt, and of the Lower Asia, and reaching from the river Euphrates, and committed to him a certain part of his forces, and of his elephants, and charged him to bring up his son Antiochus with all possible care, until he came back; and that he should conquer Judea, and take its inhabitants for slaves, and utterly destroy Jerusalem, and abolish the whole nation. And when king Antiochus had given these things in charge to Lysias, he went into Persia; and in the hundred and forty-seventh year he passed over Euphrates, and went to the superior provinces.

3. Upon this Lysias chose Ptolemy, the son of Dorymenes, and Nicanor, and Gorgias, very potent men among the king's friends, and delivered to them forty thousand foot soldiers, and seven thousand horsemen, and sent them against Judea, who came as far as the city

Emmaus, and pitched their camp in the plain country. There came also to them auxiliaries out of Syria, and the country round about; as also many of the runagate Jews. And besides these came some merchants to buy those that should be carried captives, (having bonds with them to bind those that should be made prisoners,) with that silver and gold which they were to pay for their price. And when Judas saw their camp, and how numerous their enemies were, he persuaded his own soldiers to be of good courage, and exhorted them to place their hopes of victory in God, and to make supplication to him, according to the custom of their country, clothed in sackcloth; and to show what was their usual habit of supplication in the greatest dangers, and thereby to prevail with God to grant you the victory over your enemies. So he set them in their ancient order of battle used by their forefathers, under their captains of thousands, and other officers, and dismissed such as were newly married, as well as those that had newly gained possessions, that they might not fight in a cowardly manner, out of an inordinate love of life, in order to enjoy those blessings. When he had thus disposed his soldiers, he encouraged them to fight by the following speech, which he made to them: "O my fellow soldiers, no other time remains more opportune than the present for courage and contempt of dangers; for if you now fight manfully, you may recover your liberty, which, as it is a thing of itself agreeable to all men, so it proves to be to us much more desirable, by its affording us the liberty of worshipping God. Since therefore you are in such circumstances at present, you must either recover that liberty, and so regain a happy and blessed way of living, which is that according to our laws, and the customs of our country, or to submit to the most opprobrious sufferings; nor will any seed of your nation remain if you be beat in this battle. Fight therefore manfully; and suppose that you must die, though you do not fight; but believe, that besides such glorious rewards as those of the liberty of your country, of your laws, of your religion, you shall then obtain everlasting glory. Prepare yourselves, therefore, and put yourselves into such an agreeable posture, that you may be ready to fight with the enemy as soon as it is day tomorrow morning."

4. And this was the speech which Judas made to encourage them. But when the enemy sent Gorgias, with five thousand foot and one thousand horse, that he might fall upon Judas by night, and had

for that purpose certain of the runagate Jews as guides, the son of Mattathias perceived it, and resolved to fall upon those enemies that were in their camp, now their forces were divided. When they had therefore supped in good time, and had left many fires in their camp, he marched all night to those enemies that were at Emmaus. So that when Gorgias found no enemy in their camp, but suspected that they were retired, and had hidden themselves among the mountains, he resolved to go and seek them wheresoever they were. But about break of day Judas appeared to those enemies that were at Emmaus, with only three thousand men, and those ill armed, by reason of their poverty; and when he saw the enemy very well and skillfully fortified in their camp, he encouraged the Jews, and told them that they ought to fight, though it were with their naked bodies, for that God had sometimes of old given such men strength, and that against such as were more in number, and were armed also, out of regard to their great courage. So he commanded the trumpeters to sound for the battle; and by thus falling upon the enemies when they did not expect it, and thereby astonishing and disturbing their minds, he slew many of those that resisted him, and went on pursuing the rest as far as Gadara, and the plains of Idumea, and Ashdod, and Jamnia; and of these there fell about three thousand. Yet did Judas exhort his soldiers not to be too desirous of the spoils, for that still they must have a contest and battle with Gorgias, and the forces that were with him; but that when they had once overcome them, then they might securely plunder the camp, because they were the only enemies remaining, and they expected no others. And just as he was speaking to his soldiers, Gorgias's men looked down into that army which they left in their camp, and saw that it was overthrown, and the camp burnt; for the smoke that arose from it showed them, even when they were a great way off, what had happened. When therefore those that were with Gorgias understood that things were in this posture, and perceived that those that were with Judas were ready to fight them, they also were affrighted, and put to flight; but then Judas, as though he had already beaten Gorgias's soldiers without fighting, returned and seized on the spoils. He took a great quantity of gold, and silver, and purple, and blue, and then returned home with joy, and singing hymns to God for their good success; for this victory greatly contributed to the recovery of their liberty.

5. Hereupon Lysias was confounded at the defeat of the army which he had sent, and the next year he got together sixty thousand chosen men. He also took five thousand horsemen, and fell upon Judea; and he went up to the hill country of Bethsur, a village of Judea, and pitched his camp there, where Judas met him with ten thousand men; and when he saw the great number of his enemies, he prayed to God that he would assist him, and joined battle with the first of the enemy that appeared, and beat them, and slew about five thousand of them, and thereby became terrible to the rest of them. Nay, indeed, Lysias observing the great spirit of the Jews, how they were prepared to die rather than lose their liberty, and being afraid of their desperate way of fighting, as if it were real strength, he took the rest of the army back with him, and returned to Antioch, where he listed foreigners into the service, and prepared to fall upon Judea with a greater army.

6. When therefore the generals of Antiochus's armies had been beaten so often, Judas assembled the people together, and told them, that after these many victories which God had given them, they ought to go up to Jerusalem, and purify the temple, and offer the appointed sacrifices. But as soon as he, with the whole multitude, was come to Jerusalem, and found the temple deserted, and its gates burnt down, and plants growing in the temple of their own accord, on account of its desertion, he and those that were with him began to lament, and were quite confounded at the sight of the temple; so he chose out some of his soldiers, and gave them order to fight against those guards that were in the citadel, until he should have purified the temple. When therefore he had carefully purged it, and had brought in new vessels, the candlestick, the table [of shew-bread], and the altar [of incense], which were made of gold, he hung up the veils at the gates, and added doors to them. He also took down the altar [of burnt-offering], and built a new one of stones that he gathered together, and not of such as were hewn with iron tools. So on the five and twentieth day of the month Casleu, which the Macedonians call Apeliens, they lighted the lamps that were on the candlestick, and offered incense upon the altar [of incense], and laid the loaves upon the table [of shew-bread], and offered burnt-offerings upon the new altar [of burnt-offering]. Now it so fell out, that these things were done on the very same day on which their Divine worship had fallen off, and was reduced to a profane and common use, after three years' time; for so it was, that the temple was

made desolate by Antiochus, and so continued for three years. This desolation happened to the temple in the hundred forty and fifth year, on the twenty-fifth day of the month Apeliens, and on the hundred fifty and third olympiad: but it was dedicated anew, on the same day, the twenty-fifth of the month Apeliens, on the hundred and forty-eighth year, and on the hundred and fifty-fourth olympiad. And this desolation came to pass according to the prophecy of Daniel, which was given four hundred and eight years before; for he declared that the Macedonians would dissolve that worship [for some time].

7. Now Judas celebrated the festival of the restoration of the sacrifices of the temple for eight days, and omitted no sort of pleasures thereon; but he feasted them upon very rich and splendid sacrifices; and he honored God, and delighted them by hymns and psalms. Nay, they were so very glad at the revival of their customs, when, after a long time of intermission, they unexpectedly had regained the freedom of their worship, that they made it a law for their posterity, that they should keep a festival, on account of the restoration of their temple worship, for eight days. And from that time to this we celebrate this festival, and call it Lights. I suppose the reason was, because this liberty beyond our hopes appeared to us; and that thence was the name given to that festival. Judas also rebuilt the walls round about the city, and reared towers of great height against the incursions of enemies, and set guards therein. He also fortified the city Bethsura, that it might serve as a citadel against any distresses that might come from our enemies.

8 How Judas Subdued the Nations Round About; and How Simon Beat the People of Tyre and Ptolemais; and How Judas Overcame Timotheus, and Forced Him to Fly Away, and Did Many Other Things After Joseph and Azarias Had Been Beaten

1. WHEN these things were over, the nations round about the Jews were very uneasy at the revival of their power, and rose up together, and destroyed many of them, as gaining advantage over them by laying snares for them, and making secret conspiracies against them. Judas made perpetual expeditions against these men, and endeavored to restrain them from those incursions, and to prevent the mischiefs

they did to the Jews. So he fell upon the Idumeans, the posterity of Esau, at Acrabattene, and slew a great many of them, and took their spoils. He also shut up the sons of Bean, that laid wait for the Jews; and he sat down about them, and besieged them, and burnt their towers, and destroyed the men [that were in them]. After this he went thence in haste against the Ammonites, who had a great and a numerous army, of which Timotheus was the commander. And when he had subdued them, he seized on the city Jazer, and took their wives and their children captives, and burnt the city, and then returned into Judea. But when the neighboring nations understood that he was returned, they got together in great numbers in the land of Gilead, and came against those Jews that were at their borders, who then fled to the garrison of Dathema; and sent to Judas, to inform him that Timotheus was endeavoring to take the place whither they were fled. And as these epistles were reading, there came other messengers out of Galilee, who informed him that the inhabitants of Ptolemais, and of Tyre and Sidon, and strangers of Galilee, were gotten together.

2. Accordingly Judas, upon considering what was fit to be done, with relation to the necessity both these cases required, gave order that Simon his brother should take three thousand chosen men, and go to the assistance of the Jews in Galilee, while he and another of his brothers, Jonathan, made haste into the land of Gilead, with eight thousand soldiers. And he left Joseph, the son of Zacharias, and Azarias, to be over the rest of the forces; and charged them to keep Judea very carefully, and to fight no battles with any persons whomsoever until his return. Accordingly, Simon-went into Galilee, and fought the enemy, and put them to flight, and pursued them to the very gates of Ptolemais, and slew about three thousand of them, and took the spoils of those that were slain, and those Jews whom they had made captives, with their baggage, and then returned home.

3. Now as for Judas Maccabeus, and his brother Jonathan, they passed over the river Jordan; and when they had gone three days journey, they lighted upon the Nabateans, who came to meet them peaceably, and who told them how the affairs of those in the land of Gilead stood; and how many of them were in distress, and driven into garrisons, and into the cities of Galilee; and exhorted him to make haste to go against the foreigners, and to endeavor to save his own countrymen out of their hands. To this exhortation Judas hearkened,

and returned to the wilderness; and in the first place fell upon the inhabitants of Bosor, and took the city, and beat the inhabitants, and destroyed all the males, and all that were able to fight, and burnt the city. Nor did he stop even when night came on, but he journeyed in it to the garrison where the Jews happened to be then shut up, and where Timotheus lay round the place with his army. And Judas came upon the city in the morning; and when he found that the enemy were making an assault upon the walls, and that some of them brought ladders, on which they might get upon those walls, and that others brought engines [to batter them], he bid the trumpeter to sound his trumpet, and he encouraged his soldiers cheerfully to undergo dangers for the sake of their brethren and kindred; he also parted his army into three bodies, and fell upon the backs of their enemies. But when Timotheus's men perceived that it was Maccabeus that was upon them, of both whose courage and good success in war they had formerly had sufficient experience, they were put to flight; but Judas followed them with his army, and slew about eight thousand of them. He then turned aside to a city of the foreigners called Malle, and took it, and slew all the males, and burnt the city itself. He then removed from thence, and overthrew Casphom and Bosor, and many other cities of the land of Gilead.

4. But not long after this, Timotheus prepared a great army, and took many others as auxiliaries; and induced some of the Arabians, by the promise of rewards, to go with him in this expedition, and came with his army beyond the brook, over against the city Raphon; and he encouraged his soldiers, if it came to a battle with the Jews, to fight courageously, and to hinder their passing over the brook; for he said to them beforehand, that "if they come over it, we shall be beaten." And when Judas heard that Timotheus prepared himself to fight, he took all his own army, and went in haste against Timotheus his enemy; and when he had passed over the brook, he fell upon his enemies, and some of them met him, whom he slew, and others of them he so terrified, that he compelled them to throw down their arms and fly; and some of them escaped, but some of them fled to what was called the Temple of Camaim, and hoped thereby to preserve themselves; but Judas took the city, and slew them, and burnt the temple, and so used several ways of destroying his enemies.

5. When he had done this, he gathered the Jews together, with their children and wives, and the substance that belonged to them, and was going to bring them back into Judea; but as soon as he was come to a certain city, whose name was Ephron, that lay upon the road, (and it was not possible for him to go any other way, so he was not willing to go back again,) he then sent to the inhabitants, and desired that they would open their gates, and permit them to go on their way through the city; for they had stopped up the gates with stones, and cut off their passage through it. And when the inhabitants of Ephron would not agree to this proposal, he encouraged those that were with him, and encompassed the city round, and besieged it, and, lying round it by day and night, took the city, and slew every male in it, and burnt it all down, and so obtained a way through it; and the multitude of those that were slain was so great, that they went over the dead bodies. So they came over Jordan, and arrived at the great plain, over against which is situate the city Bethshah, which is called by the Greeks Scythopolis.[20] And going away hastily from thence, they came into Judea, singing psalms and hymns as they went, and indulging such tokens of mirth as are usual in triumphs upon victory. They also offered thank-offerings, both for their good success, and for the preservation of their army, for not one of the Jews was slain in these battles.[21]

6. But as to Joseph, the son of Zacharias, and Azarias, whom Judas left generals [of the rest of his forces] at the same time when Simon was in Galilee, fighting against the people of Ptolemais, and Judas himself, and his brother Jonathan, were in the land of Gilead, did these men also affect the glory of being courageous generals in war, in order whereto they took the army that was under their command, and came to Jamnia. There Gorgias, the general of the forces of Jamnia, met them; and upon joining battle with him, they lost two thousand

---

20. The reason why Bethshah was called Scythopolis is well known from Herodotus, B. I. p. 105, and Syncellus, p. 214, that the Scythians, when they overran Asia, in the days of Josiah, seized on this city, and kept it as long as they continued in Asia, from which time it retained the name of Scythopolis, or the City of the Scythians.

21. This most providential preservation of all the religious Jews in this expedition, which was according to the will of God, is observable often among God's people, the Jews; and somewhat very like it in the changes of the four monarchies, which were also providential. See Prideaux at the years 331, 333, and 334.

of their army,[22] and fled away, and were pursued to the very borders of Judea. And this misfortune befell them by their disobedience to what injunctions Judas had given them, not to fight with any one before his return. For besides the rest of Judas's sagacious counsels, one may well wonder at this concerning the misfortune that befell the forces commanded by Joseph and Azarias, which he understood would happen, if they broke any of the injunctions he had given them. But Judas and his brethren did not leave off fighting with the Idumeans, but pressed upon them on all sides, and took from them the city of Hebron, and demolished all its fortifications, and set all its towers on fire, and burnt the country of the foreigners, and the city Marissa. They came also to Ashdod, and took it, and laid it waste, and took away a great deal of the spoils and prey that were in it, and returned to Judea.

9 *Concerning the Death of Antiochus Epiphane. How Antiochus Eupator Fought Against Juda and Besieged Him in the Temple and Afterwards Made Peace with Him and Departed; of Alcimus and Onias*

1. ABOUT this time it was that king Antiochus, as he was going over the upper countries, heard that there was a very rich city in Persia, called Elymais; and therein a very rich temple of Diana, and that it was full of all sorts of donations dedicated to it; as also weapons and breastplates, which, upon inquiry, he found had been left there by Alexander, the son of Philip, king of Macedonia. And being incited by these motives, he went in haste to Elymais, and assaulted it, and besieged it. But as those that were in it were not terrified at his assault, nor at his siege, but opposed him very courageously, he was beaten off his hopes; for they drove him away from the city, and went out and pursued after him, insomuch that he fled away as far as

22. Here is another great instance of Providence, that when, even at the very time that Simon, and Judas, and Jonathan were so miraculously preserved and blessed, in the just defense of their laws and religion, these other generals of the Jews, who went to fight for honor in a vain-glorious way, and without any commission from God, or the family he had raised up to deliver them, were miserably disappointed and defeated. See 1 Macc. 5:61, 62.

Babylon, and lost a great many of his army. And when he was grieving for this disappointment, some persons told him of the defeat of his commanders whom he had left behind him to fight against Judea, and what strength the Jews had already gotten. When this concern about these affairs was added to the former, he was confounded, and by the anxiety he was in fell into a distemper, which, as it lasted a great while, and as his pains increased upon him, so he at length perceived he should die in a little time; so he called his friends to him, and told them that his distemper was severe upon him; and confessed withal, that this calamity was sent upon him for the miseries he had brought upon the Jewish nation, while he plundered their temple, and contemned their God; and when he had said this, he gave up the ghost. Whence one may wonder at Polybius of Megalopolis, who, though otherwise a good man, yet saith that "Antiochus died because he had a purpose to plunder the temple of Diana in Persia;" for the purposing to do a thing,[23] but not actually doing it, is not worthy of punishment. But if Polybius could think that Antiochus thus lost his life on that account, it is much more probable that this king died on account of his sacrilegious plundering of the temple at Jerusalem. But we will not contend about this matter with those who may think that the cause assigned by this Polybius of Megalopolis is nearer the truth than that assigned by us.

2. However, Antiochus, before he died, called for Philip, who was one of his companions, and made him the guardian of his kingdom; and gave him his diadem, and his garment, and his ring, and charged him to carry them, and deliver them to his son Antiochus; and desired him to take care of his education, and to preserve the kingdom for him.[24] This Antiochus died in the hundred forty and ninth year; but it

---

23. Since St. Paul, a Pharisee, confesses that he had not known concupiscence, or desires, to be sinful, had not the tenth commandment said, "Thou shalt not covet," Romans 7:7, the case seems to have been much the same with our Josephus, who was of the same sect, that he had not a deep sense of the greatness of any sins that proceeded no further than the intention. However, since Josephus speaks here properly of the punishment of death, which is not intended by any law, either of God or man, for the bare intention, his words need not to be strained to mean, that sins intended, but not executed, were no sins at all.

24. No wonder that Josephus here describes Antiochus Eupator as young, and wanting tuition, when he came to the crown, since Appian informs us (Syriac. p. 177) that he was then but nine years old.

was Lysias that declared his death to the multitude, and appointed his son Antiochus to be king, (of whom at present he had the care,) and called him Eupator.

3. At this time it was that the garrison in the citadel of Jerusalem, with the Jewish runagates, did a great deal of harm to the Jews; for the soldiers that were in that garrison rushed out upon the sudden, and destroyed such as were going up to the temple in order to offer their sacrifices, for this citadel adjoined to and overlooked the temple. When these misfortunes had often happened to them, Judas resolved to destroy that garrison; whereupon he got all the people together, and vigorously besieged those that were in the citadel. This was in the hundred and fiftieth year of the dominion of the Seleucidse. So he made engines of war, and erected bulwarks, and very zealously pressed on to take the citadel. But there were not a few of the runagates who were in the place that went out by night into the country, and got together some other wicked men like themselves, and went to Antiochus the king, and desired of him that he would not suffer them to be neglected, under the great hardships that lay upon them from those of their own nation; and this because their sufferings were occasioned on his father's account, while they left the religious worship of their fathers, and preferred that which he had commanded them to follow: that there was danger lest the citadel, and those appointed to garrison it by the king, should be taken by Judas, and those that were with him, unless he would send them succors. When Antiochus, who was but a child, heard this, he was angry, and sent for his captains and his friends, and gave order that they should get an army of mercenaries together, with such men also of his own kingdom as were of an age fit for war. Accordingly, an army was collected of about a hundred thousand footmen, and twenty thousand horsemen, and thirty-two elephants.

4. So the king took this army, and marched hastily out of Antioch, with Lysias, who had the command of the whole, and came to Idumea, and thence went up to the city Bethsnra, a city that was strong, and not to be taken without great difficulty. He set about this city, and besieged it. And while the inhabitants of Bethsura courageously opposed him, and sallied out upon him, and burnt his engines of war, a great deal of time was spent in the siege. But when Judas heard of the king's coming, he raised the siege of the citadel, and met the king, and pitched his

camp in certain straits, at a place called Bethzachriah, at the distance of seventy furlongs from the enemy; but the king soon drew his forces from Bethsura, and brought them to those straits. And as soon as it was day, he put his men in battle-array, and made his elephants follow one another through the narrow passes, because they could not be set sideways by one another. Now round about every elephant there were a thousand footmen, and five hundred horsemen. The elephants also had high towers [upon their backs], and archers [in them]. And he also made the rest of his army to go up the mountains, and put his friends before the rest; and gave orders for the army to shout aloud, and so he attacked the enemy. He also exposed to sight their golden and brazen shields, so that a glorious splendor was sent from them; and when they shouted the mountains echoed again. When Judas saw this, he was not terrified, but received the enemy with great courage, and slew about six hundred of the first ranks. But when his brother Eleazar, whom they called Auran, saw the tallest of all the elephants armed with royal breastplates, and supposed that the king was upon him, he attacked him with great quickness and bravery. He also slew many of those that were about the elephant, and scattered the rest, and then went under the belly of the elephant, and smote him, and slew him; so the elephant fell upon Eleazar, and by his weight crushed him to death. And thus did this man come to his end, when he had first courageously destroyed manyof his enemies.

5. But Judas, seeing the strength of the enemy, retired to Jerusalem, and prepared to endure a siege. As for Antiochus, he sent part of his army to Bethsura, to besiege it, and with the rest of his army he came against Jerusalem; but the inhabitants of Bethsura were terrified at his strength; and seeing that their provisions grew scarce,. they delivered themselves up on the security of oaths that they should suffer no hard treatment from the king. And when Antiochus had thus taken the city, he did them no other harm than sending them out naked. He also placed a garrison of his own in the city. But as for the temple of Jerusalem, he lay at its siege a long time, while they within bravely defended it; for what engines soever the king set against them, they set other engines again to oppose them. But then their provisions failed them; what fruits of the ground they had laid up were spent and the land being not ploughed that year, continued unsowed, because it was the seventh year, on which, by our laws, we are obliged to let it lay

uncultivated. And withal, so many of the besieged ran away for want of necessaries, that but a few only were left in the temple.

6. And these happened to be the circumstances of such as were besieged in the temple. But then, because Lysias, the general of the army, and Antiochus the king, were informed that Philip was coming upon them out of Persia, and was endeavoring to get the management of public affairs to himself, they came into these sentiments, to leave the siege, and to make haste to go against Philip; yet did they resolve not to let this be known to the soldiers or to the officers: but the king commanded Lysias to speak openly to the soldiers and the officers, without saying a word about the business of Philip; and to intimate to them that the siege would be very long; that the place was very strong; that they were already in want of provisions; that many affairs of the kingdom wanted regulation; and that it was much better to make a league with the besieged, and to become friends to their whole nation, by permitting them to observe the laws of their fathers, while they broke out into this war only because they were deprived of them, and so to depart home. When Lysias had discoursed thus to them, both the army and the officers were pleased with this resolution.

7. Accordingly the king sent to Judas, and to those that were besieged with them, and promised to give them peace, and to permit them to make use of, and live according to, the laws of their fathers; and they gladly received his proposals; and when they had gained security upon oath for their performance, they went out of the temple. But when Antiochus came into it, and saw how strong the place was, he broke his oaths, and ordered his army that was there to pluck down the walls to the ground; and when he had so done, he returned to Antioch. He also carried with him Onias the high priest, who was also called Menelaus; for Lysias advised the king to slay Menelaus, if he would have the Jews be quiet, and cause him no further disturbance, for that this man was the origin of all the mischief the Jews had done them, by persuading his father to compel the Jews to leave the religion of their fathers. So the king sent Menelaus to Berea, a city of Syria, and there had him put to death, when he had been high priest ten years. He had been a wicked and an impious man; and, in order to get the government to himself, had compelled his nation to transgress their own laws. After the death of Menelaus, Alcimus, who was also called Jacimus, was made high priest. But when king Antiochus found that

Philip had already possessed himself of the government, he made war against him, and subdued him, and took him, and slew him. Now as to Onias, the son of the high priest, who, as we before informed you, was left a child when his father died, when he saw that the king had slain his uncle Menelaus, and given the high priesthood to Alcimus, who was not of the high priest stock, but was induced by Lysias to translate that dignity from his family to another house, he fled to Ptolemy, king of Egypt; and when he found he was in great esteem with him, and with his wife Cleopatra, he desired and obtained a place in the Nomus of Heliopolis, wherein he built a temple like to that at Jerusalem; of which therefore we shall hereafter give an account, in a place more proper for it.

10 *How Bacchides, the General of Demetrius's Army, Made an Expedition Against Judea, and Returned Without Success; and How Nicanor Was Sent a Little Afterward Against Judas and Perished, Together with His Army; as Also Concerning the Death of Alcimus and the Succession of Judas*

1. ABOUT the same time Demetrius, the son of Seleucus, fled away from Rome, and took Tripoli, a city of Syria, and set the diadem on his own head. He also gathered certain mercenary soldiers together, and entered into his kingdom, and was joyfully received by all, who delivered themselves up to him. And when they had taken Autiochus the king, and Lysias, they brought them to him alive; both which were immediately put to death by the command of Demetrius, when Antiochus had reigned two years, as we have already elsewhere related. But there were now many of the wicked Jewish runagates that came together to him, and with them Alcimus the high priest, who accused the whole nation, and particularly Judas and his brethren; and said that they had slain all his friends, and that those in his kingdom that were of his party, and waited for his return, were by them put to death; that these men had ejected them out of their own country, and caused them to be sojourners in a foreign land; and they desired that he would send some one of his own friends, and know from him what mischief Judas's party had done.

2. At this Demetrius was very angry, and sent Bacchides, a friend of Antiochus Epiphanes,[25] a good man, and one that had been intrusted with all Mesopotamia, and gave him an army, and committed Alcimus the high priest to his care; and gave him charge to slay Judas, and those that were with him. So Bacchides made haste, and went out of Antioch with his army; and when he was come into Judea, he sent to Judas and his brethren, to discourse with them about a league of friendship and peace, for he had a mind to take him by treachery. But Judas did not give credit to him, for he saw that he came with so great an army as men do not bring when they come to make peace, but to make war. However, some of the people acquiesced in what Bacchides caused to be proclaimed; and supposing they should undergo no considerable harm from Alcimus, who was their countryman, they went over to them; and when they had received oaths from both of them, that neither they themselves, nor those of the same sentiments, should come to any harm, they intrusted themselves with them. But Bacchides troubled not himself about the oaths he had taken, but slew threescore of them, although, by not keeping his faith with those that first went over, he deterred all the rest, who had intentions to go over to him, from doing it. But as he was gone out of Jerusalem, and was at the village called Bethzetho, he sent out, and caught many of the deserters, and some of the people also, and slew them all; and enjoined all that lived in the country to submit to Alcimus. So he left him there, with some part of the army, that he might have wherewith to keep the country in obedience and returned to Antioch to king Demetrius.

3. But Alcimus was desirous to have the dominion more firmly assured to him; and understanding that, if he could bring it about that the multitude should be his friends, he should govern with greater security, he spake kind words to them all, and discoursed to each of them after an agreeable and pleasant manner; by which means he quickly had a great body of men and an army about him, although the greater part of them were of the wicked, and the deserters. With

---

25. It is no way probable that Josephus would call Bacchidoa, that bitter and bloody enemy of the Jews, as our present copies have it, a man good, or kind, and gentle, What the author of the First Book of Maccabees, whom Josephus here follows, instead of that character, says of him, is, that he was a great man in the kingdom, and faithful to his king; which was very probably Josephus's meaning also.

these, whom he used as his servants and soldiers, he went all over the country, and slew all that he could find of Judas's party. But when Judas saw that Alcimus was already become great, and had destroyed many of the good and holy men of the country, he also went all over the country, and destroyed those that were of the other party. But when Alcimus saw that he was not able to oppose Judas, nor was equal to him in strength, he resolved to apply himself to king Demetrius for his assistance; so he came to Antioch, and irritated him against Judas, and accused him, alleging that he had undergone a great many miseries by his means, and that he would do more mischief unless he were prevented, and brought to punishment, which must be done by sending a powerful force against him.

4. So Demetrius, being already of opinion that it would be a thing pernicious to his own affairs to overlook Judas, now he was becoming so great, sent against him Nicanor, the most kind and most faithful of all his friends; for he it was who fled away with him from the city of Rome. He also gave him as many forces as he thought sufficient for him to conquer Judas withal, and bid him not to spare the nation at all. When Nicanor was come to Jerusalem, he did not resolve to fight Judas immediately, but judged it better to get him into his power by treachery; so he sent him a message of peace, and said there was no manner of necessity for them to fight and hazard themselves; and that he would give him his oath that he would do him no harm, for that he only came with some friends, in order to let him know what king Demetrius's intentions were, and what opinion he had of their nation. When Nicanor had delivered this message, Judas and his brethren complied with him, and suspecting no deceit, they gave him assurances of friendship, and received Nicanor and his army; but while he was saluting Judas, and they were talking together, he gave a certain signal to his own soldiers, upon which they were to seize upon Judas; but he perceived the treachery, and ran back to his own soldiers, and fled away with them. So upon this discovery of his purpose, and of the snares laid for Judas, Nicanor determined to make open war with him, and gathered his army together, and prepared for fighting him; and upon joining battle with him at a certain village

called Capharsalama, he beat Judas,[26] and forced him to fly to that citadel which was at Jerusalem.

5. And when Nicanor came down from the citadel unto the temple, some of the priests and elders met him, and saluted him; and showed him the sacrifices which they offered to God for the king: upon which he blasphemed, and threatened them, that unless the people would deliver up Judas to him, upon his return he would pull clown their temple. And when he had thus threatened them, he departed from Jerusalem. But the priests fell into tears out of grief at what he had said, and besought God to deliver them from their enemies But now for Nicanor, when he was gone out of Jerusalem, and was at a certain village called Bethoron, he there pitched his camp, another army out of Syria having joined him. And Judas pitched his camp at Adasa, another village, which was thirty furlongs distant from Bethoron, having no more than one thousand soldiers. And when he had encouraged them not to be dismayed at the multitude of their enemies, nor to regard how many they were against whom they were going to fight, but to consider who they themselves were, and for what great rewards they hazarded themselves, and to attack the enemy courageously, he led them out to fight, and joining battle with Nicanor, which proved to be a severe one, he overcame the enemy, and slew many of them; and at last Nicanor himself, as he was fighting gloriously, fell:—upon whose fall the army did not stay; but when they had lost their general, they were put to flight, and threw down their arms. Judas also pursued them and slew them, and gave notice by the sound of the trumpets to the neighboring villages that he had conquered the enemy; which, when the inhabitants heard, they put on their armor hastily, and met their enemies in the face as they were running away, and slew them, insomuch that not one of them escaped out of this battle, who were in number nine thousand This victory happened to fall on the thirteenth day of that month which by the Jews

---

26. Josephus's copies must have been corrupted when they here give victory to Nicanor, contrary to the words following, which imply that he who was beaten fled into the citadel, which for certain belonged to the city of David, or to Mount Zion, and was in the possession of Nicanor's garrison, and not of Judas's. As also it is contrary to the express words of Josephus's original author, 1 Macc. 7:32, who says that Nicanor lost about five thousand men, and fled to the city of David.

is called Adar and by the Macedonians Dystrus; and the Jews thereon celebrate this victory every year, and esteem it as a festival day. After which the Jewish nation were, for a while, free from wars, and enjoyed peace; but afterward they returned into their former state of wars and hazards.

6. But now as the high priest Alcimus, was resolving to pull down the wall of the sanctuary, which had been there of old time, and had been built by the holy prophets, he was smitten suddenly by God, and fell down.[27] This stroke made him fall down speechless upon the ground; and undergoing torments for many days, he at length died, when he had been high priest four years. And when he was dead, the people bestowed the high priesthood on Judas; who hearing of the power of the Romans, and that they had conquered in war Galatia, and Iberia, and Carthage, and Libya; and that, besides these, they had subdued Greece, and their kings, Perseus, and Philip, and Antiochus the Great also; he resolved to enter into a league of friendship with them. He therefore sent to Rome some of his friends, Eupolemus the son of John, and Jason the son of Eleazar, and by them desired the Romans that they would assist them, and be their friends, and would write to Demetrius that he would not fight against the Jews. So the senate received the ambassadors that came from Judas to Rome, and discoursed with them about the errand on which they came, and then granted them a league of assistance. They also made a decree concerning it, and sent a copy of it into Judea. It was also laid up in the capitol, and engraven in brass. The decree itself was this: "The decree of the senate concerning a league of assistance and friendship with the nation of the Jews. It shall not be lawful for any that are subject to the Romans to make war with the nation of the Jews, nor to assist those that do so, either by sending them corn, or ships, or money; and if any

---

27. This account of the miserable death of Alcimus, or Jac-mus, the wicked high priest, (the first that was not of the family of the high priests, and made by a vile heathen, Lysias,) before the death of Judas, and of Judas's succession to him as high priest, both here, and at the conclusion of this book, directly contradicts 1 Macc. 9:54–57, which places his death after the death of Judas, and says not a syllable of the high priesthood of Judas. How well the Roman histories agree to this account of the conquests and powerful condition of the Romans at this time, see the notes in Havercamp's edition; only that the number of the senators of Rome was then just three hundred and twenty, is, I think, only known from 1 Macc. 8:15.

attack be made upon the Jews, the Romans shall assist them, as far as they are able; and again, if any attack be made upon the Romans, the Jews shall assist them. And if the Jews have a mind to add to, or to take away any thing from, this league of assistance, that shall be done with the common consent of the Romans. And whatsoever addition shall thus be made, it shall be of force." This decree was written by Eupolemus the son of John, and by Jason the son of Eleazar,[28] when Judas was high priest of the nation, and Simon his brother was general of the army. And this was the first league that the Romans made with the Jews, and was managed after this manner.

11 *That Bacchides Was Again Sent Out Against Judas; and How Judas Fell as He Was Courageously Fighting*

1. BUT when Demetrius was informed of the death of Nicanor, and of the destruction of the army that was with him, he sent Bacchides again with an army into Judea, who marched out of Antioch, and came into Judea, and pitched his camp at Arbela, a city of Galilee; and having besieged and taken those that were there in caves, (for many of the people fled into such places,) he removed, and made all the haste he could to Jerusalem. And when he had learned that Judas had pitched his camp at a certain village whose name was Bethzetho, he led his army against him: they were twenty thousand foot-men, and two thousand horsemen. Now Judas had no more soldiers than one thousand.[29] When these saw the multitude of Bacchides's men, they were afraid, and left their camp, and fled all away, excepting eight hundred. Now when Judas was deserted by his own soldiers, and the enemy pressed upon him, and gave him no time to gather his army together, he was disposed to fight with Bacchides's army, though he

---

28. This subscription is wanting 1 Macc. 8:17, 29, and must be the words of Josephus, who by mistake thought, as we have just now seen, that Judas was at this time high priest, and accordingly then reckoned his brother Jonathan to be the general of the army, which yet he seems not to have been till after the death of Judas.

29. That this copy of Josephus, as he wrote it, had here not one thousand, but three thousand, with 1 Macc 9:5, is very plain, because though the main part ran away at first, even in Josephus, as well as in 1 Macc. 9:6, yet, as there, so here, eight hundred are said to have remained with Judas, which would be absurd, if the whole number had been no more than one thousand.

had but eight hundred men with him; so he exhorted these men to undergo the danger courageously, and encouraged them to attack the enemy. And when they said they were not a body sufficient to fight so great an army, and advised that they should retire now, and save themselves and that when he had gathered his own men together, then he should fall upon the enemy afterwards, his answer was this: "Let not the sun ever see such a thing, that I should show my back to the enemy and although this be the time that will bring me to my end, and I must die in this battle, I will rather stand to it courageously, and bear whatsoever comes upon me, than by now running away bring reproach upon my former great actions, or tarnish their glory." This was the speech he made to those that remained with him, whereby he encouraged them to attack the enemy.

2. But Bacchldes drew his army out of their camp, and put them in array for the battle. He set the horsemen on both the wings, and the light soldiers and the archers he placed before the whole army, but he was himself on the right wing. And when he had thus put his army in order of battle, and was going to join battle with the enemy, he commanded the trumpeter to give a signal of battle, and the army to make a shout, and to fall on the enemy. And when Judas had done the same, he joined battle with them; and as both sides fought valiantly, and the battle continued till sun-set, Judas saw that Bacehides and the strongest part of the army was in the right wing, and thereupon took the most courageous men with him, and ran upon that part of the army, and fell upon those that were there, and broke their ranks, and drove them into the middle, and forced them to run away, and pursued them as far as to a mountain called Aza: but when those of the left wing saw that the right wing was put to flight, they encompassed Judas, and pursued him, and came behind him, and took him into the middle of their army; so being not able to fly, but encompassed round about with enemies, he stood still, and he and those that were with him fought; and when he had slain a great many of those that came against him, he at last was himself wounded, and fell and gave up the ghost, and died in a way like to his former famous actions. When Judas was dead, those that were with him had no one whom they could regard [as their commander]; but when they saw themselves deprived of such a general, they fled. But Simon and Jonathan, Judas's brethren, received his dead body by a treaty from the enemy, and

carried it to the village of Modin, where their father had been buried, and there buried him; while the multitude lamented him many days, and performed the usual solemn rites of a funeral to him. And this was the end that Judas came to. He had been a man of valor and a great warrior, and mindful of the commands of their father Matrathins; and had undergone all difficulties, both in doing and suffering, for the liberty of his countrymen. And when his character was so excellent [while he was alive], he left behind him a glorious reputation and memorial, by gaining freedom for his nation, and delivering them from slavery under the Macedonians. And when he had retained the high priesthood three years, he died.

Book 13

Containing the Interval of Eighty-Two Years,

From the Death of Judas Maccabeus to the Death of Queen Alexandra

1 *How Jonathan Took the Government After His Brother Judas; and How He, Together with His Brother Simon, Waged War Against Bacchides*

1. BY what means the nation of the Jews recovered their freedom when they had been brought into slavery by the Macedonians, and what struggles, and how great battles, Judas, the general of their army, ran through, till he was slain as he was fighting for them, hath been related in the foregoing book; but after he was dead, all the wicked, and those that transgressed the laws of their forefathers, sprang up again in Judea, and grew upon them, and distressed them on every side. A famine also assisted their wickedness, and afflicted the country, till not a few, who by reason of their want of necessaries, and because they were not able to bear up against the miseries that both the famine and their enemies brought upon them, deserted their country, and went to the Macedonians. And now Bacchides gathered those Jews together who had apostatized from the accustomed way of living of their forefathers, and chose to live like their neighbors, and committed the care of the country to them, who also caught the friends of Judas, and those of his party, and delivered them up to Bacchides, who when he had, in the first place, tortured and tormented them at his pleasure, he, by that means, at length killed them. And when this calamity of the Jews was become so great, as they had never had experience of

the like since their return out of Babylon, those that remained of the companions of Judas, seeing that the nation was ready to be destroyed after a miserable manner, came to his brother Jonathan, and desired him that he would imitate his brother, and that care which he took of his countrymen, for whose liberty in general he died also; and that he would not permit the nation to be without a governor, especially in those destructive circumstances wherein it now was. And where Jonathan said that he was ready to die for them, and esteemed no inferior to his brother, he was appointed to be the general of the Jewish army.

2. When Bacchides heard this, and was afraid that Jonathan might be very troublesome to the king and the Macedonians, as Judas had been before him, he sought how he might slay him by treachery. But this intention of his was not unknown to Jonathan, nor to his brother Simon; but when these two were apprized of it, they took all their companions, and presently fled into that wilderness which was nearest to the city; and when they were come to a lake called Asphar, they abode there. But when Bacchides was sensible that they were in a low state, and were in that place, he hasted to fall upon them with all his forces, and pitching his camp beyond Jordan, he recruited his army. But when Jonathan knew that Bacchides Was coming upon him, he sent his brother John, who was also called Gaddis, to the Nabatean Arabs, that he might lodge his baggage with them until the battle with Bacchides should be over, for they were the Jews' friends. And the sons of Ambri laid an ambush for John from the city Medaba, and seized upon him, and upon those that were with him, and plundered all that they had with them. They also slew John, and all his companions. However, they were sufficiently punished for what they now did by John's brethren, as we shall relate presently.

3. But when Bacchides knew that Jonathan had pitched his camp among the lakes of Jordan, he observed when their sabbath day came, and then assaulted him, [as supposing that he would not fight because of the law for resting on that day]: but he exhorted his companions [to fight]; and told them that their lives were at stake, since they were encompassed by the river, and by their enemies, and had no way to escape, for that their enemies pressed upon them from before, and the river was behind them. So after he had prayed to God to give them the victory, he joined battle with the enemy, of whom he overthrew

many; and as he saw Bacchides coming up boldly to him, he stretched out his right hand to smite him; but the other foreseeing and avoiding the stroke, Jonathan with his companions leaped into the river, and swam over it, and by that means escaped beyond Jordan while the enemies did not pass over that river; but Bacchides returned presently to the citadel at Jerusalem, having lost about two thousand of his army. He also fortified many cities of Judea, whose walls had been demolished; Jericho, and Emmaus, and Betboron, and Bethel, and Tinma, and Pharatho, and Tecoa, and Gazara, and built towers in every one of these cities, and encompassed them with strong walls, that were very large also, and put garrisons into them, that they might issue out of them, and do mischief to the Jews. He also fortified the citadel at Jerusalem more than all the rest. Moreover, he took the sons of the principal Jews as pledges, and hut them up in the citadel, and in that manner guarded it.

4. About the same time one came to Jonathan, and to his brother Simon, and told them that the sons of Ambri were celebrating a marriage, and bringing the bride from the city Gabatha, who was the daughter of one of the illustrious men among the Arabians, and that the damsel was to be conducted with pomp, and splendor, and much riches: so Jonathan and Simon thinking this appeared to be the fittest time for them to avenge the death of their brother, and that they had forces sufficient for receiving satisfaction from them for his death, they made haste to Medaba, and lay in wait among the mountains for the coming of their enemies; and as soon as they saw them conducting the virgin, and her bridegroom, and such a great company of their friends with them as was to be expected at this wedding, they sallied out of their ambush, and slew them all, and took their ornaments, and all the prey that then followed them, and so returned, and received this satisfaction for their brother John from the sons of Ambri; for as well those sons themselves, as their friends, and wives, and children that followed them, perished, being in number about four hundred.

5. However, Simon and Jonathan returned to the lakes of the river, and abode there. But Bacchides, when he had secured all Judea with his garrisons, returned to the king; and then it was that the affairs of Judea were quiet for two years. But when the deserters and the wicked saw that Jonathan and those that were with him lived in the country very quietly, by reason of the peace, they sent to king Demetrius, and

excited him to send Bacchides to seize upon Jonathan, which they said was to be done without any trouble, and in one night's time; and that if they fell upon them before they were aware, they might slay them all. So the king sent Bacchides, who, when he was come into Judea, wrote to all his friends, both Jews and auxiliaries, that they should seize upon Jonathan, and bring him to him; and when, upon all their endeavors, they were not able to seize upon Jonathan, for he was sensible of the snares they laid for him, and very carefully guarded against them, Bacchides was angry at these deserters, as having imposed upon him, and upon the king, and slew fifty of their leaders: whereupon Jonathan, with his brother, and those that were with him, retired to Bethagla, a village that lay in the wilderness, out of his fear of Bacchides. He also built towers in it, and encompassed it with walls, and took care that it should be safely guarded. Upon the hearing of which Bacchides led his own army along with him, and besides took his Jewish auxiliaries, and came against Jonathan, and made an assault upon his fortifications, and besieged him many days; but Jonathan did not abate of his courage at the zeal Bacchides used in the siege, but courageously opposed him. And while he left his brother Simon in the city to fight with Bacchides, he went privately out himself into the country, and got a great body of men together of his own party, and fell upon Bacchides's camp in the night time, and destroyed a great many of them. His brother Simon knew also of this his falling upon them, because he perceived that the enemies were slain by him; so he sallied out upon them, and burnt the engines which the Macedonians used, and made a great slaughter of them. And when Bacchides saw himself encompassed with enemies, and some of them before and some behind him, he fell into despair and trouble of mind, as confounded at the unexpected ill success of this siege. However, he vented his displeasure at these misfortunes upon those deserters who sent for him from the king, as having deluded him. So he had a mind to finish this siege after a decent manner, if it were possible for him so to do, and then to return home.

6. When Jonathan understood these his intentions, he sent ambassadors to him about a league of friendship and mutual assistance, and that they might restore those they had taken captive on both sides. So Bacchides thought this a pretty decent way of retiring home, and made a league of friendship with Jonathan, when they sware that they

would not any more make war one against another. Accordingly, he restored the captives, and took his own men with him, and returned to the king at Antioch; and after this his departure, he never came into Judea again. Then did Jonathan take the opportunity of this quiet state of things, and went and lived in the city Michmash; and there governed the multitude, and punished the wicked and ungodly, and by that means purged the nation of them.

2 *How Alexander [Bala] in His War with Demetrius, Granted Jonathan Many Advantages and Appointed Him to Be High Priest and Persuaded Him to Assist Him Although Demetrius Promised Him Greater Advantages on the Other Side. Concerning the Death of Demetrius*

1. NOW in the hundred and sixtieth year, it fell out that Alexander, the son of Antiochus Epiphanes,[1] came up into Syria, and took Ptolemais the soldiers within having betrayed it to him; for they were at enmity with Demetrius, on account of his insolence and difficulty of access; for he shut himself up in a palace of his that had four towers which he had built himself, not far from Antioch and admitted nobody. He was withal slothful and negligent about the public affairs, whereby the hatred of his subjects was the more kindled against him, as we have elsewhere already related. When therefore Demetrius heard that Alexander was in Ptolemais, he took his whole army, and led it against him; he also sent ambassadors to Jonathan about a league of mutual assistance and friendship, for he resolved to be beforehand

---

1. This Alexander Bala, who certainly pretended to be the son of Antiochus Epiphanes, and was owned for such by the Jews and Romans, and many others, and yet is by several historians deemed to be a counterfeit, and of no family at all, is, however, by Josephus believed to have been the real son of that Antiochus, and by him always spoken of accordingly. And truly, since the original contemporary and authentic author of the First Book of Maccabees (10:1) calls him by his father's name, Epiphanes, and says he was the son of Antiochus, I suppose the other writers, who are all much later, are not to be followed against such evidence, though perhaps Epiphanes might have him by a woman of no family. The king of Egypt also, Philometor, soon gave him his daughter in marriage, which he would hardly have done, had he believed him to be a counterfeit, and of so very mean a birth as the later historians pretend.

with Alexander, lest the other should treat with him first, and gain assistance from him; and this he did out of the fear he had lest Jonathan should remember how ill Demetrius had formerly treated him, and should join with him in this war against him. He therefore gave orders that Jonathan should be allowed to raise an army, and should get armor made, and should receive back those hostages of the Jewish nation whom Baechides had shut up in the citadel of Jerusalem. When this good fortune had befallen Jonathan, by the concession of Demetrius, he came to Jerusalem, and read the king's letter in the audience of the people, and of those that kept the citadel. When these were read, these wicked men and deserters, who were in the citadel, were greatly afraid, upon the king's permission to Jonathan to raise an army, and to receive back the hostages. So he delivered every one of them to his own parents. And thus did Jonathan make his abode at Jerusalem, renewing the city to a better state, and reforming the buildings as he pleased; for he gave orders that the walls of the city should be rebuilt with square stones, that it might be more secure from their enemies. And when those that kept the garrisons that were in Judea saw this, they all left them, and fled to Antioch, excepting those that were in the city Bethsura, and those that were in the citadel of Jerusalem, for the greater part of these was of the wicked Jews and deserters, and on that account these did not deliver up their garrisons.

2. When Alexander knew what promises Demetrius had made Jonathan, and withal knew his courage, and what great things he had done when he fought the Macedonians, and besides what hardships he had undergone by the means of Demetrius, and of Bacchides, the general of Demetrius's army, he told his friends that he could not at present find any one else that might afford him better assistance than Jonathan, who was both courageous against his enemies, and had a particular hatred against Demetrius, as having both suffered many hard things from him, and acted many hard things against him. If therefore they were of opinion that they should make him their friend against Demetrius, it was more for their advantage to invite him to assist them now than at another time. It being therefore determined by him and his friends to send to Jonathan, he wrote to him this epistle: "King Alexander to his brother Jonathan, sendeth greeting. We have long ago heard of thy courage and thy fidelity, and for that reason have sent to thee, to make with thee a league of friendship and mutual

assistance. We therefore do ordain thee this day the high priest of the Jews, and that thou beest called my friend. I have also sent thee, as presents, a purple robe and a golden crown, and desire that, now thou art by us honored, thou wilt in like manner respect us also."

3. When Jonathan had received this letter, he put on the pontifical robe at the time of the feast of tabernacles,[2] four years after the death of his brother Judas, for at that time no high priest had been made. So he raised great forces, and had abundance of armor got ready. This greatly grieved Demetrius when he heard of it, and made him blame himself for his slowness, that he had not prevented Alexander, and got the good-will of Jonathan, but had given him time so to do. However, he also himself wrote a letter to Jonathan, and to the people, the contents whereof are these: "King Demetrius to Jonathan, and to the nation of the Jews, sendeth greeting. Since you have preserved your friendship for us, and when you have been tempted by our enemies, you have not joined yourselves to them, I both commend you for this your fidelity, and exhort you to continue in the same disposition, for which you shall be repaid, and receive rewards from us; for I will free you from the greatest part of the tributes and taxes which you formerly paid to the kings my predecessors, and to myself; and I do now set you free from those tributes which you have ever paid; and besides, I forgive you the tax upon salt, and the value of the crowns which you used to offer to me[3] and instead of the third part of the fruits [of the field], and the half of the fruits of the trees, I relinquish my part of them from this day: and as to the poll-money, which ought to be given me for every head of the inhabitants of Judea, and of the three toparchies that adjoin to Judea, Samaria, and Galilee, and Peres, that I relinquish to

---

2. Since Jonathan plainly did not put on the pontifical robes till seven or eight years after the death of his brother Judas, or not till the feast of tabernacles, in the 160th of the Seleucidm, 1 Macc. 10;21, Petitus's emendation seems here to deserve consideration, who, instead of "after four years since the death of his brother Judas," would have us read, "and therefore after eight years since the death of his brother Judas." This would tolerably well agree with the date of the Maccabees, and with Josephus's own exact chronology at the end of the twentieth book of these Antiquities, which the present text cannot be made to do.

3. Take Grotius's note here: "The Jews," says he, "were wont to present crowns to the kings [of Syria]; afterwards that gold which was paid instead of those crowns, or which was expended in making them, was called the crown gold and crown tax." On 1 Macc. 10:29.

you for this time, and for all time to come. I will also that the city of Jerusalem be holy and inviolable, and free from the tithe, and from the taxes, unto its utmost bounds. And I so far recede from my title to the citadel, as to permit Jonathan your high priest to possess it, that he may place such a garrison in it as he approves of for fidelity and good-will to himself, that they may keep it for us. I also make free all those Jews who have been made captives and slaves in my kingdom. I also give order that the beasts of the Jews be not pressed for our service; and let their sabbaths, and all their festivals, and three days before each of them, be free from any imposition. In the same manner, I set free the Jews that are inhabitants of my kingdom, and order that no injury be done them. I also give leave to such of them as are willing to list themselves in my army, that they may do it, and those as far as thirty thousand; which Jewish soldiers, wheresoever they go, shall have the same pay that my own army hath; and some of them I will place in my garrisons, and some as guards about mine own body, and as rulers over those that are in my court. I give them leave also to use the laws of their forefathers, and to observe them; and I will that they have power over the three toparchies that are added to Judea; and it shall be in the power of the high priest to take care that no one Jew shall have any other temple for worship but only that at Jerusalem. I bequeath also, out of my own revenues, yearly, for the expenses about the sacrifices, one hundred and fifty thousand [drachmae]; and what money is to spare, I will that it shall be your own. I also release to you those ten thousand drachmae which the kings received from the temple, because they appertain to the priests that minister in that temple. And whosoever shall fly to the temple at Jerusalem, or to the places thereto belonging, or who owe the king money, or are there on any other account, let them be set free, and let their goods be in safety. I also give you leave to repair and rebuild your temple, and that all be done at my expenses. I also allow you to build the walls of your city, and to erect high towers, and that they be erected at my charge. And if there be any fortified town that would be convenient for the Jewish country to have very strong, let it be so built at my expenses."

4. This was what Demetrius promised and granted to the Jews by this letter. But king Alexander raised a great army of mercenary soldiers, and of those that deserted to him out of Syria, and made an expedition against Demetrius. And when it was come to a battle,

the left wing of Demetrius put those who opposed them to flight, and pursued them a great way, and slew many of them, and spoiled their camp; but the right wing, where Demetrius happened to be, was beaten; and as for all the rest, they ran away. But Demetrius fought courageously, and slew a great many of the enemy; but as he was in the pursuit of the rest, his horse carried him into a deep bog, where it was hard to get out, and there it happened, that upon his horse's falling down, he could not escape being killed; for when his enemies saw what had befallen him, they returned back, and encompassed Demetrius round, and they all threw their darts at him; but he, being now on foot, fought bravely. But at length he received so many wounds, that he was not able to bear up any longer, but fell. And this is the end that Demetrius came to, when he had reigned eleven years,[4] as we have elsewhere related.

3 *The Friendship That Was Between Onias and Ptolemy Philometor; and How Onias Built a Temple in Egypt Like to That at Jerusalem*

1. BUT then the son of Onias the high priest, who was of the same name with his father, and who fled to king Ptolemy, who was called Philometor, lived now at Alexandria, as we have said already. When this Onias saw that Judea was oppressed by the Macedonians and their kings, out of a desire to purchase to himself a memorial and eternal fame he resolved to send to king Ptolemy and queen Cleopatra, to ask leave of them that he might build a temple in Egypt like to that at Jerusalem, and might ordain Levites and priests out of their own stock. The chief reason why he was desirous so to do, was, that he relied upon the prophet Isaiah, who lived above six hundred years before, and foretold that there certainly was to be a temple built to Almighty God in Egypt by a man that was a Jew. Onias was elevated with this prediction, and wrote the following epistle to Ptolemy and Cleopatra: "Having done many and great things for you in the affairs of the war, by the assistance of God, and that in Celesyria and Phoenicia, I came at length with the Jews to Leontopolis, and to other places of

4. Since the rest of the historians now extant give this Demetrius thirteen years, and Josephus only eleven years, Dean Prideaux does not amiss in ascribing to him the mean number twelve.

your nation, where I found that the greatest part of your people had temples in an improper manner, and that on this account they bare ill-will one against another, which happens to the Egyptians by reason of the multitude of their temples, and the difference of opinions about Divine worship. Now I found a very fit place in a castle that hath its name from the country Diana; this place is full of materials of several sorts, and replenished with sacred animals; I desire therefore that you will grant me leave to purge this holy place, which belongs to no master, and is fallen down, and to build there a temple to Almighty God, after the pattern of that in Jerusalem, and of the same dimensions, that may be for the benefit of thyself, and thy wife and children, that those Jews which dwell in Egypt may have a place whither they may come and meet together in mutual harmony one with another, and he subservient to thy advantages; for the prophet Isaiah foretold that "there should be an altar in Egypt to the Lord God;[5] and many other such things did he prophesy relating to that place."

---

5. It seems to me contrary to the opinion of Josephus, and of the moderns, both Jews and Christians, that this prophecy of Isaiah, 19:19, etc., "In that day there shall be an altar to the Lord in the midst of the land of Egypt," etc., directly foretold the building of this temple of Onias in Egypt, and was a sufficient warrant to the Jews for building it, and for worshipping the true God. the God of Israel, therein. See Authent. Rec. 11. p. 755. That God seems to have soon better accepted of the sacrifices and prayers here offered him than those at Jerusalem, see the note on ch. 10. sect. 7. And truly the marks of Jewish corruption or interpolation in this text, in order to discourage their people from approving of the Worship of God here, are very strong, and highly deserve our consideration and correction. The foregoing verse in Isaiah runs thus in our common copies, "In that day shall five cities in the land of Egypt speak the language of Canaan," [the Hebrew language; shall be full of Jews, whose sacred books were in Hebrew,] "and swear to the Lord of hosts; one" [or the first] "shall be called, The City of Destruction," Isaiah 19:18. A strange-name, "City of Destruction," upon so joyful occasion, and a name never heard of in the land of Egypt, or perhaps in any other nation. The old reading was evidently the City of the Sun, or Heliopolis; and Unkelos, in effect, and Symmachus, with the Arabic version, entirely confess that to be the true reading. The Septuagint also, though they have the text disguised in the common copies, and call it Asedek, the City of Righteousness; yet in two or three other copies the Hebrew word itself for the Sun, Achares, or Thares, is preserved. And since Onias insists with the king and queen, that Isaiah's prophecy contained many other predictions relating to this place besides the words by him recited, it is highly probable that these were especially meant by him; and that one main reason why he applied this prediction to himself, and to his prefecture of Heliopolis, which Dean Prideaux well proves was in that part of Egypt, and why he chose to build in that prefecture of Heliopolis, though otherwise an improper place,

2. And this was what Onias wrote to king Ptolemy. Now any one may observe his piety, and that of his sister and wife Cleopatra, by that epistle which they wrote in answer to it; for they laid the blame and the transgression of the law upon the head of Onias. And this was their reply: "King Ptolemy and queen Cleopatra to Onias, send greeting. We have read thy petition, wherein thou desirest leave to be given thee to purge that temple which is fallen down at Leontopolis, in the Nomus of Heliopolis, and which is named from the country Bubastis; on which account we cannot but wonder that it should be pleasing to God to have a temple erected in a place so unclean, and so full of sacred animals. But since thou sayest that Isaiah the prophet foretold this long ago, we give thee leave to do it, if it may be done according to your law, and so that we may not appear to have at all offended God herein."

3. So Onias took the place, and built a temple, and an altar to God, like indeed to that in Jerusalem, but smaller and poorer. I do not think it proper for me now to describe its dimensions or its vessels, which have been already described in my seventh book of the Wars of the Jews. However, Onias found other Jews like to himself, together with priests and Levites, that there performed Divine service. But we have said enough about this temple.

4. Now it came to pass that the Alexandrian Jews, and those Samaritans who paid their worship to the temple that was built in the days of Alexander at Mount Gerizzim, did now make a sedition one against another, and disputed about their temples before Ptolemy himself; the Jews saying that, according to the laws of Moses, the temple was to be built at Jerusalem; and the Samaritans saying that it was to be built at Gerizzim. They desired therefore the king to sit with his friends, and hear the debates about these matters, and punish those with death who were baffled. Now Sabbeus and Theodosius managed the argument for the Samaritans, and Andronicus, the son

---

was this, that the same authority that he had for building this temple in Egypt, the very same he had for building it in his own prefecture of Heliopolis also, which he desired to do, and which he did accordingly. Dean Prideaux has much ado to avoid seeing this corruption of the Hebrew; but it being in support of his own opinion about this temple, he durst not see it; and indeed he reasons here in the most injudicious manner possible. See him at the year 149.

of Messalamus, for the people of Jerusalem; and they took an oath by God and the king to make their demonstrations according to the law; and they desired of Ptolemy, that whomsoever he should find that transgressed what they had sworn to, he would put him to death. Accordingly, the king took several of his friends into the council, and sat down, in order to hear what the pleaders said. Now the Jews that were at Alexandria were in great concern for those men, whose lot it was to contend for the temple at Jerusalem; for they took it very ill that any should take away the reputation of that temple, which was so ancient and so celebrated all over the habitable earth. Now when Sabbeus and Tlteodosius had given leave to Andronicus to speak first, he began to demonstrate out of the law, and out of the successions of the high priests, how they every one in succession from his father had received that dignity, and ruled over the temple; and how all the kings of Asia had honored that temple with their donations, and with the most splendid gifts dedicated thereto. But as for that at Gerizzm, he made no account of it, and regarded it as if it had never had a being. By this speech, and other arguments, Andronicus persuaded the king to determine that the temple at Jerusalem was built according to the laws of Moses,[6] and to put Sabbeus and Theodosius to death. And these were the events that befell the Jews at Alexandria in the days of Ptolemy Philometor.

---

6. A very unfair disputation this! while the Jewish disputant, knowing that he could not properly prove out of the Pentateuch, that "the place which the Lord their God shall choose to place his name there," so often referred to in the Book of Deuteronomy, was Jerusalem any more than Gerizzim, that being not determined till the days of David, Antiq. B. VII. ch. 13. sect. 4, proves only, what the Samaritans did not deny, that the temple at Jerusalem was much more ancient, and much more celebrated and honored, than that at Gerizzim, which was nothing to the present purpose. The whole evidence, by the very oaths of both parties, being, we see, obliged to be confined to the law of Moses, or to the Pentateuch alone. However, worldly policy and interest and the multitude prevailing, the court gave sentence, as usual, on the stronger side. and poor Sabbeus and Theodosius, the Samaritan disputants, were martyred, and this, so far as appears, without any direct hearing at all, which is like the usual practice of such political courts about matters of religion. Our copies say that the body of the Jews were in a great concern about those men (in the plural) who were to dispute for their temple at Jerusalem, whereas it seems here they had but one disputant, Andronicus by name. Perhaps more were prepared to speak on the Jews' side; but the firstraying answered to his name, and overcome the Samaritans, there was necessity for any other defender of the Jerusalem temple.

Chapter 4

4 *How Alexander Honored Jonathan After an Extraordinary Manner; and How Demetrius, the Son of Demetrius, Overcame Alexander and Made a League of Friendship with Jonathan*

1. DEMETRIUS being thus slain in battle, as we have above related, Alexander took the kingdom of Syria; and wrote to Ptolemy Philometor, and desired his daughter in marriage; and said it was but just that he should be joined an affinity to one that had now received the principality of his forefathers, and had been promoted to it by God's providence, and had conquered Demetrius, and that was on other accounts not unworthy of being related to him. Ptolemy received this proposal of marriage gladly; and wrote him an answer, saluting him on account of his having received the principality of his forefathers; and promising him that he would give him his daughter in marriage; and assured him that he was coming to meet him at Ptolemais, and desired that he would there meet him, for that he would accompany her from Egypt so far, and would there marry his child to him. When Ptolemy had written thus, he came suddenly to Ptolemais, and brought his daughter Cleopatra along with him; and as he found Alexander there before him, as he desired him to come, he gave him his child in marriage, and for her portion gave her as much silver and gold as became such a king to give.

2. When the wedding was over, Alexander wrote to Jonathan the high priest, and desired him to come to Ptolemais. So when he came to these kings, and had made them magnificent presents, he was honored by them both. Alexander compelled him also to put off his own garment, and to take a purple garment, and made him sit with him in his throne; and commanded his captains that they should go with him into the middle of the city, and proclaim, that it was not permitted to any one to speak against him, or to give him any disturbance. And when the captains had thus done, those that were prepared to accuse Jonathan, and who bore him ill-will, when they saw the honor that was done him by proclamation, and that by the king's order, ran away, and were afraid lest some mischief should befall them. Nay, king Alexander was so very kind to Jonathan, that he set him down as the principal of his friends.

3. But then, upon the hundred and sixty-fifth year, Demetrius, the son of Demetrius, came from Crete with a great number of mercenary

soldiers, which Lasthenes, the Cretian, brought him, and sailed to Cilicia. This thing cast Alexander into great concern and disorder when he heard it; so he made haste immediately out of Phoenicia, and came to Antioch, that he might put matters in a safe posture there before Demetrius should come. He also left Apollonius Daus[7] governor of Celesyria, who coming to Jamnia with a great army, sent to Jonathan the high priest, and told him that it was not right that he alone should live at rest, and with authority, and not be subject to the king; that this thing had made him a reproach among all men, that he had not yet made him subject to the king. "Do not thou therefore deceive thyself, and sit still among the mountains, and pretend to have forces with thee; but if thou hast any dependence on thy strength, come down into the plain, and let our armies be compared together, and the event of the battle will demonstrate which of us is the most courageous. However, take notice, that the most valiant men of every city are in my army, and that these are the very men who have always beaten thy progenitors; but let us have the battle in such a place of the country where we may fight with weapons, and not with stones, and where there may be no place whither those that are beaten may fly."

4. With this Jonathan was irritated; and choosing himself out ten thousand of his soldiers, he went out of Jerusalem in haste, with his brother Simon, and came to Joppa, and pitched his camp on the outside of the city, because the people of Joppa had shut their gates against him, for they had a garrison in the city put there by Apollonius. But when Jonathan was preparing to besiege them, they were afraid he would take them by force, and so they opened the gates to him. But Apollonius, when he heard that Joppa was taken by Jonathan, took three thousand horsemen, and eight thousand footmen and came to Ashdod; and removing thence, he made his journey silently and slowly, and going up to Joppa, he made as if he was retiring from the place, and so drew Jonathan into the plain, as valuing himself

---

7. Of the several Apollonius about these ages, see Dean Prideaux at the year 148. This Apollonius Daus was, by his account, the son of that Apollonius who had been made governor of Celesyria and Phoenicia by Seleueus Philopater, and was himself a confidant of his son Demetrius the father, and restored to his father's government by him, but afterwards revolted from him to Alexander; but not to Demetrius the son, as he supposes.

highly upon his horsemen, and having his hopes of victory principally in them. However, Jonathan sallied out, and pursued Apollonius to Ashdod; but as soon as Apollonius perceived that his enemy was in the plain, he came back and gave him battle. But Apollonius had laid a thousand horsemen in ambush in a valley, that they might be seen by their enemies as behind them; which when Jonathan perceived, he was under no consternation, but ordering his army to stand in a square battle-array, he gave them a charge to fall on the enemy on both sides, and set them to face those that attacked them both before and behind; and while the fight lasted till the evening, he gave part of his forces to his brother Simon, and ordered him to attack the enemies; but for himself, he charged those that were with him to cover themselves with their armor, and receive the darts of the horsemen, who did as they were commanded; so that the enemy's horsemen, while they threw their darts till they had no more left, did them no harm, for the darts that were thrown did not enter into their bodies, being thrown upon the shields that were united and conjoined together, the closeness of which easily overcame the force of the darts, and they flew about without any effect. But when the enemy grew remiss in throwing their darts from morning till late at night, Simon perceived their weariness, and fell upon the body of men before him; and because his soldiers showed great alacrity, he put the enemy to flight. And when the horsemen saw that the footmen ran away, neither did they stay themselves, but they being very weary, by the duration of the fight till the evening, and their hope from the footmen being quite gone, they basely ran away, and in great confusion also, till they were separated one from another, and scattered over all the plain. Upon which Jonathan pursued them as far as Ashdod, and slew a great many of them, and compelled the rest, in despair of escaping, to fly to the temple of Dagon, which was at Ashdod; but Jonathan took the city on the first onset, and burnt it, and the villages about it; nor did he abstain from the temple of Dagon itself, but burnt it also, and destroyed those that had fled to it. Now the entire multitude of the enemies that fell in the battle, and were consumed in the temple, were eight thousand. When Jonathan therefore had overcome so great an army, he removed from Ashdod, and came to Askelon; and when he had pitched his camp without the city, the people of Askelon came out and met him, bringing him hospitable presents, and honoring him; so he accepted of their kind intentions, and returned thence to Jerusalem with a great deal of prey, which he brought thence when he conquered his enemies. But when Alexander heard that Apollonius, the general of his army, was beaten, he pretended to be glad of it, because he had fought with Jonathan his friend and ally against his directions. Accordingly, he sent to Jonathan, and gave testimony to his worth; and gave him honorary rewards, as a golden button,[8] which it is the custom to give the king's kinsmen, and allowed him Ekron and its toparchy for his own inheritance.

5. About this time it was that king Ptolemy, who was called Philometor, led an army, part by the sea, and part by land, and came to Syria, to the assistance of Alexander, who was his son-in-law; and accordingly all the cities received him willingly, as Alexander had commanded them to do, and conducted him as far as Ashdod; where they all made loud complaints about the temple of Dagon, which was burnt, and accused Jonathan of having laid it waste, and destroyed the country adjoining with fire, and slain a great number of them. Ptolemy heard these accusations, but said nothing. Jonathan also went to meet Ptolemy as far as Joppa, and obtained from him hospitable presents, and those glorious in their kinds, with all the marks of honor; and when he had conducted him as far as the river called Eleutherus, he returned again to Jerusalem.

6. But as Ptolemy was at Ptolemais, he was very near to a most unexpected destruction; for a treacherous design was laid for his life by Alexander, by the means of Ammonius, who was his friend; and as the treachery was very plain, Ptolemy wrote to Alexander, and required of him that he should bring Ammonius to condign punishment, informing him what snares had been laid for him by Ammonius, and desiring that he might be accordingly punished for it. But when Alexander did not comply with his demands, he perceived that it was he himself who laid the design, and was very angry at him. Alexander had also formerly been on very ill terms with the people of Antioch, for they had suffered very much by his means; yet did Ammonius at length undergo the punishment his insolent crimes had

---

8. Dr. Hudson here observes, that the Phoenicians and Romans used to reward such as had deserved well of them, by presenting to them a golden button. See ch. 5. sect. 4.

deserved, for he was killed in an opprobrious manner, like a woman, while he endeavored to conceal himself in a feminine habit, as we have elsewhere related.

7. Hereupon Ptolemy blamed himself for having given his daughter in marriage to Alexander, and for the league he had made with him to assist him against Demetrius; so he dissolved his relation to him, and took his daughter away from him, and immediately sent to Demetrius, and offered to make a league of mutual assistance and friendship with him, and agreed with him to give him his daughter in marriage, and to restore him to the principality of his fathers. Demetrius was well pleased with this embassage, and accepted of his assistance, and of the marriage of his daughter. But Ptolemy had still one more hard task to do, and that was to persuade the people of Antioch to receive Demetrius, because they were greatly displeased at him, on account of the injuries his father Demetrius had done them; yet did he bring this about; for as the people of Antioch hated Alexander on Ammonius's account, as we have shown already, they were easily prevailed with to cast him out of Antioch; who, thus expelled out of Antioch, came into Cilicia. Ptolemy came then to Antioch, and was made king by its inhabitants, and by the army; so that he was forced to put on two diadems, the one of Asia, the other of Egypt: but being naturally a good and a righteous man, and not desirous of what belonged to others, and besides these dispositions, being also a wise man in reasoning about futurities, he determined to avoid the envy of the Romans; so he called the people of Antioch together to an assembly, and persuaded them to receive Demetrius; and assured them that he would not be mindful of what they did to his father in case he should he now obliged by them; and he undertook that he would himself be a good monitor and governor to him, and promised that he would not permit him to attempt any bad actions; but that, for his own part, he was contented with the kingdom of Egypt. By which discourse he persuaded the people of Antioch to receive Demetrius.

8. But now Alexander made haste with a numerous and great army, and came out of Cilicia into Syria, and burnt the country belonging to Antioch, and pillaged it; whereupon Ptolemy, and his son-in-law Demetrius, brought their army against him, (for he had already given him his daughter in marriage,) and beat Alexander, and put him to flight; and accordingly he fled into Arabia. Now it happened in the

time of the battle that Ptolemy' horse, upon hearing the noise of an elephant, cast him off his back, and threw him on the ground; upon the sight of which accident, his enemies fell upon him, and gave him many wounds upon his head, and brought him into danger of death; for when his guards caught him up, he was so very ill, that for four days' time he was not able either to understand or to speak. However, Zabdiel, a prince among the Arabians, cut off Alexander's head, and sent it to Ptolemy, who recovering of his wounds, and returning to his understanding, on the fifth day, heard at once a most agreeable hearing, and saw a most agreeable sight, which were the death and the head of Alexander; yet a little after this his joy for the death of Alexander, with which he was so greatly satisfied, he also departed this life. Now Alexander, who was called Balas, reigned over Asia five years, as we have elsewhere related.

9. But when Demetrius, who was styled Nicator,[9] had taken the kingdom, he was so wicked as to treat Ptolemy's soldiers very hardly, neither remembering the league of mutual assistance that was between them, nor that he was his son-in-law and kinsman, by Cleopatra's marriage to him; so the soldiers fled from his wicked treatment to Alexandria; but Demetrius kept his elephants. But Jonathan the high priest levied an army out of all Judea, and attacked the citadel at Jerusalem, and besieged it. It was held by a garrison of Macedonians, and by some of those wicked men who had deserted the customs of their forefathers. These men at first despised the attempts of Jonathan for taking the place, as depending on its strength; but some of those wicked men went out by night, and came to Demetrius, and informed him that the citadel was besieged; who was irritated with what he heard, and took his army, and came from Antioch, against Jonathan. And when he was at Antioch, he wrote to him, and commanded him to come to him quickly to Ptolemais: upon which Jonathan did not intermit the siege of the citadel, but took with him the elders of the people, and the priests, and carried with him gold, and silver, and garments, and a great number of presents of friendship, and came to Demetrius, and presented him with them, and thereby pacified the

9. This name, Demetrius Nicator, or Demetrius the conqueror, is so written on his coins still extant, as Hudson and Spanheim inform us; the latter of whom gives us here the entire inscription, "King Demetrius the God, Philadelphus, Nicator."

king's anger. So he was honored by him, and received from him the confirmation of his high priesthood, as he had possessed it by the grants of the kings his predecessors. And when the Jewish deserters accused him, Demetrius was so far from giving credit to them, that when he petitioned him that he would demand no more than three hundred talents for the tribute of all Judea, and the three toparchies of Samaria, and Perea, and Galilee, he complied with the proposal, and gave him a letter confirming all those grants; whose contents were as follows: "King Demetrius to Jonathan his brother, and to the nation of the Jews, sendeth greeting. We have sent you a copy of that epistle which we have written to Lasthones our kinsman, that you may know its contents. "King Demetrus to Lasthenes our father, sendeth greeting. I have determined to return thanks, and to show favor to the nation of the Jews, which hath observed the rules of justice in our concerns. Accordingly, I remit to them the three prefectures, Apherims, and Lydda, and Ramatha, which have been added to Judea out of Samaria, with their appurtenances; as also what the kings my predecessors received from those that offered sacrifices in Jerusalem, and what are due from the fruits of the earth, and of the trees, and what else belongs to us; with the salt-pits, and the crowns that used to be presented to us. Nor shall they be compelled to pay any of those taxes from this time to all futurity. Take care therefore that a copy of this epistle be taken, and given to Jonathan, and be set up in an eminent place of their holy temple."' And these were the contents of this writing. And now when Demetrius saw that there was peace every where, and that there was no danger, nor fear of war, he disbanded the greatest part of his army, and diminished their pay, and even retained in pay no others than such foreigners as came up with him from Crete, and from the other islands. However, this procured him ill-will and hatred from the soldiers; on whom he bestowed nothing from this time, while the kings before him used to pay them in time of peace as they did before, that they might have their good-will, and that they might be very ready to undergo the difficulties of war, if any occasion should require it.

5 *How Trypho After He Had Beaten Demetrius Delivered the Kingdom to Antiochus the Son of Alexander, and Gained Jonathan for His Assistant; and Concerning the Actions and Embassies of Jonathan*

1. NOW there was a certain commander of Alexander's forces, an Apanemian by birth, whose name was Diodotus, and was also called Trypho, took notice the ill-will of the soldiers bare to Demetrius, and went to Malchus the Arabian, who brought up Antiochus, the son of Alexander, and told him what ill-will the army bare Demetrius, and persuaded him to give him Antiochus, because he would make him king, and recover to him the kingdom of his father. Malchus at the first opposed him in this attempt, because he could not believe him; but when Trypho lay hard at him for a long time, he over-persuaded him to comply with Trypho's intentions and entreaties. And this was the state Trypho was now in.

2. But Jonathan the high priest, being desirous to get clear of those that were in the citadel of Jerusalem, and of the Jewish deserters, and wicked men, as well as of those in all the garrisons in the country, sent presents and ambassadors to Demetrius, and entreated him to take away his soldiers out of the strong holds of Judea. Demetrius made answer, that after the war, which he was now deeply engaged in, was over, he would not only grant him that, but greater things than that also; and he desired he would send him some assistance, and informed him that his army had deserted him. So Jonathan chose out three thousand of his soldiers, and sent them to Demetrius.

3. Now the people of Antioch hated Demetrius, both on account of what mischief he had himself done them, and because they were his enemies also on account of his father Demetrius, who had greatly abused them; so they watched some opportunity which they might lay hold on to fall upon him. And when they were informed of the assistance that was coming to Demetrius from Jonathan, and considered at the same time that he would raise a numerous army, unless they prevented him, and seized upon him, they took their weapons immediately, and encompassed his palace in the way of a siege, and seizing upon all the ways of getting out, they sought to subdue their king. And when he saw that the people of Antioch were become his bitter enemies and that they were thus in arms, he took

the mercenary soldiers which he had with them, and those Jews who were sent by Jonathan, and assaulted the Antiochians; but he was overpowered by them, for they were many ten thousands, and was beaten. But when the Jews saw that the Antiochians were superior, they went up to the top of the palace, and shot at them from thence; and because they were so remote from them by their height, that they suffered nothing on their side, but did great execution on the others, as fighting from such an elevation, they drove them out of the adjoining houses, and immediately set them on fire, whereupon the flame spread itself over the whole city, and burnt it all down. This happened by reason of the closeness of the houses, and because they were generally built of wood. So the Antioehians, when they were not able to help themselves, nor to stop the fire, were put to flight. And as the Jews leaped from the top of one house to the top of another, and pursued them after that manner, it thence happened that the pursuit was so very surprising. But when the king saw that the Antiochians were were busy in saving their children and their wives, and so did not fight any longer, he fell upon them in the narrow passages, and fought them, and slew a great many of them, till at last they were forced to throw down their arms, and to deliver themselves up to Demetrius. So he forgave them this their insolent behavior, and put an end to the sedition; and when he had given rewards to the Jews out of the rich spoils he had gotten, and had returned them thanks, as the cause of his victory, he sent them away to Jerusalem to Jonathan, with an ample testimony of the assistance they had afforded him. Yet did he prove an ill man to Jonathan afterward, and broke the promises he had made; and he threatened that he would make war upon him, unless he would pay all that tribute which the Jewish nation owed to the first kings [of Syria]. And this he had done, if Trypho had not hindered him, and diverted his preparations against Jonathan to a concern for his own preservation; for he now returned out of Arabia into Syria, with the child Antiochus, for he was yet in age but a youth, and put the diadem on his head; and as the whole forces that had left Demetrius, because they had no pay, came to his assistance, he made war upon Demetrius, and joining battle with him, overcame him in the fight, and took from him both his elephants and the city Antioch.

4. Demetrius, upon this defeat, retired into Cilicia; but the child Antiochus sent ambassadors and an epistle to Jonathan, and made him

his friend and confederate, and confirmed to him the high priesthood, and yielded up to him the four prefectures which had been added to Judea. Moreover, he sent him vessels and cups of gold, and a purple garment, and gave him leave to use them. He also presented him with a golden button, and styled him one of his principal friends, and appointed his brother Simon to be the general over the forces, from the Ladder of Tyre unto Egypt. So Jonathan was so pleased with these grants made him by Antiochus, that he sent ambassadors to him and to Trypho, and professed himself to be their friend and confederate, and said he would join with him in a war against Demetrius, informing him that he had made no proper returns for the kindness he had done him; for that when he had received many marks of kindness from him, when he stood in great need of them, he, for such good turns, had requited him with further injuries.

5. So Antiochus gave Jonathan leave to raise himself a numerous army out of Syria and Phoenicia and to make war against Demetrius's generals; whereupon he went in haste to the several cities which received him splendidly indeed, but put no forces into his hands. And when he was come from thence to Askelon, the inhabitants of Askelon came and brought him presents, and met him in a splendid manner. He exhorted them, and every one of the cities of Celesyria, to forsake Demetrius, and to join with Antiochus; and, in assisting him, to endeavor to punish Demetrius for what offenses he had been guilty of against themselves; and told them there were many reasons for that their procedure, if they had a mind so to do. And when he had persuaded those cities to promise their assistance to Antiochus, he came to Gaza, in order to induce them also to be friends to Antiochus; but he found the inhabitants of Gaza much more alienated from him than he expected, for they had shut their gates against him; and although they had deserted Demetrius, they had not resolved to join themselves to Antiochus. This provoked Jonathan to besiege them, and to harass their country; for as he set a part of his army round about Gaza itself, so with the rest he overran their land, and spoiled it, and burnt what was in it. When the of Gaza saw themselves in this state of affliction, and that no assistance came to them from Demetrius, that what distressed them was at hand, but what should profit them was still at a great distance, and it was uncertain whether it would come at all or not, they thought it would be prudent conduct to leave

off any longer continuance with them, and to cultivate friendship with the other; so they sent to Jonathan, and professed they would be his friends, and afford him assistance: for such is the temper of men, that before they have had the trial of great afflictions, they do not understand what is for their advantage; but when they find themselves under such afflictions, they then change their minds, and what it had been better for them to have done before they had been at all damaged, they choose to do, but not till after they have suffered such damages. However, he made a league of friendship with them, and took from them hostages for their performance of it, and sent these hostages to Jerusalem, while he went himself over all the country, as far as Damascus.

6. But when he heard that the generals of Demetrius's forces were come to the city Cadesh with a numerous army, (the place lies between the land of the Tyrians and Galilee,)for they supposed they should hereby draw him out of Syria, in order to preserve Galilee, and that he would not overlook the Galileans, who were his own people, when war was made upon them, he went to meet them, having left Simon in Judea, who raised as great an army as he was able out of the country, and then sat down before Bethsura, and besieged it, that being the strongest place in all Judea; and a garrison of Demetrius's kept it, as we have already related. But as Simon was raising banks, and bringing his engines of war against Bethsura, and was very earnest about the siege of it, the garrison was afraid lest the place should be taken of Simon by force, and they put to the sword; so they sent to Simon, and desired the security of his oath, that they should come to no harm from him, and that they would leave the place, and go away to Demetrius. Accordingly he gave them his oath, and ejected them out of the city, and he put therein a garrison of his own.

7. But Jonathan removed out of Galilee, and from the waters which are called Gennesar, for there he was before encamped, and came into the plain that is called Asor, without knowing that the enemy was there. When therefore Demetrius's men knew a day beforehand that Jonathan was coming against them, they laid an ambush in the mountain, who were to assault him on the sudden, while they themselves met him with an army in the plain; which army, when Jonathan saw ready to engage him, he also got ready his own soldiers for the battle as well as he was able; but those that were laid in ambush

by Demetrius's generals being behind them, the Jews were afraid lest they should be caught in the midst between two bodies, and perish; so they ran away in haste, and indeed all the rest left Jonathan; but a few there were, in number about fifty, who staid with him, and with them Mattathias, the son of Absalom, and Judas, the son of Chapseus, who were commanders of the whole army. These marched boldly, and like men desperate, against the enemy, and so pushed them, that by their courage they daunted them, and with their weapons in their hands they put them to flight. And when those soldiers of Jonathan that had retired saw the enemy giving way, they got together after their flight, and pursued them with great violence; and this did they as far as Cadesh, where the camp of the enemy lay.

8. Jonathan having thus gotten a glorious victory, and slain two thousand of the enemy, returned to Jerusalem. So when he saw that all his affairs prospered according to his mind, by the providence of God, he sent ambassadors to the Romans, being desirous of renewing that friendship which their nation had with them formerly. He enjoined the same ambassadors, that, as they came back, they should go to the Spartans, and put them in mind of their friendship and kindred. So when the ambassadors came to Rome, they went into their senate, and said what they were commanded by Jonathan the high priest to say, how he had sent them to confirm their friendship. The senate then confirmed what had been formerly decreed concerning their friendship with the Jews, and gave them letters to carry to all the kings of Asia and Europe, and to the governors of the cities, that they might safely conduct them to their own country. Accordingly, as they returned, they came to Sparta, and delivered the epistle which they had received of Jonathan to them; a copy of which here follows: "Jonathan the high priest of the Jewish nation, and the senate, and body of the people of the Jews, to the ephori, and senate, and people of the Lacedemonians, send greeting. If you be well, and both your public and private affairs be agreeable to your mind, it is according to our wishes. We are well also. When in former times an epistle was brought to Onias, who was then our high priest, from Areus, who at that time was your king, by Demoteles, concerning the kindred that was between us and you, a copy of which is here subjoined, we both joyfully received the epistle, and were well pleased with Demoteles and Areus, although we did not need such a demonstration, because

we were satisfied about it from the sacred writings[10] yet did not we think fit first to begin the claim of this relation to you, lest we should seem too early in taking to ourselves the glory which is now given us by you. It is a long time since this relation of ours to you hath been renewed; and when we, upon holy and festival days, offer sacrifices to God, we pray to him for your preservation and victory. As to ourselves, although we have had many wars that have compassed us around, by reason of the covetousness of our neighbors, yet did not we determine to be troublesome either to you, or to others that were related to us; but since we have now overcome our enemies, and have occasion to send Numenius the son of Antiochus, and Antipater the son of Jason, who are both honorable men belonging to our senate, to the Romans, we gave them this epistle to you also, that they might renew that friendship which is between us. You will therefore do well yourselves to write to us, and send us an account of what you stand in need of from us, since we are in all things disposed to act according to your desires." So the Lacedemonians received the ambassadors kindly, and made a decree for friendship and mutual assistance, and sent it to them.

9. At this time there were three sects among the Jews, who had different opinions concerning human actions; the one was called the sect of the Pharisees, another the sect of the Sadducees, and the other the sect of the Essens. Now for the Pharisees,[11] they say that some

---

10. This clause is otherwise rendered in the First Book of Maccabees, 12:9, "For that we have the holy books of Scripture in our bands to comfort us." The Hebrew original being lost, we cannot certainly judge which was the truest version only the coherence favors Josephus. But if this were the Jews' meaning, that they were satisfied out of their Bible that the Jews and Lacedemonians were of kin, that part of their Bible is now lost, for we find no such assertion in our present copies.

11. Those that suppose Josephus to contradict himself in his three several accounts of the notions of the Pharisees, this here, and that earlier one, which is the largest, Of the War B. II. ch. 8. sect. 14, and that later, Antiq. B. XVIII. ch. 1. sect. 3, as if he sometimes said they introduced an absolute fatality, and denied all freedom of human actions, is almost wholly groundless if he ever, as the very learned Casaubon here truly observes, asserting, that the Pharisees were between the Essens and Sadducees, and did so far ascribe all to fate or Divine Providence as was consistent with the freedom of human actions. However, their perplexed way of talking about fate, or Providence, as overruling all things, made it commonly thought they were willing to excuse their sins by ascribing them to fate, as in the Apostolical Constitutions, B.

actions, but not all, are the work of fate, and some of them are in our own power, and that they are liable to fate, but are not caused by fate. But the sect of the Essens affirm, that fate governs all things, and that nothing befalls men but what is according to its determination. And for the Sadducees, they take away fate, and say there is no such thing, and that the events of human affairs are not at its disposal; but they suppose that all our actions are in our own power, so that we are ourselves the causes of what is good, and receive what is evil from our own folly. However, I have given a more exact account of these opinions in the second book of the Jewish War.

10. But now the generals of Demetrius being willing to recover the defeat they had had, gathered a greater army together than they had before, and came against Jonathan; but as soon as he was informed of their coming, he went suddenly to meet them, to the country of Hamoth, for he resolved to give them no opportunity of coming into Judea; so he pitched his camp at fifty furlongs' distance from the enemy, and sent out spies to take a view of their camp, and after what manner they were encamped. When his spies had given him full information, and had seized upon some of them by night, who told him the enemy would soon attack him, he, thus apprized beforehand, provided for his security, and placed watchmen beyond his camp, and kept all his forces armed all night; and he gave them a charge to be of good courage, and to have their minds prepared to fight in the night time, if they should be obliged so to do, lest their enemy's designs should seem concealed from them. But when Demetrius's commanders were informed that Jonathan knew what they intended, their counsels were disordered, and it alarmed them to find that the enemy had discovered those their intentions; nor did they expect to overcome them any other way, now they had failed in the snares they had laid for them; for should they hazard an open battle, they did not

---

VI. ch. 6. Perhaps under the same general name some difference of opinions in this point might be propagated, as is very common in all parties, especially in points of metaphysical subtilty. However, our Josephus, who in his heart was a great admirer of the piety of the Essens, was yet in practice a Pharisee, as he himself informs us, in his own Life, sect. 2. And his account of this doctrine of the Pharisees is for certain agreeable to his own opinion, who ever both fully allowed the freedom of human actions, and yet strongly believed the powerful interposition of Divine Providence. See concerning this matter a remarkable clause, Antiq. B. XVI. ch. 11. sect. 7.

think they should be a match for Jonathan's army, so they resolved to fly; and having lighted many fires, that when the enemy saw them they might suppose they were there still, they retired. When Jonathan came to give them battle in the morning in their camp, and found it deserted, and understood they were fled, he pursued them; yet he could not overtake them, for they had already passed over the river Eleutherus, and were out of danger. So when Jonathan was returned thence, he went into Arabia, and fought against the Nabateans, and drove away a great deal of their prey, and took [many] captives, and came to Damascus, and there sold off what he had taken. About the same time it was that Simon his brother went over all Judea and Palestine, as far as Askelon, and fortified the strong holds; and when he had made them very strong, both in the edifices erected, and in the garrisons placed in them, he came to Joppa; and when he had taken it, he brought a great garrison into it, for he heard that the people of Joppa were disposed to deliver up the city to Demetrius's generals.

11. When Simon and Jonathan had finished these affairs, they returned to Jerusalem, where Jonathan gathered all the people together, and took counsel to restore the walls of Jerusalem, and to rebuild the wall that encompassed the temple, which had been thrown down, and to make the places adjoining stronger by very high towers; and besides that, to build another wall in the midst of the city, in order to exclude the market-place from the garrison, which was in the citadel, and by that means to hinder them from any plenty of provisions; and moreover, to make the fortresses that were in the country much stronger and more defensible than they were before. And when these things were approved of by the multitude, as rightly proposed, Jonathan himself took care of the building that belonged to the city, and sent Simon away to make the fortresses in the country more secure than formerly. But Demetrius passed over [Euphrates], and came into Mesopotamia, as desirous to retain that country still, as well as Babylon; and when he should have obtained the dominion of the upper provinces, to lay a foundation for recovering his entire kingdom; for those Greeks and Macedonians who dwelt there frequently sent ambassadors to him, and promised, that if he would come to them, they would deliver themselves up to him, and assist him in fighting

against Arsaces,[12] the king of the Parthians. So he was elevated with these hopes, and came hastily to them, as having resolved, that if he had once overthrown the Parthians, and gotten an army of his own, he would make war against Trypho, and eject him out of Syria; and the people of that country received him with great alacrity. So he raised forces, with which he fought against Arsaces, and lost all his army, and was himself taken alive, as we have elsewhere related.

6 *How Jonathan Was Slain by Treachery; and How Thereupon the Jews Made Simon Their General and High Priest: What Courageous Actions He Also Performed Especially Against Trypho*

1. NOW when Trypho knew what had befallen Demetrius, he was no longer firm to Antiochus, but contrived by subtlety to kill him, and then take possession of his kingdom; but the fear that he was in of Jonathan was an obstacle to this his design, for Jonathan was a friend to Antiochus, for which cause he resolved first to take Jonathan out of the way, and then to set about his design relating to Antiochus; but he judging it best to take him off by deceit and treachery, came from Antioch to Bethshan, which by the Greeks is called Scythopolis, at which place Jonathan met him with forty thousand chosen men, for he thought that he came to fight him; but when he perceived that Jonathan was ready to fight, he attempted to gain him by presents and kind treatment, and gave order to his captains to obey him, and by these means was desirous to give assurance of his good-will, and to take away all suspicions out of his mind, that so he might make him careless and inconsiderate, and might take him when he was unguarded. He also advised him to dismiss his army, because there was no occasion for bringing it with him when there was no war, but all was in peace. However, he desired him to retain a few about him, and go with him to Ptolemais, for that he would deliver the city up to

12. This king, who was of the famous race of Arsaces, is bethused to call them; but by the elder author of the First Maccahere, and 1 Macc. 14:2, called by the family name Arsaces; was, the king of the Persians and Medes, according to the land but Appion says his proper name was Phraates. He is language of the Eastern nations. See Authent. Rec. Part II. also called by Josephus the king of the Parthians, as the Greeks p. 1108.

him, and would bring all the fortresses that were in the country under his dominion; and he told him that he came with those very designs.

2. Yet did not Jonathan suspect any thing at all by this his management, but believed that Trypho gave him this advice out of kindness, and with a sincere design. Accordingly, he dismissed his army, and retained no more than three thousand of them with him, and left two thousand in Galilee; and he himself, with one thousand, came with Trypho to Ptolemais. But when the people of Ptolemais had shut their gates, as it had been commanded by Trypho to do, he took Jonathan alive, and slew all that were with him. He also sent soldiers against those two thousand that were left in Galilee, in order to destroy them; but those men having heard the report of what had happened to Jonathan, they prevented the execution; and before those that were sent by Trypho came, they covered themselves with their armor, and went away out of the country. Now when those that were sent against them saw that they were ready to fight for their lives, they gave them no disturbance, but returned back to Trypho.

3. But when the people of Jerusalem heard that Jonathan was taken, and that the soldiers who were with him were destroyed, they deplored his sad fate; and there was earnest inquiry made about him by every body, and a great and just fear fell upon them, and made them sad, lest, now they were deprived of the courage and conduct of Jonathan, the nations about them should bear them ill-will; and as they were before quiet on account of Jonathan they should now rise up against them, and by making war with them, should force them into the utmost dangers. And indeed what they suspected really befell them; for when those nations heard of the death of Jonathan, they began to make war with the Jews as now destitute of a governor and Trypho himself got an army together, and had intention to go up to Judea, and make war against its inhabitants. But when Simon saw that the people of Jerusalem were terrified at the circumstances they were in, he desired to make a speech to them, and thereby to render them more resolute in opposing Trypho when he should come against them. He then called the people together into the temple, and thence began thus to encourage them: "O my countrymen, you are not ignorant that our father, myself, and my brethren, have ventured to hazard our lives, and that willingly, for the recovery of your liberty; since I have therefore such plenty of examples before me, and we of

our family have determined with ourselves to die for our laws, and our Divine worship, there shall no terror be so great as to banish this resolution from our souls, nor to introduce in its place a love of life, and a contempt of glory. Do you therefore follow me with alacrity whithersoever I shall lead you, as not destitute of such a captain as is willing to suffer, and to do the greatest things for you; for neither am I better than my brethren that I should be sparing of my own life, nor so far worse than they as to avoid and refuse what they thought the most honorable of all things,—I mean, to undergo death for your laws, and for that worship of God which is peculiar to you; I will therefore give such proper demonstrations as will show that I am their own brother; and I am so bold as to expect that I shall avenge their blood upon our enemies, and deliver you all with your wives and children from the injuries they intend against you, and, with God's assistance, to preserve your temple from destruction by them; for I see that these nations have you in contempt, as being without a governor, and that they thence are encouraged to make war against you."

4. By this speech of Simon he inspired the multitude with courage; and as they had been before dispirited through fear, they were now raised to a good hope of better things, insomuch that the whole multitude of the people cried out all at once that Simon should be their leader; and that instead of Judas and Jonathan his brethren, he should have the government over them; and they promised that they would readily obey him in whatsoever he should command them. So he got together immediately all his own soldiers that were fit for war, and made haste in rebuilding the walls of the city, and strengthening them by very high and strong towers, and sent a friend of his, one Jonathan, the son of Absalom, to Joppa, and gave him order to eject the inhabitants out of the city, for he was afraid lest they should deliver up the city to Trypho; but he himself staid to secure Jerusalem.

5. But Trypho removed from Ptoeinais with a great army, and came into Judea, and brought Jonathan with him in bonds. Simon also met him with his army at the city Adida, which is upon a hill, and beneath it lie the plains of Judea. And when Trypho knew that Simon was by the Jews made their governor, he sent to him, and would have imposed upon him by deceit and trencher, and desired, if he would have his brother Jonathan released, that he would send him a hundred talents of silver, and two of Jonathan's sons as hostages, that when he

shall be released, he may not make Judea revolt from the king; for that at present he was kept in bonds on account of the money he had borrowed of the king, and now owed it to him. But Simon was aware of the craft of Trypho; and although he knew that if he gave him the money he should lose it, and that Trypho would not set his brother free and withal should deliver the sons of Jonathan to the enemy, yet because he was afraid that he should have a calumny raised against him among the multitude as the cause of his brother's death, if he neither gave the money, nor sent Jonathan's sons, he gathered his army together, and told them what offers Trypho had made; and added this, that the offers were ensnaring and treacherous, and yet that it was more eligible to send the money and Jonathan's sons, than to be liable to the imputation of not complying with Trypho's offers, and thereby refusing to save his brother. Accordingly, Simon sent the sons of Jonathan and the money; but when Trypho had received them, he did not keep his promise, nor set Jonathan free, but took his army, and went about all the country, and resolved to go afterward to Jerusalem by the way of Idumea, while Simon went over against him with his army, and all along pitched his own camp over against his.

6. But when those that were in the citadel had sent to Trypho, and besought him to make haste and come to them, and to send them provisions, he prepared his cavalry as though he would be at Jerusalem that very night; but so great a quantity of snow fell in the night, that it covered the roads, and made them so deep, that there was no passing, especially for the cavalry. This hindered him from coming to Jerusalem; whereupon Trypho removed thence, and came into Celesyria, and falling vehemently upon the land of Gilead, he slew Jonathan there; and when he had given order for his burial, he returned himself to Antioch. However, Simon sent some to the city Basca to bring away his brother's bones, and buried them in their own city Modin; and all the people made great lamentation over him. Simon also erected a very large monument for his father and his brethren, of white and polished stone, and raised it a great height, and so as to be seen a long way off, and made cloisters about it, and set up pillars, which were of one stone apiece; a work it was wonderful to see. Moreover, he built seven pyramids also for his parents and his brethren, one for each of them, which were made very surprising, both for their largeness and beauty, and which have been preserved to

this day; and we know that it was Simon who bestowed so much zeal about the burial of Jonathan, and the building of these monuments for his relations. Now Jonathan died when he had been high priest four years[13] and had been also the governor of his nation. And these were the circumstances that concerned his death.

7. But Simon, who was made high priest by the multitude, on the very first year of his high priesthood set his people free from their slavery under the Macedonians, and permitted them to pay tribute to them no longer; which liberty and freedom from tribute they obtained after a hundred and seventy years[14] of the kingdom of the Assyrians, which was after Seleucus, who was called Nicator, got the dominion over Syria. Now the affection of the multitude towards Simon was so great, that in their contracts one with another, and in their public records, they wrote, "in the first year of Simon the benefactor and ethnarch of the Jews;" for under him they were very happy, and overcame the enemies that were round about them; for Simon overthrew the city Gazara, and Joppa, and Jamhis. He also took the citadel of Jerusalem by siege, and cast it down to the ground, that it might not be any more a place of refuge to their enemies when they

---

13. There is some error in the copies here, when no more than four years are ascribed to the high priesthood of Jonathan. We know by Josephus's last Jewish chronology, Antiq. B. XX. ch. 10., that there was an interval of seven years between the death of Alcimus, or Jacimus, the last high priest, and the real high priesthood of Jonathan, to whom yet those seven years seem here to be ascribed, as a part of them were to Judas before, Antiq. B. XII. ch. 10. sect. 6. Now since, besides these seven years interregnum in the pontificate, we are told, Antiq. B. XX. ch. 10., that Jonathan's real high priesthood lasted seven years more, these two seven years will make up fourteen years, which I suppose was Josephus's own number in this place, instead of the four in our present copies.

14. These one hundred and seventy years of the Assyrians mean no more, as Josephus explains himself here, than from the sara of Seleucus, which as it is known to have began on the 312th year before the Christian sara, from its spring in the First Book of Maccabees, and from its autumn in the Second Book of Maccabees, so did it not begin at Babylon till the next spring, on the 311th year. See Prid. at the year 312. And it is truly observed by Dr. Hudson on this place, that the Syrians and Assyrians are sometimes confounded in ancient authors, according to the words of Justin, the epitomiser of Trogus -pompeius, who says that "the Assyrians were afterward called Syrian." B. I. ch. 11. See Of the War, B. V. ch. 9. sect. 4, where the Philistines themselves, at the very south limit of Syria, in its utmost extent, are called Assyrians by Josephus as Spanheim observes.

took it, to do them a mischief, as it had been till now. And when he had done this, he thought it their best way, and most for their advantage, to level the very mountain itself upon which the citadel happened to stand, that so the temple might be higher than it. And indeed, when he had called the multitude to an assembly, he persuaded them to have it so demolished, and this by putting them in mind what miseries they had suffered by its garrison and the Jewish deserters, and what miseries they might hereafter suffer in case any foreigner should obtain the kingdom, and put a garrison into that citadel. This speech induced the multitude to a compliance, because he exhorted them to do nothing but what was for their own good: so they all set themselves to the work, and leveled the mountain, and in that work spent both day and night without any intermission, which cost them three whole years before it was removed, and brought to an entire level with the plain of the rest of the city. After which the temple was the highest of all the buildings, now the citadel, as well as the mountain whereon it stood, were demolished. And these actions were thus performed under Simon.

7 *How Simon Confederated Himself with Antiochus Pius, and Made War Against Trypho, and a Little Afterward, Against Cendebeus, the General of Antiochus's Army; as Also How Simon Was Murdered by His Son-in-Law Ptolemy, and That by Treachery*

1.[15] Now a little while after Demetrius had been carried into captivity, Trypho his governor destroyed Antiochus,[16] the son of Alexander, who was also called *The God*,[17] and this when he had reigned four years, though he gave it out that he died under the hands of the

15. It must here be diligently noted, that Josephus's copy of the First Book of Maccabees, which he had so carefully followed, and faithfully abridged, as far as the fiftieth verse of the thirteenth chapter, seems there to have ended. What few things there are afterward common to both, might probably be learned by him from some other more imperfect records. However, we must exactly observe here, what the remaining part of that book of the Maccabees informs us of, and what Josephus would never have omitted, had his copy contained so much, that this Simon the Great, the Maccabee, made a league with Antiochus Soter, the son of Demetrius Soter, and brother of the other Demetrius, who was now a captive in Parthis: that upon his coming to the crown, about the 140th year before the Christian sets, he granted great privileges to the Jewish nation, and to Simon their high priest and ethnarch; which privileges Simon seems to have taken of his own accord about three years before. In particular, he gave him leave to coin money for his country with his own stamp; and as concerning Jerusalem and the sanctuary, that they should be free, or, as the vulgar Latin hath it, "holy and free," 1 Macc. 15:6, 7, which I take to be the truer reading, as being the very words of his father's concession offered to Jonathan several years before, ch. 10:31; and Antiq. B, XIII. ch. 2. sect. 3. Now what makes this date and these grants greatly remarkable, is the state of the remaining genuine shekels of the Jews with Samaritan characters, which seem to have been (most of them at least) coined in the first four years of this Simon the Asamonean, and having upon them these words on one side, "Jerusalem the Holy;" and on the reverse, "In the Year of Freedom," 1, or 2, or 3, or 4; which shekels therefore are original monuments of these times, and undeniable marks of the truth of the history in these chapters, though it be in great measure omitted by Josephus. See Essay on the Old Test. p. 157, 158. The reason why I rather suppose that his copy of the Maccabees wanted these chapters, than that his own copies are here imperfect, is this, that all their contents are not here omitted, though much the greatest part be.

16. How Trypho killed this Antiochus the epitome of Livy informs us, ch. 53, viz. that he corrupted his physicians or surgeons, who falsely pretending to the people that he was perishing with the stone, as they cut him for it, killed him, which exactly agrees with Josephus.

17. That this Antiochus, the son of Alexader Balas, was called "The God," is evident from his coins, which Spanheim assures us bear this inscription, "King Antiochus the God, Epiphanes the Victorious."

surgeons. He then sent his friends, and those that were most intimate with him, to the soldiers, and promised that he would give them a great deal of money if they would make him king. He intimated to them that Demetrius was made a captive by the Parthians; and that Demetrius's brother Atitiochus, if he came to be king, would do them a great deal of mischief, in way of revenge for their revolting from his brother. So the soldiers, in expectation of the wealth they should get by bestowing the kingdom on Trypho, made him their ruler. However, when Trypho had gained the management of affairs, he demonstrated his disposition to be wicked; for while he was a private person, he cultivated familiarity with the multitude, and pretended to great moderation, and so drew them on artfully to whatsoever he pleased; but when he had once taken the kingdom, he laid aside any further dissimulation, and was the true Trypho; which behavior made his enemies superior to him; for the soldiery hated him, and revolted from him to Cleopatra, the wife of Demetrius, who was then shut up in Seleucia with her children. But as Antiochus, the brother of Demetrius who was called Soter, was not admitted by any of the cities on account of Trypho, Cleopatra sent to him, and invited him to marry her, and to take the kingdom. The reasons why she made this invitation were these: That her friends persuaded her to it, and that she was afraid for herself, in case some of the people of Seleucia should deliver up the city to Trypho.

2. As Antlochuswas now come to Seleucia, and his forces increased every day, he marched to fight Trypho; and having beaten him in the battle, he ejected him out of the Upper Syria into Phoenicia, and pursued him thither, and besieged him in Dora which was a fortress hard to be taken, whither he had fled. He also sent ambassadors to Simon the Jewish high priest, about a league of friendship and mutual assistance; who readily accepted of the invitation, and sent to Antiochus great sums of money and provisions for those that besieged Dora, and thereby supplied them very plentifully, so that for a little while he was looked upon as one of his most intimate friends; but still Trypho fled from Dora to Apamia, where he was taken during the siege, and put to death, when he had reigned three years.

3. However, Antiochus forgot the kind assistance that Simon had afforded him in his necessity, by reason of his covetous and wicked

disposition, and committed an army of soldiers to his friend Cendebeus, and sent him at once to ravage Judea, and to seize Simon. When Simon heard of Antiochus's breaking his league with him, although he were now in years, yet, provoked with the unjust treatment he had met with from Antiochus, and taking a resolution brisker than his age could well bear, he went like a young man to act as general of his army. He also sent his sons before among the most hardy of his soldiers, and he himself marched on with his army another way, and laid many of his men in ambushes in the narrow valleys between the mountains; nor did he fail of success in any one of his attempts, but was too hard for his enemies in every one of them. So he led the rest of his life in peace, and did also himself make a league with the Romans.

4. Now he was the ruler of the Jews in all eight years; but at a feast came to his end. It was caused by the treachery of his son-in-law Ptolemy, who caught also his wife, and two of his sons, and kept them in bonds. He also sent some to kill John the third son, whose name was Hyrcanus; but the young man perceiving them coming, he avoided the danger he was in from them,[18] and made haste into the city [Jerusalem], as relying on the good-will of the multitude, because of the benefits they had received from his father, and because of the hatred the same multitude bare to Ptolemy; so that when Ptolemy was endeavoring to enter the city by another gate, they drove him away, as having already admitted Hyrcanus.

8 Hyrcanus Receives the High Priesthood, and Ejects Ptolemy Out of the Country. Antiochus Makes War Against Hyrcanus and Afterwards Makes a League with Him

1. SO Ptolemy retired to one of the fortresses that was above Jericho, which was called Dagon. But Hyrcanus having taken the high priest-

18. Here Josephus begins to follow and to abridge the next sacred Hebrew book, styled in the end of the First Book of Maccabees, "The Chronicle of John [Hyrcanus's] high priesthood;" but in some of the Greek copies," The Fourth Book of Maccabees." A Greek version of this chronicle was extant not very long ago in the days of Sautes Pagninus, and Sixtus Senensis, at Lyons, though it seems to have been there burnt, and to be utterly lost. See Sixtus Senensis's account of it, of its many Hebraisms, and its great agreement with Josephus's abridgement, in the Authent. Rec. Part I. p. 206, 207, 208.

hood that had been his father's before, and in the first place propitiated God by sacrifices, he then made an expedition against Ptolemy; and when he made his attacks upon the place, in other points he was too hard for him, but was rendered weaker than he, by the commiseration he had for his mother and brethren, and by that only; for Ptolemy brought them upon the wall, and tormented them in the sight of all, and threatened that he would throw them down headlong, unless Hyrcanus would leave off the siege. And as he thought that so far as he relaxed as to the siege and taking of the place, so much favor did he show to those that were dearest to him by preventing their misery, his zeal about it was cooled. However, his mother spread out her hands, and begged of him that he would not grow remiss on her account, but indulge his indignation so much the more, and that he would do his utmost to take the place quickly, in order to get their enemy under his power, and then to avenge upon him what he had done to those that were dearest to himself; for that death would be to her sweet, though with torment, if that enemy of theirs might but be brought to punishment for his wicked dealings to them. Now when his mother said so, he resolved to take the fortress immediately; but when he saw her beaten, and torn to pieces, his courage failed him, and he could not but sympathize with what his mother suffered, and was thereby overcome. And as the siege was drawn out into length by this means, that year on which the Jews used to rest came on; for the Jews observe this rest every seventh year, as they do every seventh day; so that Ptolemy being for this cause released from the war,[19] he slew the brethren of Hyrcanus, and his mother; and when he had so done, he fled to Zeno, who was called Cotylas, who was then the tyrant of the city Philadelphia.

---

19. Hence we learn, that in the days of this excellent high priest, John Hyrcanus, the observation of the Sabbatic year, as Josephus supposed, required a rest from war, as did that of the weekly sabbath from work; I mean this, unless in the case of necessity, when the Jews were attacked by their enemies, in which case indeed, and in which alone, they then allowed defensive fighting to be lawful, even on the sabbath day, as we see in several places of Josephus, Antlq. B. XII. ch. 6. sect. 2; B. XIII. ch. 1. sect. 2; Of. the War, B. I. ch. 7. sect. 3. But then it must be noted, that this rest from war no way appears in the First Book of Maccabees, ch. 16., but the direct contrary; though indeed the Jews, in the days of Antiochus Epiphanes, did not venture upon fighting on the Sabbath day, even in the defense of their own lives, till the Asamoneans or Maccabees decreed so to do, 1 Macc. 2:32–41; Antiq. B. XII. ch. 6. sect. 2.

2. But Antiochus, being very uneasy at the miseries that Simon had brought upon him, he invaded Judea in the fourth years' of his reign, and the first year of the principality of Hyrcanus, in the hundred and sixty-second olympiad.[20] And when he had burnt the country, he shut up Hyrcanus in the city, which he encompassed round with seven encampments; but did just nothing at the first, because of the strength of the walls, and because of the valor of the besieged, although they were once in want of water, which yet they were delivered from by a large shower of rain, which fell at the setting of the Pleiades[21] However, about the north part of the wall, where it happened the city was upon a level with the outward ground, the king raised a hundred towers of three stories high, and placed bodies of soldiers upon them; and as he made his attacks every day, he cut a double ditch, deep and broad, and confined the inhabitants within it as within a wall; but the besieged contrived to make frequent sallies out; and if the enemy were not any where upon their guard, they fell upon them, and did them a great deal of mischief; and if they perceived them, they then retired into the city with ease. But because Hyrcanus discerned the inconvenience of so great a number of men in the city, while the provisions were the sooner spent by them, and yet, as is natural to suppose, those great numbers did nothing, he separated the useless part, and excluded them out of the city, and retained that part only which were in the flower of their age, and fit for war. However, Antiochus would not let those that were excluded go away, who therefore wandering about between the wails, and consuming away by famine, died miserably; but when the feast of tabernacles was at hand, those that were within commiserated their condition, and

---

20. Josephus's copies, both Greek and Latin, have here a gross mistake, when they say that this first year of John Hyrcanus, which we have just now seen to have been a Sabbatic year, was in the 162nd olympiad, whereas it was for certain the second year of the 161st. See the like before, B. XII. ch. 7. sect. 6.

21. This heliacal setting of the Pleiades, or seven stars, was, in the days of Hyrcanus and Josephus, early in the spring, about February, the time of the latter rain in Judea; and this, so far as I remember, is the only astronomical character of time, besides one eclipse of the moon in the reign of Herod, that we meet with in all Josephus; the Jews being little accustomed to astronomical observations, any further than for the uses of their calendar, and utterly forbidden those astrological uses which the heathens commonly made of them.

received them in again. And when Hyrcanus sent to Antiochus, and desired there might be a truce for seven days, because of the festival, be gave way to this piety towards God, and made that truce accordingly. And besides that, he sent in a magnificent sacrifice, bulls with their horns gilded,[22] with all sorts of sweet spices, and with cups of gold and silver. So those that were at the gates received the sacrifices from those that brought them, and led them to the temple, Antiochus the mean while feasting his army, which was a quite different conduct from Antiochus Epiphanes, who, when he had taken the city, offered swine upon the altar, and sprinkled the temple with the broth of their flesh, in order to violate the laws of the Jews, and the religion they derived from their forefathers; for which reason our nation made war with him, and would never be reconciled to him; but for this Antiochus, all men called him *Antiochus the Pious,* for the great zeal he had about religion.

3. Accordingly, Hyrcanus took this moderation of his kindly; and when he understood how religious he was towards the Deity, he sent an embassage to him, and desired that he would restore the settlements they received from their forefathers. So he rejected the counsel of those that would have him utterly destroy the nation,[23] by reason of their way of living, which was to others unsociable, and did not regard what they said. But being persuaded that all they did was out of a religious mind, he answered the ambassadors, that if the besieged would deliver up their arms, and pay tribute for Joppa, and the other cities which bordered upon Judea, and admit a garrison of his, on these terms he would make war against them no longer. But the Jews, although they were content with the other conditions, did not agree to admit the garrison, because they could not associate with other people, nor converse with them; yet were they willing, instead of the admission of the garrison, to give him hostages, and five hundred talents of silver; of which they paid down three hundred, and sent the hostages immediately, which king Antiochus accepted. One of those hostages was Hyrcanus's brother. But still he broke down the

---

22. Dr. Hudson tells us here, that this custom of gilding the horns of those oxen that were to be sacrificed is a known thing both in the poets and orators.

23. This account in Josephus, that the present Antiochus was persuaded, though in vain, not to make peace with the Jews, but to cut them off utterly, is fully confirmed by Diodorus Siculus, in Photiua's extracts out of his 34th Book.

fortifications that encompassed the city. And upon these conditions Antiochus broke up the siege, and departed.

4. But Hyrcanus opened the sepulcher of David, who excelled all other kings in riches, and took out of it three thousand talents. He was also the first of the Jews that, relying on this wealth, maintained foreign troops. There was also a league of friendship and mutual assistance made between them; upon which Hyrcanus admitted him into the city, and furnished him with whatsoever his army wanted in great plenty, and with great generosity, and marched along with him when he made an expedition against the Parthians; of which Nicolaus of Damascus is a witness for us; who in his history writes thus: "When Antiochus had erected a trophy at the river Lycus, upon his conquest of Indates, the general of the Parthians, he staid there two days. It was at the desire of Lyrcanus the Jew, because it was such a festival derived to them from their forefathers, whereon the law of the Jews did not allow them to travel." And truly he did not speak falsely in saying so; for that festival, which we call *Pentecost,* did then fall out to be the next day to the Sabbath. Nor is it lawful for us to journey, either on the Sabbath day, or on a festival day[24] But when Antiochus joined battle with Arsaces, the king of Parthin, he lost a great part of his army, and was himself slain; and his brother Demetrius succeeded in the kingdom of Syria, by the permission of Arsaces, who freed him from his captivity at the same time that Antiochus attacked Parthin, as we have formerly related elsewhere.

9 *How, After the Death of Antiochus, Hyrcanus Made an Expedition Against Syria, and Made a League with the Romans. Concerning the Death of King Demetrius and Alexander*

1. BUT when Hyrcanus heard of the death of Antiochus, he presently made an expedition against the cities of Syria, hoping to find them destitute of fighting men, and of such as were able to defend them. However, it was not till the sixth month that he took Medaba, and that not without the greatest distress of his army. After this he took

24. The Jews were not to march or journey on the sabbath, or on such a great festival as was equivalent to the sabbath, any farther than a sabbath day's journey, or two thousand cubits, see the note on Antiq. B. XX. ch. 8. sect. 6.

Samega, and the neighboring places; and besides these, Shechem and Gerizzim, and the nation of the Cutheans, who dwelt at the temple which resembled that temple which was at Jerusalem, and which Alexander permitted Sanballat, the general of his army, to build for the sake of Manasseh, who was son-in-law to Jaddua the high priest, as we have formerly related; which temple was now deserted two hundred years after it was built. Hyrcanus took also Dora and Marissa, cities of Idumea, and subdued all the Idumeans; and permitted them to stay in that country, if they would circumcise their genitals, and make use of the laws of the Jews; and they were so desirous of living in the country of their forefathers, that they submitted to the use of circumcision,[25] and of the rest of the Jewish ways of living; at which time therefore this befell them, that they were hereafter no other than Jews.

2. But Hyrcanus the high priest was desirous to renew that league of friendship they had with the Romans. Accordingly, he sent an embassage to them; and when the senate had received their epistle, they made a league of friendship with them, after the manner following: "Fanius, the son of Marcus, the praetor, gathered the senate together on

---

25. This account of the Idumeans admitting circumcision, and the entire Jewish law, from this time, or from the days of Hyrcanus, is confirmed by their entire history afterward. See Antiq. B. XIV. ch. 8. sect. 1; B. XV. ch. 7. sect. 9. Of the War, B. II. ch. 3. sect. 1; B. IV. ch. 4. sect. 5. This, in the opinion of Josephus, made them proselytes of justice, or entire Jews, as here and elsewhere, Antiq. B. XIV. ch. 8. sect. 1. However, Antigonus, the enemy of Herod, though Herod were derived from such a proselyte of justice for several generations, will allow him to be no more than a half Jew, B. XV. ch. 15. sect. 2. But still, take out of Dean Prideaux, at the year 129, the words of Ammouius, a grammarian, which fully confirm this account of the Idumeans in Josephus: "The Jews," says he, are such by nature, and from the beginning, whilst the Idumeans were not Jews from the beginning, but Phoenicians and Syrians; but being afterward subdued by the Jews, and compelled to be circumcised, and to unite into one nation, and be subject to the same laws, they were called Jews." Dio also says, as the Dean there quotes him, from Book XXXVI. p. 37, "That country is called Judea, and the people Jews; and this name is given also to as many others as embrace their religion, though of other nations." But then upon what foundation so good a governor as Hyrcanus took upon him to compel those Idumeans either to become Jews, or to leave the country, deserves great consideration. I suppose it was because they had long ago been driven out of the land of Edom, and had seized on and possessed the tribe of Simeon, and all the southern parts of the tribe of Judah, which was the peculiar inheritance of the worshippers of the true God without idolatry, as the reader may learn from Reland, Palestine, Part I. p. 154, 305; and from Prideaux, at the years 140 and 165.

the eighth day before the Ides of February, in the senate-house, when Lucius Manlius, the son of Lucius, of the Mentine tribe, and Caius Sempronius, the son of Caius, of the Falernian tribe, were present. The occasion was, that the ambassadors sent by the people of the Jews[26] Simon, the son of Dositheus, and Apollonius, the son of Alexander, and Diodorus, the son of Jason, who were good and virtuous men, had somewhat to propose about that league of friendship and mutual assistance which subsisted between them and the Romans, and about other public affairs, who desired that Joppa, and the havens, and Gazara, and the springs [of Jordan], and the several other cities and countries of theirs, which Antiochus had taken from them in the war, contrary to the decree of the senate, might be restored to them; and that it might not be lawful for the king's troops to pass through their country, and the countries of those that are subject to them; and that what attempts Antiochus had made during that war, without the decree of the senate, might be made void; and that they would send ambassadors, who should take care that restitution be made them of what Antiochus had taken from them, and that they should make an estimate of the country that had been laid waste in the war; and that they would grant them letters of protection to the kings and free people, in order to their quiet return home. It was therefore decreed, as to these points, to renew their league of friendship and mutual assistance with these good men, and who were sent by a good and a friendly people." But as to the letters desired, their answer was, that the senate would consult about that matter when their own affairs would give them leave; and that they would endeavor, for the time to come, that no like injury should be done to them; and that their praetor Fanius should give them money out of the public treasury to bear their expenses home. And thus did Fanius dismiss the Jewish ambassadors, and gave them money out of the public treasury; and gave the decree of the senate to those that were to conduct them, and to take care that they should return home in safety.

3. And thus stood the affairs of Hyrcanus the high priest. But as for king Demetrius, who had a mind to make war against Hyrcanus,

---

26. In this decree of the Roman senate, it seems that these ambassadors were sent from the "people of the Jews," as well as from their prince or high priest, John Hyrcanus.

there was no opportunity nor room for it, while both the Syrians and the soldiers bare ill-will to him, because he was an ill man. But when they had sent ambassadors to Ptolemy, who was called Physcon, that he would send them one of the family at Seleueus, in order to take the kingdom, and he had sent them Alexander, who was called Zebina, with an army, and there had been a battle between them, Demetrius was beaten in the fight, and fled to Cleopatra his wife, to Ptolemais; but his wife would not receive him. He went thence to Tyre, and was there caught; and when he had suffered much from his enemies before his death, he was slain by them. So Alexander took the kingdom, and made a league with Hyrcanus, who yet, when he afterward fought with Antiochus the son of Demetrius, who was called Grypus, was also beaten in the fight, and slain.

10 *How Upon the Quarrel Between Antiochus Grypus and Antiochus Cyzicenus About the Kingdom Hyrcanus Tooksamaria, and Utterly Demolished It; and How Hyrcaus Joined Himself to the Sect of the Sadducees, and Left That of the Pharisees*

1. WHEN Antiochus had taken the kingdom, he was afraid to make war against Judea, because he heard that his brother by the same mother, who was also called Antiochus, was raising an army against him out of Cyzicum; so he staid in his own land, and resolved to prepare himself for the attack he expected from his brother, who was called Cyzicenus, because he had been brought up in that city. He was the son of Antiochus that was called Soter, who died in Parthia. He was the brother of Demetrius, the father of Grypus; for it had so happened, that one and the same Cleopatra was married to two who were brethren, as we have related elsewhere. But Antiochus Cyzicenus coming into Syria, continued many years at war with his brother. Now Hyrcanus lived all this while in peace; for after the death of Antlochus, he revolted from the Macedonians,[27] nor did he any longer pay them the least regard, either as their subject or their friend; but his affairs

27. Dean Prideaux takes notice at the year 130, that Justin, in agreement with Josephus, says, "The power of the Jews was now grown so great, that after this Antiochus they would not bear any Macedonian king over them; and that they set up a government of their own, and infested Syria with great wars."

were in a very improving and flourishing condition in the times of Alexander Zebina, and especially under these brethren, for the war which they had with one another gave Hyrcanus the opportunity of enjoying himself in Judea quietly, insomuch that he got an immense quantity of money. How ever, when Antiochus Cyzicenus distressed his land, he then openly showed what he meant. And when he saw that Antiochus was destitute of Egyptian auxiliaries, and that both he and his brother were in an ill condition in the struggles they had one with another, he despised them both.

2. So he made an expedition against Samaria which was a very strong city; of whose present name Sebaste, and its rebuilding by Herod, we shall speak at a proper time; but he made his attack against it, and besieged it with a great deal of pains; for he was greatly displeased with the Samaritans for the injuries they had done to the people of Merissa, a colony of the Jews, and confederate with them, and this in compliance to the kings of Syria. When he had therefore drawn a ditch, and built a double wall round the city, which was fourscore furlongs long, he set his sons Antigonus and Arisrobulna over the siege; which brought the Samaritans to that great distress by famine, that they were forced to eat what used not to be eaten, and to call for Antiochus Cyzicenus to help them, who came readily to their assistance, but was beaten by Aristobulus; and when he was pursued as far as Scythopolis by the two brethren, he got away. So they returned to Samaria, and shut them again within the wall, till they were forced to send for the same Antiochus a second time to help them, who procured about six thousand men from Ptolemy Lathyrus, which were sent them without his mother's consent, who had then in a manner turned him out of his government. With these Egyptians Antiochus did at first overrun and ravage the country of Hyrcanus after the manner of a robber, for he durst not meet him in the face to fight with him, as not having an army sufficient for that purpose, but only from this supposal, that by thus harassing his land he should force Hyrcanus to raise the siege of Samaria; but because he fell into snares, and lost many of his soldiers therein, he went away to Tripoli, and committed the prosecution of the war against the Jews to Callimander and Epicrates.

3. But as to Callimander, he attacked the enemy too rashly, and was put to flight, and destroyed immediately; and as to Epicrates, he was

such a lover of money, that he openly betrayed Scythopolis, and other places near it, to the Jews, but was not able to make them raise the siege of Samaria. And when Hyrcanus had taken that city, which was not done till after a year's siege, he was not contented with doing that only, but he demolished it entirely, and brought rivulets to it to drown it, for he dug such hollows as might let the water run under it; nay, he took away the very marks that there had ever been such a city there. Now a very surprising thing is related of this high priest Hyrcanus, how God came to discourse with him; for they say that on the very same day on which his sons fought with Antiochus Cyzicenus, he was alone in the temple, as high priest, offering incense, and heard a voice, that his sons had just then overcome Antiochus. And this he openly declared before all the multitude upon his coming out of the temple; and it accordingly proved true; and in this posture were the affairs of Hyrcanus.

4. Now it happened at this time, that not only those Jews who were at Jerusalem and in Judea were in prosperity, but also those of them that were at Alexandria, and in Egypt and Cyprus; for Cleopatra the queen was at variance with her son Ptolemy, who was called Lathyrus, and appointed for her generals Chelcias and Ananias, the sons of that Onias who built the temple in the prefecture of Heliopolis, like to that at Jerusalem, as we have elsewhere related. Cleopatra intrusted these men with her army, and did nothing without their advice, as Strabo of Cappadocia attests, when he saith thus, "Now the greater part, both those that came to Cyprus with us, and those that were sent afterward thither, revolted to Ptolemy immediately; only those that were called Onias's party, being Jews, continued faithful, because their countrymen Chelcias and Ananias were in chief favor with the queen." These are the words of Strabo.

5. However, this prosperous state of affairs moved the Jews to envy Hyrcanus; but they that were the worst disposed to him were the Pharisees,[28] who were one of the sects of the Jews, as we have

---

28. The original of the Sadducees, as a considerable party among the Jews, being contained in this and the two following sections, take Dean Prideaux's note upon this their first public appearance, which I suppose to be true: "Hyrcanus," says be, "went over to the party of the Sadducees; that is, by embracing their doctrine against the traditions of the eiders, added to the written law, and made of equal authority with

informed you already. These have so great a power over the multitude, that when they say any thing against the king, or against the high priest, they are presently believed. Now Hyrcanus was a disciple of theirs, and greatly beloved by them. And when he once invited them to a feast, and entertained them very kindly, when he saw them in a good humor, he began to say to them, that they knew he was desirous to be a righteous man, and to do all things whereby he might please God, which was the profession of the Pharisees also. However, he desired, that if they observed him offending in any point, and going out of the right way, they would call him back and correct him. On which occasion they attested to his being entirely virtuous; with which commendation he was well pleased. But still there was one of his guests there, whose name was Eleazar, a man of an ill temper, and delighting in seditious practices. This man said," Since thou desirest to know the truth, if thou wilt be righteous in earnest, lay down the high priesthood, and content thyself with the civil government of the people," And when he desired to know for what cause he ought to lay down the high priesthood, the other replied, "We have heard it from old men, that thy mother had been a captive under the reign of Antiochus Epiphanes.[29] "This story was false, and Hyrcanus was provoked against him; and all the Pharisees had a very great indignation against him.

6. Now there was one Jonathan, a very great friend of Hyrcanus's, but of the sect of the Sadducees, whose notions are quite contrary to those of the Pharisees. He told Hyrcanus that Eleazar had cast such a reproach upon him, according to the common sentiments of all the Pharisees, and that this would be made manifest if he would but ask

---

it, but not their doctrine against the resurrection and a future state; for this cannot be supposed of so good and righteous a man as John Hyrcanus is said to be. It is most probable, that at this time the Sadducees had gone no further in the doctrines of that sect than to deny all their unwritten traditions, which the Pharisees were so fond of; for Josephus mentions no other difference at this time between them; neither doth he say that Hyrcanna went over to the Sadducees in any other particular than in the abolishing of all the traditionary constitutions of the Pharisees, which our Savior condemned as well as they." [At the year.]

29. This slander, that arose from a Pharisee, has been preserved by their successors the Rabbins to these later ages; for Dr. Hudson assures us that David Gantz, in his Chronology, S. Pr. p. 77, in Vorstius's version, relates that Hyrcanus's mother was taken captive in Mount Modinth. See ch. 13. sect. 5.

them the question, What punishment they thought this man deserved? for that he might depend upon it, that the reproach was not laid on him with their approbation, if they were for punishing him as his crime deserved. So the Pharisees made answer, that he deserved stripes and bonds, but that it did not seem right to punish reproaches with death. And indeed the Pharisees, even upon other occasions, are not apt to be severe in punishments. At this gentle sentence, Hyrcanus was very angry, and thought that this man reproached him by their approbation. It was this Jonathan who chiefly irritated him, and influenced him so far, that he made him leave the party of the Pharisees, and abolish the decrees they had imposed on the people, and to punish those that observed them. From this source arose that hatred which he and his sons met with from the multitude: but of these matters we shall speak hereafter. What I would now explain is this, that the Pharisees have delivered to the people a great many observances by succession from their fathers, which are not written in the laws of Moses; and for that reason it is that the Sadducees reject them, and say that we are to esteem those observances to be obligatory which are in the written word, but are not to observe what are derived from the tradition of our forefathers. And concerning these things it is that great disputes and differences have arisen among them, while the Sadducees are able to persuade none but the rich, and have not the populace obsequious to them, but the Pharisees have the multitude on their side. But about these two sects, and that of the Essens, I have treated accurately in the second book of Jewish affairs.

7. But when Hyrcanus had put an end to this sedition, he after that lived happily, and administered the government in the best manner for thirty-one years, and then died,[30] leaving behind him five sons.

---

30. Here ends the high priesthood, and the life of this excellent person John Hyrcanus, and together with him the holy theocracy, or Divine government of the Jewish nation, and its concomitant oracle by Urim. Now follows the profane and tyrannical Jewish monarchy, first of the Asamoneans or Maccabees, and then of Herod the Great, the Idumean, till the coming of the Messiah. See the note on Antiq. B. III. ch. 8. sect. 9. Hear Strabo's testimony on this occasion, B. XVI. p. 761, 762: "Those," says he, "that succeeded Moses continued for some time in earnest, both in righteous actions and in piety; but after a while there were others that took upon them the high priesthood, at first superstitious and afterward tyrannical persons. Such a prophet was Moses and those that succeeded him, beginning in a way not to be blamed, but

He was esteemed by God worthy of three of the greatest privileges,—the government of his nation, the dignity of the high priesthood, and prophecy; for God was with him, and enabled him to know futurities; and to foretell this in particular, that, as to his two eldest sons, he foretold that they would not long continue in the government of public affairs; whose unhappy catastrophe will be worth our description, that we may thence learn how very much they were inferior to their father's happiness.

11 *How Aristobulus, When He Had Taken the Government First of All Put a Diadem on His Head, and Was Most Barbarously Cruel to His Mother and His Brethren; and How, After He Had Slain Antigonus, He Himself Died*

1. NOW when their father Hyrcanus was dead, the eldest son Aristobulus, intending to change the government into a kingdom, for so he resolved to do, first of all put a diadem on his head, four hundred eighty and one years and three months after the people had been delivered from the Babylonish slavery, and were returned to their own country again. This Aristobulus loved his next brother Antigonus, and treated him as his equal; but the others he held in bonds. He also cast his mother into prison, because she disputed the government with him; for Hyrcanus had left her to be mistress of all. He also proceeded to that degree of barbarity, as to kill her in prison with hunger; nay, he was alienated from his brother Antigonus by calumnies, and added him to the rest whom he slew; yet he seemed to have an affection for

---

changing for the worse. And when it openly appeared that the government was become tyrannical, Alexander was the first that set up himself for a king instead of a priest; and his sons were Hyrcanus and Aristobulus." All in agreement with Josephus, excepting this, that Strabo omits the first king, Aristobulus, who reigning but a single year, seems hardly to have come to his knowledge. Nor indeed does Aristobulus, the son of Alexander, pretend that the name of king was taken before his father Alexander took it himself, Antiq. B. XIV. ch. 3. sect. 2. See also ch. 12. sect. 1, which favor Strabo also. And indeed, if we may judge from the very different characters of the Egyptian Jews under high priests, and of the Palestine Jews under kings, in the two next centuries, we may well suppose that the Divine Shechinah was removed into Egypt, and that the worshippers at the temple of Onias were better men than those at the temple of Jerusalem.

him, and made him above the rest a partner with him in the kingdom. Those calumnies he at first did not give credit to, partly because he loved him, and so did not give heed to what was said against him, and partly because he thought the reproaches were derived from the envy of the relaters. But when Antigonus was once returned from the army, and that feast was then at hand when they make tabernacles to [the honor of God,] it happened that Arlstobulus was fallen sick, and that Antigonus went up most splendidly adorned, and with his soldiers about him in their armor, to the temple to celebrate the feast, and to put up many prayers for the recovery of his brother, when some wicked persons, who had a great mind to raise a difference between the brethren, made use of this opportunity of the pompous appearance of Antigonus, and of the great actions which he had done, and went to the king, and spitefully aggravated the pompous show of his at the feast, and pretended that all these circumstances were not like those of a private person; that these actions were indications of an affectation of royal authority; and that his coming with a strong body of men must be with an intention to kill him; and that his way of reasoning was this: That it was a silly thing in him, while it was in his power to reign himself, to look upon it as a great favor that he was honored with a lower dignity by his brother.

2. Aristobulus yielded to these imputations, but took care both that his brother should not suspect him, and that he himself might not run the hazard of his own safety; so he ordered his guards to lie in a certain place that was under ground, and dark; (he himself then lying sick in the tower which was called Antonia;) and he commanded them, that in case Antigonus came in to him unarmed, they should not touch any body, but if armed, they should kill him; yet did he send to Antigonus, and desired that he would come unarmed; but the queen, and those that joined with her in the plot against Antigonus, persuaded the messenger to tell him the direct contrary: how his brother had heard that he had made himself a fine suit of armor for war, and desired him to come to him in that armor, that he might see how fine it was. So Antigonus suspecting no treachery, but depending on the good-will of his brother, came to Aristobulus armed, as he used to be, with his entire armor, in order to show it to him; but when he was come to a place which was called Strato's Tower, where the passage happened to be exceeding dark, the guards slew him; which death

of his demonstrates that nothing is stronger than envy and calumny, and that nothing does more certainly divide the good-will and natural affections of men than those passions. But here one may take occasion to wonder at one Judas, who was of the sect of the Essens,[31] and who never missed the truth in his predictions; for this man, when he saw Antigonus passing by the temple, cried out to his companions and friends, who abode with him as his scholars, in order to learn the art of foretelling things to come?" That it was good for him to die now, since he had spoken falsely about Antigonus, who is still alive, and I see him passing by, although he had foretold he should die at the place called Strato's Tower that very day, while yet the place is six hundred furlongs off, where he had foretold he should be slain; and still this day is a great part of it already past, so that he was in danger of proving a false prophet." As he was saying this, and that in a melancholy mood, the news came that Antigonus was slain in a place under ground, which itself was called also Strato's Tower, or of the same name with that Cesarea which is seated at the sea. This event put the prophet into a great disorder.

3. But Aristobulus repented immediately of this slaughter of his brother; on which account his disease increased upon him, and he was disturbed in his mind, upon the guilt of such wickedness, insomuch that his entrails were corrupted by his intolerable pain, and he vomited blood: at which time one of the servants that attended upon him, and was carrying his blood away, did, by Divine Providence, as I cannot but suppose, slip down, and shed part of his blood at the very place where there were spots of Antigonus's blood, there slain, still remaining; and when there was a cry made by the spectators, as if the servant had on purpose shed the blood on that place, Aristobulus heard it, and inquired what the matter was; and as they did not answer him, he was the more earnest to know what it was, it being natural to men to suspect that what is thus concealed is very bad: so upon his

31. Hence we learn that the Essens pretended to have ruled whereby men might foretell things to come, and that this Judas the Essen taught those rules to his scholars; but whether their pretense were of an astrological or magical nature, which yet in such religious Jews, who were utterly forbidden such arts, is no way probable, or to any Bath Col, spoken of by the later Rabbins, or otherwise, I cannot tell. See Of the War, B. II. ch. 8. sect. 12.

threatening, and forcing them by terrors to speak, they at length told him the truth; whereupon he shed many tears, in that disorder of mind which arose from his consciousness of what he had done, and gave a deep groan, and said, "I am not therefore, I perceive, to be concealed from God, in the impious and horrid crimes I have been guilty of; but a sudden punishment is coming upon me for the shedding the blood of my relations. And now, O thou most impudent body of mine, how long wilt thou retain a soul that ought to die, in order to appease the ghosts of my brother and my mother? Why dost thou not give it all up at once? And why do I deliver up my blood drop by drop to those whom I have so wickedly murdered?" In saying which last words he died, having reigned a year. He was called a lover of the Grecians; and had conferred many benefits on his own country, and made war against Iturea, and added a great part of it to Judea, and compelled the inhabitants, if they would continue in that country, to be circumcised, and to live according to the Jewish laws. He was naturally a man of candor, and of great modesty, as Strabo bears witness, in the name of Timagenes; who says thus: "This man was a person of candor, and very serviceable to the Jews; for he added a country to them, and obtained a part of the nation of the Itureans for them, and bound them to them by the bond of the circumcision of their genitals."

12 *How Alexander When He Had Taken the Government Made an Expedition Against Ptolemais, and Then Raised the Siege Out of Fear of Ptolemy Lathyrus; and How Ptolemy Made War Against Him, Because He Had Sent to Cleopatra to Persuade Her to Make War Against Ptolemy, and Yet Pretended to Be in Friendship with Him, When He Beat the Jews in the Battle*

1. WHEN Aristobulus was dead, his wife Salome, who, by the Greeks, was called Alexandra, let his brethren out of prison, (for Aristobulus had kept them in bonds, as we have said already,) and made Alexander Janneus king, who was the superior in age and in moderation. This child happened to be hated by his father as soon as he was born, and could never be permitted to come into his father's sight till he

died.[32] The occasion of which hatred is thus reported: when Hyrcanus chiefly loved the two eldest of his sons, Antigonus and Aristobutus, God appeared to him in his sleep, of whom he inquired which of his sons should be his successor. Upon God's representing to him the countenance of Alexander, he was grieved that he was to be the heir of all his goods, and suffered him to be brought up in Galilee However, God did not deceive Hyrcanus; for after the death of Aristobulus, he certainly took the kingdom; and one of his brethren, who affected the kingdom, he slew; and the other, who chose to live a private and quiet life, he had in esteem.

2. When Alexander Janneus had settled the government in the manner that he judged best, he made an expedition against Ptolemais; and having overcome the men in battle, he shut them up in the city, and sat round about it, and besieged it; for of the maritime cities there remained only Ptolemais and Gaza to be conquered, besides Strato's Tower and Dora, which were held by the tyrant Zoilus. Now while Antiochus Philometor, and Antiochus who was called Cyzicenus, were making war one against another, and destroying one another's armies, the people of Ptolemais could have no assistance from them; but when they were distressed with this siege, Zoilus, who possessed Strato's Tower and Dora, and maintained a legion of soldiers, and, on occasion of the contest between the kings, affected tyranny himself, came and brought some small assistance to the people of Ptolemais; nor indeed had the kings such a friendship for them, as that they should hope for any advantage from them. Both those kings were in the case of wrestlers, who finding themselves deficient in. strength, and yet being ashamed to yield, put off the fight by laziness, and by lying still as long as they can. The only hope they had remaining was from the kings of Egypt, and from Ptolemy Lathyrus, who now held Cyprus, and who came to Cyprus when he was driven from the government of Egypt by Cleopatra his mother. So the people of Ptolemais sent to this Ptolemy Lathyrus, and desired him to come as

32. The reason why Hyrcanus suffered not this son of his whom he did not love to come into Judea, but ordered him to be brought up in Galilee, is suggested by Dr. Hudson, that Galilee was not esteemed so happy and well cultivated a country as Judea, Matthew 26:73; John 7:52; Acts 2:7, although another obvious reason occurs also, that he was out of his sight in Galilee than he would have been in Judea.

a confederate, to deliver them, now they were in such danger, out of the hands of Alexander. And as the ambassadors gave him hopes, that if he would pass over into Syria, he would have the people of Gaza on the side of those of Ptolemais; as also they said, that Zoilus, and besides these the Sidonians, and many others, would assist them; so he was elevated at this, and got his fleet ready as soon as possible.

3. But in this interval Demenetus, one that was of abilities to persuade men to do as he would have them, and a leader of the populace, made those of Ptolemais change their opinions; and said to them, that it was better to run the hazard of being subject to the Jews, than to admit of evident slavery by delivering themselves up to a master; and besides that, to have not only a war at present, but to expect a much greater war from Egypt; for that Cleopatra would not overlook an army raised by Ptolemy for himself out of the neighborhood, but would come against them with a great army of her own, and this because she was laboring to eject her son out of Cyprus also; that as for Ptolemy, if he fail of his hopes, he can still retire to Cyprus, but that they will be left in the greatest danger possible. Now Ptolemy, although he had heard of the change that was made in the people of Ptolemais, yet did he still go on with his voyage, and came to the country called Sycamine, and there set his army on shore. This army of his, in the whole horse and foot together, were about thirty thousand, with which he marched near to Ptolemais, and there pitched his camp. But when the people of Ptolemais neither received his ambassadors, nor would hear what they had to say, he was under a very great concern.

4. But when Zoilus and the people of Gaza came to him, and desired his assistance, because their country was laid waste by the Jews, and by Alexander, Alexander raised the siege, for fear of Ptolemy: and when he had drawn off his army into his own country, he used a stratagem afterwards, by privately inviting Cleopatra to come against Ptolemy, but publicly pretending to desire a league of friendship and mutual assistance with him; and promising to give him four hundred talents of silver, he desired that, by way of requital, he would take off Zoilus the tyrant, and give his country to the Jews. And then indeed Ptolemy, with pleasure, made such a league of friendship with Alexander, and subdued Zoilus; but when he afterwards heard that he had privily sent to Cleopatra his mother, he broke the league with

him, which yet he had confirmed with an oath, and fell upon him, and besieged Ptolemais, because it would not receive him. However, leaving his generals, with some part of his forces, to go on with the siege, he went himself immediately with the rest to lay Judea waste; and when Alexander understood this to be Ptolemy's intention, he also got together about fifty thousand soldiers out of his own country; nay, as some writers have said, eighty thousand[33] He then took his army, and went to meet Ptolemy; but Ptolemy fell upon Asochis, a city of Galilee, and took it by force on the sabbath day, and there he took about ten thousand slaves, and a great deal of other prey.

5. He then tried to take Sepphoris, which was a city not far from that which was destroyed, but lost many of his men; yet did he then go to fight with Alexander; which Alexander met him at the river Jordan, near a certain place called Saphoth, [not far from the river Jordan,] and pitched his camp near to the enemy. He had however eight thousand in the first rank, which he styled Hecatontomachi, having shields of brass. Those in the first rank of Ptolemy's soldiers also had shields covered with brass. But Ptolemy's soldiers in other respects were inferior to those of Alexander, and therefore were more fearful of running hazards; but Philostephanus, the camp-master, put great courage into them, and ordered them to pass the river, which was between their camps. Nor did Alexander think fit to hinder their passage over it; for he thought, that if the enemy had once gotten the river on their back, that he should the easier take them prisoners, when they could not flee out of the battle: in the beginning of which, the acts on both sides, with their hands, and with their alacrity, were alike, and a great slaughter was made by both the armies; but Alexander was superior, till Philostephanus opportunely brought up the auxiliaries, to help those that were giving way; but as there were no auxiliaries to afford help to that part of the Jews that gave way, it fell out that they fled, and those near them did no assist them, but fled along with them.

---

33. From these, and other occasional expressions, dropped by Josephus, we may learn, that where the sacred hooks of the Jews were deficient, he had several other histories then extant, (but now most of them lost,) which he faithfully followed in his own history; nor indeed have we any other records of those times, relating to Judea, that can be compared to these accounts of Josephus, though when we do meet with authentic fragments of such original records, they almost always confirm his history.

However, Ptolemy's soldiers acted quite otherwise; for they followed the Jews, and killed them, till at length those that slew them pursued after them when they had made them all run away, and slew them so long, that their weapons of iron were blunted, and their hands quite tired with the slaughter; for the report was, that thirty thousand men were then slain. Timagenes says they were fifty thousand. As for the rest, they were part of them taken captives, and the other part ran away to their own country.

6. After this victory, Ptolemy overran all the country; and when night came on, he abode in certain villages of Judea, which when he found full of women and children, he commanded his soldiers to strangle them, and to cut them in pieces, and then to cast them into boiling caldrons, and then to devour their limbs as sacrifices. This commandment was given, that such as fled from the battle, and came to them, might suppose their enemies were cannibals, and eat men's flesh, and might on that account be still more terrified at them upon such a sight. And both Strabo and Nicholaus [of Damascus] affirm, that they used these people after this manner, as I have already related. Ptolemy also took Ptolemais by force, as we have declared elsewhere.

13 *How Alexander, Upon the League of Mutual Defense Which Cleopatra Had Agreed with Him, Made an Expedition Against Coelesyria, and Utterly Overthrew the City of Gaza; and How He Slew Many Ten Thousands of Jews That Rebelled Against Him. Also Concerning Antiochus Grypus, Seleucus Antiochus Cyziceius, and Antiochus Pius, and Others*

1. WHEN Cleopatra saw that her son was grown great, and laid Judea waste, without disturbance, and had gotten the city of Gaza under his power, she resolved no longer to overlook what he did, when he was almost at her gates; and she concluded, that now he was so much stronger than before, he would be very desirous of the dominion over the Egyptians; but she immediately marched against him, with a fleet at sea and an army of foot on land, and made Chelcias and Ananias the Jews generals of her whole army, while she sent the greatest part of

her riches, her grandchildren, and her testament, to the people of Cos[34] Cleopatra also ordered her son Alexander to sail with a great fleet to Phoenicia; and when that country had revolted, she came to Ptolemais; and because the people of Ptolemais did not receive her, she besieged the city; but Ptolemy went out of Syria, and made haste unto Egypt, supposing that he should find it destitute of an army, and soon take it, though he failed of his hopes. At this time Chelcias, one of Cleopatra's generals, happened to die in Celesyria, as he was in pursuit of Ptolemy.

2. When Cleopatra heard of her son's attempt, and that his Egyptian expedition did not succeed according to his expectations, she sent thither part of her army, and drove him out of that country; so when he was returned out of Egypt again, he abode during the winter at Gaza, in which time Cleopatra took the garrison that was in Ptolemais by siege, as well as the city; and when Alexander came to her, he gave her presents, and such marks of respect as were but proper, since under the miseries he endured by Ptolemy he had no other refuge but her. Now there were some of her friends who persuaded her to seize Alexander, and to overrun and take possession of the country, and not to sit still and see such a multitude of brave Jews subject to one man. But Ananias's counsel was contrary to theirs, who said that she would do an unjust action if she deprived a man that was her ally of that authority which belonged to him, and this a man who is related to us; "for (said he) I would not have thee ignorant of this, that what in. justice thou dost to him will make all us that are Jews to be thy enemies. This desire of Ananias Cleopatra complied with, and did no injury to Alexander, but made a league of mutual assistance with him at Scythopolis, a city of Celesyria.

3. So when Alexander was delivered from the fear he was in of Ptolemy, he presently made an expedition against Coelesyria. He also took Gadara, after a siege of ten months. He took also Areathus, a very strong fortress belonging to the inhabitants above Jordan, where Theodorus, the son of Zeno, had his chief treasure, and what

34. This city, or island, Cos, is not that remote island in the Aegean Sea, famous for the birth of the great Hippocrates, but a city or island of the same name adjoining to Egypt, mentioned both by Stephanus and Ptolemy, as Dr. Mizon informs us. Of which Cos, and the treasures there laid up by Cleopatra and the Jews, see Antiq. B. XIV. ch. 7, sect. 2.

he esteemed most precious. This Zeno fell unexpectedly upon the Jews, and slew ten thousand of them, and seized upon Alexander's baggage. Yet did not this misfortune terrify Alexander; but he made an expedition upon the maritime parts of the country, Raphia and Anthedon, (the name of which king Herod afterwards changed to Agrippias,) and took even that by force. But when Alexander saw that Ptolemy was retired from Gaza to Cyprus, and his mother Cleopatra was returned to Egypt, he grew angry at the people of Gaza, because they had invited Ptolemy to assist them, and besieged their city, and ravaged their country. But as Apollodotus, the general of the army of Gaza, fell upon the camp of the Jews by night, with two thousand foreign and ten thousand of his own forces, while the night lasted, those of Gaza prevailed, because the enemy was made to believe that it was Ptolemy who attacked them; but when day was come on, and that mistake was corrected, and the Jews knew the truth of the matter, they came back again, and fell upon those of Gaza, and slew of them about a thousand. But as those of Gaza stoutly resisted them, and would not yield for either their want of any thing, nor for the great multitude that were slain, (for they would rather suffer any hardship whatever than come under the power of their enemies,) Aretas, king of the Arabians, a person then very illustrious, encouraged them to go on with alacrity, and promised them that he would come to their assistance; but it happened that before he came Apollodotus was slain; for his brother Lysimachus envying him for the great reputation he had gained among the citizens, slew him, and got the army together, and delivered up the city to Alexander, who, when he came in at first, lay quiet, but afterward set his army upon the inhabitants of Gaza, and gave them leave to punish them; so some went one way, and some went another, and slew the inhabitants of Gaza; yet were not they of cowardly hearts, but opposed those that came to slay them, and slew as many of the Jews; and some of them, when they saw themselves deserted, burnt their own houses, that the enemy might get none of their spoils; nay, some of them, with their own hands, slew their children and their wives, having no other way but this of avoiding slavery for them; but the senators, who were in all five hundred, fled to Apollo's temple, (for this attack happened to be made as they were sitting,) whom Alexander slew; and when he had utterly overthrown their city, he returned to Jerusalem, having spent a year in that siege.

4. About this very time Antiochus, who was called Grypus, died[35] His death was caused by Heracleon's treachery, when he had lived forty-five years, and had reigned twenty-nine.[36] His son Seleucus succeeded him in the kingdom, and made war with Antiochus, his father's brother, who was called Antiochus Cyzicenus, and beat him, and took him prisoner, and slew him. But after a while Antiochus, the son of Cyzicenus, who was called Pius, came to Aradus, and put the diadem on his own head, and made war with Seleucus, and beat him, and drove him out of all Syria. But when he fled out of Syria, he came to Mopsuestia again, and levied money upon them; but the people of Mopsuestin had indignation at what he did, and burnt down his palace, and slew him, together with his friends. But when Antiochus, the son of Cyzicenus, was king of Syria, Antiochus,[37] the brother of Seleucus, made war upon him, and was overcome, and destroyed, he and his army. After him, his brother Philip put on the diadem, and reigned over some part of Syria; but Ptolemy Lathyrus sent for his fourth brother Demetrius, who was called Eucerus, from Cnidus, and made him king of Damascus. Both these brothers did Antiochus vehemently oppose, but presently died; for when he was come as an auxiliary to Laodice, queen of the Gileadites,[38] when she was making war against the Parthians, and he was fighting courageously, he fell, while Demetrius and Philip governed Syria, as hath been elsewhere related.

---

35. This account of the death of Antiochus Grypus is confirmed by Appion, Syriac. p. 132, here cited by Spanheim.

36. Porphyry says that this Antiochus Grypus reigned but twenty-six years, as Dr. Hudson observes. The copies of Josephus, both Greek and Latin, have here so grossly false a reading, Antiochus and Antoninus, or Antonius Plus, for Antiochus Pius, that the editors are forced to correct the text from the other historians, who all agree that this king's name was nothing more than Antiochus Plus.

37. These two brothers, Antiochus and Philippus are called twins by Porphyry; the fourth brother was king of Damascus: both which are the observations of Spanheim.

38. This Laodicea was a city of Gilead beyond Jordan. However, Porphyry says that this Antiochus Pius did not die in this battle; but, running away, was drowned in the river Orontes. Appian says that he, was deprived of the kingdom of Syria by Tigranes; but Porphyry makes this Laodice queen of the Calamans;—all which is noted by Spanheim. In such confusion of the later historians, we have no reason to prefer any of them before Josephus, who had more original ones before him. This reproach upon Alexander, that he was sprung from a captive, seems only the repetition of the old Pharisaical calumny upon his father, ch. 10. sect. 5.

5. As to Alexander, his own people were seditious against him; for at a festival which was then celebrated, when he stood upon the altar, and was going to sacrifice, the nation rose upon him, and pelted him with citrons [which they then had in their hands, because] the law of the Jews required that at the feast of tabernacles every one should have branches of the palm tree and citron tree; which thing we have elsewhere related. They also reviled him, as derived from a captive, and so unworthy of his dignity and of sacrificing. At this he was in a rage, and slew of them about six thousand. He also built a partition-wall of wood round the altar and the temple, as far as that partition within which it was only lawful for the priests to enter; and by this means he obstructed the multitude from coming at him. He also maintained foreigners of Pisidie and Cilicia; for as to the Syrians, he was at war with them, and so made no use of them. He also overcame the Arabians, such as the Moabites and Gileadites, and made them bring tribute. Moreover, he demolished Amathus, while Theodorus[39] durst not fight with him; but as he had joined battle with Obedas, king of the Arabians, and fell into an ambush in the places that were rugged and difficult to be traveled over, he was thrown down into a deep valley, by the multitude of the camels at Gadurn, a village of Gilead, and hardly escaped with his life. From thence he fled to Jerusalem, where, besides his other ill success, the nation insulted him, and he fought against them for six years, and slew no fewer than fifty thousand of them. And when he desired that they would desist from their ill-will to him, they hated him so much the more, on account of what had already happened; and when he had asked them what he ought to do, they all cried out, that he ought to kill himself. They also sent to Demetrius Eucerus, and desired him to make a league of mutual defense with them.

---

39. This Theodorus was the son of Zeno, and was in possession of Areathus, as we learn from sect. 3 foregoing.

14 *How Demetrius Eucerus Overcame Alexander and Yet in a Little Time Retired Out of the Country for Fear; as Also How Alexander Slew Many of the Jews and Thereby Got Clear of His Troubles. Concerning the Death of Demetrius*

1. SO Demetrius came with an army, and took those that invited him, and pitched his camp near the city Shechem; upon which Alexander, with his six thousand two hundred mercenaries, and about twenty thousand Jews, who were of his party, went against Demetrius, who had three thousand horsemen, and forty thousand footmen. Now there were great endeavors used on both sides,—Demetrius trying to bring off the mercenaries that were with Alexander, because they were Greeks, and Alexander trying to bring off the Jews that were with Demetrius. However, when neither of them could persuade them so to do, they came to a battle, and Demetrius was the conqueror; in which all Alexander's mercenaries were killed, when they had given demonstration of their fidelity and courage. A great number of Demetrius's soldiers were slain also.

2. Now as Alexander fled to the mountains, six thousand of the Jews hereupon came together [from Demetrius] to him out of pity at the change of his fortune; upon which Demetrius was afraid, and retired out of the country; after which the Jews fought against Alexander, and being beaten, were slain in great numbers in the several battles which they had; and when he had shut up the most powerful of them in the city Bethome, he besieged them therein; and when he had taken the city, and gotten the men into his power, he brought them to Jerusalem, and did one of the most barbarous actions in the world to them; for as he was feasting with his concubines, in the sight of all the city, he ordered about eight hundred of them to be crucified; and while they were living, he ordered the throats of their children and wives to be cut before their eyes. This was indeed by way of revenge for the injuries they had done him; which punishment yet was of an inhuman nature, though we suppose that he had been never so much distressed, as indeed he had been, by his wars with them, for he had by their means come to the last degree of hazard, both of his life and of his kingdom, while they were not satisfied by themselves only to fight against him, but introduced foreigners also for the same purpose; nay, at length they reduced him to that degree of necessity, that he was forced to

deliver back to the king of Arabia the land of Moab and Gilead, which he had subdued, and the places that were in them, that they might not join with them in the war against him, as they had done ten thousand other things that tended to affront and reproach him. However, this barbarity seems to have been without any necessity, on which account he bare the name of a Thracian among the Jews[40] whereupon the soldiers that had fought against him, being about eight thousand in number, ran away by night, and continued fugitives all the time that Alexander lived; who being now freed from any further disturbance from them, reigned the rest of his time in the utmost tranquillity.

3. But when Demetrius was departed out of Judea, he went to Berea, and besieged his brother Philip, having with him ten thousand footmen, and a thousand horsemen. However Strato, the tyrant of Berea, the confederate of Philip, called in Zizon, the ruler of the Arabian tribes, and Mithridates Sinax, the ruler of the Parthians, who coming with a great number of forces, and besieging Demetrius in his encampment, into which they had driven them with their arrows, they compelled those that were with him by thirst to deliver up themselves. So they took a great many spoils out of that country, and Demetrius himself, whom they sent to Mithridates, who was then king of Parthis; but as to those whom they took captives of the people of Antioch, they restored them to the Antiochinus without any reward. Now Mithridates, the king of Parthis, had Demetrius in great honor, till Demetrius ended his life by sickness. So Philip, presently after the fight was over, came to Antioch, and took it, and reigned over Syria.

---

40. This name Thracida, which the Jews gave Alexander, must, by the coherence, denote as barbarous as a Thracian, or somewhat like it; but what it properly signifies is not known.

15 *How Antiochus, Who Was Called Dionysus, and After Him Aretas Made Expeditions into Judea; as Also How Alexander Took Many Cities and Then Returned to Jerusalem, and After a Sickness of Three Years Died; and What Counsel He Gave to Alexandra*

1. AFTER this, Antiochus, who was called Dionysus,[41] and was Philip's brother, aspired to the dominion, and carne to Damascus, and got the power into his hands, and there he reigned; but as he was making war against the Arabians, his brother Philip heard of it, and came to Damascus, where Milesius, who had been left governor of the citadel, and the Damascens themselves, delivered up the city to him; yet because Philip was become ungrateful to him, and had bestowed upon him nothing of that in hopes whereof he had received him into the city, but had a mind to have it believed that it was rather delivered up out of fear than by the kindness of Milesius, and because he had not rewarded him as he ought to have done, he became suspected by him, and so he was obliged to leave Damascus again; for Milesius caught him marching out into the Hippodrome, and shut him up in it, and kept Damascus for Antiochus [Eucerus], who hearing how Philip's affairs stood, came back out of Arabia. He also came immediately, and made an expedition against Judea, with eight thousand armed footmen, and eight hundred horsemen. So Alexander, out of fear of his coming, dug a deep ditch, beginning at Chabarzaba, which is now called Antipatris, to the sea of Joppa, on which part only his army could be brought against him. He also raised a wall, and erected wooden towers, and intermediate redoubts, for one hundred and fifty furlongs in length, and there expected the coming of Antiochus; but he soon burnt them all, and made his army pass by that way into Arabia. The Arabian king [Aretas] at first retreated, but afterward appeared on the sudden with ten thousand horsemen. Antiochus gave them the meeting, and fought desperately; and indeed when he had gotten the victory, and was bringing some auxiliaries to that part of his army that was in distress, he was slain. When Antiochus was fallen, his army

41. Spanheim takes notice that this Antiochus Dionysus [the brother of Philip, and of Demetrius Eucerus, and of two otbsrs] was the fifth son of Antiochus Grypus; and that he is styled on the coins, "Antiochus, Epiphanes, Dionysus."

fled to the village Cana, where the greatest part of them perished by famine.

2. After him[42] Arems reigned over Celesyria, being called to the government by those that held Damascus, by reason of the hatred they bare to Ptolemy Menneus. He also made thence an expedition against Judea, and beat Alexander in battle, near a place called Adida; yet did he, upon certain conditions agreed on between them, retire out of Judea.

3. But Alexander marched again to the city Dios, and took it; and then made an expedition against Essa, where was the best part of Zeno's treasures, and there he encompassed the place with three walls; and when he had taken the city by fighting, he marched to Golan and Seleucia; and when he had taken these cities, he, besides them, took that valley which is called *The Valley of Antiochus,* as also the fortress of Gamala. He also accused Demetrius, who was governor of those places, of many crimes, and turned him out; and after he had spent three years in this war, he returned to his own country, when the Jews joyfully received him upon this his good success.

4. Now at this time the Jews were in possession of the following cities that had belonged to the Syrians, and Idumeans, and Phoenicians: At the sea-side, Strato's Tower, Apollonia, Joppa, Jamhis, Ashdod, Gaza, Anthedon, Raphia, and Rhinocolura; in the middle of the country, near to Idumea, Adorn, and Marissa; near the country of Samaria, Mount Carmel, and Mount Tabor, Scythopolis, and Gadara; of the country of Gaulonitis, Seleucia and Gabala; in the country of Moab, Heshbon, and Medaba, Lemba, and Oronas, Gelithon, Zorn, the valley of the Cilices, and Pollo; which last they utterly destroyed, because its inhabitants would not bear to change their religious rites for those peculiar to the Jews.[43] The Jews also possessed others of the principal cities of Syria, which had been destroyed.

---

42. This Aretas was the first king of the Arabians who took Damascus, and reigned there; which name became afterwards common to such Arabian kings, both at Petra and at Damascus, as we learn from Josephus in many places; and from St. Paul, 2 Corinthians 11:32. See the note on Antiq. B. XVI. ch. 9. sect. 4.

43. We may here and elsewhere take notice, that whatever countries or cities the Asamoneans conquered from any of the neighboring nations, or whatever countries or cities they gained from them that had not belonged to them before, they, after the days of Hyrcanus, compelled the inhabitants to leave their idolatry, and entirely to receive the law of Moses, as proselytes of justice, or else banished them into other

5. After this, king Alexander, although he fell into a distemper by hard drinking, and had a quartan ague, which held him three years, yet would not leave off going out with his army, till he was quite spent with the labors he had undergone, and died in the bounds of Ragaba, a fortress beyond Jordan. But when his queen saw that he was ready to die, and had no longer any hopes of surviving, she came to him weeping and lamenting, and bewailed herself and her sons on the desolate condition they should be left in; and said to him, "To whom dost thou thus leave me and my children, who are destitute of all other supports, and this when thou knowest how much ill-will thy nation bears thee?" But he gave her the following advice: That she need but follow what he would suggest to her, in order to retain the kingdom securely, with her children: that she should conceal his death from the soldiers till she should have taken that place; after this she should go in triumph, as upon a victory, to Jerusalem, and put some of her authority into the hands of the Pharisees; for that they would commend her for the honor she had done them, and would reconcile the nation to her for he told her they had great authority among the Jews, both to do hurt to such as they hated, and to bring advantages to those to whom they were friendly disposed; for that they are then believed best of all by the multitude when they speak any severe thing against others, though it be only out of envy at them. And he said that it was by their means that he had incurred the displeasure of the nation, whom indeed he had injured. "Do thou, therefore," said he, "when thou art come to Jerusalem, send for the leading men among them, and show them my body, and with great appearance of sincerity, give them leave to use it as they themselves please, whether they will dishonor the dead body by refusing it burial, as having severely suffered by my means, or whether in their anger they will offer any other injury to that body. Promise them also that thou wilt do nothing without them in the affairs of the kingdom. If thou dost but say this to them, I shall have the honor of a more glorious Funeral from them than thou couldst have made for me; and when it is in their power to abuse my dead

---

lands. That excellent prince, John Hyrcanus, did it to the Idumeans, as I have noted on ch. 9. sect. 1, already, who lived then in the Promised Land, and this I suppose justly; but by what right the rest did it, even to the countries or cities that were no part of that land, I do not at all know. This looks too like unjust persecution for religion.

body, they will do it no injury at all, and thou wilt rule in safety."[44] So when he had given his wife this advice, he died, after he had reigned twenty-seven years, and lived fifty years within one.

16 *How Alexandra by Gaining the Good-Will of the Pharisees, Retained the Kingdom Nine Years, and Then, Having Done Many Glorious Actions Died*

1. SO Alexandra, when she had taken the fortress, acted as her husband had suggested to her, and spake to the Pharisees, and put all things into their power, both as to the dead body, and as to the affairs of the kingdom, and thereby pacified their anger against Alexander, and made them bear goodwill and friendship to him; who then came among the multitude, and made speeches to them, and laid before them the actions of Alexander, and told them that they had lost a righteous king; and by the commendation they gave him, they brought

44. It seems, by this dying advice of Alexander Janneus to his wife, that he had himself pursued the measures of his father Hyrcanus. and taken part with the Sadducees, who kept close to the written law, against the Pharisees, who had introduced their own traditions, ch. 16. sect. 2; and that he now saw a political necessity of submitting to the Pharisees and their traditions hereafter, if his widow and family minded to retain their monarchical government or tyranny over the Jewish nation; which sect yet, thus supported, were at last in a great measure the ruin of the religion, government, and nation of the Jews, and brought them into so wicked a state, that the vengeance of God came upon them to their utter excision. Just thus did Caiaphas politically advise the Jewish sanhedrim, John 11:50, "That it was expedient for them that one man should die for the people, and that the whole nation perish not;" and this in consequence of their own political supposal, ver. 48, that, "If they let Jesus alone," with his miracles, "all men would believe on him, and the Romans would come and take away both their place and nation." Which political crucifixion of Jesus of Nazareth brought down the vengeance of God upon them, and occasioned those very Romans, of whom they seemed so much afraid, that to prevent it they put him to death, actually to "come and take away both their place and nation" within thirty-eight years afterwards. I heartily wish the politicians of Christendom would consider these and the like examples, and no longer sacrifice all virtue and religion to their pernicious schemes of government, to the bringing down the judgments of God upon themselves, and the several nations intrusted to their care. But this is a digression. I wish it were an unseasonable one also. Josephus himself several times makes such digressions, and I here venture to follow him. See one of them at the conclusion of the very next chapter.

them to grieve, and to be in heaviness for him, so that he had a funeral more splendid than had any of the kings before him. Alexander left behind him two sons, Hyrcanus and Aristobulus, but committed the kingdom to Alexandra. Now, as to these two sons, Hyrcanus was indeed unable to manage public affairs, and delighted rather in a quiet life; but the younger, Aristobulus, was an active and a bold man; and for this woman herself, Alexandra, she was loved by the multitude, because she seemed displeased at the offenses her husband had been guilty of.

2. So she made Hyrcanus high priest, because he was the elder, but much more because he cared not to meddle with politics, and permitted the Pharisees to do every thing; to whom also she ordered the multitude to be obedient. She also restored again those practices which the Pharisees had introduced, according to the traditions of their forefathers, and which her father-in-law, Hyrcanus, had abrogated. So she had indeed the name of the regent, but the Pharisees had the authority; for it was they who restored such as had been banished, and set such as were prisoners at liberty, and, to say all at once, they differed in nothing from lords. However, the queen also took care of the affairs of the kingdom, and got together a great body of mercenary soldiers, and increased her own army to such a degree, that she became terrible to the neighboring tyrants, and took hostages of them: and the country was entirely at peace, excepting the Pharisees; for they disturbed the queen, and desired that she would kill those who persuaded Alexander to slay the eight hundred men; after which they cut the throat of one of them, Diogenes; and after him they did the same to several, one after another, till the men that were the most potent came into the palace, and Aristobulus with them, for he seemed to be displeased at what was done; and it appeared openly, that if he had an opportunity, he would not permit his mother to go on so. These put the queen in mind what great dangers they had gone through, and great things they had done, whereby they had demonstrated the firmness of their fidelity to their master, insomuch that they had recieved the greatest marks of favor from him; and they begged of her, that she would not utterly blast their hopes, as it now happened, that when they had escaped the hazards that arose from their [open] enemies, they were to be cut off at home by their [private] enemies, like brute beasts, without any help whatsoever. They said also, that

if their adversaries would be satisfied with those that had been slain already, they would take what had been done patiently, on account of their natural love to their governors; but if they must expect the same for the future also, they implored of her a dismission from her service; for they could not bear to think of attempting any method for their deliverance without her, but would rather die willingly before the palace gate, in case she would not forgive them. And that it was a great shame, both for themselves and for the queen, that when they were neglected by her, they should come under the lash of her husband's enemies; for that Aretas, the Arabian king, and the monarchs, would give any reward, if they could get such men as foreign auxiliaries, to whom their very names, before their voices be heard, may perhaps be terrible; but if they could not obtain this their second request, and if she had determined to prefer the Pharisees before them, they still insisted that she would place them every one in her fortresses; for if some fatal demon hath a constant spite against Alexander's house, they would be willing to bear their part, and to live in a private station there.

3. As these men said thus, and called upon Alexander's ghost for commiseration of those already slain, and those in danger of it, all the bystanders brake out into tears. But Aristobulus chiefly made manifest what were his sentiments, and used. many reproachful expressions to his mother, [saying,] "Nay, indeed, the case is this, that they have been themselves the authors of their own calamities, who have permitted a woman who, against reason, was mad with ambition, to reign over them, when there were sons in the flower of their age fitter for it." So Alexandra, not knowing what to do with any decency, committed the fortresses to them, all but Hyrcania, and Alexandrium, and Macherus, where her principal treasures were. After a little while also, she sent her son Aristobulus with an army to Damascus against Ptolemy, who was called Menneus, who was such a bad neighbor to the city; but he did nothing considerable there, and so returned home.

4. About this time news was brought that Tigranes, the king of Armenia, had made an irruption into Syria with five hundred thousand soldiers,[45] and was coming against Judea. This news, as may well be supposed, terrified the queen and the nation. Accordingly, they sent

45. The number of five hundred thousand or even three hundred thousand, as

him many and very valuable presents, as also ambassadors, and that as he was besieging Ptolemais; for Selene the queen, the same that was also called Cleopatra, ruled then over Syria, who had persuaded the inhabitants to exclude Tigranes. So the Jewish ambassadors interceded with him, and entreated him that he would determine nothing that was severe about their queen or nation. He commended them for the respects they paid him at so great a distance, and gave them good hopes of his favor. But as soon as Ptolemais was taken, news came to Tigranes, that Lucullus, in his pursuit of Mithridates, could not light upon him, who was fled into Iberia, but was laying waste Armenia, and besieging its cities. Now when Tigranes knew this, he returned home.

5. After this, when the queen was fallen into a dangerous distemper, Aristobulus resolved to attempt the seizing of the government; so he stole away secretly by night, with only one of his servants, and went to the fortresses, wherein his friends, that were such from the days of his father, were settled; for as he had been a great while displeased at his mother's conduct, so he was now much more afraid, lest, upon her death, their whole family should be under the power of the Pharisees; for he saw the inability of his brother, who was to succeed in the government; nor was any one conscious of what he was doing but only his wife, whom he left at Jerusalem with their children. He first of all came to Agaba, where was Galestes, one of the potent men before mentioned, and was received by him. When it was day, the queen perceived that Aristobulus was fled; and for some time she supposed that his departure was not in order to make any innovation; but when messengers came one after another with the news that he had secured the first place, the second place, and all the places, for as soon as one had begun they all submitted to his disposal, then it was that the queen and the nation were in the greatest disorder, for they were aware that it would not be long ere Aristobulus would be able to settle himself firmly in the government. What they were

---

one Greek copy, with the Latin copies, have it, for Tigranes's army, that came out of Armenia into Syria and Judea, seems much too large. We have had already several such extravagant numbers in Josephus's present copies, which are not to be at all ascribed to him. Accordingly, I incline to Dr. Hudson's emendation here, which supposes them but forty thousand.

principally afraid of was this, that he would inflict punishment upon them for the mad treatment his house had had from them. So they resolved to take his wife and children into custody, and keep them in the fortress that was over the temple.[46] Now there was a mighty conflux of people that came to Aristobulus from all parts, insomuch that he had a kind of royal attendants about him; for in a little more than fifteen days he got twenty-two strong places, which gave him the opportunity of raising an army from Libanus and Trachonitis, and the monarchs; for men are easily led by the greater number, and easily submit to them. And besides this, that by affording him their assistance, when he could not expect it, they, as well as he, should have the advantages that would come by his being king, because they had been the occasion of his gaining the kingdom. Now the eiders of the Jews, and Hyrcanus with them, went in unto the queen, and desired that she would give them her sentiments about the present posture of affairs, for that Aristobulus was in effect lord of almost all the kingdom, by possessing of so many strong holds, and that it was absurd for them to take any counsel by themselves, how ill soever she were, whilst she was alive, and that the danger would be upon them in no long time. But she bid them do what they thought proper to be done; that they had many circumstances in their favor still remaining, a nation in good heart, an army, and money in their several treasuries; for that she had small concern about public affairs now, when the strength of her body already failed her.

6. Now a little while after she had said this to them, she died, when she had reigned nine years, and had in all lived seventy-three. A woman she was who showed no signs of the weakness of her sex, for she was sagacious to the greatest degree in her ambition of governing; and demonstrated by her doings at once, that her mind was fit for action, and that sometimes men themselves show the little understanding they have by the frequent mistakes they make in point of government; for she always preferred the present to futurity, and preferred the power of an imperious dominion above all things, and in

46. This fortress, castle, citadel, or tower, whither the wife and children of Aristobulus were new sent, and which overlooked the temple, could be no other than what Hyrcanus I. built, (Antiq. B. XVIII ch. 4. sect. 3,) and Herod the Great rebuilt, and called the "Tower of Antonia," Aatiq. B. XV. ch. 11. sect. 5.

comparison of that had no regard to what was good, or what was right. However, she brought the affairs of her house to such an unfortunate condition, that she was the occasion of the taking away that authority from it, and that in no long time afterward, which she had obtained by a vast number of hazards and misfortunes, and this out of a desire of what does not belong to a woman, and all by a compliance in her sentiments with those that bare ill-will to their family, and by leaving the administration destitute of a proper support of great men; and, indeed, her management during her administration while she was alive, was such as filled the palace after her death with calamities and disturbance. However, although this had been her way of governing, she preserved the nation in peace. And this is the conclusion of the affairs of, Alexandra.

Book 14

Containing the Interval of Thirty-Two Years, from the Death of Queen Alexandra to the Death of Antigonus

1 *The War Between Aristobulus and Hyrcanus About the Kingdom; and How They Made Anagreement That Aristobulus Should Be King, and Hyrcanus Live a Private Life; as Also How Hyrcanus a Little Afterward Was Persuaded by Antipater to Fly to Aretas*

1. WE have related the affairs of queen Alexandra, and her death, in the foregoing book and will now speak of what followed, and was connected with those histories; declaring, before we proceed, that we have nothing so much at heart as this, that we may omit no facts, either through ignorance or laziness;[1] for we are upon the history and explication of such things as the greatest part are unacquainted withal, because of their distance from our times; and we aim to do it with a proper beauty of style, so far as that is derived from proper words harmonically disposed, and from such ornaments of speech also as may contribute to the pleasure of our readers, that they may entertain the knowledge of what we write with some agreeable satisfaction and pleasure. But the principal scope that authors ought to aim at above all

1. Reland takes notice here, very justly, how Josephus's declaration, that it was his great concern not only to write "an agreeable, an accurate," and "a true" history, but also distinctly not to omit any thing [of consequence], either through "ignorance or laziness," implies that he could not, consistently with that resolution, omit the mention of [so famous a person as] "Jesus Christ."

the rest, is to speak accurately, and to speak truly, for the satisfaction of those that are otherwise unacquainted with such transactions, and obliged to believe what these writers inform them of.

2. Hyrcanus then began his high priesthood on the third year of the hundred and seventy-seventh olympiad, when Quintus Hortensius and Quintus Metellus, who was called Metellus of Crete, were consuls at Rome; when presently Aristobulus began to make war against him; and as it came to a battle with Hyrcanus at Jericho, many of his soldiers deserted him, and went over to his brother; upon which Hyrcanus fled into the citadel, where Aristobulus's wife and children were imprisoned by their mother, as we have said already, and attacked and overcame those his adversaries that had fled thither, and lay within the walls of the temple. So when he had sent a message to his brother about agreeing the matters between them, he laid aside his enmity to him on these conditions, that Aristobulus should be king, that he should live without intermeddling with public affairs, and quietly enjoy the estate he had acquired. When they had agreed upon these terms in the temple, and had confirmed the agreement with oaths, and the giving one an. other their right hands, and embracing one another in the sight of the whole multitude, they departed; the one, Aristobulus, to the palace; and Hyrcanus, as a private man, to the former house of Aristobulus.

3. But there was a certain friend of Hyrcanus, an Idumean, called Antipater, who was very rich, and in his nature an active and a seditious man; who was at enmity with Aristobulus, and had differences with him on account of his good-will to Hyrcanus. It is true that Nicolatls of Damascus says, that Antipater was of the stock of the principal Jews who came out of Babylon into Judea; but that assertion of his was to gratify Herod, who was his son, and who, by certain revolutions of fortune, came afterward to be king of the Jews, whose history we shall give you in its proper place hereafter. However, this Antipater was at first called Antipas,[2] and that was his father's name also; of whom they relate this: That king Alexander and his wife made

2. That the famous Antipater's or Antipas's father was also Antipater or Antipas (which two may justly be esteemed one and the same frame, the former with a Greek or Gentile, the latter with a Hebrew or Jewish termination) Josephus here assures us, though Eusebias indeed says it was Herod.

him general of all Idumea, and that he made a league of friendship with those Arabians, and Gazites, and Ascalonites, that were of his own party, and had, by many and large presents, made them his fast friends. But now this younger Antipater was suspicious of the power of Aristobulus, and was afraid of some mischief he might do him, because of his hatred to him; so he stirred up the most powerful of the Jews, and talked against him to them privately; and said that it was unjust to overlook the conduct of Aristobulus, who had gotten the government unrighteously, and ejected his brother out of it, who was the elder, and ought to retain what belonged to him by prerogative of his birth. And the same speeches he perpetually made to Hyrcanus; and told him that his own life would be in danger, unless he guarded himself, and got shut of Aristobulus; for he said that the friends of Aristobulus omitted no opportunity of advising him to kill him, as being then, and not before, sure to retain his principality. Hyrcanus gave no credit to these words of his, as being of a gentle disposition, and one that did not easily admit of calumnies against other men. This temper of his not disposing him to meddle with public affairs, and want of spirit, occasioned him to appear to spectators to be degenerous and unmanly; while. Aristo-bulus was of a contrary temper, an active man, and one of a great and generous soul.

4. Since therefore Antipater saw that Hyrcanus did not attend to what he said, he never ceased, day by day, to charge reigned crimes upon Aristobulus, and to calumniate him before him, as if he had a mind to kill him; and so, by urging him perpetually, he advised him, and persuaded him to fly to Aretas, the king of Arabia; and promised, that if he would comply with his advice, he would also himself assist him and go with him]. When Hyrcanus heard this, he said that it was for his advantage to fly away to Aretas. Now Arabia is a country that borders upon Judea. However, Hyrcanus sent Antipater first to the king of Arabia, in order to receive assurances from him, that when he should come in the manner of a supplicant to him, he would not deliver him up to his enemies. So Antipater having received such assurances, returned to Hyrcanus to Jerusalem. A while afterward he took Hyrcanus, and stole out of the city by night, and went a great journey, and came and brought him to the city called Petra, where the palace of Aretas was; and as he was a very familiar friend of that king, he persuaded him to bring back Hyrcanus into Judea, and this

persuasion he continued every day without any intermission. He also proposed to make him presents on that account. At length he prevailed with Aretas in his suit. Moreover, Hyrcanus promised him, that when he had been brought thither, and had received his kingdom, he would restore that country, and those twelve cities which his father Alexander had taken from the Arabians, which were these, Medaba, Naballo, Libias, Tharabasa, Agala, Athone, Zoar, Orone, Marissa, Rudda, Lussa, and Oruba.

2 *How Aretas and Hyrcanus Made an Expedition Against Aristobulus and Besieged Jerusalem; and How Scaurus the Roman General Raised the Siege. Concerning the Death of Onias*

1. AFTER these promises had been given to Aretas, he made an expedition against Aristobulus with an army of fifty thousand horse and foot, and beat him in the battle. And when after that victory many went over to Hyrcanus as deserters, Aristobulus was left desolate, and fled to Jerusalem; upon which the king of Arabia took all his army, and made an assault upon the temple, and besieged Aristobulus therein, the people still supporting Hyreanus, and assisting him in the siege, while none but the priests continued with Aristobulus. So Aretas united the forces of the Arabians and of the Jews together, and pressed on the siege vigorously. As this happened at the time when the feast of unleavened bread was celebrated, which we call the passover, the principal men among the Jews left the country, and fled into Egypt. Now there was one, whose name was Onias, a righteous man be was, and beloved of God, who, in a certain drought, had prayed to God to put an end to the intense heat, and whose prayers God had heard, and had sent them rain. This man had hid himself, because he saw that this sedition would last a great while. However, they brought him to the Jewish camp, and desired, that as by his prayers he had once put an end to the drought, so he would in like manner make imprecations on Aristobulus and those of his faction. And when, upon his refusal, and the excuses that he made, he was still by the multitude compelled to speak, he stood up in the midst of them, and said, "O God, the King of the whole world! since those that stand now with me are thy people, and those that are besieged are also thy priests, I beseech thee,

that thou wilt neither hearken to the prayers of those against these, nor bring to effect what these pray against those." Whereupon such wicked Jews as stood about him, as soon as he had made this prayer, stoned him to death.

2. But God punished them immediately for this their barbarity, and took vengeance of them for the murder of Onias, in the manner following: While the priests and Aristobulus were besieged, it happened that the feast called the passover was come, at which it is our custom to offer a great number of sacrifices to God; but those that were with Aristobulus wanted sacrifices, and desired that their countrymen without would furnish them with such sacrifices, and assured them they should have as much money for them as they should desire; and when they required them to pay a thousand drachmae for each head of cattle, Aristobulus and the priests willingly undertook to pay for them accordingly, and those within let down the money over the walls, and gave it them. But when the others had received it, they did not deliver the sacrifices, but arrived at that height of wickedness as to break the assurances they had given, and to be guilty of impiety towards God, by not furnishing those that wanted them with sacrifices. And when the priests found they had been cheated, and that the agreements they had made were violated, they prayed to God that he would avenge them on their countrymen. Nor did he delay that their punishment, but sent a strong and vehement storm of wind, that destroyed the fruits of the whole country, till a modius of wheat was then bought for eleven drachmae.

3. In the mean time Pompey sent Scaurus into Syria, while he was himself in Armenia, and making war with Tigranes; but when Scaurus was come to Damascus, and found that Lollins and Metellus had newly taken the city, he came himself hastily into Judea. And when he was come thither, ambassadors came to him, both from Aristobulus and Hyrcanus, and both desired he would assist them. And when both of them promised to give him money, Aristobulus four hundred talents, and Hyrcanus no less, he accepted of Aristobulus's promise, for he was rich, and had a great soul, and desired to obtain nothing but what was moderate; whereas the other was poor, and tenacious, and made incredible promises in hopes of greater advantages; for it was not the same thing to take a city that was exceeding strong and powerful, as it was to eject out of the country some fugitives, with

a greater number of Mabateans, who were no very warlike people. He therefore made an agreement with Aristobulus, for the reasons before mentioned, and took his money, and raised the siege, and ordered Aretas to depart, or else he should be declared an enemy to the Romans. So Scaurus returned to Damascus again; and Aristobulus, with a great army, made war with Aretas and Hyrcanus, and fought them at a place called Papyron, and beat them in the battle, and slew about six thousand of the enemy, with whom fell Phalion also, the brother of Antipater.

3 *How Aristobulus and Hyrcanus Came to Pompey in Order to Argue Who Ought to Have the Kingdom; and How Upon the Plight of Aristobulus to the Fortress Alexandrium Pompey Led His Army Against Him and Ordered Him to Deliver Up the Fortresses Whereof He Was Possessed*

1. A LITTLE afterward Pompey came to Damascus, and marched over Celesyria; at which time there came ambassadors to him from all Syria, and Egypt, and out of Judea also, for Aristobulus had sent him a great present, which was a golden vine[3] of the value of five hundred talents. Now Strabo of Cappadocia mentions this present in these words: "There came also an embassage out of Egypt, and a crown of the value of four thousand pieces of gold; and out of Judea there came another, whether you call it a *vine* or a *garden;* they call the thing Terpole, *the Delight.* However, we ourselves saw that present reposited at Rome,

3. This "golden vine," or "garden," seen by Strabo at Rome, has its inscription here as if it were the gift of Alexander, the father of Aristobulus, and not of Aristobulus himself, to whom yet Josephus ascribes it; and in order to prove the truth of that part of his history, introduces this testimony of Strabo; so that the ordinary copies seem to be here either erroneous or defective, and the original reading seems to have been either Aristobulus, instead of Alexander, with one Greek copy, or else "Aristobulus the son of Alexander," with the Latin copies; which last seems to me the most probable. For as to Archbishop Usher's conjectures, that Alexander made it, and dedicated it to God in the temple, and that thence Aristobulus took it, and sent it to Pompey, they are both very improbable, and no way agreeable to Josephus, who would hardly have avoided the recording both these uncommon points of history, had he known any thing of them; nor would either the Jewish nation, or even Pompey himself, then have relished such a flagrant instance of sacrilege.

in the temple of Jupiter Capitolinus, with this inscription, 'The gift of Alexander, the king of the Jews.' It was valued at five hundred talents; and the report is, that Aristobulus, the governor of the Jews, sent it."

2. In a little time afterward came ambassadors again to him, Antipater from Hyrcanus, and Nicodemus from Aristobulus; which last also accused such as had taken bribes; first Gabinius, and then Scaurus,—the one three hundred talents, and the other four hundred; by which procedure he made these two his enemies, besides those he had before. And when Pompey had ordered those that had controversies one with another to come to him in the beginning of the spring, he brought his army out of their winter quarters, and marched into the country of Damascus; and as he went along he demolished the citadel that was at Apamia, which Antiochus Cyzicenus had built, and took cognizance of the country of Ptolemy Menneus, a wicked man, and not less so than Dionysius of Tripoli, who had been beheaded, who was also his relation by marriage; yet did he buy off the punishment of his crimes for a thousand talents, with which money Pompey paid the soldiers their wages. He also conquered the place called Lysias, of which Silas a Jew was tyrant. And when he had passed over the cities of Heliopolis and Chalcis, and got over the mountain which is on the limit of Colesyria, he came from Pella to Damascus; and there it was that he heard the causes of the Jews, and of their governors Hyrcanus and Aristobulus, who were at difference one with another, as also of the nation against them both, which did not desire to be under kingly' government, because the form of government they received from their forefathers was that of subjection to the priests of that God whom they worshipped; and [they complained], that though these two were the posterity of priests, yet did they seek to change the government of their nation to another form, in order to enslave them. Hyrcanus complained, that although he were the elder brother, he was deprived of the prerogative of his birth by Aristobulus, and that he had but a small part of the country under him, Aristobulus having taken away the rest from him by force. He also accused him, that the incursions which had been made into their neighbors' countries, and the piracies that had been at sea, were owing to him; and that the nation would not have revolted, unless Aristobulus had been a man given to violence and disorder; and there were no fewer than a thousand Jews, of the best esteem among them, who confirmed

this accusation; which confirmation was procured by Antipater. But Aristobulus alleged against him, that it was Hyrcanus's own temper, which was inactive, and on that account contemptible, which caused him to be deprived of the government; and that for himself, he was necessitated to take it upon him, for fear lest it should be transferred to others. And that as to his title [of king], it was no other than what his father had taken [before him]. He also called for witnesses of what he said some persons who were both young and insolent; whose purple garments, fine heads of hair, and other ornaments, were detested [by the court], and which they appeared in, not as though they were to plead their cause in a court of justice, but as if they were marching in a pompous procession.

3. When Pompey had heard the causes of these two, and had condemned Aristobulus for his violent procedure, he then spake civilly to them, and sent them away; and told them, that when he came again into their country, he would settle all their affairs, after he had first taken a view of the affairs of the Nabateans. In the mean time, he ordered them to be quiet; and treated Aristobulus civilly, lest he should make the nation revolt, and hinder his return; which yet Aristobulus did; for without expecting any further determination, which Pompey had promised them, he went to the city Delius, and thence marched into Judea.

4. At this behavior Pompey was angry; and taking with him that army which he was leading against the Nabateans, and the auxiliaries that came from Damascus, and the other parts of Syria, with the other Roman legions which he had with him, he made an expedition against Aristobulus; but as he passed by Pella and Scythopolis, he came to Corem, which is the first entrance into Judea when one passes over the midland countries, where he came to a most beautiful fortress that was built on the top of a mountain called Alexandrium, whither Aristobulus had fled; and thence Pompey sent his commands to him, that he should come to him. Accordingly, at the persuasions of many that he would not make war with the Romans, he came down; and when he had disputed with his brother about the right to the government, he went up again to the citadel, as Pompey gave him leave to do; and this he did two or three times, as flattering himself with the hopes of having the kingdom granted him; so that he still pretended he would obey Pompey in whatsoever he commanded,

although at the same time he retired to his fortress, that he might not depress himself too low, and that he might be prepared for a war, in case it should prove as he feared, that Pompey would transfer the government to Hyrcanus. But when Pompey enjoined Aristobulus to deliver up the fortresses he held, and to send an injunction to their governors under his own hand for that purpose, for they had been forbidden to deliver them up upon any other commands, he submitted indeed to do so; but still he retired in displeasure to Jerusalem, and made preparation for war. A little after this, certain persons came out of Pontus, and informed Pompey, as he was on the way, and conducting his army against Aristobulus, that Mithridates was dead, and was slain by his son Pharmaces.

4 *How Pompey When the Citizens of Jerusalem Shut Their Gates Against Him Besieged the City and Took It by Force; as Also What Other Things He Did in Judea*

1. NOW when Pompey had pitched his camp at Jericho, (where the palm tree grows, and that balsam which is an ointment of all the most precious, which upon any incision made in the wood with a sharp stone, distills out thence like a juice,)[4] he marched in the morning to Jerusalem. Hereupon Aristobulus repented of what he was doing, and came to Pompey, had [promised to] give him money, and received him into Jerusalem, and desired that he would leave off the war, and do what he pleased peaceably. So Pompey, upon his entreaty, forgave him, and sent Gabinius, and soldiers with him, to receive the money and the city: yet was no part of this performed; but Gabinius came

4. These express testimonies of Josephus here, and Antiq. B. VIII. ch. 6. sect. 6, and B. XV. ch. 4. sect. 2, that the only balsam gardens, and the best palm trees, were, at least in his days, near Jericho and Kugaddi, about the north part of the Dead Sea, (whereabout also Alexander the Great saw the balsam drop,) show the mistake of those that understand Eusebius and Jerom as if one of those gardens were at the south part of that sea, at Zoar or Segor, whereas they must either mean another Zoar or Segor, which was between Jericho and Kugaddi, agreeably to Josephus: which yet they do not appear to do, or else they directly contradict Josephus, and were therein greatly mistaken: I mean this, unless that balsam, and the best palm trees, grew much more southward in Judea in the days of Eusebius and Jerom than they did in the days of Josephus.

back, being both excluded out of the city, and receiving none of the money promised, because Aristobulus's soldiers would not permit the agreements to be executed. At this Pompey was very angry, and put Aristobulus into prison, and came himself to the city, which was strong on every side, excepting the north, which was not so well fortified, for there was a broad and deep ditch that encompassed the city[5] and included within it the temple, which was itself encompassed about with a very strong stone wall.

2. Now there was a sedition of the men that were within the city, who did not agree what was to be done in their present circumstances, while some thought it best to deliver up the city to Pompey; but Aristobulus's party exhorted them to shut the gates, because he was kept in prison. Now these prevented the others, and seized upon the temple, and cut off the bridge which reached from it to the city, and prepared themselves to abide a siege; but the others admitted Pompey's army in, and delivered up both the city and the king's palace to him. So Pompey sent his lieutenant Piso with an army, and placed garrisons both in the city and in the palace, to secure them, and fortified the houses that joined to the temple, and all those which were more distant and without it. And in the first place, he offered terms of accommodation to those within; but when they would not comply with what was desired, he encompassed all the places thereabout with a wall, wherein Hyrcanus did gladly assist him on all occasions; but Pompey pitched his camp within [the wall], on the north part of the temple, where it was most practicable; but even on that side there were great towers, and a ditch had been dug, and a deep valley begirt it round about, for on the parts towards the city were precipices, and the bridge on which Pompey had gotten in was broken down. However, a bank was raised, day by day, with a great deal of labor, while the Romans cut down materials for it from the places round about. And when this bank was sufficiently raised, and the ditch filled up, though

5. The particular depth and breadth of this ditch, whence the stones for the wall about the temple were probably taken, are omitted in our copies of Josephus, but set down by Strabo, B. XVI. p. 763; from whom we learn that this ditch was sixty feet deep, and two hundred and fifty feet broad. However, its depth is, in the next section, said by Josephus to be immense, which exactly agrees to Strabo's description, and which numbers in Strabo are a strong confirmation of the truth of Josephus's description also.

but poorly, by reason of its immense depth, he brought his mechanical engines and battering-rams from Tyre, and placing them on the bank, he battered the temple with the stones that were thrown against it. And had it not been our practice, from the days of our forefathers, to rest on the seventh day, this bank could never have been perfected, by reason of the opposition the Jews would have made; for though our law gives us leave then to defend ourselves against those that begin to fight with us and assault us, yet does it not permit us to meddle with our enemies while they do any thing else.

3. Which thing when the Romans understood, on those days which we call Sabbaths they threw nothing at the Jews, nor came to any pitched battle with them; but raised up their earthen banks, and brought their engines into such forwardness, that they might do execution the next day. And any one may hence learn how very great piety we exercise towards God, and the observance of his laws, since the priests were not at all hindered from their sacred ministrations by their fear during this siege, but did still twice a-day, in the morning and about the ninth hour, offer their sacrifices on the altar; nor did they omit those sacrifices, if any melancholy accident happened by the stones that were thrown among them; for although the city was taken on the third month, on the day of the fast,[6] upon the hundred and seventy-ninth olympiad, when Caius Antonius and Marcus Tullius Cicero were consuls, and the enemy then fell upon them, and cut the throats of those that were in the temple; yet could not those that offered the sacrifices be compelled to run away, neither by the fear they were in of their own lives, nor by the number that were already slain, as thinking it better to suffer whatever came upon them, at their very altars, than to omit any thing that their laws required of them. And that this is not a mere brag, or an encomium to manifest a degree of our piety that was false, but is the real truth, I appeal to those that have written of the acts of Pompey; and, among them, to Strabo and

6. That is, on the 23rd of Sivan, the annual fast for the defection and idolatry of Jeroboam, "who made Israel to sin;" or possibly some other fast might fall into that month, before and in the days of Josephus.

Nicolaus [of Damascus]; and besides these two, Titus Livius, the writer of the Roman History, who will bear witness to this thing.[7]

4. But when the battering-engine was brought near, the greatest of the towers was shaken by it, and fell down, and broke down a part of the fortifications, so the enemy poured in apace; and Cornelius Faustus, the son of Sylla, with his soldiers, first of all ascended the wall, and next to him Furius the centurion, with those that followed on the other part, while Fabius, who was also a centurion, ascended it in the middle, with a great body of men after him. But now all was full of slaughter; some of the Jews being slain by the Romans, and some by one another; nay, some there were who threw themselves down the precipices, or put fire to their houses, and burnt them, as not able to bear the miseries they were under. Of the Jews there fell twelve thousand, but of the Romans very few. Absalom, who was at once both uncle and father-in-law to Aristobulus, was taken captive; and no small enormities were committed about the temple itself, which, in former ages, had been inaccessible, and seen by none; for Pompey went into it, and not a few of those that were with him also, and saw all that which it was unlawful for any other men to see but only for the high priests. There were in that temple the golden table, the holy candlestick, and the pouring vessels, and a great quantity of spices; and besides these there were among the treasures two thousand talents of sacred money: yet did Pompey touch nothing of all this,[8] on account of his regard to religion; and in this point also he acted in a manner that was worthy of his virtue. The next day he gave order to those that had the charge of the temple to cleanse it, and to

---

7. It deserves here to be noted, that this Pharisaical, superstitious notion, that offensive fighting was unlawful to Jews, even under the utmost necessity, on the Sabbath day, of which we hear nothing before the times of the Maccabees, was the proper occasion of Jerusalem's being taken by Pompey, by Sosius, and by Titus, as appears from the places already quoted in the note on Antiq. B. XIII. ch. 8. sect. 1; which scrupulous superstition, as to the observation of such a rigorous rest upon the Sabbath day, our Savior always opposed, when the Pharisaical Jews insisted on it, as is evident in many places in the New Testament, though he still intimated how pernicious that superstition might prove to them in their flight from the Romans, Matthew 25:20.

8. This is fully confirmed by the testimony of Cicero, who: says, in his oration for Flaecus, that "Cneius Pompeius, when he was conqueror, and had taken Jerusalem, did not touch any thing belonging to that temple."

bring what offerings the law required to God; and restored the high priesthood to Hyrcanus, both because he had been useful to him in other respects, and because he hindered the Jews in the country from giving Aristobulus any assistance in his war against him. He also cut off those that had been the authors of that war; and bestowed proper rewards on Faustus, and those others that mounted the wall with such alacrity; and he made Jerusalem tributary to the Romans, and took away those cities of Celesyria which the inhabitants of Judea had subdued, and put them under the government of the Roman president, and confined the whole nation, which had elevated itself so high before, within its own bounds. Moreover, he rebuilt Gadara,[9] which had been demolished a little before, to gratify Demetrius of Gadara, who was his freedman, and restored the rest of the cities, Hippos, and Scythopolis, and Pella, and Dios, and Samaria, as also Marissa, and Ashdod, and Jamnia, and Arethusa, to their own inhabitants: these were in the inland parts. Besides those that had been demolished, and also of the maritime cities, Gaza, and Joppa, and Dora, and Strato's Tower; which last Herod rebuilt after a glorious manner, and adorned with havens and temples, and changed its name to Caesarea. All these Pompey left in a state of freedom, and joined them to the province of Syria.

5. Now the occasions of this misery which came upon Jerusalem were Hyrcanus and Aristobulus, by raising a sedition one against the other; for now we lost our liberty, and became subject to the Romans, and were deprived of that country which we had gained by our arms from the Syrians, and were compelled to restore it to the Syrians. Moreover, the Romans exacted of us, in a little time, above ten thousand talents; and the royal authority, which was a dignity formerly bestowed on those that were high priests, by the right of their family, became the property of private men. But of these matters we shall treat in their proper places. Now Pompey committed Celesyria, as far as the river Euphrates and Egypt, to Scaurus, with two Roman legions, and then went away to Cilicia, and made haste to Rome. He also carried bound along with him Aristobulus and his children; for he had two daughters, and as many sons; the one of which ran away,

---

9. Of this destruction of Gadara here presupposed, and its restoration by Pompey, see the note on the War, B. I. ch. 7. sect. 7.

but the younger, Antigonus, was carried to Rome, together with his sisters.

5 *How Scaurus Made a League of Mutual Assistance with Aretas; and What Gabinius Did in Judea, After He Had Conquered Alexander, the Son of Aristobulus*

1. SCAURUS made now an expedition against Petrea, in Arabia, and set on fire all the places round about it, because of the great difficulty of access to it. And as his army was pinched by famine, Antipater furnished him with corn out of Judea, and with whatever else he wanted, and this at the command of Hyrcanus. And when he was sent to Aretas, as an ambassador by Scaurus, because he had lived with him formerly, he persuaded Aretas to give Scaurus a sum of money, to prevent the burning of his country, and undertook to be his surety for three hundred talents. So Scaurus, upon these terms, ceased to make war any longer; which was done as much at Scaurus's desire, as at the desire of Aretas.

2. Some time after this, when Alexander, the son of Aristobulus, made an incursion into Judea, Gabinius came from Rome into Syria, as commander of the Roman forces. He did many considerable actions; and particularly made war with Alexander, since Hyrcanus was not yet able to oppose his power, but was already attempting to rebuild the wall of Jerusalem, which Pompey had overthrown, although the Romans which were there restrained him from that his design. However, Alexander went over all the country round about, and armed many of the Jews, and suddenly got together ten thousand armed footmen, and fifteen hundred horsemen, and fortified Alexandrium, a fortress near to Corem, and Macherus, near the mountains of Arabia. Gabinius therefore came upon him, having sent Marcus Antonius, with other commanders, before. These armed such Romans as followed them; and, together with them, such Jews as were subject to them, whose leaders were Pitholaus and Malichus; and they took with them also their friends that were with Antipater, and met Alexander, while Gabinius himself followed with his legion. Hereupon Alexander retired to the neighborhood of Jerusalem, where they fell upon one another, and it came to a pitched battle, in which the Romans slew of their enemies about three thousand, and took a like number alive.

3. At which time Gabinius[10] came to Alexandrium, and invited those that were in it to deliver it up on certain conditions, and promised that then their former offenses should be forgiven. But as a great number of the enemy had pitched their camp before the fortress, whom the Romans attacked, Marcus Antonius fought bravely, and slew a great number, and seemed to come off with the greatest honor. So Gabinius left part of his army there, in order to take the place, and he himself went into other parts of Judea, and gave order to rebuild all the cities that he met with that had been demolished; at which time were rebuilt Samaria, Ashdod, Scythopolis, Anthedon, Raphia, and Dora; Marissa also, and Gaza, and not a few others besides. And as the men acted according to Gabinius's command, it came to pass, that at this time these cities were securely inhabited, which had been desolate for a long time.

4. When Gabinius had done thus in the country, he returned to Alexandrium; and when he urged on the siege of the place, Alexander sent an embassage to him, desiring that he would pardon his former offenses; he also delivered up the fortresses, Hyrcania and Macherus, and at last Alexandrium itself which fortresses Gabinius demolished. But when Alexander's mother, who was of the side of the Romans, as having her husband and other children at Rome, came to him, he granted her whatsoever she asked; and when he had settled matters with her, he brought Hyrcanus to Jerusalem, and committed the care of the temple to him. And when he had ordained five councils, he distributed the nation into the same number of parts. So these councils governed the people; the first was at Jerusalem, the second at Gadara, the third at Amathus, the fourth at Jericho, and the fifth at Sepphoris in Galilee. So the Jews were now freed from monarchic authority, and were governed by an aristocracy.

---

10. Dean Prideaux well observes, "That notwithstanding the clamor against Gabinius at Rome, Josephus gives him a able character, as if he had acquitted himself with honor in the charge committed to him" [in Judea]. See at the year 55.

6 *How Gabinius Caught Aristobulus After He Had Fled from Rome, and Sent Him Back to Rome Again; and Now the Same Gabinius as He Returned Out of Egypt Overcame Alexander and the Nabateans in Battle*

1. NOW Aristobulus ran away from Rome to Judea, and set about the rebuilding of Alexandrium, which had been newly demolished. Hereupon Gabinius sent soldiers against him, add for their commanders Sisenna, and Antonius, and Servilius, in order to hinder him from getting possession of the country, and to take him again. And indeed many of the Jews ran to Aristobulus, on account of his former glory, as also because they should be glad of an innovation. Now there was one Pitholaus, a lieutenant at Jerusalem, who deserted to him with a thousand men, although a great number of those that came to him were unarmed; and when Aristobulus had resolved to go to Macherus, he dismissed those people, because they were unarmed; for they could not be useful to him in what actions he was going about; but he took with him eight thousand that were armed, and marched on; and as the Romans fell upon them severely, the Jews fought valiantly, but were beaten in the battle; and when they had fought with alacrity, but were overborne by the enemy, they were put to flight; of whom were slain about five thousand, and the rest being dispersed, tried, as well as they were able, to save themselves. However, Aristobulus had with him still above a thousand, and with them he fled to Macherus, and fortified the place; and though he had had ill success, he still had good hope of his affairs; but when he had struggled against the siege for two days' time, and had received many wounds, he was brought as a captive to Gabinius, with his son Antigonus, who also fled with him from Rome. And this was the fortune of Aristobulus, who was sent back again to Rome, and was there retained in bonds, having been both king and high priest for three years and six months; and was indeed an eminent person, and one of a great soul. However, the senate let his children go, upon Gabinius's writing to them that he had promised their mother so much when she delivered up the fortresses to him; and accordingly they then returned into Judea.

2. Now when Gabinius was making an expedition against the Parthians, and had already passed over Euphrates, he changed his mind, and resolved to return into Egypt, in order to restore Ptolemy

to his kingdom.[11] This hath also been related elsewhere. However, Antipater supplied his army, which he sent against Archelaus, with corn, and weapons, and money. He also made those Jews who were above Pelusium his friends and confederates, and had been the guardians of the passes that led into Egypt. But when he came back out of Egypt, he found Syria in disorder, with seditions and troubles; for Alexander, the son of Aristobulus, having seized on the government a second time by force, made many of the Jews revolt to him; and so he marched over the country with a great army, and slew all the Romans he could light upon, and proceeded to besiege the mountain called Gerizzim, whither they had retreated.

3. But when Gabinius found Syria in such a state, he sent Antipater, who was a prudent man, to those that were seditious, to try whether he could cure them of their madness, and persuade them to return to a better mind; and when he came to them, he brought many of them to a sound mind, and induced them to do what they ought to do; but he could not restrain Alexander, for he had an army of thirty thousand Jews, and met Gabinius, and joining battle with him, was beaten, and lost ten thousand of his men about Mount Tabor.

4. So Gabinius settled the affairs which belonged to the city Jerusalem, as was agreeable to Antipater's inclination, and went against the Nabateans, and overcame them in battle. He also sent away in a friendly manner Mithridates and Orsanes, who were Parthian deserters, and came to him, though the report went abroad that they had run away from him. And when Gabinius had performed great and glorious actions, in his management of the affairs of war, he returned to Rome, and delivered the government to Crassus. Now Nicolaus of Damascus, and Strabo of Cappadocia, both describe the expeditions of Pompey and Gabinius against the Jews, while neither of them say anything new which is not in the other.

---

11. This history is best illustrated by Dr. Hudson out of Livy, who says that "A. Gabinius, the proconsul, restored Ptolemy of Pompey and Gabinius against the Jews, while neither of them say any thing new which is not in the other to his kingdom of Egypt, and ejected Archelaus, whom they had set up for king," &c. See Prid. at the years 61 and 65.

7 *How Crassus Came into Judea, and Pillaged the Temple; and Then Marched Against the Parthians and Perished, with His Army. Also How Cassius Obtained Syria, and Put a Stop to the Parthians and Then Went Up to Judea*

1. Now Crassus, as he was going upon his expedition against the Parthians, came into Judea, and carried off the money that was in the temple, which Pompey had left, being two thousand talents, and was disposed to spoil it of all the gold belonging to it, which was eight thousand talents. He also took a beam, which was made of solid beaten gold, of the weight of three hundred minae, each of which weighed two pounds and a half. It was the priest who was guardian of the sacred treasures, and whose name was Eleazar, that gave him this beam, not out of a wicked design, for he was a good and a righteous man; but being intrusted with the custody of the veils belonging to the temple, which were of admirable beauty, and of very costly workmanship, and hung down from this beam, when lie saw that Crassus was busy in gathering money, and was in fear for the entire ornaments of the temple, he gave him this beam of gold as a ransom for the whole, but this not till he had given his oath that he would remove nothing else out of the temple, but be satisfied with this only, which he should give him, being worth many ten thousand [shekels]. Now this beam was contained in a wooden beam that was hollow, but was known to no others; but Eleazar alone knew it; yet did Crassus take away this beam, upon the condition of touching nothing else that belonged to the temple, and then brake his oath, and carried away all the gold that was in the temple.

2. And let no one wonder that there was so much wealth in our temple, since all the Jews throughout the habitable earth, and those that worshipped God, nay, even those of Asia and Europe, sent their contributions to it, and this from very ancient times. Nor is the largeness of these sums without its attestation; nor is that greatness owing to our vanity, as raising it without ground to so great a height; but there are many witnesses to it, and particularly Strabo of Cappadocia, who says thus: "Mithridates sent to Cos, and took the money which queen Cleopatra had deposited there, as also eight hundred talents belonging to the Jews." Now we have no public money but only what appertains to God; and it is evident that the Asian Jews removed this

money out of fear of Mithridates; for it is not probable that those of Judea, who had a strong city and temple, should send their money to Cos; nor is it likely that the Jews who are inhabitants of Alexandria should do so neither, since they were ill no fear of Mithridates. And Strabo himself bears witness to the same thing in another place, that at the same time that Sylla passed over into Greece, in order to fight against Mithridates, he sent Lucullus to put an end to a sedition that our nation, of whom the habitable earth is full, had raised in Cyrene; where he speaks thus: "There were four classes of men among those of Cyrene; that of citizens, that of husbandmen, the third of strangers, and the fourth of Jews. Now these Jews are already gotten into all cities; and it is hard to find a place in the habitable earth that hath not admitted this tribe of men, and is not possessed by them; and it hath come to pass that Egypt and Cyrene, as having the same governors, and a great number of other nations, imitate their way of living, and maintain great bodies of these Jews in a peculiar manner, and grow up to greater prosperity with them, and make use of the same laws with that nation also. Accordingly, the Jews have places assigned them in Egypt, wherein they inhabit, besides what is peculiarly allotted to this nation at Alexandria, which is a large part of that city. There is also an ethnarch allowed them, who governs the nation, and distributes justice to them, and takes care of their contracts, and of the laws to them belonging, as if he were the ruler of a free republic. In Egypt, therefore, this nation is powerful, because the Jews were originally Egyptians, and because the land wherein they inhabit, since they went thence, is near to Egypt. They also removed into Cyrene, because that this land adjoined to the government of Egypt, as well as does Judea, or rather was formerly under the same government." And this is what Strabo says.

3. So when Crassus had settled all things as he himself pleased, he marched into Parthia, where both he himself and all his army perished, as hath been related elsewhere. But Cassius, as he fled from Rome to Syria, took possession of it, and was an impediment to the Parthians, who by reason of their victory over Crassus made incursions upon it. And as he came back to Tyre, he went up into Judea also, and fell upon Tarichee, and presently took it, and carried about thirty thousand Jews captives; and slew Pitholaus, who succeeded Aristobulus in his seditious practices, and that by the persuasion of

Antipater, who proved to have great interest in him, and was at that time in great repute with the Idumeans also: out of which nation he married a wife, who was the daughter of one of their eminent men, and her name was Cypros,[12] by whom he had four sons, Phasael, and Herod, who was afterwards made king, and Joseph, and Pheroras; and a daughter, named Salome. This Antipater cultivated also a friendship and mutual kindness with other potentates, but especially with the king of Arabia, to whom he committed his children, while he fought against Aristobulus. So Cassius removed his camp, and marched to Euphrates, to meet those that were coming to attack him, as hath been related by others.

4. But some time afterward Cesar, when he had taken Rome, and after Pompey and the senate were fled beyond the Ionian Sea, freed Aristobulus from his bonds, and resolved to send him into Syria, and delivered two legions to him, that he might set matters right, as being a potent man in that country. But Aristobulus had no enjoyment of what he hoped for from the power that was given him by Cesar; for those of Pompey's party prevented it, and destroyed him by poison; and those of Caesar's party buried him. His dead body also lay, for a good while, embalmed in honey, till Antony afterward sent it to Judea, and caused him to be buried in the royal sepulcher. But Scipio, upon Pompey's sending to him to slay Alexander, the son of Aristobulus, because the young man was accused of what offenses he had been guilty of at first against the Romans, cut off his head; and thus did he die at Antioch. But Ptolemy, the son of Menneus, who was the ruler of Chalcis, under Mount Libanus, took his brethren to him, and sent his son Philippion to Askelon to Aristobulus's wife, and desired her to send back with him her son Antigonus, and her daughters; the one of which, whose name was Alexandra, Philippion fell in love with, and married her, though afterward his father Ptolemy slew him, and married Alexandra, and continued to take care of her brethren.

---

12. Dr. Hudson observes, that the name of this wife of Antipater in Josephus was Cypros, as a Hebrew termination, but not Cypris, the Greek name for Venus, as some critics were ready to correct it.

Chapter 8

8 The Jews Become Confederates with Cesar When He Fought Against Egypt. the Glorious Actions of Antipater, and His Friendship with Caesar. the Honors Which the Jews Received from the Romans and Athenians

1. NOW after Pompey was dead, and after that victory Caesar had gained over him, Antipater, who managed the Jewish affairs, became very useful to Caesar when he made war against Egypt, and that by the order of Hyrcanus; for when Mithridates of Pergainus was bringing his auxiliaries, and was not able to continue his march through Pelusium, but obliged to stay at Askelon, Antipater came to him, conducting three thousand of the Jews, armed men. He had also taken care the principal men of the Arabians should come to his assistance; and on his account it was that all the Syrians assisted him also, as not willing to appear behindhand in their alacrity for Cesar, viz. Jamblicus the ruler, and Ptolemy his son, and Tholomy the son of Sohemus, who dwelt at Mount Libanus, and almost all the cities. So Mithridates marched out of Syria, and came to Pelusium; and when its inhabitants would not admit him, he besieged the city. Now Antipater signalized himself here, and was the first who plucked down a part of the wall, and so opened a way to the rest, whereby they might enter the city, and by this means Pelusium was taken. But it happened that the Egyptian Jews, who dwelt in the country called Onion, would not let Antipater and Mithridates, with their soldiers, pass to Caesar; but Antipater persuaded them to come over with their party, because he was of the same people with them, and that chiefly by showing them the epistles of Hyrcanus the high priest, wherein he exhorted them to cultivate friendship with Caesar, and to supply his army with money, and all sorts of provisions which they wanted; and accordingly, when they saw Antipater and the high priest of the same sentiments, they did as they were desired. And when the Jews about Memphis heard that these Jews were come over to Caesar, they also invited Mithridates to come to them; so he came and received them also into his army.

2. And when Mithridates had gone over all Delta, as the place is called, he came to a pitched battle with the enemy, near the place called the Jewish Camp. Now Mithridates had the right wing, and Antipater the left; and when it came to a fight, that wing where Mithridates was gave way, and was likely to suffer extremely, unless

Antipater had come running to him with his own soldiers along the shore, when he had already beaten the enemy that opposed him; so he delivered Mithridates, and put those Egyptians who had been too hard for him to flight. He also took their camp, and continued in the pursuit of them. He also recalled Mithridates, who had been worsted, and was retired a great way off; of whose soldiers eight hundred fell, but of Antipater's fifty. So Mithridates sent an account of this battle to Caesar, and openly declared that Antipater was the author of this victory, and of his own preservation, insomuch that Caesar commended Antipater then, and made use of him all the rest of that war in the most hazardous undertakings; he happened also to be wounded in one of those engagements

3. However, when Caesar, after some time, had finished that war, and was sailed away for Syria, he honored Antipater greatly, and confirmed Hyrcanus in the high priesthood; and bestowed on Antipater the privilege of a citizen of Rome, and a freedom from taxes every where; and it is reported by many, that Hyrcanus went along with Antipater in this expedition, and came himself into Egypt. And Strabo of Cappadocia bears witness to this, when he says thus, in the name of Aslnius: "After Mithridates had invaded Egypt, and with him Hyrcanus the high priest of the Jews." Nay, the same Strabo says thus again, in another place, in the name of Hypsicrates, that "Mithridates at first went out alone; but that Antipater, who had the care of the Jewish affairs, was called by him to Askelon, and that he had gotten ready three thousand soldiers to go along with him, and encouraged other governors of the country to go along with him also; and that Hyrcanus the high priest was also present in this expedition." This is what Strabo says.

4. But Antigonus, the son of Aristobulus, came at this time to Caesar, and lamented his father's fate; and complained, that it was by Antipater's means that Aristobulus was taken off by poison, and his brother was beheaded by Scipio, and desired that he would take pity of him who had been ejected out of that principality which was due to him. He also accused Hyrcanus and Antipater as governing the nation by violence, and offering injuries to himself. Antipater was present, and made his defense as to the accusations that were laid against him. He demonstrated that Antigonus and his party were given to innovation, and were seditious persons. He also put Caesar in

mind what difficult services he had undergone when he assisted him in his wars, and discoursed about what he was a witness of himself. He added, that Aristobulus was justly carried away to Rome, as one that was an enemy to the Romans, and could never be brought to be a friend to them, and that his brother had no more than he deserved from Scipio, as being seized in committing robberies; and that this punishment was not inflicted on him in a way of violence or injustice by him that did it.

5. When Antipater had made this speech, Caesar appointed Hyrcauus to be high priest, and gave Antipater what principality he himself should choose, leaving the determination to himself; so he made him procurator of Judea. He also gave Hyrcanus leave to raise up the walls of his own city, upon his asking that favor of him, for they had been demolished by Pompey. And this grant he sent to the consuls to Rome, to be engraven in the capitol. The decree of the senate was this that follows:[13] "Lucius Valerius, the son of Lucius the praetor, referred this to the senate, upon the Ides of December, in the temple of Concord. There were present at the writing of this decree Lucius Coponius, the son of Lucius of the Colline tribe, and Papirius of the Quirine tribe, concerning the affairs which Alexander, the son of Jason, and Numenius, the son of Antiochus, and Alexander, the son of Dositheus, ambassadors of the Jews, good and worthy men, proposed, who came to renew that league of goodwill and friendship with the Romans which was in being before. They also brought a shield of gold, as a mark of confederacy, valued at fifty thousand pieces of gold; and desired that letters might be given them, directed both to the free cities and to the kings, that their country and their havens might be at peace, and that no one among them might receive any

---

13. Take Dr. Hudson's note upon this place, which I suppose to be the truth: "Here is some mistake in Josephus; for when he had promised us a decree for the restoration of Jerusalem he brings in a decree of far greater antiquity, and that a league of friendship and union only. One may easily believe that Josephus gave order for one thing, and his amanuensis performed another, by transposing decrees that concerned the Hyrcani, and as deluded by the sameness of their names; for that belongs to the first high priest of this name, [John Hyrcanus,] which Josephus here ascribes to one that lived later [Hyrcanus, the son of Alexander Janneus]. However, the decree which he proposes to set down follows a little lower, in the collection of Raman decrees that concerned the Jews and is that dated when Caesar was consul the fifth time." See ch. 10. sect. 5.

injury. It therefore pleased [the senate] to make a league of friendship and good-will with them, and to bestow on them whatsoever they stood in need of, and to accept of the shield which was brought by them. This was done in the ninth year of Hyrcanus the high priest and ethnarch, in the month Panemus." Hyreanus also received honors from the people of Athens, as having been useful to them on many occasions. And when they wrote to him, they sent him this decree, as it here follows "Under the prutaneia and priesthood of Dionysius, the son of Esculapius, on the fifth day of the latter part of the month Panemus, this decree of the Athenians was given to their commanders, when Agathocles was archon, and Eucles, the son of Menander of Alimusia, was the scribe. In the month Munychion, on the eleventh day of the prutaneia, a council of the presidents was held in the theater. Dorotheus the high priest, and the fellow presidents with him, put it to the vote of the people. Dionysius, the son of Dionysius, gave the sentence. Since Hyrcanus, the son of Alexander, the high priest and ethnareh of the Jews, continues to bear good-will to our people in general, and to every one of our citizens in particular, and treats them with all sorts of kindness; and when any of the Athenians come to him, either as ambassadors, or on any occasion of their own, he receives them in an obliging manner, and sees that they are conducted back in safety, of which we have had several former testimonies; it is now also decreed, at the report of Theodosius, the son of Theodorus, and upon his putting the people in mind of the virtue of this man, and that his purpose is to do us all the good that is in his power, to honor him with a crown of gold, the usual reward according to the law, and to erect his statue in brass in the temple of Demus and of the Graces; and that this present of a crown shall be proclaimed publicly in the theater, in the Dionysian shows, while the new tragedies are acting; and in the Panathenean, and Eleusinian, and Gymnical shows also; and that the commanders shall take care, while he continues in his friendship, and preserves his good-will to us, to return all possible honor and favor to the man for his affection and generosity; that by this treatment it may appear how our people receive the good kindly, and repay them a suitable reward; and he may be induced to proceed in his affection towards us, by the honors we have already paid him. That ambassadors be also chosen out of all the Athenians, who shall carry this decree to him, and desire him to accept of the honors we do him, and to endeavor always to be doing some good to our city." And this shall suffice us to have spoken as to the honors that were paid by the Romans and the people of Athens to Hyrcanus.

9 *How Antipater Committed the Care of Galilee to Herod, and That of Jerusalem to Phasaelus; as Also How Herod Upon the Jews' Envy at Antipater Was Accused Before Hyrcanus*

1. NOW when Caesar had settled the affairs of Syria, he sailed away. And as soon as Antipater had conducted Caesar out of Syria, he returned to Judea. He then immediately raised up the wall which had been thrown down by Pompey; and, by coming thither, he pacified that tumult which had been in the country, and this by both threatening and advising them to be quiet; for that if they would be of Hyrcanus's side, they would live happily, and lead their lives without disturbance, and in the enjoyment of their own possessions; but if they were addicted to the hopes of what might come by innovation, and aimed to get wealth thereby, they should have him a severe master instead of a gentle governor, and Hyrcanus a tyrant instead of a king, and the Romans, together with Caesar, their bitter enemies instead of rulers, for that they would never bear him to be set aside whom they had appointed to govern. And when Antipater had said this to them, he himself settled the affairs of this country.

2. And seeing that Hyrcanus was of a slow and slothful temper, he made Phasaelus, his eldest son, governor of Jerusalem, and of the places that were about it, but committed Galilee to Herod, his next son, who was then a very young man, for he was but fifteen years of age[14] But that youth of his was no impediment to him; but as he was a youth of great mind, he presently met with an opportunity of signalizing his courage; for finding that there was one Hezekiah, a captain of a

---

14. Those who will carefully observe the several occasional numbers and chronological characters in the life and death of this Herod, and of his children, hereafter noted, will see that twenty-five years, and not fifteen, must for certain have been here Josephus's own number for the age of Herod, when he was made governor of Galilee. See ch. 23. sect. 5, and ch. 24. sect. 7; and particularly Antiq. B. XVII. ch. 8. sect. 1, where about forty-four years afterwards Herod dies an old man at about seventy.

band of robbers, who overran the neighboring parts of Syria with a great troop of them, he seized him and slew him, as well as a great number of the other robbers that were with him; for which action he was greatly beloved by the Syrians; for when they were very desirous to have their country freed from this nest of robbers, he purged it of them. So they sung songs in his commendation in their villages and cities, as having procured them peace, and the secure enjoyment of their possessions; and on this account it was that he became known to Sextus Caesar, who was a relation of the great Caesar, and was now president of Syria. Now Phasaetus, Herod's brother, was moved with emulation at his actions, and envied the fame be had thereby gotten, and became ambitious not to be behindhand with him in deserving it. So he made the inhabitants of Jerusalem bear him the greatest good-will while he held the city himself, but did neither manage its affairs improperly, nor abuse his authority therein. This conduct procured from the nation to Antipater such respect as is due to kings, and such honors as he might partake of if he were an absolute lord of the country. Yet did not this splendor of his, as frequently happens, in the least diminish in him that kindness and fidelity which he owed to Hyrcanus.

3. But now the principal men among the Jews, when they saw Antipater and his sons to grow so much in the good-will the nation bare to them, and in the revenues which they received out of Judea, and out of Hyrcanus's own wealth, they became ill-disposed to him; for indeed Antipater had contracted a friendship with the Roman emperors; and when he had prevailed with Hyrcanus to send them money, he took it to himself, and purloined the present intended, and sent it as if it were his own, and not Hyrcanus's gift to them. Hyrcanus heard of this his management, but took no care about it; nay, he rather was very glad of it. But the chief men of the Jews were therefore in fear, because they saw that Herod was a violent and bold man, and very desirous of acting tyrannically; so they came to Hyrcanus, and now accused Antipater openly, and said to him, "How long wilt thou be quiet under such actions as are now done? Or dost thou not see that Antipater and his sons have already seized upon the government, and that it is only the name of a king which is given thee? But do not thou suffer these things to be hidden from thee, nor do thou think to escape danger by being so careless of thyself and of thy kingdom; for

Antipater and his sons are not now stewards of thine affairs: do not thou deceive thyself with such a notion; they are evidently absolute lords; for Herod, Antipater's son, hath slain Hezekiah, and those that were with him, and hath thereby transgressed our law, which hath forbidden to slay any man, even though he were a wicked man, unless he had been first condemned to suffer death by the Sanhedrim[15] yet hath he been so insolent as to do this, and that without any authority from thee."

4. Upon Hyrcanus hearing this, he complied with them. The mothers also of those that had been slain by Herod raised his indignation; for those women continued every day in the temple, persuading the king and the people that Herod might undergo a trial before the Sanhedrim for what he had done. Hyrcanus was so moved by these complaints, that he summoned Herod to come to his trial for what was charged upon him. Accordingly he came; but his father had persuaded him to come not like a private man, but with a guard, for the security of his person; and that when he had settled the affairs of Galilee in the best manner he could for his own advantage, he should come to his trial, but still with a body of men sufficient for his security on his journey, yet so that he should not come with so great a force as might look like terrifying Hyrcanus, but still such a one as might not expose him naked and unguarded [to his enemies.] However, Sextus Caesar, president of Syria, wrote to Hyrcanus, and desired him to clear Herod, and dismiss him at his trial, and threatened him beforehand if he did not do it. Which epistle of his was the occasion of Hyrcanus delivering Herod from suffering any harm from the Sanhedrim, for he loved him as his own son. But when Herod stood before the Sanhedrim, with his body of men about him, he aftrighted them all, and no one of his former accusers durst after that bring any charge against him, but there was a deep silence, and nobody knew what was to be done.

---

15. It is here worth our while to remark, that none could be put to death in Judea but by the approbation of the Jewish Sanhedrim, there being an excellent provision in the law of Moses, that even in criminal causes, and particularly where life was concerned, an appeal should lie from the lesser councils of seven in the other cities to the supreme council of seventy-one at Jerusalem; and that is exactly according to our Savior's words, when he says, "It could not be that a prophet should perish out of Jerusalem," Luke 13:33.

When affairs stood thus, one whose name was Sameas,[16] a righteous man he was, and for that reason above all fear, rose up, and said, "O you that are assessors with me, and O thou that art our king, I neither have ever myself known such a case, nor do I suppose that any one of you can name its parallel, that one who is called to take his trial by us ever stood in such a manner before us; but every one, whosoever he be, that comes to be tried by this Sanhedrim, presents himself in a submissive manner, and like one that is in fear of himself, and that endeavors to move us to compassion, with his hair dishevelled, and in a black and mourning garment: but this admirable man Herod, who is accused of murder, and called to answer so heavy an accusation, stands here clothed in purple, and with the hair of his head finely trimmed, and with his armed men about him, that if we shall condemn him by our law, he may slay us, and by overbearing justice may himself escape death. Yet do not I make this complaint against Herod himself; he is to be sure more concerned for himself than for the laws; but my complaint is against yourselves, and your king, who gave him a license so to do. However, take you notice, that God is great, and that this very man, whom you are going to absolve and dismiss, for the sake of Hyrcanus, will one day punish both you and your king himself also." Nor did Sameas mistake in any part of this prediction; for when Herod had received the kingdom, he slew all the members of this Sanhedrim, and Hyrcanus himself also, excepting Sameas, for he had a great honor for him on account of his righteousness, and because, when the city was afterward besieged by Herod and Sosius, he persuaded the people to admit Herod into it; and told them that for their sins they would not be able to escape his hands:—which things will be related by us in their proper places.

5. But when Hyrcanus saw that the members of the Sanhedrim were ready to pronounce the sentence of death upon Herod, he put off the trial to another day, and sent privately to Herod, and advised him to fly out of the city, for that by this means he might escape. So he retired to Damascus, as though he fled from the king; and when he had been with Sextus Caesar, and had put his own affairs in a sure posture, he resolved to do thus; that in case he were again summoned before

16. This account, as Reland observes, is confirmed by the Talmudists, who call this Sameas, "Simeon, the son of Shetach."

the Sanhedrim to take his trial, he would not obey that summons. Hereupon the members of the Sanhedrim had great indignation at this posture of affairs, and endeavored to persuade Hyrcanus that all these things were against him; which state of matters he was not ignorant of; but his temper was so unmanly, and so foolish, that he was able to do nothing at all. But when Sextus had made Herod general of the army of Celesyria, for he sold him that post for money, Hyrcanus was in fear lest Herod should make war upon him; nor was the effect of what he feared long in coming upon him; for Herod came and brought an army along with him to fight with Hyrcanus, as being angry at the trial he bad been summoned to undergo before the Sanhedrim; but his father Antipater, and his brother [Phasaelus], met him, and hindered him from assaulting Jerusalem. They also pacified his vehement temper, and persuaded him to do no overt action, but only to affright them with threatenings, and to proceed no further against one who had given him the dignity he had: they also desired him not only to be angry that he was summoned, and obliged to come to his trial, but to remember withal how he was dismissed without condemnation, and how he ought to give Hyrcanus thanks for the same; and that he was not to regard only what was disagreeable to him, and be unthankful for his deliverance. So they desired him to consider, that since it is God that turns the scales of war, there is great uncertainty in the issue of battles, and that therefore he ought of to expect the victory when he should fight with his king, and him that had supported him, and bestowed many benefits upon him, and had done nothing itself very severe to him; for that his accusation, which was derived from evil counselors, and not from himself, had rather the suspicion of some severity, than any thing really severe in it. Herod was persuaded by these arguments, and believed that it was sufficient for his future hopes to have made a show of his strength before the nation, and done no more to it—and in this state were the affairs of Judea at this time.

10 The Honors That Were Paid the Jews; and the Leagues That Were Made by the Romans and Other Nations, with Them

1. NOW when Caesar was come to Rome, he was ready to sail into Africa to fight against Scipio and Cato, when Hyrcanus sent

ambassadors to him, and by them desired that he would ratify that league of friendship and mutual alliance which was between them, And it seems to me to be necessary here to give an account of all the honors that the Romans and their emperor paid to our nation, and of the leagues of mutual assistance they have made with it, that all the rest of mankind may know what regard the kings of Asia and Europe have had to us, and that they have been abundantly satisfied of our courage and fidelity; for whereas many will not believe what hath been written about us by the Persians and Macedonians, because those writings are not every where to be met with, nor do lie in public places, but among us ourselves, and certain other barbarous nations, while there is no contradiction to be made against the decrees of the Romans, for they are laid up in the public places of the cities, and are extant still in the capitol, and engraven upon pillars of brass; nay, besides this, Julius Caesar made a pillar of brass for the Jews at Alexandria, and declared publicly that they were citizens of Alexandria. Out of these evidences will I demonstrate what I say; and will now set down the decrees made both by the senate and by Julius Caesar, which relate to Hyrcanus and to our nation.

2. "Caius Julius Caesar, imperator and high priest, and dictator the second time, to the magistrates, senate, and people of Sidon, sendeth greeting. If you be in health, it is well. I also and the army are well. I have sent you a copy of that decree, registered on the tables, which concerns Hyrcanus, the son of Alexander, the high priest and ethnarch of the Jews, that it may be laid up among the public records; and I will that it be openly proposed in a table of brass, both in Greek and in Latin. It is as follows: I Julius Caesar, imperator the second time, and high priest, have made this decree, with the approbation of the senate. Whereas Hyrcanus, the son of Alexander the Jew, hath demonstrated his fidelity and diligence about our affairs, and this both now and in former times, both in peace and in war, as many of our generals have borne witness, and came to our assistance in the last Alexandrian war,[17] with fifteen hundred soldiers; and when he was

17. That Hyreanus was himself in Egypt, along with Antipater, at this time, to whom accordingly the bold and prudent actions of his deputy Antipater are here ascribed, as this decree of Julius Caesar supposes, we are further assured by the testimony of Strabo, already produced by Josephus, ch. 8. sect. 3.

sent by me to Mithridates, showed himself superior in valor to all the rest of that army;—for these reasons I will that Hyrcanus, the son of Alexander, and his children, be ethnarchs of the Jews, and have the high priesthood of the Jews for ever, according to the customs of their forefathers, and that he and his sons be our confederates; and that besides this, everyone of them be reckoned among our particular friends. I also ordain that he and his children retain whatsoever privileges belong to the office of high priest, or whatsoever favors have been hitherto granted them; and if at any time hereafter there arise any questions about the Jewish customs, I will that he determine the same. And I think it not proper that they should be obliged to find us winter quarters, or that any money should be required of them."

3. "The decrees of Caius Caesar, consul, containing what hath been granted and determined, are as follows: That Hyrcanus and his children bear rule over the nation of the Jews, and have the profits of the places to them bequeathed; and that he, as himself the high priest and ethnarch of the Jews, defend those that are injured; and that ambassadors be sent to Hyrcanus, the son of Alexander, the high priest of the Jews, that may discourse with him about a league of friendship and mutual assistance; and that a table of brass, containing the premises, be openly proposed in the capitol, and at Sidon, and Tyre, and Askelon, and in the temple, engraven in Roman and Greek letters: that this decree may also be communicated to the quaestors and praetors of the several cities, and to the friends of the Jews; and that the ambassadors may have presents made them; and that these decrees be sent every where."

4. "Caius Caesar, imperator, dictator, consul, hath granted, That out of regard to the honor, and virtue, and kindness of the man, and for the advantage of the senate, and of the people of Rome, Hyrcanus, the son of Alexander, both he and his children, be high priests and priests of Jerusalem, and of the Jewish nation, by the same right, and according to the same laws, by which their progenitors have held the priesthood."

5. "Caius Caesar, consul the fifth time, hath decreed, That the Jews shall possess Jerusalem, and may encompass that city with walls; and that Hyrcanus, the son of Alexander, the high priest and ethnarch of the Jews, retain it in the manner he himself pleases; and that the Jews be allowed to deduct out of their tribute, every second year the land is

let [in the Sabbatic period], a corus of that tribute; and that the tribute they pay be not let to farm, nor that they pay always the same tribute."

6. "Caius Caesar, imperator the second time, hath ordained, That all the country of the Jews, excepting Joppa, do pay a tribute yearly for the city Jerusalem, excepting the seventh, which they call the sabbatical year, because thereon they neither receive the fruits of their trees, nor do they sow their land; and that they pay their tribute in Sidon on the second year [of that sabbatical period], the fourth part of what was sown: and besides this, they are to pay the same tithes to Hyrcanus and his sons which they paid to their forefathers. And that no one, neither president, nor lieutenant, nor ambassador, raise auxiliaries within the bounds of Judea; nor may soldiers exact money of them for winter quarters, or under any other pretense; but that they be free from all sorts of injuries; and that whatsoever they shall hereafter have, and are in possession of, or have bought, they shall retain them all. It is also our pleasure that the city Joppa, which the Jews had originally, when they made a league of friendship with the Romans, shall belong to them, as it. formerly did; and that Hyrcanus, the son of Alexander, and his sons, have as tribute of that city from those that occupy the land for the country, and for what they export every year to Sidon, twenty thousand six hundred and seventy-five modii every year, the seventh year, which they call the Sabbatic year, excepted, whereon they neither plough, nor receive the product of their trees. It is also the pleasure of the senate, that as to the villages which are in the great plain, which Hyrcanus and his forefathers formerly possessed, Hyrcanus and the Jews have them with the same privileges with which they formerly had them also; and that the same original ordinances remain still in force which concern the Jews with regard to their high priests; and that they enjoy the same benefits which they have had formerly by the concession of the people, and of the senate; and let them enjoy the like privileges in Lydda. It is the pleasure also of the senate that Hyrcanus the ethnarch, and the Jews, retain those places, countries, and villages which belonged to the kings of Syria and Phoenicia, the confederates of the Romans, and which they had bestowed on them as their free gifts. It is also granted to Hyrcanus, and to his sons, and to the ambassadors by them sent to us, that in the fights between single gladiators, and in those with beasts, they shall sit among the senators to see those shows; and that when they desire an audience, they shall

be introduced into the senate by the dictator, or by the general of the horse; and when they have introduced them, their answers shall be returned them in ten days at the furthest, after the decree of the senate is made about their affairs."

7. "Caius Cqesar, imperator, dictator the fourth time, and consul the fifth time, declared to be perpetual dictator, made this speech concerning the rights and privileges of Hyrcanus, the son of Alexander, the high priest and ethnarch of the Jews. Since those imperators[18] that have been in the provinces before me have borne witness to Hyrcanus, the high priest of the Jews, and to the Jews themselves, and this before the senate and people of Rome, when the people and senate returned their thanks to them, it is good that we now also remember the same, and provide that a requital be made to Hyrcanus, to the nation of the Jews, and to the sons of Hyrcanus, by the senate and people of Rome, and that suitably to what good-will they have shown us, and to the benefits they have bestowed upon us."

8. "Julius Caius, praetor [consul] of Rome, to the magistrates, senate, and people of the Parians, sendeth greeting. The Jews of Delos, and some other Jews that sojourn there, in the presence of your ambassadors, signified to us, that, by a decree of yours, you forbid them to make use of the customs of their forefathers, and their way of sacred worship. Now it does not please me that such decrees should be made against our friends and confederates, whereby they are forbidden to live according to their own customs, or to bring in contributions for common suppers and holy festivals, while they are not forbidden so to do even at Rome itself; for even Caius Caesar, our imperator and consul, in that decree wherein he forbade the Bacchanal rioters to meet in the city, did yet permit these Jews, and these only, both to bring in their contributions, and to make their common suppers. Accordingly, when I forbid other Bacchanal rioters, I permit these Jews to gather themselves together, according to the customs and laws of their forefathers, and to persist therein. It will be therefore good for

18. Dr. Hudson justly supposes that the Roman imperators, or generals of armies, meant both here and sect. 2, who gave testimony to Hyrcanus's and the Jews' faithfulness and goodwill to the Romans before the senate and people of Rome, were principally Pompey, Scaurus, and Gabinius; of all whom Josephus had already given us the history, so far as the Jews were concerned with them.

you, that if you have made any decree against these our friends and confederates, to abrogate the same, by reason of their virtue and kind disposition towards us."

9. Now after Caius was slain, when Marcus Antonius and Publius Dolabella were consuls, they both assembled the senate, and introduced Hyrcanus's ambassadors into it, and discoursed of what they desired, and made a league of friendship with them. The senate also decreed to grant them all they desired. I add the decree itself, that those who read the present work may have ready by them a demonstration of the truth of what we say. The decree was this:

10. "The decree of the senate, copied out of the treasury, from the public tables belonging to the quaestors, when Quintus Rutilius and Caius Cornelius were quaestors, and taken out of the second table of the first class, on the third day before the Ides of April, in the temple of Concord. There were present at the writing of this decree, Lucius Calpurnius Piso of the Menenian tribe, Servius Papinins Potitus of the Lemonian tribe, Caius Caninius Rebilius of the Terentine tribe, Publius Tidetius, Lucius Apulinus, the son of Lucius, of the Sergian tribe, Flavius, the son of Lucius, of the Lemonian tribe, Publius Platins, the son of Publius, of the Papyrian tribe, Marcus Acilius, the son of Marcus, of the Mecian tribe, Lucius Erucius, the son of Lucius, of the Stellatine tribe, Mareils Quintus Plancillus, the son of Marcus, of the Pollian tribe, and Publius Serius. Publius Dolabella and Marcus Antonius, the consuls, made this reference to the senate, that as to those things which, by the decree of the senate, Caius Caesar had adjudged about the Jews, and yet had not hitherto that decree been brought into the treasury, it is our will, as it is also the desire of Publius Dolabella and Marcus Antonius, our consuls, to have these decrees put into the public tables, and brought to the city quaestors, that they may take care to have them put upon the double tables. This was done before the fifth of the Ides of February, in the temple of Concord. Now the ambassadors from Hyrcanus the high priest were these: Lysimachus, the son of Pausanias, Alexander, the son of Theodorus, Patroclus, the son of Chereas, and Jonathan the, son of Onias."

11. Hyrcanus sent also one of these ambassadors to Dolabella, who was then the prefect of Asia, and desired him to dismiss the Jews from military services, and to preserve to them the customs of

their forefathers, and to permit them to live according to them. And when Dolabella had received Hyrcanus's letter, without any further deliberation, he sent an epistle to all the Asiatics, and particularly to the city of the Ephesians, the metropolis of Asia, about the Jews; a copy of which epistle here follows:

12. "When Artermon was prytanis, on the first day of the month Leneon, Dolabella, imperator, to the senate, and magistrates, and people of the Ephesians, sendeth greeting. Alexander, the son of Theodorus, the ambassador of Hyrcanus, the son of Alexander, the high priest and ethnarch of the Jews, appeared before me, to show that his countrymen could not go into their armies, because they are not allowed to bear arms or to travel on the sabbath days, nor there to procure themselves those sorts of food which they have been used to eat from the times of their forefathers;—I do therefore grant them a freedom from going into the army, as the former prefects have done, and permit them to use the customs of their forefathers, in assembling together for sacred and religious purposes, as their law requires, and for collecting oblations necessary for sacrifices; and my will is, that you write this to the several cities under your jurisdiction."

13. And these were the concessions that Dolabella made to our nation when Hyrcanus sent an embassage to him. But Lucius the consul's decree ran thus: "I have at my tribunal set these Jews, who are citizens of Rome, and follow the Jewish religious rites, and yet live at Ephesus, free from going into the army, on account of the superstition they are under. This was done before the twelfth of the calends of October, when Lucius Lentulus and Caius Marcellus were consuls, in the presence of Titus Appius Balgus, the son of Titus, and lieutenant of the Horatian tribe; of Titus Tongins, the son of Titus, of the Crustumine tribe; of Quintus Resius, the son of Quintus; of Titus Pompeius Longinus, the son of Titus; of Catus Servilius, the son of Caius, of the Terentine tribe; of Bracchus the military tribune; of Publius Lucius Gallus, the son of Publius, of the Veturian tribe; of Caius Sentins, the son of Caius, of the Sabbatine tribe; of Titus Atilius Bulbus, the son of Titus, lieutenant and vice-praetor to the magistrates, senate, and people of the Ephesians, sendeth greeting. Lucius Lentulus the consul freed the Jews that are in Asia from going into the armies, at my intercession for them; and when I had made the same petition some time afterward to Phanius the imperator, and to Lucius Antonius

the vice-quaestor, I obtained that privilege of them also; and my will is, that you take care that no one give them any disturbance."

14. The decree of the Delians. "The answer of the praetors, when Beotus was archon, on the twentieth day of the month Thargeleon. While Marcus Piso the lieutenant lived in our city, who was also appointed over the choice of the soldiers, he called us, and many other of the citizens, and gave order, that if there be here any Jews who are Roman citizens, no one is to give them any disturbance about going into the army, because Cornelius Lentulus, the consul, freed the Jews from going into the army, on account of the superstition they are under;—you are therefore obliged to submit to the praetor." And the like decree was made by the Sardians about us also.

15. "Caius Phanius, the son of Caius, imperator and consul, to the magistrates of Cos, sendeth greeting. I would have you know that the ambassadors of the Jews have been with me, and desired they might have those decrees which the senate had made about them; which decrees are here subjoined. My will is, that you have a regard to and take care of these men, according to the senate's decree, that they may be safely conveyed home through your country."

16. The declaration of Lucius Lentulus the consul: "I have dismissed those Jews who are Roman citizens, and who appear to me to have their religious rites, and to observe the laws of the Jews at Ephesus, on account of the superstition they are under. This act was done before the thirteenth of the calends of October."

17. "Lucius Antonius, the son of Marcus, vice-quaestor, and vice-praetor, to the magistrates, senate, and people of the Sardians, sendeth greeting. Those Jews that are our fellow citizens of Rome came to me, and demonstrated that they had an assembly of their own, according to the laws of their forefathers, and this from the beginning, as also a place of their own, wherein they determined their suits and controversies with one another. Upon their petition therefore to me, that these might be lawful for them, I gave order that these their privileges be preserved, and they be permitted to do accordingly."

18. The declaration of Marcus Publius, the son of Spurius, and of Marcus, the son of Marcus, and of Lucius, the son of Publius: "We went to the proconsul, and informed him of what Dositheus, the son of Cleopatrida of Alexandria, desired, that, if he thought good, he would dismiss those Jews who were Roman citizens, and were wont to

observe the rites of the Jewish religion, on account of the superstition they were under. Accordingly, he did dismiss them. This was done before the thirteenth of the calends of October."

19. "In the month Quntius, when Lucius Lentulus and Caius Mercellus were consuls; and there were present Titus Appius Balbus, the son of Titus, lieutenant of the Horatian tribe, Titus Tongius of the Crustumine tribe, Quintus Resius, the son of Quintus, Titus Pompeius, the son of Titus, Cornelius Longinus, Caius Servilius Bracchus, the son of Caius, a military tribune, of the Terentine tribe, Publius Clusius Gallus, the son of Publius, of the Veturian tribe, Caius Teutius, the son of Caius, a milital tribune, of the EmilJan tribe, Sextus Atilius Serranus, the son of Sextus, of the Esquiline tribe, Caius Pompeius, the son of Caius, of the Sabbatine tribe, Titus Appius Menander, the son of Titus, Publius Servilius Strabo, the son of Publius, Lucius Paccius Capito, the son of Lucius, of the Colline tribe, Aulus Furius Tertius, the son of Aulus, and Appius Menus. In the presence of these it was that Lentulus pronounced this decree: I have before the tribunal dismissed those Jews that are Roman citizens, and are accustomed to observe the sacred rites of the Jews at Ephesus, on account of the superstition they are under."

20. "The magistrates of the Laodiceans to Caius Rubilius, the son of Caius, the consul, sendeth greeting. Sopater, the ambassador of Hyrcanus the high priest, hath delivered us an epistle from thee, whereby he lets us know that certain ambassadors were come from Hyrcanus, the high priest of the Jews, and brought an epistle written concerning their nation, wherein they desire that the Jews may be allowed to observe their Sabbaths, and other sacred rites, according to the laws of their forefathers, and that they may be under no command, because they are our friends and confederates, and that nobody may injure them in our provinces. Now although the Trallians there present contradicted them, and were not pleased with these decrees, yet didst thou give order that they should be observed, and informedst us that thou hadst been desired to write this to us about them. We therefore, in obedience to the injunctions we have received from thee, have received the epistle which thou sentest us, and have laid it up by itself among our public records. And as to the other things about which thou didst send to us, we will take care that no complaint be made against us."

21. "Publius Servilius, the son of Publius, of the Galban tribe, the proconsul, to the magistrates, senate, and people of the Mileslans, sendeth greeting. Prytanes, the son of Hermes, a citizen of yours, came to me when I was at Tralles, and held a court there, and informed me that you used the Jews in a way different from my opinion, and forbade them to celebrate their Sabbaths, and to perform the Sacred rites received from their forefathers, and to manage the fruits of the land, according to their ancient custom; and that he had himself been the promulger of your decree, according as your laws require: I would therefore have you know, that upon hearing the pleadings on both sides, I gave sentence that the Jews should not be prohibited to make use of their own customs."

22. The decree of those of Pergamus. "When Cratippus was prytanis, on the first day of the month Desius, the decree of the praetors was this: Since the Romans, following the conduct of their ancestors, undertake dangers for the common safety of all mankind, and are ambitious to settle their confederates and friends in happiness, and in firm peace, and since the nation of the Jews, and their high priest Hyrcanus, sent as ambassadors to them, Strato, the son of Theodatus, and Apollonius, the son of Alexander, and Eneas, the son of Antipater, and Aristobulus, the son of Amyntas, and Sosipater, the son of Philip, worthy and good men, who gave a particular account of their affairs, the senate thereupon made a decree about what they had desired of them, that Antiochus the king, the son of Antiochus, should do no injury to the Jews, the confederates of the Romans; and that the fortresses, and the havens, and the country, and whatsoever else he had taken from them, should be restored to them; and that it may be lawful for them to export their goods out of their own havens; and that no king nor people may have leave to export any goods, either out of the country of Judea, or out of their havens, without paying customs, but only Ptolemy, the king of Alexandria, because he is our confederate and friend; and that, according to their desire, the garrison that is in Joppa may be ejected. Now Lucius Pettius, one of our senators, a worthy and good man, gave order that we should take care that these things should be done according to the senate's decree; and that we should take care also that their ambassadors might return home in safety. Accordingly, we admitted Theodorus into our senate and assembly, and took the epistle out his hands, as well as

the decree of the senate. And as he discoursed with great zeal about the Jews, and described Hyrcanus's virtue and generosity, and how he was a benefactor to all men in common, and particularly to every body that comes to him, we laid up the epistle in our public records; and made a decree ourselves, that since we also are in confederacy with the Romans, we would do every thing we could for the Jews, according to the senate's decree. Theodorus also, who brought the epistle, desired of our praetors, that they would send Hyrcanus a copy of that decree, as also ambassadors to signify to him the affection of our people to him, and to exhort them to preserve and augment their friendship for us, and be ready to bestow other benefits upon us, as justly expecting to receive proper requitals from us; and desiring them to remember that our ancestors[19] were friendly to the Jews even in the days of Abraham, who was the father of all the Hebrews, as we have [also] found it set down in our public records."

23. The decree of those of Halicarnassus. "When Memnon, the son of Orestidas by descent, but by adoption of Euonymus, was priest, on the * * * day of the month Aristerion, the decree of the people, upon the representation of Marcus Alexander, was this: Since we have ever a great regard to piety towards God, and to holiness; and since we aim to follow the people of the Romans, who are the benefactors of all men, and what they have written to us about a league of friendship and mutual assistance between the Jews and our city, and that their sacred offices and accustomed festivals and assemblies may be observed by them; we have decreed, that as many men and women of the Jews as

---

19. We have here a most remarkable and authentic attestation of the citizens of Pergamus, that Abraham was the father of all the Hebrews; that their own ancestors were, in the oldest times, the friends of those Hebrews; and that the public arts of their city, then extant, confirmed the same; which evidence is too strong to be evaded by our present ignorance of the particular occasion of such ancient friendship and alliance between those people. See the like full evidence of the kindred of the Lacedemonians and the Jews; and that became they were both of the posterity of Abraham, by a public epistle of those people to the Jews, preserved in the First Book of the Maccabees, 12:19–23; and thence by Josephus, Antiq. B. XII. ch. 4 sect. 10; both which authentic records are highly valuable. It is also well worthy of observation, what Moses Chorenensis, the principal Armenian historian, informs us of, p. 83, that Arsaces, who raised the Parthian empire, was of the seed of Abraham by Chetura; and that thereby was accomplished that prediction which said, "Kings of nations shall proceed from thee," Genesis 17:6.

are willing so to do, may celebrate their Sabbaths, and perform their holy offices, according to Jewish laws; and may make their proseuchae at the sea-side, according to the customs of their forefathers; and if any one, whether he be a magistrate or private person, hindereth them from so doing, he shall be liable to a fine, to be applied to the uses of the city."

24. The decree of the Sardians. "This decree was made by the senate and people, upon the representation of the praetors: Whereas those Jews who are fellow citizens, and live with us in this city, have ever had great benefits heaped upon them by the people, and have come now into the senate, and desired of the people, that upon the restitution of their law and their liberty, by the senate and people of Rome, they may assemble together, according to their ancient legal custom, and that we will not bring any suit against them about it; and that a place may be given them where they may have their congregations, with their wives and children, and may offer, as did their forefathers, their prayers and sacrifices to God. Now the senate and people have decreed to permit them to assemble together on the days formerly appointed, and to act according to their own laws; and that such a place be set apart for them by the praetors, for the building and inhabiting the same, as they shall esteem fit for that purpose; and that those that take care of the provision for the city, shall take care that such sorts of food as they esteem fit for their eating may be imported into the city."

25. The decree of the Ephesians. "When Menophilus was prytanis, on the first day of the month Artemisius, this decree was made by the people: Nicanor, the son of Euphemus, pronounced it, upon the representation of the praetors. Since the Jews that dwell in this city have petitioned Marcus Julius Pompeius, the son of Brutus, the proconsul, that they might be allowed to observe their Sabbaths, and to act in all things according to the customs of their forefathers, without impediment from any body, the praetor hath granted their petition. Accordingly, it was decreed by the senate and people, that in this affair that concerned the Romans, no one of them should be hindered from keeping the sabbath day, nor be fined for so doing, but that they may be allowed to do all things according to their own laws."

26. Now there are many such decrees of the senate and imperators of the Romans[20] and those different from these before us, which have been made in favor of Hyrcanus, and of our nation; as also, there have been more decrees of the cities, and rescripts of the praetors, to such epistles as concerned our rights and privileges; and certainly such as are not ill-disposed to what we write may believe that they are all to this purpose, and that by the specimens which we have inserted; for since we have produced evident marks that may still be seen of the friendship we have had with the Romans, and demonstrated that those marks are engraven upon columns and tables of brass in the capitol, that axe still in being, and preserved to this day, we have omitted to set them all down, as needless and disagreeable; for I cannot suppose any one so perverse as not to believe the friendship we have had with the Romans, while they have demonstrated the same by such a great number of their decrees relating to us; nor will they doubt of our fidelity as to the rest of those decrees, since we have shown the same in those we have produced, And thus have we sufficiently explained that friendship and confederacy we at those times had with the Romans.

11 *How Marcus, Succeeded Sextus When He Had Been Slain by Bassus's Treachery; and How, After the Death of Caesar, Cassius Came into Syria, and Distressed Judea; as Also How Malichus Slew Antipater and Was Himself Slain by Herod*

1. NOW it so fell out, that about this very time the affairs of Syria were in great disorder, and this on the occasion following: Cecilius Bassus, one of Pompey's party, laid a treacherous design against Sextus Ceasar, and slew him, and then took his army, and got the management of

20. If we compare Josephus's promise in sect. 1, to produce all the public decrees of the Romans in favor of the Jews, with his excuse here for omitting many of them, we may observe, that when he came to transcribe all those decrees he had collected, he found them so numerous, that he thought he should too much tire his readers if he had attempted it, which he thought a sufficient apology for his omitting the rest of them; yet do those by him produced afford such a strong confirmation to his history, and give such great light to even the Roman antiquities themselves, that I believe the curious are not a little sorry for such his omissions.

public affairs into his own hand; so there arose a great war about Apamia, while Ceasar's generals came against him with an army of horsemen and footmen; to these Antipater also sent succors, and his sons with them, as calling to mind the kindnesses they had received from Caesar, and on that account he thought it but just to require punishment for him, and to take vengeance on the man that had murdered him. And as the war was drawn out into a great length, Marcus[21] came from Rome to take Sextus's government upon him. But Caesar was slain by Cassius and Brutus in the senate-house, after he had retained the government three years and six months. This fact however, is related elsewhere.

2. As the war that arose upon the death of Caesar was now begun, and the principal men were all gone, some one way, and some another, to raise armies, Cassius came from Rome into Syria, in order to receive the [army that lay in the] camp at Apamia; and having raised the siege, he brought over both Bassus and Marcus to his party. He then went over the cities, and got together weapons and soldiers, and laid great taxes upon those cities; and he chiefly oppressed Judea, and exacted of it seven hundred talents: but Antipater, when he saw the state to be in so great consternation and disorder, he divided the collection of that sum, and appointed his two sons to gather it; and so that part of it was to be exacted by Malichus, who was ill-disposed to him, and part by others. And because Herod did exact what is required of him from Galilee before others, he was in the greatest favor with Cassius; for he thought it a part of prudence to cultivate a friendship with the Romans, and to gain their goodwill at the expense of others; whereas the curators of the other cities, with their citizens, were sold for slaves; and Cassius reduced four cities into a state of slavery, the two most potent of which were Gophna and Emmaus; and, besides these, Lydia and Thamna. Nay, Cassius was so very angry at Malichus, that he had killed him, (for he assaulted him,) had not Hyrcanus, by the means of Antipater, sent him a hundred talents of his own, and thereby pacified his anger against him.

---

21. For Marcus, this president of Syria, sent as successor to Sextus Caesar, the Roman historians require us to read "Marcus" in Josephus, and this perpetually, both in these Antiquities, and in his History of the Wars, as the learned generally agree.

3. But after Cassius was gone out of Judea, Malichus laid snares for Antipater, as thinking that his death would-be the preservation of Hyrcanus's government; but his design was not unknown to Antipater, which when he perceived, he retired beyond Jordan, and got together an army, partly of Arabs, and partly of his own countrymen. However, Malichus, being one of great cunning, denied that he had laid any snares for him, and made his defense with an oath, both to himself and his sons; and said that while Phasaelus had a garrison in Jerusalem, and Herod had the weapons of war in his custody, he could never have a thought of any such thing. So Antipater, perceiving the distress that Malichus was in, was reconciled to him, and made an agreement with him: this was when Marcus was president of Syria; who yet perceiving that this Malichus was making a disturbance in Judea, proceeded so far that he had almost killed him; but still, at the intercession of Antipater, he saved him.

4. However, Antipater little thought that by saving Malichus he had saved his own murderer; for now Cassius and Marcus had got together an army, and intrusted the entire care of it with Herod, and made him general of the forces of Celesyria, and gave him a fleet of ships, and an army of horsemen and footmen; and promised him, that after the war was over they would make him king of Judea; for a war was already begun between Antony and the younger Caesar: but as Malichus was most afraid of Antipater, he took him out of the way; and by the offer of money, persuaded the butler of Hyrcanus, with whom they were both to feast, to kill him by poison. This being done, and he having armed men with him, settled the affairs of the city. But when Antipater's sons, Herod and Phasaelus, were acquainted with this conspiracy against their father, and had indignation at it, Malichus denied all, and utterly renounced any knowledge of the murder. And thus died Antipater, a man that had distinguished himself for piety and justice, and love to his country. And whereas one of his sons, Herod, resolved immediately to revenge their father's death, and was coming upon Malichus with an army for that purpose, the elder of his sons, Phasaelus, thought it best rather to get this man into their hands by policy, lest they should appear to begin a civil war in the country; so he accepted of Malichus's defense for himself, and pretended to believe him that he had had no hand in the violent death of Antipater his father, but erected a fine monument for him. Herod also went to

Samaria; and when he found them in great distress, he revived their spirits, and composed their differences.

5. However, a little after this, Herod, upon the approach of a festival, came with his soldiers into the city; whereupon Malichus was aftrighted, and persuaded Hyrcanus not to permit him to come into the city. Hyrcanus complied; and, for a pretense of excluding him, alleged, that a rout of strangers ought not to be admitted when the multitude were purifying themselves. But Herod had little regard to the messengers that were sent to him, and entered the city in the night time, and aftrighted Malichus; yet did he remit nothing of his former dissimulation, but wept for Antipater, and bewailed him as a friend of his with a loud voice; but Herod and his friends though, it proper not openly to contradict Malichus's hypocrisy, but to give him tokens of mutual friendship, in order to prevent his suspicion of them.

6. However, Herod sent to Cassius, and informed him of the murder of his father; who knowing what sort of man Malichus was as to his morals, sent him back word that he should revenge his father's death; and also sent privately to the commanders of his army at Tyre, with orders to assist Herod in the execution of a very just design of his. Now when Cassius had taken Laodicea, they all went together to him, and carried him garlands and money; and Herod thought that Malichus might be punished while he was there; but he was somewhat apprehensive of the thing, and designed to make some great attempt, and because his son was then a hostage at Tyre, he went to that city, and resolved to steal him away privately, and to march thence into Judea; and as Cassius was in haste to march against Antony, he thought to bring the country to revolt, and to procure the government for himself. But Providence opposed his counsels; and Herod being a shrewd man, and perceiving what his intention was, he sent thither beforehand a servant, in appearance indeed to get a supper ready, for he had said before that he would feast them all there, but in reality to the commanders of the army, whom he persuaded to go out against Malichus, with their daggers. So they went out and met the man near the city, upon the sea-shore, and there stabbed him. Whereupon Hyrcanus was so astonished at what had happened, that his speech failed him; and when, after some difficulty, he had recovered himself, he asked Herod what the matter could be, and who it was that slew Malichus; and when he said that it was done by the

command of Cassius, he commended the action; for that Malichus was a very wicked man, and one that conspired against his own country. And this was the punishment that was inflicted on Malichus for what he wickedly did to Antipater.

7. But when Cassius was marched out of Syria, disturbances arose in Judea; for Felix, who was left at Jerusalem with an army, made a sudden attempt against Phasaelus, and the people themselves rose in arms; but Herod went to Fabius, the prefect of Damascus, and was desirous to run to his brother's assistance, but was hindered by a distemper that seized upon him, till Phasaelus by himself had been too hard for Felix, and had shut him up in the tower, and there, on certain conditions, dismissed him. Phasaelus also complained of Hyrcanus, that although he had received a great many benefits from them, yet did he support their enemies; for Malichus's brother had made many places to revolt, and kept garrisons in them, and particularly Masada, the strongest fortress of them all. In the mean time, Herod was recovered of his disease, and came and took from Felix all the places he bad gotten; and, upon certain conditions, dismissed him also.

12 *Herod Ejects Antigonus, the Son of Aristobulus Out of Judea, and Gains the Friendship of Antony, Who Was Now Come into Syria, by Sending Him Much Money; on Which Account He Would Not Admit of Those That Would Have Accused Herod: And What It Was That Antony Wrote to the Tyrians in Behalf*

1. NOW[22] Ptolemy, the son of Menneus, brought back into Judea Antigonus, the son of Aristobulus, who had already raised an army, and had, by money, made Fabius to be his friend, add this because

22. In this and the following chapters the reader will easily remark, how truly Gronovius observes, in his notes on the Roman decrees in favor of the Jews, that their rights and privileges were commonly purchased of the Romans with money. Many examples of this sort, both as to the Romans and others in authority, will occur in our Josephus, both now and hereafter, and need not be taken particular notice of on the several occasions in these notes. Accordingly, the chief captain confesses to St. Paul that "with a great sum he had obtained his freedom," Acts 22:28; as had St. Paul's ancestors, very probably, purchased the like freedom for their family by money, as the same author justly concludes also.

he was of kin to him. Marion also gave him assistance. He had been left by Cassius to tyrannize over Tyre; for this Cussiris was a man that seized on Syria, and then kept it under, in the way of a tyrant. Marion also marched into Galilee, which lay in his neighborhood, and took three of his fortresses, and put garrisons into them to keep them. But when Herod came, he took all from him; but the Tyrian garrison he dismissed in a very civil manner; nay, to some of the soldiers he made presents out of the good-will he bare to that city. When he had despatched these affairs, and was gone to meet Antigonus, he joined battle with him, and beat him, and drove him out of Judea presently, when he was just come into its borders. But when he was come to Jerusalem, Hyrcanus and the people put garlands about his head; for he had already contracted an affinity with the family of Hyrcanus by having espoused a descendant of his, and for that reason Herod took the greater care of him, as being to marry the daughter of Alexander, the son of Aristobulus, add the granddaughter of Hyrcanus, by which wife he became the father of three male and two female children. He had also married before this another wife, out of a lower family of his own nation, whose name was Doris, by whom he had his eldest son Antipater.

2. Now Antonius and Caesar had beaten Cassius near Philippi, as others have related; but after the victory, Caesar went into Gaul, [Italy,] and Antony marched for Asia, who, when he was arrived at Bithynia, he had ambassadors that met him from all parts. The principal men also of the Jews came thither, to accuse Phasaelus and Herod; and they said that Hyrcanus had indeed the appearance of reigning, but that these men had all the power: but Antony paid great respect to Herod, who was come to him to make his defense against his accusers, on which account his adversaries could not so much as obtain a hearing; which favor Herod had gained of Antony by money. But still, when Antony was come to Ephesus, Hyrcanus the high priest, and our nation, sent an embassage to him, which carried a crown of gold with them, and desired that he would write to the governors of the provinces, to set those Jews free who had been carried captive by Cassius, and this without their having fought against him, and to restore them that country, which, in the days of Cassius, had been taken from them. Antony thought the Jews' desires were just, and wrote immediately to Hyrcanus, and to the Jews. He also sent, at the

same time, a decree to the Tyrians; the contents of which were to the same purpose.

3. "Marcus Antonius, imperator, to Hyrcanus the high priest and ethnarch of the Jews, sendeth greeting. It you be in health, it is well; I am also in health, with the army. Lysimachus, the son of Pausanias, and Josephus, the son of Menneus, and Alexander, the son of Theodorus, your ambassadors, met me at Ephesus, and have renewed the embassage which they had formerly been upon at Rome, and have diligently acquitted themselves of the present embassage, which thou and thy nation have intrusted to them, and have fully declared the goodwill thou hast for us. I am therefore satisfied, both by your actions and your words, that you are well-disposed to us; and I understand that your conduct of life is constant and religious: so I reckon upon you as our own. But when those that were adversaries to you, and to the Roman people, abstained neither from cities nor temples, and did not observe the agreement they had confirmed by oath, it was not only on account of our contest with them, but on account of all mankind in common, that we have taken vengeance on those who have been the authors of great injustice towards men, and of great wickedness towards the gods; for the sake of which we suppose it was that the sun turned away his light from us,[23] as unwilling to view the horrid crime they were guilty of in the case of Caesar. We have also overcome their conspiracies, which threatened the gods themselves, which Macedonia received, as it is a climate peculiarly proper for impious and insolent attempts; and we have overcome that confused rout of men, half mad with spite against us, which they got together at Philippi in Macedonia, when they seized on the places that were proper for their purpose, and, as it were, walled them round with mountains to the very sea, and where the passage was open only through a single gate. This victory we gained, because the gods had condemned those men for their wicked enterprises. Now Brutus, when he had fled as far as Philippi, was shut up by us, and became a partaker of the same perdition with Cassius; and now these

23. This clause plainly alludes to that well-known but unusual and very long darkness of the sun which happened upon the murder of Julius Cesar by Brutus and Cassius, which is greatly taken notice of by Virgil, Pliny, and other Roman authors. See Virgil's Georgics, B. I., just before the end; and Pliny's Nat. Hist. B. IL ch. 33.

have received their punishment, we suppose that we may enjoy peace for the time to come, and that Asia may be at rest from war. We therefore make that peace which God hath given us common to our confederates also, insomuch that the body of Asia is now recovered out of that distemper it was under by the means of our victory. I, therefore, bearing in mind both thee and your nation, shall take care of what may be for your advantage. I have also sent epistles in writing to the several cities, that if any persons, whether free-men or bond-men, have been sold under the spear by Caius Cassius, or his subordinate officers, they may be set free. And I will that you kindly make use of the favors which I and Dolabella have granted you. I also forbid the Tyrians to use any violence with you; and for what places of the Jews they now possess, I order them to restore them. I have withal accepted of the crown which thou sentest me."

4. "Marcus Antonius, imperator, to the magistrates, senate, and people of Tyre, sendeth greeting. The ambassadors of Hyrcanus, the high priest and ethnarch [of the Jews], appeared before me at Ephesus, and told me that you are in possession of part of their country, which you entered upon under the government of our adversaries. Since, therefore, we have undertaken a war for the obtaining the government, and have taken care to do what was agreeable to piety and justice, and have brought to punishment those that had neither any remembrance of the kindnesses they had received, nor have kept their oaths, I will that you be at peace with those that are our confederates; as also, that what you have taken by the means of our adversaries shall not be reckoned your own, but be returned to those from whom you took them; for none of them took their provinces or their armies by the gift of the senate, but they seized them by force, and bestowed them by violence upon such as became useful to them in their unjust proceedings. Since, therefore, those men have received the punishment due to them, we desire that our confederates may retain whatsoever it was that they formerly possessed without disturbance, and that you restore all the places which belong to Hyrcanus, the ethnarch of the Jews, which you have had, though it were but one day before Caius Cassius began an unjustifiable war against us, and entered into our province; nor do you use any force against him, in order to weaken him, that he may not be able to dispose of that which is his own; but if you have any contest with him about your respective rights, it shall be lawful for

you to plead your cause when we come upon the places concerned, for we shall alike preserve the rights and hear all the causes of our confederates."

5. "Marcus Antonius, imperator, to the magistrates, senate, and people of Tyre, sendeth greeting. I have sent you my decree, of which I will that ye take care that it be engraven on the public tables, in Roman and Greek letters, and that it stand engraven in the most illustrious places, that it may be read by all. Marcus Antonius, imperator, one of the triumvirate over the public affairs, made this declaration: Since Caius Cassius, in this revolt he hath made, hath pillaged that province which belonged not to him, and was held by garrisons there encamped, while they were our confederates, and hath spoiled that nation of the Jews that was in friendship with the Roman people, as in war; and since we have overcome his madness by arms, we now correct by our decrees and judicial determinations what he hath laid waste, that those things may be restored to our confederates. And as for what hath been sold of the Jewish possessions, whether they be bodies or possessions, let them be released; the bodies into that state of freedom they were originally in, and the possessions to their former owners. I also will that he who shall not comply with this decree of mine shall be punished for his disobedience; and if such a one be caught, I will take care that the offenders suffer condign punishment."

6. The same thing did Antony write to the Sidonians, and the Antiochians, and the Aradians. We have produced these decrees, therefore, as marks for futurity of the truth of what we have said, that the Romans had a great concern about our nation.

13 *How Antony Made Herod and Phasaelus Tetrarchs, After They Had Been Accused to No Purpose; and How the Parthians When They Brought Antigonus into Judea Took Hyrcanus and Phasaelus Captives. Herod's Flight; and What Afflictions Hyrcanus and Phasaelus Endured*

1. WHEN after this Antony came into Syria, Cleopatra met him in Cilicia, and brought him to fall in love with her. And there came now also a hundred of the most potent of the Jews to accuse Herod and those about him, and set the men of the greatest eloquence among

them to speak. But Messala contradicted them, on behalf of the young men, and all this in the presence of Hyrcanus, who was Herod's father-in-law[24] already. When Antony had heard both sides at Daphne, he asked Hyrcanus who they were that governed the nation best. He replied, Herod and his friends. Hereupon Antony, by reason of the old hospitable friendship he had made with his father [Antipater], at that time when he was with Gabinius, he made both Herod and Phasaelus tetrarchs, and committed the public affairs of the Jews to them, and wrote letters to that purpose. He also bound fifteen of their adversaries, and was going to kill them, but that Herod obtained their pardon.

2. Yet did not these men continue quiet when they were come back, but a thousand of the Jews came to Tyre to meet him there, whither the report was that he would come. But Antony was corrupted by the money which Herod and his brother had given him; and so he gave order to the governor of the place to punish the Jewish ambassadors, who were for making innovations, and to settle the government upon Herod; but Herod went out hastily to them, and Hyrcanus was with him, (for they stood upon the shore before the city,) and he charged them to go their ways, because great mischief would befall them if they went on with their accusation. But they did not acquiesce; whereupon the Romans ran upon them with their daggers, and slew some, and wounded more of them, and the rest fled away and went home, and lay still in great consternation. And when the people made a clamor against Herod, Antony was so provoked at it, that he slew the prisoners.

3. Now, in the second year, Pacorus, the king of Parthia's son, and Barzapharnes, a commander of the Parthians, possessed themselves of Syria. Ptolemy, the son of Menneus, also was now dead, and Lysanias his son took his government, and made a league of friendship with Antigonus, the son of Aristobulus; and in order to obtain it, made use of that commander, who had great interest in him. Now Antigonus had promised to give the Parthians a thousand talents, and five hundred women, upon condition they would take the government

---

24. We may here take notice that espousals alone were of old esteemed a sufficient foundation for affinity, Hyrcanus being here called father-in-law to Herod because his granddaughter Mariarune was betrothed to him, although the marriage was not completed till four years afterwards. See Matthew 1:16.

away from Hyrcanus, and bestow it upon him, and withal kill Herod. And although he did not give them what he had promised, yet did the Parthians make an expedition into Judea on that account, and carried Antigonus with them. Pacorus went along the maritime parts, but the commander Barzapharnes through the midland. Now the Tyrians excluded Pacorus, but the Sidontans and those of Ptolemais received him. However, Pacorus sent a troop of horsemen into Judea, to take a view of the state of the country, and to assist Antigonus; and sent also the king's butler, of the same name with himself. So when the Jews that dwelt about Mount Carmel came to Antigonus, and were ready to march with him into Judea, Antigonus hoped to get some part of the country by their assistance. The place is called Drymi; and when some others came and met them, the men privately fell upon Jerusalem; and when some more were come to them, they got together in great numbers, and came against the king's palace, and besieged it. But as Phasaelus's and Herod's party came to the other's assistance, and a battle happened between them in the market-place, the young men beat their enemies, and pursued them into the temple, and sent some armed men into the adjoining houses to keep them in, who yet being destitute of such as should support them, were burnt, and the houses with them, by the people who rose up against them. But Herod was revenged on these seditious adversaries of his a little afterward for this injury they had offered him, when he fought with them, and slew a great number of them.

4. But while there were daily skirmishes, the enemy waited for the coming of the multitude out of the country to Pentecost, a feast of ours so called; and when that day was come, many ten thousands of the people were gathered together about the temple, some in armor, and some without. Now those that came guarded both the temple and the city, excepting what belonged to the palace, which Herod guarded with a few of his soldiers; and Phasaelus had the charge of the wall, while Herod, with a body of his men, sallied out upon the enemy, who lay in the suburbs, and fought courageously, and put many ten thousands to flight, some flying into the city, and some into the temple, and some into the outer fortifications, for some such fortifications there were in that place. Phasaelus came also to his assistance; yet was Pacorus, the general of the Parthians, at the desire of Antigonus, admitted into the city, with a few of his

horsemen, under pretence indeed as if he would still the sedition, but in reality to assist Antigonus in obtaining the government. And when Phasaelus met him, and received him kindly, Pacorus persuaded him to go himself as ambassador to Barzapharnes, which was done fraudulently. Accordingly, Phasaelus, suspecting no harm, complied with his proposal, while Herod did not give his consent to what was done, because of the perfidiousness of these barbarians, but desired Phasaelus rather to fight those that were come into the city.

5. So both Hyrcanus and Phasaelus went on the embassage; but Pacorus left with Herod two hundred horsemen, and ten men, who were called the *freemen,* and conducted the others on their journey; and when they were in Galilee, the governors of the cities there met them in their arms. Barzaphanles also received them at the first with cheerfulness, and made them presents, though he afterward conspired against them; and Phasaelus, with his horsemen, were conducted to the sea-side. But when they heard that Antigonus had promised to give the Parthians a thousand talents, and five hundred women, to assist him against them, they soon had a suspicion of the barbarians. Moreover, there was one who informed them that snares were laid for them by night, while a guard came about them secretly; and they had then been seized upon, had not they waited for the seizure of Herod by the Parthians that were about Jerusalem, lest, upon the slaughter of Hyrcanus and Phasaelus, he should have an intimation of it, and escape out of their hands. And these were the circumstances they were now in; and they saw who they were that guarded them. Some persons indeed would have persuaded Phasaelus to fly away immediately on horseback, and not stay any longer; and there was one Ophellius, who, above all the rest, was earnest with him to do so; for he had heard of this treachery from Saramalla, the richest of all the Syrians at that time, who also promised to provide him ships to carry him off; for the sea was just by them. But he had no mind to desert Hyrcanus, nor bring his brother into danger; but he went to Barzapharnes, and told him he did not act justly when he made such a contrivance against them; for that if he wanted money, he would give him more than Antigonus; and besides, that it was a horrible thing to slay those that came to him upon the security of their oaths, and that when they had done them no injury. But the barbarian swore to him that there was no truth in

any of his suspicions, but that he was troubled with nothing but false proposals, and then went away to Pacorus.

6. But as soon as he was gone away, some men came and bound Hyrcanus and Phasaelus, while Phasaelus greatly reproached the Parthians for their perjury; However, that butler who was sent against Herod had it in command to get him without the walls of the city, and seize upon him; but messengers had been sent by Phasaelus to inform Herod of the perfidiousness of the Parthians. And when he knew that the enemy had seized upon them, he went to Pacorus, and to the most potent of the Parthians, as to the lord of the rest, who, although they knew the whole matter, dissembled with him in a deceitful way; and said that he ought to go out with them before the walls, and meet those which were bringing him his letters, for that they were not taken by his adversaries, but were coming to give him an account of the good success Phasaelus had had. Herod did not give credit to what they said; for he had heard that his brother was seized upon by others also; and the daughter of Hyrcanus, whose daughter he had espoused, was his monitor also [not to credit them], which made him still more suspicious of the Parthians; for although other people did not give heed to her, yet did he believe her as a woman of very great wisdom.

7. Now while the Parthians were in consultation what was fit to be done; for they did not think it proper to make an open attempt upon a person of his character; and while they put off the determination to the next day, Herod was under great disturbance of mind, and rather inclining to believe the reports he heard about his brother and the Parthians, than to give heed to what was said on the other side, he determined, that when the evening came on, he would make use of it for his flight, and not make any longer delay, as if the dangers from the enemy were not yet certain. He therefore removed with the armed men whom he had with him; and set his wives upon the beasts, as also his mother, and sister, and her whom he was about to marry, [Mariamne,] the daughter of Alexander, the son of Aristobulus, with her mother, the daughter of Hyrcanus, and his youngest brother, and all their servants, and the rest of the multitude that was with him, and without the enemy's privity pursued his way to Idumea. Nor could any enemy of his who then saw him in this case be so hardhearted, but would have commiserated his fortune, while the women drew along their infant children and left their own country, and their friends in prison, with

tears in their eyes, and sad lamentations, and in expectation of nothing but what was of a melancholy nature.

8. But for Herod himself, he raised his mind above the miserable state he was in, and was of good courage in the midst of his misfortunes; and as he passed along, he bid them every one to be of good cheer, and not to give themselves up to sorrow, because that would hinder them in their flight, which was now the only hope of safety that they had. Accordingly, they tried to bear with patience the calamity they were under, as he exhorted them to do; yet was he once almost going to kill himself, upon the overthrow of a waggon, and the danger his mother was then in of being killed; and this on two accounts, because of his great concern for her, and because he was afraid lest, by this delay, the enemy should overtake him in the pursuit: but as he was drawing his sword, and going to kill himself therewith, those that were present restrained him, and being so many in number, were too hard for him; and told him that he ought not to desert them, and leave them a prey to their enemies, for that it was not the part of a brave man to free himself from the distresses he was in, and to overlook his friends that were in the same distresses also. So he was compelled to let that horrid attempt alone, partly out of shame at what they said to him, and partly out of regard to the great number of those that would not permit him to do what he intended. So he encouraged his mother, and took all the care of her the time would allow, and proceeded on the way he proposed to go with the utmost haste, and that was to the fortress of Masada. And as he had many skirmishes with such of the Parthians as attacked him and pursued him, he was conqueror in them all.

9. Nor indeed was he free from the Jews all along as he was in his flight; for by that time he was gotten sixty furlongs out of the city, and was upon the road, they fell upon him, and fought hand to hand with him, whom he also put to flight, and overcame, not like one that was in distress and in necessity, but like one that was excellently prepared for war, and had what he wanted in great plenty. And in this very place where he overcame the Jews it was that he some time afterward build a most excellent palace, and a city round about it, and called it Herodium. And when he was come to Idumea, at a place called Thressa, his brother Joseph met him, and he then held a council to take advice about all his affairs, and what was fit to be

done in his circumstances, since he had a great multitude that followed him, besides his mercenary soldiers, and the place Masada, whither he proposed to fly, was too small to contain so great a multitude; so he sent away the greater part of his company, being above nine thousand, and bid them go, some one way, and some another, and so save themselves in Idumea, and gave them what would buy them provisions in their journey. But he took with him those that were the least encumbered, and were most intimate with him, and came to the fortress, and placed there his wives and his followers, being eight hundred in number, there being in the place a sufficient quantity of corn and water, and other necessaries, and went directly for Petra, in Arabia. But when it was day, the Parthians plundered all Jerusalem, and the palace, and abstained from nothing but Hyrcanus's money, which was three hundred talents. A great deal of Herod's money escaped, and principally all that the man had been so provident as to send into Idumea beforehand; nor indeed did what was in the city suffice the Parthians, but they went out into the country, and plundered it, and demolished the city Marissa.

10. And thus was Antigonus brought back into Judea by the king of the Parthians, and received Hyrcanus and Phasaelus for his prisoners; but he was greatly cast down because the women had escaped, whom he intended to have given the enemy, as having promised they should have them, with the money, for their reward: but being afraid that Hyrcanus, who was under the guard of the Parthians, might have his kingdom restored to him by the multitude, he cut off his ears, and thereby took care that the high priesthood should never come to him any more, because he was maimed, while the law required that this dignity should belong to none but such as had all their members entire[25] But now one cannot but here admire the fortitude of Phasaelus, who, perceiving that he was to be put to death, did not think death any terrible thing at all; but to die thus by the means of his enemy, this he thought a most pitiable and dishonorable thing; and therefore, since he had not his hands at liberty, but the bonds he was in prevented him from killing himself thereby, he dashed his head against a great stone, and thereby took away his own life, which he thought to be the

25. This law of Moses, that the priests were to be "without blemish," as to all the parts of their bodies, is in Leviticus 21:17–24

best thing he could do in such a distress as he was in, and thereby put it out of the power of the enemy to bring him to any death he pleased. It is also reported, that when he had made a great wound in his head, Antigonus sent physicians to cure it, and, by ordering them to infuse poison into the wound, killed him. However, Phasaelus hearing, before he was quite dead, by a certain woman, that his brother Herod had escaped the enemy, underwent his death cheerfully, since he now left behind him one who would revenge his death, and who was able to inflict punishment on his enemies.

14 *How Herod Got Away from the King of Arabia and Made Haste to Go into Egypt and Thence Went Away in Haste Also to Rome; and How, by Promising a Great Deal of Money to Antony He Obtained of the Senate and of Caesar to Be Made King of the Jews*

1. AS for Herod, the great miseries he was in did not discourage him, but made him sharp in discovering surprising undertakings; for he went to Malchus, king of Arabia, whom he had formerly been very kind to, in order to receive somewhat by way of requital, now he was in more than ordinary want of it, and desired he would let him have some money, either by way of loan, or as his free gift, on account of the many benefits he had received from him; for not knowing what was become of his brother, he was in haste to redeem him out of the hand of his enemies, as willing to give three hundred talents for the price of his redemption. He also took with him the son of Phasaelus, who was a child of but seven years of age, for this very reason, that he might be a hostage for the repayment of the money. But there came messengers from Malchus to meet him, by whom he was desired to be gone, for that the Parthians had laid a charge upon him not to entertain Herod. This was only a pretense which he made use of, that he might not be obliged to repay him what he owed him; and this he was further induced to by the principal men among the Arabians, that they might cheat him of what sums they had received from [his father] Antipater, and which he had committed to their fidelity. He made answer, that he did not intend to be troublesome to them by his coning thither, but that he desired only to discourse with them about certain affairs that were to him of the greatest importance.

2. Hereupon he resolved to go away, and did go very prudently the road to Egypt; and then it was that he lodged in a certain temple; for he had left a great many of his followers there. On the next day he came to Rhinocolura, and there it was that he heard what was befallen his brother. Though Malehus soon repented of what he had done, and came running after Herod; but with no manner of success, for he was gotten a very great way off, and made haste into the road to Pelusium; and when the stationary ships that lay there hindered him from sailing to Alexandria, he went to their captains, by whose assistance, and that out of much reverence of and great regard to him, he was conducted into the city [Alexandria], and was retained there by Cleopatra; yet was she not able to prevail with him to stay there, because he was making haste to Rome, even though the weather was stormy, and he was informed that the affairs of Italy were very tumultuous, and in great disorder.

3. So he set sail from thence to Pamphylia, and falling into a violent storm, he had much ado to escape to Rhodes, with the loss of the ship's burden; and there it was that two of his friends, Sappinas and Ptolemeus, met with him; and as he found that city very much damaged in the war against Cassius, though he were in necessity himself, he neglected not to do it a kindness, but did what he could to recover it to its former state. He also built there a three-decked ship, and set sail thence, with his friends, for Italy, and came to the port of Brundusium; and when he was come from thence to Rome, he first related to Antony what had befallen him in Judea, and how Phasaelus his brother was seized on by the Parthians, and put to death by them, and how Hyrcanus was detained captive by them, and how they had made Antigonus king, who had promised them a sum of money, no less than a thousand talents, with five hundred women, who were to be of the principal families, and of the Jewish stock; and that he had carried off the women by night; and that, by undergoing a great many hardships, he had escaped the hands of his enemies; as also, that his own relations were in danger of being besieged and taken, and that he had sailed through a storm, and contemned all these terrible dangers of it, in order to come, as soon as possible, to him, who was his hope and only succor at this time.

4. This account made Antony commiserate the change that had happened in Herod's condition;[26] and reasoning with himself that this was a common case among those that are placed in such great dignities, and that they are liable to the mutations that come from fortune, he was very ready to give him the assistance he desired, and this because he called to mind the friendship he had had with Antipater because Herod offered him money to make him king, as he had formerly given it him to make him tetrarch, and chiefly because of his hatred to Antigonus; for he took him to be a seditious person, and an enemy to the Romans. Caesar was also the forwarder to raise Herod's dignity, and to give him his assistance in what he desired, on account of the toils of war which he had himself undergone with Antipater his father in Egypt, and of the hospitality he had treated him withal, and the kindness he had always showed him, as also to gratify Antony, who was very zealous for Herod. So a senate was convocated; and Messala first, and then Atratinus, introduced Herod into it, and enlarged upon the benefits they had received from his father, and put them in mind of the good-will he had borne to the Romans. At the same time, they accused Antigonus, and declared him an enemy, not only because of his former opposition to them, but that he had now overlooked the Romans, and taken the government from the Parthians. Upon this the senate was irritated; and Antony informed them further, that it was for their advantage in the Parthian war that Herod should be king. This seemed good to all the senators; and so they made a decree accordingly.

5. And this was the principal instance of Antony's affection for Herod, that he not only procured him a kingdom which he did not expect, (for he did not come with an intention to ask the kingdom for himself, which he did not suppose the Romans would grant him, who used to bestow it on some of the royal family, but intended to desire it for his wife's brother, who was grandson by his father to Aristobulus, and to Hyrcanus by his mother,) but that he procured it for him so suddenly, that he obtained what he did not expect, and

---

26. Concerning the chronology of Herod, and the time when he was first made king at Rome, and concerning the time when he began his second reign, without a rival, upon the conquest and slaughter of Antigonus, both principally derived from this and the two next chapters in Josephus, see the note on sect. 6, and ch. 15. sect. 10.

departed out of Italy in so few days as seven in all. This young man [the grandson] Herod afterward took care to have slain, as we shall show in its proper place. But when the senate was dissolved, Antony and Caesar went out of the senate house with Herod between them, and with the consuls and other magistrates before them, in order to offer sacrifices, and to lay up their decrees in the capitol. Antony also feasted Herod the first day of his reign. And thus did this man receive the kingdom, having obtained it on the hundred and eighty-fourth olympiad, when Caius Domitius Calvinus was consul the second time, and Caius Asinius Pollio [the first time].

6. All this while Antigonus besieged those that were in Masada, who had plenty of all other necessaries, but were only in want of water[27] insomuch that on this occasion Joseph, Herod's brother, was contriving to run away from it, with two hundred of his dependents, to the Arabians; for he had heard that Malchus repented of the offenses he had been guilty of with regard to Herod; but God, by sending rain in the night time, prevented his going away, for their cisterns were thereby filled, and he was under no necessity of running away on that account; but they were now of good courage, and the more so, because the sending that plenty of water which they had been in want of seemed a mark of Divine Providence; so they made a sally, and fought hand to hand with Antigonus's soldiers, (with some openly, with some privately,) and destroyed a great number of them. At the same time Ventidius, the general of the Romans, was sent out of Syria, to drive the Parthians out of it, and marched after them into Judea, in pretense indeed to succor Joseph; but in reality the whole affair was no more than a stratagem, in order to get money of Antigonus; so they pitched their camp very near to Jerusalem, and stripped Antigonus of a great deal of money, and then he retired himself with the greater part of the army; but, that the wickedness he had been guilty of might be found out, he left Silo there, with a certain part of his soldiers, with whom also Antigonus cultivated an acquaintance, that he might cause him no disturbance, and was still in hopes that the Parthians would come again and defend him.

---

27. This grievous want of water at Masada, till the place had like to have been taken by the Parthians, (mentioned both here, and Of the War, B. I. ch. 15. sect. 1,) is an indication that it was now summer time.

15 *How Herod Sailed Out of Italy to Judea, and Fought with Antigonus and What Other Things Happened in Judea About That Time*

1. BY this time Herod had sailed out of Italy to Ptolemais, and had gotten together no small army, both of strangers and of his own countrymen, and marched through Galilee against Antignus. Silo also, and Ventidius, came and assisted him, being persuaded by Dellius, who was sent by Antony to assist in bringing back Herod. Now for Ventidius, he was employed in composing the disturbances that had been made in the cities by the means of the Parthians; and for Silo, he was in Judea indeed, but corrupted by Antigonus. However, as Herod went along his army increased every day, and all Galilee, with some small exception, joined him; but as he was to those that were in Masada, (for he was obliged to endeavor to save those that were in that fortress now they were besieged, because they were his relations,) Joppa was a hinderance to him, for it was necessary for him to take that place first, it being a city at variance with him, that no strong hold might be left in his enemies' hands behind him when he should go to Jerusalem. And when Silo made this a pretense for rising up from Jerusalem, and was thereupon pursued by the Jews, Herod fell upon them with a small body of men, and both put the Jews to flight and saved Silo, when he was very poorly able to defend himself; but when Herod had taken Joppa, he made haste to set free those of his family that were in Masada. Now of the people of the country, some joined him because of the friendship they had had with his father, and some because of the splendid appearance he made, and others by way of requital for the benefits they had received from both of them; but the greatest number came to him in hopes of getting somewhat from him afterward, if he were once firmly settled in the kingdom.

2. Herod had now a strong army; and as he marched on, Antigonus laid snares and ambushes in the passes and places most proper for them; but in truth he thereby did little or no damage to the enemy. So Herod received those of his family out of Masada, and the fortress Ressa, and then went on for Jerusalem. The soldiery also that was with Silo accompanied him all along, as did many of the citizens, being afraid of his power; and as soon as he had pitched his camp on the west side of the city, the soldiers that were set to guard that part shot

their arrows and threw their darts at him; and when some sallied out in a crowd, and came to fight hand to hand with the first ranks of Herod's army, he gave orders that they should, in the first place, make proclamation about the wall, that he came for the good of the people, and for the preservation of the city, and not to bear any old grudge at even his most open enemies, but ready to forget the offenses which his greatest adversaries had done him. But Antigonus, by way of reply to what Herod had caused to be proclaimed, and this before the Romans, and before Silo also, said that they would not do justly, if they gave the kingdom to Herod, who was no more than a private man, and an Idumean, i.e. a half Jew,[28] whereas they ought to bestow it on one of the royal family, as their custom was; for that in case they at present bear an ill-will to him, and had resolved to deprive him of the kingdom, as having received it from the Parthians, yet were there many others of his family that might by their law take it, and these such as had no way offended the Romans; and being of the sacerdotal family, it would be an unworthy thing to put them by. Now while they said thus one to another, and fell to reproaching one another on both sides, Antigonus permitted his own men that were upon the wall to defend themselves, who using their bows, and showing great alacrity against their enemies, easily drove them away from the towers.

3. And now it was that Silo discovered that he had taken bribes; for he set a good number of his soldiers to complain aloud of the want of provisions they were in, and to require money to buy them food; and that it was fit to let them go into places proper for winter quarters, since the places near the city were a desert, by reason that Antigonus's soldiers had carried all away; so he set the army upon removing, and endeavored to march away; but Herod pressed Silo not to depart, and exhorted Silo's captains and soldiers not to desert him, when Caesar, and Antony, and the senate had sent him thither, for that

---

28. This affirmation of Antigonus, spoken in the days of Herod, and in a manner to his face, that he was an Idumean, i.e. a half Jew, seems to me of much greater authority than that pretense of his favorite and flatterer Nicolaus of Damascus, that he derived his pedigree from Jews as far backward as the Babylonish captivity, ch. 1. sect. 3. Accordingly Josephus always esteems him an Idumean, though he says his father Antipater was of the same people with the Jews, ch. viii. sect. 1. and by birth a Jew, Antiq. B. XX. ch. 8. sect. 7; as indeed all such proselytes of justice, as the Idumeans, were in time esteemed the very same people with the Jews.

he would provide them plenty of all the things they wanted, and easily procure them a great abundance of what they required; after which entreaty, he immediately went out into the country, and left not the least pretense to Silo for his departure; for he brought an unexpected quantity of provisions, and sent to those friends of his who inhabited about Samaria to bring down corn, and wine, and oil, and cattle, and all other provisions, to Jericho, that those might be no want of a supply for the soldiers for the time to come. Antigonus was sensible of this, and sent presently over the country such as might restrain and lie in ambush for those that went out for provisions. So these men obeyed the orders of Antigonus, and got together a great number of armed men about Jericho, and sat upon the mountains, and watched those that brought the provisions. However, Herod was not idle in the mean time, for he took ten bands of soldiers, of whom five were of the Romans, and five of the Jews, with some mercenaries among them, and with some few horsemen, and came to Jericho; and as they found the city deserted, but that five hundred of them had settled themselves on the tops of the hills, with their wives and children, those he took and sent away; but the Romans fell upon the city, and plundered it, and found the houses full of all sorts of good things. So the king left a garrison at Jericho, and came back again, and sent the Roman army to take their winter quarters in the countries that were come over to him, Judea, and Galilee, and Samaria. And so much did Antigonus gain of Silo for the bribes he gave him, that part of the army should be quartered at Lydda, in order to please Antony. So the Romans laid their weapons aside, and lived in plenty of all things.

4. But Herod was not pleased with lying still, but sent out his brother Joseph against Idumea with two thousand armed footmen, and four hundred horsemen, while he himself came to Samaria, and left his mother and his other relations there, for they were already gone out of Masada, and went into Galilee, to take certain places which were held by the garrisons of Antigonus; and he passed on to Sepphoris, as God sent a snow, while Antigonus's garrisons withdrew themselves, and had great plenty of provisions. He also went thence, and resolved to destroy those robbers that dwelt in the caves, and did much mischief in the country; so he sent a troop of horsemen, and three companies of armed footmen, against them. They were very near to a village called Arbela; and on the fortieth day after, he came himself

with his whole army: and as the enemy sallied out boldly upon him, the left wing of his army gave way; but he appearing with a body of men, put those to flight who were already conquerors, and recalled his men that ran away. He also pressed upon his enemies, and pursued them as far as the river Jordan, though they ran away by different roads. So he brought over to him all Galilee, excepting those that dwelt in the caves, and distributed money to every one of his soldiers, giving them a hundred and fifty drachmae apiece, and much more to their captains, and sent them into winter quarters; at which time Silo came to him, and his commanders with him, because Antigonus would not give them provisions any longer, for he supplied them for no more than one month; nay, he had sent to all the country about, and ordered them to carry off the provisions that were there, and retire to the mountains, that the Romans might have no provisions to live upon, and so might perish by famine. But Herod committed the care of that matter to Pheroras, his youngest brother, and ordered him to repair Alexandrium also. Accordingly, he quickly made the soldiers abound with great plenty of provisions, and rebuilt Alexandrium, which had been before desolate.

5. About this time it was that Antony continued some time at Athens, and that Ventidius, who was now in Syria, sent for Silo, and commanded him to assist Herod, in the first place, to finish the present war, and then to send for their confederates for the war they were themselves engaged in; but as for Herod, he went in haste against the robbers that were in the caves, and sent Silo away to Ventidius, while he marched against them. These caves were in mountains that were exceeding abrupt, and in their middle were no other than precipices, with certain entrances into the caves, and those caves were encompassed with sharp rocks, and in these did the robbers lie concealed, with all their families about them; but the king caused certain chests to be made, in order to destroy them, and to be hung down, bound about with iron chains, by an engine, from the top of the mountain, it being not possible to get up to them, by reason of the sharp ascent of the mountains, nor to creep down to them from above. Now these chests were filled with armed men, who had long hooks in their hands, by which they might pull out such as resisted them, and then tumble them down, and kill them by so doing; but the letting the chests down proved to be a matter of great danger, because of the vast depth they

were to be let down, although they had their provisions in the chests themselves. But when the chests were let down, and not one of those in the mouths of the caves durst come near them, but lay still out of fear, some of the armed men girt on their armor, and by both their hands took hold of the chain by which the chests were let down, and went into the mouths of the caves, because they fretted that such delay was made by the robbers not daring to come out of the caves; and when they were at any of those mouths, they first killed many of those that were in the mouths with their darts, and afterwards pulled those to them that resisted them with their hooks, and tumbled them down the precipices, and afterwards went into the caves, and killed many more, and then went into their chests again, and lay still there; but, upon this, terror seized the rest, when they heard the lamentations that were made, and they despaired of escaping. However, when the night came on, that put an end to the whole work; and as the king proclaimed pardon by a herald to such as delivered themselves up to him, many accepted of the offer. The same method of assault was made use of the next day; and they went further, and got out in baskets to fight them, and fought them at their doors, and sent fire among them, and set their caves on fire, for there was a great deal of combustible matter within them. Now there was one old man who was caught within one of these caves, with seven children and a wife; these prayed him to give them leave to go out, and yield themselves up to the enemy; but he stood at the cave's mouth, and always slew that child of his who went out, till he had destroyed them every one, and after that he slew his wife, and cast their dead bodies down the precipice, and himself after them, and so underwent death rather than slavery: but before he did this, he greatly reproached Herod with the meanness of his family, although he was then king. Herod also saw what he was doing, and stretched out his hand, and offered him all manner of security for his life; by which means all these caves were at length subdued entirely.

6. And when the king had set Ptolemy over these parts of the country as his general, he went to Samaria, with six hundred horsemen, and three thousand armed footmen, as intending to fight Antigonus. But still this command of the army did not succeed well with Ptolemy, but those that had been troublesome to Galilee before attacked him, and slew him; and when they had done this, they fled among the lakes and places almost inaccessible laying waste and plundering whatsoever

they could come at in those places. But Herod soon returned, and punished them for what they had done; for some of these rebels he slew, and others of them, who had fled to the strong holds he besieged, and both slew them, and demolished their strong holds. And when he had thus put an end to their rebellion, he laid a fine upon the cities of a hundred talents.

7. In the mean time, Pacorus was fallen in a battle, and the Parthians were defeated, when Ventidius sent Macheras to the assistance of Herod, with two legions, and a thousand horsemen, while Antony encouraged him to make haste. But Macheras, at the instigation of Antigonus, without the approbation of Herod, as being corrupted by money, went about to take a view of his affairs; but Antigonus suspecting this intention of his coming, did not admit him into the city, but kept him at a distance, with throwing stones at him, and plainly showed what he himself meant. But when Macheras was sensible that Herod had given him good advice, and that he had made a mistake himself in not hearkening to that advice, he retired to the city Emmaus; and what Jews he met with he slew them, whether they were enemies or friends, out of the rage he was in at what hardships he had undergone. The king was provoked at this conduct of his, and went to Samaria, and resolved to go to Antony about these affairs, and to inform him that he stood in no need of such helpers, who did him more mischief than they did his enemies; and that he was able of himself to beat Antigonus. But Macheras followed him, and desired that he would not go to Antony; or if he was resolved to go, that he would join his brother Joseph with them, and let them fight against Antigonus. So he was reconciled to Macheras, upon his earnest entreaties. Accordingly, he left Joseph there with his army, but charged him to run no hazards, nor to quarrel with Macheras.

8. But for his own part, he made haste to Antony (who was then at the siege of Samosata, a place upon Euphrates) with his troops, both horsemen and footmen, to be auxiliaries to him. And when he came to Antioch, and met there a great number of men gotten together that were very desirous to go to Antony, but durst not venture to go, out of fear, because the barbarians fell upon men on the road, and slew many, so he encouraged them, and became their conductor upon the road. Now when they were within two days' march of Samosata, the barbarians had laid an ambush there to disturb those that came to

Antony, and where the woods made the passes narrow, as they led to the plains, there they laid not a few of their horsemen, who were to lie still until those passengers were gone by into the wide place. Now as soon as the first ranks were gone by, (for Herod brought on the rear,) those that lay in ambush, who were about five hundred, fell upon them on the sudden, and when they had put the foremost to flight, the king came riding hard, with the forces that were about him, and immediately drove back the enemy; by which means he made the minds of his own men courageous, and imboldened them to go on, insomuch that those who ran away before now returned back, and the barbarians were slain on all sides. The king also went on killing them, and recovered all the baggage, among which were a great number of beasts for burden, and of slaves, and proceeded on in his march; and whereas there were a great number of those in the woods that attacked them, and were near the passage that led into the plain, he made a sally upon these also with a strong body of men, and put them to flight, and slew many of them, and thereby rendered the way safe for those that came after; and these called Herod their savior and protector.

9. And when he was near to Samosata, Antony sent out his army in all their proper habiliments to meet him, in order to pay Herod this respect, and because of the assistance he had given him; for he had heard what attacks the barbarians had made upon him [in Judea]. He also was very glad to see him there, as having been made acquainted with the great actions he had performed upon the road. So he entertained him very kindly, and could not but admire his courage. Antony also embraced him as soon as he saw him, and saluted him after a most affectionate manner, and gave him the upper hand, as having himself lately made him a king; and in a little time Antiochus delivered up the fortress, and on that account this war was at an end; then Antony committed the rest to Sosius, and gave him orders to assist Herod, and went himself to Egypt. Accordingly, Sosius sent two legions before into Judea to the assistance of Herod, and he followed himself with the body of the army.

10. Now Joseph was already slain in Judea, in the manner following: He forgot what charge his brother Herod had given him when he went to Antony; and when he had pitched his camp among the mountains, for Macheras had lent him five regiments, with these he went hastily to Jericho, in order to reap the corn thereto belonging; and as the Roman

regiments were but newly raised, and were unskillful in war, for they were in great part collected out of Syria, he was attacked by the enemy, and caught in those places of difficulty, and was himself slain, as he was fighting bravely, and the whole army was lost, for there were six regiments slain. So when Antigonus had got possession of the dead bodies, he cut off Joseph's head, although Pheroras his brother would have redeemed it at the price of fifty talents. After which defeat, the Galileans revolted from their commanders, and took those of Herod's party, and drowned them in the lake, and a great part of Judea was become seditious; but Macheras fortified the place Gitta [in Samaria].

11. At this time messengers came to Herod, and informed him of what had been done; and when he was come to Daphne by Antioch, they told him of the ill fortune that had befallen his brother; which yet he expected, from certain visions that appeared to him in his dreams, which clearly foreshowed his brother's death. So he hastened his march; and when he came to Mount Libanus, he received about eight hundred of the men of that place, having already with him also one Roman legion, and with these he came to Ptolemais. He also marched thence by night with his army, and proceeded along Galilee. Here it was that the enemy met him, and fought him, and were beaten, and shut up in the same place of strength whence they had sallied out the day before. So he attacked the place in the morning; but by reason of a great storm that was then very violent, he was able to do nothing, but drew off his army into the neighboring villages; yet as soon as the other legion that Antony sent him was come to his assistance, those that were in garrison in the place were afraid, and deserted it in the night time. Then did the king march hastily to Jericho, intending to avenge himself on the enemy for the slaughter of his brother; and when he had pitched his tents, he made a feast for the principal commanders; and after this collation was over, and he had dismissed his guests, he retired to his own chamber; and here may one see what kindness God had for the king, for the upper part of the house fell down when nobody was in it, and so killed none, insomuch that all the people believed that Herod was beloved of God, since he had escaped such a great and surprising danger.

12. But the next day six thousand of the enemy came down from the tops of the mountains to fight the Romans, which greatly terrified them; and the soldiers that were in light armor came near, and pelted

the king's guards that were come out with darts and stones, and one of them hit him on the side with a dart. Antigonus also sent a commander against Samaria, whose name was Pappus, with some forces, being desirous to show the enemy how potent he was, and that he had men to spare in his war with them. He sat down to oppose Macheras; but Herod, when he had taken five cities, took such as were left in them, being about two thousand, and slew them, and burnt the cities themselves, and then returned to go against Pappus, who was encamped at a village called Isanas; and there ran in to him many out of Jericho and Judea, near to which places he was, and the enemy fell upon his men, so stout were they at this time, and joined battle with them, but he beat them in the fight; and in order to be revenged on them for the slaughter of his brother, he pursued them sharply, and killed them as they ran away; and as the houses were full of armed men,[29] and many of them ran as far as the tops of the houses, he got them under his power, and pulled down the roofs of the houses, and saw the lower rooms full of soldiers that were caught, and lay all on a heap; so they threw stones down upon them as they lay piled one upon another, and thereby killed them; nor was there a more frightful spectacle in all the war than this, where beyond the walls an immense multitude of dead men lay heaped one upon another. This action it was which chiefly brake the spirits of the enemy, who expected now what would come; for there appeared a mighty number of people that came from places far distant, that were now about the village, but then ran away; and had it not been for the depth of winter, which then restrained them, the king's army had presently gone to Jerusalem, as being very courageous at this good success, and the whole work had been done immediately; for Antigonus was already looking about how he might fly away and leave the city.

13. At this time the king gave order that the soldiers should go to supper, for it was late at night, while he went into a chamber to use

---

29. It may be worth our observation here, that these soldiers of Herod could not have gotten upon the tops of these houses which were full of enemies, in order to pull up the upper floors, and destroy them beneath, but by ladders from the out side; which illustrates some texts in the New Testament, by which it appears that men used to ascend thither by ladders on the outsides. See Matthew 24:17; Mark 13:15; Luke 5:19; 17:31.

the bath, for he was very weary; and here it was that he was in the greatest danger, which yet, by God's providence, he escaped; for as he was naked, and had but one servant that followed him, to be with him while he was bathing in an inner room, certain of the enemy, who were in their armor, and had fled thither, out of fear, were then in the place; and as he was bathing, the first of them came out with his naked sword drawn, and went out at the doors, and after him a second, and a third, armed in like manner, and were under such a consternation, that they did no hurt to the king, and thought themselves to have come off very well ill suffering no harm themselves in their getting out of the house. However, on the next day, he cut off the head of Pappus, for he was already slain, and sent it to Pheroras, as a punishment of what their brother had suffered by his means, for he was the man that slew him with his own hand.

14. When the rigor of winter was over, Herod removed his army, and came near to Jerusalem, and pitched his camp hard by the city. Now this was the third year since he had been made king at Rome; and as he removed his camp, and came near that part of the wall where it could be most easily assaulted, he pitched that camp before the temple, intending to make his attacks in the same manner as did Pompey. So he encompassed the place with three bulwarks, and erected towers, and employed a great many hands about the work, and cut down the trees that were round about the city; and when he had appointed proper persons to oversee the works, even while the army lay before the city, he himself went to Samaria, to complete his marriage, and to take to wife the daughter of Alexander, the son of Aristobulus; for he had betrothed her already, as I have before related.

16 *How Herod, When He Had Married Mariamne Took Jerusalem with the Assistance of Sosius by Force; and How the Government of He Asamoneans Was Put an End To*

1. AFTER the wedding was over, came Sosius through Phoenicia, having sent out his army before him over the midland parts. He also, who was their commander, came himself, with a great number of horsemen and footmen. The king also came himself from Samaria, and brought with him no small army, besides that which was there before,

for they were about thirty thousand; and they all met together at the walls of Jerusalem, and encamped at the north wall of the city, being now an army of eleven legions, armed men on foot, and six thousand horsemen, with other auxiliaries out of Syria. The generals were two: Sosius, sent by Antony to assist Herod, and Herod on his own account, in order to take the government from Antigonus, who was declared all enemy at Rome, and that he might himself be king, according to the decree of the Senate.

2. Now the Jews that were enclosed within the walls of the city fought against Herod with great alacrity and zeal (for the whole nation was gathered together); they also gave out many prophecies about the temple, and many things agreeable to the people, as if God would deliver them out of the dangers they were in; they had also carried off what was out of the city, that they might not leave any thing to afford sustenance either for men or for beasts; and by private robberies they made the want of necessaries greater. When Herod understood this, he opposed ambushes in the fittest places against their private robberies, and he sent legions of armed men to bring its provisions, and that from remote places, so that in a little time they had great plenty of provisions. Now the three bulwarks were easily erected, because so many hands were continually at work upon it; for it was summer time, and there was nothing to hinder them in raising their works, neither from the air nor from the workmen; so they brought their engines to bear, and shook the walls of the city, and tried all manner of ways to get its; yet did not those within discover any fear, but they also contrived not a few engines to oppose their engines withal. They also sallied out, and burnt not only those engines that were not yet perfected, but those that were; and when they came hand to hand, their attempts were not less bold than those of the Romans, though they were behind them in skill. They also erected new works when the former were ruined, and making mines underground, they met each other, and fought there; and making use of brutish courage rather than of prudent valor, they persisted in this war to the very last; and this they did while a mighty army lay round about them, and while they were distressed by famine and the want of necessaries, for this happened to be a Sabbatic year. The first that scaled the walls were twenty chosen men, the next were Sosius's centurions; for the first wall was taken in forty days, and the second in fifteen more, when some of the cloisters that were about

the temple were burnt, which Herod gave out to have been burnt by Antigonus, in order to expose him to the hatred of the Jews. And when the outer court of the temple and the lower city were taken, the Jews fled into the inner court of the temple, and into the upper city; but now fearing lest the Romans should hinder them from offering their daily sacrifices to God, they sent an embassage, and desired that they would only permit them to bring in beasts for sacrifices, which Herod granted, hoping they were going to yield; but when he saw that they did nothing of what he supposed, but bitterly opposed him, in order to preserve the kingdom to Antigonus, he made an assault upon the city, and took it by storm; and now all parts were full of those that were slain, by the rage of the Romans at the long duration of the siege, and by the zeal of the Jews that were on Herod's side, who were not willing to leave one of their adversaries alive; so they were murdered continually in the narrow streets and in the houses by crowds, and as they were flying to the temple for shelter, and there was no pity taken of either infants or the aged, nor did they spare so much as the weaker sex; nay, although the king sent about, and besought them to spare the people, yet nobody restrained their hand from slaughter, but, as if they were a company of madmen, they fell upon persons of all ages, without distinction; and then Antigonus, without regard to either his past or present circumstances, came down from the citadel, and fell down at the feet of Sosius, who took no pity of him, in the change of his fortune, but insulted him beyond measure, and called him Antigone [i.e. a woman, and not a man;] yet did he not treat him as if he were a woman, by letting him go at liberty, but put him into bonds, and kept him in close custody.

3. And now Herod having overcome his enemies, his care was to govern those foreigners who had been his assistants, for the crowd of strangers rushed to see the temple, and the sacred things in the temple; but the king, thinking a victory to be a more severe affliction than a defeat, if any of those things which it was not lawful to see should be seen by them, used entreaties and threatenings, and even sometimes force itself, to restrain them. He also prohibited the ravage that was made in the city, and many times asked Sosius whether the Romans would empty the city both of money and men, and leave him king of a desert; and told him that he esteemed the dominion over the whole habitable earth as by no means an equivalent satisfaction for

such a murder of his citizens'; and when he said that this plunder was justly to be permitted the soldiers for the siege they had undergone, he replied, that he would give every one their reward out of his own money; and by this means be redeemed what remained of the city from destruction; and he performed what he had promised him, for he gave a noble present to every soldier, and a proportionable present to their commanders, but a most royal present to Sosius himself, till they all went away full of money.

4. This destruction befell the city of Jerusalem when Marcus Agrippa and Caninius Gallus were consuls of Rome[30] on the hundred eighty and fifth olympiad, on the third month, on the solemnity of the fast, as if a periodical revolution of calamities had returned since that which befell the Jews under Pompey; for the Jews were taken by him on the same day, and this was after twenty-seven years' time. So when Sosius had dedicated a crown of gold to God, he marched away from Jerusalem, and carried Antigonus with him in bonds to Antony; but Herod was afraid lest Antigonus should be kept in prison [only] by

---

30. Note here, that Josephus fully and frequently assures us that there passed above three years between Herod's first obtaining the kingdom at Rome, and his second obtaining it upon the taking of Jerusalem and death of Antigonus. The present history of this interval twice mentions the army going into winter quarters, which perhaps belonged to two several winters, ch. 15. sect. 3, 4; and though Josephus says nothing how long they lay in those quarters, yet does he give such an account of the long and studied delays of Ventidius, Silo, and Macheras, who were to see Herod settled in his new kingdom, but seem not to have had sufficient forces for that purpose, and were for certain all corrupted by Antigonus to make the longest delays possible, and gives us such particular accounts of the many great actions of Herod during the same interval, as fairly imply that interval, before Herod went to Samosata, to have been very considerable. However, what is wanting in Josephus, is fully supplied by Moses Chorenensis, the Arme nian historian, in his history of that interval, B. II ch. 18., where he directly assures us that Tigranes, then king of Armenia, and the principal manager of this Parthian war, reigned two years after Herod was made king at Rome, and yet Antony did not hear of his death, in that very neighborhood, at Samosata, till he was come thither to besiege it; after which Herod brought him an army, which was three hundred and forty miles' march, and through a difficult country, full of enemies also, and joined with him in the siege of Samosata till that city was taken; then Herod and Sosins marched back with their large armies the same number of three hundred and forty miles; and when, in a little time, they sat down to besiege Jerusalem, they were not able to take it but by a siege of five months. All which put together, fully supplies what is wanting in Josephus, and secures the entire chronology of these times beyond contradiction.

Antony, and that when he was carried to Rome by him, he might get his cause to be heard by the senate, and might demonstrate, as he was himself of the royal blood, and Herod but a private man, that therefore it belonged to his sons however to have the kingdom, on account of the family they were of, in case he had himself offended the Romans by what he had done. Out of Herod's fear of this it was that he, by giving Antony a great deal of money, endeavored to persuade him to have Antigonus slain, which if it were once done, he should be free from that fear. And thus did the government of the Asamoneans cease, a hundred twenty and six years after it was first set up. This family was a splendid and an illustrious one, both on account of the nobility of their stock, and of the dignity of the high priesthood, as also for the glorious actions their ancestors had performed for our nation; but these men lost the government by their dissensions one with another, and it came to Herod, the son of Antipater, who was of no more than a vulgar family, and of no eminent extraction, but one that was subject to other kings. And this is what history tells us was the end of the Asamonean family.

Book 15

Containing the Interval of Eighteen Years, from the Death of Antigonus to the Finishing of the Temple by Herod

1 *Concerning Pollio and Sameas. Herod Slays the Principal of Antigonus's Friends, and Spoils the City of Its Wealth. Antony Beheads Antigonus*

1. HOW Sosius and Herod took Jerusalem by force; and besides that, how they took Antigonus captive, has been related by us in the foregoing book. We will now proceed in the narration. And since Herod had now the government of all Judea put into his hands, he promoted such of the private men in the city as had been of his party, but never left off avenging and punishing every day those that had chosen to be of the party of his enemies. But Pollio the Pharisee, and Sameas, a disciple of his, were honored by him above all the rest; for when Jerusalem was besieged, they advised the citizens to receive Herod, for which advice they were well requited. But this Pollio, at the time when Herod was once upon his trial of life and death, foretold, in way of reproach, to Hyrcanus and the other judges, how this Herod, whom they suffered now to escape, would afterward inflict punishment on them all; which had its completion in time, while God fulfilled the words he had spoken.

2. At this time Herod, now he had got Jerusalem under his power, carried off all the royal ornaments, and spoiled the wealthy men of what they had gotten; and when, by these means, he had heaped together a great quantity of silver and gold, he gave it all to Antony,

and his friends that were about him. He also slew forty-five of the principal men of Antigonus's party, and set guards at the gates of the city, that nothing might be carried out together with their dead bodies. They also searched the dead, and whatsoever was found, either of silver or gold, or other treasure, it was carried to the king; nor was there any end of the miseries he brought upon them; and this distress was in part occasioned by the covetousness of the prince regent, who was still in want of more, and in part by the Sabbatic year, which was still going on, and forced the country to lie still uncultivated, since we are forbidden to sow our land in that year. Now when Antony had received Antigonus as his captive, he determined to keep him against his triumph; but when he heard that the nation grew seditious, and that, out of their hatred to Herod, they continued to bear good-will to Antigonus, he resolved to behead him at Antioch, for otherwise the Jews could no way be brought to be quiet. And Strabo of Cappadocia attests to what I have said, when he thus speaks: "Antony ordered Antigonus the Jew to be brought to Antioch, and there to be beheaded. And this Antony seems to me to have been the very first man who beheaded a king, as supposing he could no other way bend the minds of the Jews so as to receive Herod, whom he had made king in his stead; for by no torments could they he forced to call him king, so great a fondness they had for their former king; so he thought that this dishonorable death would diminish the value they had for Antigonus's memory, and at the same time would diminish the hatred they bare to Herod." Thus far Strabo.

2 *How Hyrcanus Was Set at Liberty by the Parthians, and Returned to Herod; and What Alexandra Did When She Heard That Ananelus Was Made High Priest*

1. NOW after Herod was in possession of the kingdom, Hyrcanus the high priest, who was then a captive among the Parthians, came to him again, and was set free from his captivity, in the manner following: Barzapharnes and Pacorus, the generals of the Parthians, took Hyreanus, who was first made high priest and afterward king, and Herod's brother, Phasaelus captives, and were them away into Parthis. Phasaelus indeed could not bear the reproach of being in

bonds; and thinking that death with glory was better than any life whatsoever, he became his own executioner, as I have formerly related.

2. But when Hyrcanus was brought into Parthia the king Phraates treated him after a very gentle manner, as having already learned of what an illustrious family he was; on which account he set him free from his bonds, and gave him a habitation at Babylon,[1] where there were Jews in great numbers. These Jews honored Hyrcanus as their high priest and king, as did all the Jewish nation that dwelt as far as Euphrates; which respect was very much to his satisfaction. But when he was informed that Herod had received the kingdom, new hopes came upon him, as having been himself still of a kind disposition towards him, and expecting that Herod would bear in mind what favor be had received from him; and when he was upon his trial, and when he was in danger that a capital sentence would be pronounced against him, he delivered him from that danger, and from all punishment. Accordingly, he talked of that matter with the Jew that came often to him with great affection; but they endeavored to retain him among them, and desired that he would stay with them, putting him in mind of the kind offices and honors they did him, and that those honors they paid him were not at all inferior to what they could pay to either their high priests or their kings; and what was a greater motive to determine him, they said, was this, that he could not have those dignities [in Judea] because of that maim in his body, which had been inflicted on him by Antigonus; and that kings do not use to requite men for those kindnesses which they received when they were private persons, the height of their fortune making usually no small changes in them.

3. Now although they suggested these arguments to him for his own advantage, yet did Hyrcanus still desire to depart. Herod also wrote to him, and persuaded him to desire of Phraates, and the Jews that were there, that they should not grudge him the royal authority, which he should have jointly with himself, for that now was the proper

---

1. The city here called "Babylon" by Josephus, seems to be one which was built by some of the Seleucidae upon the Tigris, which long after the utter desolation of old Babylon was commonly so called, and I suppose not far from Seleueia; just as the latter adjoining city Bagdat has been and is often called by the same old name of Babylon till this very day.

time for himself to make him amends for the favors he had received from him, as having been brought up by him, and saved by him also, as well as for Hyrcanus to receive it. And as he wrote thus to Hyrcanus, so did he send also Saramallas, his ambassador, to Phraates, and many presents with him, and desired him in the most obliging way that he would be no hinderance to his gratitude towards his benefactor. But this zeal of Herod's did not flow from that principle, but because he had been made governor of that country without having any just claim to it, he was afraid, and that upon reasons good enough, of a change in his condition, and so made what haste he could to get Hyrcanus into his power, or indeed to put him quite out of the way; which last thing he compassed afterward.

4. Accordingly, when Hyrcanus came, full of assurance, by the permission of the king of Parthia, and at the expense of the Jews, who supplied him with money, Herod received him with all possible respect, and gave him the upper place at public meetings, and set him above all the rest at feasts, and thereby deceived him. He called him his father, and endeavored, by all the ways possible, that he might have no suspicion of any treacherous design against him. He also did other things, in order to secure his government, which yet occasioned a sedition in his own family; for being cautious how he made any illustrious person the high priest of God,[2] he sent for an obscure priest out of Babylon, whose name was Ananelus, and bestowed the high priesthood upon him.

5. However, Alexandra, the daughter of Hyrcanus, and wife of Alexander, the son of Aristobulus the king, who had also brought Alexander [two] children, could not bear this indignity. Now this

---

2. Here we have an eminent example of Herod's worldly and profane politics, when by the abuse of his unlawful and usurped power, to make whom he pleased high priest, in the person of Ananelus, he occasioned such disturbances in his kingdom, and in his own family, as suffered him to enjoy no lasting peace or tranquillity ever afterward; and such is frequently the effect of profane court politics about matters of religion in other ages and nations. The Old Testament is full of the miseries of the people of the Jews derived from such court politics, especially in and after the days of Jeroboam the son of Nebat, "who made Israel to sin;" who gave the most pernicious example of it; who brought on the grossest corruption of religion by it; and the punishment of whose family for it was most remarkable. The case is too well known to stand in need of particular citations.

son was one of the greatest comeliness, and was called Aristobulus; and the daughter, Mariamne, was married to Herod, and eminent for her beauty also. This Alexandra was much disturbed, and took this indignity offered to her son exceeding ill, that while be was alive, any one else should be sent for to have the dignity of the high priesthood conferred upon him. Accordingly, she wrote to Cleopatra (a musician assisting her in taking care to have her letters carried) to desire her intercession with Antony, in order to gain the high priesthood for her son.

6. But as Antony was slow in granting this request, his friend Dellius[3] came into Judea upon some affairs; and when he saw Aristobulus, he stood in admiration at the tallness and handsomeness of the child, and no less at Mariarune, the king's wife, and was open in his commendations of Alexandra, as the mother of most beautiful children. And when she came to discourse with him, he persuaded her to get pictures drawn of them both, and to send them to Antony, for that when he saw them, he would deny her nothing that she should ask. Accordingly, Alexandra was elevated with these words of his, and sent the pictures to Antony. Dellius also talked extravagantly, and said that these children seemed not derived from men, but from some god or other. His design in doing so was to entice Antony into lewd pleasures with them, who was ashamed to send for the damsel, as being the wife of Herod, and avoided it, because of the reproaches he should have from Cleopatra on that account; but he sent, in the most decent manner he could, for the young man; but added this withal, unless he thought it hard upon him so to do. When this letter was brought to Herod, he did not think it safe for him to send one so handsome as was Aristobulus, in the prime of his life, for he was sixteen years of age, and of so noble a family, and particularly not to Antony, the principal man among the Romans, and one that would abuse him in his amours, and besides, one that openly indulged himself in such pleasures as his power allowed him without control. He therefore wrote back to him, that if this boy should only go out of the country, all would be in a state of war and uproar, because the Jews were in hopes of a change in the government, and to have another king over them.

---

3. Of this wicked Dellius, see the note on the War, B. I. ch. 15. sect. 3.

7. When Herod had thus excused himself to Antony, he resolved that he would not entirely permit the child or Alexandra to be treated dishonorably; but his wife Mariamne lay vehemently at him to restore the high priesthood to her brother; and he judged it was for his advantage so to do, because if he once had that dignity, he could not go out of the country. So he called his friends together, and told them that Alexandra privately conspired against his royal authority, and endeavored, by the means of Cleopatra, so to bring it about, that he might be deprived of the government, and that by Antony's means this youth might have the management of public affairs in his stead; and that this procedure of hers was unjust, since she would at the same time deprive her daughter of the dignity she now had, and would bring disturbances upon the kingdom, for which he had taken a great deal of pains, and had gotten it with extraordinary hazards; that yet, while he well remembered her wicked practices, he would not leave off doing what was right himself, but would even now give the youth the high priesthood; and that he formerly set up Ananelus, because Aristobulus was then so very young a child. Now when he had said this, not at random, but as he thought with the best discretion he had, in order to deceive the women, and those friends whom he had taken to consult withal, Alexandra, out of the great joy she had at this unexpected promise, and out of fear from the suspicions she lay under, fell a weeping; and made the following apology for herself; and said, that as to the [high] priesthood, she was very much concerned for the disgrace her son was under, and so did her utmost endeavors to procure it for him; but that as to the kingdom, she had made no attempts, and that if it were offered her [for her son], she would not accept it; and that now she would be satisfied with her son's dignity, while he himself held the civil government, and she had thereby the security that arose from his peculiar ability in governing to all the remainder of her family; that she was now overcome by his benefits, and thankfully accepted of this honor showed by him to her son, and that she would hereafter be entirely obedient. And she desired him to excuse her, if the nobility of her family, and that freedom of acting which she thought that allowed her, had made her act too precipitately and imprudently in this matter. So when they had spoken thus to one another, they came to an agreement, and all suspicions, so far as appeared, were vanished away.

Chapter 3

3 *How Herod Upon His Making Aristobulus High Priest Took Care That He Should Be Murdered in a Little Time; and What Apology He Made to Antony About Aristobulus; as Also Concerning Joseph and Mariamne*

1. SO king Herod immediately took the high priesthood away from Ananelus, who, as we said before, was not of this country, but one of those Jews that had been carried captive beyond Euphrates; for there were not a few ten thousands of this people that had been carried captives, and dwelt about Babylonia, whence Ananelus came. He was one of the stock of the high priests[4] and had been of old a particular friend of Herod; and when he was first made king, he conferred that dignity upon him, and now put him out of it again, in order to quiet the troubles in his family, though what he did was plainly unlawful, for at no other time [of old] was any one that had once been in that dignity deprived of it. It was Antiochus Epiphanes who first brake that law, and deprived Jesus, and made his brother Onias high priest in his stead. Aristobulus was the second that did so, and took that dignity from his brother [Hyrcanus]; and this Herod was the third, who took that high office away [from Arianflus], and gave it to this young man, Aristobulus, in his stead.

2. And now Herod seemed to have healed the divisions in his family; yet was he not without suspicion, as is frequently the case, of people seeming to be reconciled to one another, but thought that, as Alexandra had already made attempts tending to innovations, so did he fear that she would go on therein, if she found a fit opportunity for so doing; so he gave a command that she should dwell in the palace,

4. When Josephus says here that this Ananelus, the new high priest, was "of the stock of the high priests," and since he had been just telling us that he was a priest of an obscure family or character, ch. 2. sect. 4, it is not at all probable that he could so soon say that he was "of the stock of the high priests." However, Josephus here makes a remarkable observation, that this Ananelus was the third that was ever unjustly and wickedly turned out of the high priesthood by the civil power, no king or governor having ventured to do so, that Josephus knew of, but that heathen tyrant and persecutor Antiochus Epiphanes; that barbarous parricide Aristobulus, the first that took royal authority among the Maccabees; and this tyrant king Herod the Great, although afterward that infamous practice became frequent, till the very destruction of Jerusalem, when the office of high priesthood was at an end.

and meddle with no public affairs. Her guards also were so careful, that nothing she did in private life every day was concealed. All these hardships put her out of patience, by little and little and she began to hate Herod; for as she had the pride of a woman to the utmost degree, she had great indignation at this suspicious guard that was about her, as desirous rather to undergo any thing that could befall her, than to be deprived of her liberty of speech, and, under the notion of an honorary guard, to live in a state of slavery and terror. She therefore sent to Cleopatra, and made a long complaint of the circumstances she was in, and entreated her to do her utmost for her assistance. Cleopatra hereupon advised her to take her son with her, and come away immediately to her into Egypt. This advice pleased her; and she had this contrivance for getting away: She got two coffins made, as if they were to carry away two dead bodies and put herself into one, and her son into the other and gave orders to such of her servants as knew of her intentions to carry them away in the night time. Now their road was to be thence to the sea-side and there was a ship ready to carry them into Egypt. Now Aesop, one of her servants, happened to fall upon Sabion, one of her friends, and spake of this matter to him, as thinking he had known of it before. When Sabion knew this, (who had formerly been an enemy of Herod, and been esteemed one of those that laid snares for and gave the poison to [his father] Antipater,) he expected that this discovery would change Herod's hatred into kindness; so he told the king of this private stratagem of Alexandra: whereupon be suffered her to proceed to the execution of her project, and caught her in the very fact; but still he passed by her offense; and though he had a great mind to do it, he durst not inflict any thing that was severe upon her, for he knew that Cleopatra would not bear that he should have her accused, on account of her hatred to him; but made a show as if it were rather the generosity of his soul, and his great moderation, that made him forgive them. However, he fully proposed to himself to put this young man out of the way, by one means or other; but he thought he might in probability be better concealed in doing it, if he did it not presently, nor immediately after what had lately happened.

3. And now, upon the approach of the feast of tabernacles, which is a festival very much observed among us, he let those days pass over, and both he and the rest of the people were therein very merry;

yet did the envy which at this time arose in him cause him to make haste to do what lie was about, and provoke him to it; for when this youth Aristobulus, who was now in the seventeenth year of his age, went up to the altar, according to the law, to offer the sacrifices, and this with the ornaments of his high priesthood, and when he performed the sacred offices,[5] he seemed to be exceedingly comely, and taller than men usually were at that age, and to exhibit in his countenance a great deal of that high family he was sprung from,—a warm zeal and affection towards him appeared among the people, and the memory of the actions of his grandfather Aristobulus was fresh in their minds; and their affections got so far the mastery of them, that they could not forbear to show their inclinations to him. They at once rejoiced and were confounded, and mingled with good wishes their joyful acclamations which they made to him, till the good-will of the multitude was made too evident; and they more rashly proclaimed the happiness they had received from his family than was fit under a monarchy to have done. Upon all this, Herod resolved to complete what he had intended against the young man. When therefore the festival was over, and he was feasting at Jericho[6] with Alexandra, who entertained them there, he was then very pleasant with the young man, and drew him into a lonely place, and at the same time played with him in a juvenile and ludicrous manner. Now the nature of that place was hotter than ordinary; so they went out in a body, and of a sudden, and in a vein of madness; and as they stood by the fish-ponds, of which there were large ones about the house, they went to cool themselves [by bathing], because it was in the midst of a hot day. At first they were only spectators of Herod's servants and acquaintance as they were swimming; but after a while, the young man, at the instigation of Herod, went into the water among them, while such of Herod's acquaintance, as he had appointed to do it, dipped him as he was swimming, and plunged him under water, in the dark of the evening, as if it had been done in sport only; nor did they desist till he was

---

5. This entirely confutes the Talmudists, who pretend that no one under twenty years of age could officiate as high priest among the Jews.

6. A Hebrew chronicle, cited by Reland, says this drowning was at Jordan, not at Jericho, and this even when he quote Josephus. I suspect the transcriber of the Hebrew chronicle mistook the name, and wrote Jordan for Jericho.

entirely suffocated. And thus was Aristobulus murdered, having lived no more in all than eighteen years,[7] and kept the high priesthood one year only; which high priesthood Ananelus now recovered again.

4. When this sad accident was told the women, their joy was soon changed to lamentation, at the sight of the dead body that lay before them, and their sorrow was immoderate. The city also [of Jerusalem], upon the spreading of this news, were in very great grief, every family looking on this calamity as if it had not belonged to another, but that one of themselves was slain. But Alexandra was more deeply affected, upon her knowledge that he had been destroyed [on purpose]. Her sorrow was greater than that of others, by her knowing how the murder was committed; but she was under the necessity of bearing up under it, out of her prospect of a greater mischief that might otherwise follow; and she oftentimes came to an inclination to kill herself with her own hand, but still she restrained herself, in hopes she might live long enough to revenge the unjust murder thus privately committed; nay, she further resolved to endeavor to live longer, and to give no occasion to think she suspected that her son was slain on purpose, and supposed that she might thereby be in a capacity of revenging it at a proper opportunity. Thus did she restrain herself, that she might not be noted for entertaining any such suspicion. However, Herod endeavored that none abroad should believe that the child's death was caused by any design of his; and for this purpose he did not only use the ordinary signs of sorrow, but fell into tears also, and exhibited a real confusion of soul; and perhaps his affections were overcome on this occasion, when he saw the child's countenance so young and so beautiful, although his death was supposed to tend to his own security. So far at least this grief served as to make some apology for him; and as for his funeral, that he took care should be very magnificent, by making great preparation for a sepulcher to lay his body in, and providing a great quantity of spices, and burying many ornaments together with him, till the very women, who were in such deep sorrow, were astonished at it, and received in this way some consolation.

---

7. The reading of one of Josephus's Greek MSS. seems here to be right, that Aristobulus was "not eighteen years old" when he was drowned, for he was not seventeen when he was made high priest, ch. 2. sect. 6, ch. 3. sect. 3, and he continued in that office but one year, as in the place before us.

5. However, no such things could overcome Alexandra's grief; but the remembrance of this miserable case made her sorrow, both deep and obstinate. Accordingly, she wrote an account of this treacherous scene to Cleopatra, and how her son was murdered; but Cleopatra, as she had formerly been desirous to give her what satisfaction she could, and commiserating Alexandra's misfortunes, made the case her own, and would not let Antony be quiet, but excited him to punish the child's murder; for that it was an unworthy thing that Herod, who had been by him made king of a kingdom that no way belonged to him, should be guilty of such horrid crimes against those that were of the royal blood in reality. Antony was persuaded by these arguments; and when he came to Laodicea, he sent and commanded Herod to come and make his defense, as to what he had done to Aristobulus, for that such a treacherous design was not well done, if he had any hand in it. Herod was now in fear, both of the accusation, and of Cleopatra's ill-will to him, which was such that she was ever endeavoring to make Antony hate him. He therefore determined to obey his summons, for he had no possible way to avoid it. So he left his uncle Joseph procurator for his government, and for the public affairs, and gave him a private charge, that if Antony should kill him, he also should kill Mariamne immediately; for that he had a tender affection for this his wife, and was afraid of the injury that should be offered him, if, after his death, she, for her beauty, should be engaged to some other man: but his intimation was nothing but this at the bottom, that Antony had fallen in love with her, when he had formerly heard somewhat of her beauty. So when Herod had given Joseph this charge, and had indeed no sure hopes of escaping with his life, he went away to Antony.

6. But as Joseph was administering the public affairs of the kingdom, and for that reason was very frequently with Mariamne, both because his business required it, and because of the respects he ought to pay to the queen, he frequently let himself into discourses about Herod's kindness, and great affection towards her; and when the women, especially Alexandra, used to turn his discourses into feminine raillery, Joseph was so over-desirous to demonstrate the kings inclinations, that he proceeded so far as to mention the charge he had received, and thence drew his demonstration, that Herod was not able to live without her; and that if he should come to any ill end, he could not endure a separation from her, even after he was dead. Thus

spake Joseph. But the women, as was natural, did not take this to be an instance of Herod's strong affection for them, but of his severe usage of them, that they could not escape destruction, nor a tyrannical death, even when he was dead himself. And this saying [of Joseph] was a foundation for the women's severe suspicions about him afterwards.

7. At this time a report went about the city Jerusalem among Herod's enemies, that Antony had tortured Herod, and put him to death. This report, as is natural, disturbed those that were about the palace, but chiefly the women; upon which Alexandra endeavored to persuade Joseph to go out of the palace, and fly away with them to the ensigns of the Roman legion, which then lay encamped about the city, as a guard to the kingdom, under the command of Julius; for that by this means, if any disturbance should happen about the palace, they should be in greater security, as having the Romans favorable to them; and that besides, they hoped to obtain the highest authority, if Antony did but once see Mariamne, by whose means they should recover the kingdom, and want nothing which was reasonable for them to hope for, because of their royal extraction.

8. But as they were in the midst of these deliberations, letters were brought from Herod about all his affairs, and proved contrary to the report, and of what they before expected; for when he was come to Antony, he soon recovered his interest with him, by the presents he made him, which he had brought with him from Jerusalem; and he soon induced him, upon discoursing with him, to leave off his indignation at him, so that Cleopatra's persuasions had less force than the arguments and presents he brought to regain his friendship; for Antony said that it was not good to require an account of a king, as to the affairs of his government, for at this rate he could be no king at all, but that those who had given him that authority ought to permit him to make use of it. He also said the same things to Cleopatra, that it would be best for her not busily to meddle with the acts of the king's government. Herod wrote an account of these things, and enlarged upon the other honors which he had received from Antony; how he sat by him at his hearing causes, and took his diet with him every day, and that he enjoyed those favors from him, notwithstanding the reproaches that Cleopatra so severely laid against him, who having a great desire of his country, and earnestly entreating Antony that the kingdom might be given to her, labored with her utmost diligence to

have him out of the way; but that he still found Antony just to him, and had no longer any apprehensions of hard treatment from him; and that he was soon upon his return, with a firmer additional assurance of his favor to him, in his reigning and managing public affairs; and that there was no longer any hope for Cleopatra's covetous temper, since Antony had given her Celesyria instead of what she had desired; by which means he had at once pacified her, and got clear of the entreaties which she made him to have Judea bestowed upon her.

9. When these letters were brought, the women left off their attempt for flying to the Romans, which they thought of while Herod was supposed to be dead; yet was not that purpose of theirs a secret; but when the king had conducted Antony on his way against the Partnians, he returned to Judea, when both his sister Salome and his mother informed him of Alexandra's intentions. Salome also added somewhat further against Joseph, though it was no more than a calumny, that he had often had criminal conversation with Mariamne. The reason of her saying so was this, that she for a long time bare her ill-will; for when they had differences with one another, Mariamne took great freedoms, and reproached the rest for the meanness of their birth. But Herod, whose affection to Mariamne was always very warm, was presently disturbed at this, and could not bear the torments of jealousy, but was still restrained from doing any rash thing to her by the love he had for her; yet did his vehement affection and jealousy together make him ask Mariamne by herself about this matter of Joseph; but she denied it upon her oath, and said all that an innocent woman could possibly say in her own defense; so that by little and little the king was prevailed upon to drop the suspicion, and left off his anger at her; and being overcome with his passion for his wife, he made an apology to her for having seemed to believe what he had heard about her, and returned her a great many acknowledgments of her modest behavior, and professed the extraordinary affection and kindness he had for her, till at last, as is usual between lovers, they both fell into tears, and embraced one another with a most tender affection. But as the king gave more and more assurances of his belief of her fidelity, and endeavored to draw her to a like confidence in him, Marianme said, Yet was not that command thou gavest, that if any harm came to thee from Antony, I, who had been no occasion of it, should perish with thee, a sign of thy love to me?" When these words

were fallen from her, the king was shocked at them, and presently let her go out of his arms, and cried out, and tore his hair with his own hands, and said, that "now he had an evident demonstration that Joseph had had criminal conversation with his wife; for that he would never have uttered what he had told him alone by himself, unless there had been such a great familiarity and firm confidence between them. And while he was in this passion he had like to have killed his wife; but being still overborne by his love to her, he restrained this his passion, though not without a lasting grief and disquietness of mind. However, he gave order to slay Joseph, without permitting him to come into his sight; and as for Alexandra, he bound her, and kept her in custody, as the cause of all this mischief.

4 *How Cleopatra, When She Had Gotten from Antony Some Parts of Judea and Arabia Came into Judea; and How Herod Gave Her Many Presents and Conducted Her on Her Way Back to Egypt*

1. NOW at this time the affairs of Syria were in confusion by Cleopatra's constant persuasions to Antony to make an attempt upon every body's dominions; for she persuaded him to take those dominions away from their several princes, and bestow them upon her; and she had a mighty influence upon him, by reason of his being enslaved to her by his affections. She was also by nature very covetous, and stuck at no wickedness. She had already poisoned her brother, because she knew that he was to be king of Egypt, and this when he was but fifteen years old; and she got her sister Arsinoe to be slain, by the means of Antony, when she was a supplicant at Diana's temple at Ephesus; for if there were but any hopes of getting money, she would violate both temples and sepulchers. Nor was there any holy place that was esteemed the most inviolable, from which she would not fetch the ornaments it had in it; nor any place so profane, but was to suffer the most flagitious treatment possible from her, if it could but contribute somewhat to the covetous humor of this wicked creature: yet did not all this suffice so extravagant a woman, who was a slave to her lusts, but she still imagined that she wanted every thing she could think of, and did her utmost to gain it; for which reason she hurried Antony on perpetually to deprive others of their dominions, and give them to

her. And as she went over Syria with him, she contrived to get it into her possession; so he slew Lysanias, the son of Ptolemy, accusing him of his bringing the Parthians upon those countries. She also petitioned Antony to give her Judea and Arabia; and, in order thereto, desired him to take these countries away from their present governors. As for Antony, he was so entirely overcome by this woman, that one would not think her conversation only could do it, but that he was some way or other bewitched to do whatsoever she would have him; yet did the grossest parts of her injustice make him so ashamed, that he would not always hearken to her to do those flagrant enormities she would have persuaded him to. That therefore he might not totally deny her, nor, by doing every thing which she enjoined him, appear openly to be an ill man, he took some parts of each of those countries away from their former governors, and gave them to her. Thus he gave her the cities that were within the river Eleutherus, as far as Egypt, excepting Tyre and Sidon, which he knew to have been free cities from their ancestors, although she pressed him very often to bestow those on her also.

2. When Cleopatra had obtained thus much, and had accompanied Antony in his expedition to Armenia as far as Euphrates, she returned back, and came to Apamia and Damascus, and passed on to Judea, where Herod met her, and farmed of her parts of Arabia, and those revenues that came to her from the region about Jericho. This country bears that balsam, which is the most precious drug that is there, and grows there alone. The place bears also palm trees, both many in number, and those excellent in their kind. When she was there, and was very often with Herod, she endeavored to have criminal conversation with the king; nor did she affect secrecy in the indulgence of such sort of pleasures; and perhaps she had in some measure a passion of love to him; or rather, what is most probable, she laid a treacherous snare for him, by aiming to obtain such adulterous conversation from him: however, upon the whole, she seemed overcome with love to him. Now Herod had a great while borne no good-will to Cleopatra, as knowing that she was a woman irksome to all; and at that time he thought her particularly worthy of his hatred, if this attempt proceeded out of lust; he had also thought of preventing her intrigues, by putting her to death, if such were her endeavors. However, he refused to comply with her proposals, and called a counsel of his friends to consult with them whether he should not kill her, now he

had her in his power; for that he should thereby deliver all those from a multitude of evils to whom she was already become irksome, and was expected to be still so for the time to come; and that this very thing would be much for the advantage of Antony himself, since she would certainly not be faithful to him, in case any such season or necessity should come upon him as that he should stand in need of her fidelity. But when he thought to follow this advice, his friends would not let him; and told him that, in the first place, it was not right to attempt so great a thing, and run himself thereby into the utmost danger; and they laid hard at him, and begged of him to undertake nothing rashly, for that Antony would never bear it, no, not though any one should evidently lay before his eyes that it was for his own advantage; and that the appearance of depriving him of her conversation, by this violent and treacherous method, would probably set his affections more on a flame than before. Nor did it appear that he could offer any thing of tolerable weight in his defense, this attempt being against such a woman as was of the highest dignity of any of her sex at that time in the world; and as to any advantage to be expected from such an undertaking, if any such could be supposed in this case, it would appear to deserve condemnation, on account of the insolence he must take upon him in doing it: which considerations made it very plain that in so doing he would find his government filled with mischief, both great and lasting, both to himself and his posterity, whereas it was still in his power to reject that wickedness she would persuade him to, and to come off honorably at the same time. So by thus affrighting Herod, and representing to him the hazard he must, in all probability, run by this undertaking, they restrained him from it. So he treated Cleopatra kindly, and made her presents, and conducted her on her way to Egypt.

3. But Antony subdued Armenia, and sent Artabazes, the son of Tigranes, in bonds, with his children and procurators, to Egypt, and made a present of them, and of all the royal ornaments which he had taken out of that kingdom, to Cleopatra. And Artaxias, the eldest of his sons, who had escaped at that time, took the kingdom of Armenia; who yet was ejected by Archclaus and Nero Caesar, when they restored Tigranes, his younger brother, to that kingdom; but this happened a good while afterward.

4. But then, as to the tributes which Herod was to pay Cleopatra for that country which Antony had given her, he acted fairly with her, as deeming it not safe for him to afford any cause for Cleopatra to hate him. As for the king of Arabia, whose tribute Herod had undertaken to pay her, for some time indeed he paid him as much as came to two hundred talents; but he afterwards became very niggardly and slow in his payments, and could hardly be brought to pay some parts of it, and was not willing to pay even them without some deductions.

5 *How Herod Made War with the King of Arabia, and After They Had Fought Many Battles, at Length Conquered Him, and Was Chosen by the Arabs to Be Governor of That Nation; as Also Concerning a Great Earthquake*

1. HEREUPON Herod held himself ready to go against the king of Arabia, because of his ingratitude to him, and because, after all, he would do nothing that was just to him, although Herod made the Roman war an occasion of delaying his own; for the battle at Actium was now expected, which fell into the hundred eighty and seventh olympiad, where Caesar and Antony were to fight for the supreme power of the world; but Herod having enjoyed a country that was very fruitful, and that now for a long time, and having received great taxes, and raised great armies therewith, got together a body of men, and carefully furnished them with all necessaries, and designed them as auxiliaries for Antony. But Antony said he had no want of his assistance; but he commanded him to punish the king of Arabia; for he had heard both from him, and from Cleopatra, how perfidious he was; for this was what Cleopatra desired, who thought it for her own advantage that these two kings should do one another as great mischief as possible. Upon this message from Antony, Herod returned back, but kept his army with him, in order to invade Arabia immediately. So when his army of horsemen and footmen was ready, he marched to Diospolis, whither the Arabians came also to meet them, for they were not unapprized of this war that was coming upon them; and after a great battle had been fought, the Jews had the victory. But afterward there were gotten together another numerous army of the Arabians, at Cana, which is a place of Celesyria. Herod was informed

of this beforehand; so he came marching against them with the greatest part of the forces he had; and when he was come near to Cana, he resolved to encamp himself; and he cast up a bulwark, that he might take a proper season for attacking the enemy; but as he was giving those orders, the multitude of the Jews cried out that he should make no delay, but lead them against the Arabians. They went with great spirit, as believing they were in very good order; and those especially were so that had been in the former battle, and had been conquerors, and had not permitted their enemies so much as to come to a close fight with them. And when they were so tumultuous, and showed such great alacrity, the king resolved to make use of that zeal the multitude then exhibited; and when he had assured them he would not be behindhand with them in courage, he led them on, and stood before them all in his armor, all the regiments following him in their several ranks: whereupon a consternation fell upon the Arabians; for when they perceived that the Jews were not to be conquered, and were full of spirit, the greater part of them ran away, and avoided fighting; and they had been quite destroyed, had not Anthony fallen upon the Jews, and distressed them; for this man was Cleopatra's general over the soldiers she had there, and was at enmity with Herod, and very wistfully looked on to see what the event of the battle would be. He had also resolved, that in case the Arabians did any thing that was brave and successful, he would lie still; but in case they were beaten, as it really happened, he would attack the Jews with those forces he had of his own, and with those that the country had gotten together for him. So he fell upon the Jews unexpectedly, when they were fatigued, and thought they had already vanquished the enemy, and made a great slaughter of them; for as the Jews had spent their courage upon their known enemies, and were about to enjoy themselves in quietness after their victory, they were easily beaten by these that attacked them afresh, and in particular received a great loss in places where the horses could not be of service, and which were very stony, and where those that attacked them were better acquainted with the places than themselves. And when the Jews had suffered this loss, the Arabians raised their spirits after their defeat, and returning back again, slew those that were already put to flight; and indeed all sorts of slaughter were now frequent, and of those that escaped, a few only returned into the camp. So king Herod, when he despaired of the battle, rode up to them to bring them assistance; yet did he not come time enough to do them any service, though he labored hard to do it; but the Jewish camp was taken; so that the Arabians had unexpectedly a most glorious success, having gained that victory which of themselves they were no way likely to have gained, and slaying a great part of the enemy's army: whence afterward Herod could only act like a private robber, and make excursions upon many parts of Arabia, and distress them by sudden incursions, while he encamped among the mountains, and avoided by any means to come to a pitched battle; yet did he greatly harass the enemy by his assiduity, and the hard labor he took in this matter. He also took great care of his own forces, and used all the means he could to restore his affairs to their old state.

2. At this time it was that the fight happened at Actium, between Octavius Caesar and Antony, in the seventh year of the reign of Herod[8] and then it was also that there was an earthquake in Judea, such a one as had not happened at any other time, and which earthquake brought a great destruction upon the cattle in that country. About ten thousand men also perished by the fall of houses; but the army, which lodged in the field, received no damage by this sad accident. When the Arabians were informed of this, and when those that hated the Jews, and pleased themselves with aggravating the reports, told them of it, they raised their spirits, as if their enemy's country was quite overthrown, and the men were utterly destroyed, and thought there now remained nothing that could oppose them. Accordingly, they took the Jewish ambassadors, who came to them after all this had happened, to make peace with them, and slew them, and came with great alacrity against their army; but the Jews durst not withstand them, and were so cast down by the calamities they were under, that they took no care of their affairs, but gave up themselves to despair; for they had no hope that they should be upon a level again with them in battles, nor obtain any assistance elsewhere, while their affairs at home were in such great distress also. When matters were in this condition, the king persuaded

---

8. The reader is here to take notice, that this seventh year of the reign of Herod, and all the other years of his reign, in Josephus, are dated from the death of Antigonus, or at the soonest from the conclusion of Antigonus, and the taking of Jerusalem a few months before, and never from his first obtaining the kingdom at Rome, above three years before, as some have very weakly and injudiciously done.

the commanders by his words, and tried to raise their spirits, which were quite sunk; and first he endeavored to encourage and embolden some of the better sort beforehand, and then ventured to make a speech to the multitude, which he had before avoided to do, lest he should find them uneasy thereat, because of the misfortunes which had happened; so he made a consolatory speech to the multitude, in the manner following:

3. "You are not unacquainted, my fellow soldiers, that we have had, not long since, many accidents that have put a stop to what we are about, and it is probable that even those that are most distinguished above others for their courage can hardly keep up their spirits in such circumstances; but since we cannot avoid fighting, and nothing that hath happened is of such a nature but it may by ourselves be recovered into a good state, and this by one brave action only well performed, I have proposed to myself both to give you some encouragement, and, at the same time, some information; both which parts of my design will tend to this point; that you may still continue in your own proper fortitude. I will then, in the first place, demonstrate to you that this war is a just one on our side, and that on this account it is a war of necessity, and occasioned by the injustice of our adversaries; for if you be once satisfied of this, it will be a real cause of alacrity to you; after which I will further demonstrate, that the misfortunes we are under are of no great consequence, and that we have the greatest reason to hope for victory. I shall begin with the first, and appeal to yourselves as witnesses to what I shall say. You are not ignorant certainly of the wickedness of the Arabians, which is to that degree as to appear incredible to all other men, and to include somewhat that shows the grossest barbarity and ignorance of God. The chief things wherein they have affronted us have arisen from covetousness and envy; and they have attacked us in an insidious manner, and on the sudden. And what occasion is there for me to mention many instances of such their procedure? When they were in danger of losing their own government of themselves, and of being slaves to Cleopatra, what others were they that freed them from that fear? for it was the friendship. I had with Antony, and the kind disposition he was in towards us, that hath been the occasion that even these Arabians have not been utterly undone, Antony being unwilling to undertake any thing which might be suspected by us of unkindness: but when he had

a mind to bestow some parts of each of our dominions on Cleopatra, I also managed that matter so, that by giving him presents of my own, I might obtain a security to both nations, while I undertook myself to answer for the money, and gave him two hundred talents, and became surety for those two hundred more which were imposed upon the land that was subject to this tribute; and this they have defrauded us of, although it was not reasonable that Jews should pay tribute to any man living, or allow part of their land to be taxable; but although that was to be, yet ought we not to pay tribute for these Arabians, whom we have ourselves preserved; nor is it fit that they, who have professed (and that with great integrity and sense of our kindness) that it is by our means that they keep their principality, should injure us, and deprive us of what is our due, and this while we have been still not their enemies, but their friends. And whereas observation of covenants takes place among the bitterest enemies, but among friends is absolutely necessary, this is not observed among these men, who think gain to be the best of all things, let it be by any means whatsoever, and that injustice is no harm, if they may but get money by it: is it therefore a question with you, whether the unjust are to be punished or not? when God himself hath declared his mind that so it ought to be, and hath commanded that we ever should hate injuries and injustice, which is not only just, but necessary, in wars between several nations; for these Arabians have done what both the Greeks and barbarians own to be an instance of the grossest wickedness, with regard to our ambassadors, which they have beheaded, while the Greeks declare that such ambassadors are sacred and inviolable.[9] And for ourselves, we have learned from God the most excellent of our doctrines, and the most holy part of our law, by angels or ambassadors; for this name brings God to the knowledge of mankind, and is sufficient to reconcile enemies one to another. What wickedness then can be greater than the slaughter of ambassadors, who come to treat about doing what is right? And when such have been their actions, how is it possible they can either live securely in common life, or be successful in war? In my

9. Herod says here, that as ambassadors were sacred when they carried messages to others, so did the laws of the Jews derive a sacred authority by being delivered from God by angels, [or Divine ambassadors,] which is St. Paul's expression about the same laws, Galatians 3:19; Hebrews 2;2.

opinion, this is impossible; but perhaps some will say, that what is holy, and what is righteous, is indeed on our side, but that the Arabians are either more courageous or more numerous than we are. Now, as to this, in the first place, it is not fit for us to say so, for with whom is what is righteous, with them is God himself; now where God is, there is both multitude and courage. But to examine our own circumstances a little, we were conquerors in the first battle; and when we fought again, they were not able to oppose us, but ran away, and could not endure our attacks or our courage; but when we had conquered them, then came Athenion, and made war against us without declaring it; and pray, is this an instance of their manhood? or is it not a second instance of their wickedness and treachery? Why are we therefore of less courage, on account of that which ought to inspire us with stronger hopes? and why are we terrified at these, who, when they fight upon the level, are continually beaten, and when they seem to be conquerors, they gain it by wickedness? and if we suppose that any one should deem them to be men of real courage, will not he be excited by that very consideration to do his utmost against them? for true valor is not shown by fighting against weak persons, but in being able to overcome the most hardy. But then if the distresses we are ourselves under, and the miseries that have come by the earthquake, hath aftrighted any one, let him consider, in the first place, that this very thing will deceive the Arabians, by their supposal that what hath befallen us is greater than it really is. Moreover, it is not right that the same thing that emboldens them should discourage us; for these men, you see, do not derive their alacrity from any advantageous virtue of their own, but from their hope, as to us, that we are quite cast down by our misfortunes; but when we boldly march against them, we shall soon pull down their insolent conceit of themselves, and shall gain this by attacking them, that they will not be so insolent when we come to the battle; for our distresses are not so great, nor is what hath happened all indication of the anger of God against us, as some imagine; for such things are accidental, and adversities that come in the usual course of things; and if we allow that this was done by the will of God, we must allow that it is now over by his will also, and that he is satisfied with what hath already happened; for had he been willing to afflict us still more thereby, he had not changed his mind so soon. And as for the war we are engaged in, he hath himself demonstrated that he is willing it should go on, and that he knows it to be a just war; for while some of the people in the country have perished, all you who were in arms have suffered nothing, but are all preserved alive; whereby God makes it plain to us, that if you had universally, with your children and wives, been in the army, it had come to pass that you had not undergone any thing that would have much hurt you. Consider these things, and, what is more than all the rest, that you have God at all times for your Protector; and prosecute these men with a just bravery, who, in point of friendship, are unjust, in their battles perfidious, towards ambassadors impious, and always inferior to you in valor."

4. When the Jews heard this speech, they were much raised in their minds, and more disposed to fight than before. So Herod, when he had offered the sacrifices appointed by the law[10] made haste, and took them, and led them against the Arabians; and in order to that passed over Jordan, and pitched his camp near to that of the enemy. He also thought fit to seize upon a certain castle that lay in the midst of them, as hoping it would be for his advantage, and would the sooner produce a battle; and that if there were occasion for delay, he should by it have his camp fortified; and as the Arabians had the same intentions upon that place, a contest arose about it; at first they were but skirmishes, after which there came more soldiers, and it proved a sort of fight, and some fell on both sides, till those of the Arabian side were beaten and retreated. This was no small encouragement to the Jews immediately; and when Herod observed that the enemy's army was disposed to any thing rather than to come to an engagement, he ventured boldly to attempt the bulwark itself, and to pull it to pieces,

10. This piece of religion, the supplicating God with sacrifices, by Herod, before he went to this fight with the Arabians, taken notice of also in the first book of the War, ch. 19. sect. 5, is worth remarking, because it is the only example of this nature, so far as I remember, that Josephus ever mentions in all his large and particular accounts of this Herod; and it was when he had been in mighty distress, and discouraged by a great defeat of his former army, and by a very great earthquake in Judea, such times of affliction making men most religious; nor was he disappointed of his hopes here, but immediately gained a most signal victory over the Arabians, while they who just before had been so great victors, and so much elevated upon the earthquake in Judea as to venture to slay the Jewish ambassadors, were now under a strange consternation, and hardly able to fight at all.

and so to get nearer to their camp, in order to fight them; for when they were forced out of their trenches, they went out in disorder, and had not the least alacrity, or hope of victory; yet did they fight hand to hand, because they were more in number than the Jews, and because they were in such a disposition of war that they were under a necessity of coming on boldly; so they came to a terrible battle, while not a few fell on each side. However, at length the Arabians fled; and so great a slaughter was made upon their being routed, that they were not only killed by their enemies, but became the authors of their own deaths also, and were trodden down by the multitude, and the great current of people in disorder, and were destroyed by their own armor; so five thousand men lay dead upon the spot, while the rest of the multitude soon ran within the bulwark for safety, but had no firm hope of safety, by reason of their want of necessaries, and especially of water. The Jews pursued them, but could not get in with them, but sat round about the bulwark, and watched any assistance that would get in to them, and prevented any there, that had a mind to it, from running away.

5. When the Arabians were in these circumstances, they sent ambassadors to Herod, in the first place, to propose terms of accommodation, and after that to offer him, so pressing was their thirst upon them, to undergo whatsoever he pleased, if he would free them from their present distress; but he would admit of no ambassadors, of no price of redemption, nor of any other moderate terms whatever, being very desirous to revenge those unjust actions which they had been guilty of towards his nation. So they were necessitated by other motives, and particularly by their thirst, to come out, and deliver themselves up to him, to be carried away captives; and in five days' time the number of four thousand were taken prisoners, while all the rest resolved to make a sally upon their enemies, and to fight it out with them, choosing rather, if so it must be, to die therein, than to perish gradually and ingloriously. When they had taken this resolution, they came out of their trenches, but could no way sustain the fight, being too much disabled, both in mind and body, and having not room to exert themselves, and thought it an advantage to be killed, and a misery to survive; so at the first onset there fell about seven thousand of them, after which stroke they let all the courage they had put on before fall, and stood amazed at Herod's warlike spirit under his own

calamities; so for the future they yielded, and made him ruler of their nation; whereupon he was greatly elevated at so seasonable a success, and returned home, taking great authority upon him, on account of so bold and glorious an expedition as he had made.

6 *How Herod Slew Hyrcanus and Then Hasted Away to Caesar, and Obtained the Kingdom from Him Also; and How a Little Time Afterward, He Entertained Caesar in a Most Honorable Manner*

1. HEROD'S other affairs were now very prosperous, and he was not to be easily assaulted on any side. Yet did there come upon him a danger that would hazard his entire dominions, after Antony had been beaten at the battle of Actium by Caesar [Octarian]; for at that time both Herod's enemies and friends despaired of his affairs, for it was not probable that he would remain without punishment, who had showed so much friendship for Antony. So it happened that his friends despaired, and had no hopes of his escape; but for his enemies, they all outwardly appeared to be troubled at his case, but were privately very glad of it, as hoping to obtain a change for the better. As for Herod himself he saw that there was no one of royal dignity left but Hyrcanus, and therefore he thought it would be for his advantage not to suffer him to be an obstacle in his way any longer; for that in case he himself survived, and escaped the danger he was in, he thought it the safest way to put it out of the power of such a man to make any attempt against him, at such junctures of affairs, as was more worthy of the kingdom than himself; and in case he should be slain by Caesar, his envy prompted him to desire to slay him that would otherwise be king after him.

2. While Herod had these things in his mind, there was a certain occasion afforded him: for Hyrcanus was of so mild a temper, both then and at other times, that he desired not to meddle with public affairs, nor to concern himself with innovations, but left all to fortune, and contented himself with what that afforded him: but Alexandra [his daughter] was a lover of strife, and was exceeding desirous of a change of the government, and spake to her father not to bear for ever Herod's injurious treatment of their family, but to anticipate their future hopes, as he safely might; and desired him to write about these

matters to Malchus, who was then governor of Arabia, to receive them, and to secure them [from Herod], for that if they went away, and Herod's affairs proved to be as it was likely they would be, by reason of Caesar's enmity to him, they should then be the only persons that could take the government; and this, both on account of the royal family they were of, and on account of the good disposition of: the multitude to them. While she used these persuasions, Hyrcanus put off her suit; but as she showed that she was a woman, and a contentious woman too, and would not desist either night or day, but would always be speaking to him about these matters, and about Herod's treacherous designs, she at last prevailed with him to intrust Dositheus, one of his friends, with a letter, wherein his resolution was declared; and he desired the Arabian governor to send to him some horsemen, who should receive him, and conduct him to the lake Asphaltites, which is from the bounds of Jerusalem three hundred furlongs: and he did therefore trust Dositheus with this letter, because he was a careful attendant on him, and on Alexandra, and had no small occasions to bear ill-will to Herod; for he was a kinsman of one Joseph, whom he had slain, and a brother of those that were formerly slain at Tyre by Antony: yet could not these motives induce Dositheus to serve Hyrcanus in this affair; for, preferring the hopes he had from the present king to those he had from him, he gave Herod the letter. So he took his kindness in good part, and bid him besides do what he had already done, that is, go on in serving him, by rolling up the epistle and sealing it again, and delivering it to Malchus, and then to bring back his letter in answer to it; for it would be much better if he could know Malchus's intentions also. And when Dositheus was very ready to serve him in this point also, the Arabian governor returned back for answer, that he would receive Hyrcanus, and all that should come with him, and even all the Jews that were of his party; that he would, moreover, send forces sufficient to secure them in their journey; and that he should be in no want of any thing he should desire. Now as soon as Herod had received this letter, he immediately sent for Hyrcanus, and questioned him about the league he had made with Malchus; and when he denied it, he showed his letter to the Sanhedrim, and put the man to death immediately.

3. And this account we give the reader, as it is contained in the commentaries of king Herod: but other historians do not agree with

them, for they suppose that Herod did not find, but rather make, this an occasion for thus putting him to death, and that by treacherously laying a snare for him; for thus do they write: That Herod and he were once at a treat, and that Herod had given no occasion to suspect [that he was displeased at him], but put this question to Hyrcanus, Whether he had received any letters from Malchus? and when he answered that he had received letters, but those of salutation only; and when he asked further, whether he had not received any presents from him? and when he had replied that he had received no more than four horses to ride on, which Malchus had sent him; they pretended that Herod charged these upon him as the crimes of bribery and treason, and gave order that he should be led away and slain. And in order to demonstrate that he had been guilty of no offense, when he was thus brought to his end, they alleged how mild his temper had been, and that even in his youth he had never given any demonstration of boldness or rashness, and that the case was the same when he came to be king, but that he even then committed the management of the greatest part of public affairs to Antipater; and that he was now above fourscore years old, and knew that Herod's government was in a secure state. He also came over Euphrates, and left those who greatly honored him beyond that river, though he were to be entirely under Herod's government; and that it was a most incredible thing that he should enterprise any thing by way of innovation, and not at all agreeable to his temper, but that this was a plot of Herod's contrivance.

4. And this was the fate of Hyrcanus; and thus did he end his life, after he had endured various and manifold turns of fortune in his lifetime. For he was made high priest of the Jewish nation in the beginning of his mother Alexandra's reign, who held the government nine years; and when, after his mother's death, he took the kingdom himself, and held it three months, he lost it, by the means of his brother Aristobulus. He was then restored by Pompey, and received all sorts of honor from him, and enjoyed them forty years; but when he was again deprived by Antigonus, and was maimed in his body, he was made a captive by the Parthians, and thence returned home again after some time, on account of the hopes that Herod had given him; none of which came to pass according to his expectation, but he still conflicted with many misfortunes through the whole course of his life; and, what was the heaviest calamity of all, as we have related already, he came

to an end which was undeserved by him. His character appeared to be that of a man of a mild and moderate disposition, and suffered the administration of affairs to be generally done by others under him. He was averse to much meddling with the public, nor had shrewdness enough to govern a kingdom. And both Antipater and Herod came to their greatness by reason of his mildness; and at last he met with such an end from them as was not agreeable either to justice or piety.

5. Now Herod, as soon as he had put Hyrcanus out of the way, made haste to Caesar; and because he could not have any hopes of kindness from him, on account of the friendship he had for Antony, he had a suspicion of Alexandra, lest she should take this opportunity to bring the multitude to a revolt, and introduce a sedition into the affairs of the kingdom; so he committed the care of every thing to his brother Pheroras, and placed his mother Cypros, and his sister [Salome], and the whole family at Masada, and gave him a charge, that if he should hear any sad news about him, he should take care of the government. But as to Mariamne his wife, because of the misunderstanding between her and his sister, and his sister's mother, which made it impossible for them to live together, he placed her at Alexandrium, with Alexandra her mother, and left his treasurer Joseph and Sohemus of Iturea to take care of that fortress. These two had been very faithful to him from the beginning, and were now left as a guard to the women. They also had it in charge, that if they should hear any mischief had befallen him, they should kill them both, and, as far as they were able, to preserve the kingdom for his sons, and for his brother Pheroras.

6. When he had given them this charge, he made haste to Rhodes, to meet Caesar; and when he had sailed to that city, he took off his diadem, but remitted nothing else of his usual dignity. And when, upon his meeting him, he desired that he would let him speak to him, he therein exhibited a much more noble specimen of a great soul; for he did not betake himself to supplications, as men usually do upon such occasions, nor offered him any petition, as if he were an offender; but, after an undaunted manner, gave an account of what he had done; for he spake thus to Caesar: That he had the greatest friendship for Antony, and did every thing he could that he might attain the government; that he was not indeed in the army with him, because the Arabians had diverted him; but that he had sent him both money

and corn, which was but too little in comparison of what he ought to have done for him; "for if a man owns himself to be another's friend, and knows him to be a benefactor, he is obliged to hazard every thing, to use every faculty of his soul, every member of his body, and all the wealth he hath, for him, in which I confess I have been too deficient. However, I am conscious to myself, that so far I have done right, that I have not deserted him upon his defeat at Actium; nor upon the evident change of his fortune have I transferred my hopes from him to another, but have preserved myself, though not as a valuable fellow soldier, yet certainly as a faithful counselor, to Antony, when I demonstrated to him that the only way that he had to save himself, and not to lose all his authority, was to slay Cleopatra; for when she was once dead, there would be room for him to retain his authority, and rather to bring thee to make a composition with him, than to continue at enmity any longer. None of which advises would he attend to, but preferred his own rash resolution before them, which have happened unprofitably for him, but profitably for thee. Now, therefore, in case thou determinest about me, and my alacrity in serving Antony, according to thy anger at him, I own there is no room for me to deny what I have done, nor will I be ashamed to own, and that publicly too, that I had a great kindness for him. But if thou wilt put him out of the case, and only examine how I behave myself to my benefactors in general, and what sort of friend I am, thou wilt find by experience that we shall do and be the same to thyself, for it is but changing the names, and the firmness of friendship that we shall bear to thee will not be disapproved by thee."

7. By this speech, and by his behavior, which showed Caesar the frankness of his mind, he greatly gained upon him, who was himself of a generous and magnificent temper, insomuch that those very actions, which were the foundation of the accusation against him, procured him Caesar's good-will. Accordingly, he restored him his diadem again; and encouraged him to exhibit himself as great a friend to himself as he had been to Antony, and then had him in great esteem. Moreover, he added this, that Quintus Didius had written to him that Herod had very readily assisted him in the affair of the gladiators. So when he had obtained such a kind reception, and had, beyond all his hopes, procured his crown to be more entirely and firmly settled upon him than ever by Caesar's donation, as well as by that decree of the Romans, which Caesar took care to procure for his greater

security, he conducted Caesar on his way to Egypt, and made presents, even beyond his ability, to both him and his friends, and in general behaved himself with great magnanimity. He also desired that Caesar would not put to death one Alexander, who had been a companion of Antony; but Caesar had sworn to put him to death, and so he could not obtain that his petition. And now he returned to Judea again with greater honor and assurance than ever, and affrighted those that had expectations to the contrary, as still acquiring from his very dangers greater splendor than before, by the favor of God to him. So he prepared for the reception of Caesar, as he was going out of Syria to invade Egypt; and when he came, he entertained him at Ptolemais with all royal magnificence. He also bestowed presents on the army, and brought them provisions in abundance. He also proved to be one of Caesar's most cordial friends, and put the army in array, and rode along with Caesar, and had a hundred and fifty men, well appointed in all respects, after a rich and sumptuous manner, for the better reception of him and his friends. He also provided them with what they should want, as they passed over the dry desert, insomuch that they lacked neither wine nor water, which last the soldiers stood in the greatest need of; and besides, he presented Caesar with eight hundred talents, and procured to himself the good-will of them all, because he was assisting to them in a much greater and more splendid degree than the kingdom he had obtained could afford; by which means he more and more demonstrated to Caesar the firmness of his friendship, and his readiness to assist him; and what was of the greatest advantage to him was this, that his liberality came at a seasonable time also. And when they returned again out of Egypt, his assistances were no way inferior to the good offices he had formerly done them.

7 *How Herod Slew Sohemus and Mariamne and Afterward Alexandra and Costobarus, and His Most Intimate Friends, and at Last the Sons of Babbas Also*

1. HOWEVER, when he came into his kingdom again, he found his house all in disorder, and his wife Mariamne and her mother Alexandra very uneasy; for as they supposed (what was easy to be supposed) that they were not put into that fortress [Alexandrium]

for the security of their persons, but as into a garrison for their imprisonment, and that they had no power over any thing, either of others or of their own affairs, they were very uneasy; and Mariamne supposing that the king's love to her was but hypocritical, and rather pretended (as advantageous to himself) than real, she looked upon it as fallacious. She also was grieved that he would not allow her any hopes of surviving him, if he should come to any harm himself. She also recollected what commands he had formerly given to Joseph, insomuch that she endeavored to please her keepers, and especially Sohemus, as well apprized how all was in his power. And at the first Sohemus was faithful to Herod, and neglected none of the things he had given him in charge; but when the women, by kind words and liberal presents, had gained his affections over to them, he was by degrees overcome, and at length discovered to them all the king's injunctions, and this on that account principally, that he did not so much as hope he would come back with the same authority he had before; so that he thought he should both escape any danger from him, mid supposed that he did hereby much gratify the women, who were likely not to be overlooked in the settling of the government; nay, that they would be able to make him abundant recompense, since they must either reign themselves, or be very near to him that should reign. He had a further ground of hope also, that though Herod should have all the success he could wish for, and should return again, he could not contradict his wife in what she desired, for he knew that the king's fondness for his wife was inexpressible. These were the motives that drew Sohemus to discover what injunctions had been given him. So Mariamne was greatly displeased to hear that there was no end of the dangers she was under from Herod, and was greatly uneasy at it, and wished that he might obtain no favors [from Caesar], and esteemed it almost an insupportable task to live with him any longer; and this she afterward openly declared, without concealing her resentment.

2. And now Herod sailed home with joy, at the unexpected good success he had had; and went first of all, as was proper, to this his wife, and told her, and her only, the good news, as preferring her before the rest, on account of his fondness for her, and the intimacy there had been between them, and saluted her; but so it happened, that as he told her of the good success he had had, she was so far from rejoicing at it, that she rather was sorry for it; nor was she able

to conceal her resentments, but, depending on her dignity, and the nobility of her birth, in return for his salutations, she gave a groan, and declared evidently that she rather grieved than rejoiced at his success, and this till Herod was disturbed at her, as affording him, not only marks of her suspicion, but evident signs of her dissatisfaction. This much troubled him, to see that this surprising hatred of his wife to him was not concealed, but open; and he took this so ill, and yet was so unable to bear it, on account of the fondness he had for her, that he could not continue long in any one mind, but sometimes was angry at her, and sometimes reconciled himself to her; but by always changing one passion for another, he was still in great uncertainty, and thus was he entangled between hatred and love, and was frequently disposed to inflict punishment on her for her insolence towards him; but being deeply in love with her in his soul, he was not able to get quit of this woman. In short, as he would gladly have her punished, so was he afraid lest, ere he were aware, he should, by putting her to death, bring a heavier punishment upon himself at the same time.

3. When Herod's sister and mother perceived that he was in this temper with regard to Mariamne they thought they had now got an excellent opportunity to exercise their hatred against her and provoked Herod to wrath by telling him, such long stories and calumnies about her, as might at once excite his hatred and his jealousy. Now, though he willingly enough heard their words, yet had not he courage enough to do any thing to her as if he believed them; but still he became worse and worse disposed to her, and these ill passions were more and more inflamed on both sides, while she did not hide her disposition towards him, and he turned his love to her into wrath against her. But when he was just going to put this matter past all remedy, he heard the news that Caesar was the victor in the war, and that Antony and Cleopatra were both dead, and that he had conquered Egypt; whereupon he made haste to go to meet Caesar, and left the affairs of his family in their present state. However, Mariamne recommended Sohemus to him, as he was setting out on his journey, and professed that she owed him thanks for the care he had taken of her, and asked of the king for him a place in the government; upon which an honorable employment was bestowed upon him accordingly. Now when Herod was come into Egypt, he was introduced to Caesar with great freedom, as already a friend of his, and received very great favors from him; for he made him

a present of those four hundred Galatians who had been Cleopatra's guards, and restored that country to him again, which, by her means, had been taken away from him. He also added to his kingdom Gadara, Hippos, and Samaria; and, besides those, the maritime cities, Gaza, and Anthedon, and Joppa, and Strato's Tower.

4. Upon these new acquisitions, he grew more magnificent, and conducted Caesar as far as Antioch; but upon his return, as much as his prosperity was augmented by the foreign additions that had been made him, so much the greater were the distresses that came upon him in his own family, and chiefly in the affair of his wife, wherein he formerly appeared to have been most of all fortunate; for the affection he had for Mariamne was no way inferior to the affections of such as are on that account celebrated in history, and this very justly. As for her, she was in other respects a chaste woman, and faithful to him; yet had she somewhat of a woman rough by nature, and treated her husband imperiously enough, because she saw he was so fond of her as to be enslaved to her. She did not also consider seasonably with herself that she lived under a monarchy, and that she was at another's disposal, and accordingly would behave herself after a saucy manner to him, which yet he usually put off in a jesting way, and bore with moderation and good temper. She would also expose his mother and his sister openly, on account of the meanness of their birth, and would speak unkindly of them, insomuch that there was before this a disagreement and unpardonable hatred among the women, and it was now come to greater reproaches of one another than formerly, which suspicions increased, and lasted a whole year after Herod returned from Caesar. However, these misfortunes, which had been kept under some decency for a great while, burst out all at once upon such an occasion as was now offered; for as the king was one day about noon lain down on his bed to rest him, he called for Mariamne, out of the great affection he had always for her. She came in accordingly, but would not lie down by him; and when he was very desirous of her company, she showed her contempt of him; and added, by way of reproach, that he had caused her father and her brother to be slain.[11] And when he took this injury very unkindly, and was ready to use violence to her, in a precipitate manner, the king's sister Salome,

11. Whereas Mariamne is here represented as reproaching: Herod with the murder

observing that he was more than ordinarily disturbed, sent in to the king his cup-bearer, who had been prepared long beforehand for such a design, and bid him tell the king how Mariamne had persuaded him to give his assistance in preparing a love potion for him; and if he appeared to be greatly concerned, and to ask what that love potion was, to tell him that she had the potion, and that he was desired only to give it him; but that in case he did not appear to be much concerned at this potion, to let the thing drop; and that if he did so, no harm should thereby come to him. When she had given him these instructions, she sent him in at this time to make such a speech. So he went in, after a composed manner, to gain credit to what he should say, and yet somewhat hastily, and said that Mariamne had given him presents, and persuaded him to give him a love potion. And when this moved the king, he said that this love potion was a composition that she had given him, whose effects he did not know, which was the reason of his resolving to give him this information, as the safest course he could take, both for himself and for the king. When Herod heard what he said, and was in an ill disposition before, his indignation grew more violent; and he ordered that eunuch of Mariamne, who was most faithful to her, to be brought to torture about this potion, as well knowing it was not possible that any thing small or great could be done without him. And when the man was under the utmost agonies, he could say nothing concerning the thing he was tortured about, but so far he knew, that Mariamne's hatred against him was occasioned by somewhat that Sohemus had said to her. Now as he was saying this, Herod cried out aloud, and said that Sohemus, who had been at all other times most faithful to him, and to his government, would not have betrayed what injunctions he had given him, unless he had had a nearer conversation than ordinary with Mariamne. So he gave order that Sohemus should be seized on and slain immediately; but he allowed his wife to take her trial; and got together those that were most faithful to him, and laid an elaborate accusation against her for

---

of her father [Alexander], as well as her brother [Aristobulus], while it was her grandfather Hyrcanus, and not her father Alexander, whom he caused to be slain, (as Josephus himself informs us, ch. 6. sect. 2,) we must either take Zonaras's reading, which is here grandfather, rightly, or else we must, as before, ch. 1. sect. 1, allow a slip of Josephus's pen or memory in the place before us.

this love potion and composition, which had been charged upon her by way of calumny only. However, he kept no temper in what he said, and was in too great a passion for judging well about this matter. Accordingly, when the court was at length satisfied that he was so resolved, they passed the sentence of death upon her; but when the sentence was passed upon her, this temper was suggested by himself, and by some others of the court, that she should not be thus hastily put to death, but be laid in prison in one of the fortresses belonging to the kingdom: but Salome and her party labored hard to have the woman put to death; and they prevailed with the king to do so, and advised this out of caution, lest the multitude should be tumultuous if she were suffered to live; and thus was Mariamne led to execution.

5. When Alexandra observed how things went, and that there were small hopes that she herself should escape the like treatment from Herod, she changed her behavior to quite the reverse of what might have been expected from her former boldness, and this after a very indecent manner; for out of her desire to show how entirely ignorant she was of the crimes laid against Mariamne, she leaped out of her place, and reproached her daughter in the hearing of all the people; and cried out that she had been an ill woman, and ungrateful to her husband, and that her punishment came justly upon her for such her insolent behavior, for that she had not made proper returns to him who had been their common benefactor. And when she had for some time acted after this hypocritical manner, and been so outrageous as to tear her hair, this indecent and dissembling behavior, as was to be expected, was greatly condemned by the rest of the spectators, as it was principally by the poor woman who was to suffer; for at the first she gave her not a word, nor was discomposed at her peevishness, and only looked at her, yet did she out of a greatness of soul discover her concern for her mother's offense, and especially for her exposing herself in a manner so unbecoming her; but as for herself, she went to her death with an unshaken firmness of mind, and without changing the color of her face, and thereby evidently discovered the nobility of her descent to the spectators, even in the last moments of her life.

6. And thus died Mariamne, a woman of an excellent character, both for chastity and greatness of soul; but she wanted moderation, and had too much of contention in her nature; yet had she all that can be said in the beauty of her body, and her majestic appearance in conversation;

and thence arose the greatest part of the occasions why she did not prove so agreeable to the king, nor live so pleasantly with him, as she might otherwise have done; for while she was most indulgently used by the king, out of his fondness for her, and did not expect that he could do any hard thing to her, she took too unbounded a liberty. Moreover, that which most afflicted her was, what he had done to her relations, and she ventured to speak of all they had suffered by him, and at last greatly provoked both the king's mother and sister, till they became enemies to her; and even he himself also did the same, on whom alone she depended for her expectations of escaping the last of punishments.

7. But when she was once dead, the king's affections for her were kindled in a more outrageous manner than before, whose old passion for her we have already described; for his love to her was not of a calm nature, nor such as we usually meet with among other husbands; for at its commencement it was of an enthusiastic kind, nor was it by their long cohabitation and free conversation together brought under his power to manage; but at this time his love to Mariamne seemed to seize him in such a peculiar manner, as looked like Divine vengeance upon him for the taking away her life; for he would frequently call for her, and frequently lament for her in a most indecent manner. Moreover, he bethought him of every thing he could make use of to divert his mind from thinking of her, and contrived feasts and assemblies for that purpose, but nothing would suffice; he therefore laid aside the administration of public affairs, and was so far conquered by his passion, that he would order his servants to call for Mariamne, as if she were still alive, and could still hear them. And when he was in this way, there arose a pestilential disease, and carried off the greatest part of the multitude, and of his best and most esteemed friends, and made all men suspect that this was brought upon them by the anger of God, for the injustice that had been done to Mariamne. This circumstance affected the king still more, till at length he forced himself to go into desert places, and there, under pretense of going a hunting, bitterly afflicted himself; yet had he not borne his grief there many days before he fell into a most dangerous distemper himself: he had an inflammation upon him, and a pain in the hinder part of his head, joined with madness; and for the remedies that were used, they did him no good at all, but proved contrary to his case, and

so at length brought him to despair. All the physicians also that were about him, partly because the medicines they brought for his recovery could not at all conquer the disease, and partly because his diet could be no other than what his disease inclined him to, desired him to eat whatever he had a mind to, and so left the small hopes they had of his recovery in the power of that diet, and committed him to fortune. And thus did his distemper go on, while he was at Samaria, now called Sebaste.

8. Now Alexandra abode at this time at Jerusalem; and being informed what condition Herod was in, she endeavored to get possession of the fortified places that were about the city, which were two, the one belonging to the city itself, the other belonging to the temple; and those that could get them into their hands had the whole nation under their power, for without the command of them it was not possible to offer their sacrifices; and to think of leaving on those sacrifices is to every Jew plainly impossible, who are still more ready to lose their lives than to leave off that Divine worship which they have been wont to pay unto God. Alexandra, therefore, discoursed with those that had the keeping of these strong holds, that it was proper for them to deliver the same to her, and to Herod's sons, lest, upon his death, any other person should seize upon the government; and that upon his recovery none could keep them more safely for him than those of his own family. These words were not by them at all taken in good part; and as they had been in former times faithful [to Herod], they resolved to continue so more than ever, both because they hated Alexandra, and because they thought it a sort of impiety to despair of Herod's recovery while he was yet alive, for they had been his old friends; and one of them, whose name was Achiabus, was his cousin-german. They sent messengers therefore to acquaint him with Alexandra's design; so he made no longer delay, but gave orders to have her slain; yet was it still with difficulty, and after he had endured great pain, that he got clear of his distemper. He was still sorely afflicted, both in mind and body, and made very uneasy, and readier than ever upon all occasions to inflict punishment upon those that fell under his hand. He also slew the most intimate of his friends, Costobarus, and Lysimachus, and Cadias, who was also called Antipater; as also Dositheus, and that upon the following occasion.

9. Costobarus was an Idumean by birth, and one of principal dignity among them, and one whose ancestors had been priests to the Koze, whom the Idumeans had [formerly] esteemed as a god; but after Hyrcanus had made a change in their political government, and made them receive the Jewish customs and law, Herod made Costobarus governor of Idumea and Gaza, and gave him his sister Salome to wife; and this was upon the slaughter of [his uncle] Joseph, who had that government before, as we have related already. When Costobarus had gotten to be so highly advanced, it pleased him and was more than he hoped for, and he was more and more puffed up by his good success, and in a little while he exceeded all bounds, and did not think fit to obey what Herod, as their ruler, commanded him, or that the Idumeans should make use of the Jewish customs, or be subject to them. He therefore sent to Cleopatra, and informed her that the Idumeans had been always under his progenitors, and that for the same reason it was but just that she should desire that country for him of Antony, for that he was ready to transfer his friendship to her; and this he did, not because he was better pleased to be under Cleopatra's government, but because he thought that, upon the diminution of Herod's power, it would not be difficult for him to obtain himself the entire government over the Idumeans, and somewhat more also; for he raised his hopes still higher, as having no small pretenses, both by his birth and by these riches which he had gotten by his constant attention to filthy lucre; and accordingly it was not a small matter that he aimed at. So Cleopatra desired this country of Antony, but failed of her purpose. An account of this was brought to Herod, who was thereupon ready to kill Costobarus; yet, upon the entreaties of his sister and mother, he forgave him, and vouchsafed to pardon him entirely; though he still had a suspicion of him afterward for this his attempt.

10. But some time afterward, when Salome happened to quarrel with Costobarus, she sent him a bill of divorce[12] and dissolved her

12. Here is a plain example of a Jewish lady giving a bill of divorce to her husband, though in the days of Josephus it was not esteemed lawful for a woman so to do. See the like among the Parthians, Antiq. B. XVIII. ch. 9. sect. 6. However, the Christian law, when it allowed divorce for adultery, Matthew 5:32, allowed the innocent wife to divorce her guilty husband, as well as the innocent husband to divorce his guilty

marriage with him, though this was not according to the Jewish laws; for with us it is lawful for a husband to do so; but a wife; if she departs from her husband, cannot of herself be married to another, unless her former husband put her away. However, Salome chose to follow not the law of her country, but the law of her authority, and so renounced her wedlock; and told her brother Herod, that she left her husband out of her good-will to him, because she perceived that he, with Antipater, and Lysimachus, and Dositheus, were raising a sedition against him; as an evidence whereof, she alleged the case of the sons of Babas, that they had been by him preserved alive already for the interval of twelve years; which proved to be true. But when Herod thus unexpectedly heard of it, he was greatly surprised at it, and was the more surprised, because the relation appeared incredible to him. As for the fact relating to these sons of Babas, Herod had formerly taken great pains to bring them to punishment, as being enemies to his government; but they were now forgotten by him, on account of the length of time [since he had ordered them to be slain]. Now the cause of his ill-will and hatred to them arose hence, that while Antigonus was king, Herod, with his army, besieged the city of Jerusalem, where the distress and miseries which the besieged endured were so pressing, that the greater number of them invited Herod into the city, and already placed their hopes on him. Now the sons of Babas were of great dignity, and had power among the multitude, and were faithful to Antigonus, and were always raising calumnies against Herod, and encouraged the people to preserve the government to that royal family which held it by inheritance. So these men acted thus politically, and, as they thought, for their own advantage; but when the city was taken, and

---

wife, as we learn from the shepherd of Hermas, Mand. B. IV., and from: the second apology of Justin Martyr, where a persecution was brought upon the Christians upon such a divorce; and I think the Roman laws permitted it at that time, as well as the laws of Christianity. Now this Babas, who was one of the race of the Asamoneans or Maccabees, as the latter end of this section informs us, is related by the Jews, as Dr. Hudson here remarks, to have been so eminently religious in the Jewish way, that, except the day following the tenth of Tisri, the great day of atonement, when he seems to have supposed all his sins entirely forgiven, he used every day of the whole year to offer a sacrifice for his sins of ignorance, or such as he supposed he had been guilty of, but did not distinctly remember. See somewhat like it of Agrippa the Great, Antiq. B. XIX. ch. 3. sect. 3, and Job 1:4, 5.

Herod had gotten the government into his hands, and Costobarus was appointed to hinder men from passing out at the gates, and to guard the city, that those citizens that were guilty, and of the party opposite to the king, might not get out of it, Costobarus, being sensible that the sons of Babas were had in respect and honor by the whole multitude, and supposing that their preservation might be of great advantage to him in the changes of government afterward, he set them by themselves, and concealed them in his own farms; and when the thing was suspected, he assured Herod upon oath that he really knew nothing of that matter, and so overcame the suspicions that lay upon him; nay, after that, when the king had publicly proposed a reward for the discovery, and had put in practice all sorts of methods for searching out this matter, he would not confess it; but being persuaded that when he had at first denied it, if the men were found, he should not escape unpunished, he was forced to keep them secret, not only out of his good-will to them, but out of a necessary regard to his own preservation also. But when the king knew the thing, by his sister's information, he sent men to the places where he had the intimation they were concealed, and ordered both them, and those that were accused as guilty with them, to be slain, insomuch that there were now none at all left of the kindred of Hyrcanus, and the kingdom was entirely in Herod's own power, and there was nobody remaining of such dignity as could put a stop to what he did against the Jewish laws.

8 *How Ten Men of the Citizens [of Jerusalem] Made a Conspiracy Against Herod, for the Foreign Practices He Had Introduced, Which Was a Transgression of the Laws of Their Country. Concerning the Building of Sebaste and Cesarea, and Other Edifices of Herod*

1. ON this account it was that Herod revolted from the laws of his country, and corrupted their ancient constitution, by the introduction of foreign practices, which constitution yet ought to have been preserved inviolable; by which means we became guilty of great wickedness afterward, while those religious observances which used to lead the multitude to piety were now neglected; for, in the first

place, he appointed solemn games to be celebrated every fifth year, in honor of Caesar, and built a theater at Jerusalem, as also a very great amphitheater in the plain. Both of them were indeed costly works, but opposite to the Jewish customs; for we have had no such shows delivered down to us as fit to be used or exhibited by us; yet did he celebrate these games every five years, in the most solemn and splendid manner. He also made proclamation to the neighboring countries, and called men together out of every nation. The wrestlers also, and the rest of those that strove for the prizes in such games, were invited out of every land, both by the hopes of the rewards there to be bestowed, and by the glory of victory to be there gained. So the principal persons that were the most eminent in these sorts of exercises were gotten together, for there were very great rewards for victory proposed, not only to those that performed their exercises naked, but to those that played the musicians also, and were called Thymelici; and he spared no pains to induce all persons, the most famous for such exercises, to come to this contest for victory. He also proposed no small rewards to those who ran for the prizes in chariot races, when they were drawn by two, or three, or four pair of horses. He also imitated every thing, though never so costly or magnificent, in other nations, out of an ambition that he might give most public demonstration of his grandeur. Inscriptions also of the great actions of Caesar, and trophies of those nations which he had conquered in his wars, and all made of the purest gold and silver, encompassed the theater itself; nor was there any thing that could be subservient to his design, whether it were precious garments, or precious stones set in order, which was not also exposed to sight in these games. He had also made a great preparation of wild beasts, and of lions themselves in great abundance, and of such other beasts as were either of uncommon strength, or of such a sort as were rarely seen. These were prepared either to fight with one another, or that men who were condemned to death were to fight with them. And truly foreigners were greatly surprised and delighted at the vastness of the expenses here exhibited, and at the great dangers that were here seen; but to natural Jews, this was no better than a dissolution of those customs for which they had so great a veneration.[13] It appeared also no better than an instance of barefaced

---

13. These grand plays, and shows, and Thymelici, or music meetings, and chariot races, when the chariots were drawn by two, three, or four pair of horses, etc.,

impiety, to throw men to wild beasts, for the affording delight to the spectators; and it appeared an instance of no less impiety, to change their own laws for such foreign exercises: but, above all the rest, the trophies gave most distaste to the Jews; for as they imagined them to be images, included within the armor that hung round about them, they were sorely displeased at them, because it was not the custom of their country to pay honors to such images.

2. Nor was Herod unacquainted with the disturbance they were under; and as he thought it unseasonable to use violence with them, so he spake to some of them by way of consolation, and in order to free them from that superstitious fear they were under; yet could not he satisfy them, but they cried out with one accord, out of their great uneasiness at the offenses they thought he had been guilty of, that although they should think of bearing all the rest yet would they never bear images of men in their city, meaning the trophies, because this was disagreeable to the laws of their country. Now when Herod saw them in such a disorder, and that they would not easily change their resolution unless they received satisfaction in this point, he called to him the most eminent men among them, and brought them upon the theater, and showed them the trophies, and asked them what sort of things they took these trophies to be; and when they cried out that they were the images of men, he gave order that they should be stripped of these outward ornaments which were about them, and showed them the naked pieces of wood; which pieces of wood, now without any ornament, became matter of great sport and laughter to them, because they had before always had the ornaments of images themselves in derision.

3. When therefore Herod had thus got clear of the multitude, and had dissipated the vehemency of passion under which they had been, the greatest part of the people were disposed to change their conduct, and not to be displeased at him any longer; but still some of them

---

instituted by Herod in his theatres, were still, as we see here, looked on by the sober Jews as heathenish sports, and tending to corrupt the manners of the Jewish nation, and to bring them in love with paganish idolatry, and paganish conduct of life, but to the dissolution of the law of Moses, and accordingly were greatly and justly condemned by them, as appears here and every where else in Josephus. Nor is the case of our modern masquerades, plays, operas, and the like "pomps and vanities of this wicked world," of any better tendency under Christianity.

continued in their displeasure against him, for his introduction of new customs, and esteemed the violation of the laws of their country as likely to be the origin of very great mischiefs to them, so that they deemed it an instance of piety rather to hazard themselves [to be put to death], than to seem as if they took no notice of Herod, who, upon the change he had made in their government, introduced such customs, and that in a violent manner, which they had never been used to before, as indeed in pretense a king, but in reality one that showed himself an enemy to their whole nation; on which account ten men that were citizens [of Jerusalem] conspired together against him, and sware to one another to undergo any dangers in the attempt, and took daggers with them under their garments [for the purpose of killing Herod]. Now there was a certain blind man among those conspirators who had thus sworn to one another, on account of the indignation he had against what he heard to have been done; he was not indeed able to afford the rest any assistance in the undertaking, but was ready to undergo any suffering with them, if so be they should come to any harm, insomuch that he became a very great encourager of the rest of the undertakers.

4. When they had taken this resolution, and that by common consent, they went into the theater, hoping that, in the first place, Herod himself could not escape them, as they should fall upon him so unexpectedly; and supposing, however, that if they missed him, they should kill a great many of those that were about him; and this resolution they took, though they should die for it, in order to suggest to the king what injuries he had done to the multitude. These conspirators, therefore, standing thus prepared beforehand, went about their design with great alacrity; but there was one of those spies of Herod, that were appointed for such purposes, to fish out and inform him of any conspiracies that should be made against him, who found out the whole affair, and told the king of it, as he was about to go into the theater. So when he reflected on the hatred which he knew the greatest part of the people bore him, and on the disturbances that arose upon every occasion, he thought this plot against him not to be improbable. Accordingly, he retired into his palace, and called those that were accused of this conspiracy before him by their several names; and as, upon the guards falling upon them, they were caught in the very fact, and knew they could not escape, they prepared themselves for their

ends with all the decency they could, and so as not at all to recede from their resolute behavior, for they showed no shame for what they were about, nor denied it; but when they were seized, they showed their daggers, and professed that the conspiracy they had sworn to was a holy and pious action; that what they intended to do was not for gain, or out of any indulgence to their passions, but principally for those common customs of their country, which all the Jews were obliged to observe, or to die for them. This was what these men said, out of their undaunted courage in this conspiracy. So they were led away to execution by the king's guards that stood about them, and patiently underwent all the torments inflicted on them till they died. Nor was it long before that spy who had discovered them was seized on by some of the people, out of the hatred they bore to him; and was not only slain by them, but pulled to pieces, limb from limb, and given to the dogs. This execution was seen by many of the citizens, yet would not one of them discover the doers of it, till upon Herod's making a strict scrutiny after them, by bitter and severe tortures, certain women that were tortured confessed what they had seen done; the authors of which fact were so terribly punished by the king, that their entire families were destroyed for this their rash attempt; yet did not the obstinacy of the people, and that undaunted constancy they showed in the defense of their laws, make Herod any easier to them, but he still strengthened himself after a more secure manner, and resolved to encompass the multitude every way, lest such innovations should end in an open rebellion.

5. Since, therefore, he had now the city fortified by the palace in which he lived, and by the temple which had a strong fortress by it, called Antonia, and was rebuilt by himself, he contrived to make Samaria a fortress for himself also against all the people, and called it Sebaste, supposing that this place would be a strong hold against the country, not inferior to the former. So he fortified that place, which was a day's journey distant from Jerusalem, and which would be useful to him in common, to keep both the country and the city in awe. He also built another fortress for the whole nation; it was of old called Strato's Tower, but was by him named Cesarea. Moreover, he chose out some select horsemen, and placed them ill the great plain; and built [for them] a place in Galilee, called Gaba with Hesebonitis, in Perea. And these were the places which he particularly built, while

he always was inventing somewhat further for his own security, and encompassing the whole nation with guards, that they might by no means get from under his power, nor fall into tumults, which they did continually upon any small commotion; and that if they did make any commotions, he might know of it, while some of his spies might be upon them from the neighborhood, and might both be able to know what they were attempting, and to prevent it. And when he went about building the wall of Samaria, he contrived to bring thither many of those that had been assisting to him in his wars, and many of the people in that neighborhood also, whom he made fellow citizens with the rest. This he did out of an ambitious desire of building a temple, and out of a desire to make the city more eminent than it had been before; but principally because he contrived that it might at once be for his own security, and a monument of his magnificence. He also changed its name, and called it Sebaste. Moreover, he parted the adjoining country, which was excellent in its kind, among the inhabitants of Samaria, that they might be in a happy condition, upon their first coming to inhabit. Besides all which, he encompassed the city with a wall of great strength, and made use of the acclivity of the place for making its fortifications stronger; nor was the compass of the place made now so small as it had been before, but was such as rendered it not inferior to the most famous cities; for it was twenty furlongs in circumference. Now within, and about the middle of it, he built a sacred place, of a furlong and a half [in circuit], and adorned it with all sorts of decorations, and therein erected a temple, which was illustrious on account of both its largeness and beauty. And as to the several parts of the city, he adorned them with decorations of all sorts also; and as to what was necessary to provide for his own security, he made the walls very strong for that purpose, and made it for the greatest part a citadel; and as to the elegance of the building, it was taken care of also, that he might leave monuments of the fineness of his taste, and of his beneficence, to future ages.

9 *Concerning the Famine That Happened in Judea and Syria; and How Herod, After He Had Married Another Wife, Rebuilt Cesarea, and Other Grecian Cities*

1. NOW on this very year, which was the thirteenth year of the reign of Herod, very great calamities came upon the country; whether they were derived from the anger of God, or whether this misery returns again naturally in certain periods of time[14] for, in the first place, there were perpetual droughts, and for that reason the ground was barren, and did not bring forth the same quantity of fruits that it used to produce; and after this barrenness of the soil, that change of food which the want of corn occasioned produced distempers in the bodies of men, and a pestilential disease prevailed, one misery following upon the back of another; and these circumstances, that they were destitute both of methods of cure and of food, made the pestilential distemper, which began after a violent manner, the more lasting. The destruction of men also after such a manner deprived those that surived of all their courage, because they had no way to provide remedies sufficient for the distresses they were in. When therefore the fruits of that year were spoiled, and whatsoever they had laid up beforehand was spent, there was no foundation of hope for relief remaining, but the misery, contrary to what they expected still increased upon them; and this not only on that year, while they had nothing for themselves left [at the end of it], but what seed they had sown perished also, by reason of the ground not yielding its fruits on the second year.[15] This distress they were in made them also, out of necessity, to eat many things that did not use to be eaten; nor was

---

14. Here we have an eminent example of the language of Josephus in his writing to Gentiles, different from that when he wrote to Jews; in his writing to whom he still derives all such judgments from the anger of God; but because he knew many of the Gentiles thought they might naturally come in certain periods, he complies with them in the following sentence. See the note on the War. B. I. ch. 33. sect. 2.

15. This famine for two years that affected Judea and Syria, the thirteenth mid fourteenth years of Herod, which are the twenty-third and twenty-fourth years before the Christian era, seems to have been more terrible during this time than was that in the days of Jacob, Genesis 41., 42. And what makes the comparison the more remarkable is this, that now, as well as then, the relief they had was from Egypt also; then from Joseph the governor of Egypt, under Pharaoh king of Egypt; and now from Petronius the prefect of Egypt, under Augustus the Roman emperor. See almost the

the king himself free from this distress any more than other men, as being deprived of that tribute he used to have from the fruits of the ground, and having already expended what money he had, in his liberality to those whose cities he had built; nor had he any people that were worthy of his assistance, since this miserable state of things had procured him the hatred of his subjects: for it is a constant rule, that misfortunes are still laid to the account of those that govern.

2. In these circumstances he considered with himself how to procure some seasonable help; but this was a hard thing to be done, while their neighbors had no food to sell them; and their money also was gone, had it been possible to purchase a little food at a great price. However, he thought it his best way, by all means, not to leave off his endeavors to assist his people; so he cut off the rich furniture that was in his palace, both of silver and gold, insomuch that he did not spare the finest vessels he had, or those that were made with the most elaborate skill of the artificers, but sent the money to Petronius, who had been made prefect of Egypt by Caesar; and as not a few had already fled to him under their necessities, and as he was particularly a friend to Herod, and desirous to have his subjects preserved, he gave leave to them in the first place to export corn, and assisted them every way, both in purchasing and exporting the same; so that he was the principal, if not the only person, who afforded them what help they had. And Herod taking care the people should understand that this help came from himself, did thereby not only remove the ill opinion of those that formerly hated him, but gave them the greatest demonstration possible of his good-will to them, and care of them; for, in the first place, as for those who were able to provide their own food, he distributed to them their proportion of corn in the exactest manner; but for those many that were not able, either by reason of their old age, or any other infirmity, to provide food for themselves, he made this provision for them, the bakers should make their bread ready for them. He also took care that they might not be hurt by the dangers of winter,

---

like case, Antiq. B. XX. ch. 2. sect. 6. It is also well worth our observation here, that these two years were a Sabbatic year, and a year of jubilee, for which Providence, during the theocracy, used to provide a triple crop beforehand; but became now, when the Jews had forfeited that blessing, the greatest years of famine to them ever since the days of Ahab, 1 Kings 17., 18.

since they were in great want of clothing also, by reason of the utter destruction and consumption of their sheep and goats, till they had no wool to make use of, nor any thing else to cover themselves withal. And when he had procured these things for his own subjects, he went further, in order to provide necessaries for their neighbors, and gave seed to the Syrians, which thing turned greatly to his own advantage also, this charitable assistance being afforded most seasonably to their fruitful soil, so that every one had now a plentiful provision of food. Upon the whole, when the harvest of the land was approaching, he sent no fewer than fifty thousand men, whom he had sustained, into the country; by which means he both repaired the afflicted condition of his own kingdom with great generosity and diligence, and lightened the afflictions of his neighbors, who were under the same calamities; for there was nobody who had been in want that was left destitute of a suitable assistance by him; nay, further, there were neither any people, nor any cities, nor any private men, who were to make provision for the multitudes, and on that account were in want of support, and had recourse to him, but received what they stood in need of, insomuch that it appeared, upon a computation, that the number of cori of wheat, of ten attic medimni apiece, that were given to foreigners, amounted to ten thousand, and the number that was given in his own kingdom was about fourscore thousand. Now it happened that this care of his, and this seasonable benefaction, had such influence on the Jews, and was so cried up among other nations, as to wipe off that old hatred which his violation of some of their customs, during his reign, had procured him among all the nation, and that this liberality of his assistance in this their greatest necessity was full satisfaction for all that he had done of that nature, as it also procured him great fame among foreigners; and it looked as if these calamities that afflicted his land, to a degree plainly incredible, came in order to raise his glory, and to be to his great advantage; for the greatness of his liberality in these distresses, which he now demonstrated beyond all expectation, did so change the disposition of the multitude towards him, that they were ready to suppose he had been from the beginning not such a one as they had found him to be by experience, but such a one as the care he had taken of them in supplying their necessities proved him now to be.

3. About this time it was that he sent five hundred chosen men out of the guards of his body as auxiliaries to Caesar, whom Aelius

Gallus[16] led to the Red Sea, and who were of great service to him there. When therefore his affairs were thus improved, and were again in a flourishing condition, he built himself a palace in the upper city, raising the rooms to a very great height, and adorning them with the most costly furniture of gold, and marble scats, and beds; and these were so large that they could contain very many companies of men. These apartments were also of distinct magnitudes, and had particular names given them; for one apartment was called Caesar's, another Agrippa's. He also fell in love again, and married another wife, not suffering his reason to hinder him from living as he pleased. The occasion of this his marriage was as follows: There was one Simon, a citizen of Jerusalem, the son of one Boethus, a citizen of Alexandria, and a priest of great note there; this man had a daughter, who was esteemed the most beautiful woman of that time; and when the people of Jerusalem began to speak much in her commendation, it happened that Herod was much affected with what was said of her; and when he saw the damsel, he was smitten with her beauty, yet did he entirely reject the thoughts of using his authority to abuse her, as believing, what was the truth, that by so doing he should be stigmatized for violence and tyranny; so he thought it best to take the damsel to wife. And while Simon was of a dignity too inferior to be allied to him, but still too considerable to be despised, he governed his inclinations after the most prudent manner, by augmenting the dignity of the family, and making them more honorable; so he immediately deprived Jesus, the son of Phabet, of the high priesthood, and conferred that dignity on Simon, and so joined in affinity with him [by marrying his daughter].

4. When this wedding was over, he built another citadel in that place where he had conquered file Jews when he was driven out of his government, and Antigonus enjoyed it. This citadel is distant from Jerusalem about threescore furlongs. It was strong by nature, and fit for such a building. It is a sort of a moderate hill, raised to a further height by the hand of man, till it was of the shape of a woman's breast. It is encompassed with circular towers, and hath a strait ascent up to it,

16. This Aelius Gallus seems to be no other than that Aelius Lagus whom Dio speaks of as conducting an expedition that was about this time made into Arabia Felix, according to Betarius, who is here cited by Spanheim. See a full account of this expedition in Prideaux, at the years 23 and 24.

which ascent is composed of steps of polished stones, in number two hundred. Within it are royal and very rich apartments, of a structure that provided both for security and for beauty. About the bottom there are habitations of such a structure as are well worth seeing, both on other accounts, and also on account of the water which is brought thither from a great way off, and at vast expenses, for the place itself is destitute of water. The plain that is about this citadel is full of edifices, not inferior to any city in largeness, and having the hill above it in the nature of a castle.

5. And now, when all Herod's designs had succeeded according to his hopes, he had not the least suspicion that any troubles could arise in his kingdom, because he kept his people obedient, as well by the fear they stood in of him, for he was implacable in the infliction of his punishments, as by the provident care he had showed towards them, after the most magnanimous manner, when they were under their distresses. But still he took care to have external security for his government as a fortress against his subjects; for the orations he made to the cities were very fine, and full of kindness; and he cultivated a seasonable good understanding with their governors, and bestowed presents on every one of them, inducing them thereby to be more friendly to him, and using his magnificent disposition so as his kingdom might be the better secured to him, and this till all his affairs were every way more and more augmented. But then this magnificent temper of his, and that submissive behavior and liberality which he exercised towards Caesar, and the most powerful men of Rome, obliged him to transgress the customs of his nation, and to set aside many of their laws, and by building cities after an extravagant manner, and erecting temples,—not in Judea indeed, for that would not have been borne, it being forbidden for us to pay any honor to images, or representations of animals, after the manner of the Greeks; but still he did thus in the country [properly] out of our bounds, and in the cities thereof[17] The apology which he made to the Jews for these

---

17. One may here take notice, that how tyrannical and extravagant soever Herod were in himself, and in his Grecian cities, as to those plays, and shows, and temples for idolatry, mentioned above, ch. 8. sect. 1, and here also; yet durst even he introduce very few of them into the cities of the Jews, who, as Josephus here notes, would not even then have borne them, so zealous were they still for many of the laws

things was this: That all was done, not out of his own inclinations, but by the commands and injunctions of others, in order to please Caesar and the Romans, as though he had not the Jewish customs so much in his eye as he had the honor of those Romans, while yet he had himself entirely in view all the while, and indeed was very ambitious to leave great monuments of his government to posterity; whence it was that he was so zealous in building such fine cities, and spent such vast sums of money upon them.

6. Now upon his observation of a place near the sea, which was very proper for containing a city, and was before called Strato's Tower, he set about getting a plan for a magnificent city there, and erected many edifices with great diligence all over it, and this of white stone. He also adorned it with most sumptuous palaces and large edifices for containing the people; and what was the greatest and most laborious work of all, he adorned it with a haven, that was always free from the waves of the sea. Its largeness was not less than the Pyrmum [at Athens], and had towards the city a double station for the ships. It was of excellent workmanship; and this was the more remarkable for its being built in a place that of itself was not suitable to such noble structures, but was to be brought to perfection by materials from other places, and at very great expenses. This city is situate in Phoenicia, in the passage by sea to Egypt, between Joppa and Dora, which are lesser maritime cities, and not fit for havens, on account of

---

of Moses, even under so tyrannical a government as this was of Herod the Great; which tyrannical government puts me naturally in mind of Dean Prideaux's honest reflection upon the like ambition after such tyrannical power in Pompey and Caesar: "One of these (says he, at the year 60) could not bear an equal, nor the other a superior; and through this ambitions humor and thirst after more power in these two men, the whole Roman empire being divided into two opposite factions, there was produced hereby the most destructive war that ever afflicted it; and the like folly too much reigns in all other places. Could about thirty men be persuaded to live at home in peace, without enterprising upon the rights of each other, for the vain glory of conquest, and the enlargement of power, the whole world might be at quiet; but their ambition, their follies, and their humor, leading them constantly to encroach upon and quarrel with each other, they involve all that are under them in the mischiefs thereof; and many thousands are they which yearly perish by it; so that it may almost raise a doubt, whether the benefit which the world receives from government be sufficient to make amends for the calamities which it suffers from the follies, mistakes, and real-administrations of those that manage it."

the impetuous south winds that beat upon them, which rolling the sands that come from the sea against the shores, do not admit of ships lying in their station; but the merchants are generally there forced to ride at their anchors in the sea itself. So Herod endeavored to rectify this inconvenience, and laid out such a compass towards the land as might be sufficient for a haven, wherein the great ships might lie in safety; and this he effected by letting down vast stones of above fifty feet in length, not less than eighteen in breadth, and nine in depth, into twenty fathom deep; and as some were lesser, so were others bigger than those dimensions. This mole which he built by the sea-side was two hundred feet wide, the half of which was opposed to the current of the waves, so as to keep off those waves which were to break upon them, and so was called Procymatia, or the first breaker of the waves; but the other half had upon it a wall, with several towers, the largest of which was named Drusus, and was a work of very great excellence, and had its name from Drusus, the son-in-law of Caesar, who died young. There were also a great number of arches where the mariners dwelt. There was also before them a quay, [or landing place,] which ran round the entire haven, and was a most agreeable walk to such as had a mind to that exercise; but the entrance or mouth of the port was made on the north quarter, on which side was the stillest of the winds of all in this place: and the basis of the whole circuit on the left hand, as you enter the port, supported a round turret, which was made very strong, in order to resist the greatest waves; while on the right hand, as you enter, stood two vast stones, and those each of them larger than the turret, which were over against them; these stood upright, and were joined together. Now there were edifices all along the circular haven, made of the politest stone, with a certain elevation, whereon was erected a temple, that was seen a great way off by those that were sailing for that haven, and had in it two statues, the one of Rome, the other of Caesar. The city itself was called Cesarea, which was also itself built of fine materials, and was of a fine structure; nay, the very subterranean vaults and cellars had no less of architecture bestowed on them than had the buildings above ground. Some of these vaults carried things at even distances to the haven and to the sea; but one of them ran obliquely, and bound all the rest together, that both the rain and the filth of the citizens were together carried off with ease, and the sea itself, upon the flux of the tide from without, came into the city, and washed it all clean. Herod also built therein a theater of stone; and on the south quarter, behind the port, an amphitheater also, capable of holding a vast number of men, and conveniently situated for a prospect to the sea. So this city was thus finished in twelve years;[18] during which time the king did not fail to go on both with the work, and to pay the charges that were necessary.

10 *How Herod Sent His Sons to Rome; How Also He Was Accused by Zenodorus and the Gadarens, but Was Cleared of What They Accused Him of and Withal Gained to Himself the Good-Will of Caesar. Concerning the Pharisees, the Essens and Manahem*

1. WHEN Herod was engaged in such matters, and when he had already re-edified Sebaste, [Samaria,] he resolved to send his sons Alexander and Aristobulus to Rome, to enjoy the company of Caesar; who, when they came thither, lodged at the house of Pollio,[19] who was very fond of Herod's friendship; and they had leave to lodge in Caesar's own palace, for he received these sons of Herod with all humanity, and gave Herod leave to give his, kingdom to which of his sons he pleased; and besides all this, he bestowed on him Trachon, and Batanea, and Auranitis, which he gave him on the occasion following: One Zenodorus[20] had hired what was called the house of Lysanias, who, as he was not satisfied with its revenues, became a partner with the robbers that inhabited the Trachonites, and so procured himself a larger income; for the inhabitants of those places lived in a mad way, and pillaged the country of the Damascenes, while Zenodorus did not restrain them, but partook of the prey they acquired. Now as

---

18. Cesarea being here said to be rebuilt and adorned in twelve years, and soon afterwards in ten years, Antiq. B. XVI. ch. 5. sect. 1, there must be a mistake in one of the places as to the true number, but in which of them it is hard positively to determine.

19. This Pollio, with whom Herod's sons lived at Rome, was not Pollio the Pharisee, already mentioned by Josephus, ch. 1. sect. 1, and again presently after this, ch. 10. sect. 4; but Asinine Pollo, the Roman, as Spanheim here observes.

20. The character of this Zenodorus is so like that of a famous robber of the same name in Strabo, and that about this very country, and about this very time also, that I think Dr. Hudson hardly needed to have put a overlaps to his determination that they were the same.

the neighboring people were hereby great. sufferers, they complained to Varro, who was then president [of Syria], and entreated him to write to Caesar about this injustice of Zenodorus. When these matters were laid before Caesar, he wrote back to Varro to destroy those nests of robbers, and to give the land to Herod, that so by his care the neighboring countries might be no longer disturbed with these doings of the Trachonites; for it was not an easy firing to restrain them, since this way of robbery had been their usual practice, and they had no other way to get their living, because they had neither any city of their own, nor lands in their possession, but only some receptacles and dens in the earth, and there they and their cattle lived in common together. However, they had made contrivances to get pools of water, and laid up corn in granaries for themselves, and were able to make great resistance, by issuing out on the sudden against any that attacked them; for the entrances of their caves were narrow, in which but one could come in at a time, and the places within incredibly large, and made very wide but the ground over their habitations was not very high, but rather on a plain, while the rocks are altogether hard and difficult to be entered upon, unless any one gets into the plain road by the guidance of another, for these roads are not straight, but have several revolutions. But when these men are hindered from their wicked preying upon their neighbors, their custom is to prey one upon another, insomuch that no sort of injustice comes amiss to them. But when Herod had received this grant from Caesar, and was come into this country, he procured skillful guides, and put a stop to their wicked robberies, and procured peace and quietness to the neighboring people.

2. Hereupon Zenodorus was grieved, in the first place, because his principality was taken away from him; and still more so, because he envied Herod, who had gotten it; So he went up to Rome to accuse him, but returned back again without success. Now Agrippa was [about this time] sent to succeed Caesar in the government of the countries beyond the Ionian Sea, upon whom Herod lighted when he was wintering about Mitylene, for he had been his particular friend and companion, and then returned into Judea again. However, some of the Gadarens came to Agrippa, and accused Herod, whom he sent back bound to the king without giving them the hearing. But still the Arabians, who of old bare ill-will to Herod's government, were

nettled, and at that time attempted to raise a sedition in his dominions, and, as they thought, upon a more justifiable occasion; for Zenodorus, despairing already of success as to his own affairs, prevented [his enemies], by selling to those Arabians a part of his principality, called Auranitis, for the value of fifty talents; but as this was included in the donations of Caesar, they contested the point with Herod, as unjustly deprived of what they had bought. Sometimes they did this by making incursions upon him, and sometimes by attempting force against him, and sometimes by going to law with him. Moreover, they persuaded the poorer soldiers to help them, and were troublesome to him, out of a constant hope that they should reduce the people to raise a sedition; in which designs those that are in the most miserable circumstances of life are still the most earnest; and although Herod had been a great while apprized of these attempts, yet did not he indulge any severity to them, but by rational methods aimed to mitigate things, as not willing to give any handle for tumults.

3. Now when Herod had already reigned seventeen years, Caesar came into Syria; at which time the greatest part of the inhabitants of Gadara clamored against Herod, as one that was heavy in his injunctions, and tyrannical. These reproaches they mainly ventured upon by the encouragement of Zenodorus, who took his oath that he would never leave Herod till he had procured that they should be severed from Herod's kingdom, and joined to Caesar's province. The Gadarens were induced hereby, and made no small cry against him, and that the more boldly, because those that had been delivered up by Agrippa were not punished by Herod, who let them go, and did them no harm; for indeed he was the principal man in the world who appeared almost inexorable in punishing crimes in his own family, but very generous in remitting the offenses that were committed elsewhere. And while they accused Herod of injuries, and plunderings, and subversions of temples, he stood unconcerned, and was ready to make his defense. However, Caesar gave him his right hand, and remitted nothing of his kindness to him, upon this disturbance by the multitude; and indeed these things were alleged the first day, but the hearing proceeded no further; for as the Gadarens saw the inclination of Caesar and of his assessors, and expected, as they had reason to do, that they should be delivered up to the king, some of them, out of a dread of the torments they might undergo, cut their

own throats in the night time, and some of them threw themselves down precipices, and others of them cast themselves into the river, and destroyed themselves of their own accord; which accidents seemed a sufficient condemnation of the rashness and crimes they had been guilty of; whereupon Caesar made no longer delay, but cleared Herod from the crimes he was accused of. Another happy accident there was, which was a further great advantage to Herod at this time; for Zenodorus's belly burst, and a great quantity of blood issued from him in his sickness, and he thereby departed this life at Antioch in Syria; so Caesar bestowed his country, which was no small one, upon Herod; it lay between Trachon and Galilee, and contained Ulatha, and Paneas, and the country round about. He also made him one of the procurators of Syria, and commanded that they should do every thing with his approbation; and, in short, he arrived at that pitch of felicity, that whereas there were but two men that governed the vast Roman empire, first Caesar, and then Agrippa, who was his principal favorite, Caesar preferred no one to Herod besides Agrippa, and Agrippa made no one his greater friend than Herod besides Caesar. And when he had acquired such freedom, he begged of Caesar a tetrarchy[21] for his brother Pheroras, while he did himself bestow upon him a revenue of a hundred talents out of his own kingdom, that in case he came to any harm himself, his brother might be in safety, and that his sons might not have dominion over him. So when he had conducted Caesar to the sea, and was returned home, he built him a most beautiful temple, of the whitest stone, in Zenodorus's country, near the place called Panlure. This is a very fine cave in a mountain, under which there is a great cavity in the earth, and the cavern is abrupt, and prodigiously deep, and frill of a still water; over it hangs a vast mountain; and under the caverns arise the springs of the river Jordan. Herod adorned this place, which was already a very remarkable one, still further by the erection of this temple, which he dedicated to Caesar.

4. At which time Herod released to his subjects the third part of their taxes, under pretense indeed of relieving them, after the dearth

21. A tetrarchy properly and originally denoted the fourth part of an entire kingdom or country, and a tetrarch one that was ruler of such a fourth part, which always implies somewhat less extent of dominion and power than belong to a kingdom and to a king.

they had had; but the main reason was, to recover their good-will, which he now wanted; for they were uneasy at him, because of the innovations he had introduced in their practices, of the dissolution of their religion, and of the disuse of their own customs; and the people every where talked against him, like those that were still more provoked and disturbed at his procedure; against which discontents he greatly guarded himself, and took away the opportunities they might have to disturb him, and enjoined them to be always at work; nor did he permit the citizens either to meet together, or to walk or eat together, but watched every thing they did, and when any were caught, they were severely punished; and many there were who were brought to the citadel Hyrcania, both openly and secretly, and were there put to death; and there were spies set every where, both in the city and in the roads, who watched those that met together; nay, it is reported that he did not himself neglect this part of caution, but that he would oftentimes himself take the habit of a private man, and mix among the multitude, in the night time, and make trial what opinion they had of his government: and as for those that could no way be reduced to acquiesce under his scheme of government, he prosecuted them all manner of ways; but for the rest of the multitude, he required that they should be obliged to take an oath of fidelity to him, and at the same time compelled them to swear that they would bear him good-will, and continue certainly so to do, in his management of the government; and indeed a great part of them, either to please him, or out of fear of him, yielded to what he required of them; but for such as were of a more open and generous disposition, and had indignation at the force he used to them, he by one means or other made away, with them. He endeavored also to persuade Pollio the Pharisee, and Satneas, and the greatest part of their scholars, to take the oath; but these would neither submit so to do, nor were they punished together with the rest, out of the reverence he bore to Pollio. The Essens also, as we call a sect of ours, were excused from this imposition. These men live the same kind of life as do those whom the Greeks call Pythagoreans, concerning whom I shall discourse more fully elsewhere. However, it is but fit to set down here the reasons wherefore Herod had these Essens in such honor, and thought higher of them than their mortal nature required; nor will this account be unsuitable to the nature of this history, as it will show the opinion men had of these Essens.

5. Now there was one of these Essens, whose name was Manahem, who had this testimony, that he not only conducted his life after an excellent manner, but had the foreknowledge of future events given him by God also. This man once saw Herod when he was a child, and going to school, and saluted him as king of the Jews; but he, thinking that either he did not know him, or that he was in jest, put him in mind that he was but a private man; but Manahem smiled to himself, and clapped him on his backside with his hand, and said," However that be, thou wilt be king, and wilt begin thy reign happily, for God finds thee worthy of it. And do thou remember the blows that Manahem hath given thee, as being a signal of the change of thy fortune. And truly this will be the best reasoning for thee, that thou love justice [towards men], and piety towards God, and clemency towards thy citizens; yet do I know how thy whole conduct will be, that thou wilt not be such a one, for thou wilt excel all men in happiness, and obtain an everlasting reputation, but wilt forget piety and righteousness; and these crimes will not be concealed from God, at the conclusion of thy life, when thou wilt find that he will be mindful of them, and punish time for them." Now at that time Herod did not at all attend to what Manahem said, as having no hopes of such advancement; but a little afterward, when he was so fortunate as to be advanced to the dignity of king, and was in the height of his dominion, he sent for Manahem, and asked him how long he should reign. Manahem did not tell him the full length of his reign; wherefore, upon that silence of his, he asked him further, whether he should reign ten years or not? He replied, "Yes, twenty, nay, thirty years;" but did not assign the just determinate limit of his reign. Herod was satisfied with these replies, and gave Manahem his hand, and dismissed him; and from that time he continued to honor all the Essens. We have thought it proper to relate these facts to our readers, how strange soever they be, and to declare what hath happened among us, because many of these Essens have, by their excellent virtue, been thought worthy of this knowledge of Divine revelations.

Chapter 11

11 *How Herod Rebuilt the Temple and Raised It Higher and Made It More Magnificent Than It Was Before; as Also Concerning That Tower Which He Called Antonia*

1. AND now Herod, in the eighteenth year of his reign, and after the acts already mentioned, undertook a very great work, that is, to build of himself the temple of God,[22] and make it larger in compass, and to raise it to a most magnificent altitude, as esteeming it to be the most glorious of all his actions, as it really was, to bring it to perfection; and that this would be sufficient for an everlasting memorial of him; but as he knew the multitude were not ready nor willing to assist him in so vast a design, he thought to prepare them first by making a speech to them, and then set about the work itself; so he called them together, and spake thus to them: "I think I need not speak to you, my countrymen, about such other works as I have done since I came to the kingdom, although I may say they have been performed in such a manner as to bring more security to you than glory to myself; for I have neither been negligent in the most difficult times about what tended to ease your necessities, nor have the buildings. I have made been so proper to preserve me as yourselves from injuries; and I imagine that, with God's assistance, I have advanced the nation of the Jews to a degree of happiness which they never had before; and for the particular edifices belonging to your own country, and your own cities, as also to those cities that we have lately acquired, which we have erected and greatly adorned, and thereby augmented the dignity of your nation, it seems to me a needless task to enumerate them to you, since you well know them yourselves; but as to that undertaking which I have a mind to set about at present, and which will be a work of the greatest piety and excellence that can possibly be undertaken by

22. We may here observe, that the fancy of the modern Jews, in calling this temple, which was really the third of their temples, the second temple, followed so long by later Christians, seems to be without any solid foundation. The reason why the Christians here followed the Jews is, because of the prophecy of Haggai, 2:6–9, which they expound of the Messiah's coning to the second or Zorobabel's temple, of which they suppose this of Herod to be only a continuation; which is meant, I think, of his coming to the fourth and last temple, of that future, largest, and most glorious one, described by Ezekiel; whence I take the former notion, how general soever, to be a great mistake. See Lit. Accorap. of Proph. p. 2.

us, I will now declare it to you. Our fathers, indeed, when they were returned from Babylon, built this temple to God Almighty, yet does it want sixty cubits of its largeness in altitude; for so much did that first temple which Solomon built exceed this temple; nor let any one condemn our fathers for their negligence or want of piety herein, for it was not their fault that the temple was no higher; for they were Cyrus, and Darius the son of Hystaspes, who determined the measures for its rebuilding; and it hath been by reason of the subjection of those fathers of ours to them and to their posterity, and after them to the Macedonians, that they had not the opportunity to follow the original model of this pious edifice, nor could raise it to its ancient altitude; but since I am now, by God's will, your governor, and I have had peace a long time, and have gained great riches and large revenues, and, what is the principal filing of all, I am at amity with and well regarded by the Romans, who, if I may so say, are the rulers of the whole world, I will do my endeavor to correct that imperfection, which hath arisen from the necessity of our affairs, and the slavery we have been under formerly, and to make a thankful return, after the most pious manner, to God, for what blessings I have received from him, by giving me this kingdom, and that by rendering his temple as complete as I am able."

2. And this was the speech which Herod made to them; but still this speech aftrighted many of the people, as being unexpected by them; and because it seemed incredible, it did not encourage them, but put a damp upon them, for they were afraid that he would pull down the whole edifice, and not be able to bring his intentions to perfection for its rebuilding; and this danger appeared to them to be very great, and the vastness of the undertaking to be such as could hardly be accomplished. But while they were in this disposition, the king encouraged them, and told them he would not pull down their temple till all things were gotten ready for building it up entirely again. And as he promised them this beforehand, so he did not break his word with them, but got ready a thousand waggons, that were to bring stones for the building, and chose out ten thousand of the most skillful workmen, and bought a thousand sacerdotal garments for as many of the priests, and had some of them taught the arts of stone-cutters, and others of carpenters, and then began to build; but this not till every thing was well prepared for the work.

3. So Herod took away the old foundations, and laid others, and erected the temple upon them, being in length a hundred cubits, and in height twenty additional cubits, which [twenty], upon the sinking of their foundations[23] fell down; and this part it was that we resolved to raise again in the days of Nero. Now the temple was built of stones that were white and strong, and each of their length was twenty-five cubits, their height was eight, and their breadth about twelve; and the whole structure, as also the structure of the royal cloister, was on each side much lower, but the middle was much higher, till they were visible to those that dwelt in the country for a great many furlongs, but chiefly to such as lived over against them, and those that approached to them. The temple had doors also at the entrance, and lintels over them, of the same height with the temple itself. They were adorned with embroidered veils, with their flowers of purple, and pillars interwoven; and over these, but under the crown-work, was spread out a golden vine, with its branches hanging down from a great height, the largeness and fine workmanship of which was a surprising sight to the spectators, to see what vast materials there were, and with what great skill the workmanship was done. He also encompassed the entire temple with very large cloisters, contriving them to be in a due proportion thereto; and he laid out larger sums of money upon them than had been done before him, till it seemed that no one else had so greatly adorned the temple as he had done. There was a large wall to both the cloisters, which wall was itself the most prodigious work that was ever heard of by man. The hill was a rocky ascent, that

---

23. Some of our modem students in architecture have made a strange blunder here, when they imagine that Josephus affirms the entire foundations of the temple or holy house sunk down into the rocky mountain on which it stood no less than twenty cubits, whereas he is clear that they were the foundations of the additional twenty cubits only above the hundred (made perhaps weak on purpose, and only for show and grandeur) that sunk or fell down, as Dr. Hudson rightly understands him; nor is the thing itself possible in the other sense. Agrippa's preparation for building the inner parts of the temple twenty cubits higher (History of the War, B. V. ch. 1. sect. 5) must in all probability refer to this matter, since Josephus says here, that this which had fallen down was designed to be raised up again under Nero, under whom Agrippa made that preparation. But what Josephus says presently, that Solomon was the first king of the Jews, appears by the parallel place, Antiq. B. XX. ch. 9. sect. 7, and other places, to be meant only the first of David's posterity, and the first builder of the temple.

declined by degrees towards the east parts of the city, till it came to an elevated level. This hill it was which Solomon, who was the first of our kings, by Divine revelation, encompassed with a wall; it was of excellent workmanship upwards, and round the top of it. He also built a wall below, beginning at the bottom, which was encompassed by a deep valley; and at the south side he laid rocks together, and bound them one to another with lead, and included some of the inner parts, till it proceeded to a great height, and till both the largeness of the square edifice and its altitude were immense, and till the vastness of the stones in the front were plainly visible on the outside, yet so that the inward parts were fastened together with iron, and preserved the joints immovable for all future times. When this work [for the foundation] was done in this manner, and joined together as part of the hill itself to the very top of it, he wrought it all into one outward surface, and filled up the hollow places which were about the wall, and made it a level on the external upper surface, and a smooth level also. This hill was walled all round, and in compass four furlongs, [the distance of] each angle containing in length a furlong: but within this wall, and on the very top of all, there ran another wall of stone also, having, on the east quarter, a double cloister, of the same length with the wall; in the midst of which was the temple itself. This cloister looked to the gates of the temple; and it had been adorned by many kings in former times; and round about the entire temple were fixed the spoils taken from barbarous nations; all these had been dedicated to the temple by Herod, with the addition of those he had taken from the Arabians.

4. Now on the north side [of the temple] was built a citadel, whose walls were square, and strong, and of extraordinary firmness. This citadel was built by the kings of the Asamonean race, who were also high priests before Herod, and they called it the Tower, in which were reposited the vestments of the high priest, which the high priest only put on at the time when he was to offer sacrifice. These vestments king Herod kept in that place; and after his death they were under the power of the Romans, until the time of Tiberius Caesar; under whose reign Vitellius, the president of Syria, when he once came to Jerusalem, and had been most magnificently received by the multitude, he had a mind to make them some requital for the kindness they had shewn him; so, upon their petition to have those holy vestments in their

own power, he wrote about them to Tiberius Caesar, who granted his request: and this their power over the sacerdotal vestments continued with the Jews till the death of king Agrippa; but after that, Cassius Longinus, who was president of Syria, and Cuspius Fadus, who was procurator of Judea, enjoined the Jews to reposit those vestments in the tower of Antonia, for that they ought to have them in their power, as they formerly had. However, the Jews sent ambassadors to Claudius Caesar, to intercede with him for them; upon whose coming, king Agrippa, junior, being then at Rome, asked for and obtained the power over them from the emperor, who gave command to Vitellius, who was then commander in Syria, to give it them accordingly. Before that time they were kept under the seal of the high priest, and of the treasurers of the temple; which treasurers, the day before a festival, went up to the Roman captain of the temple guards, and viewed their own seal, and received the vestments; and again, when the festival was over, they brought it to the same place, and showed the captain of the temple guards their seal, which corresponded with his seal, and reposited them there. And that these things were so, the afflictions that happened to us afterwards [about them] are sufficient evidence. But for the tower itself, when Herod the king of the Jews had fortified it more firmly than before, in order to secure and guard the temple, he gratified Antonius, who was his friend, and the Roman ruler, and then gave it the name of the Tower of Antonia.

5. Now in the western quarters of the enclosure of the temple there were four gates; the first led to the king's palace, and went to a passage over the intermediate valley; two more led to the suburbs of the city; and the last led to the other city, where the road descended down into the valley by a great number of steps, and thence up again by the ascent for the city lay over against the temple in the manner of a theater, and was encompassed with a deep valley along the entire south quarter; but the fourth front of the temple, which was southward, had indeed itself gates in its middle, as also it had the royal cloisters, with three walks, which reached in length from the east valley unto that on the west, for it was impossible it should reach any farther: and this cloister deserves to be mentioned better than any other under the sun; for while the valley was very deep, and its bottom could not be seen, if you looked from above into the depth, this further vastly high elevation of the cloister stood upon that height, insomuch

that if any one looked down from the top of the battlements, or down both those altitudes, he would be giddy, while his sight could not reach to such an immense depth. This cloister had pillars that stood in four rows one over against the other all along, for the fourth row was interwoven into the wall, which [also was built of stone]; and the thickness of each pillar was such, that three men might, with their arms extended, fathom it round, and join their hands again, while its length was twenty-seven feet, with a double spiral at its basis; and the number of all the pillars [in that court] was a hundred and sixty-two. Their chapiters were made with sculptures after the Corinthian order, and caused an amazement [to the spectators], by reason of the grandeur of the whole. These four rows of pillars included three intervals for walking in the middle of this cloister; two of which walks were made parallel to each other, and were contrived after the same manner; the breadth of each of them was thirty feet, the length was a furlong, and the height fifty feet; but the breadth of the middle part of the cloister was one and a half of the other, and the height was double, for it was much higher than those on each side; but the roofs were adorned with deep sculptures in wood, representing many sorts of figures. The middle was much higher than the rest, and the wall of the front was adorned with beams, resting upon pillars, that were interwoven into it, and that front was all of polished stone, insomuch that its fineness, to such as had not seen it, was incredible, and to such as had seen it, was greatly amazing. Thus was the first enclosure. In the midst of which, and not far from it, was the second, to be gone up to by a few steps: this was encompassed by a stone wall for a partition, with an inscription, which forbade any foreigner to go in under pain of death. Now this inner enclosure had on its southern and northern quarters three gates [equally] distant one from another; but on the east quarter, towards the sun-rising, there was one large gate, through which such as were pure came in, together with their wives; but the temple further inward in that gate was not allowed to the women; but still more inward was there a third [court of the] temple, whereinto it was not lawful for any but the priests alone to enter. The temple itself was within this; and before that temple was the altar, upon which we offer our sacrifices and burnt-offerings to God. Into none of these three did king Herod enter,[24] for he was forbidden, because he was not a priest. However, he took care of the cloisters and the outer enclosures, and these he built in eight years.

6. But the temple itself was built by the priests in a year and six months; upon which all the people were full of joy; and presently they returned thanks, in the first place, to God; and in the next place, for the alacrity the king had showed. They feasted and celebrated this rebuilding of the temple: and for the king, he sacrificed three hundred oxen to God, as did the rest every one according to his ability; the number of which sacrifices is not possible to set down, for it cannot be that we should truly relate it; for at the same time with this celebration for the work about the temple fell also the day of the king's inauguration, which he kept of an old custom as a festival, and it now coincided with the other, which coincidence of them both made the festival most illustrious.

7. There was also an occult passage built for the king; it led from Antonia to the inner temple, at its eastern gate; over which he also erected for himself a tower, that he might have the opportunity of a subterraneous ascent to the temple, in order to guard against any sedition which might be made by the people against their kings. It is also reported,[25] that during the time that the temple was building, it did not rain in the daytime, but that the showers fell in the nights, so that the work was not hindered. And this our fathers have delivered

---

24. "Into none Of these three did king Herod enter," i.e. 1. Not into the court of the priests; 2. Nor into the holy house itself; 3. Nor into the separate place belonging to the altar, as the words following imply; for none but priests, or their attendants the Levites, might come into any of them. See Antiq. B. XVI. ch. 4. sect. 6, when Herod goes into the temple, and makes a speech in it to the people, but that could only be into the court of Israel, whither the people could come to hear him.

25. This tradition which Josephus here mentions, as delivered down from fathers to their children, of this particular remarkable circumstance relating to the building of Herod's temple, is a demonstration that such its building was a known thing in Judea at this time. He was born about forty-six years after it is related to have been finished, and might himself have seen and spoken with some of the builders themselves, and with a great number of those that had seen it building. The doubt therefore about the truth of this history of the pulling down and rebuilding this temple by Herod, which some weak people have indulged, was not then much greater than it soon may be, whether or not our St. Paul's church in London was burnt down in the fire of London, A.D. 1666, and rebuilt by Sir Christopher Wren a little afterward.

to us; nor is it incredible, if any one have regard to the manifestations of God. And thus was performed the work of the rebuilding of the temple.

Book 16

Containing the Interval of Twelve Years, from the Finishing of the Temple by Herod to the Death of Alexander and Aristobulus

1 *A Law of Herod's About, Thieves. Salome and Pheroras Calumniate Alexander and Aristobulus, Upon Their Return from Rome for Whom Yet Herod Provides Wives*

1. AS king Herod was very zealous in the administration of his entire government, and desirous to put a stop to particular acts of injustice which were done by criminals about the city and country, he made a law, no way like our original laws, and which he enacted of himself, to expose house-breakers to be ejected out of his kingdom; which punishment was not only grievous to be borne by the offenders, but contained in it a dissolution of the customs of our forefathers; for this slavery to foreigners, and such as did not live after the manner of Jews, and this necessity that they were under to do whatsoever such men should command, was an offense against our religious settlement, rather than a punishment to such as were found to have offended, such a punishment being avoided in our original laws; for those laws ordain, that the thief shall restore fourfold; and that if he have not so much, he shall be sold indeed, but not to foreigners, nor so that he be under perpetual slavery, for he must have been released after six years. But this law, thus enacted, in order to introduce a severe and illegal punishment, seemed to be a piece of insolence of Herod, when he did not act as a king, but as a tyrant, and thus contemptuously, and without any regard to his subjects, did he venture to introduce such

a punishment. Now this penalty, thus brought into practice, was like Herod's other actions, and became a part of his accusation, and an occasion of the hatred he lay under.

2. Now at this time it was that he sailed to Italy, as very desirous to meet with Caesar, and to see his sons who lived at Rome; and Caesar was not only very obliging to him in other respects, but delivered him his sons again, that he might take them home with him, as having already completed themselves in the sciences; but as soon as the young men were come from Italy, the multitude were very desirous to see them, and they became conspicuous among them all, as adorned with great blessings of fortune, and having the countenances of persons of royal dignity. So they soon appeared to be the objects of envy to Salome, the king's sister, and to such as had raised calumnies against Mariamne; for they were suspicious, that when these came to the government, they should be punished for the wickedness they had been guilty of against their mother; so they made this very fear of theirs a motive to raise calumnies against them also. They gave it out that they were not pleased with their father's company, because he had put their mother to death, as if it were not agreeable to piety to appear to converse with their mother's murderer. Now, by carrying these stories; that had indeed a true foundation [in the fact], but were only built on probabilities as to the present accusation, they were able to do them mischief, and to make Herod take away that kindness from his sons which he had before borne to them; for they did not say these things to him openly, but scattered abroad such words, among the rest of the multitude; from which words, when carried to Herod, he was induced [at last] to hate them, and which natural affection itself, even in length of time, was not able to overcome; yet was the king at that time in a condition to prefer the natural affection of a father before all the suspicions and calumnies his sons lay under. So he respected them as he ought to do, and married them to wives, now they were of an age suitable thereto. To Aristobulus he gave for a wife Bernice, Salome's daughter; and to Alexander, Glaphyra, the daughter of Archelaus, king of Cappadocia.

Chapter 2

2 *How Herod Twice Sailed to Agrippa; and How Upon the Complaint in Ionia Against the Greeks Agrippa Confirmed the Laws to Them*

1. WHEN Herod had despatched these affairs, and he understood that Marcus Agrippa had sailed again out of Italy into Asia, he made haste to him, and besought him to come to him into his kingdom, and to partake of what he might justly expect from one that had been his guest, and was his friend. This request he greatly pressed, and to it Agrippa agreed, and came into Judea; whereupon Herod omitted nothing that might please him. He entertained him in his new-built cities, and showed him the edifices he had built, and provided all sorts of the best and most costly dainties for him and his friends, and that at Sebaste and Cesarea, about that port that he had built, and at the fortresses which he had erected at great expenses, Alexandrium, and Herodium, and Hyrcania. He also conducted him to the city Jerusalem, where all the people met him in their festival garments, and received him with acclamations. Agrippa also offered a hecatomb of sacrifices to God; and feasted the people, without omitting any of the greatest dainties that could be gotten. He also took so much pleasure there, that he abode many days with them, and would willingly have staid longer, but that the season of the year made him make haste away; for as winter was coming on, he thought it not safe to go to sea later, and yet he was of necessity to return again to Ionia.

2. So Agrippa went away, when Herod had bestowed on him, and on the principal of those that were with him, many presents; but king Herod, when he had passed the winter in his own dominions, made haste to get to him again in the spring, when he knew he designed to go to a campaign at the Bosptiorus. So when he had sailed by Rhodes and by Cos, he touched at Lesbos, as thinking he should have overtaken Agrippa there; but he was taken short here by a north wind, which hindered his ship from going to the shore; so he continued many days at Chius, and there he kindly treated a great many that came to him, and obliged them by giving them royal gifts. And when he saw that the portico of the city was fallen down, which as it was overthrown in the Mithridatic war, and was very large and fine building, so was it not so easy to rebuild that as it was the rest, yet did he furnish a sum not only large enough for that purpose, but what was more than sufficient to finish the building; and ordered them not

to overlook that portico, but to rebuild it quickly, that so the city might recover its proper ornaments. And when the high winds were laid, he sailed to Mytilene, and thence to Byzantium; and when he heard that Agrippa was sailed beyond the Cyanean rocks, he made all the haste possible to overtake him, and came up with him about Sinope, in Pontus. He was seen sailing by the ship-men most unexpectedly, but appeared to their great joy; and many friendly salutations there were between them, insomuch that Agrippa thought he had received the greatest marks of the king's kindness and humanity towards him possible, since the king had come so long a voyage, and at a very proper season, for his assistance, and had left the government of his own dominions, and thought it more worth his while to come to him. Accordingly, Herod was all in all to Agrippa, in the management of the war, and a great assistant in civil affairs, and in giving him counsel as to particular matters. He was also a pleasant companion for him when he relaxed himself, and a joint partaker with him in all things; ill troubles because of his kindness, and in prosperity because of the respect Agrippa had for him. Now as soon as those affairs of Pontus were finished, for whose sake Agrippa was sent thither, they did not think fit to return by sea, but passed through Paphlagonia and Cappadocia; they then traveled thence over great Phrygia, and came to Ephesus, and then they sailed from Ephesus to Samos. And indeed the king bestowed a great many benefits on every city that he came to, according as they stood in need of them; for as for those that wanted either money or kind treatment, he was not wanting to them; but he supplied the former himself out of his own expenses: he also became an intercessor with Agrippa for all such as sought after his favor, and he brought things so about, that the petitioners failed in none of their suits to him, Agrippa being himself of a good disposition, and of great generosity, and ready to grant all such requests as might be advantageous to the petitioners, provided they were not to the detriment of others. The inclination of the king was of great weight also, and still excited Agrippa, who was himself ready to do good; for he made a reconciliation between the people of Ilium, at whom he was angry, and paid what money the people of Chius owed Caesar's procurators, and discharged them of their tributes; and helped all others, according as their several necessities required.

3. But now, when Agrippa and Herod were in Ionia, a great multitude of Jews, who dwelt in their cities, came to them, and laying hold of the opportunity and the liberty now given them, laid before them the injuries which they suffered, while they were not permitted to use their own laws, but were compelled to prosecute their law-suits, by the ill usage of the judges, upon their holy days, and were deprived of the money they used to lay up at Jerusalem, and were forced into the army, and upon such other offices as obliged them to spend their sacred money; from which burdens they always used to be freed by the Romans, who had still permitted them to live according to their own laws. When this clamor was made, the king desired of Agrippa that he would hear their cause, and assigned Nicolaus, one of his friends, to plead for those their privileges. Accordingly, when Agrippa had called the principal of the Romans, and such of the kings and rulers as were there, to be his assessors, Nicolaus stood up, and pleaded for the Jews, as follows: "It is of necessity incumbent on such as are in distress to have recourse to those that have it in their power to free them from those injuries they lie under; and for those that now are complainants, they approach you with great assurance; for as they have formerly often obtained your favor, so far as they have even wished to have it, they now only entreat that you, who have been the donors, will take care that those favors you have already granted them may not be taken away from them. We have received these favors from you, who alone have power to grant them, but have them taken from us by such as are no greater than ourselves, and by such as we know are as much subjects as we are; and certainly, if we have been vouchsafed great favors, it is to our commendation who have obtained them, as having been found deserving of such great favors; and if those favors be but small ones, it would be barbarous for the donors not to confirm them to us. And for those that are the hinderance of the Jews, and use them reproachfully, it is evident that they affront both the receivers, while they will not allow those to be worthy men to whom their excellent rulers themselves have borne their testimony, and the donors, while they desire those favors already granted may be abrogated. Now if any one should ask these Gentiles themselves, which of the two things they would choose to part with, their lives, or the customs of their forefathers, their solemnities, their sacrifices, their festivals, which they celebrated in honor of those they suppose to be

gods? I know very well that they would choose to suffer any thing whatsoever rather than a dissolution of any of the customs of their forefathers; for a great many of them have rather chosen to go to war on that account, as very solicitous not to transgress in those matters. And indeed we take an estimate of that happiness which all mankind do now enjoy by your means from this very thing, that we are allowed every one to worship as our own institutions require, and yet to live [in peace]; and although they would not be thus treated themselves, yet do they endeavor to compel others to comply with them, as if it were not as great an instance of impiety profanely to dissolve the religious solemnities of any others, as to be negligent in the observation of their own towards their gods. And let us now consider the one of these practices. Is there any people, or city, or community of men, to whom your government and the Roman power does not appear to be the greatest blessing '. Is there any one that can desire to make void the favors they have granted? No one is certainly so mad; for there are no men but such as have been partakers of their favors, both public and private; and indeed those that take away what you have granted, can have no assurance but every one of their own grants made them by you may be taken from them also; which grants of yours can yet never be sufficiently valued; for if they consider the old governments under kings, together with your present government, besides the great number of benefits which this government hath bestowed on them, in order to their happiness, this is instead of all the rest, that they appear to be no longer in a state of slavery, but of freedom. Now the privileges we desire, even when we are in the best circumstances, are not such as deserve to be envied, for we are indeed in a prosperous state by your means, but this is only in common with others; and it is no more than this which we desire, to preserve our religion without any prohibition; which as it appears not in itself a privilege to be envied us, so it is for the advantage of those that grant it to us; for if the Divinity delights in being honored, it must delight in those that permit them to be honored. And there are none of our customs which are inhuman, but all tending to piety, and devoted to the preservation of justice; nor do we conceal those injunctions of ours by which we govern our lives, they being memorials of piety, and of a friendly conversation among men. And the seventh day we set apart from labor; it is dedicated to the learning of our customs and laws,[1] we thinking it proper to reflect on them, as well as on any [good] thing else, in order to our avoiding of sin. If any one therefore examine into our observances, he will find they are good in themselves, and that they are ancient also, though some think otherwise, insomuch that those who have received them cannot easily be brought to depart from them, out of that honor they pay to the length of time they have religiously enjoyed them and observed them. Now our adversaries take these our privileges away in the way of injustice; they violently seize upon that money of ours which is owed to God, and called sacred money, and this openly, after a sacrilegious manner; and they impose tributes upon us, and bring us before tribunals on holy days, and then require other like debts of us, not because the contracts require it, and for their own advantage, but because they would put an affront on our religion, of which they are conscious as well as we, and have indulged themselves in an unjust, and to them involuntary, hatred; for your government over all is one, tending to the establishing of benevolence, and abolishing of ill-will among such as are disposed to it. This is therefore what we implore from thee, most excellent Agrippa, that we may not be ill-treated; that we may not be abused; that we may not be hindered from making use of our own customs, nor be despoiled of our goods, nor be forced by these men to do what we ourselves force nobody to do; for these privileges of ours are not only according to justice, but have formerly been granted us by you. And we are able to read to you many decrees of the senate, and the tables that contain them, which are still extant in the capitol, concerning these things, which it is evident were granted after you had experience of our fidelity towards you, which ought to be valued, though no such fidelity had been; for you have hitherto preserved what people were in possession of, not to us only, but almost to all men, and have added greater advantages than they could have hoped for, and thereby your government is become a great advantage to them. And if any one were able to enumerate the prosperity you have conferred on

1. We may here observe the ancient practice of the Jews, of dedicating the sabbath day, not to idleness, but to the learning their sacred rites and religious customs, and to the meditation on the law of Moses; the like to which we meet with elsewhere in Josephus also against Apion, B. I. sect. 22.

every nation, which they possess by your means, he could never put an end to his discourse; but that we may demonstrate that we are not unworthy of all those advantages we have obtained, it will be sufficient for us, to say nothing of other things, but to speak freely of this king who now governs us, and is now one of thy assessors; and indeed in what instance of good-will, as to your house, hath he been deficient? What mark of fidelity to it hath he omitted? What token of honor hath he not devised? What occasion for his assistance of you hath he not regarded at the very first? What hindereth; therefore, but that your kindnesses may be as numerous as his so great benefits to you have been? It may also perhaps be fit not here to pass over in silence the valor of his father Antipater, who, when Caesar made an expedition into Egypt, assisted him with two thousand armed men, and proved inferior to none, neither in the battles on land, nor in the management of the navy; and what need I say any thing of how great weight those soldiers were at that juncture? or how many and how great presents they were vouchsafed by Caesar? And truly I ought before now to have mentioned the epistles which Caesar wrote to the senate; and how Antipater had honors, and the freedom of the city of Rome, bestowed upon him; for these are demonstrations both that we have received these favors by our own deserts, and do on that account petition thee for thy confirmation of them, from whom we had reason to hope for them, though they had not been given us before, both out of regard to our king's disposition towards you, and your disposition towards him. And further, we have been informed by those Jews that were there with what kindness thou camest into our country, and how thou offeredst the most perfect sacrifices to God, and honoredst him with remarkable vows, and how thou gavest the people a feast, and acceptedst of their own hospitable presents to thee. We ought to esteem all these kind entertainments made both by our nation and to our city, to a man who is the ruler and manager of so much of the public affairs, as indications of that friendship which thou hast returned to the Jewish nation, and which hath been procured them by the family of Herod. So we put thee in mind of these things in the presence of the king, now sitting by thee, and make our request for no more but this, that what you have given us yourselves you will not see taken away by others from us."

4. When Nicolaus had made this speech, there was no opposition made to it by the Greeks, for this was not an inquiry made, as in a court of justice, but an intercession to prevent violence to be offered to the Jews any longer; nor did the Greeks make any defense of themselves, or deny what it was supposed they had done. Their pretense was no more than this, that while the Jews inhabited in their country, they were entirely unjust to them [in not joining in their worship] but they demonstrated their generosity in this, that though they worshipped according to their institutions, they did nothing that ought to grieve them. So when Agrippa perceived that they had been oppressed by violence, he made this answer: That, on account of Herod's good-will and friendship, he was ready to grant the Jews whatsoever they should ask him, and that their requests seemed to him in themselves just; and that if they requested any thing further, he should not scruple to grant it them, provided they were no way to the detriment of the Roman government; but that while their request was no more than this, that what privileges they had already given them might not be abrogated, he confirmed this to them, that they might continue in the observation of their own customs, without any one offering them the least injury. And when he had said thus, he dissolved the assembly; upon which Herod stood up and saluted him, and gave him thanks for the kind disposition he showed to them. Agrippa also took this in a very obliging manner, and saluted him again, and embraced him in his arms; after which he went away from Lesbos; but the king determined to sail from Samos to his own country; and when he had taken his leave of Agrippa, he pursued his voyage, and landed at Cesarea in a few days' time, as having favorable winds; from whence he went to Jerusalem, and there gathered all the people together to an assembly, not a few being there out of the country also. So he came to them, and gave them a particular account of all his journey, and of the affairs of all the Jews in Asia, how by his means they would live without injurious treatment for the time to come. He also told them of the entire good fortune he had met with and how he had administered the government, and had not neglected any thing which was for their advantage; and as he was very joyful, he now remitted to them the fourth part of their taxes for the last year. Accordingly, they were so pleased with his favor and speech to them, that they went their ways with great gladness, and wished the king all manner of happiness.

3 *How Great Disturbances Arose in Herods Family on His Preferring Antipater His Eldest Son Before the Rest, Till Alexander Took That Injury Very Heinously*

1. BUT now the affairs in Herod's family were in more and more disorder, and became more severe upon him, by the hatred of Salome to the young men [Alexander and Aristobulus], which descended as it were by inheritance [from their mother Mariamne]; and as she had fully succeeded against their mother, so she proceeded to that degree of madness and insolence, as to endeavor that none of her posterity might be left alive, who might have it in their power to revenge her death. The young men had also somewhat of a bold and uneasy disposition towards their father occasioned by the remembrance of what their mother had unjustly suffered, and by their own affectation of dominion. The old grudge was also renewed; and they east reproaches on Salome and Pheroras, who requited the young men with malicious designs, and actually laid treacherous snares for them. Now as for this hatred, it was equal on both sides, but the manner of exerting that hatred was different; for as for the young men, they were rash, reproaching and affronting the others openly, and were inexperienced enough to think it the most generous to declare their minds in that undaunted manner; but the others did not take that method, but made use of calumnies after a subtle and a spiteful manner, still provoking the young men, and imagining that their boldness might in time turn to the offering violence to their father; for inasmuch as they were not ashamed of the pretended crimes of their mother, nor thought she suffered justly, these supposed that might at length exceed all bounds, and induce them to think they ought to be avenged on their father, though it were by despatching him with their own hands. At length it came to this, that the whole city was full of their discourses, and, as is usual in such contests, the unskilfulness of the young men was pitied; but the contrivance of Salome was too hard for them, and what imputations she laid upon them came to be believed, by means of their own conduct; for they who were so deeply affected with the death of their mother, that while they said both she and themselves were in a miserable case, they vehemently complained of her pitiable end, which indeed was truly such, and said that they were themselves in a

pitiable case also, because they were forced to live with those that had been her murderers, and to be partakers with them.

2. These disorders increased greatly, and the king's absence abroad had afforded a fit opportunity for that increase; but as soon as Herod was returned, and had made the forementioned speech to the multitude, Pheroras and Salome let fill words immediately as if he were in great danger, and as if the young men openly threatened that they would not spare him any longer, but revenge their mother's death upon him. They also added another circumstance, that their hopes were fixed on Archclaus, the king of Cappadocia, that they should be able by his means to come to Caesar, and accuse their father. Upon hearing such things, Herod was immediately disturbed; and indeed was the more astonished, because the same things were related to him by some others also. He then called to mind his former calamity, and considered that the disorders in his family had hindered him from enjoying any comfort from those that were dearest to him or from his wife whom he loved so well; and suspecting that his future troubles would soon be heavier and greater than those that were past, he was in great confusion of mind; for Divine Providence had in reality conferred upon him a great many outward advantages for his happiness, even beyond his hopes; but the troubles he had at home were such as he never expected to have met with, and rendered him unfortunate; nay, both sorts came upon him to such a degree as no one could imagine, and made it a doubtful question, whether, upon the comparison of both, he ought to have exchanged so great a success of outward good things for so great misfortunes at home, or whether he ought not to have chosen to avoid the calamities relating to his family, though he had, for a compensation, never been possessed of the admired grandeur of a kingdom.

3. As he was thus disturbed and afflicted, in order to depress these young men, he brought to court another of his sons, that was born to him when he was a private man; his name was Antipater; yet did he not then indulge him as he did afterwards, when he was quite overcome by him, and let him do every thing as he pleased, but rather with a design of depressing the insolence of the sons of Marianme, and managing this elevation of his so, that it might be for a warning to them; for this bold behavior of theirs [he thought] would not be so great, if they were once persuaded that the succession to

the kingdom did not appertain to them alone, or must of necessity come to them. So he introduced Antipater as their antagonist, and imagined that he made a good provision for discouraging their pride, and that after this was done to the young men, there might be a proper season for expecting these to be of a better disposition; but the event proved otherwise than he intended, for the young men thought he did them a very great injury; and as Antipater was a shrewd man, when he had once obtained this degree of freedom, and began to expect greater things than he had before hoped for, he had but one single design in his head, and that was to distress his brethren, and not at all to yield to them the pre-eminence, but to keep close to his father, who was already alienated from them by the calumnies he had heard about them, and ready to be wrought upon in any way his zeal against them should advise him to pursue, that he might be continually more and more severe against them. Accordingly, all the reports that were spread abroad came from him, while he avoided himself the suspicion as if those discoveries proceeded from him; but he rather chose to make use of those persons for his assistants that were unsuspected, and such as might be believed to speak truth by reason of the good-will they bore to the king; and indeed there were already not a few who cultivated a friendship with Antipater, in hopes of gaining somewhat by him, and these were the men who most of all persuaded Herod, because they appeared to speak thus out of their good-will to him: and with these joint accusations, which from various foundations supported one another's veracity, the young men themselves afforded further occasions to Antipater also; for they were observed to shed tears often, on account of the injury that was offered them, and had their mother in their mouths; and among their friends they ventured to reproach their father, as not acting justly by them; all which things were with an evil intention reserved in memory by Antipater against a proper opportunity; and when they were told to Herod, with aggravations, increased the disorder so much, that it brought a great tumult into the family; for while the king was very angry at imputations that were laid upon the sons of Mariamne, and was desirous to humble them, he still increased the honor that he had bestowed on Antipater, and was at last so overcome by his persuasions, that he brought his mother to court also. He also wrote frequently to Caesar in favor of him, and more earnestly recommended him to his care particularly. And when Agrippa was returning to Rome, after he had finished his ten years' government in Asia.[2] Herod sailed from Judea; and when he met with him, he had none with him but Antipater, whom he delivered to Agrippa, that he might take him along with him, together with many presents, that so he might become Caesar's friend, insomuch that things already looked as if he had all his father's favor, and that the young men were already entirely rejected from any hopes of the kingdom.

4 *How During Antipater's Abode at Rome, Herod Brought Alexander and Aristobulus Before Caesar and Accused Them. Alexander's Defense of Himself Before Caesar and Reconciliation to His Father*

1. AND now what happened during Antipater's absence augmented the honor to which he had been promoted, and his apparent eminence above his brethren; for he had made a great figure in Rome, because Herod had sent recommendations of him to all his friends there; only he was grieved that he was not at home, nor had proper opportunities of perpetually calumniating his brethren; and his chief fear was, lest his father should alter his mind, and entertain a more favorable opinion of the sons of Mariamne; and as he had this in his mind, he did not desist from his purpose, but continually sent from Rome any such stories as he hoped might grieve and irritate his father against his brethren, under pretense indeed of a deep concern for his preservation, but in truth such as his malicious mind dictated, in order to purchase a greater hope of the succession, which yet was already great in itself: and thus he did till he had excited such a degree of anger in Herod, that he was already become very ill-disposed towards the young men; but still while he delayed to exercise so violent a disgust against them, and that he might not either be too remiss or too rash, and so offend, he thought it best to sail to Rome, and there accuse his sons before Caesar, and not indulge himself in any such crime as might be heinous enough to be suspected of impiety. But as he was going up to Rome, it happened that he made such haste as to

---

2. This interval of ten years for the duration of Marcus Agrippa's government in Asia seems to be true, and agreeable to the Roman history. See Usher's Annals at A.M. 3392.

meet with Caesar at the city Aquilei[3] so when he came to the speech of Caesar, he asked for a time for hearing this great cause, wherein he thought himself very miserable, and presented his sons there, and accused them of their mad actions, and of their attempts against him: That they were enemies to him; and by all the means they were able, did their endeavors to show their hatred to their own father, and would take away his life, and so obtain his kingdom, after the most barbarous manner: that he had power from Caesar to dispose of it, not by necessity, but by choice, to him who shall exercise the greatest piety towards him; while these my sons are not so desirous of ruling, as they are, upon a disappointment thereof, to expose their own life, if so be they may but deprive their father of his life; so wild and polluted is their mind by time become, out of their hatred to him: that whereas he had a long time borne this his misfortune, he was now compelled to lay it before Caesar, and to pollute his ears with such language, while he himself wants to know what severity they have ever suffered from him, or what hardships he hath ever laid upon them to make them complain of him; and how they can think it just that he should not be lord of that kingdom which he in a long time, and with great danger, had gained, and not allow him to keep it and dispose of it to him who should deserve best; and this, with other advantages, he proposes as a reward for the piety of such a one as will hereafter imitate the care he hath taken of it, and that such a one may gain so great a requital as that is: and that it is an impious thing for them to pretend to meddle with it beforehand; for he who hath ever the kingdom in his view, at the same time reckons upon procuring the death of his father, because otherwise he cannot come at the government: that as for himself, he had hitherto given them all that he was able, and what was agreeable to such as are subject to the royal authority, and the sons of a king; what ornaments they wanted, with servants and delicate fare, and had married them

3. Although Herod met Augustus at Aquilei, yet was this accusation of his sons deferred till they came to Rome, as sect. 3 assures us, and as we are particularly informed in the History of the War, B. I. ch. 23. sect. 3; though what he here says belonged distinctly to Alexander, the elder brother, I mean his being brought to Rome, is here justly extended to both the brothers, and that not only in our copies, but in that of Zonaras also; nor is there reason to doubt but they were both at this solemn hearing by Augustus, although the defense was made by Alexander alone, who was the eldest brother, and one that could speak very well.

into the most illustrious families, the one [Aristobulus] to his sister's daughter, but Alexander to the daughter of king Archelaus; and, what was the greatest favor of all, when their crimes were so very bad, and he had authority to punish them, yet had he not made use of it against them, but had brought them before Caesar, their common benefactor, and had not used the severity which, either as a father who had been impiously abused, or as a king who had been assaulted treacherously, he might have done, but made them stand upon a level with him in judgment: that, however, it was necessary that all this should not be passed over without punishment, nor himself live in the greatest fears; nay, that it was not for their own advantage to see the light of the sun after what they have done, although they should escape at this time, since they had done the vilest things, and would certainly suffer the greatest punishments that ever were known among mankind.

2. These were the accusations which Herod laid with great vehemency against his sons before Caesar. Now the young men, both while he was speaking, and chiefly at his concluding, wept, and were in confusion. Now as to themselves, they knew in their own conscience they were innocent; but because they were accused by their father, they were sensible, as the truth was, that it was hard for them to make their apology, since though they were at liberty to speak their minds freely as the occasion required, and might with force and earnestness refute the accusation, yet was it not now decent so to do. There was therefore a difficulty how they should be able to speak; and tears, and at length a deep groan, followed, while they were afraid, that if they said nothing, they should seem to be in this difficulty from a consciousness of guilt,—nor had they any defense ready, by reason of their youth, and the disorder they were under; yet was not Caesar unapprized, when he looked upon them in the confusion they were in, that their delay to make their defense did not arise from any consciousness of great enormities, but from their unskilfulness and modesty. They were also commiserated by those that were there in particular; and they moved their father's affections in earnest till he had much ado to conceal them.

3. But when they saw there was a kind disposition arisen both in him and in Caesar, and that every one of the rest did either shed tears, or at least did all grieve with them, the one of them, whose name was Alexander, called to his father, and attempted to answer

his accusation, and said, "O father, the benevolence thou hast showed to us is evident, even in this very judicial procedure, for hadst thou had any pernicious intentions about us, thou hadst not produced us here before the common savior of all, for it was in thy power, both as a king and as a father, to punish the guilty; but by thus bringing us to Rome, and making Caesar himself a witness to what is done, thou intimatest that thou intendest to save us; for no one that hath a design to slay a man will bring him to the temples, and to the altars; yet are our circumstances still worse, for we cannot endure to live ourselves any longer, if it be believed that we have injured such a father; nay, perhaps it would be worse for us to live with this suspicion upon us, that we have injured him, than to die without such guilt. And if our open defense may be taken to be true, we shall be happy, both in pacifying thee, and in escaping the danger we are in; but if this calumny so prevails, it is more than enough for us that we have seen the sun this day; which why should we see, if this suspicion be fixed upon us? Now it is easy to say of young men, that they desire to reign; and to say further, that this evil proceeds from the case of our unhappy mother. This is abundantly sufficient to produce our present misfortune out of the former; but consider well, whether such an accusation does not suit all such young men, and may not be said of them all promiscuously; for nothing can hinder him that reigns, if he have children, and their mother be dead, but the father may have a suspicion upon all his sons, as intending some treachery to him; but a suspicion is not sufficient to prove such an impious practice. Now let any man say, whether we have actually and insolently attempted any such thing, whereby actions otherwise incredible use to be made credible? Can any body prove that poison hath been prepared? or prove a conspiracy of our equals, or the corruption of servants, or letters written against thee? though indeed there are none of those things but have sometimes been pretended by way of calumny, when they were never done; for a royal family that is at variance with itself is a terrible thing; and that which thou callest a reward of piety often becomes, among very wicked men, such a foundation of hope, as makes them leave no sort of mischief untried. Nor does any one lay any wicked practices to our charge; but as to calumnies by hearsay, how can he put an end to them, who will not hear what we have to say? Have we talked with too great freedom? Yes; but not against thee, for that would be unjust, but against those that never conceal any thing that is spoken to them. Hath either of us lamented our mother? Yes; but not because she is dead, but because she was evil spoken of by those that had no reason so to do. Are we desirous of that dominion which we know our father is possessed of? For what reason can we do so? If we already have royal honors, as we have, should not we labor in vain? And if we have them not, yet are not we in hopes of them? Or supposing that we had killed thee, could we expect to obtain thy kingdom? while neither the earth would let us tread upon it, nor the sea let us sail upon it, after such an action as that; nay, the religion of all your subjects, and the piety of the whole nation, would have prohibited parricides from assuming the government, and from entering into that most holy temple which was built by thee[4] But suppose we had made light of other dangers, can any murderer go off unpunished while Caesar is alive? We are thy sons, and not so impious or so thoughtless as that comes to, though perhaps more unfortunate than is convenient for thee. But in case thou neither findest any causes of complaint, nor any treacherous designs, what sufficient evidence hast thou to make such a wickedness of ours credible? Our mother is dead indeed, but then what befell her might be an instruction to us to caution, and not an incitement to wickedness. We are willing to make a larger apology for ourselves; but actions never done do not admit of discourse. Nay, we will make this agreement with thee, and that before Caesar, the lord of all, who is now a mediator between us, If thou, O father, canst bring thyself, by the evidence of truth, to have a mind free from suspicion concerning us let us live, though even then we shall live in an unhappy way, for to be accused of great acts of wickedness, though falsely, is a terrible thing; but if thou hast any fear remaining, continue thou on in thy pious life, we will give this reason for our own conduct; our life is not so desirable to us as to desire to have it, if it tend to the harm of our father who gave it us."

---

4. Since some prejudiced men have indulged a wild suspicion, as we have supposed already, Antiq. B. XV. ch. 11. sect. 7, that Josephus's history of Herod's rebuilding the temple is no better than a fable, it may not be amiss to take notice of this occasional clause in the speech of Alexander before his father Herod, in his and his brother's vindication, which mentions the temple as known by every body to have been built by Herod.

4. When Alexander had thus spoken, Caesar, who did not before believe so gross a calumny, was still more moved by it, and looked intently upon Herod, and perceived he was a little confounded: the persons there present were under an anxiety about the young men, and the fame that was spread abroad made the king hated, for the very incredibility of the calumny, and the commiseration of the flower of youth, the beauty of body, which were in the young men, pleaded for assistance, and the more so on this account, that Alexander had made their defense with dexterity and prudence; nay, they did not themselves any longer continue in their former countenances, which had been bedewed with tears, and cast downwards to the ground, but now there arose in them hope of the best; and the king himself appeared not to have had foundation enough to build such an accusation upon, he having no real evidence wherewith to correct them. Indeed he wanted some apology for making the accusation; but Caesar, after some delay, said, that although the young men were thoroughly innocent of that for which they were calumniated, yet had they been so far to blame, that they had not demeaned themselves towards their father so as to prevent that suspicion which was spread abroad concerning them. He also exhorted Herod to lay all such suspicions aside, and to be reconciled to his sons; for that it was not just to give any credit to such reports concerning his own children; and that this repentance on both sides might still heal those breaches that had happened between them, and might improve that their good-will to one another, whereby those on both sides, excusing the rashness of their suspicions, might resolve to bear a greater degree of affection towards each other than they had before. After Caesar had given them this admonition, he beckoned to the young men. When therefore they were disposed to fall down to make intercession to their father, he took them up, and embraced them, as they were in tears, and took each of them distinctly in his arms, till not one of those that were present, whether free-man or slave, but was deeply affected with what they saw.[5]

---

5. See John 2:20. See also another speech of Herod's own to the young men that pulled down his golden eagle from the front of the temple, where he takes notice how the building of the temple cost him a vast sum; and that the Asamoneans, in those one hundred and twenty-five years they held the government, were not able to perform so great a work, to the honor of God, as this was, Antiq. B. XVII. ch. 6. sect. 3.

5. Then did they return thanks to Caesar, and went away together; and with them went Antipater, with an hypocritical pretense that he rejoiced at this reconciliation. And in the last days they were with Caesar, Herod made him a present of three hundred talents, as he was then exhibiting shows and largesses to the people of Rome; and Caesar made him a present of half the revenue of the copper mines in Cyprus, and committed the care of the other half to him, and honored him with other gifts and incomes; and as to his own kingdom, he left it in his own power to appoint which of his sons he pleased for his successor, or to distribute it in parts to every one, that the dignity might thereby come to them all. And when Herod was disposed to make such a settlement immediately, Caesar said he would not give him leave to deprive himself, while he was alive, of the power over his kingdom, or over his sons.

6. After this, Herod returned to Judea again. But during his absence no small part of his dominion about Trachon had revolted, whom yet the commanders he left there had vanquished, and compelled to a submission again. Now as Herod was sailing with his sons, and was come over against Cilicia, to [the island] Eleusa, which hath now changed its name for Sebaste, he met with Archelaus, king of Cappadocia, who received him kindly, as rejoicing that he was reconciled to his sons, and that the accusation against Alexander, who had married his daughter, was at an end. They also made one another such presents as it became kings to make, From thence Herod came to Judea and to the temple, where he made a speech to the people concerning what had been done in this his journey. He also discoursed to them about Caesar's kindness to him, and about as many of the particulars he had done as he thought it for his advantage other people should be acquainted with. At last he turned his speech to the admonition of his sons; and exhorted those that lived at court, and the multitude, to concord; and informed them that his sons were to reign after him; Antipater first, and then Alexander and Aristobulus, the sons of Mariamne: but he desired that at present they should all have regard to himself, and esteem him king and lord of all, since he was not yet hindered by old age, but was in that period of life when he must be the most skillful in governing; and that he was not deficient in other arts of management that might enable him to govern the kingdom well, and to rule over his children also. He further told

the rulers under him, and the soldiery, that in case they would look upon him alone, their life would be led in a peaceable manner, and they would make one another happy. And when he had said this, he dismissed the assembly. Which speech was acceptable to the greatest part of the audience, but not so to them all; for the contention among his sons, and the hopes he had given them, occasioned thoughts and desires of innovations among them.

5 *How Herod Celebrated the Games That Were to Return Every Fifth Year Upon the Building of Cesarea; and How He Built and Adorned Many Other Places After a Magnificent Manner; and Did Many Other Actions Gloriously*

1. ABOUT this time it was that Cesarea Sebaste, which he had built, was finished. The entire building being accomplished: in the tenth year, the solemnity of it fell into the twenty-eighth year of Herod's reign, and into the hundred and ninety-second olympiad. There was accordingly a great festival and most sumptuous preparations made presently, in order to its dedication; for he had appointed a contention in music, and games to be performed naked. He had also gotten ready a great number of those that fight single combats, and of beasts for the like purpose; horse races also, and the most chargeable of such sports and shows as used to be exhibited at Rome, and in other places. He consecrated this combat to Caesar, and ordered it to be celebrated every fifth year. He also sent all sorts of ornaments for it out of his own furniture, that it might want nothing to make it decent; nay, Julia, Caesar's wife, sent a great part of her most valuable furniture [from Rome], insomuch that he had no want of any thing. The sum of them all was estimated at five hundred talents. Now when a great multitude was come to that city to see the shows, as well as the ambassadors whom other people sent, on account of the benefits they had received from Herod, he entertained them all in the public inns, and at public tables, and with perpetual feasts; this solemnity having in the day time the diversions of the fights, and in the night time such merry meetings as cost vast sums of money, and publicly demonstrated the generosity of his soul; for in all his undertakings he was ambitious to exhibit what exceeded whatsoever had been done before of the same kind. And it

is related that Caesar and Agrippa often said, that the dominions of Herod were too little for the greatness of his soul; for that he deserved to have both all the kingdom of Syria, and that of Egypt also.

2. After this solemnity and these festivals were over, Herod erected another city in the plain called Capharsaba, where he chose out a fit place, both for plenty of water and goodness of soil, and proper for the production of what was there planted, where a river encompassed the city itself, and a grove of the best trees for magnitude was round about it: this he named Antipatris, from his father Antipater. He also built upon another spot of ground above Jericho, of the same name with his mother, a place of great security and very pleasant for habitation, and called it Cypros. He also dedicated the finest monuments to his brother Phasaelus, on account of the great natural affection there had been between them, by erecting a tower in the city itself, not less than the tower of Pharos, which he named Phasaelus, which was at once a part of the strong defenses of the city, and a memorial for him that was deceased, because it bare his name. He also built a city of the same name in the valley of Jericho, as you go from it northward, whereby he rendered the neighboring country more fruitful by the cultivation its inhabitants introduced; and this also he called Phasaelus.

3. But as for his other benefits, it is impossible to reckon them up, those which he bestowed on cities, both in Syria and in Greece, and in all the places he came to in his voyages; for he seems to have conferred, and that after a most plentiful manner, what would minister to many necessities, and the building of public works, and gave them the money that was necessary to such works as wanted it, to support them upon the failure of their other revenues: but what was the greatest and most illustrious of all his works, he erected Apollo's temple at Rhodes, at his own expenses, and gave them a great number of talents of silver for the repair of their fleet. He also built the greatest part of the public edifices for the inhabitants of Nicopolis, at Actium;[6] and for the Antiochinus, the inhabitants of the principal city of Syria, where a broad street cuts through the place lengthways, he built cloisters

6. Dr. Hudson here gives us the words of Suetonius concerning this Nicopolis, when Augustus rebuilt it: "And that the memory of the victory at Actium might be celebrated the more afterward, he built Nicopolis at Actium, and appointed public shows to be there exhibited every fifth year." In August, sect. 18.

along it on both sides, and laid the open road with polished stone, and was of very great advantage to the inhabitants. And as to the olympic games, which were in a very low condition, by reason of the failure of their revenues, he recovered their reputation, and appointed revenues for heir maintenance, and made that solemn meeting more venerable, as to the sacrifices and other ornaments; and by reason of this vast liberality, he was generally declared in their inscriptions to be one of the perpetual managers of those games.

4. Now some there are who stand amazed at the diversity of Herod's nature and purposes; for when we have respect to his magnificence, and the benefits which he bestowed on all mankind, there is no possibility for even those that had the least respect for him to deny, or not openly to confess, that he had a nature vastly beneficent; but when any one looks upon the punishments he inflicted, and the injuries he did, not only to his subjects, but to his nearest relations, and takes notice of his severe and unrelenting disposition there, he will be forced to allow that he was brutish, and a stranger to all humanity; insomuch that these men suppose his nature to be different, and sometimes at contradiction with itself; but I am myself of another opinion, and imagine that the occasion of both these sort of actions was one and the same; for being a man ambitious of honor, and quite overcome by that passion, he was induced to be magnificent, wherever there appeared any hopes of a future memorial, or of reputation at present; and as his expenses were beyond his abilities, he was necessitated to be harsh to his subjects; for the persons on whom he expended his money were so many, that they made him a very bad procurer of it; and because he was conscious that he was hated by those under him, for the injuries he did them, he thought it not an easy thing to amend his offenses, for that it was inconvenient for his revenue; he therefore strove on the other side to make their ill-will an occasion of his gains. As to his own court, therefore, if any one was not very obsequious to him in his language, and would not confess himself to be his slave, or but seemed to think of any innovation in his government, he was not able to contain himself, but prosecuted his very kindred and friends, and punished them as if they were enemies and this wickedness he undertook out of a desire that he might be himself alone honored. Now for this, my assertion about that passion of his, we have the greatest evidence, by what he did to honor Caesar and Agrippa, and

his other friends; for with what honors he paid his respects to them who were his superiors, the same did he desire to be paid to himself; and what he thought the most excellent present he could make another, he discovered an inclination to have the like presented to himself. But now the Jewish nation is by their law a stranger to all such things, and accustomed to prefer righteousness to glory; for which reason that nation was not agreeable to him, because it was out of their power to flatter the king's ambition with statues or temples, or any other such performances; And this seems to me to have been at once the occasion of Herod's crimes as to his own courtiers and counselors, and of his benefactions as to foreigners and those that had no relation to him.

6 *An Embassage in Cyrene and Asia to Caesar, Concerning the Complaints They Had to Make Against the Greeks; with Copies of the Epistles Which Caesar and Agrippa Wrote to the Cities for Them*

1. Now the cities ill-treated the Jews in Asia, and all those also of the same nation which lived ill Libya, which joins to Cyrene, while the former kings had given them equal privileges with the other citizens; but the Greeks affronted them at this time, and that so far as to take away their sacred money, and to do them mischief on other particular occasions. When therefore they were thus afflicted, and found no end of their barbarous treatment they met with among the Greeks, they sent ambassadors to Caesar on those accounts, who gave them the same privileges as they had before, and sent letters to the same purpose to the governors of the provinces, copies of which I subjoin here, as testimonials of the ancient favorable disposition the Roman emperors had towards us.

2. "Caesar Augustus, high priest and tribune of the people, ordains thus: Since the nation of the Jews hath been found grateful to the Roman people, not only at this time, but in time past also, and chiefly Hyrcanus the high priest, under my father[7] Caesar the emperor, it seemed good to me and my counselors, according to the sentence

7. Augustus here calls Julius Caesar his father, though by birth he was only his uncle, on account of his adoption by him. See the same Antiq. B. XIV. ch. 14. sect. 4.

and oath of the people of Rome, that the Jews have liberty to make use of their own customs, according to the law of their forefathers, as they made use of them under Hyrcanus the high priest of the Almighty God; and that their sacred money be not touched, but be sent to Jerusalem, and that it be committed to the care of the receivers at Jerusalem; and that they be not obliged to go before any judge on the sabbath day, nor on the day of the preparation to it, after the ninth hour.[8] But if any one be caught stealing their holy books, or their sacred money, whether it be out of the synagogue or public school, he shall be deemed a sacrilegious person, and his goods shall be brought into the public treasury of the Romans. And I give order that the testimonial which they have given me, on account of my regard to that piety which I exercise toward all mankind, and out of regard to Caius Marcus Censorinus, together with the present decree, be proposed in that most eminent place which hath been consecrated to me by the community of Asia at Ancyra. And if any one transgress any part of what is above decreed, he shall be severely punished." This was inscribed upon a pillar in the temple of Caesar.

3. "Caesar to Norbanus Flaccus, sendeth greeting. Let those Jews, how many soever they be, who have been used, according to their ancient custom, to send their sacred money to Jerusalem, do the same freely." These were the decrees of Caesar.

4. Agrippa also did himself write after the manner following, on behalf of the Jews: "Agrippa, to the magistrates, senate, and people of the Ephesians, sendeth greeting. I will that the care and custody of the sacred money that is carried to the temple at Jerusalem be left to the Jews of Asia, to do with it according to their ancient custom; and that such as steal that sacred money of the Jews, and fly to a sanctuary, shall be taken thence and delivered to the Jews, by the same law that sacrilegious persons are taken thence. I have also written to Sylvanus the praetor, that no one compel the Jews to come before a judge on the sabbath day."

5. "Marcus Agrippa to the magistrates, senate, and people of Cyrene, sendeth greeting. The Jews of Cyrene have interceded with

8. This is authentic evidence that the Jews, in the days of Augustus, began to prepare for the celebration of the sabbath at the ninth hour on Friday, as the tradition of the elders did, it seems, then require of them.

me for the performance of what Augustus sent orders about to Flavius, the then praetor of Libya, and to the other procurators of that province, that the sacred money may be sent to Jerusalem freely, as hath been their custom from their forefathers, they complaining that they are abused by certain informers, and under pretense of taxes which were not due, are hindered from sending them, which I command to be restored without any diminution or disturbance given to them. And if any of that sacred money in the cities be taken from their proper receivers, I further enjoin, that the same be exactly returned to the Jews in that place."

6. "Caius Norbanus Flaccus, proconsul, to the magistrates of the Sardians, sendeth greeting. Caesar hath written to me, and commanded me not to forbid the Jews, how many soever they be, from assembling together according to the custom of their forefathers, nor from sending their money to Jerusalem. I have therefore written to you, that you may know that both Caesar and I would have you act accordingly."

7. Nor did Julius Antonius, the proconsul, write otherwise. "To the magistrates, senate, and people of the Ephesians, sendeth greeting. As I was dispensing justice at Ephesus, on the Ides of February, the Jews that dwell in Asia demonstrated to me that Augustus and Agrippa had permitted them to use their own laws and customs, and to offer those their first-fruits, which every one of them freely offers to the Deity on account of piety, and to carry them in a company together to Jerusalem without disturbance. They also petitioned me that I also would confirm what had been granted by Augustus and Agrippa by my own sanction. I would therefore have you take notice, that according to the will of Augustus and Agrippa, I permit them to use and do according to the customs of their forefathers without disturbance."

8. I have been obliged to set down these decree because the present history of our own acts will go generally among the Greeks; and I have hereby demonstrated to them that we have formerly been in great esteem, and have not been prohibited by those governors we were under from keeping any of the laws of our forefathers; nay, that we have been supported by them, while we followed our own religion, and the worship we paid to God; and I frequently make mention of these decrees, in order to reconcile other people to us, and to take away the causes of that hatred which unreasonable men bear to us.

As for our customs[9] there is no nation which always makes use of the same, and in every city almost we meet with them different from one another; but natural justice is most agreeable to the advantage of all men equally, both Greeks and barbarians, to which our laws have the greatest regard, and thereby render us, if we abide in them after a pure manner, benevolent and friendly to all men; on which account we have reason to expect the like return from others, and to inform them that they ought not to esteem difference of positive institutions a sufficient cause of alienation, but [join with us in] the pursuit of virtue and probity, for this belongs to all men in common, and of itself alone is sufficient for the preservation of human life. I now return to the thread of my history.

7 *How, Upon Herod's Going Down into David's Sepulcher, the Sedition in His Family Greatly Increased*

1. AS for Herod, he had spent vast sums about the cities, both without and within his own kingdom; and as he had before heard that Hyrcanus, who had been king before him, had opened David's sepulcher, and taken out of it three thousand talents of silver, and that there was a much greater number left behind, and indeed enough to suffice all his wants, he had a great while an intention to make the attempt; and at this time he opened that sepulcher by night, and went into it, and endeavored that it should not be at all known in the city, but took only his most faithful friends with him. As for any money, he found none, as Hyrcanus had done, but that furniture of gold, and those precious goods that were laid up there; all which he took away. However, he had a great desire to make a more diligent search, and to go farther in, even as far as the very bodies of David and Solomon; where two of his guards were slain, by a flame that burst out upon those that went in, as the report was. So he was terribly aftrighted,

9. The remaining part of this chapter is remarkable, as justly distinguishing natural justice, religion, and morality, from positive institutions in all countries, and evidently preferring the former before the latter, as did the true prophets of God always under the Old Testament, and Christ and his New; whence Josephus seems to have been at this time nearer Christianity than were the Scribes and Pharisees of his age; who, as we know from the New Testament, were entirely of a different opinion and practice.

and went out, and built a propitiatory monument of that fright he had been in; and this of white stone, at the mouth of the sepulcher, and that at great expense also. And even Nicolaus[10] his historiographer makes mention of this monument built by Herod, though he does not mention his going down into the sepulcher, as knowing that action to be of ill repute; and many other things he treats of in the same manner in his book; for he wrote in Herod's lifetime, and under his reign, and so as to please him, and as a servant to him, touching upon nothing but what tended to his glory, and openly excusing many of his notorious crimes, and very diligently concealing them. And as he was desirous to put handsome colors on the death of Mariamne and her sons, which were barbarous actions in the king, he tells falsehoods about the incontinence of Mariamne, and the treacherous designs of his sons upon him; and thus he proceeded in his whole work, making a pompous encomium upon what just actions he had done, but earnestly apologizing for his unjust ones. Indeed, a man, as I said, may have a great deal to say by way of excuse for Nicolaus; for he did not so properly write this as a history for others, as somewhat that might be subservient to the king himself. As for ourselves, who come of a family nearly allied to the Asamonean kings, and on that account have an honorable place, which is the priesthood, we think it indecent to say any thing that is false about them, and accordingly we have described their actions after an unblemished and upright manner. And although we reverence many of Herod's posterity, who still reign, yet do we pay a greater regard to truth than to them, and this though it sometimes happens that we incur their displeasure by so doing.

2. And indeed Herod's troubles in his family seemed to be augmented by reason of this attempt he made upon David's sepulcher; whether Divine vengeance increased the calamities he lay under, in order to render them incurable, or whether fortune made an assault upon him, in those cases wherein the seasonableness of the cause

10. It is here worth our observation, how careful Josephus was as to the discovery of truth in Herod's history, since he would not follow Nicolaus of Damascus himself, so great an historian, where there was great reason to suspect that he flattered Herod; which impartiality in history Josephus here solemnly pro fesses, and of which impartiality he has given more demonstrations than almost any historian whomsoever; but as to Herod's taking great wealth out of David's sepulcher, though I cannot prove it, yet do I strongly suspect it from this very history.

made it strongly believed that the calamities came upon him for his impiety; for the tumult was like a civil war in his palace, and their hatred towards one another was like that where each one strove to exceed another in calumnies. However, Antipater used stratagems perpetually against his brethren, and that very cunningly; while abroad he loaded them with accusations, but still took upon him frequently to apologize for them, that this apparent benevolence to them might make him be believed, and forward his attempts against them; by which means he, after various manners, circumvented his father, who believed all that he did was for his preservation. Herod also recommended Ptolemy, who was a great director of the affairs of his kingdom, to Antipater; and consulted with his mother about the public affairs also. And indeed these were all in all, and did what they pleased, and made the king angry against any other persons, as they thought it might be to their own advantage; but still the sons of Marianme were in a worse and worse condition perpetually; and while they were thrust out, and set in a more dishonorable rank, who yet by birth were the most noble, they could not bear the dishonor. And for the women, Glaphyra, Alexander's wife, the daughter of Archclaus, hated Salome, both because of her love to her husband, and because Glaphyra seemed to behave herself somewhat insolently towards Salome's daughter, who was the wife of Aristobulus, which equality of hers to herself Glaphyra took very impatiently.

3. Now, besides this second contention that had fallen among them, neither did the king's brother Pheroras keep himself out of trouble, but had a particular foundation for suspicion and hatred; for he was overcome with the charms of his wife, to such a degree of madness, that he despised the king's daughter, to whom he had been betrothed, and wholly bent his mind to the other, who had been but a servant. Herod also was grieved by the dishonor that was done him, because he had bestowed many favors upon him, and had advanced him to that height of power that he was almost a partner with him in the kingdom, and saw that he had not made him a due return for his labors, and esteemed himself unhappy on that account. So upon Pheroras's unworthy refusal, he gave the damsel to Phasaelus's son; but after some time, when he thought the heat of his brother's affections was over, he blamed him for his former conduct, and desired him to take his second daughter, whose name was Cypros. Ptolemy also advised

him to leave off affronting his brother, and to forsake her whom he had loved, for that it was a base thing to be so enamored of a servant, as to deprive himself of the king's good-will to him, and become an occasion of his trouble, and make himself hated by him. Pheroras knew that this advice would be for his own advantage, particularly because he had been accused before, and forgiven; so he put his wife away, although he already had a son by her, and engaged to the king that he would take his second daughter, and agreed that the thirtieth day after should be the day of marriage; and sware he would have no further conversation with her whom he had put away; but when the thirty days were over, he was such a slave to his affections, that he no longer performed any thing he had promised, but continued still with his former wife. This occasioned Herod to grieve openly, and made him angry, while the king dropped one word or other against Pheroras perpetually; and many made the king's anger an opportunity for raising calumnies against him. Nor had the king any longer a single quiet day or hour, but occasions of one fresh quarrel or another arose among his relations, and those that were dearest to him; for Salome was of a harsh temper, and ill-natured to Mariamne's sons; nor would she suffer her own daughter, who was the wife of Aristobulus, one of those young men, to bear a good-will to her husband, but persuaded her to tell her if he said any thing to her in private, and when any misunderstandings happened, as is common, she raised a great many suspicions out of it; by which means she learned all their concerns, and made the damsel ill-natured to the young man. And in order to gratify her mother, she often said that the young men used to mention Mariamne when they were by themselves; and that they hated their father, and were continually threatening, that if they had once got the kingdom, they would make Herod's sons by his other wives country schoolmasters, for that the present education which was given them, and their diligence in learning, fitted them for such an employment. And as for the women, whenever they saw them adorned with their mother's clothes, they threatened, that instead of their present gaudy apparel, they should be clothed in sackcloth, and confined so closely that they should not see the light of the sun. These stories were presently carried by Salome to the king, who was troubled to hear them, and endeavored to make up matters; but these suspicions afflicted him, and becoming more and more uneasy, he believed every body against every body. However, upon his rebuking his sons, and hearing the defense they made for themselves, he was easier for a while, though a little afterwards much worse accidents came upon him.

4. For Pheroras came to Alexander, the husband of Glaphyra, who was the daughter of Archelaus, as we have already told you, and said that he had heard from Salome that Herod has enamored on Glaphyra, and that his passion for her was incurable. When Alexander heard that, he was all on fire, from his youth and jealousy; and he interpreted the instances of Herod's obliging behavior to her, which were very frequent, for the worse, which came from those suspicions he had on account of that word which fell from Pheroras; nor could he conceal his grief at the thing, but informed him what word: Pheroras had said. Upon which Herod was in a greater disorder than ever; and not bearing such a false calumny, which was to his shame, was much disturbed at it; and often did he lament the wickedness of his domestics, and how good he had been to them, and how ill requitals they had made him. So he sent for Pheroras, and reproached him, and said, "Thou vilest of all men! art thou come to that unmeasurable and extravagant degree of ingratitude, as not only to suppose such things of me, but to speak of them? I now indeed perceive what thy intentions are. It is not thy only aim to reproach me, when thou usest such words to my son, but thereby to persuade him to plot against me, and get me destroyed by poison. And who is there, if he had not a good genius at his elbow, as hath my son, but would not bear such a suspicion of his father, but would revenge himself upon him? Dost thou suppose that thou hast only dropped a word for him to think of, and not rather hast put a sword into his hand to slay his father? And what dost thou mean, when thou really hatest both him and his brother, to pretend kindness to them, only in order to raise a reproach against me, and talk of such things as no one but such an impious wretch as thou art could either devise in their mind, or declare in their words? Begone, thou art such a plague to thy benefactor and thy brother, and may that evil conscience of thine go along with thee; while I still overcome my relations by kindness, and am so far from avenging myself of them, as they deserve, that I bestow greater benefits upon them than they are worthy of."

5. Thus did the king speak. Whereupon Pheroras, who was caught in the very act of his villainy, said that "it was Salome who was the framer of this plot, and that the words came from her." But as soon as she heard that, for she was at hand, she cried out, like one that would be believed, that no such thing ever came out of her mouth; that they all earnestly endeavored to make the king hate her, and to make her away, because of the good-will she bore to Herod, and because she was always foreseeing the dangers that were coming upon him, and that at present there were more plots against him than usual; for while she was the only person who persuaded her brother to put away the wife he now had, and to take the king's daughter, it was no wonder if she were hated by him. As she said this, and often tore her hair, and often beat her breast, her countenance made her denial to be believed; but the peverseness of her manners declared at the same time her dissimulation in these proceedings; but Pheroras was caught between them, and had nothing plausible to offer in his own defense, while he confessed that he had said what was charged upon him, but was not believed when he said he had heard it from Salome; so the confusion among them was increased, and their quarrelsome words one to another. At last the king, out of his hatred to his brother and sister, sent them both away; and when he had commended the moderation of his son, and that he had himself told him of the report, he went in the evening to refresh himself. After such a contest as this had fallen out among them, Salome's reputation suffered greatly, since she was supposed to have first raised the calumny; and the king's wives were grieved at her, as knowing she was a very ill-natured woman, and would sometimes be a friend, and sometimes an enemy, at different seasons: so they perpetually said one thing or another against her; and somewhat that now fell out made them the bolder in speaking against her.

6. There was one Obodas, king of Arabia, an inactive and slothful man in his nature; but Sylleus managed most of his affairs for him. He was a shrewd man, although he was but young, and was handsome withal. This Sylleus, upon some occasion coining to Herod, and supping with him, saw Salome, and set his heart upon her; and understanding that she was a widow, he discoursed with her. Now because Salome was at this time less in favor with her brother, she looked upon Sylleus with some passion, and was very earnest to be

married to him; and on the days following there appeared many, and those very great, indications of their agreement together. Now the women carried this news to the king, and laughed at the indecency of it; whereupon Herod inquired about it further of Pheroras, and desired him to observe them at supper, how their behavior was one toward another; who told him, that by the signals which came from their heads and their eyes, they both were evidently in love. After this, Sylleus the Arabian being suspected, went away, but came again in two or three months afterwards, as it were on that very design, and spake to Herod about it, and desired that Salome might be given him to wife; for that his affinity might not be disadvantageous to his affairs, by a union with Arabia, the government of which country was already in effect under his power, and more evidently would be his hereafter. Accordingly, when Herod discoursed with his sister about it, and asked her whether she were disposed to this match, she immediately agreed to it. But when Sylleus was desired to come over to the Jewish religion, and then he should marry her, and that it was impossible to do it on any other terms, he could not bear that proposal, and went his way; for he said, that if he should do so, he should be stoned by the Arabs. Then did Pheroras reproach Salome for her incontinency, as did the women much more; and said that Sylleus had debauched her. As for that damsel which the king had betrothed to his brother Pheroras, but he had not taken her, as I have before related, because he was enamored on his former wife, Salome desired of Herod she might be given to her son by Costobarus; which match he was very willing to, but was dissuaded from it by Pheroras, who pleaded that this young man would not be kind to her, since his father had been slain by him, and that it was more just that his son, who was to be his successor in the tetrarchy, should have her. So he begged his pardon, and persuaded him to do so. Accordingly the damsel, upon this change of her espousals, was disposal of to this young man, the son of Pheroras, the king giving for her portion a hundred talents.

Chapter 8

8 *How Herod Took Up Alexander and Bound Him; Whom Yet Archelaus King of Cappadocia Reconciled to His Father Herod Again*

1. BUT still the affairs of Herod's family were no better, but perpetually more troublesome. Now this accident happened, which arose from no decent occasion, but proceeded so far as to bring great difficulties upon him. There were certain eunuchs which the king had, and on account of their beauty was very fond of them; and the care of bringing him drink was intrusted to one of them; of bringing him his supper, to another; and of putting him to bed, to the third, who also managed the principal affairs of the government; and there was one told the king that these eunuchs were corrupted by Alexander the king's son with great sums of money. And when they were asked whether Alexander had had criminal conversation with them, they confessed it, but said they knew of no further mischief of his against his father; but when they were more severely tortured, and were in the utmost extremity, and the tormentors, out of compliance with Antipater, stretched the rack to the very utmost, they said that Alexander bare great ill-will and innate hatred to his father; and that he told them that Herod despaired to live much longer; and that, in order to cover his great age, he colored his hair black, and endeavored to conceal what would discover how old he was; but that if he would apply himself to him, when he should attain the kingdom, which, in spite of his father, could come to no one else, he should quickly have the first place in that kingdom under him, for that he was now ready to take the kingdom, not only as his birthright, but by the preparations he had made for obtaining it, because a great many of the rulers, and a great many of his friends, were of his side, and those no ill men neither, ready both to do and to suffer whatsoever should come on that account.

2. When Herod heard this confession, he was all over anger and fear, some parts seeming to him reproachful, and some made him suspicious of dangers that attended him, insomuch that on both accounts he was provoked, and bitterly afraid lest some more heavy plot was laid against him than he should be then able to escape from; whereupon he did not now make an open search, but sent about spies to watch such as he suspected, for he was now overrun with suspicion and hatred against all about him; and indulging abundance

of those suspicions, in order to his preservation, he continued to suspect those that were guiltless; nor did he set any bounds to himself, but supposing that those who staid with him had the most power to hurt him, they were to him very frightful; and for those that did not use to come to him, it seemed enough to name them [to make them suspected], and he thought himself safer when they were destroyed. And at last his domestics were come to that pass, that being no way secure of escaping themselves, they fell to accusing one another, and imagining that he who first accused another was most likely to save himself; yet when any had overthrown others, they were hated; and they were thought to suffer justly who unjustly accused others, and they only thereby prevented their own accusation; nay, they now executed their own private enmities by this means, and when they were caught, they were punished in the same way. Thus these men contrived to make use of this opportunity as an instrument and a snare against their enemies; yet when they tried it, were themselves caught also in the same snare which they laid for others: and the king soon repented of what he had done, because he had no clear evidence of the guilt of those whom he had slain; and yet what was still more severe in him, he did not make use of his repentance, in order to leave off doing the like again, but in order to inflict the same punishment upon their accusers.

3. And in this state of disorder were the affairs of the palace; and he had already told many of his friends directly that they ought not to appear before him, her come into the palace; and the reason of this injunction was, that [when they were there], he had less freedom of acting, or a greater restraint on himself on their account; for at this time it was that he expelled Andromachus and Gamellus, men who had of old been his friends, and been very useful to him in the affairs of his kingdom, and been of advantage to his family, by their embassages and counsels; and had been tutors to his sons, and had in a manner the first degree of freedom with him. He expelled Andromachus, because his son Demetrius was a companion to Alexander; and Gamellus, because he knew that he wished him well, which arose from his having been with him in his youth, when he was at school, and absent at Rome. These he expelled out of his palace, and was willing enough to have done worse by them; but that he might not seem to take such liberty against men of so great reputation, he contented himself

with depriving them of their dignity, and of their power to hinder his wicked proceedings.

4. Now it was Antipater who was the cause of all this; who when he knew what a mad and licentious way of acting his father was in, and had been a great while one of his counselors, he hurried him on, and then thought he should bring him to do somewhat to purpose, when every one that could oppose him was taken away. When therefore Andromachus and his friends were driven away, and had no discourse nor freedom with the king any longer, the king, in the first place, examined by torture all whom he thought to be faithful to Alexander, Whether they knew of any of his attempts against him; but these died without having any thing to say to that matter, which made the king more zealous [after discoveries], when he could not find out what evil proceedings he suspected them of. As for Antipater, he was very sagacious to raise a calumny against those that were really innocent, as if their denial was only their constancy and fidelity [to Alexander], and thereupon provoked Herod to discover by the torture of great numbers what attempts were still concealed. Now there was a certain person among the many that were tortured, who said that he knew that the young man had often said, that when he was commended as a tall man in his body, and a skillful marksman, and that in his other commendable exercises he exceeded all men, these qualifications given him by nature, though good in themselves, were not advantageous to him, because his father was grieved at them, and envied him for them; and that when he walked along with his father, he endeavored to depress and shorten himself, that he might not appear too tall; and that when he shot at any thing as he was hunting, when his father was by, he missed his mark on purpose, for he knew how ambitious his father was of being superior in such exercises. So when the man was tormented about this saying, and had ease given his body after it, he added, that he had his brother Aristobulus for his assistance, and contrived to lie in wait for their father, as they were hunting, and kill him; and when they had done so to fly to Rome, and desire to have the kingdom given them. There were also letters of the young man found, written to his brother, wherein he complained that his father did not act justly in giving Antipater a country, whose [yearly] revenues amounted to two hundred talents. Upon these confessions Herod presently thought he had somewhat

to depend on, in his own opinion, as to his suspicion about his sons; so he took up Alexander and bound him: yet did he still continue to be uneasy, and was not quite satisfied of the truth of what he had heard; and when he came to recollect himself, he found that they had only made juvenile complaints and contentions, and that it was an incredible thing, that when his son should have slain him, he should openly go to Rome [to beg the kingdom]; so he was desirous to have some surer mark of his son's wickedness, and was very solicitous about it, that he might not appear to have condemned him to be put in prison too rashly; so he tortured the principal of Alexander's friends, and put not a few of them to death, without getting any of the things out of them which he suspected. And while Herod was very busy about this matter, and the palace was full of terror and trouble, one of the younger sort, when he was in the utmost agony, confessed that Alexander had sent to his friends at Rome, and desired that he might be quickly invited thither by Caesar, and that he could discover a plot against him; that Mithridates, the king of Parthia, was joined in friendship with his father against the Romans, and that he had a poisonous potion ready prepared at Askelori.

5. To these accusations Herod gave credit, and enjoyed hereby, in his miserable case, some sort of consolation, in excuse of his rashness, as fiattering himself with finding things in so bad a condition; but as for the poisonous potion, which he labored to find, he could find none. As for Alexander, he was very desirous to aggravate the vast misfortunes he was under, so he pretended not to deny the accusations, but punished the rashness of his father with a greater crime of his own; and perhaps he was willing to make his father ashamed of his easy belief of such calumnies: he aimed especially, if he could gain belief to his story, to plague him and his whole kingdom; for he wrote four letters, and sent them to him, that he did not need to torture any more persons, for he had plotted against him; and that he had for his partners Pheroras and the most faithful of his friends; and that Salome came in to him by night, and that she lay with him whether he would or not; and that all men were come to be of one mind, to make away with him as soon as they could, and so get clear of the continual fear they were in from him. Among these were accused Ptolemy and Sapinnius, who were the most faithful friends to the king. And what more can be said, but that those who before were the

most intimate friends, were become wild beasts to one another, as if a certain madness had fallen upon them, while there was no room for defense or refutation, in order to the discovery of the truth, but all were at random doomed to destruction; so that some lamented those that were in prison, some those that were put to death, and others lamented that they were in expectation of the same miseries; and a melancholy solitude rendered the kingdom deformed, and quite the reverse to that happy state it was formerly in. Herod's own life also was entirely disturbed; and because he could trust nobody, he was sorely punished by the expectation of further misery; for he often fancied in his imagination that his son had fallen upon him, or stood by him with a sword in his hand; and thus was his mind night and day intent upon this thing, and revolved it over and over, no otherwise than if he were under a distraction. And this was the sad condition Herod was now in.

6. But when Archelaus, king of Cappadocia, heard of the state that Herod was in, and being in great distress about his daughter, and the young man [her husband], and grieving with Herod, as with a man that was his friend, on account of so great a disturbance as he was under, he came [to Jerusalem] on purpose to compose their differences; and when he found Herod in such a temper, he thought it wholly unseasonable to reprove him, or to pretend that he had done any thing rashly, for that he should thereby naturally bring him to dispute the point with him, and by still more and more apologizing for himself to be the more irritated: he went, therefore, another way to work, in order to correct the former misfortunes, and appeared angry at the young man, and said that Herod had been so very mild a man, that he had not acted a rash part at all. He also said he would dissolve his daughter's marriage with Alexander, nor could in justice spare his own daughter, if she were conscious of any thing, and did not inform Herod of it. When Archelaus appeared to be of this temper, and otherwise than Herod expected or imagined, and, for the main, took Herod's part, and was angry on his account, the king abated of his harshness, and took occasion from his appearing to have acted justly hitherto, to come by degrees to put on the affection of a father, and was on both sides to be pitied; for when some persons refuted the calumnies that were laid on the young man, he was thrown into a passion; but when Archclaus joined in the accusation, he was dissolved into tears and sorrow after

an affectionate manner. Accordingly, he desired that he would not dissolve his son's marriage, and became not so angry as before for his offenses. So when Archclaus had brought him to a more moderate temper, he transferred the calumnies upon his friends; and said it must be owing to them that so young a man, and one unacquainted with malice, was corrupted; and he supposed that there was more reason to suspect the brother than the soft. Upon which Herod was very much displeased at Pheroras, who indeed now had no one that could make a reconciliation between him and his brother. So when he saw that Archclaus had the greatest power with Herod, he betook himself to him in the habit of a mourner, and like one that had all the signs upon him of an undone man. Upon this Archclaus did not overlook the intercession he made to him, nor yet did he undertake to change the king's disposition towards him immediately; and he said that it was better for him to come himself to the king, and confess himself the occasion of all; that this would make the king's anger not to be extravagant towards him, and that then he would be present to assist him. When he had persuaded him to this, he gained his point with both of them; and the calumnies raised against the young man were, beyond all expectation, wiped off. And Archclaus, as soon as he had made the reconciliation, went then away to Cappadocia, having proved at this juncture of time the most acceptable person to Herod in the world; on which account he gave him the richest presents, as tokens of his respects to him; and being on other occasions magnanimous, he esteemed him one of his dearest friends. He also made an agreement with him that he would go to Rome, because he had written to Caesar about these affairs; so they went together as far as Antioch, and there Herod made a reconciliation between Archclaus and Titus, the president of Syria, who had been greatly at variance, and so returned back to Judea.

9 *Concerning the Revolt of the Trachonites; How Sylleus Accused Herod Before Caesar; and How Herod, When Caesar Was Angry at Him, Resolved to Send Nicolaus to Rome*

1. WHEN Herod had been at Rome, and was come back again, a war arose between him and the Arabians, on the occasion following: The

inhabitants of Trachonitis, after Caesar had taken the country away from Zenodorus, and added it to Herod, had not now power to rob, but were forced to plough the land, and to live quietly, which was a thing they did not like; and when they did take that pains, the ground did not produce much fruit for them. However, at the first the king would not permit them to rob, and so they abstained from that unjust way of living upon their neighbors, which procured Herod a great reputation for his care. But when he was sailing to Rome, it was at that time when he went to accuse his son Alexander, and to commit Antipater to Caesar's protection, the Trachonites spread a report as if he were dead, and revolted from his dominion, and betook themselves again to their accustomed way of robbing their neighbors; at which time the king's commanders subdued them during his absence; but about forty of the principal robbers, being terrified by those that had been taken, left the country, and retired into Arabia, Sylleus entertaining them, after he had missed of marrying Salome, and gave them a place of strength, in which they dwelt. So they overran not only Judea, but all Celesyria also, and carried off the prey, while Sylleus afforded them places of protection and quietness during their wicked practices. But when Herod came back from Rome, he perceived that his dominions had greatly suffered by them; and since he could not reach the robbers themselves, because of the secure retreat they had in that country, and which the Arabian government afforded them, and yet being very uneasy at the injuries they had done him, he went all over Trachonitis, and slew their relations; whereupon these robbers were more angry than before, it being a law among them to be avenged on the murderers of their relations by all possible means; so they continued to tear and rend every thing under Herod's dominion with impunity. Then did he discourse about these robberies to Saturninus and Volumnius, and required that they should be punished; upon which occasion they still the more confirmed themselves in their robberies, and became more numerous, and made very great disturbances, laying waste the countries and villages that belonged to Herod's kingdom, and killing those men whom they caught, till these unjust proceedings came to be like a real war, for the robbers were now become about a thousand;—at which Herod was sore displeased, and required the robbers, as well as the money which he had lent Obodas, by Sylleus, which was sixty talents, and since the time of payment was now past, he desired to have it paid him; but Sylleus, who had laid Obodas aside, and managed all by himself, denied that the robbers were in Arabia, and put off the payment of the money; about which there was a hearing before Saturninus and Volumnius, who were then the presidents of Syria.[11] At last he, by their means, agreed, that within thirty days' time Herod should be paid his money, and that each of them should deliver up the other's subjects reciprocally. Now, as to Herod, there was not one of the other's subjects found in his kingdom, either as doing any injustice, or on any other account, but it was proved that the Arabians had the robbers amongst them.

2. When this day appointed for payment of the money was past, without Sylleus's performing any part of his agreement, and he was gone to Rome, Herod demanded the payment of the money, and that the robbers that were in Arabia should be delivered up; and, by the permission of Saturninus and Volumnius, executed the judgment himself upon those that were refractory. He took an army that he had, and let it into Arabia, and in three days' time marched seven mansions; and when he came to the garrison wherein the robbers were, he made an assault upon them, and took them all, and demolished the place, which was called Raepta, but did no harm to any others. But as the Arabians came to their assistance, under Naceb their captain, there ensued a battle, wherein a few of Herod's soldiers, and Naceb, the captain of the Arabians, and about twenty of his soldiers, fell, while the rest betook themselves to flight. So when he had brought these to punishment, he placed three thousand Idumeans in Trachonitis, and thereby restrained the robbers that were there. He also sent an account to the captains that were about Phoenicia, and demonstrated that he had done nothing but what he ought to do, in punishing the refractory Arabians, which, upon an exact inquiry, they found to be no more than what was true.

3. However, messengers were hasted away to Sylleus to Rome, and informed him what had been done, and, as is usual, aggravated every thing. Now Sylleus had already insinuated himself into the knowledge of Caesar, and was then about the palace; and as soon as he heard of

---

11. These joint presidents of Syria, Saturninus and Volumnius, were not perhaps of equal authority, but the latter like a procurator under the former, as the very learned Noris and Pagi, and with them Dr. Hudson, determine.

these things, he changed his habit into black, and went in, and told Caesar that Arabia was afflicted with war, and that all his kingdom was in great confusion, upon Herod's laying it waste with his army; and he said, with tears in his eyes, that two thousand five hundred of the principal men among the Arabians had been destroyed, and that their captain Nacebus, his familiar friend and kinsman, was slain; and that the riches that were at Raepta were carried off; and that Obodas was despised, whose infirm state of body rendered him unfit for war; on which account neither he, nor the Arabian army, were present. When Sylleus said so, and added invidiously, that he would not himself have come out of the country, unless he had believed that Caesar would have provided that they should all have peace one with another, and that, had he been there, he would have taken care that the war should not have been to Herod's advantage; Caesar was provoked when this was said, and asked no more than this one question, both of Herod's friends that were there, and of his own friends, who were come from Syria, Whether Herod had led an army thither? And when they were forced to confess so much, Caesar, without staying to hear for what reason he did it, and how it was done, grew very angry, and wrote to Herod sharply. The sum of his epistle was this, that whereas of old he had used him as his friend, he should now use him as his subject. Sylleus also wrote an account of this to the Arabians, who were so elevated with it, that they neither delivered up the robbers that had fled to them, nor paid the money that was due; they retained those pastures also which they had hired, and kept them without paying their rent, and all this because the king of the Jews was now in a low condition, by reason of Caesar's anger at him. Those of Trachonitis also made use of this opportunity, and rose up against the Idumean garrison, and followed the same way of robbing with the Arabians, who had pillaged their country, and were more rigid in their unjust proceedings, not only in order to get by it, but by way of revenge also.

4. Now Herod was forced to bear all this, that confidence of his being quite gone with which Caesar's favor used to inspire him; for Caesar would not admit so much as an embassage from him to 'make an apology for him; and when they came again, he sent them away without success. So he was cast into sadness and fear; and Sylleus's circumstances grieved him exceedingly, who was now believed by Caesar, and was present at Rome, nay, sometimes aspiring higher.

Now it came to pass that Obodas was dead; and Aeneas, whose name was afterward changed to Aretas,[12] took the government, for Sylleus endeavored by calumnies to get him turned out of his principality, that he might himself take it; with which design he gave much money to the courtiers, and promised much money to Caesar, who indeed was angry that Aretas had not sent to him first before he took the kingdom; yet did Aeneas send an epistle and presents to Caesar, and a golden crown, of the weight of many talents. Now that epistle accused Sylleus as having been a wicked servant, and having killed Obodas by poison; and that while he was alive, he had governed him as he pleased; and had also debauched the wives of the Arabians; and had borrowed money, in order to obtain the dominion for himself: yet did not Caesar give heed to these accusations, but sent his ambassadors back, without receiving any of his presents. But in the mean time the affairs of Judea and Arabia became worse and worse, partly because of the anarchy they were under, and partly because, as bad as they were, nobody had power to govern them; for of the two kings, the one was not yet confirmed in his kingdom, and so had not authority sufficient to restrain the evil-doers; and as for Herod, Caesar was immediately angry at him for having avenged himself, and so he was compelled to bear all the injuries that were offered him. At length, when he saw no end of the mischief which surrounded him, he resolved to send ambassadors to Rome again, to see whether his friends had prevailed to mitigate Caesar, and to address themselves to Caesar himself; and the ambassador he sent thither was Nicolans of Damascus.

10 *How Eurycles Falsely Accused Herod's Sons; and How Their Father Bound Them, and Wrote to Caesar About Them. of Sylleus and How He Was Accused by Nicolaus*

1. THE disorders about Herod's family and children about this time grew much worse; for it now appeared certain, nor was it unforeseen before-hand, that fortune threatened the greatest and most insupportable misfortunes possible to his kingdom. Its progress and augmentation at this time arose on the occasion following: One Eurycles, a

12. This Aretas was now become so established a name for the kings of Arabia, [at Petra and Damascus,] that when the crown came to this Aeneas, he changed his name to Aretas, as Havercamp here justly observes. See Antiq. B. XIII. ch. 15. sect, 2.

Lacedemonian, (a person of note there, but a man of a perverse mind, and so cunning in his ways of voluptuousness and flattery, as to indulge both, and yet seem to indulge neither of them,) came in his travels to Herod, and made him presents, but so that he received more presents from him. He also took such proper seasons for insinuating himself into his friendship, that he became one of the most intimate of the king's friends. He had his lodging in Antipater's house; but he had not only access, but free conversation, with Alexander, as pretending to him that he was in great favor with Archclaus, the king of Cappadocia; whence he pretended much respect to Glaphyra, and in an occult manner cultivated a friendship with them all; but always attending to what was said and done, that he might be furnished with calumnies to please them all. In short, he behaved himself so to every body in his conversation, as to appear to be his particular friend, and he made others believe that his being any where was for that person's advantage. So he won upon Alexander, who was but young; and persuaded him that he might open his grievances to him with assurance and with nobody else. So he declared his grief to him, how his father was alienated from him. He related to him also the affairs of his mother, and of Antipater; that he had driven them from their proper dignity, and had the power over every thing himself; that no part of this was tolerable, since his father was already come to hate them; and he added, that he would neither admit them to his table, nor to his conversation. Such were the complaints, as was but natural, of Alexander about the things that troubled him; and these discourses Eurycles carried to Antipater, and told him he did not inform him of this on his own account, but that being overcome by his kindness, the great importance of the thing obliged him to do it; and he warned him to have a care of Alexander, for that what he said was spoken with vehemency, and that, in consequence of what he said, he would certainly kill him with his own hand. Whereupon Antipater, thinking him to be his friend by this advice, gave him presents upon all occasions, and at length persuaded him to inform Herod of what he had heard. So when he related to the king Alexander's ill temper, as discovered by the words he had heard him speak, he was easily believed by him; and he thereby brought the king to that pass, turning him about by his words, and irritating him, till he increased his hatred to him and made him implacable, which he showed at that very time, for he immediately gave Eurycles a present of fifty talents; who, when he had gotten them, went to Archclaus, king of Cappadocia, and commended Alexander before him, and told him that he had been many ways of advantage to him, in making a reconciliation between him and his father. So he got money from him also, and went away, before his pernicious practices were found out; but when Eurycles was returned to Lacedemon, he did not leave off doing mischief; and so, for his many acts of injustice, he was banished from his own country.

2. But as for the king of the Jews, he was not now in the temper he was in formerly towards Alexander and Aristobulus, when he had been content with the hearing their calumnies when others told him of them; but he was now come to that pass as to hate them himself, and to urge men to speak against them, though they did not do it of themselves. He also observed all that was said, and put questions, and gave ear to every one that would but speak, if they could but say any thing against them, till at length he heard that Euaratus of Cos was a conspirator with Alexander; which thing to Herod was the most agreeable and sweetest news imaginable.

3. But still a greater misfortune came upon the young men; while the calumnies against them were continually increased, and, as a man may say, one would think it was every one's endeavor to lay some grievous thing to their charge, which might appear to be for the king's preservation. There were two guards of Herod's body, who were in great esteem for their strength and tallness, Jucundus and Tyrannus; these men had been cast off by Herod, who was displeased at them; these now used to ride along with Alexander, and for their skill in their exercises were in great esteem with him, and had some gold and other gifts bestowed on them. Now the king having an immediate suspicion of those men, had them tortured, who endured the torture courageously for a long time; but at last confessed that Alexander would have persuaded them to kill Herod, when he was in pursuit of the wild beasts, that it might be said he fell from his horse, and was run through with his own spear, for that he had once such a misfortune formerly. They also showed where there was money hidden in the stable under ground; and these convicted the king's chief hunter, that he had given the young men the royal hunting spears and weapons to Alexander's dependents, at Alexander's command.

4. After these, the commander of the garrison of Alexandrium was caught and tortured; for he was accused to have promised to receive the young men into his fortress, and to supply them with that money of the king's which was laid up in that fortress, yet did not he acknowledge any thing of it himself; but his son came ill, and said it was so, and delivered up the writing, which, so far as could be guessed, was in Alexander's hand. Its contents were these: "When we have finished, by God's help, all that we have proposed to do, we will come to you; but do your endeavors, as you have promised, to receive us into your fortress." After this writing was produced, Herod had no doubt about the treacherous designs of his sons against him. But Alexander said that Diophantus the scribe had imitated his hand, and that the paper was maliciously drawn up by Antipater; for Diophantus appeared to be very cunning in such practices; and as he was afterward convicted of forging other papers, he was put to death for it.

5. So the king produced those that had been tortured before the multitude at Jericho, in order to have them accuse the young men, which accusers many of the people stoned to death; and when they were going to kill Alexander and Aristobulus likewise, the king would not permit them to do so, but restrained the multitude, by the means of Ptolemy and Pheroras. However, the young men were put under a guard, and kept in custody, that nobody might come at them; and all that they did or said was watched, and the reproach and fear they were in was little or nothing different from those of condemned criminals: and one of them, who was Aristobulus, was so deeply affected, that he brought Salome, who was his aunt, and his mother-in-law, to lament with him for his calamities, and to hate him who had suffered things to come to that pass; when he said to her, "Art thou not in danger of destruction also, while the report goes that thou hadst disclosed beforehand all our affairs to Syllcus, when thou wast in hopes of being married to him?" But she immediately carried these words to her brother. Upon this he was out of patience, and gave command to bind him; and enjoined them both, now they were kept separate one from the other, to write down the ill things they had done against their father, and bring the writings to him, So when this was enjoined them, they wrote this, that they had laid no treacherous designs, nor made any preparations against their father, but that they had intended to

fly away; and that by the distress they were in, their lives being now uncertain and tedious to them.

6. About this time there came an ambassador out of Cappadocia from Archelaus, whose name was Melas; he was one of the principal rulers under him. So Herod, being desirous to show Archelaus's ill-will to him, called for Alexander, as he was in his bonds, and asked him again concerning his fight, whether and how they had resolved to retire Alexander replied, To Archclaus, who had promised to send them away to Rome; but that they had no wicked nor mischievous designs against their father, and that nothing of that nature which their adversaries had charged upon them was true; and that their desire was, that he might have examined Tyrannus and Jucundus more strictly, but that they had been suddenly slain by the means of Antipater, who put his own friends among the multitude [for that purpose].

7. When this was said, Herod commanded that both Alexander and Melas should be carried to Glaphyra, Archelaus's daughter, and that she should be asked, whether she did not know somewhat of Alexander's treacherous designs against Herod? Now as soon as they were come to her, and she saw Alexander in bonds, she beat her head, and in a great consternation gave a deep and moving groan. The young man also fell into tears. This was so miserable a spectacle to those present, that, for a great while, they were not able to say or to do any thing; but at length Ptolemy, who was ordered to bring Alexander, bid him say whether his wife was conscious of his actions. He replied, "How is it possible that she, whom I love better than my own soul, and by whom I have had children, should not know what I do?" Upon which she cried out that she knew of no wicked designs of his; but that yet, if her accusing herself falsely would tend to his preservation, she would confess it all. Alexander replied, "There is no such wickedness as those (who ought the least of all so to do) suspect, which either I have imagined, or thou knowest of, but this only, that we had resolved to retire to Archelaus, and from thence to Rome." Which she also confessed. Upon which Herod, supposing that Archelaus's ill-will to him was fully proved, sent a letter by Olympus and Volumnius; and bid them, as they sailed by, to touch at Eleusa of Cilicia, and give Archelaus the letter. And that when they had ex-postulated with him, that he had a hand in his son's treacherous design against him, they

should from thence sail to Rome; and that, in case they found Nicolaus had gained any ground, and that Caesar was no longer displeased at him, he should give him his letters, and the proofs which he had ready to show against the young men. As to Archelaus, he made his defense for himself, that he had promised to receive the young men, because it was both for their own and their father's advantage so to do, lest some too severe procedure should be gone upon in that anger and disorder they were in on occasion of the present suspicions; but that still he had not promised to send them to Caesar; and that he had not promised any thing else to the young men that could show any ill-will to him.

8. When these ambassadors were come to Rome, they had a fit opportunity of delivering their letters to Caesar, because they found him reconciled to Herod; for the circumstances of Nicolaus's embassage had been as follows: As soon as he was come to Rome, and was about the court, he did not first of all set about what he was come for only, but he thought fit also to accuse Sylleus. Now the Arabians, even before he came to talk with them, were quarrelling one with another; and some of them left Sylleus's party, and joining themselves to Nicolaus, informed him of all the wicked things that had been done; and produced to him evident demonstrations of the slaughter of a great number of Obodas's friends by Sylleus; for when these men left Sylleus, they had carried off with them those letters whereby they could convict him. When Nicolaus saw such an opportunity afforded him, he made use of it, in order to gain his own point afterward, and endeavored immediately to make a reconciliation between Caesar and Herod; for he was fully satisfied, that if he should desire to make a defense for Herod directly, he should not be allowed that liberty; but that if he desired to accuse Sylleus, there would an occasion present itself of speaking on Herod's behalf. So when the cause was ready for a hearing, and the day was appointed, Nicolaus, while Aretas's ambassadors were present, accused Sylleus, and said that he imputed to him the destruction of the king [Obodas], and of many others of the Arabians; that he had borrowed money for no good design; and he proved that he had been guilty of adultery, not only with the Arabian, but Reinan women also. And. he added, that above all the rest he had alienated Caesar from Herod, and that all that he had said about the actions of Herod were falsities. When Nicolaus was come to this topic, Caesar stopped him from going on, and desired him only to

speak to this affair of Herod, and to show that he had not led an army into Arabia, nor slain two thousand five hundred men there, nor taken prisoners, nor pillaged the country. To which Nicolaus made this answer: "I shall principally demonstrate, that either nothing at all, or but a very little, of those imputations are true, of which thou hast been informed; for had they been true, thou mightest justly have been still more angry at Herod." At this strange assertion Caesar was very attentive; and Nicolaus said that there was a debt due to Herod of five hundred talents, and a bond, wherein it was written, that if the time appointed be lapsed, it should be lawful to make a seizure out of any part of his country. "As for the pretended army," he said, "it was no army, but a party sent out to require the just payment of the money; that this was not sent immediately, nor so soon as the bond allowed, but that Sylleus had frequently come before Saturninus and Volumnius, the presidents of Syria; and that at last he had sworn at Berytus, by thy fortune,[13] that he would certainly pay the money within thirty days, and deliver up the fugitives that were under his dominion. And that when Sylleus had performed nothing of this, Herod came again before the presidents; and upon their permission to make a seizure for his money, he, with difficulty, went out of his country with a party of soldiers for that purpose. And this is all the war which these men so tragically describe; and this is the affair of the expedition into Arabia. And how can this be called a war, when thy presidents permitted it, the covenants allowed it, and it was not executed till thy name, O Caesar, as well as that of the other gods, had been profaned? And now I must speak in order about the captives. There were robbers that dwelt in Trachonitis; at first their number was no more than forty, but they became more afterwards, and they escaped the punishment Herod would have inflicted on them, by making Arabia their refuge. Sylleus received them, and supported them with food, that they might be mischievous to all mankind, and gave them a country to inhabit, and himself received the gains they made by robbery; yet did he promise that he would deliver up these men, and that by the same oaths and same time that he sware and

13. This oath, by the fortune of Caesar, was put to Polycarp, a bishop of Smyrna, by the Roman governor, to try whether he were a Christian, as they were then esteemed who refused to swear that oath. Martyr. Polycarp, sect. 9.

fixed for payment of his debt: nor can he by any means show that any other persons have at this time been taken out of Arabia besides these, and indeed not all these neither, but only so many as could not conceal themselves. And thus does the calumny of the captives, which hath been so odiously represented, appear to be no better than a fiction and a lie, made on purpose to provoke thy indignation; for I venture to affirm that when the forces of the Arabians came upon us, and one or two of Herod's party fell, he then only defended himself, and there fell Nacebus their general, and in all about twenty-five others, and no more; whence Sylleus, by multiplying every single soldier to a hundred, he reckons the slain to have been two thousand five hundred."

9. This provoked Caesar more than ever. So he turned to Sylleus full of rage, and asked him how many of the Arabians were slain. Hereupon he hesitated, and said he had been imposed upon. The covenants also were read about the money he had borrowed, and the letters of the presidents of Syria, and the complaints of the several cities, so many as had been injured by the robbers. The conclusion was this, that Sylleus was condemned to die, and that Caesar was reconciled to Herod, and owned his repentance for what severe things he had written to him, occasioned by calumny, insomuch that he told Sylleus, that he had compelled him, by his lying account of things, to be guilty of ingratitude against a man that was his friend. At the last all came to this, Sylleus was sent away to answer Herod's suit, and to repay the debt that he owed, and after that to be punished [with death]. But still Caesar was offended with Aretas, that he had taken upon himself the government, without his consent first obtained, for he had determined to bestow Arabia upon Herod; but that the letters he had sent hindered him from so doing; for Olympus and Volumnius, perceiving that Caesar was now become favorable to Herod, thought fit immediately to deliver him the letters they were commanded by Herod to give him concerning his sons. When Caesar had read them, he thought it would not be proper to add another government to him, now he was old, and in an ill state with relation to his sons, so he admitted Aretas's ambassadors; and after he had just reproved him for his rashness, in not tarrying till he received the kingdom from him, he accepted of his presents, and confirmed him in his government.

11 *How Herod, by Permission from Caesar Accused His Sons Before an Assembly of Judges at Berytus; and What Tero Suffered for Using a Boundless and Military Liberty of Speech. Concerning Also the Death of the Young Men and Their Burial at Alexandrium*

1. SO Caesar was now reconciled to Herod, and wrote thus to him: That he was grieved for him on account of his sons; and that in case they had been guilty of any profane and insolent crimes against him, it would behoove him to punish them as parricides, for which he gave him power accordingly; but if they had only contrived to fly away, he would have him give them an admonition, and not proceed to extremity with them. He also advised him to get an assembly together, and to appoint some place near Berytus,[14] which is a city belonging to the Romans, and to take the presidents of Syria, and Archelaus king of Cappadocia, and as many more as he thought to be illustrious for their friendship to him, and the dignities they were in, and determine what should be done by their approbation. These were the directions that Caesar gave him. Accordingly Herod, when the letter was brought to him, was immediately very glad of Caesar's reconciliation to him, and very glad also that he had a complete authority given him over his sons. And it strangely came about, that whereas before, in his adversity, though he had indeed showed himself severe, yet had he not been very rash nor hasty in procuring the destruction of his sons; he now, in his prosperity, took advantage of this change for the better, and the freedom he now had, to exercise his hatred against them after an unheard of manner; he therefore sent and called as many as he thought fit to this assembly, excepting Archclaus; for as for him, he either hated him, so that he would not invite him, or he thought he would be an obstacle to his designs.

2. When the presidents, and the rest that belonged to the cities, were come to Berytus, he kept his sons in a certain village belonging

---

14. What Josephus relates Augustus to have here said, that Berytus was a city belonging to the Romans, is confirmed by Spanheim's notes here: "It was," says he, "a colony placed there by Augustus. Whence Ulpian, De Gens. bel. L. T. XV. The colony of Berytus was rendered famous by the benefits of Caesar; and thence it is that, among the coins of Augustus, we meet with some having this inscription: The happy colony of Augustus at Berytua"

to Sidon, called Platana, but near to this city, that if they were called, he might produce them, for he did not think fit to bring them before the assembly: and when there were one hundred and fifty assessors present, Herod came by himself alone, and accused his sons, and that in such a way as if it were not a melancholy accusation, and not made but out of necessity, and upon the misfortunes he was under; indeed, in such a way as was very indecent for a father to accuse his sons, for he was very vehement and disordered when he came to the demonstration of the crime they were accused of, and gave the greatest signs of passion and barbarity: nor would he suffer the assessors to consider of the weight of the evidence, but asserted them to be true by his own authority, after a manner most indecent in a father against his sons, and read himself what they themselves had written, wherein there was no confession of any plots or contrivances against him, but only how they had contrived to fly away, and containing withal certain reproaches against him, on account of the ill-will he bare them; and when he came to those reproaches, he cried out most of all, and exaggerated what they said, as if they had confessed the design against him, and took his oath that he had rather lose his life than hear such reproachful words. At last he said that he had sufficient authority, both by nature and by Caesar's grant to him, [to do what he thought fit]. He also added an allegation of a law of their country, which enjoined this: That if parents laid their hands on the head of him that was accused, the standers by were obliged to cast stones at him, and thereby to slay him; which though he were ready to do in his own country and kingdom, yet did he wait for their determination; and yet they came thither not so much as judges, to condemn them for such manifest designs against him, whereby he had almost perished by his sons' means, but as persons that had an opportunity of showing their detestation of such practices, and declaring how unworthy a thing it must be in any, even the most remote, to pass over such treacherous designs [without punishment].

3. When the king had said this, and the young men had not been produced to make any defense for themselves, the assessors perceived there was no room for equity and reconciliation, so they confirmed his authority. And in the first place, Saturninus, a person that had been consul, and one of great dignity, pronounced his sentence, but with great moderation and trouble; and said that he condemned Herod's

sons, but did not think they should be put to death. He had sons of his own, and to put one's son to death is a greater misfortune than any other that could befall him by their means. After him Saturninus's sons, for he had three sons that followed him, and were his legates, pronounced the same sentence with their father. On the contrary, Volumnius's sentence was to inflict death on such as had been so impiously undutiful to their father; and the greatest part of the rest said the same, insomuch that the conclusion seemed to be, that the young men were condemned to die. Immediately after this Herod came away from thence, and took his sons to Tyre, where Nicolaus met him in his voyage from Rome; of whom he inquired, after he had related to him what had passed at Berytus, what his sentiments were about his sons, and what his friends at Rome thought of that matter. His answer was, "That what they had determined to do to thee was impious, and that thou oughtest to keep them in prison; and if thou thinkest any thing further necessary, thou mayst indeed so punish them, that thou mayst not appear to indulge thy anger more than to govern thyself by judgment; but if thou inclinest to the milder side, thou mayst absolve them, lest perhaps thy misfortunes be rendered incurable; and this is the opinion of the greatest part of thy friends at Rome also." Whereupon Herod was silent, and in great thoughtfulness, and bid Nicolaus sail along with him.

4. Now as they came to Cesarea, every body was there talking of Herod's sons, and the kingdom was in suspense, and the people in great expectation of what would become of them; for a terrible fear seized upon all men, lest the ancient disorders of the family should come to a sad conclusion, and they were in great trouble about their sufferings; nor was it without danger to say any rash thing about this matter, nor even to hear another saying it, but men's pity was forced to be shut up in themselves, which rendered the excess of their sorrow very irksome, but very silent yet was there an old soldier of Herod's, whose name was Tero, who had a son of the same age with Alexander, and his friend, who was so very free as openly to speak out what others silently thought about that matter; and was forced to cry out often among the multitude, and said, in the most unguarded manner, that truth was perished, and justice taken away from men, while lies and ill-will prevailed, and brought such a mist before public affairs, that the offenders were not able to see the greatest mischiefs that can

befall men. And as he was so bold, he seemed not to have kept himself out of danger, by speaking so freely; but the reasonableness of what he said moved men to regard him as having behaved himself with great manhood, and this at a proper time also, for which reason every one heard what he said with pleasure; and although they first took care of their own safety by keeping silent themselves, yet did they kindly receive the great freedom he took; for the expectation they were in of so great an affliction, put a force upon them to speak of Tero whatsoever they pleased.

5. This man had thrust himself into the king's presence with the greatest freedom, and desired to speak with him by himself alone, which the king permitted him to do, where he said this: "Since I am not able, O king, to bear up under so great a concern as I am under, I have preferred the use of this bold liberty that I now take, which may be for thy advantage, if thou mind to get any profit by it, before my own safety. Whither is thy understanding gone, and left thy soul empty? Whither is that extraordinary sagacity of thine gone whereby thou hast performed so many and such glorious-actions? Whence comes this solitude, and desertion of thy friends and relations? Of which I cannot but determine that they are neither thy friends nor relations, while they overlook such horrid wickedness in thy once happy kingdom. Dost not thou perceive what is doing? Wilt thou slay these two young men, born of thy queen, who are accomplished with every virtue in the highest degree, and leave thyself destitute in thy old age, but exposed to one son, who hath very ill managed the hopes thou hast given him,' and to relations, whose death thou hast so often resolved on thyself? Dost not thou take notice, that the very silence of the multitude at once sees the crime, and abhors the fact? The whole army and the officers have commiseration on the poor unhappy youths, and hatred to those that are the actors in this matter." These words the king heard, and for some time with good temper. But what can one say? When Tero plainly touched upon the bad behavior and perfidiousness of his domestics, he was moved at it; but Tero went on further, and by degrees used an unbounded military freedom of speech, nor was he so well disciplined as to accommodate himself to the time. So Herod was greatly disturbed, and seeming to be rather reproached by this speech, than to be hearing what was for his advantage, while he learned thereby that both the soldiers abhorred the thing he was about, and

the officers had indignation at it, he gave order that all whom Tero had named, and Tero himself, should be bound and kept in prison.

6. When this was over, one Trypho, who was the king's barber, took the opportunity, and came and told the king, that Tero would often have persuaded him, when he trimmed him with a razor, to cut his throat, for that by this means he should be among the chief of Alexander's friends, and receive great rewards from him. When he had said this, the king gave order that Tero, and his son, and the barber should be tortured, which was done accordingly; but while Tero bore up himself, his son seeing his father already in a sad case, and had no hope of deliverance, and perceiving what would be the consequence of his terrible sufferings, said, that if the king would free him and his father from these torments for what he should say, he would tell the truth. And when the king had given his word to do so, he said that there was an agreement made, that Tero should lay violent hands on the king, because it was easy for him to come when he was alone; and that if, when he had done the thing, he should suffer death for it, as was not unlikely, it would be an act of generosity done in favor of Alexander. This was what Tero's son said, and thereby freed his father from the distress he was in; but uncertain it is whether he had been thus forced to speak what was true, or whether it were a contrivance of his, in order to procure his own and his father's deliverance from their miseries.

7. As for Herod, if he had before any doubt about the slaughter of his sons, there was now no longer any room left in his soul for it; but he had banished away whatsoever might afford him the least suggestion of reasoning better about this matter, so he already made haste to bring his purpose to a conclusion. He also brought out three hundred of the officers that were under an accusation, as also Tero and his son, and the barber that accused them before an assembly, and brought an accusation against them all; whom the multitude stoned with whatsoever came to hand, and thereby slew them. Alexander also and Aristobulus were brought to Sebaste, by their father's command, and there strangled; but their dead bodies were in the night time carried to Alexandraum, where their uncle by the mother's side, and the greatest part of their ancestors, had been deposited.

8.[15] And now perhaps it may not seem unreasonable to some, that such an inveterate hatred might increase so much [on both sides], as to proceed further, and overcome nature; but it may justly deserve consideration, whether it be to be laid to the charge of the young men, that they gave such an occasion to their father's anger, and led him to do what he did, and by going on long in the same way put things past remedy, and brought him to use them so unmercifully; or whether it be to be laid to the father's charge, that he was so hard-hearted, and so very tender in the desire of government, and of other things that would tend to his glory, that tae would take no one into a partnership with him, that so whatsoever he would have done himself might continue immovable; or, indeed, whether fortune have not greater power than all prudent reasonings; whence we are persuaded that human actions are thereby determined beforehand by an inevitable necessity, and we call her Fate, because there is nothing which is not done by her; wherefore I suppose it will be sufficient to compare this notion with that other, which attribute somewhat to ourselves, and renders men not unaccountable for the different conducts of their lives, which notion is no other than the philosophical determination of our ancient law. Accordingly, of the two other causes of this sad event, any body may lay the blame on the young men, who acted by youthful vanity, and pride of their royal birth, that they should bear to hear the calumnies that were raised against their father, while certainly they were not equitable judges of the actions of his life, but ill-natured in suspecting, and intemperate in speaking of it, and on both accounts easily caught by those that observed them, and revealed them to gain favor; yet cannot their father be thought worthy excuse, as to that horrid impiety which he was guilty of about them, while he ventured, without any certain evidence of their treacherous designs against him, and without any proofs that they had made preparations for such attempt, to kill his own sons, who were of very comely bodies, and the great darlings of other men, and no way deficient in their conduct, whether it were in hunting, or in warlike exercises, or in speaking upon occasional topics of discourse; for in all these they were skillful,

15. The reader is here to note, that this eighth section is entirely wanting in the old Latin version, as Spanheim truly observes; nor is there any other reason for it, I suppose, than the great difficulty of an exact translation.

and especially Alexander, who was the eldest; for certainly it had been sufficient, even though he had condemned them, to have kept them alive in bonds, or to let them live at a distance from his dominions in banishment, while he was surrounded by the Roman forces, which were a strong security to him, whose help would prevent his suffering any thing by a sudden onset, or by open force; but for him to kill them on the sudden, in order to gratify a passion that governed him, was a demonstration of insufferable impiety. He also was guilty of so great a crime in his older age; nor will the delays that he made, and the length of time in which the thing was done, plead at all for his excuse; for when a man is on a sudden amazed, and in commotion of mind, and then commits a wicked action, although this be a heavy crime, yet is it a thing that frequently happens; but to do it upon deliberation, and after frequent attempts, and as frequent puttings-off, to undertake it at last, and accomplish it, was the action of a murderous mind, and such as was not easily moved from that which is evil. And this temper he showed in what he did afterward, when he did not spare those that seemed to be the best beloved of his friends that were left, wherein, though the justice of the punishment caused those that perished to be the less pitied, yet was the barbarity of the man here equal, in that he did not abstain from their slaughter also. But of those persons we shall have occasion to discourse more hereafter.

Book 17

Containing the Interval of Fourteen Years, from the Death of Alexander and Aristobulus to the Banishment of Archelaus

1 *How Antipater Was Hated by All the Nation [of the Jews] for the Slaughter of His Brethren; and How, for That Reason He Got into Peculiar Favor with His Friends at Rome, by Giving Them Many Presents; as He Did Also with Saturninus, the President of Syria and the Governors Who Were under Him; and Concerning Herod's Wives and Children*

1. WHEN Antipater had thus taken off his brethren, and had brought his father into the highest degree of impiety, till he was haunted with furies for what he had done, his hopes did not succeed to his mind, as to the rest of his life; for although he was delivered from the fear of his brethren being his rivals as to the government, yet did he find it a very hard thing, and almost impracticable, to come at the kingdom, because the hatred of the nation against him on that account was become very great; and besides this very disagreeable circumstance, the affair of the soldiery grieved him still more, who were alienated from him, from which yet these kings derived all the safety which they had, whenever they found the nation desirous of innovation: and all this danger was drawn upon him by his destruction of his brethren. However, he governed the nation jointly with his father, being indeed no other than a king already; and he was for that very reason trusted, and the more firmly depended on, for the which he ought himself to

have been put to death, as appearing to have betrayed his brethren out of his concern for the preservation of Herod, and not rather out of his ill-will to them, and, before them, to his father himself: and this was the accursed state he was in. Now all Antipater's contrivances tended to make his way to take off Herod, that he might have nobody to accuse him in the vile practices he was devising: and that Herod might have no refuge, nor any to afford him their assistance, since they must thereby have Antipater for their open enemy; insomuch that the very plots he had laid against his brethren were occasioned by the hatred he bore his father. But at this time he was more than ever set upon the execution of his attempts against Herod, because if he were once dead, the government would now be firmly secured to him; but if he were suffered to live any longer, he should be in danger, upon a discovery of that wickedness of which he had been the contriver, and his father would of necessity then become his enemy. And on this account it was that he became very bountiful to his father's friends, and bestowed great sums on several of them, in order to surprise men with his good deeds, and take off their hatred against him. And he sent great presents to his friends at Rome particularly, to gain their good-will; and above all to Saturninus, the president of Syria. He also hoped to gain the favor of Saturninus's brother with the large presents he bestowed on him; as also he used the same art to [Salome] the king's sister, who had married one of Herod's chief friends. And when he counterfeited friendship to those with whom he conversed, he was very subtle in gaining their belief, and very cunning to hide his hatred against any that he really did hate. But he could not impose upon his aunt, who understood him of a long time, and was a woman not easily to be deluded, especially while she had already used all possible caution in preventing his pernicious designs. Although Antipeter's uncle by the mother's side was married to her daughter, and this by his own connivance and management, while she had before been married to Aristobulus, and while Salome's other daughter by that husband was married to the son of Calleas; yet that marriage was no obstacle to her, who knew how wicked he was, in her discovering his designs, as her former kindred to him could not prevent her hatred of him. Now Herod had compelled Salome, while she was in love with Sylleus the Arabian, and had taken a fondness for him, to marry Alexas; which match was by her submitted to at the instance of Julia, who persuaded

Salome not to refuse it, lest she should herself be their open enemy, since Herod had sworn that he would never be friends with Salome, if she would not accept of Alexas for her husband; so she submitted to Julia as being Caesar's wife; and besides that, she advised her to nothing but what was very much for her own advantage. At this time also it was that Herod sent back king Archelaus's daughter, who had been Alexander's wife, to her father, returning the portion he had with her out of his own estate, that there might be no dispute between them about it.

2. Now Herod brought up his sons' children with great care; for Alexander had two sons by Glaphyra; and Aristobulus had three sons by Bernice, Salome's daughter, and two daughters; and as his friends were once with him, he presented the children before them; and deploring the hard fortune of his own sons, he prayed that no such ill fortune would befall these who were their children, but that they might improve in virtue, and obtain what they justly deserved, and might make him amends for his care of their education. He also caused them to be betrothed against they should come to the proper age of marriage; the elder of Alexander's sons to Pheroras's daughter, and Antipater's daughter to Aristobulus's eldest son. He also allotted one of Aristobulus's daughters to Antipater's son, and Aristobulus's other daughter to Herod, a son of his own, who was born to him by the high priest's daughter; for it is the ancient practice among us to have many wives at the same time. Now the king made these espousals for the children, out of commiseration of them now they were fatherless, as endeavoring to render Antipater kind to them by these intermarriages. But Antipater did not fail to bear the same temper of mind to his brothers' children which he had borne to his brothers themselves; and his father's concern about them provoked his indignation against them upon this supposal, that they would become greater than ever his brothers had been; while Archclaus, a king, would support his daughter's sons, and Pheroras, a tetrarch, would accept of one of the daughters as a wife to his son. What provoked him also was this, that all the multitude would so commiserate these fatherless children, and so hate him [for making them fatherless], that all would come out, since they were no strangers to his vile disposition towards his brethren. He contrived, therefore, to overturn his father's settlements, as thinking it a terrible thing that they should be so related to him,

and be so powerful withal. So Herod yielded to him, and changed his resolution at his entreaty; and the determination now was, that Antipater himself should marry Aristobulus's daughter, and Antipater's son should marry Pheroras's daughter. So the espousals for the marriages were changed after this manner, even without the king's real approbation.

3. Now Herod[1] the king had at this time nine wives; one of them Antipater's mother, and another the high priest's daughter, by whom he had a son of his own name. He had also one who was his brother's daughter, and another his sister's daughter; which two had no children. One of his wives also was of the Samaritan nation, whose sons were Antipas and Archelaus, and whose daughter was Olympias; which daughter was afterward married to Joseph, the king's brother's son; but Archelaus and Antipas were brought up with a certain private man at Rome. Herod had also to wife Cleopatra of Jerusalem, and by her he had his sons Herod and Philip; which last was also brought up at Rome. Pallas also was one of his wives, which bare him his son Phasaelus. And besides these, he had for his wives Phedra and E1pis, by whom he had his daughters Roxana and Salome. As for his elder daughters by the same mother with Alexander and Aristobulus, and whom Pheroras neglected to marry, he gave the one in marriage to Antipater, the king's sister's son, and the other to Phasaelus, his brother's son. And this was the posterity of Herod.

2 *Concerning Zamaris, the Babylonian Jew; Concerning the Plots Laid by Antipater Against His Father; and Somewhat About the Pharisees*

1. AND now it was that Herod, being desirous of securing himself on the side of the Trachonites, resolved to build a village as large as a city for the Jews, in the middle of that country, which might make his own country difficult to be assaulted, and whence he might be at

---

1. Those who have a mind to know all the family and descendants of Antipater the Idumean, and of Herod the Great, his son, and have a memory to preserve them all distinctly, may consult Josephus, Antiq. B. XVIII. ch. 5. sect. 4; and Of the War, B. I. ch. 28. sect. 4; in Havercamp's edition, p. 336; and Spanheim, lb. p. 402—405; and Reland, Paleslin. Part I. p. 178, 176.

hand to make sallies upon them, and do them a mischief. Accordingly, when he understood that there was a man that was a Jew come out of Babylon, with five hundred horsemen, all of whom could shoot their arrows as they rode on horde-back, and, with a hundred of his relations, had passed over Euphrates, and now abode at Antioch by Daphne of Syria, where Saturninus, who was then president, had given them a place for habitation, called Valatha, he sent for this man, with the multitude that followed him, and promised to give him land in the toparchy called Batanea, which country is bounded with Trachonitis, as desirous to make that his habitation a guard to himself. He also engaged to let him hold the country free from tribute, and that they should dwell entirely without paying such customs as used to be paid, and gave it him tax-free.

2. The Babylonian was reduced by these offers to come hither; so he took possession of the land, and built in it fortresses and a village, and named it Bathyra. Whereby this man became a safeguard to the inhabitants against the Trachonites, and preserved those Jews who came out of Babylon, to offer their sacrifices at Jerusalem, from being hurt by the Trachonite robbers; so that a great number came to him from all those parts where the ancient Jewish laws were observed, and the country became full of people, by reason of their universal freedom from taxes. This continued during the life of Herod; but when Philip, who was [tetrarch] after him, took the government, he made them pay some small taxes, and that for a little while only; and Agrippa the Great, and his son of the same name, although they harassed them greatly, yet would they not take their liberty away. From whom, when the Romans have now taken the government into their own hands, they still gave them the privilege of their freedom, but oppress them entirely with the imposition of taxes. Of which matter I shall treat more accurately in the progress of this history.[2]

3. At length Zamaris the Babylonian, to whom Herod had given that country for a possession, died, having lived virtuously, and left children of a good character behind him; one of whom was Jacim, who was famous for his valor, and taught his Babylonians how to ride their horses; and a troop of them were guards to the forementioned kings. And when Jacim was dead in his old age, he left a son, whose name

2. This is now wanting.

was Philip, one of great strength in his hands, and in other respects also more eminent for his valor than any of his contemporaries; on which account there was a confidence and firm friendship between him and king Agrippa. He had also an army which he maintained as great as that of a king, which he exercised and led wheresoever lie had occasion to march.

4. When the affairs of Herod were in the condition I have described, all the public affairs depended upon Antipater; and his power was such, that he could do good turns to as many as he pleased, and this by his father's concession, in hopes of his good-will and fidelity to him; and this till he ventured to use his power still further, because his wicked designs were concealed from his father, and he made him believe every thing he said. He was also formidable to all, not so much on account of the power and authority he had, as for the shrewdness of his vile attempts beforehand; but he who principally cultivated a friendship with him was Pheroras, who received the like marks of his friendship; while Antipater had cunningly encompassed him about by a company of women, whom he placed as guards about him; for Pheroras was greatly enslaved to his wife, and to her mother, and to her sister; and this notwithstanding the hatred he bare them for the indignities they had offered to his virgin daughters. Yet did he bear them, and nothing was to be done without the women, who had got this man into their circle, and continued still to assist each other in all things, insomuch that Antipater was entirely addicted to them, both by himself and by his mother; for these four women,[3] said all one and the same thing; but the opinions of Pheroras and Antipater were different in some points of no consequence. But the king's sister [Salome] was their antagonist, who for a good while had looked about all their affairs, and was apprized that this their friendship was made in order to do Herod some mischief, and was disposed to inform the king of it. And since these people knew that their friendship was very disagreeable to Herod, as tending to do him a mischief, they contrived that their meetings should not be discovered; so they pretended to hate one another, and to abuse one another when time served, and especially when Herod was present, or when any one was there that would tell him: but still their intimacy was firmer than ever, when

3. Pheroras's wife, and her mother and sister, and Doris, Antipater's mother.

they were private. And this was the course they took. But they could not conceal from Salome neither their first contrivance, when they set about these their intentions, nor when they had made some progress in them; but she searched out every thing; and, aggravating the relations to her brother, declared to him, as well their secret assemblies and compotations, as their counsels taken in a clandestine manner, which if they were not in order to destroy him, they might well enough have been open and public. But to appearance they are at variance, and speak about one another as if they intended one another a mischief, but agree so well together when they are out of the sight of the multitude; for when they are alone by themselves, they act in concert, and profess that they will never leave off their friendship, but will fight against those from whom they conceal their designs. And thus did she search out these things, and get a perfect knowledge of them, and then told her brother of them, who understood also of himself a great deal of what she said, but still durst not depend upon it, because of the suspicions he had of his sister's calumnies. For there was a certain sect of men that were Jews, who valued themselves highly upon the exact skill they had in the law of their fathers, and made men believe they were highly favored by God, by whom this set of women were inveigled. These are those that are called the sect of the Pharisees, who were in a capacity of greatly opposing kings. A cunning sect they were, and soon elevated to a pitch of open fighting and doing mischief. Accordingly, when all the people of the Jews gave assurance of their good-will to Caesar, and to the king's government, these very men did not swear, being above six thousand; and when the king imposed a fine upon them, Pheroras's wife paid their fine for them. In order to requite which kindness of hers, since they were believed to have the foreknowledge of things to come by Divine inspiration, they foretold how God had decreed that Herod's government should cease, and his posterity should be deprived of it; but that the kingdom should come to her and Pheroras, and to their children. These predictions were not concealed from Salome, but were told the king; as also how they had perverted some persons about the palace itself; so the king slew such of the Pharisees as were principally accused, and Bagoas the eunuch, and one Carus, who exceeded all men of that time in comeliness, and one that was his catamite. He slew also all those of his own family who had consented to what the Pharisees foretold; and for Bagoas, he had been puffed up by them, as though he should be named the father and the benefactor of him who, by the prediction, was foretold to be their appointed king; for that this king would have all things in his power, and would enable Bagoas to marry, and to have children of his own body begotten.

3 *Concerning the Enmity Between Herod and Pheroras; How Herod Sent Antipater to Caesar; and of the Death of Pheroras*

1. WHEN Herod had punished those Pharisees who had been convicted of the foregoing crimes, he gathered an assembly together of his friends, and accused Pheroras's wife; and ascribing the abuses of the virgins to the impudence of that woman, brought an accusation against her for the dishonor she had brought upon them: that she had studiously introduced a quarrel between him and his brother, and, by her ill temper, had brought them into a state of war, both by her words and actions; that the fines which he had laid had not been paid, and the offenders had escaped punishment by her means; and that nothing which had of late been done had been done without her; "for which reason Pheroras would do well, if he would of his own accord, and by his own command, and not at my entreaty, or as following my opinion, put this his wife away, as one that will still be the occasion of war between thee and me. And now, Pheroras, if thou valuest thy relation to me, put this wife of thine away; for by this means thou wilt continue to be a brother to me, and wilt abide in thy love to me." Then said Pheroras, (although he was pressed hard by the former words,) that as he would not do so unjust a thing as to renounce his brotherly relation to him, so would he not leave off his affection for his wife; that he would rather choose to die than to live, and be deprived of a wife that was so dear unto him. Hereupon Herod put off his anger against Pheroras on these accounts, although he himself thereby underwent a very uneasy punishment. However, he forbade Antipater and his mother to have any conversation with Pheroras, and bid them to take care to avoid the assemblies of the women; which they promised to do, but still got together when occasion served, and both Ptieroras and Antipater had their own merry meetings. The report went also, that Antipater had criminal conversation with Pheroras's wife, and that they were brought together by Antipater's mother.

2. But Antipater had now a suspicion of his father, and was afraid that the effects of his hatred to him might increase; so he wrote to his friends at Rome, and bid them to send to Herod, that he would immediately send Antipater to Caesar; which when it was done, Herod sent Antipater thither, and sent most noble presents along with him; as also his testament, wherein Antipater was appointed to be his successor; and that if Antipater should die first, his son [Herod Philip] by the high priest's daughter should succeed. And, together with Antipater, there went to Rome Sylleus the Arabian, although he had done nothing of all that Caesar had enjoined him. Antipater also accused him of the same crimes of which he had been formerly accused by Herod. Sylleus was also accused by Aretas, that without his consent he had slain many of the chief of the Arabians at Petra; and particularly Soemus, a man that deserved to be honored by all men; and that he had slain Fabatus, a servant of Caesar. These were the things of which Sylleus was accused, and that on the occasion following: There was one Corinthus, belonging to Herod, of the guards of the king's body, and one who was greatly trusted by him. Sylleus had persuaded this man with the offer of a great sum of money to kill Herod; and he had promised to do it. When Fabatus had been made acquainted with this, for Sylleus had himself told him of it, he informed the king of it; who caught Corinthus, and put him to the torture, and thereby got out of him the whole conspiracy. He also caught two other Arabians, who were discovered by Corinthus; the one the head of a tribe, and the other a friend to Sylleus, who both were by the king brought to the torture, and confessed that they were come to encourage Corinthus not to fail of doing what he had undertaken to do; and to assist him with their own hands in the murder, if need should require their assistance. So Saturninns, upon Herod's discovering the whole to him, sent them to Rome.

3. At this time Herod commanded Pheroras, that since he was so obstinate in his affection for his wife, he should retire into his own tetrarchy; which he did very willingly, and sware many oaths that he would not come again till he heard that Herod was dead. And indeed when, upon a sickness of the king, he was desired to come to him before he died, that he might intrust him with some of his injunctions, he had such a regard to his oath, that he would not come to him; yet did not Herod so retain his hatred to Pheroras, but remitted of

his purpose [not to see him], which he before had, and that for such great causes as have been already mentioned: but as soon as he began to be ill, he came to him, and this without being sent for; and when he was dead, he took care of his funeral, and had his body brought to Jerusalem, and buried there, and appointed a solemn mourning for him. This [death of Pheroras] became the origin of Antipater's misfortunes, although he were already sailed for Rome, God now being about to punish him for the murder of his brethren, I will explain the history of this matter very distinctly, that it may be for a warning to mankind, that they take care of conducting their whole lives by the rules of virtue.

4 *Pheroras's Wife Is Accused by His Freedmen, as Guilty of Poisoning Him; and How Herod, Upon Examining; of the Matter by Torture Found the Poison; but So That It Had Been Prepared for Himself by His Son Antipater; and Upon an Inquiry by Torture He Discovered the Dangerous Designs of Antipater*

1. AS soon as Pheroras was dead, and his funeral was over, two of Pheroras's freed-men, who were much esteemed by him, came to Herod, and entreated him not to leave the murder of his brother without avenging it, but to examine into such an unreasonable and unhappy death. When he was moved with these words, for they seemed to him to be true, they said that Pheroras supped with his wife the day before he fell sick, and that a certain potion was brought him in such a sort of food as he was not used to eat; but that when he had eaten, he died of it: that this potion was brought out of Arabia by a woman, under pretense indeed as a love-potion, for that was its name, but in reality to kill Pheroras; for that the Arabian women are skillful in making such poisons: and the woman to whom they ascribe this was confessedly a most intimate friend of one of Sylleus's mistresses; and that both the mother and the sister of Pheroras's wife had been at the places where she lived, and had persuaded her to sell them this potion, and had come back and brought it with them the day before that his supper. Hereupon the king was provoked, and put the women slaves to the torture, and some that were free with them; and as the fact did not yet appear, because none of them would confess it, at length

one of them, under the utmost agonies, said no more but this, that she prayed that God would send the like agonies upon Antipater's mother, who had been the occasion of these miseries to all of them. This prayer induced Herod to increase the women's tortures, till thereby all was discovered; their merry meetings, their secret assemblies, and the disclosing of what he had said to his son alone unto Pheroras's[4] women. (Now what Herod had charged Antipater to conceal, was the gift of a hundred talents to him not to have any conversation with Pheroras.) And what hatred he bore to his father; and that he complained to his mother how very long his father lived; and that he was himself almost an old man, insomuch that if the kingdom should come to him, it would not afford him any great pleasure; and that there were a great many of his brothers, or brothers' children, bringing up, that might have hopes of the kingdom as well as himself, all which made his own hopes of it uncertain; for that even now, if he should himself not live, Herod had ordained that the government should be conferred, not on his son, but rather on a brother. He also had accused the king of great barbarity, and of the slaughter of his sons; and that it was out of the fear he was under, lest he should do the like to him, that made him contrive this his journey to Rome, and Pheroras contrive to go to his own tetrarchy.[5]

2. These confessions agreed with what his sister had told him, and tended greatly to corroborate her testimony, and to free her from the suspicion of her unfaithfulness to him. So the king having satisfied himself of the spite which Doris, Antipater's mother, as well as himself, bore to him, took away from her all her fine ornaments, which were worth many talents, and then sent her away, and entered into friendship with Pheroras's women. But he who most of all irritated the king against his son was one Antipater, the procurator of Antipater

---

4. His wife, her mother, and sister.

5. It seems to me, by this whole story put together, that Pheroras was not himself poisoned, as is commonly supposed; for Antipater had persuaded him to poison Herod, ch. v. sect. 1, which would fall to the ground if he wore himself poisoned; nor could the poisoning of Pheroras serve any design that appears now going forward; it was only the supposal of two of his freed-men, that this love-potion, or poison, which they knew was brought to Pheroras's wife, was made use of for poisoning him; whereas it appears to have been brought for her husband to poison Herod withal, as the future examinations demonstrate.

the king's son, who, when he was tortured, among other things, said that Antipater had prepared a deadly potion, and given it to Pheroras, with his desire that he would give it to his father during his absence, and when he was too remote to have the least suspicion cast upon him thereto relating; that Antiphilus, one of Antipater's friends, brought that potion out of Egypt; and that it was sent to Pheroras by Thendion, the brother of the mother of Antipater, the king's son, and by that means came to Pheroras's wife, her husband having given it her to keep. And when the king asked her about it, she confessed it; and as she was running to fetch it, she threw herself down from the house-top; yet did she not kill herself, because she fell upon her feet; by which means, when the king had comforted her, and had promised her and her domestics pardon, upon condition of their concealing nothing of the truth from him, but had threatened her with the utmost miseries if she proved ungrateful [and concealed any thing]: so she promised, and swore that she would speak out every thing, and tell after what manner every thing was done; and said what many took to be entirely true, that the potion was brought out of Egypt by Antiphilus; and that his brother, who was a physician, had procured it; and that" when Thendion brought it us, she kept it upon Pheroras's committing it to her; and that it was prepared by Antipater for thee. When, therefore, Pheroras was fallen sick, and thou camest to him and tookest care of him, and when he saw the kindness thou hadst for him, his mind was overborne thereby. So he called me to him, and said to me, 'O woman! Antipater hath circumvented me in this affair of his father and my brother, by persuading me to have a murderous intention to him, and procuring a potion to be subservient thereto; do thou, therefore, go and fetch my potion, (since my brother appears to have still the same virtuous disposition towards me which he had formerly, and I do not expect to live long myself, and that I may not defile my forefathers by the murder of a brother,) and burn it before my face:' that accordingly she immediately brought it, and did as her husband bade her; and that she burnt the greatest part of the potion; but that a little of it was left, that if the king, after Pheroras's death, should treat her ill, she might poison herself, and thereby get clear of her miseries." Upon her saying thus, she brought out the potion, and the box in which it was, before them all. Nay, there was another brother of Antiphilus, and his mother also, who, by the extremity of pain and torture, confessed the same things, and owned the box [to be that which had been brought out of Egypt]. The high priest's daughter also, who was the king's wife, was accused to have been conscious of all this, and had resolved to conceal it; for which reason Herod divorced her, and blotted her son out of his testament, wherein he had been mentioned as one that was to reign after him; and he took the high priesthood away from his father-in-law, Simeon the son of Boethus, and appointed Matthias the son of Theophilus, who was born at Jerusalem, to be high priest in his room.

3. While this was doing, Bathyllus also, Antipater's freed-man, came from Rome, and, upon the torture, was found to have brought another potion, to give it into the hands of Antipater's mother, and of Pheroras, that if the former potion did not operate upon the king, this at least might carry him off. There came also letters from Herod's friends at Rome, by the approbation and at the suggestion of Antipater, to accuse Archelaus and Philip, as if they calumniated their father on account of the slaughter of Alexander and Aristobulus, and as if they commiserated their deaths, and as if, because they were sent for home, (for their father had already recalled them,) they concluded they were themselves also to be destroyed. These letters had been procured by great rewards by Antipater's friends; but Antipater himself wrote to his father about them, and laid the heaviest things to their charge; yet did he entirely excuse them of any guilt, and said they were but young men, and so imputed their words to their youth. But he said that he had himself been very busy in the affair relating to Sylleus, and in getting interest among the great men; and on that account had bought splendid ornaments to present them withal, which cost him two hundred talents. Now one may wonder how it came about, that while so many accusations were laid against him in Judea during seven months before this time, he was not made acquainted with any of them. The causes of which were, that the roads were exactly guarded, and that men hated Antipater; for there was nobody who would run any hazard himself to gain him any advantages.

5 *Antipater's Navigation from Rome to His Father; and How He Was Accused by Nicolaus of Damascus and Condemned to Die by His Father, and by Quintilius Varus, Who Was Then President of Syria; and How He Was Then Bound Till Caesar Should Be Informed of His Cause*

1. NOW Herod, upon Antipater's writing to him, that having done all that he was to do, and this in the manner he was to do it, he would suddenly come to him, concealed his anger against him, and wrote back to him, and bid him not delay his journey, lest any harm should befall himself in his absence. At the same time also he made some little complaint about his mother, but promised that he would lay those complaints aside when he should return. He withal expressed his entire affection for him, as fearing lest he should have some suspicion of him, and defer his journey to him; and lest, while he lived at Rome, he should lay plots for the kingdom, and, moreover, do somewhat against himself. This letter Antipater met with in Cilicia; but had received an account of Pheroras's death before at Tarentum. This last news affected him deeply; not out of any affection for Pheroras, but because he was dead without having murdered his father, which he had promised him to do. And when he was at Celenderis in Cilicia, he began to deliberate with himself about his sailing home, as being much grieved with the ejection of his mother. Now some of his friends advised him that he should tarry a while some where, in expectation of further information. But others advised him to sail home without delay; for that if he were once come thither, he would soon put an end to all accusations, and that nothing afforded any weight to his accusers at present but his absence. He was persuaded by these last, and sailed on, and landed at the haven called Sebastus, which Herod had built at vast expenses in honor of Caesar, and called Sebastus. And now was Antipater evidently in a miserable condition, while nobody came to him nor saluted him, as they did at his going away, with good wishes of joyful acclamations; nor was there now any thing to hinder them from entertaining him, on the contrary, with bitter curses, while they supposed he was come to receive his punishment for the murder of his brethren.

2. Now Quintilius Varus was at this time at Jerusalem, being sent to succeed Saturninus as president of Syria, and was come as an

assessor to Herod, who had desired his advice in his present affairs; and as they were sitting together, Antipater came upon them, without knowing any thing of the matter; so he came into the palace clothed in purple. The porters indeed received him in, but excluded his friends. And now he was in great disorder, and presently understood the condition he was in, while, upon his going to salute his father, he was repulsed by him, who called him a murderer of his brethren, and a plotter of destruction against himself, and told him that Varus should be his auditor and his judge the very next day; so he found that what misfortunes he now heard of were already upon him, with the greatness of which he went away in confusion; upon which his mother and his wife met him, (which wife was the daughter of Antigonus, who was king of the Jews before Herod,) from whom he learned all circumstances which concerned him, and then prepared himself for his trial.

3. On the next day Varus and the king sat together in judgment, and both their friends were also called in, as also the king's relations, with his sister Salome, and as many as could discover any thing, and such as had been tortured; and besides these, some slaves of Antipater's mother, who were taken up a little before Antipater's coming, and brought with them a written letter, the sum of which was this: That he should not come back, because all was come to his father's knowledge; and that Caesar was the only refuge he had left to prevent both his and her delivery into his father's hands. Then did Antipater fall down at his father's feet, and besought him not to prejudge his cause, but that he might be first heard by his father, and that his father would keep himself unprejudiced. So Herod ordered him to be brought into the midst, and then lamented himself about his children, from whom he had suffered such great misfortunes; and because Antipater fell upon him in his old age. He also reckoned up what maintenance and what education he had given them; and what seasonable supplies of wealth he had afforded them, according to their own desires; none of which favors had hindered them from contriving against him, and from bringing his very life into danger, in order to gain his kingdom, after an impious manner, by taking away his life before the course of nature, their father's wishes, or justice required that that kingdom should come to them; and that he wondered what hopes could elevate Antipater to such a pass as to be hardy enough to attempt such things;

that he had by his testament in writing declared him his successor in the government; and while he was alive, he was in no respect inferior to him, either in his illustrious dignity, or in power and authority, he having no less than fifty talents for his yearly income, and had received for his journey to Rome no fewer than thirty talents. He also objected to him the case of his brethren whom he had accused; and if they were guilty, he had imitated their example; and if not, he had brought him groundless accusations against his near relations; for that he had been acquainted with all those things by him, and by nobody else, and had done what was done by his approbation, and whom he now absolved from all that was criminal, by becoming the inheritor of the guilt of such their parricide.

4. When Herod had thus spoken, he fell a weeping, and was not able to say any more; but at his desire Nicolaus of Damascus, being the king's friend, and always conversant with him, and acquainted with whatsoever he did, and with the circumstances of his affairs, proceeded to what remained, and explained all that concerned the demonstrations and evidences of the facts. Upon which Antipater, in order to make his legal defense, turned himself to his father, and enlarged upon the many indications he had given of his good-will to him; and instanced in the honors that had been done him, which yet had not been done, had he not deserved them by his virtuous concern about him; for that he had made provision for every thing that was fit to be foreseen beforehand, as to giving him his wisest advice; and whenever there was occasion for the labor of his own hands, he had not grudged any such pains for him. And that it was almost impossible that he, who had delivered his father from so many treacherous contrivances laid against him, should be himself in a plot against him, and so lose all the reputation he had gained for his virtue, by his wickedness which succeeded it; and this while he had nothing to prohibit him, who was already appointed his successor, to enjoy the royal honor with his father also at present; and that there was no likelihood that a person who had the one half of that authority without any danger, and with a good character, should hunt after the whole with infamy and danger, and this when it was doubtful whether he could obtain it or not; and when he saw the sad example of his brethren before him, and was both the informer and the accuser against them, at a time when they might not otherwise have been

discovered; nay, was the author of the punishment inflicted upon them, when it appeared evidently that they were guilty of a wicked attempt against their father; and that even the contentions there were in the king's family were indications that he had ever managed affairs out of the sincerest affection to his father. And as to what he had done at Rome, Caesar was a witness thereto, who yet was no more to be imposed upon than God himself; of whose opinions his letters sent hither are sufficient evidence; and that it was not reasonable to prefer the calumnies of such as proposed to raise disturbances before those letters; the greatest part of which calumnies had been raised during his absence, which gave scope to his enemies to forge them, which they had not been able to do if he had been there. Moreover he showed the weakness of the evidence obtained by torture, which was commonly false, because the distress men are in under such tortures naturally obliges them to say many things in order to please those that govern them. He also offered himself to the torture.

5. Hereupon there was a change observed in the assembly, while they greatly pitied Antipater, who by weeping and putting on a countenance suitable to his sad case made them commiserate the same, insomuch that his very enemies were moved to compassion; and it appeared plainly that Herod himself was affected in his own mind, although he was not willing it should be taken notice of. Then did Nicolaus begin to prosecute what the king had begun, and that with great bitterness; and summed up all the evidence which arose from the tortures, or from the testimonies. He principally and largely cried up the king's virtues, which he had exhibited in the maintenance and education of his sons; while he never could gain any advantage thereby, but still fell from one misfortune to another. Although he owned that he was not so much surprised with that thoughtless behavior of his former sons, who were but young, and were besides corrupted by wicked counselors, who were the occasion of their wiping out of their minds the righteous dictates of nature, and this out of a desire of coming to the government sooner than they ought to do; yet that he could not but justly stand amazed at the horrid wickedness of Antipater, who, although he had not only had great benefits bestowed on him by his father, enough to tame his reason, yet could not be more tamed than the most envenomed serpents; whereas even those creatures admit of some mitigation, and will not

bite their benefactors, while Antipater hath not let the misfortunes of his brethren be any hinderance to him, but he hath gone on to imitate their barbarity notwithstanding. "Yet wast thou, O Antipater! (as thou hast thyself confessed,) the informer as to what wicked actions they had done, and the searcher out of the evidence against them, and the author of the punishment they underwent upon their detection. Nor do we say this as accusing thee for being so zealous in thy anger against them, but are astonished at thy endeavors to imitate their profligate behavior; and we discover thereby that thou didst not act thus for the safety of thy father, but for the destruction of thy brethren, that by such outside hatred of their impiety thou mightest be believed a lover of thy father, and mightest thereby get thee power enough to do mischief with the greatest impunity; which design thy actions indeed demonstrate. It is true, thou tookest thy brethren off, because thou didst convict theft of their wicked designs; but thou didst not yield up to justice those who were their partners; and thereby didst make it evident to all men that thou madest a covenant with them against thy father, when thou chosest to be the accuser of thy brethren, as desirous to gain to thyself alone this advantage of laying plots to kill thy father, and so to enjoy double pleasure, which is truly worthy of thy evil disposition, which thou has openly showed against thy brethren; on which account thou didst rejoice, as having done a most famous exploit, nor was that behavior unworthy of thee. But if thy intention were otherwise, thou art worse than they: while thou didst contrive to hide thy treachery against thy father, thou didst hate them, not as plotters against thy father, for in that case thou hadst not thyself fallen upon the like crime, but as successors of his dominions, and more worthy of that succession than thyself. Thou wouldst kill thy father after thy brethren, lest thy lies raised against them might be detected; and lest thou shouldst suffer what punishment thou hadst deserved, thou hadst a mind to exact that punishment of thy unhappy father, and didst devise such a sort of uncommon parricide as the world never yet saw. For thou who art his son didst not only lay a treacherous design against thy father, and didst it while he loved thee, and had been thy benefactor, had made thee in reality his partner in the kingdom, and had openly declared thee his successor, while thou wast not forbidden to taste the sweetness of authority already, and hadst the firm hope of what was future by thy father's determination, and the security of a written testament; but, for certain, thou didst not measure these things according to thy father's various disposition, but according to thy own thoughts and inclinations; and was desirous to take the part that remained away from thy too indulgent father, and soughtest to destroy him with thy deeds, whom thou in words pretendedst to preserve. Nor wast thou content to be wicked thyself, but thou filledst thy mother's head with thy devices, and raised disturbances among thy brethren, and hadst the boldness to call thy father a wild beast; while thou hadst thyself a mind more cruel than any serpent, whence thou sentest out that poison among thy nearest kindred and greatest benefactors, and invitedst them to assist thee and guard thee, and didst hedge thyself in on all sides, by the artifices of both men and women, against an old man, as though that mind of thine was not sufficient of itself to support so great a hatred as thou baredst to him. And here thou appearest, after the tortures of free-men, of domestics, of men and women, which have been examined on thy account, and after the informations of thy fellow conspirators, as making haste to contradict the truth; and hast thought on ways not only how to take thy father out of the world, but to disannul that written law which is against thee, and the virtue of Varus, and the nature of justice; nay, such is that impudence of thine on which thou confidest, that thou desirest to be put to the torture thyself, while thou allegest that the tortures of those already examined thereby have made them tell lies; that those that have been the deliverers of thy father may not be allowed to have spoken the truth; but that thy tortures may be esteemed the discoverers of truth. Wilt not thou, O Varus! deliver the king from the injuries of his kindred? Wilt not thou destroy this wicked wild beast, which hath pretended kindness to his father, in order to destroy his brethren; while yet he is himself alone ready to carry off the kingdom immediately, and appears to be the most bloody butcher to him of them all? for thou art sensible that parricide is a general injury both to nature and to common life, and that the intention of parricide is not inferior to its perpetration; and he who does not punish it is injurious to nature itself."

6. Nicolaus added further what belonged to Antipater's mother, and whatsoever she had prattled like a woman; as also about the predictions and the sacrifices relating to the king; and whatsoever Antipater had done lasciviously in his cups and his amours among Pheroras's women; the examination upon torture; and whatsoever

concerned the testimonies of the witnesses, which were many, and of various kinds; some prepared beforehand, and others were sudden answers, which further declared and confirmed the foregoing evidence. For those men who were not acquainted with Antipater's practices, but had concealed them out of fear, when they saw that he was exposed to the accusations of the former witnesses, and that his great good fortune, which had supported him hitherto, had now evidently betrayed him into the hands of his enemies, who were now insatiable in their hatred to him, told all they knew of him. And his ruin was now hastened, not so much by the enmity of those that were his accusers, as by his gross, and impudent, and wicked contrivances, and by his ill-will to his father and his brethren; while he had filled their house with disturbance, and caused them to murder one another; and was neither fair in his hatred, nor kind in his friendship, but just so far as served his own turn. Now there were a great number who for a long time beforehand had seen all this, and especially such as were naturally disposed to judge of matters by the rules of virtue, because they were used to determine about affairs without passion, but had been restrained from making any open complaints before; these, upon the leave now given them, produced all that they knew before the public. The demonstrations also of these wicked facts could no way be disproved, because the many witnesses there were did neither speak out of favor to Herod, nor were they obliged to keep what they had to say silent, out of suspicion of any danger they were in; but they spake what they knew, because they thought such actions very wicked, and that Antipater deserved the greatest punishment; and indeed not so much for Herod's safety, as on account of the man's own wickedness. Many things were also said, and those by a great number of persons, who were no way obliged to say them, insomuch that Antipater, who used generally to be very shrewd in his lies and impudence, was not able to say one word to the contrary. When Nicolaus had left off speaking, and had produced the evidence, Varus bid Antipater to betake himself to the making his defense, if he had prepared any thing whereby it might appear that he was not guilty of the crimes he was accused of; for that, as he was himself desirous, so did he know that his father was in like manner desirous also, to have him found entirely innocent. But Antipater fell down on his face, and appealed to God and to all men for testimonials of his innocency, desiring that God would declare, by some evident signals, that he had not laid any plot against his father. This being the usual method of all men destitute of virtue, that when they set about any wicked undertakings, they fall to work according to their own inclinations, as if they believed that God was unconcerned in human affairs; but when once they are found out, and are in danger of undergoing the punishment due to their crimes, they endeavor to overthrow all the evidence against them by appealing to God; which was the very thing which Antipater now did; for whereas he had done everything as if there were no God in the world, when he was on all sides distressed by justice, and when he had no other advantage to expect from any legal proofs, by which he might disprove the accusations laid against him, he impudently abused the majesty of God, and ascribed it to his power that he had been preserved hitherto; and produced before them all what difficulties he had ever undergone in his bold acting for his father's preservation.

7. So when Varus, upon asking Antipater what he had to say for himself, found that he had nothing to say besides his appeal to God, and saw that there was no end of that, he bid them bring the potion before the court, that he might see what virtue still remained in it; and when it was brought, and one that was condemned to die had drank it by Varus's command, he died presently. Then Varus got up, and departed out of the court, and went away the day following to Antioch, where his usual residence was, because that was the palace of the Syrians; upon which Herod laid his son in bonds. But what were Varus's discourses to Herod was not known to the generality, and upon what words it was that he went away; though it was also generally supposed that whatsoever Herod did afterward about his son was done with his approbation. But when Herod had bound his son, he sent letters to Rome to Caesar about him, and such messengers withal as should, by word of mouth, inform Caesar of Antipater's wickedness. Now at this very time there was seized a letter of Antiphilus, written to Antipater out of Egypt (for he lived there); and when it was opened by the king, it was found to contain what follows: "I have sent thee Acme's letter, and hazarded my own life; for thou knowest that I am in danger from two families, if I be discovered. I wish thee good success in thy affair." These were the contents of this letter; but the king made inquiry about the other letter also, for it did

not appear; and Antiphilus's slave, who brought that letter which had been read, denied that he had received the other. But while the king was in doubt about it, one of Herod's friends seeing a seam upon the inner coat of the slave, and a doubling of the cloth, (for he had two coats on,) he guessed that the letter might be within that doubling; which accordingly proved to be true. So they took out the letter, and its contents were these: "Acme to Antipater. I have written such a letter to thy father as thou desiredst me. I have also taken a copy and sent it, as if it came from Salome, to my lady [Livia]; which, when thou readest, I know that Herod Will punish Salome, as plotting against him?' Now this pretended letter of Salome to her lady was composed by Antipater, in the name of Salome, as to its meaning, but in the words of Acme. The letter was this: "Acme to king Herod. I have done my endeavor that nothing that is done against thee should be concealed from thee. So, upon my finding a letter of Salome written to my lady against thee, I have written out a copy, and sent it to thee; with hazard to myself, but for thy advantage. The reason why she wrote it was this, that she had a mind to be married to Sylleus. Do thou therefore tear this letter in pieces, that I may not come into danger of my life." Now Acme had written to Antipater himself, and informed him, that, in compliance with his command, she had both herself written to Herod, as if Salome had laid a sudden plot entirely against him, and had herself sent a copy of an epistle, as coming from Salome to her lady. Now Acme was a Jew by birth, and a servant to Julia, Caesar's wife; and did this out of her friendship for Antipater, as having been corrupted by him with a large present of money, to assist in his pernicious designs against his father and his aunt.

8. Hereupon Herod was so amazed at the prodigious wickedness of Antipater, that he was ready to have ordered him to be slain immediately, as a turbulent person in the most important concerns, and as one that had laid a plot not only against himself, but against his sister also, and even corrupted Caesar's own domestics. Salome also provoked him to it, beating her breast, and bidding him kill her, if he could produce any credible testimony that she had acted in that manner. Herod also sent for his son, and asked him about this matter, and bid him contradict if he could, and not suppress any thing he had to say for himself; and when he had not one word to say, he asked him, since he was every way caught in his villainy, that he would

make no further delay, but discover his associates in these his wicked designs. So he laid all upon Antiphilus, but discovered nobody else. Hereupon Herod was in such great grief, that he was ready to send his son to Rome to Caesar, there to give an account of these his wicked contrivances. But he soon became afraid, lest he might there, by the assistance of his friends, escape the danger he was in; so he kept him bound as before, and sent more ambassadors and letters [to Rome] to accuse his son, and an account of what assistance Acme had given him in his wicked designs, with copies of the epistles before mentioned.

6 *Concerning the Disease That Herod Fell into and the Sedition Which the Jews Raised Thereupon; with the Punishment of the Seditious*

1. NOW Herod's ambassadors made haste to Rome; but sent, as instructed beforehand, what answers they were to make to the questions put to them. They also carried the epistles with them. But Herod now fell into a distemper, and made his will, and bequeathed his kingdom to [Antipas], his youngest son; and this out of that hatred to Archclaus and Philip, which the calumnies of Antipater had raised against them. He also bequeathed a thousand talents to Caesar, and five hundred to Julia, Caesar's wife, to Caesar's children, and friends and freedmen. He also distributed among his sons and their sons his money, his revenues, and his lands. He also made Salome his sister very rich, because she had continued faithful to him in all his circumstances, and was never so rash as to do him any harm; and as he despaired of recovering, for he was about the seventieth year of his age, he grew fierce, and indulged the bitterest anger upon all occasions; the cause whereof was this, that he thought himself despised, and that the nation was pleased with his misfortunes; besides which, he resented a sedition which some of the lower sort of men excited against him, the occasion of which was as follows.

2. There was one Judas, the son of Saripheus, and Mattbias, the son of Margalothus, two of the most eloquent men among the Jews, and the most celebrated interpreters of the Jewish laws, and men well beloved by the people, because of their education of their youth; for all those that were studious of virtue frequented their lectures

every day. These men, when they found that the king's distemper was incurable, excited the young men that they would pull down all those works which the king had erected contrary to the law of their fathers, and thereby obtain the rewards which the law will confer on them for such actions of piety; for that it was truly on account of Herod's rashness in making such things as the law had forbidden, that his other misfortunes, and this distemper also, which was so unusual among mankind, and with which he was now afflicted, came upon him; for Herod had caused such things to be made which were contrary to the law, of which he was accused by Judas and Matthias; for the king had erected over the great gate of the temple a large golden eagle, of great value, and had dedicated it to the temple. Now the law forbids those that propose to live according to it, to erect images[6] or representations of any living creature. So these wise men persuaded [their scholars] to pull down the golden eagle; alleging, that although they should incur any danger, which might bring them to their deaths, the virtue of the action now proposed to them would appear much more advantageous to them than the pleasures of life; since they would die for the preservation and observation of the law of their fathers; since they would also acquire an everlasting fame and commendation; since they would be both commended by the present generation, and leave an example of life that would never be forgotten to posterity; since that common calamity of dying cannot be avoided by our living so as to escape any such dangers; that therefore it is a right thing for those who are in love with a virtuous conduct, to wait for that fatal hour by such behavior as may carry them out of the world with praise and honor; and that this will alleviate death to a great degree, thus to come at it by the performance of brave actions, which bring us into danger of it; and at the same time to leave that reputation behind them to their children, and to all their relations, whether they be men or women, which will be of great advantage to them afterward.

3. And with such discourses as this did these men excite the young men to this action; and a report being come to them that the king was dead, this was an addition to the wise men's persuasions; so, in the very middle of the day, they got upon the place, they pulled down the

6. That the making of images, without an intention to worship them, was not unlawful to the Jews, see the note on Antiq. B VIII. ch. 7. sect. 5.

eagle, and cut it into pieces with axes, while a great number of the people were in the temple. And now the king's captain, upon hearing what the undertaking was, and supposing it was a thing of a higher nature than it proved to be, came up thither, having a great band of soldiers with him, such as was sufficient to put a stop to the multitude of those who pulled down what was dedicated to God; so he fell upon them unexpectedly, and as they were upon this bold attempt, in a foolish presumption rather than a cautious circumspection, as is usual with the multitude, and while they were in disorder, and incautious of what was for their advantage; so he caught no fewer than forty of the young men, who had the courage to stay behind when the rest ran away, together with the authors of this bold attempt, Judas and Matthius, who thought it an ignominious thing to retire upon his approach, and led them to the king. And when they were come to the king, and he asked them if they had been so bold as to pull down what he had dedicated to God, "Yes, (said they,) what was contrived we contrived, and what hath been performed we performed it, and that with such a virtuous courage as becomes men; for we have given our assistance to those things which were dedicated to the majesty of God, and we have provided for what we have learned by hearing the law; and it ought not to be wondered at, if we esteem those laws which Moses had suggested to him, and were taught him by God, and which he wrote and left behind him, more worthy of observation than thy commands. Accordingly we will undergo death, and all sorts of punishments which thou canst inflict upon us, with pleasure, since we are conscious to ourselves that we shall die, not for any unrighteous actions, but for our love to religion." And thus they all said, and their courage was still equal to their profession, and equal to that with which they readily set about this undertaking. And when the king had ordered them to be bound, he sent them to Jericho, and called together the principal men among the Jews; and when they were come, he made them assemble in the theater, and because he could not himself stand, he lay upon a couch, and enumerated the many labors that he had long endured on their account, and his building of the temple, and what a vast charge that was to him; while the Asamoneans, during the hundred and twenty-five years of their government, had not been able to perform any so great a work for the honor of God as that was; that he had also adorned it with very valuable donations, on which account he hoped that he had left himself a memorial, and procured himself a reputation after his death. He then cried out, that these men had not abstained from affronting him, even in his lifetime, but that in the very day time, and in the sight of the multitude, they had abused him to that degree, as to fall upon what he had dedicated, and in that way of abuse had pulled it down to the ground. They pretended, indeed, that they did it to affront him; but if any one consider the thing truly, they will find that they were guilty of sacrilege against God therein.

4. But the people, on account of Herod's barbarous temper, and for fear he should be so cruel and to inflict punishment on them, said what was done was done without their approbation, and that it seemed to them that the actors might well be punished for what they had done. But as for Herod, he dealt more mildly with others [of the assembly] but he deprived Matthias of the high priesthood, as in part an occasion of this action, and made Joazar, who was Matthias's wife's brother, high priest in his stead. Now it happened, that during the time of the high priesthood of this Matthias, there was another person made high priest for a single day, that very day which the Jews observed as a fast. The occasion was this: This Matthias the high priest, on the night before that day when the fast was to be celebrated, seemed, in a dream,[7] to have conversation with his wife; and because he could not officiate himself on that account, Joseph, the son of Ellemus, his kinsman, assisted him in that sacred office. But Herod deprived this Matthias of the high priesthood, and burnt the other Matthias, who had raised the sedition, with his companions, alive. And that very night there was an eclipse of the moon.[8]

---

7. This fact, that one Joseph was made high priest for a single day, on occasion of the action here specified, that befell Matthias, the real high priest, in his sleep, the night before the great day of expiation, is attested to both in the Mishna and Talmud, as Dr. Hudson here informs us. And indeed, from this fact, thus fully attested, we may confute that pretended rule in the Talmud here mentioned, and endeavored to be excused lay Reland, that the high priest was not suffered to sleep the night before that great day of expiation; which watching would surely rather unfit him for the many important duties he was to perform on that solemn day, than dispose him duly to perform them. Nor do such Talmudical rules, when unsupported by better evidence, much less when contradicted there by, seem to me of weight enough to deserve that so great a man as Reland should spend his time in endeavors at their vindication.

8. This eclipse of the moon (which is the only eclipse of either of the luminaries

5. But now Herod's distemper greatly increased upon him after a severe manner, and this by God's judgment upon him for his sins; for a fire glowed in him slowly, which did not so much appear to the touch outwardly, as it augmented his pains inwardly; for it brought upon him a vehement appetite to eating, which he could not avoid to supply with one sort of food or other. His entrails were also ex-ulcerated, and the chief violence of his pain lay on his colon; an aqueous and transparent liquor also had settled itself about his feet, and a like matter afflicted him at the bottom of his belly. Nay, further, his privy-member was putrefied, and produced worms; and when he sat upright, he had a difficulty of breathing, which was very loathsome, on account of the stench of his breath, and the quickness of its returns; he had also convulsions in all parts of his body, which increased his strength to an insufferable degree. It was said by those who pretended to divine, and who were endued with wisdom to foretell such things, that God inflicted this punishment on the king on account of his great impiety; yet was he still in hopes of recovering, though his afflictions seemed greater than any one could bear. He also sent for physicians, and did not refuse to follow what they prescribed for his assistance, and went beyond the river Jordan, and bathed himself in the warm baths that were at Callirrhoe, which, besides their other general virtues, were also fit to drink; which water runs into the lake called Asphaltiris. And when the physicians once thought fit to have him bathed in a vessel full of oil, it was supposed that he was just dying; but upon the lamentable cries of his domestics, he revived; and having no longer the least hopes of recovering, he gave order that every soldier should be paid fifty drachmae; and he also gave a great deal to their commanders, and to his friends, and came again to Jericho, where he grew so choleric, that it brought him to do all things like a madman; and though he were near his death, he contrived the following wicked designs. He commanded that all the principal men of the entire Jewish nation, wheresoever they lived, should be called

---

mentioned by our Josephus in any of his writings) is of the greatest consequence for the determination of the time for the death of Herod and Antipater, and for the birth and entire chronology of Jesus Christ. It happened March 13th, in the year of the Julian period 4710, and the 4th year before the Christian era. See its calculation by the rules of astronomy, at the end of the Astronomical Lectures, edit. Lat. p. 451, 452.

to him. Accordingly, they were a great number that came, because the whole nation was called, and all men heard of this call, and death was the penalty of such as should despise the epistles that were sent to call them. And now the king was in a wild rage against them all, the innocent as well as those that had afforded ground for accusations; and when they were come, he ordered them to be all shut up in the hyppodrome,[9] and sent for his sister Salome, and her husband Alexas, and spake thus to them: "I shall die in a little time, so great are my pains; which death ought to be cheerfully borne, and to be welcomed by all men; but what principally troubles me is this, that I shall die without being lamented, and without such mourning as men usually expect at a king's death. For that he was not unacquainted with the temper of the Jews, that his death would be a thing very desirable, and exceedingly acceptable to them, because during his lifetime they were ready to revolt from him, and to abuse the donations he had dedicated to God that it therefore was their business to resolve to afford him some alleviation of his great sorrows on this occasion; for that if they do not refuse him their consent in what he desires, he shall have a great mourning at his funeral, and such as never had any king before him; for then the whole nation would mourn from their very soul, which otherwise would be done in sport and mockery only. He desired therefore, that as soon as they see he hath given up the ghost, they shall place soldiers round the hippodrome, while they do not know that he is dead; and that they shall not declare his death to the multitude till this is done, but that they shall give orders to have those that are in custody shot with their darts; and that this slaughter of them all will cause that he shall not miss to rejoice on a double account; that as he is dying, they will make him secure that his will shall be executed in what he charges them to do; and that he shall have the honor of a memorable mourning at his funeral. So he deplored his condition, with tears in his eyes, and obtested them by the kindness due from them, as of his kindred, and by the faith they owed to God, and begged of them that they would not hinder him of this honorable mourning at his funeral. So they promised him not to transgress his commands.

6. Now any one may easily discover the temper of this man's mind, which not only took pleasure in doing what he had done formerly

---

9. A place for the horse-races.

against his relations, out of the love of life, but by those commands of his which savored of no humanity; since he took care, when he was departing out of this life, that the whole nation should be put into mourning, and indeed made desolate of their dearest kindred, when he gave order that one out of every family should be slain, although they had done nothing that was unjust, or that was against him, nor were they accused of any other crimes; while it is usual for those who have any regard to virtue to lay aside their hatred at such a time, even with respect to those they justly esteemed their enemies.

7 *Herod Has Thoughts of Killing Himself with His Own Hand; and a Little Afterwards He Orders Antipater to Be Slain*

1. AS he was giving these commands to his relations, there came letters from his ambassadors, who had been sent to Rome unto Caesar, which, when they were read, their purport was this: That Acme was slain by Caesar, out of his indignation at what hand, she had in Antipater's wicked practices; and that as to Antipater himself, Caesar left it to Herod to act as became a father and a king, and either to banish him, or to take away his life, which he pleased. When Herod heard this, he was some-what better, out of the pleasure he had from the contents of the letters, and was elevated at the death of Acme, and at the power that was given him over his son; but as his pains were become very great, he was now ready to faint for want of somewhat to eat; so he called for an apple and a knife; for it was his custom formerly to pare the apple himself, and soon afterwards to cut it, and eat it. When he had got the knife, he looked about, and had a mind to stab himself with it; and he had done it, had not his first cousin, Achiabus, prevented him, and held his hand, and cried out loudly. Whereupon a woeful lamentation echoed through the palace, and a great tumult was made, as if the king were dead. Upon which Antipater, who verily believed his father was deceased, grew bold in his discourse, as hoping to be immediately and entirely released from his bonds, and to take the kingdom into his hands without any more ado; so he discoursed with the jailer about letting him go, and in that case promised him great things, both now and hereafter, as if that were the only thing now in question. But the jailer did not only refuse to do what Antipater would have him, but

informed the king of his intentions, and how many solicitations he had had from him [of that nature]. Hereupon Herod, who had formerly no affection nor good-will towards his son to restrain him, when he heard what the jailer said, he cried out, and beat his head, although he was at death's door, and raised himself upon his elbow, and sent for some of his guards, and commanded them to kill Antipater without tiny further delay, and to do it presently, and to bury him in an ignoble manner at Hyrcania.

8 Concerning Herod's Death, and Testament, and Burial

1. AND now Herod altered his testament upon the alteration of his mind; for he appointed Antipas, to whom he had before left the kingdom, to be tetrarch of Galilee and Perea, and granted the kingdom to Archclaus. He also gave Gaulonitis, and Trachonitis, and Paneas to Philip, who was his son, but own brother to Archclaus[10] by the name of a tetrarchy; and bequeathed Jarnnia, and Ashdod, and Phasaelis to Salome his sister, with five hundred thousand [drachmae] of silver that was coined. He also made provision for all the rest of his kindred, by giving them sums of money and annual revenues, and so left them all in a wealthy condition. He bequeathed also to Caesar ten millions [of drachmae] of coined money, besides both vessels of gold and silver, and garments exceeding costly, to Julia, Caesar's wife; and to certain others, five millions. When he had done these things, he died, the fifth day after he had caused Antipater to be slain; having reigned, since he had procured Antigonus to be slain, thirty-four years; but since he had been declared king by the Romans, thirty-seven.[11] A man he was

---

10. When it is here said that Philip the tetrarch, and Archelaus the king, or ethnarch, were own brother, or genuine brothers, if those words mean own brothers, or born of the same father and mother, there must be here some mistake; because they had indeed the same father, Herod, but different mothers; the former Cleopatra, and Archclaus Malthace. They were indeed brought up together privately at Rome like when he went to have his kingdom confirmed to him at Rome, ch. 9. sect. 5; and Of the War, B. II. ch. 2. sect. 1; which intimacy is perhaps all that Josephus intended by the words before us.

11. These numbers of years for Herod's reign, 34 and 37, are the very same with those, Of the War, B. I. ch. 33. sect. 8, and are among the principal chronological characters belonging to the reign or death of Herod. See Harm. p. 150—155.

of great barbarity towards all men equally, and a slave to his passion; but above the consideration of what was right; yet was he favored by fortune as much as any man ever was, for from a private man he became a king; and though he were encompassed with ten thousand dangers, he got clear of them all, and continued his life till a very old age. But then, as to the affairs of his family and children, in which indeed, according to his own opinion, he was also very fortunate, because he was able to conquer his enemies, yet, in my opinion, he was herein very unfortunate.

2. But then Salome and Alexas, before the king's death was made known, dismissed those that were shut up in the hippodrome, and told them that the king ordered them to go away to their own lands, and take care of their own affairs, which was esteemed by the nation a great benefit. And now the king's death was made public, when Salome and Alexas gathered the soldiery together in the amphitheater at Jericho; and the first thing they did was, they read Herod's letter, written to the soldiery, thanking them for their fidelity and good-will to him, and exhorting them to afford his son Archelaus, whom he had appointed for their king, like fidelity and good-will. After which Ptolemy, who had the king's seal intrusted to him, read the king's testament, which was to be of force no otherwise than as it should stand when Caesar had inspected it; so there was presently an acclamation made to Archelaus, as king; and the soldiers came by bands, and their commanders with them, and promised the same good-will to him, and readiness to serve him, which they had exhibited to Herod; and they prayed God to be assistant to him.

3. After this was over, they prepared for his funeral, it being Archelaus's care that the procession to his father's sepulcher should be very sumptuous. Accordingly, he brought out all his ornaments to adorn the pomp of the funeral. The body was carried upon a golden bier, embroidered with very precious stones of great variety, and it was covered over with purple, as well as the body itself; he had a diadem upon his head, and above it a crown of gold: he also had a scepter in his right hand. About the bier were his sons and his numerous relations; next to these was the soldiery, distinguished according to their several countries and denominations; and they were put into the following order: First of all went his guards, then the band of Thracians, and after them the Germans; and next the band of Galatians,

every one in their habiliments of war; and behind these marched the whole army in the same manner as they used to go out to war, and as they used to be put in array by their muster-masters and centurions; these were followed by five hundred of his domestics carrying spices. So they went eight furlongs[12] to Herodium; for there by his own command he was to be buried. And thus did Herod end his life.

4. Now Archelaus paid him so much respect, as to continue his mourning till the seventh day; for so many days are appointed for it by the law of our fathers. And when he had given a treat to the multitude, and left off his motoring, he went up into the temple; he had also acclamations and praises given him, which way soever he went, every one striving with the rest who should appear to use the loudest acclamations. So he ascended a high elevation made for him, and took his seat, in a throne made of gold, and spake kindly to the multitude, and declared with what joy he received their acclamations, and the marks of the good-will they showed to him; and returned them thanks that they did not remember the injuries his father had done them to his disadvantage; and promised them he would endeavor not to be behindhand with them in rewarding their alacrity in his service, after a suitable manner; but that he should abstain at present from the name of king, and that he should have the honor of that dignity, if Caesar should confirm and settle that testament which his father had made; and that it was on this account, that when the army would have put the diadem on him at Jericho, he would not accept of that honor, which is usually so much desired, because it was not yet evident that he who was to be principally concerned in bestowing it would give it him; although, by his acceptance of the government, he should not want the ability of rewarding their kindness to him and that it should be his endeavor, as to all things wherein they were concerned, to prove in every respect better than his father. Whereupon the multitude, as it is usual with them, supposed that the first days of those that enter upon such governments declare the intentions of those that accept them; and so by how much Archelaus spake the more gently and civilly to

12. At eight stadia or furlongs a-day, as here, Herod's funeral, conducted to Herodium, which lay at the distance from Jericho, where he died, of 200 stadia or furlongs, Of the War, B. 1. ch. 33. sect. 9, must have taken up no less than twenty-five days.

them, by so much did they more highly commend him, and made application to him for the grant of what they desired. Some made a clamor that he would ease them of some of their annual payments; but others desired him to release those that were put into prison by Herod, who were many, and had been put there at several times; others of them required that he would take away those taxes which had been severely laid upon what was publicly sold and bought. So Archelaus contradicted them in nothing, since he pretended to do all things so as to get the good-will of the multitude to him, as looking upon that good-will to be a great step towards his preservation of the government. Hereupon he went and offered sacrifice to God, and then betook himself to feast with his friends.

9 *How the People Raised a Sedition Against Archelaus, and How He Sailed to Rome*

1. AT this time also it was that some of the Jews got together out of a desire of innovation. They lamented Matthias, and those that were slain with him by Herod, who had not any respect paid them by a funeral mourning, out of the fear men were in of that man; they were those who had been condemned for pulling down the golden eagle. The people made a great clamor and lamentation hereupon, and cast out some reproaches against the king also, as if that tended to alleviate the miseries of the deceased. The people assembled together, and desired of Archelaus, that, in way of revenge on their account, he would inflict punishment on those who had been honored by Herod; and that, in the first and principal place, he would deprive that high priest whom Herod had made, and would choose one more agreeable to the law, and of greater purity, to officiate as high priest. This was granted by Archelaus, although he was mightily offended at their importunity, because he proposed to himself to go to Rome immediately to look after Caesar's determination about him. However, he sent the general of his forces to use persuasions, and to tell them that the death which was inflicted on their friends was according to the law; and to represent to them that their petitions about these things were carried to a great height of injury to him; that the time was not now proper for such petitions, but required their unanimity until such

time as he should be established in the government by the consent of Caesar, and should then be come back to them; for that he would then consult with them in common concerning the purport of their petitions; but that they ought at present to be quiet, lest they should seem seditious persons.

2. So when the king had suggested these things, and instructed his general in what he was to say, be sent him away to the people; but they made a clamor, and would not give him leave to speak, and put him in danger of his life, and as many more as were desirous to venture upon saying openly any thing which might reduce them to a sober mind, and prevent their going on in their present courses, because they had more concern to have all their own wills performed than to yield obedience to their governors; thinking it to be a thing insufferable, that, while Herod was alive, they should lose those that were most dear to them, and that when he was dead, they could not get the actors to be punished. So they went on with their designs after a violent manner, and thought all to be lawful and right which tended to please them, and being unskillful in foreseeing what dangers they incurred; and when they had suspicion of such a thing, yet did the present pleasure they took in the punishment of those they deemed their enemies overweigh all such considerations; and although Archelaus sent many to speak to them, yet they treated them not as messengers sent by him, but as persons that came of their own accord to mitigate their anger, and would not let one of them speak. The sedition also was made by such as were in a great passion; and it was evident that they were proceeding further in seditious practices, by the multitude running so fast upon them.

3. Now, upon the approach of that feast of unleavened bread, which the law of their fathers had appointed for the Jews at this time, which feast is called the Passover[13] and is a memorial of their deliverance out of Egypt, when they offer sacrifices with great alacrity; and when they are required to slay more sacrifices in number than at any other festival; and when an innumerable multitude came thither out of the country, nay, from beyond its limits also, in order to worship God, the seditious lamented Judas and Matthias, those teachers of the laws,

13. This passover, when the sedition here mentioned was moved against Archelaus, was not one, but thirteen months after the eclipse of the moon already mentioned.

and kept together in the temple, and had plenty of food, because these seditious persons were not ashamed to beg it. And as Archelaus was afraid lest some terrible thing should spring up by means of these men's madness, he sent a regiment of armed men, and with them a captain of a thousand, to suppress the violent efforts of the seditious before the whole multitude should be infected with the like madness; and gave them this charge, that if they found any much more openly seditious than others, and more busy in tumultuous practices, they should bring them to him. But those that were seditious on account of those teachers of the law, irritated the people by the noise and clamors they used to encourage the people in their designs; so they made an assault upon the soldiers, and came up to them, and stoned the greatest part of them, although some of them ran away wounded, and their captain among them; and when they had thus done, they returned to the sacrifices which were already in their hands. Now Archelaus thought there was no way to preserve the entire government but by cutting off those who made this attempt upon it; so he sent out the whole army upon them, and sent the horsemen to prevent those that had their tents without the temple from assisting those that were within the temple, and to kill such as ran away from the footmen when they thought themselves out of danger; which horsemen slew three thousand men, while the rest went to the neighboring mountains. Then did Archelaus order proclamation to be made to them all, that they should retire to their own homes; so they went away, and left the festival, out of fear of somewhat worse which would follow, although they had been so bold by reason of their want of instruction. So Archelaus went down to the sea with his mother, and took with him Nicolaus and Ptolemy, and many others of his friends, and left Philip his brother as governor of all things belonging both to his own family and to the public. There went out also with him Salome, Herod's sister who took with her, her children, and many of her kindred were with her; which kindred of hers went, as they pretended, to assist Archelaus in gaining the kingdom, but in reality to oppose him, and chiefly to make loud complaints of what he had done in the temple. But Sabinus, Caesar's steward for Syrian affairs, as he was making haste into Judea to preserve Herod's effects, met with Archclaus at Caesarea; but Varus (president of Syria) came at that time, and restrained him from meddling with them, for he was there as sent for by Archceaus, by the means of Ptolemy. And Sabinus, out of regard to Varus, did neither seize upon any of the castles that were among the Jews, nor did he seal up the treasures in them, but permitted Archelaus to have them, until Caesar should declare his resolution about them; so that, upon this his promise, he tarried still at Cesarea. But after Archelaus was sailed for Rome, and Varus was removed to Antioch, Sabinus went to Jerusalem, and seized on the king's palace. He also sent for the keepers of the garrisons, and for all those that had the charge of Herod's effects, and declared publicly that he should require them to give an account of what they had; and he disposed of the castles in the manner he pleased; but those who kept them did not neglect what Archelaus had given them in command, but continued to keep all things in the manner that had been enjoined them; and their pretense was, that they kept them all for Caesar,

4. At the same time also did Antipas, another of Herod's sons, sail to Rome, in order to gain the government; being buoyed up by Salome with promises that he should take that government; and that he was a much honester and fitter man than Archelaus for that authority, since Herod had, in his former testament, deemed him the worthiest to be made king, which ought to be esteemed more valid than his latter testament. Antipas also brought with him his mother, and Ptolemy the brother of Nicolaus, one that had been Herod's most honored friend, and was now zealous for Antipas; but it was Ireneus the orator, and one who, on account of his reputation for sagacity, was intrusted with the affairs of the kingdom, who most of all encouraged him to attempt to gain the kingdom; by whose means it was, that when some advised him to yield to Archelaus, as to his elder brother, and who had been declared king by their father's last will, he would not submit so to do. And when he was come to Rome, all his relations revolted to him; not out of their good-will to him, but out of their hatred to Archelaus; though indeed they were most of all desirous of gaining their liberty, and to be put under a Roman governor; but if there were too great an opposition made to that, they thought Antipas preferable to Archelaus, and so joined with him, in order to procure the kingdom for him. Sabinus also, by letters, accused Archelaus to Caesar.

5. Now when Archelaus had sent in his papers to Caesar, wherein he pleaded his right to. the kingdom, and his father's testament, with the accounts of Herod's money, and with Ptolemy, who brought

Herod's seal, he so expected the event; but when Caesar had read these papers, and Varus's and Sabinus's letters, with the accounts of the money, and what were the annual incomes of the kingdom, and understood that Antipas had also sent letters to lay claim to the kingdom, he summoned his friends together, to know their opinions, and with them Caius, the son of Agrippa, and of Julia his daughter, whom he had adopted, and took him, and made him sit first of all, and desired such as pleased to speak their minds about the affairs now before them. Now Antipater, Salome's son, a very subtle orator, and a bitter enemy to Archelaus, spake first to this purpose: That it was ridiculous in Archelaus to plead now to have the kingdom given him, since he had, in reality, taken already the power over it to himself, before Caesar had granted it to him; and appealed to those bold actions of his, in destroying so many at the Jewish festival; and if the men had acted unjustly, it was but fit the punishing of them should have been reserved to those that were out of the country, but had the power to punish them, and not been executed by a man that, if he pretended to be a king, he did an injury to Caesar, by usurping that authority before it was determined for him by Caesar; but if he owned himself to be a private person, his case was much worse, since he who was putting in for the kingdom could by no means expect to have that power granted him, of which he had already deprived Caesar [by taking it to himself]. He also touched sharply upon him, and appealed to his changing the commanders in the army, and his sitting in the royal throne beforehand, and his determination of law-suits; all done as if he were no other than a king. He appealed also to his concessions to those that petitioned him on a public account, and indeed doing such things, than which he could devise no greater if he had been already settled in the kingdom by Caesar. He also ascribed to him the releasing of the prisoners that were in the hippodrome, and many other things, that either had been certainly done by him, or were believed to be done, and easily might be believed to have been done, because they were of such a nature as to be usually done by young men, and by such as, out of a desire of ruling, seize upon the government too soon. He also charged him with his neglect of the funeral mourning for his father, and with having merry meetings the very night in which he died; and that it was thence the multitude took the handle of raising a tumult: and if Archelaus could thus requite his dead father, who had bestowed such benefits upon him, and bequeathed such great things to him, by pretending to shed tears for him in the day time, like an actor on the stage, but every night making mirth for having gotten the government, he would appear to be the same Archelaus with regard to Caesar, if he granted him the kingdom, which he hath been to his father; since he had then dancing and singing, as though an enemy of his were fallen, and not as though a man were carried to his funeral, that was so nearly related, and had been so great a benefactor to him. But he said that the greatest crime of all was this, that he came now before Caesar to obtain the government by his grant, while he had before acted in all things as he could have acted if Caesar himself, who ruled all, had fixed him firmly in the government. And what he most aggravated in his pleading was the slaughter of those about the temple, and the impiety of it, as done at the festival; and how they were slain like sacrifices themselves, some of whom were foreigners, and others of their own country, till the temple was full of dead bodies: and all this was done, not by an alien, but by one who pretended to the lawful title of a king, that he might complete the wicked tyranny which his nature prompted him to, and which is hated by all men. On which account his father never so much as dreamed of making him his successor in the kingdom, when he was of a sound mind, because he knew his disposition; and in his former and more authentic testament, he appointed his antagonist Antipas to succeed; but that Archelaus was called by his father to that dignity when he was in a dying condition, both of body and mind; while Antipas was called when he was ripest in his judgment, and of such strength of body as made him capable of managing his own affairs: and if his father had the like notion of him formerly that he hath now showed, yet hath he given a sufficient specimen what a king he is likely to be, when he hath [in effect] deprived Caesar of that power of disposing of the kingdom, which he justly hath, and hath not abstained from making a terrible slaughter of his fellow citizens in the temple, while lie was but a private person.

6. So when Antipater had made this speech, and had confirmed what he had said by producing many witnesses from among Archelaus's own relations, he made an end of his pleading. Upon which Nicolaus arose up to plead for Archelaus, and said, "That what had been done at the temple was rather to be attributed to the mind of those that

had been killed, than to the authority of Archelaus; for that those who were the authors of such things are not only wicked in the injuries they do of themselves, but in forcing sober persons to avenge themselves upon them. Now it is evident that what these did in way of opposition was done under pretense, indeed, against Archelaus, but in reality against Caesar himself, for they, after an injurious manner, attacked and slew those who were sent by Archelaus, and who came only to put a stop to their doings. They had no regard, either to God or to the festival, whom Antipater yet is not ashamed to patronize, whether it be out of his indulgence of an enmity to Archelaus, or out of his hatred of virtue and justice. For as to those who begin such tumults, and first set about such unrighteous actions, they are the men who force those that punish them to betake themselves to arms even against their will. So that Antipater in effect ascribes the rest of what was done to all those who were of counsel to the accusers; for nothing which is here accused of injustice has been done but what was derived from them as its authors; nor are those things evil in themselves, but so represented only in order to do harm to Archelaus. Such is these men's inclination to do an injury to a man that is of their kindred, their father's benefactor, and familiarity acquainted with them, and that hath ever lived in friendship with them; for that, as to this testament, it was made by the king when he was of a sound mind, and so ought to be of more authority than his former testament; and that for this reason, because Caesar is therein left to be the judge and disposer of all therein contained; and for Caesar, he will not, to be sure, at all imitate the unjust proceedings of those men, who, during Herod's whole life, had on all occasions been joint partakers of power with him, and yet do zealously endeavor to injure his determination, while they have not themselves had the same regard to their kinsman [which Archelaus had]. Caesar will not therefore disannul the testament of a man whom he had entirely supported, of his friend and confederate, and that which is committed to him in trust to ratify; nor will Caesar's virtuous and upright disposition, which is known and uncontested through all the habitable world, imitate the wickedness of these men in condemning a king as a madman, and as having lost his reason, while he hath bequeathed the succession to a good son of his, and to one who flies to Caesar's upright determination for refuge. Nor can Herod at any time have been mistaken in his judgment about a successor, while he showed so much prudence as to submit all to Caesar's determination."

7. Now when Nicolaus had laid these things before Caesar, he ended his plea; whereupon Caesar was so obliging to Archelaus, that he raised him up when he had cast himself down at his feet, and said that he well deserved the kingdom; and he soon let them know that he was so far moved in his favor, that he would not act otherwise than his father's testament directed, and than was for the advantage of Archelaus. However, while he gave this encouragement to Archelaus to depend on him securely, he made no full determination about him; and when the assembly was broken up, he considered by himself whether he should confirm the kingdom to Archelaus, or whether he should part it among all Herod's posterity; and this because they all stood in need of much assistance to support them.

10 *A Sedition Against Sabinus; and How Varus Brought the Authors of It to Punishment*

1. BUT before these things could be brought to a settlement, Malthace, Archelaus's mother, fell into a distemper, and died of it; and letters came from Varus, the president of Syria, which informed Caesar of the revolt of the Jews; for after Archlaus was sailed, the whole nation was in a tumult. So Varus, since he was there himself, brought the authors of the disturbance to punishment; and when he had restrained them for the most part from this sedition, which was a great one, he took his journey to Antiocli, leaving one legion of his army at Jerusalem to keep the Jews quiet, who were now very fond of innovation. Yet did not this at all avail to put an end to that their sedition; for after Varus was gone away, Sabinus, Caesar's procurator, staid behind, and greatly distressed the Jews, relying on the forces that were left there that they would by their multitude protect him; for he made use of them, and armed them as his guards, thereby so oppressing the Jews, and giving them so great disturbance, that at length they rebelled; for he used force in seizing the citadels, and zealously pressed on the search after the king's money, in order to seize upon it by force, on account of his love of gain and his extraordinary covetousness.

2. But on the approach of pentecost, which is a festival of ours, so called from the days of our forefathers, a great many ten thousands

of men got together; nor did they come only to celebrate the festival, but out of their indignation at the madness of Sabinus, and at the injuries he offered them. A great number there was of Galileans, and Idumeans, and many men from Jericho, and others who had passed over the river Jordan, and inhabited those parts. This whole multitude joined themselves to all the rest, and were more zealous than the others in making an assault on Sabinus, in order to be avenged on him; so they parted themselves into three bands, and encamped themselves in the places following:—some of them seized on the hippodrome and of the other two bands, one pitched themselves from the northern part of the temple to the southern, on the east quarter; but the third band held the western part of the city, where the king's palace was. Their work tended entirely to besiege the Romans, and to enclose them on all sides. Now Sabinus was afraid of these men's number, and of their resolution, who had little regard to their lives, but were very desirous not to be overcome, while they thought it a point of puissance to overcome their enemies; so he sent immediately a letter to Varus, and, as he used to do, was very pressing with him, and entreated him to come quickly to his assistance, because the forces he had left were in imminent danger, and would probably, in no long time, be seized upon, and cut to pieces; while he did himself get up to the highest tower of the fortress Phasaelus, which had been built in honor of Phasaelus, king Herod's brother, and called so when the Parthians had brought him to his death.[14] So Sabinus gave thence a signal to the Romans to fall upon the Jews, although he did not himself venture so much as to come down to his friends, and thought he might expect that the others should expose themselves first to die on account of his avarice. However, the Romans ventured to make a sally out of the place, and a terrible battle ensued; wherein, though it is true the Romans beat their adversaries, yet were not the Jews daunted in their resolutions, even when they had the sight of that terrible slaughter that was made of them; but they went round about, and got upon those cloisters which encompassed the outer court of the temple, where a great fight was still continued, and they cast stones at the Romans, partly with their hands, and partly with slings, as being much used to those exercises. All the archers also in array did

---

14. See Antiq. B. XIV. ch. 13. sect. 10; and Of the War; B. II. ch. 12. sect. 9.

the Romans a great deal of mischief, because they used their hands dexterously from a place superior to the others, and because the others were at an utter loss what to do; for when they tried to shoot their arrows against the Jews upwards, these arrows could not reach them, insomuch that the Jews were easily too hard for their enemies. And this sort of fight lasted a great while, till at last the Romans, who were greatly distressed by what was done, set fire to the cloisters so privately, that those that were gotten upon them did not perceive it. This fire[15] being fed by a great deal of combustible matter, caught hold immediately on the roof of the cloisters; so the wood, which was full of pitch and wax, and whose gold was laid on it with wax, yielded to the flame presently, and those vast works, which were of the highest value and esteem, were destroyed utterly, while those that were on the roof unexpectedly perished at the same time; for as the roof tumbled down, some of these men tumbled down with it, and others of them were killed by their enemies who encompassed them. There was a great number more, who, out of despair of saving their lives, and out of astonishment at the misery that surrounded them, did either cast themselves into the fire, or threw themselves upon their swords, and so got out of their misery. But as to those that retired behind the same way by which they ascended, and thereby escaped, they were all killed by the Romans, as being unarmed men, and their courage failing them; their wild fury being now not able to help them, because they were destitute of armor, insomuch that of those that went up to the top of the roof, not one escaped. The Romans also rushed through the fire, where it gave them room so to do, and seized on that treasure where the sacred money was reposited; a great part of which was stolen by the soldiers, and Sabinus got openly four hundred talents.

3. But this calamity of the Jews' friends, who fell in this battle, grieved them, as did also this plundering of the money dedicated to God in the temple. Accordingly, that body of them which continued best together, and was the most warlike, encompassed the palace,

15. These great devastations made about the temple here, and Of the War, B. II. ch. 3. sect. 3, seem not to have been full re-edified in the days of Nero; till whose time there were eighteen thousand workmen continually employed in rebuilding and repairing that temple, as Josephus informs us, Antiq. B. XX. ch. 9. sect. 7. See the note on that place.

and threatened to set fire to it, and kill all that were in it. Yet still they commanded them to go out presently, and promised, that if they would do so, they would not hurt them, nor Sabinus neither; at which time the greatest part of the king's troops deserted to them, while Rufus and Gratus, who had three thousand of the most warlike of Herod's army with them, who were men of active bodies, went over to the Romans. There was also a band of horsemen under the command of Ruffis, which itself went over to the Romans also. However, the Jews went on with the siege, and dug mines under the palace walls, and besought those that were gone over to the other side not to be their hinderance, now they had such a proper opportunity for the recovery of their country's ancient liberty; and for Sabinus, truly he was desirous of going away with his soldiers, but was not able to trust himself with the enemy, on account of what mischief he had already done them; and he took this great [pretended] lenity of theirs for an argument why he should not comply with them; and so, because he expected that Varus was coming, he still bore the siege.

4. Now at this time there were ten thousand other disorders in Judea, which were like tumults, because a great number put themselves into a warlike posture, either out of hopes of gain to themselves, or out of enmity to the Jews. In particular, two thousand of Herod's old soldiers, who had been already disbanded, got together in Judea itself, and fought against the king's troops, although Achiabus, Herod's first cousin, opposed them; but as he was driven out of the plains into the mountainous parts by the military skill of those men, he kept himself in the fastnesses that were there, and saved what he could.

5. There was also Judas,[16] the son of that Ezekias who had been

---

16. Unless this Judas, the son of Ezekias, be the same with that Theudas, mentioned Acts 5:36, Josephus must have omitted him; for that other Thoualas, whom he afterward mentions, under Fadus the Roman governor, B. XX. ch. 5. sect. 1, is much too late to correspond to him that is mentioned in the Acts. The names Theudas, Thaddeus, and Judas differ but little. See Archbishop Usher's Annals at A.M. 4001. However, since Josephus does not pretend to reckon up the heads of all those ten thousand disorders in Judea, which he tells us were then abroad, see sect. 4 and 8, the Theudas of the Acts might be at the head of one of those seditions, though not particularly named by him. Thus he informs us here, sect. 6, and Of the War, B. II. ch. 4. Sect. 2, that certain of the seditious came and burnt the royal palace at Amsthus, or Betharamphta, upon the river Jordan. Perhaps their leader, who is not named by Josephus, might be this Theudas.

head of the robbers; which Ezekias was a very strong man, and had with great dificulty been caught by Herod. This Judas, having gotten together a multitude of men of a profligate character about Sepphoris in Galilee, made an assault upon the palace [there,] and seized upon all the weapons that were laid up in it, and with them armed every one of those that were with him, and carried away what money was left there; and he became terrible to all men, by tearing and rending those that came near him; and all this in order to raise himself, and out of an ambitious desire of the royal dignity; and he hoped to obtain that as the reward not of his virtuous skill in war, but of his extravagance in doing injuries.

6. There was also Simon, who had been a slave of Herod the king, but in other respects a comely person, of a tall and robust body; he was one that was much superior to others of his order, and had had great things committed to his care. This man was elevated at the disorderly state of things, and was so bold as to put a diadem on his head, while a certain number of the people stood by him, and by them he was declared to be a king, and thought himself more worthy of that dignity than any one else. He burnt down the royal palace at Jericho, and plundered what was left in it. He also set fire to many other of the king's houses in several places of the country, and utterly destroyed them, and permitted those that were with him to take what was left in them for a prey; and he would have done greater things, unless care had been taken to repress him immediately; for Gratus, when he had joined himself to some Roman soldiers, took the forces he had with him, and met Simon, and after a great and a long fight, no small part of those that came from Perea, who were a disordered body of men, and fought rather in a bold than in a skillful manner, were destroyed; and although Simon had saved himself by flying away through a certain valley, yet Gratus overtook him, and cut off his head. The royal palace also at Amathus, by the river Jordan, was burnt down by a party of men that were got together, as were those belonging to Simon. And thus did a great and wild fury spread itself over the nation, because they had no king to keep the multitude in good order, and because those foreigners who came to reduce the seditious to sobriety did, on the contrary, set them more in a flame, because of the injuries they offered them, and the avaricious management of their affairs.

7. But because Athronges, a person neither eminent by the dignity of his progenitors, nor for any great wealth he was possessed of, but one that had in all respects been a shepherd only, and was not known by any body; yet because he was a tall man, and excelled others in the strength of his hands, he was so bold as to set up for king. This man thought it so sweet a thing to do more than ordinary injuries to others, that although he should be killed, he did not much care if he lost his life in so great a design. He had also four brethren, who were tall men themselves, and were believed to be superior to others in the strength of their hands, and thereby were encouraged to aim at great things, and thought that strength of theirs would support them in retaining the kingdom. Each of these ruled over a band of men of their own; for those that got together to them were very numerous. They were every one of them also commanders; but when they came to fight, they were subordinate to him, and fought for him, while he put a diadem about his head, and assembled a council to debate about what things should be done, and all things were done according to his pleasure. And this man retained his power a great while; he was also called king, and had nothing to hinder him from doing what he pleased. He also, as well as his brethren, slew a great many both of the Romans and of the king's forces, an managed matters with the like hatred to each of them. The king's forces they fell upon, because of the licentious conduct they had been allowed under Herod's government; and they fell upon the Romans, because of the injuries they had so lately received from them. But in process of time they grew more cruel to all sorts of men, nor could any one escape from one or other of these seditions, since they slew some out of the hopes of gain, and others from a mere custom of slaying men. They once attacked a company of Romans at Emmaus, who were bringing corn and weapons to the army, and fell upon Arius, the centurion, who commanded the company, and shot forty of the best of his foot soldiers; but the rest of them were aftrighted at their slaughter, and left their dead behind them, but saved themselves by the means of Gratus, who came with the king's troops that were about him to their assistance. Now these four brethren continued the war a long while by such sort of expeditions, and much grieved the Romans; but did their own nation also a great deal of mischief. Yet were they afterwards subdued; one of them in a fight with Gratus, another with Ptolemy; Archelaus also took the eldest of them prisoner; while the last

of them was so dejected at the other's misfortune, and saw so plainly that he had no way now left to save himself, his army being worn away with sickness and continual labors, that he also delivered himself up to Archclaus, upon his promise and oath to God [to preserve his life.] But these things came to pass a good while afterward.

8. And now Judea was full of robberies; and as the several companies of the seditious lighted upon any one to head them, he was created a king immediately, in order to do mischief to the public. They were in some small measure indeed, and in small matters, hurtful to the Romans; but the murders they committed upon their own people lasted a long while.

9. As soon as Varus was once informed of the state of Judea by Sabinus's writing to him, he was afraid for the legion he had left there; so he took the two other legions, (for there were three legions in all belonging to Syria,) and four troops of horsemen, with the several auxiliary forces which either the kings or certain of the tetrarchs afforded him, and made what haste he could to assist those that were then besieged in Judea. He also gave order that all that were sent out for this expedition, should make haste to Ptolemais. The citizens of Berytus also gave him fifteen hundred auxiliaries as he passed through their city. Aretas also, the king of Arabia Petrea, out of his hatred to Herod, and in order to purchase the favor of the Romans, sent him no small assistance, besides their footmen and horsemen; and when he had now collected all his forces together, he committed part of them to his son, and to a friend of his, and sent them upon an expedition into Galilee, which lies in the neighborhood of Ptolemais; who made an attack upon the enemy, and put them to flight, and took Sepphoris, and made its inhabitants slaves, and burnt the city. But Varus himself pursued his march for Samaria with his whole army; yet did not he meddle with the city of that name, because it had not at all joined with the seditious; but pitched his camp at a certain village that belonged to Ptolemy, whose name was Arus, which the Arabians burnt, out of their hatred to Herod, and out of the enmity they bore to his friends; whence they marched to another village, whose name was Sampho, which the Arabians plundered and burnt, although it was a fortified and a strong place; and all along this march nothing escaped them, but all places were full of fire and of slaughter. Emmaus was also burnt by Varus's order, after its inhabitants had deserted it, that he might

avenge those that had there been destroyed. From thence he now marched to Jerusalem; whereupon those Jews whose camp lay there, and who had besieged the Roman legion, not bearing the coming of this army, left the siege imperfect: but as to the Jerusalem Jews, when Varus reproached them bitterly for what had been done, they cleared themselves of the accusation, and alleged that the conflux of the people was occasioned by the feast; that the war was not made with their approbation, but by the rashness of the strangers, while they were on the side of the Romans, and besieged together with them, rather than having any inclination to besiege them. There also came beforehand to meet Varus, Joseph, the cousin-german of king Herod, as also Gratus and Rufus, who brought their soldiers along with them, together with those Romans who had been besieged; but Sabinus did not come into Varus's presence, but stole out of the city privately, and went to the sea-side.

10. Upon this, Varus sent a part of his army into the country, to seek out those that had been the authors of the revolt; and when they were discovered, he punished some of them that were most guilty, and some he dismissed: now the number of those that were crucified on this account were two thousand. After which he disbanded his army, which he found no way useful to him in the affairs he came about; for they behaved themselves very disorderly, and disobeyed his orders, and what Varus desired them to do, and this out of regard to that gain which they made by the mischief they did. As for himself, when he was informed that ten thousand Jews had gotten together, he made haste to catch them; but they did not proceed so far as to fight him, but, by the advice of Achiabus, they came together, and delivered themselves up to him: hereupon Varus forgave the crime of revolting to the multitude, but sent their several commanders to Caesar, many of whom Caesar dismissed; but for the several relations of Herod who had been among these men in this war, they were the only persons whom he punished, who, without the least regard to justice, fought against their own kindred.

11 *An Embassage to Caesar; and How Caesar Confirmed Herod's Testament*

1. SO when Varus had settled these affairs, and had placed the former legion at Jerusalem, he returned back to Antioch; but as for Archelaus, he had new sources of trouble come upon him at Rome, on the occasions following: for an embassage of the Jews was come to Rome, Varus having permitted the nation to send it, that they might petition for the liberty of living by their own laws.[17] Now the number of the ambassadors that were sent by the authority of the nation were fifty, to which they joined above eight thousand of the Jews that were at Rome already. Hereupon Caesar assembled his friends, and the chief men among the Romans, in the temple of Apollo,[18] which he had built at a vast charge; whither the ambassadors came, and a multitude of the Jews that were there already came with them, as did also Archelaus and his friends; but as for the several kinsmen which Archelaus had, they would not join themselves with him, out of their hatred to him; and yet they thought it too gross a thing for them to assist the ambassadors [against him], as supposing it would be a disgrace to them in Caesar's opinion to think of thus acting in opposition to a man of their own kindred. Philip[19] also was come hither out of Syria, by the persuasion of Varus, with this principal intention to assist his brother [Archelaus]; for Varus was his great friend: but still so, that if there should any change happen in the form of government, (which Varus suspected there would,) and if any distribution should be made on account of the number that desired the liberty of living by their own laws, that he might not be disappointed, but might have his share in it.

2. Now upon the liberty that was given to the Jewish ambassadors to speak, they who hoped to obtain a dissolution of kingly government betook themselves to accuse Herod of his iniquities; and they declared that he was indeed in name a king, but that he had taken to himself that uncontrollable authority which tyrants exercise over their subjects, and had made use of that authority for the destruction of

17. See Of the War, B. II. ch. 2. sect. 3.
18. See the note, Of the War, B. II. ch. 6. sect. 1.
19. He was tetrarch afterward.

the Jews, and did not abstain from making many innovations among them besides, according to his own inclinations; and that whereas there were a great many who perished by that destruction he brought upon them, so many indeed as no other history relates, they that survived were far more miserable than those that suffered under him; not only by the anxiety they were in from his looks and disposition towards them, but from the danger their estates were in of being taken away by him. That he did never leave off adorning these cities that lay in their neighborhood, but were inhabited by foreigners; but so that the cities belonging to his own government were ruined, and utterly destroyed that whereas, when he took the kingdom, it was in an extraordinary flourishing condition, he had filled the nation with the utmost degree of poverty; and when, upon unjust pretenses, he had slain any of the nobility, he took away their estates; and when he permitted any of them to live, he condemned them to the forfeiture of what they possessed. And besides the annual impositions which he laid upon every one of them, they were to make liberal presents to himself, to his domestics and friends, and to such of his slaves as were vouchsafed the favor of being his tax-gatherers, because there was no way of obtaining a freedom from unjust violence without giving either gold or silver for it. That they would say nothing of the corruption of the chastity of their virgins, and the reproach laid on their wives for incontinency, and those things acted after an insolent and inhuman manner; because it was not a smaller pleasure to the sufferers to have such things concealed, than it would have been not to have suffered them. That Herod had put such abuses upon them as a wild beast would not have put on them, if he had power given him to rule over us; and that although their nation had passed through many subversions and alterations of government, their history gave no account of any calamity they had ever been under, that could be compared with this which Herod had brought upon their nation; that it was for this reason that they thought they might justly and gladly salute Archelaus as king, upon this supposition, that whosoever should be set over their kingdom, he would appear more mild to them than Herod had been; and that they had joined with him in the mourning for his father, in order to gratify him, and were ready to oblige him in other points also, if they could meet with any degree of moderation from him; but that he seemed to be afraid lest he should not be deemed Herod's own son;

and so, without any delay, he immediately let the nation understand his meaning, and this before his dominion was well established, since the power of disposing of it belonged to Caesar, who could either give it to him or not, as he pleased. That he had given a specimen of his future virtue to his subjects, and with what kind of moderation and good administration he would govern them, by that his first action, which concerned them, his own citizens, and God himself also, when he made the slaughter of three thousand of his own countrymen at the temple. How then could they avoid the just hatred of him, who, to the rest of his barbarity, hath added this as one of our crimes, that we have opposed and contradicted him in the exercise of his authority? Now the main thing they desired was this: That they might be delivered from kingly and the like forms of government,[20] and might be added to Syria, and be put under the authority of such presidents of theirs as should be sent to them; for that it would thereby be made evident, whether they be really a seditious people, and generally fond of innovations, or whether they would live in an orderly manner, if they might have governors of any sort of moderation set over them.

3. Now when the Jews had said this, Nicolaus vindicated the kings from those accusations, and said, that as for Herod, since he had never been thus accused all the time of his life, it was not fit for those that might have accused him of lesser crimes than those now mentioned, and might have procured him to be punished during his lifetime, to bring an accusation against him now he is dead. He also attributed the actions of Archlaus to the Jews' injuries to him, who, affecting to govern contrary to the laws, and going about to kill those that

20. If any one compare that Divine prediction concerning the tyrannical power which Jewish kings would exercise over them, if they would be so foolish as to prefer it before their ancient theocracy or aristocracy, 1 Samuel 8:1–22; Antiq. B. VI. ch. 4. sect. 4, he will soon find that it was superabundantly fulfilled in the days of Herod, and that to such a degree, that the nation now at last seem sorely to repent of such their ancient choice, in opposition to God's better choice for them, and had much rather be subject to even a pagan Roman government, and their deputies, than to be any longer under the oppression of the family of Herod; which request of theirs Augustus did not now grant them, but did it for the one half of that nation in a few years afterward, upon fresh complaints made by the Jews against Archelaus, who, under the more humble name of an ethnarch, which Augustus only would now allow him, soon took upon him the insolence and tyranny of his father king Herod, as the remaining part of this book will inform us, and particularly ch. 13. sect. 2.

would have hindered them from acting unjustly, when they were by him punished for what they had done, made their complaints against him; so he accused them of their attempts for innovation, and of the pleasure they took in sedition, by reason of their not having learned to submit to justice and to the laws, but still desiring to be superior in all things. This was the substance of what Nicolaus said.

4. When Caesar had heard these pleadings, he dissolved the assembly; but a few days afterwards he appointed Archelaus, not indeed to be king of the whole country, but ethnarch of the one half of that which had been subject to Herod, and promised to give him the royal dignity hereafter, if he governed his part virtuously. But as for the other half, he divided it into two parts, and gave it to two other of Herod's sons, to Philip and to Antipas, that Antipas who disputed with Archelaus for the whole kingdom. Now to him it was that Peres and Galilee paid their tribute, which amounted annually to two hundred talents,[21] while Batanea, with Trachonitis, as well as Auranitis, with a certain part of what was called the *House of Zenodorus*,[22] paid the tribute of one hundred talents to Philip; but Idumea, and Judea, and the country

---

21. This is not true. See Antiq. B. XIV. ch. 9. sect. 3, 4; and ch. 12. sect. 2; and ch. 13. sect. 1, 2. Antiq. B. XV. ch. 3. sect. 5; and ch. 10. sect. 2, 3. Antiq. B. XVI. ch. 9. sect. 3. Since Josephus here informs us that Archelaus had one half of the kingdom of Herod, and presently informs us further that Archelaus's annual income, after an abatement of one quarter for the present, was 600 talents, we may therefore ga ther pretty nearly what was Herod the Great's yearly income, I mean about 1600 talents, which, at the known value of 3000 shekels to a talent, and about 2s. 10d. to a shekel, in the days of Josephus, see the note on Antiq. B. III. ch. 8. sect. 2, amounts to 680,000 sterling per annum; which income, though great in itself, bearing no proportion to his vast expenses every where visible in Josephus, and to the vast sums he left behind him in his will, ch. 8. sect. 1, and ch. 12. sect. 1, the rest must have arisen either from his confiscation of those great men's estates whom he put to death, or made to pay fine for the saving of their lives, or from some other heavy methods of oppression which such savage tyrants usually exercise upon their miserable subjects; or rather from these several methods not together, all which yet seem very much too small for his expenses, being drawn from no larger a nation than that of the Jews, which was very populous, but without the advantage of trade to bring them riches; so that I cannot but strongly suspect that no small part of this his wealth arose from another source; I mean from some vast sums he took out of David's sepulcher, but concealed from the people. See the note on Antiq. B. VII. ch. 15. sect. 3.

22. Take here a very useful note of Grotias, on Luke 3:1, here quoted by Dr. Hudson: "When Josephus says that some part of the house (or possession) of Zenodorus (i.e. Abilene) was allotted to Philip, he thereby declares that the larger part of it belonged

of Samaria paid tribute to Archelaus, but had now a fourth part of that tribute taken off by the order of Caesar, who decreed them that mitigation, because they did not join in this revolt with the rest of the multitude. There were also certain of the cities which paid tribute to Archelaus: Strato's Tower and Sebaste, with Joppa and Jerusalem; for as to Gaza, and Gadara, and Hippos, they were Grecian cities, which Caesar separated from his government, and added them to the province of Syria. Now the tribute-money that came to Archelaus every year from his own dominions amounted to six hundred talents.

5. And so much came to Herod's sons from their father's inheritance. But Salome, besides what her brother left her by his testament, which were Jamnia, and Ashdod, and Phasaelis, and five hundred thousand [drachmae] of coined silver, Caesar made her a present of a royal habitation at Askelo; in all, her revenues amounted to sixty talents by the year, and her dwelling-house was within Archelaus's government. The rest also of the king's relations received what his testament allotted them. Moreover, Caesar made a present to each of Herod's two virgin daughters, besides what their father left them, of two hundred and fifty thousand [drachmae] of silver, and married them to Pheroras's sons: he also granted all that was bequeathed to himself to the king's sons, which was one thousand five hundred talents, excepting a few of the vessels, which he reserved for himself; and they were acceptable to him, not so much for the great value they were of, as because they were memorials of the king to him.

---

to another. This other was Lysanias, whom Luke mentions, of the posterity of that Lysanias who was possessed of the same country called Abilene, from the city Abila, and by others Chalcidene, from the city Chaleis, when the government of the East was under Antonius, and this after Ptolemy, the son of Menneus; from which Lysanias this country came to be commonly called the Country of Lysanias; and as, after the death of the former Lyanias, it was called the tetrarchy of Zenodorus, so, after the death of Zenodorus, or when the time for which he hired it was ended. when another Lysanias, of the same name with the former, was possessed of the same country, it began to be called the Tetrarchy of Lysanias." However, since Josephus elsewhere (Antiq. B. XX. ch. 7. sect. 1) clearly distinguishes Abilene from Cilalcidcue, Groius must be here so far mistaken.

12 *Concerning a Spurious Alexander*

1. WHEN these affairs had been thus settled by Caesar, a certain young man, by birth a Jew, but brought up by a Roman freed-man in the city Sidon, ingrafted himself into the kindred of Herod, by the resemblance of his countenance, which those that saw him attested to be that of Alexander, the son of Herod, whom he had slain; and this was an incitement to him to endeavor to obtain the government; so he took to him as an assistant a man of his own country, (one that was well acquainted with the affairs of the palace, but, on other accounts, an ill man, and one whose nature made him capable of causing great disturbances to the public, and one that became a teacher of such a mischievous contrivance to the other,) and declared himself to be Alexander, and the son of Herod, but stolen away. by one of those that were sent to slay him, who, in reality, slew other men, in order to deceive the spectators, but saved both him and his brother Aristobulus. Thus was this man elated, and able to impose on those that came to him; and when he was come to Crete, he made all the Jews that came to discourse with him believe him [to be Alexander]. And when he had gotten much money which had been presented to him there, he passed over to Melos, where he got much more money than he had before, out of the belief they had that he was of the royal family, and their hopes that he would recover his father's principality, and reward his benefactors; so he made haste to Rome, and was conducted thither by those strangers who entertained him. He was also so fortunate, as, upon his landing at Dicearchia, to bring the Jews that were there into the same delusion; and not only other people, but also all those that had been great with Herod, or had a kindness for him, joined themselves to this man as to their king. The cause of it was this, that men were glad of his pretenses, which were seconded by the likeness of his countenance, which made those that had been acquainted with Alexander strongly to believe that he was no other but the very same person, which they also confirmed to others by oath; insomuch that when the report went about him that he was coming to Rome, the whole multitude of the Jews that were there went out to meet him, ascribing it to Divine Providence that he has so unexpectedly escaped, and being very joyful on account of his mother's family. And when he was come, he was carried in a royal litter through the streets; and all

the ornaments about him were such as kings are adorned withal; and this was at the expense of those that entertained him. The multitude also flocked about him greatly, and made mighty acclamations to him, and nothing was omitted which could be thought suitable to such as had been so unexpectedly preserved.

2. When this thing was told Caesar, he did not believe it, because Herod was not easily to be imposed upon in such affairs as were of great concern to him; yet, having some suspicion it might be so, he sent one Celadus, a freed-man of his, and one that had conversed with the young men themselves, and bade him bring Alexander into his presence; so he brought him, being no more accurate in judging about him than the rest of the multitude. Yet did not he deceive Caesar; for although there was a resemblance between him and Alexander, yet was it not so exact as to impose on such as were prudent in discerning; for this spurious Alexander had his hands rough, by the labors he had been put to and instead of that softness of body which the other had, and this as derived from his delicate and generous education, this man, for the contrary reason, had a rugged body. When, therefore, Caesar saw how the master and the scholar agreed in this lying story, and in a bold way of talking, he inquired about Aristobulus, and asked what became of him who (it seems) was stolen away together with him, and for what reason it was that he did not come along with him, and endeavor to recover that dominion which was due to his high birth also. And when he said that he had been left in the isle of Crete, for fear of the dangers of the sea, that, in case any accident should come to himself, the posterity of Mariamne might not utterly perish, but that Aristobulus might survive, and punish those that laid such treacherous designs against them; and when he persevered in his affirmations, and the author of the imposture agreed in supporting it, Caesar took the young man by himself, and said to him, "If thou wilt not impose upon me, thou shalt have this for thy reward, that thou shalt escape with thy life; tell me, then, who thou art, and who it was that had boldness enough to contrive such a cheat as this. For this contrivance is too considerable a piece of villainy to be undertaken by one of thy age." Accordingly, because he had no other way to take, he told Caesar the contrivance, and after what manner and by whom it was laid together. So Caesar, upon observing the spurious Alexander to be a strong active man, and fit to work with his hands, that he might

not break his promise to him, put him among those that were to row among the mariners, but slew him that induced him to do what he had done; for as for the people of Melos, he thought them sufficiently punished, in having thrown away so much of their money upon this spurious Alexander. And such was the ignominious conclusion of this bold contrivance about the spurious Alexander.

13 *How Archelaus Upon a Second Accusation, Was Banished to Vienna*

1. WHEN Archelaus was entered on his ethnarchy, and was come into Judea, he accused Joazar, the son of Boethus, of assisting the seditious, and took away the high priesthood from him, and put Eleazar his brother in his place. He also magnificently rebuilt the royal palace that had been at Jericho, and he diverted half the water with which the village of Neara used to be watered, and drew off that water into the plain, to water those palm trees which he had there planted: he also built a village, and put his own name upon it, and called it Archelais. Moreover, he transgressed the law of our fathers[23] and married Glaphyra, the daughter of Archelaus, who had been the wife of his brother Alexander, which Alexander had three children by her, while it was a thing detestable among the Jews to marry the brother's wife. Nor did this Eleazar abide long in the high priesthood, Jesus, the son of Sie, being put in his room while he was still living.

2. But in the tenth year of Archelaus's government, both his brethren, and the principal men of Judea and Samaria, not being able to bear his barbarous and tyrannical usage of them, accused him before Caesar, and that especially because they knew he had broken the commands of Caesar, which obliged him to behave himself with moderation among them. Whereupon Caesar, when he heard it, was very angry, and called for Archelaus's steward, who took care of his affairs at Rome, and whose name was Archelaus also; and thinking it beneath him to write to Archelaus, he bid him sail away as soon as possible, and bring him to us: so the man made haste in his voyage,

23. Spanheim seasonably observes here, that it was forbidden the Jews to marry their brother's wife when she had children by her first husband, and that Zonaras (cites, or) interprets the clause before us accordingly.

and when he came into Judea, he found Archelaus feasting with his friends; so he told him what Caesar had sent him about, and hastened him away. And when he was come [to Rome], Caesar, upon hearing what certain accusers of his had to say, and what reply he could make, both banished him, and appointed Vienna, a city of Gaul, to be the place of his habitation, and took his money away from him.

3. Now, before Archelaus was gone up to Rome upon this message, he related this dream to his friends: That he saw ears of corn, in number ten, full of wheat, perfectly ripe, which ears, as it seemed to him, were devoured by oxen. And when he was awake and gotten up, because the vision appeared to beof great importance to him, he sent for the diviners, whose study was employed about dreams. And while some were of one opinion, and some of another, (for all their interpretations did not agree,) Simon, a man of the sect of the Essens, desired leave to speak his mind freely, and said that the vision denoted a change in the affairs of Archelaus, and that not for the better; that oxen, because that animal takes uneasy pains in his labors, denoted afflictions, and indeed denoted, further, a change of affairs, because that land which is ploughed by oxen cannot remain in its former state; and that the ears of corn being ten, determined the like number of years, because an ear of corn grows in one year; and that the time of Archelaus's government was over. And thus did this man expound the dream. Now on the fifth day after this dream came first to Archelaus, the other Archelaus, that was sent to Judea by Caesar to call him away, came hither also.

4. The like accident befell Glaphyra his wife, who was the daughter of king Archelaus, who, as I said before, was married, while she was a virgin, to Alexander, the son of Herod, and brother of Archelaus; but since it fell out so that Alexander was slain by his father, she was married to Juba, the king of Lybia; and when he was dead, and she lived in widowhood in Cappadocia with her father, Archclaus divorced his former wife Mariamne, and married her, so great was his affection for this Glphyra; who, during her marriage to him, saw the following dream: She thought she saw Alexander standing by her, at which she rejoiced, and embraced him with great affection; but that he complained o her, and said, O Glaphyra! thou provest that saying to be true, which assures us that women are not to be trusted. Didst not thou pledge thy faith to me? and wast not thou married to me when

thou wast a virgin? and had we not children between us? Yet hast thou forgotten the affection I bare to thee, out of a desire of a second husband. Nor hast thou been satisfied with that injury thou didst me, but thou hast been so bold as to procure thee a third husband to lie by thee, and in an indecent and imprudent manner hast entered into my house, and hast been married to Archelaus, thy husband and my brother. However, I will not forget thy former kind affection for me, but will set thee free from every such reproachful action, and cause thee to be mine again, as thou once wast. When she had related this to her female companions, in a few days' time she departed this life.

5. Now I did not think these histories improper for the present discourse, both because my discourse now is concerning kings, and otherwise also on account of the advantage hence to be drawn, as well for the confirmation of the immortality of the soul, as of the providence of God over human affairs, I thought them fit to be set down; but if any one does not believe such relations, let him indeed enjoy his own opinion, but let him not hinder another that would thereby encourage himself in virtue. So Archelaus's country was laid to the province of Syria; and Cyrenius, one that had been consul, was sent by Caesar to take account of people's effects in Syria, and to sell the house of Archelaus.

Book 18

Containing the Interval of Thirty-Two Years, from the Banishment of Archelus to the Departure from Babylon

1 *How Cyrenius Was Sent by Caesar to Make a Taxation of Syria and Judea; and How Coponius Was Sent to Be Procurator of Judea; Concerning Judas of Galilee and Concerning the Sects That Were Among the Jews*

1. NOW Cyrenius, a Roman senator, and one who had gone through other magistracies, and had passed through them till he had been consul, and one who, on other accounts, was of great dignity, came at this time into Syria, with a few others, being sent by Caesar to be a judge of that nation, and to take an account of their substance. Coponius also, a man of the equestrian order, was sent together with him, to have the supreme power over the Jews. Moreover, Cyrenius came himself into Judea, which was now added to the province of Syria, to take an account of their substance, and to dispose of Archelaus's money; but the Jews, although at the beginning they took the report of a taxation heinously, yet did they leave off any further opposition to it, by the persuasion of Joazar, who was the son of Beethus, and high priest; so they, being over-pesuaded by Joazar's words, gave an account of their estates, without any dispute about it. Yet was there one Judas, a Gaulonite,[1] of a city whose name was

1. Since St. Luke once, Acts 5:37, and Josephus four several times, once here, sect. 6; and B. XX. ch. 5. sect. 2; Of the War, B. II. ch. 8. sect. 1; and ch. 17. sect. 8, calls

Gamala, who, taking with him Sadduc,[2] a Pharisee, became zealous to draw them to a revolt, who both said that this taxation was no better than an introduction to slavery, and exhorted the nation to assert their liberty; as if they could procure them happiness and security for what they possessed, and an assured enjoyment of a still greater good, which was that of the honor and glory they would thereby acquire for magnanimity. They also said that God would not otherwise be assisting to them, than upon their joining with one another in such councils as might be successful, and for their own advantage; and this especially, if they would set about great exploits, and not grow weary in executing the same; so men received what they said with pleasure, and this bold attempt proceeded to a great height. All sorts of misfortunes also sprang from these men, and the nation was infected with this doctrine to an incredible degree; one violent war came upon us after another, and we lost our friends which used to alleviate our pains; there were also very great robberies and murder of our principal men. This was done in pretense indeed for the public welfare, but in reality for the hopes of gain to themselves; whence arose seditions, and from them murders of men, which sometimes fell

---

this Judas, who was the pestilent author of that seditious doctrine and temper which brought the Jewish nation to utter destruction, a Galilean; but here (sect. 1) Josephus calls him a Gaulonite, of the city of Gamala; it is a great question where this Judas was born, whether in Galilee on the west side, or in Gaulonitis on the east side, of the river Jordan; while, in the place just now cited out of the Antiquities, B. XX. ch. 5. sect. 2, he is not only called a Galilean, but it is added to his story, "as I have signified in the books that go before these," as if he had still called him a Galilean in those Antiquities before, as well as in that particular place, as Dean Aldrich observes, Of the War, B. II. ch. 8. sect. 1. Nor can one well imagine why he should here call him a Gaulonite, when in the 6th sect. following here, as well as twice Of the War, he still calls him a Galilean. As for the city of Gamala, whence this Judas was derived, it determines nothing, since there were two of that name, the one in Gaulonitis, the other in Galilee. See Reland on the city or town of that name.

2. It seems not very improbable to me that this Sadduc, the Pharisee, was the very same man of whom the Rabbins speak, as the unhappy, but undesigning, occasion of the impiety or infidelity of the Sadducees; nor perhaps had the men this name of Sadducees till this very time, though they were a distinct sect long before. See the note on B. XIII. ch. 10. sect 5; and Dean Prideaux, as there quoted. Nor do we, that I know of, find the least footsteps of such impiety or infidelity of these Sadducees before this time, the Recognitions assuring us that they began about the days of John the Baptist; B. 1. ch. 54. See note above.

on those of their own people, (by the madness of these men towards one another, while their desire was that none of the adverse party might be left,) and sometimes on their enemies; a famine also coming upon us, reduced us to the last degree of despair, as did also the taking and demolishing of cities; nay, the sedition at last increased so high, that the very temple of God was burnt down by their enemies' fire. Such were the consequences of this, that the customs of our fathers were altered, and such a change was made, as added a mighty weight toward bringing all to destruction, which these men occasioned by their thus conspiring together; for Judas and Sadduc, who excited a fourth philosophic sect among us, and had a great many followers therein, filled our civil government with tumults at present, and laid the foundations of our future miseries, by this system of philosophy, which we were before unacquainted withal, concerning which I will discourse a little, and this the rather because the infection which spread thence among the younger sort, who were zealous for it, brought the public to destruction.

2. The Jews had for a great while had three sects of philosophy peculiar to themselves; the sect of the Essens, and the sect of the Sadducees, and the third sort of opinions was that of those called Pharisees; of which sects, although I have already spoken in the second book of the Jewish War, yet will I a little touch upon them now.

3. Now, for the Pharisees, they live meanly, and despise delicacies in diet; and they follow the conduct of reason; and what that prescribes to them as good for them they do; and they think they ought earnestly to strive to observe reason's dictates for practice. They also pay a respect to such as are in years; nor are they so bold as to contradict them in any thing which they have introduced; and when they determine that all things are done by fate, they do not take away the freedom from men of acting as they think fit; since their notion is, that it hath pleased God to make a temperament, whereby what he wills is done, but so that the will of man can act virtuously or viciously. They also believe that souls have an immortal rigor in them, and that under the earth there will be rewards or punishments, according as they have lived virtuously or viciously in this life; and the latter are to be detained in an everlasting prison, but that the former shall have power to revive and live again; on account of which doctrines they are able greatly to persuade the body of the people; and whatsoever they do about Divine worship,

prayers, and sacrifices, they perform them according to their direction; insomuch that the cities give great attestations to them on account of their entire virtuous conduct, both in the actions of their lives and their discourses also.

4. But the doctrine of the Sadducees is this: That souls die with the bodies; nor do they regard the observation of any thing besides what the law enjoins them; for they think it an instance of virtue to dispute with those teachers of philosophy whom they frequent: but this doctrine is received but by a few, yet by those still of the greatest dignity. But they are able to do almost nothing of themselves; for when they become magistrates, as they are unwillingly and by force sometimes obliged to be, they addict themselves to the notions of the Pharisees, because the multitude would not otherwise bear them.

5. The doctrine of the Essens is this: That all things are best ascribed to God. They teach the immortality of souls, and esteem that the rewards of righteousness are to be earnestly striven for; and when they send what they have dedicated to God into the temple, they do not offer sacrifices[3] because they have more pure lustrations of their own; on which account they are excluded from the common court of the temple, but offer their sacrifices themselves; yet is their course of life better than that of other men; and they entirely addict themselves to husbandry. It also deserves our admiration, how much they exceed all other men that addict themselves to virtue, and this in righteousness; and indeed to such a degree, that as it hath never appeared among any other men, neither Greeks nor barbarians, no, not for a little time, so hath it endured a long while among them. This is demonstrated by that institution of theirs, which will not suffer any thing to hinder them from having all things in common; so that a rich man enjoys no more of his own wealth than he who hath nothing at all. There are about four thousand men that live in this way, and neither marry wives, nor are desirous to keep servants; as thinking the latter tempts

---

3. It seems by what Josephus says here, and Philo himself elsewhere, Op. p. 679, that these Essens did not use to go to the Jewish festivals at Jerusalem, or to offer sacrifices there, which may be one great occasion why they are never mentioned in the ordinary books of the New Testament; though, in the Apostolical Constitutions, they are mentioned as those that observed the customs of their forefathers, and that without any such ill character laid upon them as is there laid upon the other sects among that people.

men to be unjust, and the former gives the handle to domestic quarrels; but as they live by themselves, they minister one to another. They also appoint certain stewards to receive the incomes of their revenues, and of the fruits of the ground; such as are good men and priests, who are to get their corn and their food ready for them. They none of them differ from others of the Essens in their way of living, but do the most resemble those Dacae who are called Polistae[4] [dwellers in cities].

6. But of the fourth sect of Jewish philosophy, Judas the Galilean was the author. These men agree in all other things with the Pharisaic notions; but they have an inviolable attachment to liberty, and say that God is to be their only Ruler and Lord. They also do not value dying any kinds of death, nor indeed do they heed the deaths of their relations and friends, nor can any such fear make them call any man lord. And since this immovable resolution of theirs is well known to a great many, I shall speak no further about that matter; nor am I afraid that any thing I have said of them should be disbelieved, but rather fear, that what I have said is beneath the resolution they show when they undergo pain. And it was in Gessius Florus's time that the nation began to grow mad with this distemper, who was our procurator, and who occasioned the Jews to go wild with it by the abuse of his authority, and to make them revolt from the Romans. And these are the sects of Jewish philosophy.

2 *Now Herod and Philip Built Several Cities in Honor of Caesar. Concerning the Succession of Priests and Procurators; as Also What Befell Phraates and the Parthians*

1. WHEN Cyrenius had now disposed of Archelaus's money, and when the taxings were come to a conclusion, which were made in the thirty-seventh year of Caesar's victory over Antony at Actium, he deprived Joazar of the high priesthood, which dignity had been conferred on him by the multitude, and he appointed Ananus, the son of Seth, to be high priest; while Herod and Philip had each of them

4. Who these Polistae in Josephus, or in Strabo. among the Pythagoric Dacae, were, it is not easy to determine. Scaliger offers no improbable conjecture, that some of these Dacae lived alone, like monks, in tents or caves; but that others of them lived together in built cities, and thence were called by such names as implied the same.

received their own tetrarchy, and settled the affairs thereof. Herod also built a wall about Sepphoris, (which is the security of all Galilee,) and made it the metropolis of the country. He also built a wall round Betharamphtha, which was itself a city also, and called it Julias, from the name of the emperor's wife. When Philip also had built Paneas, a city at the fountains of Jordan, he named it Cesarea. He also advanced the village Bethsaids, situate at the lake of Gennesareth, unto the dignity of a city, both by the number of inhabitants it contained, and its other grandeur, and called it by the name of Julias, the same name with Caesar's daughter.

2. As Coponius, who we told you was sent along with Cyrenius, was exercising his office of procurator, and governing Judea, the following accidents happened. As the Jews were celebrating the feast of unleavened bread, which we call the Passover, it was customary for the priests to open the temple-gates just after midnight. When, therefore, those gates were first opened, some of the Samaritans came privately into Jerusalem, and threw about dead men's bodies, in the cloisters; on which account the Jews afterward excluded them out of the temple, which they had not used to do at such festivals; and on other accounts also they watched the temple more carefully than they had formerly done. A little after which accident Coponius returned to Rome, and Marcus Ambivius came to be his successor in that government; under whom Salome, the sister of king Herod, died, and left to Julia, [Caesar's wife,] Jamnia, all its toparchy, and Phasaelis in the plain, and Arehelais, where is a great plantation of palm trees, and their fruit is excellent in its kind. After him came Annius Rufus, under whom died Caesar, the second emperor of the Romans, the duration of whose reign was fifty-seven years, besides six months and two days (of which time Antonius ruled together with him fourteen years; but the duration of his life was seventy-seven years); upon whose death Tiberius Nero, his wife Julia's son, succeeded. He was now the third emperor; and he sent Valerius Gratus to be procurator of Judea, and to succeed Annius Rufus. This man deprived Ananus of the high priesthood, and appointed Ismael, the son of Phabi, to be high priest. He also deprived him in a little time, and ordained Eleazar, the son of Ananus, who had been high priest before, to be high priest; which office, when he had held for a year, Gratus deprived him of it, and gave the high priesthood to Simon, the son of Camithus; and when

he had possessed that dignity no longer than a year, Joseph Caiaphas was made his successor. When Gratus had done those things, he went back to Rome, after he had tarried in Judea eleven years, when Pontius Pilate came as his successor.

3. And now Herod the tetrarch, who was in great favor with Tiberius, built a city of the same name with him, and called it Tiberias. He built it in the best part of Galilee, at the lake of Gennesareth. There are warm baths at a little distance from it, in a village named Emmaus. Strangers came and inhabited this city; a great number of the inhabitants were Galileans also; and many were necessitated by Herod to come thither out of the country belonging to him, and were by force compelled to be its inhabitants; some of them were persons of condition. He also admitted poor people, such as those that were collected from all parts, to dwell in it. Nay, some of them were not quite free-men, and these he was benefactor to, and made them free in great numbers; but obliged them not to forsake the city, by building them very good houses at his own expenses, and by giving them land also; for he was sensible, that to make this place a habitation was to transgress the Jewish ancient laws, because many sepulchers were to be here taken away, in order to make room for the city Tiberias[5] whereas our laws pronounce that such inhabitants are unclean for seven days.[6]

4. About this time died Phraates, king of the Parthians, by the treachery of Phraataces his son, upon the occasion following: When Phraates had had legitimate sons of his own, he had also an Italian maid-servant, whose name was Thermusa, who had been formerly sent to him by Julius Caesar, among other presents. He first made her his concubine; but he being a great admirer of her beauty, in process of time having a son by her, whose name was Phraataces, he made her his legitimate wife, and had a great respect for her. Now she was able to persuade him to do any thing that she said, and was earnest

5. We may here take notice, as well as in the parallel parts of the books Of the War, B. II. ch. 9. sect. 1, that after the death of Herod the Great, and the succession of Archclaus, Josephus is very brief in his accounts of Judea, till near his own time. I suppose the reason is, that after the large history of Nicolaus of Damascus, including the life of Herod, and probably the succession and first actions of his sons, he had but few good histories of those times before him.

6. Numbers 19:11–14.

in procuring the government of Parthia for her son; but still she saw that her endeavors would not succeed, unless she could contrive how to remove Phraates's legitimate sons [out of the kingdom;] so she persuaded him to send those his sons as pledges of his fidelity to Rome; and they were sent to Rome accordingly, because it was not easy for him to contradict her commands. Now while Phraataces was alone brought up in order to succeed in the government, he thought it very tedious to expect that government by his father's donation [as his successor]; he therefore formed a treacherous design against his father, by his mother's assistance, with whom, as the report went, he had criminal conversation also. So he was hated for both these vices, while his subjects esteemed this [wicked] love of his mother to be no way inferior to his parricide; and he was by them, in a sedition, expelled out of the country before he grew too great, and died. But as the best sort of Parthians agreed together that it was impossible they should be governed without a king, while also it was their constant practice to choose one of the family of Arsaces, [nor did their law allow of any others; and they thought this kingdom had been sufficiently injured already by the marriage with an Italian concubine, and by her issue,] they sent ambassadors, and called Orodes [to take the crown]; for the multitude would not otherwise have borne them; and though he was accused of very great cruelty, and was of an untractable temper, and prone to wrath, yet still he was one of the family of Arsaces. However, they made a conspiracy against him, and slew him, and that, as some say, at a festival, and among their sacrifices; (for it is the universal custom there to carry their swords with them;) but, as the more general report is, they slew him when they had drawn him out a hunting. So they sent ambassadors to Rome, and desired they would send one of those that were there as pledges to be their king. Accordingly, Vonones was preferred before the rest, and sent to them (for he seemed capable of such great fortune, which two of the greatest kingdoms under the sun now offered him, his own and a foreign one). However, the barbarians soon changed their minds, they being naturally of a mutable disposition, upon the supposal that this man was not worthy to be their governor; for they could not think of obeying the commands of one that had been a slave, (for so they called those that had been hostages,) nor could they bear the ignominy of that name; and this was the more intolerable, because then the Parthians must have such a king set over them, not by right of war, but in time of peace. So they presently invited Artabanus, king of Media, to be their king, he being also of the race of Arsaces. Artabanus complied with the offer that was made him, and came to them with an army. So Vonones met him; and at first the multitude of the Parthians stood on this side, and he put his army in array; but Artabanus was beaten, and fled to the mountains of Media. Yet did he a little after gather a great army together, and fought with Vonones, and beat him; whereupon Vonones fled away on horseback, with a few of his attendants about him, to Seleucia [upon Tigris]. So when Artabanus had slain a great number, and this after he had gotten the victory by reason of the very great dismay the barbarians were in, he retired to Ctesiphon with a great number of his people; and so he now reigned over the Parthians. But Vonones fled away to Armenia; and as soon as he came thither, he had an inclination to have the government of the country given him, and sent ambassadors to Rome [for that purpose]. But because Tiberius refused it him, and because he wanted courage, and because the Parthian king threatened him, and sent ambassadors to him to denounce war against him if he proceeded, and because he had no way to take to regain any other kingdom, (for the people of authority among the Armenians about Niphates joined themselves to Artabanus,) he delivered up himself to Silanus, the president of Syria, who, out of regard to his education at Rome, kept him in Syria, while Artabanus gave Armenia to Orodes, one of his own sons.

5. At this time died Antiochus, the king of Commagene; whereupon the multitude contended with the nobility, and both sent ambassadors to [Rome]; for the men of power were desirous that their form of government might be changed into that of a [Roman] province; as were the multitude desirous to be under kings, as their fathers had been. So the senate made a decree that Germanicus should be sent to settle the affairs of the East, fortune hereby taking a proper opportunity for depriving him of his life; for when he had been in the East, and settled all affairs there, his life was taken away by the poison which Piso gave him, as hath been related elsewhere.[7]

7. This citation is now wanting.

3 *Sedition of the Jews Against Pontius Pilate. Concerning Christ, and What Befell Paulina and the Jews at Rome,*

1. BUT now Pilate, the procurator of Judea, removed the army from Cesarea to Jerusalem, to take their winter quarters there, in order to abolish the Jewish laws. So he introduced Caesar's effigies, which were upon the ensigns, and brought them into the city; whereas our law forbids us the very making of images; on which account the former procurators were wont to make their entry into the city with such ensigns as had not those ornaments. Pilate was the first who brought those images to Jerusalem, and set them up there; which was done without the knowledge of the people, because it was done in the night time; but as soon as they knew it, they came in multitudes to Cesarea, and interceded with Pilate many days that he would remove the images; and when he would not grant their requests, because it would tend to the injury of Caesar, while yet they persevered in their request, on the sixth day he ordered his soldiers to have their weapons privately, while he came and sat upon his judgment-seat, which seat was so prepared in the open place of the city, that it concealed the army that lay ready to oppress them; and when the Jews petitioned him again, he gave a signal to the soldiers to encompass them routed, and threatened that their punishment should be no less than immediate death, unless they would leave off disturbing him, and go their ways home. But they threw themselves upon the ground, and laid their necks bare, and said they would take their death very willingly, rather than the wisdom of their laws should be transgressed; upon which Pilate was deeply affected with their firm resolution to keep their laws inviolable, and presently commanded the images to be carried back from Jerusalem to Cesarea.

2. But Pilate undertook to bring a current of water to Jerusalem, and did it with the sacred money, and derived the origin of the stream from the distance of two hundred furlongs. However, the Jews[8] were

---

8. These Jews, as they are here called, whose blood Pilate shed on this occasion, may very well be those very Galilean Jews, "whose blood Pilate had mingled with their sacrifices," Luke 13:1, 2; these tumults being usually excited at some of the Jews' great festivals, when they slew abundance of sacrifices, and the Galileans being commonly much more busy in such tumults than those of Judea and Jerusalem, as we

not pleased with what had been done about this water; and many ten thousands of the people got together, and made a clamor against him, and insisted that he should leave off that design. Some of them also used reproaches, and abused the man, as crowds of such people usually do. So he habited a great number of his soldiers in their habit, who carried daggers under their garments, and sent them to a place where they might surround them. So he bid the Jews himself go away; but they boldly casting reproaches upon him, he gave the soldiers that signal which had been beforehand agreed on; who laid upon them much greater blows than Pilate had commanded them, and equally punished those that were tumultuous, and those that were not; nor did they spare them in the least: and since the people were unarmed, and were caught by men prepared for what they were about, there were a great number of them slain by this means, and others of them ran away wounded. And thus an end was put to this sedition.

3. Now there was about this time Jesus, a wise man, if it be lawful to call him a man; for he was a doer of wonderful works, a teacher of such men as receive the truth with pleasure. He drew over to him both many of the Jews and many of the Gentiles. He was [the] Christ. And when Pilate, at the suggestion of the principal men amongst us, had condemned him to the cross,[9] those that loved him at the first did not forsake him; for he appeared to them alive again the third day;[10] as the divine prophets had foretold these and ten thousand other wonderful things concerning him. And the tribe of Christians, so named from him, are not extinct at this day.

---

learn from the history of Archelaus, Antiq. B. XVII. ch. 9. sect. 3 and ch. 10. sect. 2, 9; though, indeed, Josephus's present copies say not one word of "those eighteen upon whom the tower in Siloam fell, and slew them," which the 4th verse of the same 13th chapter of St. Luke informs us of. But since our gospel teaches us, Luke 23:6, 7, that "when Pilate heard of Galilee, he asked whether Jesus were a Galilean. And as soon as he knew that he belonged to Herod's jurisdiction, he sent him to Herod;" and ver. 12, "The same day Pilate and Herod were made friends together for before they had been at enmity between themselves;" take the very probable key of this matter in the words of the learned Noldius, de Herod. No. 219: "The cause of the enmity between Herod and Pilate (says he) seems to have been this, that Pilate had intermeddled with the tetrarch's jurisdiction, and had slain some of his Galilean subjects, Luke 13:1; and, as he was willing to correct that error, he sent Christ to Herod at this time."

9. A.D. 33, April 3.

10. April 5.

4. About the same time also another sad calamity put the Jews into disorder, and certain shameful practices happened about the temple of Isis that was at Rome. I will now first take notice of the wicked attempt about the temple of Isis, and will then give an account of the Jewish affairs. There was at Rome a woman whose name was Paulina; one who, on account of the dignity of her ancestors, and by the regular conduct of a virtuous life, had a great reputation: she was also very rich; and although she was of a beautiful countenance, and in that flower of her age wherein women are the most gay, yet did she lead a life of great modesty. She was married to Saturninus, one that was every way answerable to her in an excellent character. Decius Mundus fell in love with this woman, who was a man very high in the equestrian order; and as she was of too great dignity to be caught by presents, and had already rejected them, though they had been sent in great abundance, he was still more inflamed with love to her, insomuch that he promised to give her two hundred thousand Attic drachmae for one night's lodging; and when this would not prevail upon her, and he was not able to bear this misfortune in his amours, he thought it the best way to famish himself to death for want of food, on account of Paulina's sad refusal; and he determined with himself to die after such a manner, and he went on with his purpose accordingly. Now Mundus had a freed-woman, who had been made free by his father, whose name was Ide, one skillful in all sorts of mischief. This woman was very much grieved at the young man's resolution to kill himself, (for he did not conceal his intentions to destroy himself from others,) and came to him, and encouraged him by her discourse, and made him to hope, by some promises she gave him, that he might obtain a night's lodging with Paulina; and when he joyfully hearkened to her entreaty, she said she wanted no more than fifty thousand drachmae for the entrapping of the woman. So when she had encouraged the young man, and gotten as much money as she required, she did not take the same methods as had been taken before, because she perceived that the woman was by no means to be tempted by money; but as she knew that she was very much given to the worship of the goddess Isis, she devised the following stratagem: She went to some of Isis's priests, and upon the strongest assurances [of concealment], she persuaded them by words, but chiefly by the offer of money, of twenty-five thousand drachmae in hand, and as

much more when the thing had taken effect; and told them the passion of the young man, and persuaded them to use all means possible to beguile the woman. So they were drawn in to promise so to do, by that large sum of gold they were to have. Accordingly, the oldest of them went immediately to Paulina; and upon his admittance, he desired to speak with her by herself. When that was granted him, he told her that he was sent by the god Anubis, who was fallen in love with her, and enjoined her to come to him. Upon this she took the message very kindly, and valued herself greatly upon this condescension of Anubis, and told her husband that she had a message sent her, and was to sup and lie with Anubis; so he agreed to her acceptance of the offer, as fully satisfied with the chastity of his wife. Accordingly, she went to the temple, and after she had supped there, and it was the hour to go to sleep, the priest shut the doors of the temple, when, in the holy part of it, the lights were also put out. Then did Mundus leap out, (for he was hidden therein,) and did not fail of enjoying her, who was at his service all the night long, as supposing he was the god; and when he was gone away, which was before those priests who knew nothing of this stratagem were stirring, Paulina came early to her husband, and told him how the god Anubis had appeared to her. Among her friends, also, she declared how great a value she put upon this favor, who partly disbelieved the thing, when they reflected on its nature, and partly were amazed at it, as having no pretense for not believing it, when they considered the modesty and the dignity of the person. But now, on the third day after what had been done, Mundus met Paulina, and said, "Nay, Paulina, thou hast saved me two hundred thousand drachmae, which sum thou sightest have added to thy own family; yet hast thou not failed to be at my service in the manner I invited thee. As for the reproaches thou hast laid upon Mundus, I value not the business of names; but I rejoice in the pleasure I reaped by what I did, while I took to myself the name of Anubis." When he had said this, he went his way. But now she began to come to the sense of the grossness of what she had done, and rent her garments, and told her husband of the horrid nature of this wicked contrivance, and prayed him not to neglect to assist her in this case. So he discovered the fact to the emperor; whereupon Tiberius inquired into the matter thoroughly by examining the priests about it, and ordered them to be crucified, as well as Ide, who was the occasion of their perdition, and who had contrived the whole matter, which was so injurious to the woman. He also demolished the temple of Isis, and gave order that her statue should be thrown into the river Tiber; while he only banished Mundus, but did no more to him, because he supposed that what crime he had committed was done out of the passion of love. And these were the circumstances which concerned the temple of Isis, and the injuries occasioned by her priests. I now return to the relation of what happened about this time to the Jews at Rome, as I formerly told you I would.

5. There was a man who was a Jew, but had been driven away from his own country by an accusation laid against him for transgressing their laws, and by the fear he was under of punishment for the same; but in all respects a wicked man. He, then living at Rome, professed to instruct men in the wisdom of the laws of Moses. He procured also three other men, entirely of the same character with himself, to be his partners. These men persuaded Fulvia, a woman of great dignity, and one that had embraced the Jewish religion, to send purple and gold to the temple at Jerusalem; and when they had gotten them, they employed them for their own uses, and spent the money themselves, on which account it was that they at first required it of her. Whereupon Tiberius, who had been informed of the thing by Saturninus, the husband of Fulvia, who desired inquiry might be made about it, ordered all the Jews to be banished out of Rome; at which time the consuls listed four thousand men out of them, and sent them to the island Sardinia; but punished a greater number of them, who were unwilling to become soldiers, on account of keeping the laws of their forefathers.[11] Thus were these Jews banished out of

11. Of the banishment of these four thousand Jews into Sardinia by Tiberius, see Suetonlus in Tiber. sect. 36. But as for Mr. Reland's note here, which supposes that Jews could not, consistently with their laws, be soldiers, it is contradicted by one branch of the history before us, and contrary to innumerable instances of their fighting, and proving excellent soldiers in war; and indeed many of the best of them, and even under heathen kings themselves, did so; those, I mean, who allowed them their rest on the sabbath day, and other solemn festivals, and let them live according to their own laws, as Alexander the Great and the Ptolemies of Egypt did. It is true, they could not always obtain those privileges, and then they got executed as well as they could, or sometimes absolutely refused to fight, which seems to have been the case here, as to the major part of the Jews now banished, but nothing more. See several of the Roman decrees in their favor as to such matters, B. XIV. ch. 10.

the city by the wickedness of four men.

4 *How the Samaritans Made a Tumult and Pilate Destroyed Many of Them; How Pilate Was Accused and What Things Were Done by Vitellius Relating to the Jews and the Parthians*

1. BUT the nation of the Samaritans did not escape without tumults. The man who excited them to it was one who thought lying a thing of little consequence, and who contrived every thing so that the multitude might be pleased; so he bid them to get together upon Mount Gerizzim, which is by them looked upon as the most holy of all mountains, and assured them, that when they were come thither, he would show them those sacred vessels which were laid under that place, because Moses put them there[12] So they came thither armed, and thought the discourse of the man probable; and as they abode at a certain village, which was called Tirathaba, they got the rest together to them, and desired to go up the mountain in a great multitude together; but Pilate prevented their going up, by seizing upon file roads with a great band of horsemen and foot-men, who fell upon those that were gotten together in the village; and when it came to an action, some of them they slew, and others of them they put to flight, and took a great many alive, the principal of which, and also the most potent of those that fled away, Pilate ordered to be slain.

2. But when this tumult was appeased, the Samaritan senate sent an embassy to Vitellius, a man that had been consul, and who was now president of Syria, and accused Pilate of the murder of those that were killed; for that they did not go to Tirathaba in order to revolt from the Romans, but to escape the violence of Pilate. So Vitellius sent Marcellus, a friend of his, to take care of the affairs of Judea, and ordered Pilate to go to Rome, to answer before the emperor to

---

12. Since Moses never came himself beyond Jordan, nor particularly to Mount Gerizzim, and since these Samaritans have a tradition among them, related here by Dr. Hudson, from Reland, who was very skillful in Jewish and Samaritan learning, that in the days of Uzzi or Ozis the high priest, 1 Chronicles 6:6; the ark and other sacred vessels were, by God's command, laid up or hidden in Mount Gerizzim, it is highly probable that this was the foolish foundation the present Samaritans went upon, in the sedition here described.

the accusations of the Jews. So Pilate, when he had tarried ten years in Judea, made haste to Rome, and this in obedience to the orders of Vitellius, which he durst not contradict; but before he could get to Rome Tiberius was dead.

3. But Vitellius came into Judea, and went up to Jerusalem; it was at the time of that festival which is called the Passover. Vitellius was there magnificently received, and released the inhabitants of Jerusalem from all the taxes upon the fruits that were bought and sold, and gave them leave to have the care of the high priest's vestments, with all their ornaments, and to have them under the custody of the priests in the temple, which power they used to have formerly, although at this time they were laid up in the tower of Antonia, the citadel so called, and that on the occasion following: There was one of the [high] priests, named Hyrcanus; and as there were many of that name, he was the first of them; this man built a tower near the temple, and when he had so done, he generally dwelt in it, and had these vestments with him, because it was lawful for him alone to put them on, and he had them there reposited when he went down into the city, and took his ordinary garments; the same things were continued to be done by his sons, and by their sons after them. But when Herod came to be king, he rebuilt this tower, which was very conveniently situated, in a magnificent manner; and because he was a friend to Antonius, he called it by the name of Antonia. And as he found these vestments lying there, he retained them in the same place, as believing, that while he had them in his custody, the people would make no innovations against him. The like to what Herod did was done by his son Archelaus, who was made king after him; after whom the Romans, when they entered on the government, took possession of these vestments of the high priest, and had them reposited in a stone-chamber, under the seal of the priests, and of the keepers of the temple, the captain of the guard lighting a lamp there every day; and seven days before a festival[13]

13. This mention of the high priest's sacred garments received seven days before a festival, and purified in those days against a festival, as having been polluted by being in the custody of heathens, in Josephus, agrees well with the traditions of the Talmudists, as Reland here observes. Nor is there any question but the three feasts here mentioned were the passover, pentecost, and feast of tabernacles; and the fast so called by way of distinction, as Acts 27:9, was the great day of expiation.

they were delivered to them by the captain of the guard, when the high priest having purified them, and made use of them, laid them up again in the same chamber where they had been laid up before, and this the very next day after the feast was over. This was the practice at the three yearly festivals, and on the fast day; but Vitellius put those garments into our own power, as in the days of our forefathers, and ordered the captain of the guard not to trouble himself to inquire where they were laid, or when they were to be used; and this he did as an act of kindness, to oblige the nation to him. Besides which, he also deprived Joseph, who was also called Caiaphas, of the high priesthood, and appointed Jonathan the son of Ananus, the former high priest, to succeed him. After which, he took his journey back to Antioch.

4. Moreover, Tiberius sent a letter to Vitellius, and commanded him to make a league of friendship with Artabanus, the king of Parthia; for while he was his enemy, he terrified him, because he had taken Armenia away from him, lest he should proceed further, and told him he should no otherwise trust him than upon his giving him hostages, and especially his son Artabanus. Upon Tiberius's writing thus to Vitellius, by the offer of great presents of money, he persuaded both the king of Iberia and the king of Albania to make no delay, but to fight against Artabanus; and although they would not do it themselves, yet did they give the Scythians a passage through their country, and opened the Caspian gates to them, and brought them upon Artabanus. So Armenia was again taken from the Parthians, and the country of Parthis was filled with war, and the principal of their men were slain, and all things were in disorder among them: the king's son also himself fell in these wars, together with. many ten thousands of his army. Vitellius had also sent such great sums of money to Artabanus's father's kinsmen and friends, that he had almost procured him to be slain by the means of those bribes which they had taken. And when Artabanus perceived that the plot laid against him was not to be avoided, because it was laid by the principal men, and those a great many in number, and that it would certainly take effect,—when he had estimated the number of those that were truly faithful to him, as also of those who were already corrupted, but were deceitful in the kindness they professed to him, and were likely, upon trial, to go over to his enemies, he made his escape to the upper provinces, where he

afterwards raised a great army out of the Dahae and Sacre, and fought with his enemies, and retained his principality.

5. When Tiberius had heard of these things, he desired to have a league of friendship made between him and Artabanus; and when, upon this invitation, he received the proposal kindly, Artabanus and Vitellius went to Euphrates, and as a bridge was laid over the river, they each of them came with their guards about them, and met one another on the midst of the bridge. And when they had agreed upon the terms of peace Herod, the tetrarch erected a rich tent on the midst of the passage, and made them a feast there. Artabanus also, not long afterward, sent his son Darius as an hostage, with many presents, among which there was a man seven cubits tall, a Jew he was by birth, and his name was Eleazar, who, for his tallness, was called a giant. After which Vitellius went to Antioch, and Artabanus to Babylon; but Herod [the tetrarch] being desirous to give Caesar the first information that they had obtained hostages, sent posts with letters, wherein he had accurately described all the particulars, and had left nothing for the consular Vitellius to inform him of. But when Vitellius's letters were sent, and Caesar had let him know that he was acquainted with the affairs already, because Herod had given him an account of them before, Vitellius was very much troubled at it; and supposing that he had been thereby a greater sufferer than he really was, he kept up a secret anger upon this occasion, till he could be revenged on him, which he was after Caius had taken the government.

6. About this time it was that Philip, Herod's brother, departed this life, in the twentieth year of the reign of Tiberius,[14] after he had been tetrarch of Trachonitis and Gaulanitis, and of the nation of the Bataneans also, thirty-seven years. He had showed himself a person of moderation and quietness in the conduct of his life and government; he constantly lived in that country which was subject to him; he used

---

14. This calculation, from all Josephus's Greek copies, is exactly right; for since Herod died about September, in the fourth year before the Christian era, and Tiberius began, as is well known, Aug. 19, A.D. 14, it is evident that the thirty-seventh year of Philip, reckoned from his father's death, was the twentieth of Tiberius, or near the end of A.D. 33, [the very year of our Savior's death also,] or, however, in the beginning of the next year, A.D. 34. This Philip the tetrarch seems to have been the best of all the posterity of Herod, for his love of peace, and his love of justice.

An excellent example this.

to make his progress with a few chosen friends; his tribunal also, on which he sat in judgment, followed him in his progress; and when any one met him who wanted his assistance, he made no delay, but had his tribunal set down immediately, wheresoever he happened to be, and sat down upon it, and heard his complaint: he there ordered the guilty that were convicted to be punished, and absolved those that had been accused unjustly. He died at Julias; and when he was carried to that monument which he had already erected for himself beforehand, he was buried with great pomp. His principality Tiberius took, (for he left no sons behind him,) and added it to the province of Syria, but gave order that the tributes which arose from it should be collected, and laid up in his tetrachy.

5 *Herod the Tetrarch Makes War with Aretas, the King of Arabia, and Is Beaten by Him as Also Concerning the Death of John the Baptist. How Vitellius Went Up to Jerusalem; Together with Some Account of Agrippa and of the Posterity of Herod the Great*

1. ABOUT this time Aretas (the king of Arabia Petres) and Herod had a quarrel on the account following: Herod the tetrarch had, married the daughter of Aretas, and had lived with her a great while; but when he was once at Rome, he lodged with Herod,[15] who was his brother indeed, but not by the same mother; for this Herod was the son of the high priest Sireoh's daughter. However, he fell in love with Herodias, this last Herod's wife, who was the daughter of Aristobulus their brother, and the sister of Agrippa the Great. This man ventured to talk to her about a marriage between them; which address, when she admitted, an agreement was made for her to change her habitation,

15. This Herod seems to have had the additional name of Philip, as Antipus was named Herod-Antipas: and as Antipus and Antipater seem to be in a manner the very same name, yet were the names of two sons of Herod the Great; so might Philip the tetrarch and this Herod-Philip be two different sons of the same father, all which Grotias observes on Matthew 14:3. Nor was it, as I with Grotias and others of the Philip the tetrarch, but this Herod-Philip, whose wife Herod the tetrarch had married, and that in her first husband's lifetime, and when her first husband had issue by her-; for which adulterous and incestuous marriage John the Baptist justly reproved Herod the tetrarch, and for which reproof Salome, the daughter of Herodias by her first husband Herod-Philip, who was still alive, occasioned him to be unjustly beheaded.

and come to him as soon as he should return from Rome: one article of this marriage also was this, that he should divorce Aretas's daughter. So Antipus, when he had made this agreement, sailed to Rome; but when he had done there the business he went about, and was returned again, his wife having discovered the agreement he had made with Herodias, and having learned it before he had notice of her knowledge of the whole design, she desired him to send her to Macherus, which is a place in the borders of the dominions of Aretas and Herod, without informing him of any of her intentions. Accordingly Herod sent her thither, as thinking his wife had not perceived any thing; now she had sent a good while before to Macherus, which was subject to her father and so all things necessary for her journey were made ready for her by the general of Aretas's army; and by that means she soon came into Arabia, under the conduct of the several generals, who carried her from one to another successively; and she soon came to her father, and told him of Herod's intentions. So Aretas made this the first occasion of his enmity between him and Herod, who had also some quarrel with him about their limits at the country of Gamalitis. So they raised armies on both sides, and prepared for war, and sent their generals to fight instead of themselves; and when they had joined battle, all Herod's army was destroyed by the treachery of some fugitives, who, though they were of the tetrarchy of Philip, joined with Aretas's army. So Herod wrote about these affairs to Tiberius, who being very angry at the attempt made by Aretas, wrote to Vitellius to make war upon him, and either to take him alive, and bring him to him in bonds, or to kill him, and send him his head. This was the charge that Tiberius gave to the president of Syria.

2. Now some of the Jews thought that the destruction of Herod's army came from God, and that very justly, as a punishment of what he did against John, that was called the Baptist: for Herod slew him, who was a good man, and commanded the Jews to exercise virtue, both as to righteousness towards one another, and piety towards God, and so to come to baptism; for that the washing [with water] would be acceptable to him, if they made use of it, not in order to the putting away [or the remission] of some sins [only], but for the purification of the body; supposing still that the soul was thoroughly purified beforehand by righteousness. Now when [many] others came in crowds about him, for they were very greatly moved [or pleased] by

hearing his words, Herod, who feared lest the great influence John had over the people might put it into his power and inclination to raise a rebellion, (for they seemed ready to do any thing he should advise,) thought it best, by putting him to death, to prevent any mischief he might cause, and not bring himself into difficulties, by sparing a man who might make him repent of it when it would be too late. Accordingly he was sent a prisoner, out of Herod's suspicious temper, to Macherus, the castle I before mentioned, and was there put to death. Now the Jews had an opinion that the destruction of this army was sent as a punishment upon Herod, and a mark of God's displeasure to him.

3. So Vitellius prepared to make war with Aretas, having with him two legions of armed men; he also took with him all those of light armature, and of the horsemen which belonged to them, and were drawn out of those kingdoms which were under the Romans, and made haste for Petra, and came to Ptolemais. But as he was marching very busily, and leading his army through Judea, the principal men met him, and desired that he would not thus march through their land; for that the laws of their country would not permit them to overlook those images which were brought into it, of which there were a great many in their ensigns; so he was persuaded by what they said, and changed that resolution of his which he had before taken in this matter. Whereupon he ordered the army to march along

the great plain, while he himself, with Herod the tetrarch and his friends, went up to Jerusalem to offer sacrifice to God, an ancient festival of the Jews being then just approaching; and when he had been there, and been honorably entertained by the multitude of the Jews, he made a stay there for three days, within which time he deprived Jonathan of the high priesthood, and gave it to his brother Theophilus. But when on the fourth day letters came to him, which informed him of the death of Tiberius, he obliged the multitude to take an oath of fidelity to Caius; he also recalled his army, and made them every one go home, and take their winter quarters there, since, upon the devolution of the empire upon Caius, he had not the like authority of making this war which he had before. It was also reported, that when Aretas heard of the coming of Vitellius to fight him, he said, upon his consulting the diviners, that it was impossible that this army of Vitellius's could enter Petra; for that one of the rulers would die, either he that gave orders for the war, or he that was marching at the other's desire, in order to be subservient to his will, or else he against whom this army is prepared. So Vitellius truly retired to Antioch; but Agrippa, the son of Aristobulus, went up to Rome, a year before the death of Tiberius, in order to treat of some affairs with the emperor, if he might be permitted so to do. I have now a mind to describe Herod and his family, how it fared with them, partly because it is suitable to this history to speak of that matter, and partly because this thing is a demonstration of the interposition of Providence, how a multitude of children is of no advantage, no more than any other strength that mankind set their hearts upon, besides those acts of piety which are done towards God; for it happened, that, within the revolution of a hundred years, the posterity of Herod, which were a great many in number, were, excepting a few, utterly destroyed.[16] One may well apply this for the instruction of mankind, and learn thence how unhappy they were: it will also show us the history of Agrippa, who, as he was a person most worthy of admiration, so was he from a private man, beyond all the expectation of those that knew him, advanced to great power and authority. I have said something of them formerly, but I shall now also speak accurately about them.

4. Herod the Great had two daughters by Mariamne, the [grand] daughter of Hyrcanus; the one was Salampsio, who was married to Phasaelus, her first cousin, who was himself the son of Phasaelus, Herod's brother, her father making the match; the other was Cypros, who was herself married also to her first cousin Antipater, the son of Salome, Herod's sister. Phasaelus had five children by Salampsio; Antipater, Herod, and Alexander, and two daughters, Alexandra and Cypros; which last Agrippa, the son of Aristobulus, married; and Timius of Cyprus married Alexandra; he was a man of note, but had by her no children. Agrippa had by Cypros two sons and three daughters, which daughters were named Bernice, Mariarune, and Drusius; but the names of the sons were Agrippa and Drusus, of

16. Whether this sudden extinction of almost the entire lineage of Herod the Great, which was very numerous, as we are both here and in the next section informed, was not in part as a punishment for the gross incests they were frequently guilty of, in marrying their own nephews and nieces, well deserves to be considered. See Leviticus 18:6, 7; 21:10; and Noldius, De Herod, No. 269, 270.

which Drusus died before he came to the years of puberty; but their father, Agrippa, was brought up with his other brethren, Herod and Aristobulus, for these were also the sons of the son of Herod the Great by Bernice; but Bernice was the daughter of Costobarus and of Salome, who was Herod's sister. Aristobulus left these infants when he was slain by his father, together with his brother Alexander, as we have already related. But when they were arrived at years of puberty, this Herod, the brother of Agrippa, married Mariamne, the daughter of Olympias, who was the daughter of Herod the king, and of Joseph, the son of Joseph, who was brother to Herod the king, and had by her a son, Aristobulus; but Aristobulus, the third brother of Agrippa, married Jotape, the daughter of Sampsigeramus, king of Emesa; they had a daughter who was deaf, whose name also was Jotape; and these hitherto were the children of the male line. But Herodias, their sister, was married to Herod [Philip], the son of Herod the Great, who was born of Mariamne, the daughter of Simon the high priest, who had a daughter, Salome; after whose birth Herodias took upon her to confound the laws of our country, and divorced herself from her husband while he was alive, and was married to Herod [Antipas], her husband's brother by the father's side, he was tetrarch of Galilee; but her daughter Salome was married to Philip, the son of Herod, and tetrarch of Trachonitis; and as he died childless, Aristobulus, the son of Herod, the brother of Agrippa, married her; they had three sons, Herod, Agrippa, and Aristobulus; and this was the posterity of Phasaelus and Salampsio. But the daughter of Antipater by Cypros was Cypros, whom Alexas Selcias, the son of Alexas, married; they had a daughter, Cypros; but Herod and Alexander, who, as we told you, were the brothers of Antipater, died childless. As to Alexander, the son of Herod the king, who was slain by his father, he had two sons, Alexander and Tigranes, by the daughter of Archelaus, king of Cappadocia. Tigranes, who was king of Armenia, was accused at Rome, and died childless; Alexander had ason of the same name with his brother Tigranes, and was sent to take possession of the kingdom of Armenia by Nero; he had a son, Alexander, who married Jotape,[17] the daughter of Antiochus, the king of Commagena; Vespasian made

17. There are coins still extant of this Eraess, as Spanheim informs us. Spanheim also informs us of a coin still extant of this Jotape, daughter of the king of Commageus.

him king of an island in Cilicia. But these descendants of Alexander, soon after their birth, deserted the Jewish religion, and went over to that of the Greeks. But for the rest of the daughters of Herod the king, it happened that they died childless. And as these descendants of Herod, whom we have enumerated, were in being at the same time that Agrippa the Great took the kingdom, and I have now given an account of them, it now remains that I relate the several hard fortunes which befell Agrippa, and how he got clear of them, and was advanced to the greatest height of dignity and power.

6 *Of the Navigation of King Agrippa to Rome, to Tiberius Caesar; and Now Upon His Being Accused by His Own Freed-Man, He Was Bound; How Also He, Was Set at Liberty by Caius, After Tiberius's Death and Was Made King of the Tetrarchy of Philip*

1. A LITTLE before the death of Herod the king, Agrippa lived at Rome, and was generally brought up and conversed with Drusus, the emperor Tiberius's son, and contracted a friendship with Antonia, the wife of Drusus the Great, who had his mother Bernice in great esteem, and was very desirous of advancing her son. Now as Agrippa was by nature magnanimous and generous in the presents he made, while his mother was alive, this inclination of his mind did not appear, that he might be able to avoid her anger for such his extravagance; but when Bernice was dead, and he was left to his own conduct, he spent a great deal extravagantly in his daily way of living, and a great deal in the immoderate presents he made, and those chiefly among Caesar's freed-men, in order to gain their assistance, insomuch that he was, in a little time, reduced to poverty, and could not live at Rome any longer. Tiberius also forbade the friends of his deceased son to come into his sight, because on seeing them he should be put in mind of his son, and his grief would thereby be revived.

2. For these reasons he went away from Rome, and sailed to Judea, but in evil circumstances, being dejected with the loss of that money which he once had, and because he had not wherewithal to pay his creditors, who were many in number, and such as gave him no room for escaping them. Whereupon he knew not what to do; so, for shame of his present condition, he retired to a certain tower, at

Malatha, in Idumea, and had thoughts of killing himself; but his wife Cypros perceived his intentions, and tried all sorts of methods to divert him from his taking such a course; so she sent a letter to his sister Herodias, who was now the wife of Herod the tetrarch, and let her know Agrippa's present design, and what necessity it was which drove him thereto, and desired her, as a kinswoman of his, to give him her help, and to engage her husband to do the same, since she saw how she alleviated these her husband's troubles all she could, although she had not the like wealth to do it withal. So they sent for him, and allotted him Tiberias for his habitation, and appointed him some income of money for his maintenance, and made him a magistrate of that city, by way of honor to him. Yet did not Herod long continue in that resolution of supporting him, though even that support was not sufficient for him; for as once they were at a feast at Tyre, and in their cups, and reproaches were cast upon one another, Agrippa thought that was not to be borne, while Herod hit him in the teeth with his poverty, and with his owing his necessary food to him. So he went to Flaccus, one that had been consul, and had been a very great friend to him at Rome formerly, and was now president of Syria.

3. Hereupon Flaccus received him kindly, and he lived with him. Flaccus had also with him there Aristobulus, who was indeed Agrippa's brother, but was at variance with him; yet did not their enmity to one another hinder the friendship of Flaccus to them both, but still they were honorably treated by him. However, Aristobulus did not abate of his ill-will to Agrippa, till at length he brought him into ill terms with Flaccus; the occasion of bringing on which estrangement was this: The Damascens were at difference with the Sidonians about their limits, and when Flaccus was about to hear the cause between them, they understood that Agrippa had a mighty influence upon him; so they desired that he would be of their side, and for that favor promised him a great deal of money; so he was zealous in assisting the Damascens as far as he was able. Now Aristobulus had gotten intelligence of this promise of money to him, and accused him to Flaccus of the same; and when, upon a thorough examination of the matter, it appeared plainly so to be, he rejected Agrippa out of the number of his friends. So he was reduced to the utmost necessity, and came to Ptolemais; and because he knew not where else to get a livelihood, he thought to sail to Italy; but as he was restrained from so doing by want of

money, he desired Marsyas, who was his freed-man, to find some method for procuring him so much as he wanted for that purpose, by borrowing such a sum of some person or other. So Marsyas desired of Peter, who was the freed-man of Bernice, Agrippa's mother, and by the right of her testament was bequeathed to Antonia, to lend so much upon Agrippa's own bond and security; but he accused Agrippa of having defrauded him of certain sums of money, and so obliged Marsyas, when he made the bond of twenty thousand Attic drachmae, to accept of twenty-five hundred drachma as[18] less than what he desired, which the other allowed of, because he could not help it. Upon the receipt of this money, Agrippa came to Anthedon, and took shipping, and was going to set sail; but Herennius Capito, who was the procurator of Jamhis, sent a band of soldiers to demand of him three hundred thousand drachmae of silver, which were by him owing to Caesar's treasury while he was at Rome, and so forced him to stay. He then pretended that he would do as he bid him; but when night came on, he cut his cables, and went off, and sailed to Alexandria, where he desired Alexander the alabarch[19] to lend him two hundred thousand drachmae; but he said he would not lend it to him, but would not refuse it to Cypros, as greatly astonished at her affection to her husband, and at the other instances of her virtue; so she undertook to repay it. Accordingly, Alexander paid them five talents at Alexandria, and promised to pay them the rest of that sum at Dicearchia [Puteoli]; and this he did out of the fear he was in that Agrippa would soon spend it. So this Cypros set her husband free, and dismissed him to go on with his navigation to Italy, while she and her children departed for Judea.

4. And now Agrippa was come to Puteoli, whence he wrote a letter to Tiberius Caesar, who then lived at Capreae, and told him that he was come so far in order to wait on him, and to pay him a visit; and desired that he would give him leave to come over to Caprein: so Tiberius made no difficulty, but wrote to him in an obliging way in other respects; and withal told him he was glad of his safe return,

---

18. Spanheim observes, that we have here an instance of the Attic quantity of use-money, which was the eighth part of the original sum, or 12 per cent., for such is the proportion of 2500 to 20,000.

19. The governor of the Jews there.

and desired him to come to Capreae; and when he was come, he did not fail to treat him as kindly as he had promised him in his letter to do. But the next day came a letter to Caesar from Herennius Capito, to inform him that Agrippa had borrowed three hundred thousand drachmae, and not pad it at the time appointed; but when it was demanded of him, he ran away like a fugitive, out of the places under his government, and put it out of his power to get the money of him. When Caesar had read this letter, he was much troubled at it, and gave order that Agrippa should be excluded from his presence until he had paid that debt: upon which he was no way daunted at Caesar's anger, but entreated Antonia, the mother of Germanicus, and of Claudius, who was afterward Caesar himself, to lend him those three hundred thousand drachmae, that he might not be deprived of Tiberius's friendship; so, out of regard to the memory of Bernice his mother, (for those two women were very familiar with one another,) and out of regard to his and Claudius's education together, she lent him the money; and, upon the payment of this debt, there was nothing to hinder Tiberius's friendship to him. After this, Tiberius Caesar recommended to him his grandson,[20] and ordered that he should always accompany him when he went abroad. But upon Agrippa's kind reception by Antonia, he betook him to pay his respects to Caius, who was her grandson, and in very high reputation by reason of the good-will they bare his father. Now there was one Thallus, a freed-man of Caesar, of whom he borrowed a million of drachmae, and thence repaid Antonia the debt he owed her; and by sending the overplus in paying his court to Caius, became a person of great authority with him.

5. Now as the friendship which Agrippa had for Caius was come to a great height, there happened some words to pass between them, as they once were in a chariot together, concerning Tiberius; Agrippa praying [to God] (for they two sat by themselves) that Tiberius might soon go off the stage, and leave the government to Caius, who was in every respect more worthy of it. Now Eutychus, who was Agrippa's freed-man, and drove his chariot, heard these words, and at that time said nothing of them; but when Agrippa accused him of stealing some garments of his, (which was certainly true,) he ran away from him;

20. Tiberius, junior of Germanicus.

but when he was caught, and brought before Piso, who was governor of the city, and the man was asked why he ran away, be replied, that he had somewhat to say to Caesar, that tended to his security and preservation: so Piso bound him, and sent him to Capreae. But Tiberius, according to his usual custom, kept him still in bonds, being a delayer of affairs, if ever there was any other king or tyrant that was so; for he did not admit ambassadors quickly, and no successors were despatched away to governors or procurators of the provinces that had been formerly sent, unless they were dead; whence it was that he was so negligent in hearing the causes of prisoners; insomuch that when he was asked by his friends what was the reason of his delay in such cases, he said that he delayed to hear ambassadors, lest, upon their quick dismission, other ambassadors should be appointed, and return upon him; and so he should bring trouble upon himself in their public reception and dismission: that he permitted those governors who had been sent once to their government [to stay there a long while], out of regard to the subjects that were under them; for that all governors are naturally disposed to get as much as they can; and that those who are not to fix there, but to stay a short time, and that at an uncertainty when they shall be turned out, do the more severely hurry themselves on to fleece the people; but that if their government be long continued to them; they are at last satiated with the spoils, as having gotten a vast deal, and so become at length less sharp in their pillaging; but that if successors are sent quickly, the poor subjects, who are exposed to them as a prey, will not be able to bear the new ones, while they shall not have the same time allowed them wherein their predecessors had filled themselves, and so grew more unconcerned about getting more; and this because they are removed before they have had time [for their oppressions]. He gave them an example to show his meaning: A great number of flies came about the sore places of a man that had been wounded; upon which one of the standers-by pitied the man's misfortune, and thinking he was not able to drive those flies away himself, was going to drive them away for him; but he prayed him to let them alone: the other, by way of reply, asked him the reason of such a preposterous proceeding, in preventing relief from his present misery; to which he answered, "If thou drivest these flies away, thou wilt hurt me worse; for as these are already full of my blood, they do not crowd about me, nor pain me so much as before, but are somewhat more remiss, while the fresh ones that come almost famished, and find me quite tired down already, will be my destruction. For this cause, therefore, it is that I am myself careful not to send such new governors perpetually to those my subjects, who are already sufficiently harassed by many oppressions, as may, like these flies, further distress them; and so, besides their natural desire of gain, may have this additional incitement to it, that they expect to be suddenly deprived of that pleasure which they take in it." And, as a further attestation to what I say of the dilatory nature of Tiberius, I appeal to this his practice itself; for although he was emperor twenty-two years, he sent in all but two procurators to govern the nation of the Jews, Gratus, and his successor in the government, Pilate. Nor was he in one way of acting with respect to the Jews, and in another with respect to the rest of his subjects. He further informed them, that even in the hearing of the causes of prisoners, he made such delays, because immediate death to those that must be condemned to die would be an alleviation of their present miseries, while those wicked wretches have not deserved any such favor; "but I do it, that, by being harassed with the present calamity, they may undergo greater misery."

6. On this account it was that Eutychus could not obtain a bearing, but was kept still in prison. However, some time afterward, Tiberius came from Capreae to Tusculanum, which is about a hundred furlongs from Rome. Agrippa then desired of Antonia that she would procure a hearing for Eutychus, let the matter whereof he accused him prove what it would. Now Antonia was greatly esteemed by Tiberius on all accounts, from the dignity of her relation to him, who had been his brother Drusus's wife, and from her eminent chastity;[21] for though

21. This high commendation of Antonia for marrying but once, given here, and supported elsewhere; Antiq. B. XVII. ch. 13. sect. 4, and this, notwithstanding the strongest temptations, shows how honorable single marriages were both among the Jews and Romans, in the days of Josephus and of the apostles, and takes away much of that surprise which the modern Protestants have at those laws of the apostles, where no widows, but those who had been the wives of one husband only, are taken into the church list; and no bishops, priests, or deacons are allowed to marry more than once, without leaving off to officiate as clergymen any longer. See Luke 2:36; 1 Timothy 5:11, 12; 3:2, 12; Titus 1:10; Constit. Apost. B. II. sect. 1, 2; B. VI. sect. 17; Can. B. XVII,; Grot. in Luc. ii. 36; and Resports. ad Consult. Cassand. p. 44; and Cotelet. in Constit. B. VI. sect. 17. And note, that Tertullian owns this law against second marriages of the

she was still a young woman, she continued in her widowhood, and refused all other matches, although Augustus had enjoined her to be married to somebody else; yet did she all along preserve her reputation free from reproach. She had also been the greatest benefactress to Tiberius, when there was a very dangerous plot laid against him by Sejanus, a man who had been her husband's friend, and wire had the greatest authority, because he was general of the army, and when many members of the senate and many of the freed-men joined with him, and the soldiery was corrupted, and the plot was come to a great height. Now Sejanus had certainly gained his point, had not Antonia's boldness been more wisely conducted than Sejanus's malice; for when she had discovered his designs against Tiberius, she wrote him an exact account of the whole, and gave the letter to Pallas, the most faithful of her servants, and sent him to Caprere to Tiberius, who, when he understood it, slew Sejanus and his confederates; so that Tiberius, who had her in great esteem before, now looked upon her with still greater respect, and depended upon her in all things. So when Tiberius was desired by this Antonia to examine Eutychus, he answered, "If indeed Eutychus hath falsely accused Agrippa in what he hath said of him, he hath had sufficient punishment by what I have done to him already; but if, upon examination, the accusation appears to be true, let Agrippa have a care, lest, out of desire of punishing his freed-man, he do not rather bring a punishment upon himself." Now when Antonia told Agrippa of this, he was still much more pressing that the matter might be examined into; so Antonia, upon Agrippa's lying hard at her continually to beg this favor, took the following opportunity: As Tiberius lay once at his ease upon his sedan, and was carried about, and Caius, her grandson, and Agrippa, were before him after dinner she walked by the sedan, and desired him to call Eutychus, and have him examined; to which he replied, "O Antonia! the gods are my witnesses that I am induced to do what I am going to do, not

clergy had been once at least executed in his time; and heavily complains elsewhere, that the breach thereof had not been always punished by the catholics, as it ought to have been. Jerome, speaking of the ill reputation of marrying twice, says, that no such person could be chosen into the clergy in his days; which Augustine testifies also; and for Epiphanius, rather earlier, he is clear and full to the same purpose, and says that law obtained over the whole catholic church in his days,—as the places in the forecited authors inform us.

by my own inclination, but because I am forced to it by thy prayers." When he had said this, he ordered Macro, who succeeded Sejanus, to bring Eutychus to him; accordingly, without any delay, he was brought. Then Tiberius asked him what he had to say against a man who had given him his liberty. Upon which he said, "O my lord! this Caius, and Agrippa with him, were once riding in a chariot, when I sat at their feet, and, among other discourses that passed, Agrippa said to Caius, Oh that the day would once come when this old fellow will dies and name thee for the governor of the habitable earth! for then this Tiberius, his grandson, would be no hinderance, but would be taken off by thee, and that earth would be happy, and I happy also." Now Tiberius took these to be truly Agrippa's words, and bearing a grudge withal at Agrippa, because, when he had commanded him to pay his respects to Tiberius, his grandson, and the son of Drusus, Agrippa had not paid him that respect, but had disobeyed his commands, and transferred all his regard to Caius; he said to Macro, "Bind this man." But Macro, not distinctly knowing which of them it was whom he bid him bind, and not expecting that he would have any such thing done to Agrippa, he forbore, and came to ask more distinctly what it was that he said. But when Caesar had gone round the hippodrome, he found Agrippa standing: "For certain," said he, "Macro, this is the man I meant to have bound;" and when he still asked, "Which of these is to be bound?" he said "Agrippa." Upon which Agrippa betook himself to make supplication for himself, putting him in mind of his son, with whom he was brought up, and of Tiberius [his grandson] whom he had educated; but all to no purpose; for they led him about bound even in his purple garments. It was also very hot weather, and they had but little wine to their meal, so that he was very thirsty; he was also in a sort of agony, and took this treatment of him heinously: as he therefore saw one of Caius's slaves, whose name was Thaumastus, carrying some water in a vessel, he desired that he would let him drink; so the servant gave him some water to drink, and he drank heartily, and said, "O thou boy! this service of thine to me will be for thy advantage; for if I once get clear of these my bonds, I will soon procure thee thy freedom of Caius who has not been wanting to minister to me now I am in bonds, in the same manner as when I was in my former state and dignity." Nor did he deceive him in what he promised him, but made him amends for what he had now done; for when afterward Agrippa was come to the kingdom, he took particular care of Thaumastus, and got him his liberty from Caius, and made him the steward over his own estate; and when he died, he left him to Agrippa his son, and to Bernice his daughter, to minister to them in the same capacity. The man also grew old in that honorable post, and therein died. But all this happened a good while later.

7. Now Agrippa stood in his bonds before the royal palace, and leaned on a certain tree for grief, with many others,. who were in bonds also; and as a certain bird sat upon the tree on which Agrippa leaned, (the Romans call this bird bubo,) [an owl,] one of those that were bound, a German by nation, saw him, and asked a soldier who that man in purple was; and when he was informed that his name was Agrippa, and that he was by nation a Jew, and one of the principal men of that nation, he asked leave of the soldier to whom he was bound,[22] to let him come nearer to him, to speak with him; for that he had a mind to inquire of him about some things relating to his country; which liberty, when he had obtained, and as he stood near him, he said thus to him by an interpreter: "This sudden change of thy condition, O young man! is grievous to thee, as bringing on thee a manifold and very great adversity; nor wilt thou believe me, when I foretell how thou wilt get clear of this misery which thou art now under, and how Divine Providence will provide for thee. Know therefore (and I appeal to my own country gods, as well as to the gods of this place, who have awarded these bonds to us) that all I am going to say about thy concerns shall neither be said for favor nor bribery, nor out of an endeavor to make thee cheerful without cause; for such predictions, when they come to fail, make the grief at last, and in earnest, more bitter than if the party had never heard of any such thing. However, though I run the hazard of my own self, I think it fit to declare to thee the prediction of the gods. It cannot be that thou shouldst long continue in these bonds; but thou wilt soon be delivered from them, and wilt be promoted to the highest dignity and power, and thou wilt be envied by all those who now pity thy hard fortune; and thou wilt be happy till thy death, and wilt leave

---

22. Dr. Hudson here takes notice, out of Seneca, Epistle V. that this was the custom of Tiberius, to couple the prisoner and the soldier that guarded him together in the same chain.

thine happiness to the children whom thou shalt have. But do thou remember, when thou seest this bird again, that thou wilt then live but five days longer. This event will be brought to pass by that God who hath sent this bird hither to be a sign unto thee. And I cannot but think it unjust to conceal from thee what I foreknow concerning thee, that, by thy knowing beforehand what happiness is coming upon thee, thou mayst not regard thy present misfortunes. But when this happiness shall actually befall thee, do not forget what misery I am in myself, but endeavor to deliver me." So when the German had said this, he made Agrippa laugh at him as much as he afterwards appeared worthy of admiration. But now Antonia took Agrippa's misfortune to heart: however, to speak to Tiberius on his behalf, she took to be a very difficult thing, and indeed quite impracticable, as to any hope of success; yet did she procure of Macro, that the soldiers that kept him should be of a gentle nature, and that the centurion who was over them and was to diet with him, should be of the same disposition, and that he might have leave to bathe himself every day, and that his freed-men and friends might come to him, and that other things that tended to ease him might be indulged him. So his friend Silas came in to him, and two of his freed-men, Marsyas and Stechus, brought him such sorts of food as he was fond of, and indeed took great care of him; they also brought him garments, under pretense of selling them; and when night came on, they laid them under him; and the soldiers assisted them, as Macro had given them order to do beforehand. And this was Agrippa's condition for six months' time, and in this case were his affairs.

8. But for Tiberius, upon his return to Caprein, he fell sick. At first his distemper was but gentle; but as that distemper increased upon him, he had small or no hopes of recovery. Hereupon he bid Euodus, who was that freed-man whom he most of all respected, to bring the children[23] to him, for that he wanted to talk to them before he died. Now he had at present no sons of his own alive for Drusus, who was his only son, was dead; but Drusus's son Tiberius was still living, whose additional name was Gemellus: there was also living Caius, the son of Germanicus, who was the son[24] of his brother [Drusus]. He was

23. Tiberius his own grandson, and Caius his brother Drusus's grandson.

24. So I correct Josephus's copy, which calls Germanicus his brother, who was his brother's son.

now grown up, and had a liberal education, and was well improved by it, and was in esteem and favor with the people, on account of the excellent character of his father Germanicus, who had attained the highest honor among the multitude, by the firmness of his virtuous behavior, by the easiness and agreeableness of his conversing with the multitude, and because the dignity he was in did not hinder his familiarity with them all, as if they were his equals; by which behavior he was not only greatly esteemed by the people and the senate, but by every one of those nations that were subject to the Romans; some of which were affected when they came to him with the gracefulness of their reception by him, and others were affected in the same manner by the report of the others that had been with him; and, upon his death, there was a lamentation made by all men; not such a one as was to be made in way of flattery to their rulers, while they did but counterfeit sorrow, but such as was real; while every body grieved at his death, as if they had lost one that was near to them. And truly such had been his easy conversation with men, that it turned greatly to the advantage of his son among all; and, among others, the soldiery were so peculiarly affected to him, that they reckoned it an eligible thing, if need were, to die themselves, if he might but attain to the government.

9. But when Tiberius had given order to Euodus to bring the children to him the next day in the morning, he prayed to his country gods to show him a manifest signal which of those children should come to the government; being very desirous to leave it to his son's son, but still depending upon what God should foreshow concerning them more than upon his own opinion and inclination; so he made this to be the omen, that the government should be left to him who should come to him first the next day. When he had thus resolved within himself, he sent to his grandson's tutor, and ordered him to bring the child to him early in the morning, as supposing that God would permit him to be made emperor. But God proved opposite to his designation; for while Tiberius was thus contriving matters, and as soon as it was at all day, he bid Euodus to call in that child which should be there ready. So he went out, and found Caius before the door, for Tiberius was not yet come, but staid waiting for his breakfast; for Euodus knew nothing of what his lord intended; so he said to Caius, "Thy father calls thee," and then brought him in. As soon as Tiberius saw Caius, and not before, he reflected on the power of God, and how the

ability of bestowing the government on whom he would was entirely taken from him; and thence he was not able to establish what he had intended. So he greatly lamented that his power of establishing what he had before contrived was taken from him, and that his grandson Tiberius was not only to lose the Roman empire by his fatality, but his own safety also, because his preservation would now depend upon such as would be more potent than himself, who would think it a thing not to be borne, that a kinsman should live with them, and so his relation would not be able to protect him; but he would be feared and bated by him who had the supreme authority, partly on account of his being next to the empire, and partly on account of his perpetually contriving to get the government, both in order to preserve himself, and to be at the head of affairs also. Now Tiberius had been very much given to astrology,[25] and the calculation of nativities, and had spent his life in the esteem of what predictions had proved true, more than those whose profession it was. Accordingly, when he once saw Galba coming in to him, he said to his most intimate friends, that there came in a man that would one day have the dignity of the Roman empire. So that this Tiberius was more addicted to all such sorts of diviners than any other of the Roman emperors, because he had found them to have told him truth in his own affairs. And indeed he was now in great distress upon this accident that had befallen him, and was very much grieved at the destruction of his son's son, which he foresaw, and complained of himself, that he should have made use of such a method of divination beforehand, while it was in his power to have died without grief by this knowledge of futurity; whereas he was now tormented by his foreknowledge of the misfortune of such as were dearest to him, and must die under that torment. Now although he was disordered at this unexpected revolution of the government to those for whom he did not intend it, he spake thus to Caius, though unwillingly, and against his own inclination: "O child! although Tiberius be nearer related to me than thou art, I, by my own determination, and the conspiring suffrage of the gods, do give and put into thy hand the Roman empire; and I desire thee never to be unmindful when thou comest to it, either of my kindness to thee, who

25. This is a known thing among the Roman historians and poets, that Tiberius was greatly given to astrology and divination.

set thee in so high a dignity, or of thy relation to Tiberius. But as thou knowest that I am, together with and after the gods, the procurer of so great happiness to thee; so I desire that thou wilt make me a return for my readiness to assist thee, and wilt take care of Tiberius because of his near relation to thee. Besides which, thou art to know, that while Tiberius is alive, he will be a security to thee, both as to empire and as to thy own preservation; but if he die, that will be but a prelude to thy own misfortunes; for to be alone under the weight of such vast affairs is very dangerous; nor will the gods suffer those actions which are unjustly done, contrary to that law which directs men to act otherwise, to go off unpunished." This was the speech which Tiberius made, which did not persuade Caius to act accordingly, although he promised so to do; but when he was settled in the government, he took off this Tiberius, as was predicted by the other Tiberius; as he was also himself, in no long time afterward, slain by a secret plot laid against him.

10. So when Tiberius had at this time appointed Caius to be his successor, he outlived but a few days, and then died, after he had held the government twenty-two years five months and three days. Now Caius was the fourth emperor. But when the Romans understood that Tiberius was dead, they rejoiced at the good news, but had not courage to believe it; not because they were unwilling it should be true, for they would have given huge sums of money that it might be so, but because they were afraid, that if they had showed their joy when the news proved false, their joy should be openly known, and they should be accused for it, and be thereby undone. For this Tiberius had brought a vast number of miseries on the best families of the Romans, since he was easily inflamed with passion in all cases, and was of such a temper as rendered his anger irrevocable, till he had executed the same, although he had taken a hatred against men without reason; for he was by nature fierce in all the sentences he gave, and made death the penalty for the lightest offenses; insomuch that when the Romans heard the rumor about his death gladly, they were restrained from the enjoyment of that pleasure by the dread of such miseries as they foresaw would follow, if their hopes proved ill-grounded. Now Marsyas, Agrippa's freed-man, as soon as he heard of Tiberius's death, came running to tell Agrippa the news; and finding him going out to the bath, he gave him a nod, and said, in the Hebrew

tongue, "The lion[26] is dead;" who, understanding his meaning, and being ovejoyed at the news, "Nay," said he, "but all sorts of thanks and happiness attend thee for this news of thine; only I wish that what thou sayest may prove true." Now the centurion who was set to keep Agrippa, when he saw with what haste Marsyas came, and what joy Agrippa had from what he said, he had a suspicion that his words implied some great innovation of affairs, and he asked them about what was said. They at first diverted the discourse; but upon his further pressing, Agrippa, without more ado, told him, for he was already become his friend; so he joined with him in that pleasure which this news occasioned, because it would be fortunate to Agrippa, and made him a supper. But as they were feasting, and the cups went about, there came one who said that Tiberius was still alive, and would return to the city ill a few days. At which news the centurion was exceedingly troubled, because he had done what might cost him his life, to have treated so joyfully a prisoner, and this upon the news of the death of Caesar; so he thrust Agrippa from the couch whereon he lay, and said, "Dost thou think to cheat me by a lie about the emperor without punishment? and shalt not thou pay for this thy malicious report at the price of thine head?" When he had so said, he ordered Agrippa to be bound again, (for he had loosed him before,) and kept a severer guard over him than formerly, and in that evil condition was Agrippa that night; but the next day the rumor increased in the city, and confirmed the news that Tiberius was certainly dead; insomuch that men durst now openly and freely talk about it; nay, some offered sacrifices on that account. Several letters also came from Caius; one of them to the senate, which informed them of the death of Tiberius, and of his own entrance on the government; another to Piso, the governor of the city, which told him the same thing. He also gave order that Agrippa should be removed out of the camp, and go to that house where he lived before he was put in prison; so that he was now out of fear as to his own affairs; for although he was still in custody, yet it was now with ease to his own affairs. Now, as soon as Caius was

26. This name of a lion is often given to tyrants, especially by the such Agrippa, and probably his freed-man Marsyas, in effect were, Ezekiel 19:1, 9; Esther 4:9 2 Timothy 4:17. They are also sometimes compared to or represented by wild beasts, of which the lion is the principal, Daniel 7:3, 8; Apoc. 13:1, 2.

come to Rome, and had brought Tiberius's dead body with him, and had made a sumptuous funeral for him, according to the laws of his country, he was much disposed to set Agrippa at liberty that very day; but Antonia hindered him, not out of any ill-will to the prisoner, but out of regard to decency in Caius, lest that should make men believe that he received the death of Tiberius with pleasure, when he loosed one whom he had bound immediately. However, there did not many days pass ere he sent for him to his house, and had him shaved, and made him change his raiment; after which he put a diadem upon his head, and appointed him to be king of the tetrarchy of Philip. He also gave him the tetrarchy of Lysanias,[27] and changed his iron chain for a golden one of equal weight. He also sent Marullus to be procurator of Judea.

11. Now, in the second year of the reign of Caius Caesar, Agrippa desired leave to be given him to sail home, and settle the affairs of his government; and he promised to return again, when he had put the rest in order, as it ought to be put. So, upon the emperor's permission, he came into his own country, and appeared to them all unexpectedly as asking, and thereby demonstrated to the men that saw him the power of fortune, when they compared his former poverty with his present happy affluence; so some called him a happy man, and others could not well believe that things were so much changed with him for the better.

7 How Herod the Tetrarch Was Banished

1. BUT Herodias, Agrippa's sister, who now lived as wife to that Herod who was tetrarch of Galilee and Peres, took this authority of her brother in an envious manner, particularly when she saw that he had a greater dignity bestowed on him than her husband had; since, when he ran away, it was because he was not able to pay his debts; and now he was come back, he was in a way of dignity, and of great good fortune. She was therefore grieved and much displeased at so great a mutation of his affairs; and chiefly when she saw him marching

27. Although Caius now promised to give Agrippa the tetrarchy of Lysanias, yet was it not actually conferred upon him till the reign of Claudius, as we learn, Antiq. B. XIX, ch. 5. sect. 1.

among the multitude with the usual ensigns of royal authority, she was not able to conceal how miserable she was, by reason of the envy she had towards him; but she excited her husband, and desired him that he would sail to Rome, to court honors equal to his; for she said that she could not bear to live any longer, while Agrippa, the son of that Aristobulus who was condemned to die by his father, one that came to her husband in such extreme poverty, that the necessaries of life were forced to be entirely supplied him day by day; and when he fled away from his creditors by sea, he now returned a king; while he was himself the son of a king, and while the near relation he bare to royal authority called upon him to gain the like dignity, he sat still, and was contented with a privater life. "But then, Herod, although thou wast formerly not concerned to be in a lower condition than thy father from whom thou wast derived had been, yet do thou now seek after the dignity which thy kinsman hath attained to; and do not thou bear this contempt, that a man who admired thy riches should he in greater honor than thyself, nor suffer his poverty to show itself able to purchase greater things than our abundance; nor do thou esteem it other than a shameful thing to be inferior to one who, the other day, lived upon thy charity. But let us go to Rome, and let us spare no pains nor expenses, either of silver or gold, since they cannot be kept for any better use than for the obtaining of a kingdom."

2. But for Herod, he opposed her request at this time, out of the love of ease, and having a suspicion of the trouble he should have at Rome; so he tried to instruct her better. But the more she saw him draw back, the more she pressed him to it, and desired him to leave no stone unturned in order to be king; and at last she left not off till she engaged him, whether he would or not, to be of her sentiments, because he could no otherwise avoid her importunity. So he got all things ready, after as sumptuous a manner as he was able, and spared for nothing, and went up to Rome, and took Herodias along with him. But Agrippa, when he was made sensible of their intentions and preparations, he also prepared to go thither; and as soon as he heard they set sail, he sent Fortunatus, one of his freed-men, to Rome, to carry presents to the emperor, and letters against Herod, and to give Caius a particular account of those matters, if he should have any opportunity. This man followed Herod so quick, and had so prosperous a voyage, and came so little after Herod, that while Herod was with Caius, he came

himself, and delivered his letters; for they both sailed to Dicearchia, and found Caius at Bairn, which is itself a little city of Campania, at the distance of about five furlongs from Dicearchia. There are in that place royal palaces, with sumptuous apartments, every emperor still endeavoring to outdo his predecessor's magnificence; the place also affords warm baths, that spring out of the ground of their own accord, which are of advantage for the recovery of the health of those that make use of them; and, besides, they minister to men's luxury also. Now Caius saluted Herod, for he first met with him, and then looked upon the letters which Agrippa had sent him, and which were written in order to accuse Herod; wherein he accused him, that he had been in confederacy with Sejanus against Tiberius's and that he was now confederate with Artabanus, the king of Parthia, in opposition to the government of Caius; as a demonstration of which he alleged, that he had armor sufficient for seventy thousand men ready in his armory. Caius was moved at this information, and asked Herod whether what was said about the armor was true; and when he confessed there was such armor there, for he could not deny the same, the truth of it being too notorious, Caius took that to be a sufficient proof of the accusation, that he intended to revolt. So he took away from him his tetrarchy, and gave it by way of addition to Agrippa's kingdom; he also gave Herod's money to Agrippa, and, by way of punishment, awarded him a perpetual banishment, and appointed Lyons, a city of Gaul, to be his place of habitation. But when he was informed that Herodias was Agrippa's sister, he made her a present of what money was her own, and told her that it was her brother who prevented her being put under the same calamity with her husband. But she made this reply: "Thou, indeed, O emperor! actest after a magnificent manner, and as becomes thyself in what thou offerest me; but the kindness which I have for my husband hinders me from partaking of the favor of thy gift; for it is not just that I, who have been made a partner in his prosperity, should forsake him in his misfortunes." Hereupon Caius was angry at her, and sent her with Herod into banishment, and gave her estate to Agrippa. And thus did God punish Herodias for her envy at her brother, and Herod also for giving ear to the vain discourses of a woman. Now Caius managed public affairs with great magnanimity during the first and second year of his reign, and behaved himself with such moderation, that he gained the good-will of the Romans themselves, and of his other subjects. But, in process of time, he went beyond the bounds of human nature in his conceit of himself, and by reason of the vastness of his dominions made himself a god, and took upon himself to act in all things to the reproach of the Deity itself.

8 *Concerning the Embassage of the Jews to Caius;*[28] and How Caius Sent Petronius into Syria to Make War Against the Jews, Unless They Would Receive His Statue

1. THERE was now a tumult arisen at Alexandria, between the Jewish inhabitants and the Greeks; and three ambassadors were chosen out of each party that were at variance, who came to Caius. Now one of these ambassadors from the people of Alexandria was Apion,[29] who uttered many blasphemies against the Jews; and, among other things that he said, he charged them with neglecting the honors that belonged to Caesar; for that while all who were subject to the Roman empire built altars and temples to Caius, and in other regards universally received him as they received the gods, these Jews alone thought it a dishonorable thing for them to erect statues in honor of him, as well as to swear by his name. Many of these severe things were said by Apion, by which he hoped to provoke Caius to anger at the Jews, as he was likely to be. But Philo, the principal of the Jewish embassage, a man eminent on all accounts, brother to Alexander the alabarch,[30] and

---

28. Regarding instances of the interpositions of Providence, as have been always very rare among the other idolatrous nations, but of old very many among the posterity of Abraham, the worshippers of the true God; nor do these seem much inferior to those in the Old Testament, which are the more remarkable, because, among all their other follies and vices, the Jews were not at this time idolaters; and the deliverances here mentioned were done in order to prevent their relapse into that idolatry.

29. Josephus here assures us that the ambassadors from Alexandria to Caius were on each part no more than three in number, for the Jews, and for the Gentiles, which are but six in all; whereas Philo, who was the principal ambassador from the Jews, as Josephus here confesses, (as was Apion for the Gentiles,) says, the Jews' ambassadors were themselves no fewer than live, towards the end of his legation to Caius; which, if there be no mistake in the copies, must be supposed the truth; nor, in that case, would Josephus have contradicted so authentic a witness, had he seen that account of Philo's; which that he ever did does not appear.

30. This Alexander, the alabarch, or governor of the Jews, at Alexandria, and brother to Philo, is supposed by Bishop Pearson, in Act. Apost. p. 41,42, to be the same with

one not unskillful in philosophy, was ready to betake himself to make his defense against those accusations; but Caius prohibited him, and bid him begone; he was also in such a rage, that it openly appeared he was about to do them some very great mischief. So Philo being thus affronted, went out, and said to those Jews who were about him, that they should be of good courage, since Caius's words indeed showed anger at them, but in reality had already set God against himself.

2. Hereupon Caius, taking it very heinously that he should be thus despised by the Jews alone, sent Petronius to be president of Syria, and successor in the government to Vitellius, and gave him order to make an invasion into Judea, with a great body of troops; and if they would admit of his statue willingly, to erect it in the temple of God; but if they were obstinate, to conquer them by war, and then to do it. Accordingly, Petronius took the government of Syria, and made haste to obey Caesar's epistle. He got together as great a number of auxiliaries as he possibly could, and took with him two legions of the Roman army, and came to Ptolemais, and there wintered, as intending to set about the war in the spring. He also wrote word to Caius what he had resolved to do, who commended him for his alacrity, and ordered him to go on, and to make war with them, in case they would not obey his commands. But there came many ten thousands of the Jews to Petronius, to Ptolemais, to offer their petitions to him, that he would not compel them to transgress and violate the law of their forefathers; "but if," said they, "thou art entirely resolved to bring this statue, and erect it, do thou first kill us, and then do what thou hast resolved on; for while we are alive we cannot permit such things as are forbidden us to be done by the authority of our legislator, and by our forefathers' determination that such prohibitions are instances of virtue." But Petronius was angry at them, and said, "If indeed I were myself emperor, and were at liberty to follow my own inclination, and then had designed to act thus, these your words would be justly spoken to me; but now Caesar hath sent to me, I am under the necessity of being subservient to his decrees, because a disobedience to them will bring upon me inevitable destruction." Then the Jews replied, "Since, therefore, thou art so disposed, O Petronius! that thou wilt not

---

that Alexander who is mentioned by St. Luke, as of the kindred of the high priests, Acts 4:6.

disobey Caius's epistles, neither will we transgress the commands of our law; and as we depend upon the excellency of our laws, and, by the labors of our ancestors, have continued hitherto without suffering them to be transgressed, we dare not by any means suffer ourselves to be so timorous as to transgress those laws out of the fear of death, which God hath determined are for our advantage; and if we fall into misfortunes, we will bear them, in order to preserve our laws, as knowing that those who expose themselves to dangers have good hope of escaping them, because God will stand on our side, when, out of regard to him, we undergo afflictions, and sustain the uncertain turns of fortune. But if we should submit to thee, we should be greatly reproached for our cowardice, as thereby showing ourselves ready to transgress our law; and we should incur the great anger of God also, who, even thyself being judge, is superior to Caius."

3. When Petronius saw by their words that their determination was hard to be removed, and that, without a war, he should not be able to be subservient to Caius in the dedication of his statue, and that there must be a great deal of bloodshed, he took his friends, and the servants that were about him, and hasted to Tiberias, as wanting to know in what posture the affairs of the Jews were; and many ten thousands of the Jews met Petronius again, when he was come to Tiberias. These thought they must run a mighty hazard if they should have a war with the Romans, but judged that the transgression of the law was of much greater consequence, and made supplication to him, that he would by no means reduce them to such distresses, nor defile their city with the dedication of the statue. Then Petronius said to them, "Will you then make war with Caesar, without considering his great preparations for war, and your own weakness?" They replied, "We will not by any means make war with him, but still we will die before we see our laws transgressed." So they threw themselves down upon their faces, and stretched out their throats, and said they were ready to be slain; and this they did for forty days together, and in the mean time left off the tilling of their ground, and that while the season of the year required them to sow it.[31] Thus they continued firm in their

31. What Josephus here, and sect. 6, relates as done by the Jews seed time, is in Philo, "not far off the time when the corn was ripe," who, as Le Clerc notes, differ

resolution, and proposed to themselves to die willingly, rather than to see the dedication of the statue.

4. When matters were in this state, Aristobulus, king Agrippa's brother, and Heleias the Great, and the other principal men of that family with them, went in unto Petronius, and besought him, that since he saw the resolution of the multitude, he would not make any alteration, and thereby drive them to despair; but would write to Caius, that the Jews had an insuperable aversion to the reception of the statue, and how they continued with him, and left of the tillage off their ground: that they were not willing to go to war with him, because they were not able to do it, but were ready to die with pleasure, rather than suffer their laws to be transgressed: and how, upon the land's continuing unsown, robberies would grow up, on the inability they would be under of paying their tributes; and that Caius might be thereby moved to pity, and not order any barbarous action to be done to them, nor think of destroying the nation: that if he continues inflexible in his former opinion to bring a war upon them, he may then set about it himself. And thus did Aristobulus, and the rest with him, supplicate Petronius. So Petronius,[32] partly on account of the pressing instances which Aristobulus and the rest with him made, and because of the great consequence of what they desired, and the earnestness wherewith they made their supplication,—partly on account of the firmness of the opposition made by the Jews, which he saw, while he thought it a terrible thing for him to be such a slave to the madness of Caius, as to slay so many ten thousand men, only because of their religious disposition towards God, and after that to pass his life in expectation of punishment; Petronius, I say, thought it much better to send to Caius, and to let him know how intolerable it was to him to bear the anger he might have against him for not serving him sooner,

---

here one from the other. This is another indication that Josephus, when he wrote this account, had not seen Philo's Legat. ad Caiurn, otherwise he would hardly trove herein differed from him.

32. This. Publius Petronius was after this still president of Syria, under Cladius, and, at the desire of Agrippa, published a severe decree against the inhabitants of Dora, who, in a sort of intitation of Caius, had set op a statue of Claudius in a Jewish synagogue there. This decree is extant, B. XIX. ch. 6. sect. 3, and greatly confirms the present accounts of Josephus, as do the other decrees of Claudius, relating to the like Jewish affairs, B. XIX. ch. 5. sect. 2, 3, to which I refer the inquisitive reader.

in obedience to his epistle, for that perhaps he might persuade him; and that if this mad resolution continued, he might then begin the war against them; nay, that in case he should turn his hatred against himself, it was fit for virtuous persons even to die for the sake of such vast multitudes of men. Accordingly, he determined to hearken to the petitioners in this matter.

5. He then called the Jews together to Tiberias, who came many ten thousands in number; he also placed that army he now had with him opposite to them; but did not discover his own meaning, but the commands of the emperor, and told them that his wrath would, without delay, be executed on such as had the courage to disobey what he had commanded, and this immediately; and that it was fit for him, who had obtained so great a dignity by his grant, not to contradict him in any thing:—"yet," said he, "I do not think it just to have such a regard to my own safety and honor, as to refuse to sacrifice them for your preservation, who are so many in number, and endeavor to preserve the regard that is due to your law; which as it hath come down to you from your forefathers, so do you esteem it worthy of your utmost contention to preserve it: nor, with the supreme assistance and power of God, will I be so hardy as to suffer your temple to fall into contempt by the means of the imperial authority. I will, therefore, send to Caius, and let him know what your resolutions are, and will assist your suit as far as I am able, that you may not be exposed to suffer on account of the honest designs you have proposed to yourselves; and may God be your assistant, for his authority is beyond all the contrivance and power of men; and may he procure you the preservation of your ancient laws, and may not he be deprived, though without your consent, of his accustomed honors. But if Caius be irritated, and turn the violence of his rage upon me, I will rather undergo all that danger and that affliction that may come either on my body or my soul, than see so many of you to perish, while you are acting in so excellent a manner. Do you, therefore, every one of you, go your way about your own occupations, and fall to the cultivation of your ground; I will myself send to Rome, and will not refuse to serve you in all things, both by myself and by my friends."

6. When Petronius had said this, and had dismissed rite assembly of the Jews, he desired the principal of them to take care of their husbandry, and to speak kindly to the people, and encourage them

to have good hope of their affairs. Thus did he readily bring the multitude to be cheerful again. And now did God show his presence to Petronius, and signify to him that he would afford him his assistance in his whole design; for he had no sooner finished the speech that he made to the Jews, but God sent down great showers of rain, contrary to human expectation;[33] for that day was a clear day, and gave no sign, by the appearance of the sky, of any rain; nay, the whole year had been subject to a great drought, and made men despair of any water from above, even when at any time they saw the heavens overcast with clouds; insomuch that when such a great quantity of rain came, and that in an unusual manner, and without any other expectation of it, the Jews hoped that Petronius would by no means fail in his petition for them. But as to Petronius, he was mightily surprised when he perceived that God evidently took care of the Jews, and gave very plain signs of his appearance, and this to such a degree, that those that were in earnest much inclined to the contrary had no power left to contradict it. This was also among those other particulars which he wrote to Caius, which all tended to dissuade him, and by all means to entreat him not to make so many ten thousands of these men go distracted; whom, if he should slay, (for without war they would by no means suffer the laws of their worship to be set aside,) he would lose the revenue they paid him, and would be publicly cursed by them for all future ages. Moreover, that God, who was their Governor, had shown his power most evidently on their account, and that such a power of his as left no room for doubt about it. And this was the business that Petronius was now engaged in.

7. But king Agrippa, who now lived at Rome, was more and more in the favor of Caius; and when he had once made him a supper, and was careful to exceed all others, both in expenses and in such preparations as might contribute most to his pleasure; nay, it was so far from the ability of others, that Caius himself could never equal,

33. Josephus here uses the solemn New Testament words, the presence and appearance of God, for the extraordinary manifestation of his power and providence to Petronius, by sending rain in a time of distress, immediately upon the resolution he had taken to preserve the temple unpolluted, at the hazard of his own life, without any other miraculous appearance at all in that case; which well deserves to be taken notice of here, and greatly illustrates several texts, both in the Old and New Testament.

much less exceed it (such care had he taken beforehand to exceed all men, and particularly. to make all agreeable to Caesar); hereupon Caius admired his understanding and magnificence, that he should force himself to do all to please him, even beyond such expenses as he could bear, and was desirous not to be behind Agrippa in that generosity which he exerted in order to please him. So Caius, when he had drank wine plentifully, and was merrier than ordinary, said thus during the feast, when Agrippa had drunk to him: "I knew before now how great a respect thou hast had for me, and how great kindness thou hast shown me, though with those hazards to thyself, which thou underwentest under Tiberius on that account; nor hast thou omitted any thing to show thy good-will towards us, even beyond thy ability; whence it would be a base thing for me to be conquered by thy affection. I am therefore desirous to make thee amends for every thing in which I have been formerly deficient; for all that I have bestowed on thee, that may be called my gifts, is but little. Everything that may contribute to thy happiness shall be at thy service, and that cheerfully, and so far as my ability will reach."[34] And this was what Caius said to Agrippa, thinking be would ask for some large country, or the revenues of certain cities. But although he had prepared beforehand what he would ask, yet had he not discovered his intentions, but made this answer to Caius immediately: That it was not out of any expectation of gain that he formerly paid his respects to him, contrary to the commands of Tiberius, nor did he now do any thing relating to him out of regard to his own advantage, and in order to receive any thing from him; that the gifts he had already bestowed upon him were great, and beyond the hopes of even a craving man; for although they may be beneath thy power, [who art the donor,] yet are they greater than my inclination and dignity, who am the receiver. And as Caius was astonished at Agrippa's inclinations, and still the more pressed him to make his request for somewhat which he might gratify him with, Agrippa replied, "Since thou, O my lord! declarest such is thy readiness to grant, that I am worthy of thy gifts, I will ask nothing relating to my own felicity; for what thou hast already bestowed on me has made me excel therein; but I desire somewhat which may make

---

34. This behavior of Caius to Agrippa is very like that of Herod Antipas, his uncle, to Herodias, Agrippa's sister, about it John the Baptist, Matthew 14:6—11.

thee glorious for piety, and render the Divinity assistant to thy designs, and may be for an honor to me among those that inquire about it, as showing that I never once fail of obtaining what I desire of thee; for my petition is this, that thou wilt no longer think of the dedication of that statue which thou hast ordered to be set up in the Jewish temple by Petronius."

8. And thus did Agrippa venture to cast the die upon this occasion, so great was the affair in his opinion, and in reality, though he knew how dangerous a thing it was so to speak; for had not Caius approved of it, it had tended to no less than the loss of his life. So Caius, who was mightily taken with Agrippa's obliging behavior, and on other accounts thinking it a dishonorable thing to be guilty of falsehood before so many witnesses, in points wherein he had with such alacrity forced Agrippa to become a petitioner, and that it would look as if he had already repented of what he had said, and because he greatly admired Agrippa's virtue, in not desiring him at all to augment his own dominions, either with larger revenues, or other authority, but took care of the public tranquillity, of the laws, and of the Divinity itself, he granted him what he had requested. He also wrote thus to Petronius, commending him for his assembling his army, and then consulting him about these affairs. "If therefore," said' he," thou hast already erected my statue, let it stand; but if thou hast not yet dedicated it, do not trouble thyself further about it, but dismiss thy army, go back, and take care of those affairs which I sent thee about at first, for I have now no occasion for the erection of that statue. This I have granted as a favor to Agrippa, a man whom I honor so very greatly, that I am not able to contradict what he would have, or what he desired me to do for him." And this was what Caius wrote to Petronius, which was before he received his letter, informing him that the Jews were very ready to revolt about the statue, and that they seemed resolved to threaten war against the Romans, and nothing else. When therefore Caius was much displeased that any attempt should be made against his government as he was a slave to base and vicious actions on all occasions, and had no regard to What was virtuous and honorable, and against whomsoever he resolved to show his anger, and that for any cause whatsoever, he suffered not himself to be restrained by any admonition, but thought the indulging his anger to be a real pleasure, he wrote thus to Petronius: "Seeing thou esteemest

the presents made thee by the Jews to be of greater value than my commands, and art grown insolent enough to be subservient to their pleasure, I charge thee to become thy own judge, and to consider what thou art to do, now thou art under my displeasure; for I will make thee an example to the present and to all future ages, that they. may not dare to contradict the commands of their emperor."

9. This was the epistle which Caius wrote to. Petronius; but Petronius did not receive it while Caius was alive, that ship which carried it sailing so slow, that other letters came to Petronius before this, by which he understood that Caius was dead; for God would not forget the dangers Petronius had undertaken on account of the Jews, and of his own honor. But when he had taken Caius away, out of his indignation of what he had so insolently attempted in assuming to himself divine worship, both Rome and all that dominion conspired with Petronius, especially those that were of the senatorian order, to give Caius his due reward, because he had been unmercifully severe to them; for he died not long after he had written to Petronius that epistle which threatened him with death. But as for the occasion of his death, and the nature of the plot against him, I shall relate them in the progress of this narration. Now that epistle which informed Petronius of Caius's death came first, and a little afterward came that which commanded him to kill himself with his own hands. Whereupon he rejoiced at this coincidence as to the death of Caius, and admired God's providence, who, without the least delay, and immediately, gave him a reward for the regard he had to the temple, and the assistance he afforded the Jews for avoiding the dangers they were in. And by this means Petronius escaped that danger of death, which he could not foresee.

9 *What Befell the Jews That Were in Babylon on Occasion of Asineus and Anileus, Two Brethren,*

1. A VERY sad calamity now befell the Jews that were in Mesopotamia, and especially those that dwelt in Babylonia. Inferior it was to none of the calamities which had gone before, and came together with a great slaughter of them, and that greater than any upon record before; concerning all which I shall speak accurately, and shall explain

the occasions whence these miseries came upon them. There was a city of Babylonia called Neerda; not only a ver populous one, but one that had a good and a large territory about it, and, besides its other advantages, full of men also. It was, besides, not easily to be assaulted by enemies, from the river Euphrates encompassing it all round, and from the wails that were built about it. There was also the city Nisibis, situate on the same current of the river. For which reason the Jews, depending on the natural strength of these places, deposited in them that half shekel which every one, by the custom of our country, offers unto God, as well as they did other things devoted to him; for they made use of these cities as a treasury, whence, at a proper time, they were transmitted to Jerusalem; and many ten thousand men undertook the carriage of those donations, out of fear of the ravages of the Parthians, to whom the Babylonians were then subject. Now there were two men, Asineus and Anileus, of the city Neerda by birth, and brethren to one another. They were destitute of a father, and their mother put them to learn the art of weaving curtains, it not being esteemed disgrace among them for men to be weavers of cloth. Now he that taught them that art, and was set over them, complained that they came too late to their work, and punished them with stripes; but they took this just punishment as an affront, and carried off all the weapons which were kept in that house, which were not a few, and went into a certain place where was a partition of the rivers, and was a place naturally very fit for the feeding of cattle, and for preserving such fruits as were usually laid up against winter. The poorest sort of the young men also resorted to them, whom they armed with the weapons they had gotten, and became their captains; and nothing hindered them from being their leaders into mischief; for as soon as they were become invincible, and had built them a citadel, they sent to such as fed cattle, and ordered them to pay them so much tribute out of them as might be sufficient for their maintenance, proposing also that they would be their friends, if they would submit to them, and that they would defend them from all their other enemies on every side, but that they would kill the cattle of those that refused to obey them. So they hearkened to their proposals, (for they could do nothing else,) and sent them as many sheep as were required of them; whereby their forces grew greater, and they became lords over all they pleased, because they marched suddenly, and did them a mischief, insomuch that every body who had to do with them chose to pay them respect; and they became formidable to such as came to assault them, till the report about them came to the ears of the king of Parthia himself.

2. But when the governor of Babylonia understood this, and had a mind to put a stop to them before they grew greater, and before greater mischiefs should arise from them, he got together as great an army as he could, both of Parthians and Babylonians, and marched against them, thinking to attack them and destroy them before any one should carry them the news that he had got an army together. He then encamped at a lake, and lay still; but on the next day (it was the sabbath, which is among the Jews a day of rest from all sorts of work) he supposed that the enemy would not dare to fight him thereon, but that he would take them and carry them away prisoners, without fighting. He therefore proceeded gradually, and thought to fall upon them on the sudden. Now Asineus was sitting with the rest, and their weapons lay by them; upon which he said, "Sirs, I hear a neighing of horses; not of such as are feeding, but such as have men on their backs; I also hear such a noise of their bridles, that I am afraid that some enemies are coming upon us to encompass us round. However, let somebody go to look about, and make report of what reality there is in the present state of things; and may what I have said prove a false alarm." And when he had said this, some of them went out to spy out what was the matter; and they came again immediately, and said to him, that "neither hast thou been mistaken in telling us what our enemies were doing, nor will those enemies permit us to be injurious to people any longer. We are caught by their intrigues like brute beasts, and there is a large body of cavalry marching upon us, while we are destitute of hands to defend ourselves withal, because we are restrained from doing it by the prohibition of our law, which obliges us to rest [on this day]." But Asiueus did not by any means agree with the opinion of his spy as to what was to be done, but thought it more agreeable to the law to pluck up their spirits in this necessity they were fallen into, and break their law by avenging themselves, although they should die in the action, than by doing nothing to please their enemies in submitting to be slain by them. Accordingly, he took up his weapons, and infused courage into those that were with him to act as courageously as himself. So they fell upon their enemies, and slew

a great many of them, because they despised them and came as to a certain victory, and put the rest to flight.

3. But when the news of this fight came to the king of Parthia, he was surprised at the boldness of these brethren, and was desirous to see them, and speak with them. He therefore sent the most trusty of all his guards to say thus to them: "That king Artsbanus, although he had been unjustly treated by you, who have made an attempt against his government, yet hath he more regard to your courageous behavior, than to the anger he bears to you, and hath sent me to give you his right hand[35] and security; and he permits you to come to him safely, and without any violence upon the road; and he wants to have you address yourselves to him as friends, without meaning any guile or deceit to you. He also promises to make you presents, and to pay you those respects which will make an addition of his power to your courage, and thereby be of advantage to you." Yet did Asineus himself put off his journey thither, but sent his brother Anileus with all such presents as he could procure. So he went, and was admitted to the king's presence; and when Artabanus saw Anileus coming alone, he inquired into the reason why Asineus avoided to come along with him; and when he understood that he was afraid, and staid by the lake, he took an oath, by the gods of his country, that he would do them no harm, if they came to him upon the assurances he gave them, and gave him his right hand. This is of the greatest force there with all these barbarians, and affords a firm security to those who converse with them; for none of them will deceive you when once they have given you their right hands, nor will any one doubt of their fidelity, when that is once given, even though they were before suspected of injustice. When Artabanus had done this, he sent away Anileus to persuade his brother to come to him. Now this the king did, because he wanted to curb his own governors of provinces by the courage of these Jewish brethren, lest they should make a league with them; for they were ready for a revolt, and were disposed to rebel, had they been sent on an expedition against them. He was also afraid, lest when he was

35. The joining of the right hands was esteemed among the Peoians [and Parthians] in particular a most inviolable obligation to fidelity, as Dr. Hudson here observes, and refers to the commentary on Justin, B. XI. ch. 15., for its confirmation. We often meet with the like use of it in Josephus.

engaged in a war, in order to subdue those governors of provinces that had revolted, the party of Asineus, and those in Babylonia, should be augmented, and either make war upon him, when they should hear of that revolt, or if they should be disappointed in that case, they would not fail of doing further mischief to him.

4. When the king had these intentions, he sent away Anileus, and Anileus prevailed on his brother [to come to the king], when he had related to him the king's good-will, and the oath that he had taken. Accordingly, they made haste to go to Artsbanus, who received them when they were come with pleasure, and admired Asineus's courage in the actions he had done, and this because he was a little man to see to, and at first sight appeared contemptible also, and such as one might deem a person of no value at all. He also said to his friends, how, upon the comparison, he showed his soul to be in all respects superior to his body; and when, as they were drinking together, he once showed Asineus to Abdagases, one of the generals of his army, and told him his name, and described the great courage he was of in war, and Abdagases had desired leave to kill him, and thereby to inflict on him a punishment for those injuries he had done to the Parthian government, the king replied, "I will never give thee leave to kill a man who hath depended on my faith, especially not after I have sent him my right hand, and endeavored to gain his belief by oaths made by the gods. But if thou be a truly warlike man, thou standest not in need of my perjury. Go thou then, and avenge the Parthian government; attack this man, when he is returned back, and conquer him by the forces that are under thy command, without my privity." Hereupon the king called for Asineus, and said to him, "It is time for thee, O thou young man! to return home, and not provoke the indignation of my generals in this place any further, lest they attempt to murder thee, and that without my approbation. I commit to thee the country of Babylonia in trust, that it may, by thy care, be preserved free from robbers, and from other mischiefs. I have kept my faith inviolable to thee, and that not in trifling affairs, but in those that concerned thy safety, and do therefore deserve thou shouldst be kind to me." When he had said this, and given Asineus some presents, he sent him away immediately; who, when he was come home, built fortresses, and became great in a little time, and managed things with such courage and success, as no other person, that had no higher a beginning, ever did before him.

Those Parthian governors also, who were sent that way, paid him great respect; and the honor that was paid him by the Babylonians seemed to them too small, and beneath his deserts, although he were in no small dignity and power there; nay, indeed, all the affairs of Mesopotamia depended upon him, and he more and more flourished in this happy condition of his for fifteen years.

5. But as their affairs were in so flourishing a state, there sprang up a calamity among them on the following occasion. When once they had deviated from that course of virtue whereby they had gained so great power, they affronted and transgressed the laws of their forefathers, and fell under the dominion of their lusts and pleasures. A certain Parthian, who came as general of an army into those parts, had a wife following him, who had a vast reputation for other accomplishments, and particularly was admired above all other women for her beauty. Anileus, the brother of Asineus, either heard of that her beauty from others, or perhaps saw her himself also, and so became at once her lover and her enemy; partly because he could not hope to enjoy this woman but by obtaining power over her as a captive, and partly because he thought he could not conquer his inclinations for her. As soon therefore as her husband had been declared an enemy to them, and was fallen in the battle, the widow of the deceased was married to this her lover. However, this woman did not come into their house without producing great misfortunes, both to Anileus himself, and to Asineus also; but brought great mischiefs upon them on the occasion following. Since she was led away captive, upon the death of her husband, she concealed the images of those gods which were their country gods, common to her husband and to herself: now it was the custom[36] of that country for all to have the idols they worship in their own houses, and to carry them along with them when they go into a foreign land; agreeable to which custom of theirs she carried her idols with her. Now at first she performed her worship to them privately;

36. This custom of the Mesopotamians to carry their household gods along with them wherever they traveled is as old as the days of Jacob, when Rachel his wife did the same, Genesis 31:19, 30–35; nor is it to pass here unobserved, what great miseries came on these Jews, because they suffered one of their leaders to marry an idolatrous wife, contrary to the law of Moses. Of which matter see the note on B. XIX. ch. 5. sect. 3.

but when she was become Anileus's married wife, she worshipped them in her accustomed manner, and with the same appointed ceremonies which she used in her former husband's days; upon which their most esteemed friends blamed him at first, that he did not act after the manner of the Hebrews, nor perform what was agreeable to their laws, in marrying a foreign wife, and one that transgressed the accurate appointments of their sacrifices and religious ceremonies; that he ought to consider, lest, by allowing himself in many pleasures of the body, he might lose his principality, on account of the beauty of a wife, and that high authority which, by God's blessing, he had arrived at. But when they prevailed not at all upon him, he slew one of them for whom he had the greatest respect, because of the liberty he took with him; who, when he was dying, out of regard to the laws, imprecated a punishment upon his murderer Anileus, and upon Asineus also, and that all their companions might come to a like end from their enemies; upon the two first as the principal actors of this wickedness, and upon the rest as those that would not assist him when he suffered in the defense of their laws. Now these latter were sorely grieved, yet did they tolerate these doings, because they remembered that they had arrived at their present happy state by no other means than their fortitude. But when they also heard of the worship of those gods whom the Parthians adore, they thought the injury that Anileus offered to their laws was to be borne no longer; and a greater number of them came to Asineus, and loudly complained of Aniteus, and told him that it had been well that he had of himself seen what was advantageous to them; but that however it was now high time to correct what had been done amiss, before the crime that had been committed proved the ruin of himself and all the rest of them. They added, that the marriage of this woman was made without their consent, and without a regard to their old laws; and that the worship which this woman paid [to her gods] was a reproach to the God whom they worshipped. Now Asineus was sensible of his brother's offense, that it had been already the cause of great mischiefs, and would be so for the time to come; yet did he tolerate the same from the good-will he had to so near a relation, and forgiving it to him, on account that his brother was quite overborne by his wicked inclinations. But as more and more still came about him every day, and the clamors about it became greater, he at length spake to Anileus about these clamors, reproving him for his former actions, and desiring him for the future to leave them off, and send the woman back to her relations. But nothing was gained by these reproofs; for as the woman perceived what a tumult was made among the people on her account, and was afraid for Anileus, lest he should come to any harm for his love to her, she infused poison into Asineus's food, and thereby took him off, and was now secure of prevailing, when her lover was to be judge of what should be done about her.

6. So Anileus took the government upon himself alone, and led his army against the villages of Mithridates, who was a man of principal authority in Parthin, and had married king Artabanus's daughter; he also plundered them, and among that prey was found much money, and many slaves, as also a great number of sheep, and many other things, which, when gained, make men's condition happy. Now when Mithridates, who was there at this time, heard that his villages were taken, he was very much displeased to find that Anileus had first begun to injure him, and to affront him in his present dignity, when he had not offered any injury to him beforehand; and he got together the greatest body of horsemen he was able, and those out of that number which were of an age fit for war, and came to fight Anileus; and when he was arrived at a certain village of his own, he lay still there, as intending to fight him on the day following, because it was the sabbath, the day on which the Jews rest. And when Anileus was informed of this by a Syrian stranger of another village, who not only gave him an exact account of other circumstances, but told him where Mithridates would have a feast, he took his supper at a proper time, and marched by night, with an intent of falling upon the Parthians while they were unaprrized what they should do; so he fell upon them about the fourth watch of the night, and some of them he slew while they were asleep, and others he put to flight, and took Mithridates alive, and set him naked upon an ass[37] which, among the Parthians, is esteemed the greatest reproach possible. And when he had brought him into a wood with such a resolution, and his friends desired him to

37. This custom, in Syria and Mesopotamia, of setting men upon an ass, by way of disgrace, is still kept up at Damascus in Syria; where, in order to show their despite against the Christians, the Turks will not suffer them to hire horses, but asses only, when they go abroad to see the country, as Mr. Maundrell assures us, p. 128.

kill Mithridates, he soon told them his own mind to the contrary, and said that it was not right to kill a man who was of one of the principal families among the Parthians, and greatly honored with matching into the royal family; that so far as they had hitherto gone was tolerable; for although they had injured Mithridates, yet if they preserved his life, this benefit would be remembered by him to the advantage of those that gave it him; but that if be were once put to death, the king would not be at rest till he had made a great slaughter of the Jews that dwelt at Babylon; "to whose safety we ought to have a regard, both on account of our relation to them, and because if any misfortune befall us, we have no other place to retire to, since he hath gotten the flower of their youth under him." By this thought, and this speech of his made in council, he persuaded them to act accordingly; so Mithridates was let go. But when he was got away, his wife reproached him, that although he was son-in-law to the king, he neglected to avenge himself on those that had injured him, while he took no care about it, but was contented to have been made a captive by the Jews, and to have escaped them; and she bid him either to go back like a man of courage, or else she sware by the gods of their royal family that she would certainly dissolve her marriage with him. Upon which, partly because he could not bear the daily trouble of her taunts, and partly because he was afraid of her insolence, lest she should in earnest dissolve their marriage, he unwillingly, and against his inclinations, got together again as great an army as he could, and marched along with them, as himself thinking it a thing not to be borne any longer, that he, a Parthian, should owe his preservation to the Jews, when they had been too hard for him in the war.

7. But as soon as Anileus understood that Mithridates was marching with a great army against him, he thought it too ignominious a thing to tarry about the lakes, and not to take the first opportunity of meeting his enemies, and he hoped to have the same success, and to beat their enemies as they did before; as also he ventured boldly upon the like attempts. Accordingly, he led out his army, and a great many more joined themselves to that army, in order to betake themselves to plunder the people, and in order to terrify the enemy again by their numbers. But when they had marched ninety furlongs, while the road had been through dry [and sandy] places, and about the midst of the day, they were become very thirsty; and Mithridates

appeared, and fell upon them, as they were in distress for want of water, on which account, and on account of the time of the day, they were not able to bear their weapons. So Anileus and his men were put to an ignominious rout, while men in despair were to attack those that were fresh and in good plight; so a great slaughter was made, and many ten thousand men fell. Now Anileus, and all that stood firm about him, ran away as fast as they were able into a wood, and afforded Mithridates the pleasure of having gained a great victory over them. But there now came in to Anileus a conflux of bad men, who regarded their own lives very little, if they might but gain some present ease, insomuch that they, by thus coming to him, compensated the multitude of those that perished in the fight. Yet were not these men like to those that fell, because they were rash, and unexercised in war; however, with these he came upon the villages of the Babylonians, and a mighty devastation of all things was made there by the injuries that Anileus did them. So the Babylonians, and those that had already been in the war, sent to Neerda to the Jews there, and demanded Anileus. But although they did not agree to their demands, (for if they had been willing to deliver him up, it was not in their power so to do,) yet did they desire to make peace with them. To which the other replied, that they also wanted to settle conditions of peace with them, and sent men together with the Babylonians, who discoursed with Anileus about them. But the Babylonians, upon taking a view of his situation, and having learned where Anileus and his men lay, fell secretly upon them as they were drunk and fallen asleep, and slew all that they caught of them, without any fear, and killed Anileus himself also.

8. The Babylonians were now freed from Anileus's heavy incursions, which had been a great restraint to the effects of that hatred they bore to the Jews; for they were almost always at variance, by reason of the contrariety of their laws; and which party soever grew boldest before the other, they assaulted the other: and at this time in particular it was, that upon the ruin of Anileus's party, the Babylonians attacked the Jews, which made those Jews so, vehemently to resent the injuries they received from the Babylonians, that being neither able to fight them, nor bearing to live with them, they went to Seleucia, the principal city of those parts, which was built by Seleucus Nicator. It was inhabited by many of the Macedonians, but by more of the Grecians;

not a few of the Syrians also dwelt there; and thither did the Jews fly, and lived there five years, without any misfortunes. But on the sixth year, a pestilence came upon these at Babylon, which occasioned new removals of men's habitations out of that city; and because they came to Seleucia, it happened that a still heavier calamity came upon them on that account which I am going to relate immediately.

9. Now the way of living of the people of Seleucia, which were Greeks and Syrians, was commonly quarrelsome, and full of discords, though the Greeks were too hard for the Syrians. When, therefore, the Jews were come thither, and dwelt among them, there arose a sedition, and the Syrians were too hard for the other, by the assistance of the Jews, who are men that despise dangers, and very ready to fight upon any occasion. Now when the Greeks had the worst in this sedition, and saw that they had but one way of recovering their former authority, and that was, if they could prevent the agreement between the Jews and the Syrians, they every one discoursed with such of the Syrians as were formerly their acquaintance, and promised they would be at peace and friendship with them. Accordingly, they gladly agreed so to do; and when this was done by the principal men of both nations, they soon agreed to a reconciliation; and when they were so agreed, they both knew that the great design of such their union would be their common hatred to the Jews. Accordingly, they fell upon them, and slew about fifty thousand of them; nay, the Jews were all destroyed, excepting a few who escaped, either by the compassion which their friends or neighbors afforded them, in order to let them fly away. These retired to Ctesiphon, a Grecian city, and situate near to Seleucia, where the king [of Parthia] lives in winter every year, and where the greatest part of his riches are reposited; but the Jews had here no certain settlement, those of Seleucia having little concern for the king's honor. Now the whole nation of the Jews were in fear both of the Babylonians and of the Seleucians, because all the Syrians that live in those places agreed with the Seleucians in the war against the Jews; so the most of them gathered themselves together, and went to Neerda and Nisibis, and obtained security there by the strength of those cities; besides which their inhabitants, who were a great many, were all warlike men. And this was the state of the Jews at this time in Babylonia.

Book 19

Containing the Interval of Three Years and a Half, from the Departure Out of Babylon to Fadus, the Roman Procurator

1 *How Caius*[1] Was Slain by Cherea

1. NOW this Caius[2] did not demonstrate his madness in offering injuries only to the Jews at Jerusalem, or to those that dwelt in the neighborhood; but suffered it to extend itself through all the earth and sea, so far as was in subjection to the Romans, and filled it with ten thousand mischiefs; so many indeed in number as no former history relates. But Rome itself felt the most dismal effects of what he did, while he deemed that not to be any way more honorable than the rest of the cities; but he pulled and hauled its other citizens, but especially the senate, and particularly the nobility, and such as had been dignified by illustrious ancestors; he also had ten thousand devices against such of the equestrian order, as it was styled, who

---

1. In this and the three next chapters we have, I think, a larger and more distinct account of the slaughter of Caius, and the succession of Claudius, than we have of any such ancient facts whatsoever elsewhere. Some of the occasions of which probably were, Josephus's bitter hatred against tyranny, and the pleasure he took in giving the history of the slaughter of such a barbarous tyrant as was this Caius Caligula, as also the deliverance his own nation had by that slaughter, of which he speaks sect. 2, together with the great intimacy he had with Agrippa, junior, whose father was deeply concerned in the advancement of Claudius, upon the death of Caius; from which Agrippa, junior, Josephus might be fully informed Of his history.

2. Called Caligula by the Romans.

were esteemed by the citizens equal in dignity and wealth with the senators, because out of them the senators were themselves chosen; these he treated after all ignominious manner, and removed them out of his way, while they were at once slain, and their wealth plundered, because he slew men generally in order to seize on their riches. He also asserted his own divinity, and insisted on greater honors to be paid him by his subjects than are due to mankind. He also frequented that temple of Jupiter which they style the Capitol, which is with them the most holy of all their temples, and had boldness enough to call himself the brother of Jupiter. And other pranks he did like a madman; as when he laid a bridge from the city Dicearchia, which belongs to Campania, to Misenum, another city upon the sea-side, from one promontory to another, of the length of thirty furlongs, as measured over the sea. And this was done because he esteemed it to be a most tedious thing to row over it in a small ship, and thought withal that it became him to make that bridge, since he was lord of the sea, and might oblige it to give marks of obedience as well as the earth; so he enclosed the whole bay within his bridge, and drove his chariot over it; and thought that, as he was a god, it was fit for him to travel over such roads as this was. Nor did he abstain from the plunder of any of the Grecian temples, and gave order that all the engravings and sculptures, and the rest of the ornaments of the statues and donations therein dedicated, should be brought to him, saying that the best things ought to be set no where but in the best place, and that the city of Rome was that best place. He also adorned his own house and his gardens with the curiosities brought from those temples, together with the houses he lay at when he traveled all over Italy; whence he did not scruple to give a command that the statue of Jupiter Olympius, so called because he was honored at the Olympian games by the Greeks, which was the work of Phidias the Athenian, should be brought to Rome. Yet did not he compass his end, because the architects told Memmius Regulus, who was commanded to remove that statue of Jupiter, that the workmanship was such as would be spoiled, and would not bear the removal. It was also reported that Memmius, both on that account, and on account of some such mighty prodigies as are of an incredible nature, put off the taking it down, and wrote to Caius those accounts, as his apology for not having done what his epistle required of him; and that when he was thence in danger of perishing, he was saved by Caius being dead himself, before he had put him to death.

2. Nay, Caius's madness came to this height, that when he had a daughter born, he carried her into the capitol, and put her upon the knees of the statue, and said that the child was common to him and to Jupiter, and determined that she had two fathers, but which of these fathers were the greatest he left undetermined; and yet mankind bore him in such his pranks. He also gave leave to slaves to accuse their masters of any crimes whatsoever they pleased; for all such accusations were terrible, because they were in great part made to please him, and at his suggestion, insomuch that Pollux, Claudius's slave, had the boldness to lay an accusation against Claudius himself; and Caius was not ashamed to be present at his trial of life and death, to hear that trial of his own uncle, in hopes of being able to take him off, although he did not succeed to his mind. But when he had filled the whole habitable world which he governed with false accusations and miseries, and had occasioned the greatest insults of slaves against their masters, who indeed in a great measure ruled them, there were many secret plots now laid against him; some in anger, and in order for men to revenge themselves, on account of the miseries they had already undergone from him; and others made attempts upon him, in order to take him off before they should fall into such great miseries, while his death came very fortunately for the preservation of the laws of all men, and had a great influence upon the public welfare; and this happened most happily for our nation in particular, which had almost utterly perished if he had not been suddenly slain. And I confess I have a mind to give a full account of this matter particularly, because it will afford great assurance of the power of God, and great comfort to those that are under afflictions, and wise caution to those who think their happiness will never end, nor bring them at length to the most lasting miseries, if they do not conduct their lives by the principles of virtue.

3. Now there were three several conspiracies made in order to take off Caius, and each of these three were conducted by excellent persons. Emilius Regulus, born at Corduba in Spain, got some men together, and was desirous to take Caius off, either by them or by himself. Another conspiracy there was laid by them, under the conduct of Cherea Cassius, the tribune [of the Pretorian band].

Minucianus Annins was also one of great consequence among those that were prepared to oppose his tyranny. Now the several occasions of these men's several hatred and conspiracy against Caius were these: Regulus had indignation and hatred against all injustice, for he had a mind naturally angry, and bold, and free, which made him not conceal his counsels; so he communicated them to many of his friends, and to others who seemed to him persons of activity and vigor: Minucianus entered into this conspiracy, because of the injustice done to Lepidus his particular friend, and one of the best character of all the citizens, whom Caius had slain, as also because he was afraid of himself, since Caius's wrath tended to the slaughter of all alike: and for Cherea, he came in, because he thought it a deed worthy of a free ingenuous man to kill Caius, and was ashamed of the reproaches he lay under from Caius, as though he were a coward; as also because he was himself in danger every day from his friendship with him, and the observance he paid him. These men proposed this attempt to all the rest that were concerned, who saw the injuries that were offered them, and were desirous that Caius's slaughter might succeed by their mutual assistance of one another, and they might themselves escape being killed by the taking off Caius; that perhaps they should gain their point; and that it would be a happy thing, if they should gain it, to approve themselves to so many excellent persons, as earnestly wished to be partakers with them in their design for the delivery of the city and of the government, even at the hazard of their own lives. But still Cherea was the most zealous of them all, both out of a desire of getting himself the greatest name, and also by reason of his access to Caius's presence with less danger, because he was tribune, and could therefore the more easily kill him.

4. Now at this time came on the horse-races [Circensian games]; the view of which games was eagerly desired by the people of Rome, for they come with great alacrity into the hippodrome [circus] at such times, and petition their emperors, in great multitudes, for what they stand in need of; who usually did not think fit to deny them their requests, but readily and gratefully granted them. Accordingly, they most importunately desired that Caius would now ease them in their tributes, and abate somewhat of the rigor of their taxes imposed upon them; but he would not hear their petition; and when their clamors increased, he sent soldiers some one way and some another, and gave

order that they should lay hold on those that made the clamors, and without any more ado bring them out, and put them to death. These were Caius's commands, and those who were commanded executed the same; and the number of those who were slain on this occasion was very great. Now the people saw this, and bore it so far, that they left off clamoring, because they saw with their own eyes that this petition to be relieved, as to the payment of their money, brought immediate death upon them. These things made Cherea more resolute to go on with his plot, in order to put an end to this barbarity of Caius against men. He then at several times thought to fall upon Caius, even as he was feasting; yet did he restrain himself by some considerations; not that he had any doubt on him about killing him, but as watching for a proper season, that the attempt might not be frustrated, but that he might give the blow so as might certainly gain his purpose.

5. Cherea had been in the army a long time, yet was he not pleased with conversing so much with Caius. But Caius had set him to require the tributes, and other dues, which, when not paid in due time, were forfeited to Caesar's treasury; and he had made some delays in requiring them, because those burdens had been doubled, and had rather indulged his own mild disposition than performed Caius's command; nay, indeed, be provoked Caius to anger by his sparing men, and pitying the hard fortunes of those from whom he demanded the taxes; and Caius upbraided him with his sloth and effeminacy in being so long about collecting the taxes. And indeed he did not only affront him in other respects, but when he gave him the watchword of the day, to whom it was to be given by his place, he gave him feminine words, and those of a nature very reproachful; and these watchwords he gave out, as having been initiated in the secrets of certain mysteries, which he had been himself the author of. Now although he had sometimes put on women's clothes, and had been wrapt in some embroidered garments to them belonging, and done a great many other things, in order to make the company mistake him for a woman; yet did he, by way of reproach, object the like womanish behavior to Cherea. But when Cherea received the watchword from him, he had indignation at it, but had greater indignation at the delivery of it to others, as being laughed at by those that received it; insomuch that his fellow tribunes made him the subject of their drollery; for they would foretell that he would bring them some of

his usual watchwords when he was about to take the watchword from Caesar, and would thereby make him ridiculous; on which accounts he took the courage of assuming certain partners to him, as having just reasons for his indignation against Caius. Now there was one Pompedius, a senator, and one who had gone through almost all posts in the government, but otherwise an Epicurean, and for that reason loved to lead an inactive life. Now Timidius, an enemy of his, had informed Caius that he had used indecent reproaches against him, and he made use of Quintilia for a witness to them; a woman she was much beloved by many that frequented the theater, and particularly by Pompedius, on account of her great beauty. Now this woman thought it a horrible thing to attest to an accusation that touched the life of her lover, which was also a lie. Timidius, however, wanted to have her brought to the torture. Caius was irritated at this reproach upon him, and commanded Cherea, without any delay, to torture Quintilia, as he used to employ Cherea in such bloody matters, and those that required the torture, because he thought he would do it the more barbarously, in order to avoid that imputation of effeminacy which he had laid upon him. But Quintilia, when she was brought to the rack, trod upon the foot of one of her associates, and let him know that he might be of good courage, and not be afraid of the consequence of her tortures, for that she would bear them with magnanimity. Cherea tortured this woman after a cruel manner; unwillingly indeed, but because he could not help it. He then brought her, without being in the least moved at what she had suffered, into the presence of Caius, and that in such a state as was sad to behold; and Caius, being somewhat affected with the sight of Quintilia, who had her body miserably disordered by the pains she had undergone, freed both her and Pompedius of the crime laid to their charge. He also gave her money to make her an honorable amends, and comfort her for that maiming of her body which she had suffered, and for her glorious patience under such insufferable torments.

6. This matter sorely grieved Cherea, as having been the cause, as far as he could, or the instrument, of those miseries to men, which seemed worthy of consolation to Caius himself; on which account he said to Clement and to Papinius, (of whom Clement was general of the army, and Papinius was a tribune,) "To be sure, O Clement, we have no way failed in our guarding the emperor; for as to those that

have made conspiracies against his government, some have been slain by our care and pains, and some have been by us tortured, and this to such a degree, that he hath himself pitied them. How great then is our virtue in submitting to conduct his armies!" Clement held his peace, but showed the shame he was under in obeying Caius's orders, both by his eyes and his blushing countenance, while he thought it by no means right to accuse the emperor in express words, lest their own safety should be endangered thereby. Upon which Cherea took courage, and spake to him without fear of the dangers that were before him, and discoursed largely of the sore calamities under which the city and the government then labored, and said, "We may indeed pretend in words that Caius is the person unto whom the cause of such miseries ought to be imputed; but, in the opinion of such as are able to judge uprightly, it is I, O Clement! and this Papinius, and before us thou thyself, who bring these tortures upon the Romans, and upon all mankind. It is not done by our being subservient to the commands of Caius, but it is done by our own consent; for whereas it is in our power to put an end to the life of this man, who hath so terribly injured the citizens and his subjects, we are his guard in mischief, and his executioners instead of his soldiers, and are the instruments of his cruelty. We bear these weapons, not for our liberty, not for the Roman government, but only for his preservation, who hath enslaved both their bodies and their minds; and we are every day polluted with the blood that we shed, and the torments we inflict upon others; and this we do, till somebody becomes Caius's instrument in bringing the like miseries upon ourselves. Nor does he thus employ us because he hath a kindness for us, but rather because he hath a suspicion of us, as also because when abundance more have been killed, (for Caius will set no bounds to his wrath, since he aims to do all, not out of regard to justice, but to his own pleasure,) we shall also ourselves be exposed to his cruelty; whereas we ought to be the means of confirming the security and liberty of all, and at the same time to resolve to free ourselves from dangers.

7. Hereupon Clement openly commended Cherea's intentions, but bid him hold his tongue; for that in case his words should get out among many, and such things should be spread abroad as were fit to be concealed, the plot would come to be discovered before it was executed, and they should be brought to punishment; but that they

should leave all to futurity, and the hope which thence arose, that some fortunate event would come to their assistance; that, as for himself, his age would not permit him to make any attempt in that case. "However, although perhaps I could suggest what may be safer than what thou, Cherea, hast contrived and said, yet trow is it possible for any one to suggest what is more for thy reputation?" So Clement went his way home, with deep reflections on what he had heard, and what he had himself said. Cherea also was under a concern, and went quickly to Cornelius Sabinus, who was himself one of the tribunes, and whom he otherwise knew to be a worthy man, and a lover of liberty, and on that account very uneasy at the present management of public affairs, he being desirous to come immediately to the execution of what had been determined, and thinking it right for him to propose it to the other, and afraid lest Clement should discover them, and besides looking upon delays and puttings off to be the next to desisting from the enterprise.

8. But as all was agreeable to Sabinus, who had himself, equally without Cherea, the same design, but had been silent for want of a person to whom he could safely communicate that design; so having now met with one, who not only promised to conceal what he heard, but who had already opened his mind to him, he was much more encouraged, and desired of Cherea that no delay might be made therein. Accordingly they went to Minucianus, who was as virtuous a man, and as zealous to do glorious actions, as themselves, and suspected by Caius on occasion of the slaughter of Lepidus; for Minucianus and Lepidus were intimate friends, and both in fear of the dangers that they were under; for Caius was terrible to all the great men, as appearing ready to act a mad part towards each of them in particular, and towards all of: them in general; and these men were afraid of one another, while they were yet uneasy at the posture of affairs, but avoided to declare their mind and their hatred against Caius to one another, out of fear of the dangers they might be in thereby, although they perceived by other means their mutual hatred against Caius, and on that account were not averse to a mutual kindness one towards another.

9. When Minuetanus and Cherea had met together, and saluted one another, (as they had been used on former conversations to give the upper hand to Minucianus, both on account of his eminent dignity, for he was the noblest of all the citizens, and highly commended by all

men, especially when he made speeches to them,) Minuetanus began first, and asked Cherea, What was the watchword he had received that day from Caius; for the affront which was offered Cherea, in giving the watchwords, was famous over the city. But Cherea made no delay so long as to reply to that question, out of the joy he had that Minueianus would have such confidence in him as to discourse with him. "But do thou," said he, "give me the watchword of liberty. And I return thee my thanks that thou hast so greatly encouraged me to exert myself after an extraordinary manner; nor do I stand in need of many words to encourage me, since both thou and I are of the same mind, and partakers of the same resolutions, and this before we have conferred together. I have indeed but one sword girt on, but this one will serve us both. Come on, therefore, let us set about the work. Do thou go first, if thou hast a mind, and bid me follow thee; or else I will go first, and thou shalt assist me, and we will assist one another, and trust one another. Nor is there a necessity for even one sword to such as have a mind disposed to such works, by which mind the sword uses to be successful. I am zealous about this action, nor am I solicitous what I may myself undergo; for I can not at leisure to consider the dangers that may come upon myself, so deeply am I troubled at the slavery our once free country is now under, and at the contempt cast upon our excellent laws, and at the destruction which hangs over all men, by the means of Caius. I wish that I may be judged by thee, and that thou mayst esteem me worthy of credit in these matters, seeing we are both of the same opinion, and there is herein no difference between us."

10. When Minucianus saw the vehemency with which Cherea delivered himself, he gladly embraced him, and encouraged him in his bold attempt, commending him, and embracing him; so he let him go with his good wishes; and some affirm that he thereby confirmed Minuclanus in the prosecution of what had been agreed among them; for as Cherea entered into the court, the report runs, that a voice came from among the multitude to encourage him, which bid him finish what he was about, and take the opportunity that Providence afforded; and that Cherea at first suspected that some one of the conspirators had betrayed him, and he was caught, but at length perceived that it

was by way of exhortation. Whether somebody[3] that was conscious of what he was about, gave a signal for his encouragement, or whether it was God himself, who looks upon the actions of men, that encouraged him to go on boldly in his design, is uncertain. The plot was now communicated to a great many, and they were all in their armor; some of the conspirators being senators, and some of the equestrian order, and as many of the soldiery as were made acquainted with it; for there was not one of them who would not reckon it a part of his happiness to kill Caius; and on that account they were all very zealous in the affair, by what means soever any one could come at it, that he might not be behindhand in these virtuous designs, but might be ready with all his alacrity or power, both by words and actions, to complete this slaughter of a tyrant. And besides these, Callistus also, who was a freed-man of Caius, and was the only man that had arrived at the greatest degree of power under him,—such a power, indeed, as was in a manner equal to the power of the tyrant himself, by the dread that all men had of him, and by the great riches he had acquired; for he took bribes most plenteously, and committed injuries without bounds, and was more extravagant in the use of his power in unjust proceedings than any other. He also knew the disposition of Caius to be implacable, and never to be turned from what he had resolved on. He had withal many other reasons why he thought himself in danger, and the vastness of his wealth was not one of the least of them; on which account he privately ingratiated himself with Claudius, and transferred his courtship to him, out of this hope, that in case, upon the removal of Caius, the government should come to him, his interest in such changes should lay a foundation for his preserving his dignity under him, since he laid in beforehand a stock of merit, and did Claudius good offices in his promotion. He had also the boldness to pretend that he had been persuaded to make away with Claudius, by poisoning him, but had still invented ten thousand excuses for delaying to do it. But it seems probable to me that Callistus only counterfeited this, in order to ingratiate himself with Claudius; for if

---

3. Just such a voice as this is related to be came, and from an unknown original also, to the famous Polycarp, as he was going to martyrdom, bidding him "play the man;" as the church of Smyrna assures us in their account of that his martyrdom, sect. 9.

Caius had been in earnest resolved to take off Claudius, he would not have admitted of Callistus's excuses; nor would Callistus, if he had been enjoined to do such an act as was desired by Caius, have put it off; nor if he had disobeyed those injunctions of his master, had he escaped immediate punishment; while Claudius was preserved from the madness of Caius by a certain Divine providence, and Callistus pretended to such a piece of merit as he no way deserved.

11. However, the execution of Cherea's designs was put off from day to day, by the sloth of many therein concerned; for as to Cherea himself, he would not willingly make any delay in that execution, thinking every time a fit time for it; for frequent opportunities offered themselves; as when Caius went up to the capitol to sacrifice for his daughter, or when he stood upon his royal palace, and threw gold and silver pieces of money among the people, he might be pushed down headlong, because the top of the palace, that looks towards the market-place, was very high; and also when he celebrated the mysteries, which he had appointed at that time; for he was then no way secluded from the people, but solicitous to do every thing carefully and decently, and was free from all suspicion that he should be then assaulted by any body; and although the gods should afford him no divine assistance to enable him to take away his life, yet had he strength himself sufficient to despatch Caius, even without a sword. Thus was Chorea angry at his fellow conspirators, for fear they should suffer a proper opportunity to pass by; and they were themselves sensible that he had just cause to be angry at them, and that his eagerness was for their advantage; yet did they desire he would have a little longer patience, lest, upon any disappointment they might meet with, they should put the city into disorder, and an inquisition should be made after the conspiracy, and should render the courage of those that were to attack Caius without success, while he would then secure himself more carefully than ever against them; that it would therefore be the best to set about the work when the shows were exhibited in the palace. These shows were acted in honor of that Caesar[4] who first of all changed the popular government, and

4. Here Josephus supposes that it was Augustus, and not Julius Caesar, who first changed the Roman commonwealth into a monarchy; for these shows were in honor of Augustus, as we shall learn in the next section.

transferred it to himself; galleries being fixed before the palace, where the Romans that were patricians became spectators, together with their children and their wives, and Caesar himself was to be also a spectator; and they reckoned, among those many ten thousands who would there be crowded into a narrow compass, they should have a favorable opportunity to make their attempt upon him as he came in, because his guards that should protect him, if any of them should have a mind to do it, would not here be able to give him any assistance.

12. Cherea consented to this delay; and when the shows were exhibited, it was resolved to do the work the first day. But fortune, which allowed a further delay to his slaughter, was too hard for their foregoing resolution; and as three days of the regular times for these shows were now over, they had much ado to get the business done on the last day. Then Cherea called the conspirators together, and spake thus to them: "So much time passed away without effort is a reproach to us, as delaying to go through such a virtuous design as we are engaged in; but more fatal will this delay prove if we be discovered, and the design be frustrated; for Caius will then become more cruel in his unjust proceedings. Do we not see how long we deprive all our friends of their liberty, and give Caius leave still to tyrannize over them? while we ought to have procured them security for the future, and, by laying a foundation for the happiness of others, gain to ourselves great admiration and honor for all time to come." Now while the conspirators had nothing tolerable to say by way of contradiction, and yet did not quite relish what they were doing, but stood silent and astonished, he said further, "O my brave comrades! why do we make such delays? Do not you see that this is the last day of these shows, and that Caius is about to go to sea? for he is preparing to sail to Alexandria, in order to see Egypt. Is it therefore for your honor to let a man go out of your hands who is a reproach to mankind, and to permit him to go, after a pompous manner, triumphing both at land and sea? Shall not we be justly ashamed of ourselves, if we give leave to some Egyptian or other, who shall think his injuries insufferable to free-men, to kill him? As for myself, I will no longer bear your stow proceedings, but will expose myself to the dangers of the enterprise this very day, and bear cheerfully whatsoever shall be the consequence of the attempt; nor, let them be ever so great, will I put them off any longer: for, to a wise and courageous man, what can be more miserable

than that, while I am alive, any one else should kill Caius, and deprive me of the honor of so virtuous an action?"

13. When Cherea had spoken thus, he zealously set about the work, and inspired courage into the rest to go on with it, and they were all eager to fall to it without further delay. So he was at the palace in the morning, with his equestrian sword girt on him; for it was the custom that the tribunes should ask for the watchword with their swords on, and this was the day on which Cherea was, by custom, to receive the watchword; and the multitude were already come to the palace, to be soon enough for seeing the shows, and that in great crowds, and one tumultuously crushing another, while Caius was delighted with this eagerness of the multitude; for which reason there was no order observed in the seating men, nor was any peculiar place appointed for the senators, or for the equestrian order; but they sat at random, men and women together, and free-men were mixed with the slaves. So Caius came out in a solemn manner, and offered sacrifice to Augustus Caesar, in whose honor indeed these shows were celebrated. Now it happened, upon the fall of a certain priest, that the garment of Asprenas, a senator, was filled with blood, which made Caius laugh, although this was an evident omen to Asprenas, for he was slain at the same time with Caius. It is also related that Caius was that day, contrary to his usual custom, so very affable and good-natured in his conversation, that every one of those that were present were astonished at it. After the sacrifice was over, Caius betook himself to see the shows, and sat down for that purpose, as did also the principal of his friends sit near him. Now the parts of the theater were so fastened together, as it used to be every year, in the manner following: It had two doors, the one door led to the open air, the other was for going into, or going out of, the cloisters, that those within the theater might not be thereby disturbed; but out of one gallery there went an inward passage, parted into partitions also, which led into another gallery, to give room to the combatants and to the musicians to go out as occasion served. When the multitude were set down, and Cherea, with the other tribunes, were set down also, and the right corner of the theater was allotted to Caesar, one Vatinius, a senator, commander of the praetorian band, asked of Cluvius, one that sat by him, and was of consular dignity also, whether he had heard any thing of news, or not? but took care that nobody should hear what he

said; and when Cluvius replied, that he had heard no news, "Know then," said Vatinius, "that the game of the slaughter of tyrants is to be played this dav." But Cluvius replied "O brave comrade hold thy peace, lest some other of the Achaians hear thy tale." And as there was abundance of autumnal fruit thrown among the spectators, and a great number of birds, that were of great value to such as possessed them, on account of their rareness, Caius was pleased with the birds fighting for the fruits, and with the violence wherewith the spectators seized upon them: and here he perceived two prodigies that happened there; for an actor was introduced, by whom a leader of robbers was crucified, and the pantomime brought in a play called Cinyras, wherein he himself was to be slain, as well as his daughter Myrrha, and wherein a great deal of fictitious blood was shed, both about him that was crucified, and also about Cinyras. It was also confessed that this was the same day wherein Pausanias, a friend of Philip, the son of Amyntas, who was king of Macedonia, slew him, as he was entering into the theater. And now Caius was in doubt whether he should tarry to the end of the shows, because it was the last day, or whether he should not go first to the bath, and to dinner, and then return and sit down as before. Hereupon Minucianus, who sat over Caius, and was afraid that the opportunity should fail them, got up, because he saw Cherea was already gone out, and made haste out, to confirm him in his resolution; but Caius took hold of his garment, in an obliging way, and said to him, "O brave man! whither art thou going?" Whereupon, out of reverence to Caesar, as it seemed, he sat down again; but his fear prevailed over him, and in a little time he got up again, and then Caius did no way oppose his going out, as thinking that he went out to perform some necessities of nature. And Asprenas, who was one of the confederates, persuaded Caius to go out to the bath, and to dinner, and then to come in again, as desirous that what had been resolved on might be brought to a conclusion immediately.

14. So Cherea's associates placed themselves in order, as the time would permit them, and they were obliged to labor hard, that the place which was appointed them should not be left by them; but they had an indignation at the tediousness of the delays, and that what they were about should be put off any longer, for it was already about the

ninth[5] hour of the day; and Cherea, upon Caius's tarrying so long, had a great mind to go in, and fall upon him in his seat, although he foresaw that this could not be done without much bloodshed, both of the senators, and of those of the equestrian order that were present; and although he knew this must happen, yet had he a great mind to do so, as thinking it a right thing to procure security and freedom to all, at the expense of such as might perish at the same time. And as they were just going back into the entrance to the theater, word was brought them that Caius was arisen, whereby a tumult was made; hereupon the conspirators thrust away the crowd, under pretense as if Caius was angry at them, but in reality as desirous to have a quiet place, that should have none in it to defend him, while they set about Caius's slaughter. Now Claudius, his uncle, was gone out before, and Marcus Vinicius his sister's husband, as also Valellus of Asia; whom though they had had such a mind to put out of their places, the reverence to their dignity hindered them so to do; then followed Caius, with Paulus Arruntius: and because Caius was now gotten within the palace, he left the direct road, along which those his servants stood that were in waiting, and by which road Claudius had gone out before, Caius turned aside into a private narrow passage, in order to go to the place for bathing, as also in order to take a view of the boys that came out of Asia, who were sent thence, partly to sing hymns in these mysteries which were now celebrated, and partly to dance in the Pyrrhic way of dancing upon the theatres. So Cherea met him, and asked him for the watchword; upon Caius's giving him one of his ridiculous words, he immediately reproached him, and drew his sword, and gave him a terrible stroke with it, yet was not this stroke mortal. And although there be those that say it was so contrived on purpose by Chorea, that Caius should not be killed at one blow, but should be punished more severely by a multitude of wounds; yet does this story appear to me incredible, because the fear men are under in such actions does not allow them to use their reason. And if Cherea was of that mind, I esteem him the greatest of all fools, in pleasing himself in his spite against Caius, rather than immediately procuring safety to himself and to his confederates from the dangers they were in, because

5. Suetonius says Caius was slain about the seventh hour of the day, the ninth. The series of the narration favors Josephus.

there might many things still happen for helping Caius's escape, if he had not already given up the ghost; for certainly Cherea would have regard, not so much to the punishment of Caius, as to the affliction himself and his friends were in, while it was in his power, after such success, to keep silent, and to escape the wrath of Caius's defenders, and not to leave it to uncertainty whether he should gain the end he aimed at or not, and after an unreasonable manner to act as if he had a mind to ruin himself, and lose the opportunity that lay before him. But every body may guess as he please about this matter. However, Caius was staggered with the pain that the blow gave him; for the stroke of the sword falling in the middle, between the shoulder and the neck, was hindered by the first bone of the breast from proceeding any further. Nor did he either cry out, (in such astonishment was he,) nor did he call out for any of his friends; whether it were that he had no confidence in them, or that his mind was otherwise disordered, but he groaned under the pain he endured, and presently went forward and fled; when Cornelius Sabinus, who was already prepared in his mind so to do, thrust him down upon his knee, where many of them stood round about him, and struck him with their swords; and they cried out, and encouraged one another all at once to strike him again; but all agree that Aquila gave him the finishing stroke, which directly killed him. But one may justly ascribe this act to Cherea; for although many concurred in the act itself, yet was he the first contriver of it, and began long before all the rest to prepare for it, and was the first man that boldly spake of it to the rest; and upon their admission of what he said about it, he got the dispersed conspirators together; he prepared every thing after a prudent manner, and by suggesting good advice, showed himself far superior to the rest, and made obliging speeches to them, insomuch that he even compelled them all to go on, who otherwise had not courage enough for that purpose; and when opportunity served to use his sword in hand, he appeared first of all ready so to do, and gave the first blow in this virtuous slaughter; he also brought Caius easily into the power of the rest, and almost killed him himself, insomuch that it is but just to ascribe all that the rest did to the advice, and bravery, and labors of the hands of Cherea.

15. Thus did Caius come to his end, and lay dead, by the many wounds which had been given him. Now Cherea and his associates, upon Caius's slaughter, saw that it was impossible for them to save

themselves, if they should all go the same way, partly on account of the astonishment they were under; for it was no small danger they had incurred by killing an emperor, who was honored and loved by the madness of the people, especially when the soldiers were likely to make a bloody inquiry after his murderers. The passages also were narrow wherein the work was done, which were also crowded with a great multitude of Caius's attendants, and of such of the soldiers as were of the emperor's guard that day; whence it was that they went by other ways, and came to the house of Germanicus, the father of Caius, whom they had now killed (which house adjoined to the palace; for while the edifice was one, it was built in its several parts by those particular persons who had been emperors, and those parts bare the names of those that built them or the name of him who had begun to build its parts). So they got away from the insults of the multitude, and then were for the present out of danger, that is, so long as the misfortune which had overtaken the emperor was not known. The Germans were the first who perceived that Caius was slain. These Germans were Caius's guard, and carried the name of the country whence they were chosen, and composed the Celtic legion. The men of that country are naturally passionate, which is commonly the temper of some other of the barbarous nations also, as being not used to consider much about what they do; they are of robust bodies and fall upon their enemies as soon as ever they are attacked by them; and which way soever they go, they perform great exploits. When, therefore, these German guards understood that Caius was slain, they were very sorry for it, because they did not use their reason in judging about public affairs, but measured all by the advantages themselves received, Caius being beloved by them because of the money he gave them, by which he had purchased their kindness to him; so they drew their swords, and Sabinus led them on. He was one of the tribunes, not by the means of the virtuous actions of his pro genitors, for he bad been a gladiator, but he had obtained that post in the army by his having a robust body. So these Germans marched along the houses in quest of Caesar's murderers, and cut Asprenas to pieces, because he was the first man they fell upon, and whose garment it was that the blood of the sacrifices stained, as I have said already, and which foretold that this his meeting the soldiers would not be for his good. Then did Norbanus meet them, who was one of the principal nobility of and could show many generals of armies among his ancestors; but they paid no regard to his dignity; yet was he of such great strength, that he wrested the sword of the first of those that assaulted him out of his hands, and appeared plainly not to be willing to die without a struggle for his life, until he was surrounded by a great number of assailants, and died by the multitude of the wounds which they gave him. The third man was Anteius, a senator, and a few others with him. He did not meet with these Germans by chance, as the rest did before, but came to show his hatred to Caius, and because he loved to see Caius lie dead with his own eyes, and took a pleasure in that sight; for Caius had banished Anteius's father, who was of the same name with himself, and being not satisfied with that, he sent out his soldiers, and slew him; so he was come to rejoice at the sight of him, now he was dead. But as the house was now all in a tumult, when he was aiming to hide himself, he could not escape that accurate search which the Germans made, while they barbarously slew those that were guilty, and those that were not guilty, and this equally also. And thus were these [three] persons slain.

16. But when the rumor that Caius was slain reached the theater, they were astonished at it, and could not believe it; even some that entertained his destruction with great pleasure, and were more desirous of its happening than almost any other faction that could come to them, were under such a fear, that they could not believe it. There were also those who greatly distrusted it, because they were unwilling that any such thing should come to Caius, nor could believe it, though it were ever so true, because they thought no man could possibly so much power as to kill Caius. These were the women, and the children, and the slaves, and some of the soldiery. This last sort had taken his pay, and in a manner tyrannized with him, and had abused the best of the citizens, in being subservient to his unjust commands, in order to gain honors and advantages to themselves; but for the women and the youth, they had been inveigled with shows, and the fighting of the gladiators, and certain distributions of flesh-meat among them, which things them pretense were designed for the pleasing of multitude, but in reality to satiate the barbarous cruelty and madness of Caius. The slaves also were sorry, because they were by Caius allowed to accuse and to despise their masters, and they could have recourse to his assistance when they had unjustly

affronted them; for he was very easy in believing them against their masters, even when they the city, accused them falsely; and if they would discover what money their masters had, they might soon obtain both riches and liberty, as the rewards of their accusations, because the reward of these informers was the eighth[6] part of the criminal's substance. As to the nobles, although the report appeared credible to some of them, either because they knew of the plot beforehand, or because they wished it might be true; however, they concealed not only the joy they had at the relation of it, but that they had heard any thing at all about it. These last acted so out of the fear they had, that if the report proved false, they should be punished, for having so soon let men know their minds. But those that knew Caius was dead, because they were partners with the conspirators, they concealed all still more cautiously, as not knowing one another's minds; and fearing lest they should speak of it to some of those to whom the continuance of tyranny was advantageous; and if Caius should prove to be alive, they might be informed against, and punished. And another report went about, that although Caius had been wounded indeed, yet was not he dead, but alive still, and under the physician's hands. Nor was any one looked upon by another as faithful enough to be trusted, and to whom any one would open his mind; for he was either a friend to Caius, and therefore suspected to favor his tyranny, or he was one that hated him, who therefore might be suspected to deserve the less credit, because of his ill-will to him. Nay, it was said by some (and this indeed it was that deprived the nobility of their hopes, and made them sad) that Caius was in a condition to despise the dangers he had been in, and took no care of healing his wounds, but was gotten away into the market-place, and, bloody as he was, was making an harangue to the people. And these were the conjectural reports of those that were so unreasonable as to endeavor to raise tumults, which they turned different ways, according to the opinions of the bearers. Yet did they not leave their seats, for fear of being accused, if they should go out before the rest; for they should not be sentenced according to the real

6. The rewards proposed by the Roman laws to informers was sometimes an eigth partm as Spanheim assures us, from the criminal's goods, as here, and sometimes a fourth part.

intention with which they went out, but according to the supposals of the accusers and of the judges.

17. But now a multitude of Germans had surrounded the theater with their swords drawn: all the spectators looked for nothing but death, and at every one coming in a fear seized upon them, as if they were to be cut in pieces immediately; and in great distress they were, as neither having courage enough to go out of the theater, nor believing themselves safe from dangers if they tarried there. And when the Germans came upon them, the cry was so great, that the theater rang again with the entreaties of the spectators to the soldiers, pleading that they were entirely ignorant of every thing that related to such seditious contrivances, and that if there were any sedition raised, they knew nothing of it; they therefore begged that they would spare them, and not punish those that had not the least hand in such bold crimes as belonged to other persons, while they neglected to search after such as had really done whatsoever it be that hath been done. Thus did these people appeal to God, and deplore their infelicity with shedding of tears, and beating their faces, and said every thing that the most imminent danger and the utmost concern for their lives could dictate to them. This brake the fury of the soldiers, and made them repent of what they minded to do to the spectators, which would have been the greatest instance of cruelty. And so it appeared to even these savages, when they had once fixed the heads of those that were slain with Asprenas upon the altar; at which sight the spectators were sorely afflicted, both upon the consideration of the dignity of the persons, and out of a commiseration of their sufferings; nay, indeed, they were almost in as great disorder at the prospect of the danger themselves were in, seeing it was still uncertain whether they should entirely escape the like calamity. Whence it was that such as thoroughly and justly hated Caius could yet no way enjoy the pleasure of his death, because they were themselves in jeopardy of perishing together with him; nor had they hitherto any firm assurance of surviving.

18. There was at this time one Euaristus Arruntius, a public crier in the market, and therefore of a strong and audible voice, who vied in wealth with the richest of the Romans, and was able to do what he pleased in the city, both then and afterward. This man put himself into the most mournful habit he could, although he had a greater hatred against Caius than any one else; his fear and his wise contrivance to

gain his safety taught him so to do, and prevailed over his present pleasure; so he put on such a mournful dress as he would have done had he lost his dearest friends in the world; this man came into the theater, and informed them of the death of Caius, and by this means put an end to that state of ignorance the men had been in. Arruntius also went round about the pillars, and called out to the Germans, as did the tribunes with him, bidding them put up their swords, and telling them that Caius was dead. And this proclamation it was plainly which saved those that were collected together in the theater, and all the rest who any way met the Germans; for while they had hopes that Caius had still any breath in him, they abstained from no sort of mischief; and such an abundant kindness they still had for Caius, that they would willingly have prevented the plot against him, and procured his escape from so sad a misfortune, at the expense of their own lives. But they now left off the warm zeal they had to punish his enemies, now they were fully satisfied that Caius was dead, because it was now in vain for them to show their zeal and kindness to him, when he who should reward them was perished. They were also afraid that they should be punished by the senate, if they should go on in doing such injuries; that is, in case the authority of the supreme governor should revert to them. And thus at length a stop was put, though not without difficulty, to that rage which possessed the Germans on account of Caius's death.

19. But Cherea was so much afraid for Minucianus, lest he should light upon the Germans now they were in their fury, that he went and spike to every one of the soldiers, and prayed them to take care of his preservation, and made himself great inquiry about him, lest he should have been slain. And for Clement, he let Minucianus go when he was brought to him, and, with many other of the senators, affirmed the action was right, and commended the virtue of those that contrived it, and had courage enough to execute it; and said that "tyrants do indeed please themselves and look big for a while, upon having the power to act unjustly; but do not however go happily out of the world, because they are hated by the virtuous; and that Caius, together with all his unhappiness, was become a conspirator against himself, before these other men who attacked him did so; and by becoming intolerable, in setting aside the wise provision the laws had made, taught his dearest friends to treat him as an enemy; insomuch

that although in common discourse these conspirators were those that slew Caius, yet that, in reality, he lies now dead as perishing by his own self."

20. Now by this time the people in the theatre were arisen from their seats, and those that were within made a very great disturbance; the cause of which was this, that the spectators were too hasty in getting away. There was also one Aleyon, a physician, who hurried away, as if to cure those that were wounded, and under that pretense he sent those that were with him to fetch what things were necessary for the healing of those wounded persons, but in reality to get them clear of the present dangers they were in. Now the senate, during this interval, had met, and the people also assembled together in the accustomed form, and were both employed in searching after the murderers of Caius. The people did it very zealously, but the senate in appearance only; for there was present Valerius of Asia, one that had been consul; this man went to the people, as they were in disorder, and very uneasy that they could not yet discover who they were that had murdered the emperor; he was then earnestly asked by them all who it was that had done it. He replied, "I wish I had been the man." The consuls[7] also published an edict, wherein they accused Caius, and gave order to the people then got together, and to the soldiers, to go home; and gave the people hopes of the abatement of the oppressions they lay under; and promised the soldiers, if they lay quiet as they used to do, and would not go abroad to do mischief unjustly, that they would bestow rewards upon them; for there was reason to fear lest the city might suffer harm by their wild and ungovernable behavior, if they should once betake themselves to spoil the citizens, or plunder the temples. And now the whole multitude of the senators were assembled together, and especially those that had conspired to take away the life of Caius, who put on at this time an air of great assurance, and appeared with great magnanimity, as if the administration of the public affairs were already devolved upon them.

---

7. These consuls are named in the War of the Jews, B. II. ch. 11. sect; 1, Sentius Saturninus and Pomponius Secundus, as Spanheim notes here. The speech of the former of them is set down in the next chapter, sect. 2.

2 *How the Senators Determined to Restore the Democracy; but the Soldiers Were for Preserving the Monarchy, Concerning the Slaughter of Caius's Wife and Daughter. a Character of Caius's Morals*

1. WHEN the public affairs were in this posture, Claudius was on the sudden hurried away out of his house; for the soldiers had a meeting together; and when they had debated about what was to be done, they saw that a democracy was incapable of managing such a vast weight of public affairs; and that if it should be set up, it would not be for their advantage; and in case any one of those already in the government should obtain the supreme power, it would in all respects be to their grief, if they were not assisting to him in this advancement; that it would therefore be right for them, while the public affairs were unsettled, to choose Claudius emperor, who was uncle to the deceased Caius, and of a superior dignity and worth to every one of those that were assembled together in the senate, both on account of the virtues of his ancestors, and of the learning he had acquired in his education; and who, if once settled in the empire, would reward them according to their deserts, and bestow largesses upon them. These were their consultations, and they executed the same immediately. Claudius was therefore seized upon suddenly by the soldiery. But Cneas Sentins Saturninns, although he understood that Claudius was seized, and that he intended to claim the government, unwillingly indeed in appearance, but in reality by his own free consent, stood up in the senate, and, without being dismayed, made an exhortatory oration to them, and such a one indeed as was fit for men of freedom and generosity, and spake thus:

2. "Although it be a thing incredible, O Romans! because of the great length of time, that so unexpected an event hath happened, yet are we now in possession of liberty. How long indeed this will last is uncertain, and lies at the disposal of the gods, whose grant it is; yet such it is as is sufficient to make us rejoice, and be happy for the present, although we may soon be deprived of it; for one hour is sufficient to those that are exercised in virtue, wherein we may live with a mind accountable only to ourselves, in our own country, now free, and governed by such laws as this country once flourished under. As for myself, I cannot remember our former time of liberty, as being

born after it was gone; but I am beyond measure filled with joy at the thoughts of our present freedom. I also esteem those that were born and bred up in that our former liberty happy men, and that those men are worthy of no less esteem than the gods themselves who have given us a taste of it in this age; and I heartily wish that this quiet enjoyment of it, which we have at present, might continue to all ages. However, this single day may suffice for our youth, as well as for us that are in years. It will seem an age to our old men, if they might die during its happy duration: it may also be for the instruction of the younger sort, what kind of virtue those men, from whose loins we are derived, were exercised in. As for ourselves, our business is, during the space of time, to live virtuously, than which nothing can be more to our advantage; which course of virtue it is alone that can preserve our liberty; for as to our ancient state, I have heard of it by the relations of others; but as to our later state, during my lifetime, I have known it by experience, and learned thereby what mischiefs tyrannies have brought upon this commonwealth, discouraging all virtue, and depriving persons of magnanimity of their liberty, and proving the teachers of flattery and slavish fear, because it leaves the public administration not to be governed by wise laws, but by the humor of those that govern. For since Julius Caesar took it into his head to dissolve our democracy, and, by overbearing the regular system of our laws, to bring disorders into our administration, and to get above right and justice, and to be a slave to his own inclinations, there is no kind of misery but what hath tended to the subversion of this city; while all those that have succeeded him have striven one with another to overthrow the ancient laws of their country, and have left it destitute of such citizens as were of generous principles, because they thought it tended to their safety to have vicious men to converse withal, and not only to break the spirits of those that were best esteemed for their virtue, but to resolve upon. their utter destruction. Of all which emperors, who have been many in number, and who laid upon us insufferable hardships during the times of their government, this Caius, who hath been slain today, hath brought more terrible calamities upon us than did all the rest, not only by exercising his ungoverned rage upon his fellow citizens, but also upon his kindred and friends, and alike upon all others, and by inflicting still greater miseries upon them, as punishments, which they never deserved, he being equally furious against men and against the gods. For tyrants are not content to gain their sweet pleasure, and this by acting injuriously, and in the vexation they bring both upon men's estates and their wives; but they look upon that to be their principal advantage, when they can utterly overthrow the entire families of their enemies; while all lovers of liberty are the enemies of tyranny. Nor can those that patiently endure what miseries they bring on them gain their friendship; for as they are conscious of the abundant mischiefs they have brought on these men, and how magnanimously they have borne their hard fortunes, they cannot but be sensible what evils they have done, and thence only depend on security from what they are suspicious of, if it may be in their power to take them quite out of the world. Since, then, we are now gotten clear of such great misfortunes, and are only accountable to one another, (which form of government affords us the best assurance of our present concord, and promises us the best security from evil designs, and will be most for our own glory in settling the city in good order,) you ought, every one of you in particular, to make provision for his own, and in general for the public utility: or, on the contrary, they may declare their dissent to such things as have been proposed, and this without any hazard of danger to come upon them, because they have now no lord set over them, who, without fear of punishment, could do mischief to the city, and had an uncontrollable power to take off those that freely declared their opinions. Nor has any thing so much contributed to this increase of tyranny of late as sloth, and a timorous forbearance of contradicting the emperor's will; while men had an over-great inclination to the sweetness of peace, and had learned to live like slaves; and as many of us as either heard of intolerable calamities that happened at a distance from us, or saw the miseries that were near us, out of the dread of dying virtuously, endured a death joined with the utmost infamy. We ought, then, in the first place, to decree the greatest honors we are able to those that have taken off the tyrant, especially to Cherea Cassius; for this one man, with the assistance of the gods, hath, by his counsel and by his actions, been the procurer of our liberty. Nor ought we to forget him now we have recovered our liberty, who, under the foregoing tyranny, took counsel beforehand, and beforehand hazarded himself for our liberties; but ought to decree him proper honors, and thereby freely declare that he from the beginning acted with our approbation. And certainly it is a very excellent thing, and what becomes free-men, to requite their benefactors, as this man hath been a benefactor to us all, though not at all like Cassius and Brutus, who slew Caius Julius [Caesar]; for those men laid the foundations of sedition and civil wars in our city; but this man, together with his slaughter of the tyrant, hath set our city free from all those sad miseries which arose from the tyranny."[8]

3. And this was the purport of Sentius's oration,[9] which was received with pleasure by the senators, and by as many of the equestrian order as were present. And now one Trebellius Maximus rose up hastily, and took off Sentius's finger a ring, which had a stone, with the image of Caius engraven upon it, and which, in his zeal in speaking, and his earnestness in doing what he was about, as it was supposed, he had forgotten to take off himself. This sculpture was broken immediately. But as it was now far in the night, Cherea demanded of the consuls the watchword, who gave him this word, Liberty. These facts were the subjects of admiration to themselves, and almost incredible; for it was a hundred years since the democracy had been laid aside, when this giving the watchword returned to the consuls; for before the city was subject to tyrants, they were the commanders of the soldiers. But when Cherea had received that watchword, he delivered it to those who were on the senate's side, which were four regiments, who esteemed the government without emperors to be preferable to tyranny. So these went away with their tribunes. The people also now departed very joyful, full of hope and of courage, as having recovered their former democracy, and were no longer under an emperor; and Cherea was in very great esteem with them.

4. And now Cherea was very uneasy that Caius's daughter and wife were still alive, and that all his family did not perish with him, since

---

8. In this oration of Sentius Saturninus, we may see the great value virtuous men put upon public liberty, and the sad misery they underwent, while they were tyrannized over by such emperors as Caius. See Josephus's own short but pithy reflection at the end of the chapter: "So difficult," says he, "it is for those to obtain the virtue that is necessary to a wise man, who have the absolute power to do what they please without control."

9. Hence we learn that, in the opinion of Saturninus, the sovereign authority of the consuls and senate had been taken away just a hundred years before the death of Caius, A.D. 41, or in the sixtieth year before the Christian saga, when the first triumvirate began under Caesar, Pompey, and Crassus.

whosoever was left of them must be left for the ruin of the city and of the laws. Moreover, in order to finish this matter with the utmost zeal, and in order to satisfy his hatred of Caius, he sent Julius Lupus, one of the tribunes, to kill Caius's wife and daughter. They proposed this office to Lupus as to a kinsman of Clement, that he might be so far a partaker of this murder of the tyrant, and might rejoice in the virtue of having assisted his fellow citizens, and that he might appear to have been a partaker with those that were first in their designs against him. Yet did this action appear to some of the conspirators to be too cruel, as to this using such severity to a woman, because Caius did more indulge his own ill-nature than use her advice in all that he did; from which ill-nature it was that the city was in so desperate a condition with the miseries that were brought on it, and the flower of the city was destroyed. But others accused her of giving her consent to these things; nay, they ascribed all that Caius had done to her as the cause of it, and said she had given a potion to Caius, which had made him obnoxious to her, and had tied him down to love her by such evil methods; insomuch that she, having rendered him distracted, was become the author of all the mischiefs that had befallen the Romans, and that habitable world which was subject to them. So that at length it was determined that she must die; nor could those of the contrary opinion at all prevail to have her saved; and Lupus was sent accordingly. Nor was there any delay made in executing what he went about, but he was subservient to those that sent him on the first opportunity, as desirous to be no way blameable in what might be done for the advantage of the people. So when he was come into the palace, he found Cesonia, who was Caius's wife, lying by her husband's dead body, which also lay down on the ground, and destitute of all such things as the law allows to the dead, and all over herself besmeared with the blood of her husband's wounds, and bewailing the great affliction she was under, her daughter lying by her also; and nothing else was heard in these her circumstances but her complaint of Caius, as if he had not regarded what she had often told him of beforehand; which words of hers were taken in a different sense even at that time, and are now esteemed equally ambiguous by those that hear of them, and are still interpreted according to the different inclinations of people. Now some said that the words denoted that she had advised him to leave off his mad behavior and his barbarous cruelty to the citizens, and to govern the public with moderation and virtue, lest he should perish by the same way, upon their using him as he had used them. But some said, that as certain words had passed concerning the conspirators, she desired Caius to make no delay, but immediately to put them all to death, and this whether they were guilty or not, and that thereby he would be out of the fear of any danger; and that this was what she reproached him for, when she advised him so to do, but he was too slow and tender in the matter. And this was what Cesonia said, and what the opinions of men were about it. But when she saw Lupus approach, she showed him Caius's dead body, and persuaded him to come nearer, with lamentation and tears; and as she perceived that Lupus was in disorder, and approached her in order to execute some design disagreeable to himself, she was well aware for what purpose he came, and stretched out her naked throat, and that very cheerfully to him, bewailing her case, like one that utterly despaired of her life, and bidding him not to boggle at finishing the tragedy they had resolved upon relating to her. So she boldly received her death's wound at the hand of Lupus, as did the daughter after her. So Lupus made haste to inform Cherea of what he had done.

5. This was the end of Caius, after he had reigned four years, within four months. He was, even before he came to be emperor, ill-natured, and one that had arrived at the utmost pitch of wickedness; a slave to his pleasures, and a lover of calumny; greatly affected by every terrible accident, and on that account of a very murderous disposition where he durst show it. He enjoyed his exorbitant power to this only purpose, to injure those who least deserved it, with unreasonable insolene and got his wealth by murder and injustice. He labored to appear above regarding either what was divine or agreeable to the laws, but was a slave to the commendations of the populace; and whatsoever the laws determined to be shameful, and punished, that he esteemed more honorable than what was virtuous. He was unmindful of his friends, how intimate soever, and though they were persons of the highest character; and if he was once angry at any of them, he would inflict punishment upon them on the smallest occasions, and esteemed every man that endeavored to lead a virtuous life his enemy. And whatsoever he commanded, he would not admit of any contradiction to his inclinations; whence it was that he had criminal

conversation with his own sister;[10] from which occasion chiefly it was also that a bitter hatred first sprang up against him among the citizens, that sort of incest not having been known of a long time; and so this provoked men to distrust him, and to hate him that was guilty of it. And for any great or royal work that he ever did, which might be for the present and for future ages, nobody can name any such, but only the haven that he made about Rhegium and Sicily, for the reception of the ships that brought corn from Egypt; which was indeed a work without dispute very great in itself, and of very great advantage to the navigation. Yet was not this work brought to perfection by him, but was the one half of it left imperfect, by reason of his want of application to it; the cause of which was this, that he employed his studies about useless matters, and that by spending his money upon such pleasures as concerned no one's benefit but his own, he could not exert his liberality in things that were undeniably of great consequence. Otherwise he was an excellent orator, and thoroughly acquainted with the Greek tongue, as well as with his own country or Roman language. He was also able, off-hand and readily, to give answers to compositions made by others, of considerable length and accuracy. He was also more skillful in persuading others to very great things than any one else, and this from a natural affability of temper, which had been improved by much exercise and pains-taking; for as he was the grandson[11] of the brother of Tiberius, whose successor he was, this was a strong inducement to his acquiring of learning, because Tiberius aspired after the highest pitch of that sort of reputation; and Caius aspired after the like glory for eloquence, being induced thereto by the letters of his kinsman and his emperor. He was also among the first rank of his own citizens. But the advantages he received from his learning did not countervail the mischief he brought upon himself in the exercise of his authority; so difficult it is for those to obtain the

---

10. Spanheim here notes from Suetonius, that the name of Caius's sister with whom he was guilty of incest, was Drusilla and that Suetonius adds, he was guilty of the same crime with all his sisters also. He notes further, that Suetonius omits the mention of the haven for ships, which our author esteems the only public work for the good of the present and future ages which Caius left behind him, though in an imperfect condition.

11. This Caius was the son of that excellent person Germanicus, who was the son of Drusus, the brother of Tiberius the emperor.

virtue that is necessary for a wise man, who have the absolute power to do what they please without control. At the first he got himself such friends as were in all respects the most worthy, and was greatly beloved by them, while he imitated their zealous application to the learning and to the glorious actions of the best men; but when he became insolent towards them, they laid aside the kindness they had for him, and began to hate him; from which hatred came that plot which they raised against him, and wherein he perished.

3 *How Claudius Was Seized Upon and Brought Out of His House and Brought to the Camp; and How the Senate Sent an Embassage to Him*

1. NOW Claudius, as I said before, went out of that way along which Caius was gone; and as the family was in a mighty disorder upon the sad accident of the murder of Caius, he was in great distress how to save himself, and was found to have hidden himself in a certain narrow place,[12] though he had no other occasion for suspicion of any dangers, besides the dignity of his birth; for while he was a private man, he behaved himself with moderation, and was contented with his present fortune, applying himself to learning, and especially to that of the Greeks, and keeping himself entirely clear from every thing that might bring on any disturbance. But as at this time the multitude were under a consternation, and the whole palace was full of the soldiers' madness, and the very emperor's guards seemed under the like fear and disorder with private persons, the band called *pretorian,* which was the purest part of the army, was in consultation what was to be done at this juncture. Now all those that were at this consultation had little regard to the punishment Caius had suffered, because he justly deserved such his fortune; but they were rather considering their own circumstances, how they might take the best care of themselves, especially while the Germans were busy in punishing the murderers of Caius; which yet was rather done to gratify their own savage temper, than for the good of the public; all which things disturbed Claudius,

---

12. The first place Claudius came to was inhabited, and called Herincure, as Spanheim here informs us from Suetonius, in Claud. ch. 10.

who was afraid of his own safety, and this particularly because he saw the heads of Asprenas and his partners carried about. His station had been on a certain elevated place, whither a few steps led him, and whither he had retired in the dark by himself. But when Gratus, who was one of the soldiers that belonged to the palace, saw him, but did not well know by his countenance who he was, because it was dark, though he could well judge that it was a man who was privately there on some design, he came nearer to him; and when Claudius desired that he would retire, be discovered who he was, and owned him to be Claudius. So he said to his followers, "This is a Germanicus;[13] come on, let us choose him for our emperor." But when Claudius saw they were making preparations for taking him away by force, and was afraid they would kill him, as they had killed Caius, he besought them to spare him, putting them in mind how quietly he had demeaned himself, and that he was unacquainted with what had been done. Hereupon Gratus smiled upon him, and took him by the right hand, and said, "Leave off, sir, these low thoughts of saving yourself, while you ought to have greater thoughts, even of obtaining the empire, which the gods, out of their concern for the habitable world, by taking Caius out of the way, commit to thy virtuous conduct. Go to, therefore, and accept of the throne of thy ancestors." So they took him up and carried him, because he was not then able to go on foot, such was his dread and his joy at what was told him.

2. Now there was already gathered together about Gratus a great number of the guards; and when they saw Claudius carried off, they looked with a sad countenance, as supposing that he was carried to execution for the mischiefs that had been lately done; while yet they thought him a man who never meddled with public affairs all his life long, and one that had met with no contemptible dangers under the reign of Caius; and some of them thought it reasonable that the consuls should take cognizance of these matters; and as still more and more of the soldiery got together, the crowd about him ran away, and Claudius could hardly go on, his body was then so weak; and

13. How Claudius, another son of Drusus, which Drusus was the father of Germanicus, could be here himself called Germanicus, Suetonius informs us, when he assures us that, by a decree of the senate, the surname of Germanicus was bestowed upon Drusus, and his posterity also.—In Claud. ch. 1.

those who carried his sedan, upon an inquiry that was made about his being carried off, ran away and saved themselves, as despairing of their Lord's preservation. But when they were come into the large court of the palace, (which, as the report goes about it, was inhabited first of all the parts of the city of Rome,) and had just reached the public treasury, many more soldiers came about him, as glad to see Claudius's face, and thought it exceeding right to make him emperor, on account of their kindness for Germanicus, who was his brother, and had left behind him a vast reputation among all that were acquainted with him. They reflected also on the covetous temper of the leading men of the senate, and what great errors they had been guilty of when the senate had the government formerly; they also considered the impossibility of such an undertaking, as also what dangers they should be in, if the government should come to a single person, and that such a one should possess it as they had no hand in advancing, and not to Claudius, who would take it as their grant, and as gained by their good-will to him, and would remember the favors they had done him, and would make them a sufficient recompense for the same.

3. These were the discourses the soldiers had one with another by themselves, and they communicated them to all such as came in to them. Now those that inquired about this matter willingly embraced the invitation that was made them to join with the rest; so they carried Claudius into the camp, crowding about him as his guard, and encompassing him about, one chairman still succeeding another, that their vehement endeavors might not be hindered. But as to the populace and senators, they disagreed in their opinions. The latter were very desirous to recover their former dignity, and were zealous to get clear of the slavery that had been brought on them by the injurious treatment of the tyrants, which the present opportunity afforded them; but for the people, who were envious against them, and knew that the emperors were capable of curbing their covetous temper, and were a refuge from them, they were very glad that Claudius had been seized upon, and brought to them, and thought that if Claudius were made emperor, he would prevent a civil war, such as there was in the days of Pompey. But when the senate knew that Claudius was brought into the camp by the soldiers, they sent to him those of their body which had the best character for their virtues, that they might inform him that he ought to do nothing by violence, in order to gain the

government; that he who was a single person, one either already or hereafter to be a member of their body, ought to yield to the senate, which consisted of so great a number; that he ought to let the law take place in the disposal of all that related to the public order, and to remember how greatly the former tyrants had afflicted their city, and what dangers both he and they had escaped under Caius; and that he ought not to hate the heavy burden of tyranny, when the injury is done by others, while he did himself willfully treat his country after a mad and insolent manner; that if he would comply with them, and demonstrate that his firm resolution was to live quietly and virtuously, he would have the greatest honors decreed to him that a free people could bestow; and by subjecting himself to the law, would obtain this branch of commendation, that he acted like a man of virtue, both as a ruler and a subject; but that if he would act foolishly, and learn no wisdom by Caius's death, they would not permit him to go on; that a great part of the army was got together for them, with plenty of weapons, and a great number of slaves, which they could make use of; that good hope was a great matter in such cases, as was also good fortune; and that the gods would never assist any others but those that undertook to act with virtue and goodness, who can be no other than such as fight for the liberty of their country.

4. Now these ambassadors, Veranius and Brocchus, who were both of them tribunes of the people, made this speech to Claudius; and falling down upon their knees, they begged of him that he would not throw the city into wars and misfortunes; but when they saw what a multitude of soldiers encompassed and guarded Claudius, and that the forces that were with the consuls were, in comparison of them, perfectly inconsiderable, they added, that if he did desire the government, he should accept of it as given by the senate; that he would prosper better, and be happier, if he came to it, not by the injustice, but by the good-will of those that would bestow it upon him.

4 *What Things King Agrippa Did for Claudius; and How Claudius When He Had Taken the Government Commanded the Murderers of Caius to Be Slain*

1. NOW Claudius, though he was sensible after what an insolent manner the senate had sent to him yet did he, according to their

advice, behave himself for the present with moderation; but not so far that he could not recover himself out of his fright; so he was encouraged [to claim the government] partly by the boldness of the soldiers, and partly by the persuasion of king Agrippa, who exhorted him not to let such a dominion slip out of his hands, when it came thus to him of its own accord. Now this Agrippa, with relation to Caius, did what became one that had been so much honored by him; for he embraced Caius's body after he was dead, and laid it upon a bed, and covered it as well as he could, and went out to the guards, and told them that Caius was still alive; but he said that they should call for physicians, since he was very ill of his wounds. But when he had learned that Claudius was carried away violently by the soldiers, he rushed through the crowd to him, and when he found that he was in disorder, and ready to resign up the government to the senate, he encouraged him, and desired him to keep the government; but when he had said this to Claudius, he retired home. And upon the senate's sending for him, he anointed his head with ointment, as if he had lately accompanied with his wife, and had dismissed her, and then came to them: he also asked of the senators what Claudius did; who told him the present state of affairs, and then asked his opinion about the settlement of the public. He told them in words that he was ready to lose his life for the honor of the senate, but desired them to consider what was for their advantage, without any regard to what was most agreeable to them; for that those who grasp at government will stand in need of weapons and soldiers to guard them, unless they will set up without any preparation for it, and so fall into danger. And when the senate replied that they would bring in weapons in abundance, and money, and that as to an army, a part of it was already collected together for them, and they would raise a larger one by giving the slaves their liberty,—Agrippa made answer, "O senators! may you be able to compass what you have a mind to; yet will I immediately tell you my thoughts, because they tend to your preservation. Take notice, then, that the army which will fight for Claudius hath been long exercised in warlike affairs; but our army will be no better than a rude multitude of raw men, and those such as have been unexpectedly made free from slavery, and ungovernable; we must then fight against those that are skillful in war, with men who know not so much as how to draw their swords. So that my opinion is, that we should send some persons to Claudius, to persuade him to lay down the government; and I am ready to be one of your ambassadors."

2. Upon this speech of Agrippa, the senate complied with him, and he was sent among others, and privately informed Claudius of the disorder the senate was in, and gave him instructions to answer them in a somewhat commanding strain, and as one invested with dignity and authority. Accordingly, Claudius said to the ambassadors, that he did not wonder the senate had no mind to have an emperor over them, because they had been harassed by the barbarity of those that had formerly been at the head of their affairs; but that they should taste of an equitable government under him, and moderate times, while he should only he their ruler in name, but the authority should be equally common to them all; and since he had passed through many and various scenes of life before their eyes, it would be good for them not to distrust him. So the ambassadors, upon their hearing this his answer, were dismissed. But Claudius discoursed with the army which was there gathered together, who took oaths that they would persist in their fidelity to him; Upon which he gave the guards every man five thousand[14] drachmae a-piece, and a proportionable quantity to their captains, and promised to give the same to the rest of the armies wheresoever they were.

3. And now the consuls called the senate together into the temple of Jupiter the Conqueror, while it was still night; but some of those senators concealed themselves in the city, being uncertain what to do, upon the hearing of this summons; and some of them went out of the city to their own farms, as foreseeing whither the public affairs were going, and despairing of liberty; nay, these supposed it much better for them to be slaves without danger to themselves, and to live a lazy and inactive life, than by claiming the dignity of their forefathers, to run the hazard of their own safety. However, a hundred and no more were gotten together; and as they were in consultation about the present

14. This number of drachmae to be distributed to each private soldier, five thousand drachmae, equal to twenty thousand sesterces, or one hundred and sixty-one pounds sterling, seems much too large, and directly contradicts Suetonius, ch. 10., who makes them in all but fifteen sesterces, or two shillings and four pence. Yet might Josephus have this number from Agrippa, junior, though I doubt the thousands, or at least the hundreds, have been added by the transcribers, of which we have had several examples already in Josephus.

posture of affairs, a sudden clamor was made by the soldiers that were on their side, desiring that the senate would choose them an emperor, and not bring the government into ruin by setting up a multitude of rulers. So they fully declared themselves to be for the giving the government not to all, but to one; but they gave the senate leave to look out for a person worthy to be set over them, insomuch that now the affairs of the senate were much worse than before, because they had not only failed in the recovery of their liberty, which they boasted themselves of, but were in dread of Claudius also. Yet were there those that hankered after the government, both on account of the dignity of their families and that accruing to them by their marriages; for Marcus Minucianus was illustrious, both by his own nobility, and by his having married Julia, the sister of Caius, who accordingly was very ready to claim the government, although the consuls discouraged him, and made one delay after another in proposing it: that Minucianus also, who was one of Caius's murderers, restrained Valerius of Asia from thinking of such things; and a prodigious slaughter there had been, if leave had been given to these men to set up for themselves, and oppose Claudius. There were also a considerable number of gladiators besides, and of those soldiers who kept watch by night in the city, and rowers of ships, who all ran into the camp; insomuch that, of those who put in for the government, some left off their pretensions in order to spare the city, and others out of fear for their own persons.

4. But as soon as ever it was day, Cherea, and those that were with him, came into the senate, and attempted to make speeches to the soldiers. However, the multitude of those soldiers, when they saw that they were making signals for silence with their hands, and were ready to begin to speak to them, grew tumultuous, and would not let them speak at all, because they were all zealous to be under a monarchy; and they demanded of the senate one for their ruler, as not enduring any longer delays: but the senate hesitated about either their own governing, or how they should themselves be governed, while the soldiers would not admit them to govern, and the murderers of Caius would not permit the soldiers to dictate to them. When they were in these circumstances, Cherea was not able to contain the anger he had, and promised, that if they desired an emperor, he would give them one, if any one would bring him the watchword from Eutychus. Now this Eutychus was charioteer of the green-band faction, styled

Prasine, and a great friend of Caius, who used to harass the soldiery with building stables for the horses, and spent his time in ignominious labors, which occasioned Cherea to reproach them with him, and to abuse them with much other scurrilous language; and told them he would bring them the head of Claudius; and that it was an amazing thing, that, after their former madness, they should commit their government to a fool. Yet were not they moved with his words, but drew their swords, and took up their ensigns, and went to Claudius, to join in taking the oath of fidelity to him. So the senate were left without any body to defend them, and the very consuls differed nothing from private persons. They were also under consternation and sorrow, men not knowing what would become of them, because Claudius was very angry at them; so they fell a reproaching one another, and repented of what they had done. At which juncture Sabinus, one of Caius's murderers, threatened that he would sooner come into the midst of them and kill himself, than consent to make Claudius emperor, and see slavery returning upon them; he also abused Cherea for loving his life too well, while he who was the first in his contempt of Caius, could think it a good thin to live, when, even by all that they had done for the recovery of their liberty, they found it impossible to do it. But Cherea said he had no manner of doubt upon him about killing himself; that yet he would first sound the intentions of Claudius before he did it.

5. These were the debates [about the senate]; but in the camp every body was crowding on all sides to pay their court to Claudius; and the other consul, Quintus Pomponhis, was reproached by the soldiery, as having rather exhorted the senate to recover their liberty; whereupon they drew their swords, and were going to assault him, and they had done it, if Claudius had not hindered them, who snatched the consul out of the danger he was in, and set him by him. But he did not receive that part of the senate which was with Quintus in the like honorable manner; nay, some of them received blows, and were thrust away as they came to salute Claudius; nay, Aponius went away wounded, and they were all in danger. However, king Agrippa went up to Claudius, and desired he would treat the senators more gently; for if any mischief should come to the senate, he would have no others over whom to rule. Claudius complied with him, and called the senate together into the palace, and was carried thither himself through the city, while the soldiery conducted him, though this was to the great

vexation of the multitude; for Cherea and Sabinus, two of Caius's murderers, went in the fore-front of them, in an open manner, while Pollio, whom Claudius, a little before, had made captain of his guards, had sent them an epistolary edict, to forbid them to appear in public. Then did Claudius, upon his coming to the palace, get his friends together, and desired their suffrages about Cherea. They said that the work he had done was a glorious one; but they accused him the he did it of perfidiousness, and thought it just to inflict the punishment [of death] upon him, to discountenance such actions for the time to come. So Cherea was led to his execution, and Lupus and many other Romans with him. Now it is reported that Cherea bore this calamity courageously; and this not only by the firmness of his own behavior under it, but by the reproaches he laid upon Lupus, who fell into tears; for when Lupus laid his garment aside, and complained of the cold[15] he said, that cold was never hurtful to Lupus [i.e. a wolf] And as a great many men went along with them to see the sight, when Cherea came to the place, he asked the soldier who was to be their executioner, whether this office was what he was used to, or whether this was the first time of his using his sword in that manner, and desired him to bring him that very sword with which he himself slew Caius.[16] So he

15. This piercing cold here complained of by Lupus agrees well to the time of the year when Claudius began his reign; it being for certain about the months of November, December, or January, and most probably a few days after January the twenty-fourth, and a few days before the Roman Parentalia.

16. It is both here and elsewhere very remarkable, that the murders of the vilest tyrants, who yet highly deserved to die, when those murderers were under oaths, or other the like obligations of fidelity to them, were usually revenged, and the murderers were cut off themselves, and that after a remarkable manner; and this sometimes, as in the present case, by those very persons who were not sorry for such murders, but got kingdoms by them. The examples are very numerous, both in sacred and profane histories, and seem generally indications of Divine vengeance on such murderers. Nor is it unworthy of remark, that such murderers of tyrants do it usually on such ill principles, in such a cruel manner, and as ready to involve the innocent with the guilty, which was the case here, ch. 1. sect. 14, and ch. 2. sect. 4, as justly deserved the Divine vengeance upon them. Which seems to have been the case of Jehu also, when, besides the house of Ahab, for whose slaughter he had a commission from God, without any such commission, any justice or commiseration, he killed Ahab's great men, and acquaintance, and priests, and forty-two of the kindred of Ahaziah, 2 Kings 10:11–14. See Hosea 1:4. I do not mean here to condemn Ehud or Judith, or the like executioners of God's vengeance on those wicked tyrants who had

was happily killed at one stroke. But Lupus did not meet with such good fortune in going out of the world, since he was timorous, and had many blows leveled at his neck, because he did not stretch it out boldly [as he ought to have done].

6. Now, a few days after this, as the Parental solemnities were just at hand, the Roman multitude made their usual oblations to their several ghosts, and put portions into the fire in honor of Cherea, and besought him to be merciful to them, and not continue his anger against them for their ingratitude. And this was the end of the life that Cherea came to. But for Sabinus, although Claudius not only set him at liberty, but gave him leave to retain his former command in the army, yet did he think it would be unjust in him to fail of performing his obligations to his fellow confederates; so he fell upon his sword, and killed himself, the wound reaching up to the very hilt of the sword.

5 *How Claudius Restored to Agrippa His Grandfathers Kingdoms and Augmented His Dominions; and How He Published an Edict in Behalf*

1. NOW when Claudius had taken out of the way all those soldiers whom he suspected, which he did immediately, he published an edict, and therein confirmed that kingdom to Agrippa which Caius had given him, and therein commended the king highly. He also made all addition to it of all that country over which Herod, who was his grandfather, had reigned, that is, Judea and Samaria; and this he restored to him as due to his family. But for Abila[17] of Lysanias, and all

---

unjustly oppressed God's own people under their theocracy; who, as they appear still to have had no selfish designs nor intentions to slay the innocent, so had they still a Divine commission, or a Divine impulse, which was their commission for what they did, Judges 3:15, 19, 20; Judith 9:2; Test. Levi. sect. 5, in Authent. Rec. p. 312. See also page 432.

17. Here St. Luke is in some measure confirmed, when he reforms us, ch. 3:1, that Lysanias was some time before tetrarch of Abilene, whose capital was Abila; as he is further confirmed by Ptolemy, the great geographer, which Spanheim here observes, when he calls that city Abila of Lysanias. See the note on B. XVII. ch. 11. sect. 4; and Prid. at the years 36 and 22. I esteem this principality to have belonged to the land of Canaan originally, to have been the burying-place of Abel, and referred to as such, Matthew 23:35; Luke 11:51. See Authent. Rec. Part. II. p. 883—885.

that lay at Mount Libanus, he bestowed them upon him, as out of his own territories. He also made a league with this Agrippa, confirmed by oaths, in the middle of the forum, in the city of Rome: he also took away from Antiochus that kingdom which he was possessed of, but gave him a certain part of Cilicia and Commagena: he also set Alexander Lysimachus, the alabarch, at liberty, who had been his old friend, and steward to his mother Antonia, but had been imprisoned by Caius, whose son [Marcus] married Bernice, the daughter of Agrippa. But when Marcus, Alexander's son, was dead, who had married her when she was a virgin, Agrippa gave her in marriage to his brother Herod, and begged for him of Claudius the kingdom of Chalcis.

2. Now about this time there was a sedition between the Jews and the Greeks, at the city of Alexandria; for when Caius was dead, the nation of the Jews, which had been very much mortified under the reign of Caius, and reduced to very great distress by the people of Alexandria, recovered itself, and immediately took up their arms to fight for themselves. So Claudius sent an order to the president of Egypt to quiet that tumult; he also sent an edict, at the requests of king Agrippa and king Herod, both to Alexandria and to Syria, whose contents were as follows: "Tiberius Claudius Caesar Augustus Germanicus, high priest, and tribune of the people, ordains thus: Since I am assured that the Jews of Alexandria, called Alexandrians, have been joint inhabitants in the earliest times with the Alexandrians, and have obtained from their kings equal privileges with them, as is evident by the public records that are in their possession, and the edicts themselves; and that after Alexandria had been subjected to our empire by Augustus, their rights and privileges have been preserved by those presidents who have at divers times been sent thither; and that no dispute had been raised about those rights and privileges, even when Aquila was governor of Alexandria; and that when the Jewish ethnarch was dead, Augustus did not prohibit the making such ethnarchs, as willing that all men should be so subject [to the Romans] as to continue in the observation of their own customs, and not be forced to transgress the ancient rules of their own country religion; but that, in the time of Caius, the Alexandrians became insolent towards the Jews that were among them, which Caius, out of his great madness and want of understanding, reduced the nation of the Jews very low, because they would not transgress the religious worship of their

country, and call him a god: I will therefore that the nation of the Jews be not deprived of their rights and privileges, on account of the madness of Caius; but that those rights and privileges which they formerly enjoyed be preserved to them, and that they may continue in their own customs. And I charge both parties to take very great care that no troubles may arise after the promulgation of this edict."

3. And such were the contents of this edict on behalf of the Jews that was sent to Alexandria. But the edict that was sent into the other parts of the habitable earth was this which follows: "Tiberius Claudius Caesar Augustus Germanicus, high priest, tribune of the people, chosen consul the second time, ordains thus: Upon the petition of king Agrippa and king Herod, who are persons very dear to me, that I would grant the same rights and privileges should be preserved to the Jews which are in all the Roman empire, which I have granted to those of Alexandria, I very willingly comply therewith; and this grant I make not only for the sake of the petitioners, but as judging those Jews for whom I have been petitioned worthy of such a favor, on account of their fidelity and friendship to the Romans. I think it also very just that no Grecian city should be deprived of such rights and privileges, since they were preserved to them under the great Augustus. It will therefore be fit to permit the Jews, who are in all the world under us, to keep their ancient customs without being hindered so to do. And I do charge them also to use this my kindness to them with moderation, and not to show a contempt of the superstitious observances of other nations, but to keep their own laws only. And I will that this decree of mine be engraven on tables by the magistrates of the cities, and colonies, and municipal places, both those within Italy and those without it, both kings and governors, by the means of the ambassadors, and to have them exposed to the public for full thirty days, in such a place whence it may plainly be read from the ground.[18]

---

18. This form was so known and frequent among the Romans, as Dr. Hudson here tells us from the great Selden, that it used to be thus represented at the bottom of their edicts by the initial letters only, U. D. P. R. L. P, Unde De Plano Recte Lege Possit; "Whence it may be plainly read from the ground."

6 *What Things Were Done by Agrippa at Jerusalem When He Was Returned Back into Judea; and What It Was That Petronius Wrote to the Inhabitants of Doris, in Behalf*

1. NOW Claudius Caesar, by these decrees of his which were sent to Alexandria, and to all the habitable earth, made known what opinion he had of the Jews. So he soon sent Agrippa away to take his kingdom, now he was advanced to a more illustrious dignity than before, and sent letters to the presidents and procurators of the provinces that they should treat him very kindly. Accordingly, he returned in haste, as was likely he would, now lie returned in much greater prosperity than he had before. He also came to Jerusalem, and offered all the sacrifices that belonged to him, and omitted nothing which the law required;[19] on which account he ordained that many of the Nazarites should have their heads shorn. And for the golden chain which had been given him by Caius, of equal weight with that iron chain wherewith his royal hands had been bound, he hung it up within the limits of the temple, over the treasury,[20] that it might be a memorial of the severe fate he had lain under, and a testimony of his change for the better; that it might be a demonstration how the greatest prosperity may have a fall, and that God sometimes raises up what is fallen down: for this chain thus dedicated afforded a document to all men, that king Agrippa had been once bound in a chain for a small cause, but recovered his former dignity again; and a little while afterward got out of his bonds, and was advanced to be a more illustrious king than he was before. Whence men may understand that all that partake of human nature, how great soever they are, may fall; and that those that fall may gain their former illustrious dignity again.

---

19. Josephus shows, both here and ch. 7. sect. 3, that he had a much greater opinion of king Agrippa I. than Simon the learned Rabbi, than the people of Cesarea and Sebaste, ch. 7. sect. 4; and ch. 9. sect. 1; and indeed than his double-dealing between the senate and Claudius, ch. 4. sect. 2, than his slaughter of James the brother of John, and his imprisonment of Peter, or his vain-glorious behavior before he died, both in Acts 12:13; and here, ch. 4. sect. 1, will justify or allow. Josephus's character was probably taken from his son Agrippa, junior.

20. This treasury-chamber seems to have been the very same in which our Savior taught, and where the people offered their charity money for the repairs or other uses of the temple, Mark 12:41, etc.; Luke 22:1; John 8:20.

2. And when Agrippa had entirely finished all the duties of the Divine worship, he removed Theophilus, the son of Ananus, from the high priesthood, and bestowed that honor of his on Simon the son of Boethus, whose name was also Cantheras whose daughter king Herod married, as I have related above. Simon, therefore, had the [high] priesthood with his brethren, and with his father, in like manner as the sons of Simon, the son of Onias, who were three, had it formerly under the government of the Macedonians, as we have related in a former book.

3. When the king had settled the high priesthood after this manner, he returned the kindness which the inhabitants of Jerusalem had showed him; for he released them from the tax upon houses, every one of which paid it before, thinking it a good thing to requite the tender affection of those that loved him. He also made Silas the general of his forces, as a man who had partaken with him in many of his troubles. But after a very little while the young men of Doris, preferring a rash attempt before piety, and being naturally bold and insolent, carried a statue of Caesar into a synagogue of the Jews, and erected it there. This procedure of theirs greatly provoked Agrippa; for it plainly tended to the dissolution of the laws of his country. So he came without delay to Publius Petronius, who was then president of Syria, and accused the people of Doris. Nor did he less resent what was done than did Agrippa; for he judged it a piece of impiety to transgress the laws that regulate the actions of men. So he wrote the following letter to the people of Doris in an angry strain: "Publius Petronius, the president under Tiberius Claudius Caesar Augustus Germanicus, to the magistrates of Doris, ordains as follows: Since some of you have had the boldness, or madness rather, after the edict of Claudius Caesar Augustus Germanicus was published, for permitting the Jews to observe the laws of their country, not to obey the same, but have acted in entire opposition thereto, as forbidding the Jews to assemble together in the synagogue, by removing Caesar's statue, and setting it up therein, and thereby have offended not only the Jews, but the emperor himself, whose statue is more commodiously placed in his own temple than in a foreign one, where is the place of assembling together; while it is but a part of natural justice, that every one should have the power over the place belonging peculiarly to themselves, according to the determination of Caesar,—to say nothing of my own

determination, which it would be ridiculous to mention after the emperor's edict, which gives the Jews leave to make use of their own customs, as also gives order that they enjoy equally the rights of citizens with the Greeks themselves,—I therefore ordain that Proculus Vitellius, the centurion, bring those men to me, who, contrary to Augustus's edict, have been so insolent as to do this thing, at which those very men, who appear to be of principal reputation among them, have an indignation also, and allege for themselves, 'that it was not done with their consent, but by the violence of the multitude, that they may give an account of what hath been done. I also exhort the principal magistrates among them, unless they have a mind to have this action esteemed to be done with their consent, to inform the centurion of those that were guilty of it, and take care that no handle be hence taken for raising a sedition or quarrel among them; which those seem to me to treat after who encourage such doings; while both I myself, and king Agrippa, for whom I have the highest honor, have nothing more under our care, than that the nation of the Jews may have no occasion given them of getting together, under the pretense of avenging themselves, and become tumultuous. And that it may be more publicly known what Augustus hath resolved about this whole matter, I have subjoined those edicts which he hath lately caused to be published at Alexandria, and which, although they may be well known to all, yet did king Agrippa, for whom I have the highest honor, read them at that time before my tribunal, and pleaded that the Jews ought not to be deprived of those rights which Augustus hath granted them. I therefore charge you, that you do not, for the time to come, seek for any occasion of sedition or disturbance, but that every one be allowed to follow their own religious customs."

4. Thus did Petronius take care of this matter, that such a breach of the law might be corrected, and that no such thing might be attempted afterwards against the Jews. And now king Agrippa took the [high] priesthood away from Simon Cantheras, and put Jonathan, the son of Ananus, into it again, and owned that he was more worthy of that dignity than the other. But this was not a thing acceptable to him, to recover that his former dignity. So he refused it, and said, "O king! I rejoice in the honor that thou hast for me, and take it kindly that thou wouldst give me such a dignity of thy own inclinations, although God hath judged that I am not at all worthy of the high priesthood. I am

satisfied with having once put on the sacred garments; for I then put them on after a more holy manner than I should now receive them again. But if thou desirest that a person more worthy than myself should have this honorable employment, give me leave to name thee such a one. I have a brother that is pure from all sin against God, and of all offenses against thyself; I recommend him to thee, as one that is fit for this dignity." So the king was pleased with these words of his, and passed by Jonathan, and, according to his brother's desire, bestowed the high priesthood upon Matthias. Nor was it long before Marcus succeeded Petronius, as president of Syria.

7 *Concerning Silas and on What Account It Was That King Agrippa Was Angry at Him. How Agrippa Began to Encompass Jerusalem with a Wall; and What Benefits He Bestowed on the Inhabitants of Berytus*

1. NOW Silas, the general of the king's horse, because he had been faithful to him under all his misfortunes, and had never refused to be a partaker with him in any of his dangers, but had oftentimes undergone the most hazardous dangers for him, was full of assurance, and thought he might expect a sort of equality with the king, on account of the firmness of the friendship he had showed to him. Accordingly, he would no where let the king sit as his superior, and took the like liberty in speaking to him upon all occasions, till he became troublesome to the king, when they were merry together, extolling himself beyond measure, and oft putting the king in mind of the severity of fortune he had undergone, that he might, by way of ostentation, demonstrate What zeal he had showed in his service; and was continually harping upon this string, what pains he had taken for him, and much enlarged still upon that subject. The repetition of this so frequently seemed to reproach the king, insomuch that he took this ungovernable liberty of talking very ill at his hands. For the commemoration of times when men have been under ignominy, is by no means agreeable to them; and he is a very silly man who is perpetually relating to a person what kindness he had done him. At last, therefore, Silas had so thoroughly provoked the king's indignation, that he acted rather out of passion than good consideration, and did not only turn Silas out of his place,

as general of his horse, but sent him in bonds into his own country. But the edge of his anger wore off by length of time, and made room for more just reasonings as to his judgment about this man; and he considered how many labors he had undergone for his sake. So when Agrippa was solemnizing his birth-day, and he gave festival entertainments to all his subjects, he sent for Silas on the sudden to be his guest. But as he was a very frank man, he thought he had now a just handle given him to be angry; which he could not conceal from those that came for him, but said to them, "What honor is this the king invites me to, which I conclude will soon be over? For the king hath not let me keep those original marks of the good-will I bore him, which I once had from him; but he hath plundered me, and that unjustly also. Does he think that I can leave off that liberty of speech, which, upon the consciousness of my deserts, I shall use more loudly than before, and shall relate how many misfortunes I have been delivered from; how many labors I have undergone for him, whereby I procured him deliverance and respect; as a reward for which I have borne the hardships of bonds and a dark prison? I shall never forget this usage. Nay, perhaps, my very soul, when it is departed out of the body, will not forget the glorious actions I did on his account." This was the clamor he made, and he ordered the messengers to tell it to the king. So he perceived that Silas was incurable in his folly, and still suffered him to lie in prison.

2. As for the walls of Jerusalem, that were adjoining to the new city [Bezetha], he repaired them at the expense of the public, and built them wider in breadth, and higher in altitude; and he had made them too strong for all human power to demolish, unless Marcus, the then president of Syria, had by letter informed Claudius Caesar of what he was doing. And when Claudius had some suspicion of attempts for innovation, he sent to Agrippa to leave off the building of those walls presently. So he obeyed, as not thinking it proper to contradict Claudius.

3. Now this king was by nature very beneficent and liberal in his gifts, and very ambitious to oblige people with such large donations; and he made himself very illustrious by the many chargeable presents he made them. He took delight in giving, and rejoiced in living with good reputation. He was not at all like that Herod who reigned before him; for that Herod was ill-natured, and severe in his punishments,

and had no mercy on them that he hated; and every one perceived that he was more friendly to the Greeks than to the Jews; for he adorned foreign cities with large presents in money; with building them baths and theatres besides; nay, in some of those places he erected temples, and porticoes in others; but he did not vouchsafe to raise one of the least edifices in any Jewish city, or make them any donation that was worth mentioning. But Agrippa's temper was mild, and equally liberal to all men. He was humane to foreigners, and made them sensible of his liberality. He was in like manner rather of a gentle and compassionate temper. Accordingly, he loved to live continually at Jerusalem, and was exactly careful in the observance of the laws of his country. He therefore kept himself entirely pure; nor did any day pass over his head without its appointed sacrifice.

4. However, there was a certain mall of the Jewish nation at Jerusalem, who appeared to be very accurate in the knowledge of the law. His name was Simon. This man got together an assembly, while the king was absent at Cesarea, and had the insolence to accuse him as not living holily, and that he might justly be excluded out of the temple, since it belonged only to native Jews. But the general of Agrippa's army informed him that Simon had made such a speech to the people. So the king sent for him; and as he was sitting in the theater, he bid him sit down by him, and said to him with a low and gentle voice, "What is there done in this place that is contrary to the law?" But he had nothing to say for himself, but begged his pardon. So the king was more easily reconciled to him than one could have imagined, as esteeming mildness a better quality in a king than anger, and knowing that moderation is more becoming in great men than passion. So he made Simon a small present, and dismissed him.

5. Now as Agrippa was a great builder in many places, he paid a peculiar regard to the people of Berytus; for he erected a theater for them, superior to many others of that sort, both in Sumptuousness and elegance, as also an amphitheater, built at vast expenses; and besides these, he built them baths and porticoes, and spared for no costs in any of his edifices, to render them both handsome and large. He also spent a great deal upon their dedication, and exhibited shows upon them, and brought thither musicians of all sorts, and such as made the most delightful music of the greatest variety. He also showed his magnificence upon the theater, in his great number of gladiators; and

there it was that he exhibited the several antagonists, in order to please the spectators; no fewer indeed than seven hundred men to fight with seven hundred other men[21] and allotted all the malefactors he had for this exercise, that both the malefactors might receive their punishment, and that this operation of war might be a recreation in peace. And thus were these criminals all destroyed at once.

8 *What Other Acts Were Done by Agrippa Until His Death; and After What Manner He Died*

1. WHEN Agrippa had finished what I have above related at Berytus, he removed to Tiberias, a city of Galilee. Now he was in great esteem among other kings. Accordingly there came to him Antiochus, king of Commalena, Sampsigeratnus, king of Emesa, and Cotys, who was king of the Lesser Armenia, and Polemo, who was king of Pontus, as also Herod his brother, who was king of Chalcis. All these he treated with agreeable entertainments, and after an obliging manner, and so as to exhibit the greatness of his mind, and so as to appear worthy of those respects which the kings paid to him, by coming thus to see him. However, while these kings staid with him, Marcus, the president of Syria, came thither. So the king, in order to preserve the respect that was due to the Romans, went out of the city to meet him, as far as seven furlongs. But this proved to be the beginning of a difference between him and Marcus; for he took with him in his chariot those other kings as his assessors. But Marcus had a suspicion what the meaning could be of so great a friendship of these kings one with another, and did not think so close an agreement of so many potentates to be for the interest of the Romans. He therefore sent some of his domestics to every one of them, and enjoined them to go their ways home without further delay. This was very ill taken by Agrippa, who after that became his enemy. And now he took the high priesthood away from Matthias, and made Elioneus, the son of Cantheras, high priest in his stead.

2. Now when Agrippa had reigned three years over all Judea, he came to the city Cesarea, which was formerly called Strato's Tower;

---

21. A strange number of condemned criminals to be under the sentence of death at once; no fewer, it seems, than one thousand four hundred!

and there he exhibited shows in honor of Caesar, upon his being informed that there was a certain festival celebrated to make vows for his safety. At which festival a great multitude was gotten together of the principal persons, and such as were of dignity through his province. On the second day of which shows he put on a garment made wholly of silver, and of a contexture truly wonderful, and came into the theater early in the morning; at which time the silver of his garment being illuminated by the fresh reflection of the sun's rays upon it, shone out after a surprising manner, and was so resplendent as to spread a horror over those that looked intently upon him; and presently his flatterers cried out, one from one place, and another from another, (though not for his good,) that he was a god; and they added, "Be thou merciful to us; for although we have hitherto reverenced thee only as a man, yet shall we henceforth own thee as superior to mortal nature." Upon this the king did neither rebuke them, nor reject their impious flattery. But as he presently afterward looked up, he saw an owl[22] sitting on a certain rope over his head, and immediately understood that this bird was the messenger of ill tidings, as it had

---

22. We have a mighty cry made here by some critics, as the great Eusebius had on purpose falsified this account of Josephus, so as to make it agree with the parallel account in the Acts of the Apostles, because the present copies of his citation of it, Hist. Eceles. B. II. ch. 10., omit the words an owl—on a certain rope, which Josephus's present copies retain, and only have the explicatory word or angel; as if he meant that angel of the Lord which St. Luke mentions as smiting Herod, Acts 12:23, and not that owl which Josephus called an angel or messenger, formerly of good, but now of bad news, to Agrippa. This accusation is a somewhat strange one in the case of the great Eusebius, who is known to have so accurately and faithfully produced a vast number of other ancient records, and particularly not a few out of our Josephus also, without any suspicion of prevarication. Now, not to allege how uncertain we are whether Josephus's and Eusebius's copies of the fourth century were just like the present in this clause, which we have no distinct evidence of, the following words, preserved still in Eusebius, will not admit of any such exposition: "This [bird] (says Eusebius) Agrippa presently perceived to be the cause of ill fortune, as it was once of good fortune, to him;" which can only belong to that bird, the owl, which as it had formerly foreboded his happy deliverance from imprisonment, Antiq. B. XVIII. ch. 6. sect. 7, so was it then foretold to prove afterward the unhappy forerunner of his death in five days' time. If the improper words signifying cause, be changed for Josephus's proper word angel or messenger, and the foregoing words, be inserted, Esuebius's text will truly represent that in Josephus. Had this imperfection been in some heathen author that was in good esteem with our modern critics, they would have readily corrected these as barely errors in the copies; but being in an ancient

once been the messenger of good tidings to him; and fell into the deepest sorrow. A severe pain also arose in his belly, and began in a most violent manner. He therefore looked upon his friends, and said, "I, whom you call a god, am commanded presently to depart this life; while Providence thus reproves the lying words you just now said to me; and I, who was by you called immortal, am immediately to be hurried away by death. But I am bound to accept of what Providence allots, as it pleases God; for we have by no means lived ill, but in a splendid and happy manner." When he said this, his pain was become violent. Accordingly he was carried into the palace, and the rumor went abroad every where, that he would certainly die in a little time. But the multitude presently sat in sackcloth, with their wives and children, after the law of their country, and besought God for the king's recovery. All places were also full of mourning and lamentation. Now the king rested in a high chamber, and as he saw them below lying prostrate on the ground, he could not himself forbear weeping. And when he had been quite worn out by the pain in his belly for five days, he departed this life, being in the fifty-fourth year of his age, and in the seventh year of his reign; for he reigned four years under Caius Caesar, three of them were over Philip's tetrarchy only, and on the fourth he had that of Herod added to it; and he reigned, besides those, three years under the reign of Claudius Caesar; in which time he reigned over the forementioned countries, and also had Judea added to them, as well as Samaria and Cesarea. The revenues that he received out of them were very great, no less than twelve millions of drachme.[23] Yet did he borrow great sums from others; for he was so very liberal that his expenses exceeded his incomes, and his generosity was boundless.[24]

Christian writer, not so well relished by many of those critics, nothing will serve but the ill-grounded supposal of willful corruption and prevarication.

23. This sum of twelve millions of drachmae, which is equal to three millions of shekels, i.e. at 2s. 10d. a shekel, equal to four hundred and twenty-five thousand pounds sterling, was Agrippa the Great's yearly income, or about three quarters of his grandfather Herod's income; he having abated the tax upon houses at Jerusalem, ch. 6. sect. 3, and was not so tyrannical as Herod had been to the Jews. See the note on Antiq. B. XVII. ch. 11. sect. 4. A large sum this! but not, it seems, sufficient for his extravagant expenses.

24. Reland takes notice here, not improperly, that Josephus omits the reconciliation

3. But before the multitude were made acquainted with Agrippa's being expired, Herod the king of Chalcis, and Helcias the master of his horse, and the king's friend, sent Aristo, one of the king's most faithful servants, and slew Silas, who had been their enemy, as if it had been done by the king's own command.

9 *What Things Were Done After the Death of Agrippa; and How Claudius, on Account of the Youth and Unskilfulness of Agrippa, Junior, Sent Cuspius Fadus to Be Procurator of Judea, and of the Entire Kingdom*

1. AND thus did king Agrippa depart this life. But he left behind him a son, Agrippa by name, a youth in the seventeenth year of his age, and three daughters; one of which, Bernice, was married to Herod, his father's brother, and was sixteen years old; the other two, Mariamne and Drusilla, were still virgins; the former was ten years old, and Drusilla six. Now these his daughters were thus espoused by their father; Marlatone to Julius Archclaus Epiphanes, the son of Antiochus, the son of Chelcias; and Drusilla to the king of Commagena. But when it was known that Agrippa was departed this life, the inhabitants of Cesarea and of Sebaste forgot the kindnesses he had bestowed on them, and acted the part of the bitterest enemies; for they cast such reproaches upon the deceased as are not fit to be spoken of; and so many of them as were then soldiers, which were a great number, went to his house, and hastily carried off the statues[25] of this king's daughters, and all at once carried them into the brothel-houses, and when they had set them on the tops of those houses, they abused them to the utmost of their power, and did such things to them as are too indecent to be related. They also laid themselves down in public places, and celebrated general feastings, with garlands on their heads, and with ointments and libations to Charon, and drinking to

---

of this Herod Agrippa to the Tyrians and Sidoninus, by the means of Blastus the king's chamberlain, mentioned Acts 12:20. Nor is there any history in the world so complete, as to omit nothing that other historians take notice of, unless the one be taken out of the other, and accommodated to it.

25. Photius, who made an extract out of this section, says they were not the statues or images, but the ladies themselves, who were thus basely abused by the soldiers.

one another for joy that the king was expired. Nay, they were not only unmindful of Agrippa, who had extended his liberality to them in abundance, but of his grandfather Herod also, who had himself rebuilt their cities, and had raised them havens and temples at vast expenses.

2. Now Agrippa, the son of the deceased, was at Rome, and brought up with Claudius Caesar. And when Caesar was informed that Agrippa was dead, and that the inhabitants of Sebaste and Cesarea had abused him, he was sorry for the first news, and was displeased with the ingratitude of those cities. He was therefore disposed to send Agrippa, junior, away presently to succeed his father in the kingdom, and was willing to confirm him in it by his oath. But those freed-men and friends of his, who had the greatest authority with him, dissuaded him from it, and said that it was a dangerous experiment to permit so large a kingdom to come under the government of so very young a man, and one hardly yet arrived at years of discretion, who would not be able to take sufficient care of its administration; while the weight of a kingdom is heavy enough to a grown man. So Caesar thought what they said to be reasonable. Accordingly he sent Cuspins Fadus to be procurator of Judea, and of the entire kingdom, and paid that respect to the eceased as not to introduce Marcus, who had been at variance with him, into his kingdom. But he determined, in the first place, to send orders to Fadus, that he should chastise the inhabitants of Cesarca and Sebaste for those abuses they had offered to him that was deceased, and their madness towards his daughters that were still alive; and that he should remove that body of soldiers that were at Cesarea and Sebaste, with the five regiments, into Pontus, that they might do their military duty there; and that he should choose an equal number of soldiers out of the Roman legions that were in Syria, to supply their place. Yet were not those that had such orders actually removed; for by sending ambassadors to Claudius, they mollified him, and got leave to abide in Judea still; and these were the very men that became the source of very great calamities to the Jews in after-times, and sowed the seeds of that war which began under Florus; whence it was that when Vespasian had subdued the country, he removed them out of his province, as we shall relate hereafter.

Book 20

Containing the Interval of Twenty-Two Years, from Fadus the Procurator to Florus

1 *A Sedition of the Philadelphians Against the Jews; and Also Concerning the Vestments of the High Priest*

1. UPON the death of king Agrippa, which we have related in the foregoing book, Claudius Caesar sent Cassius Longinus as successor to Marcus, out of regard to the memory of king Agrippa, who had often desired of him by letters, while be was alive, that he would not suffer Marcus to be any longer president of Syria. But Fadus, as soon as he was come procurator into Judea, found quarrelsome doings between the Jews that dwelt in Perea, and the people of Philadelphia, about their borders, at a village called Mia, that was filled with men of a warlike temper; for the Jews of Perea had taken up arms without the consent of their principal men, and had destroyed many of the Philadelphians. When Fadus was informed of this procedure, it provoked him very much that they had not left the determination of the matter to him, if they thought that the Philadelphians had done them any wrong, but had rashly taken up arms against them. So he seized upon three of their principal men, who were also the causes of this sedition, and ordered them to be bound, and afterwards had one of them slain, whose name was Hannibal; and he banished the other two, Areram and Eleazar. Tholomy also, the arch robber, was, after some time, brought to him bound, and slain, but not till he had done a world of mischief to Idumea and the Arabians. And indeed, from that time, Judea was cleared of robberies by the care

and providence of Fadus. He also at this time sent for the high priests and the principal citizens of Jerusalem, and this at the command of the emperor, and admonished them that they should lay up the long garment and the sacred vestment, which it is customary for nobody but the high priest to wear, in the tower of Antonia, that it might be under the power of the Romans, as it had been formerly. Now the Jews durst not contradict what he had said, but desired Fadus, however, and Longinus, (which last was come to Jerusalem, and had brought a great army with him, out of a fear that the [rigid] injunctions of Fadus should force the Jews to rebel,) that they might, in the first place, have leave to send ambassadors to Caesar, to petition him that they may have the holy vestments under their own power; and that, in the next place, they would tarry till they knew what answer Claudius would give to that their request. So they replied, that they would give them leave to send their ambassadors, provided they would give them their sons as pledges [for their peaceable behavior]. And when they had agreed so to do, and had given them the pledges they desired, the ambassadors were sent accordingly. But when, upon their coming to Rome, Agrippa, junior, the son of the deceased, understood the reason why they came, (for he dwelt with Claudius Caesar, as we said before,) he besought Caesar to grant the Jews their request about the holy vestments, and to send a message to Fadus accordingly.

2. Hereupon Claudius called for the ambassadors; and told them that he granted their request; and bade them to return their thanks to Agrippa for this favor, which had been bestowed on them upon his entreaty. And besides these answers of his, he sent the following letter by them: "Claudius Caesar Germanicus, tribune of the people the fifth time, and designed consul the fourth time, and imperator the tenth time, the father of his country, to the magistrates, senate, and people, and the whole nation of the Jews, sendeth greeting. Upon the presentation of your ambassadors to me by Agrippa, my friend, whom I have brought up, and have now with me, and who is a person of very great piety, who are come to give me thanks for the care I have taken of your nation, and to entreat me, in an earnest and obliging manner, that they may have the holy vestments, with the crown belonging to them, under their power,—I grant their request, as that excellent person Vitellius, who is very dear to me, had done before me. And I have complied with your desire, in the first place,

out of regard to that piety which I profess, and because I would have every one worship God according to the laws of their own country; and this I do also because I shall hereby highly gratify king Herod, and Agrippa, junior, whose sacred regards to me, and earnest good-will to you, I am well acquainted with, and with whom I have the greatest friendship, and whom I highly esteem, and look on as persons of the best character. Now I have written about these affairs to Cuspius Fadus, my procurator. The names of those that brought me your letter are Cornelius, the son of Cero, Trypho, the son of Theudio, Dorotheus, the son of Nathaniel, and John, the son of Jotre. This letter is dated before the fourth of the calends of July, when Ruffis and Pompeius Sylvanus are consuls."

3. Herod also, the brother of the deceased Agrippa, who was then possessed of the royal authority over Chalcis, petitioned Claudius Caesar for the authority over the temple, and the money of the sacred treasure, and the choice of the high priests, and obtained all that he petitioned for. So that after that time this authority continued among all his descendants till the end of the war[1] Accordingly, Herod removed the last high priest, called Cimtheras, and bestowed that dignity on his successor Joseph, the son of Cantos.

2 *How Helena the Queen of Adiabene and Her Son Izates, Embraced the Jewish Religion; and How Helena Supplied the Poor with Corn, When There Was a Great Famine at Jerusalem*

1. ABOUT this time it was that Helena, queen of Adiabene, and her son Izates, changed their course of life, and embraced the Jewish customs, and this on the occasion following: Monobazus, the king of Adiabene, who had also the name of Bazeus, fell in love with his sister Helena, and took her to be his wife, and begat her with child. But as he was in bed with her one night, he laid his hand upon his wife's belly, and fell asleep, and seemed to hear a voice, which bid him take his hand

---

1. Here is some error in the copies, or mistake in Josephus; for the power of appointing high priests, alter Herod king of Chalcis was dead, and Agrippa, junior, was made king of Chalcis in his room, belonged to him; and he exercised the same all along till Jerusalem was destroyed, as Josephus elsewhere informs us, ch. 8. sect. 11; ch. 9. sect. 1, 4, 6, 7.

off his wife's belly, and not hurt the infant that was therein, which, by God's providence, would be safely born, and have a happy end. This voice put him into disorder; so he awaked immediately, and told the story to his wife; and when his son was born, he called him Izates. He had indeed Monobazus, his elder brother, by Helena also, as he had other sons by other wives besides. Yet did he openly place all his affections on this his only begotten[2] son Izates, which was the origin of that envy which his other brethren, by the same father, bore to him; while on this account they hated him more and more, and were all under great affliction that their father should prefer Izates before them. Now although their father was very sensible of these their passions, yet did he forgive them, as not indulging those passions out of an ill disposition, but out of a desire each of them had to be beloved by their father. However, he sent Izates, with many presents, to Abennerig, the king of Charax-Spasini, and that out of the great dread he was in about him, lest he should come to some misfortune by the hatred his brethren bore him; and he committed his son's preservation to him. Upon which Abennerig gladly received the young man, and had a great affection for him, and married him to his own daughter, whose name was Samacha: he also bestowed a country upon him, from which he received large revenues.

2. But when Monobazus was grown old, and saw that he had but a little time to live, he had a mind to come to the sight of his son before he died. So he sent for him, and embraced him after the most affectionate manner, and bestowed on him the country called Carra; it was a soil that bare amomum in great plenty: there are also in it the remains of that ark, wherein it is related that Noah escaped the deluge, and where they are still shown to such as are desirous to see them.[3] Accordingly, Izates abode in that country until his father's death. But the very day that Monobazus died, queen Helena sent for all the grandees, and governors of the kingdom, and for those that

---

2. Josephus here uses the word monogene, an only begotten son, for no other than one best beloved, as does both the Old and New Testament, I mean where there were one or more sons besides, Genesis 22:2; Hebrew 11:17. See the note on B. I. ch. 13. sect. 1.

3. It is here very remarkable, that the remains of Noah's ark were believed to be still in being in the days of Josephus. See the note on B. I. ch. 3. sect. 5.

had the armies committed to their command; and when they were come, she made the following speech to them: "I believe you are not unacquainted that my husband was desirous Izates should succeed him in the government, and thought him worthy so to do. However, I wait your determination; for happy is he who receives a kingdom, not from a single person only, but from the willing suffrages of a great many." This she said, in order to try those that were invited, and to discover their sentiments. Upon the hearing of which, they first of all paid their homage to the queen, as their custom was, and then they said that they confirmed the king's determination, and would submit to it; and they rejoiced that Izates's father had preferred him before the rest of his brethren, as being agreeable to all their wishes: but that they were desirous first of all to slay his brethren and kinsmen, that so the government might come securely to Izates; because if they were once destroyed, all that fear would be over which might arise from their hatred and envy to him. Helena replied to this, that she returned them her thanks for their kindness to herself and to Izates; but desired that they would however defer the execution of this slaughter of Izates's brethren till he should be there himself, and give his approbation to it. So since these men had not prevailed with her, when they advised her to slay them, they exhorted her at least to keep them in bonds till he should come, and that for their own security; they also gave her counsel to set up some one whom she could put the greatest trust in, as a governor of the kingdom in the mean time. So queen Helena complied with this counsel of theirs, and set up Monobazus, the eldest son, to be king, and put the diadem upon his head, and gave him his father's ring, with its signet; as also the ornament which they call Sampser, and exhorted him to administer the affairs of the kingdom till his brother should come; who came suddenly upon hearing that his father was dead, and succeeded his brother Monobazus, who resigned up the government to him.

3. Now, during the time Izates abode at Charax-Spasini, a certain Jewish merchant, whose name was Ananias, got among the women that belonged to the king, and taught them to worship God according to the Jewish religion. He, moreover, by their means, became known to Izates, and persuaded him, in like manner, to embrace that religion; he also, at the earnest entreaty of Izates, accompanied him when he was sent for by his father to come to Adiabene; it also happened that

Helena, about the same time, was instructed by a certain other Jew and went over to them. But when Izates had taken the kingdom, and was come to Adiabene, and there saw his brethren and other kinsmen in bonds, he was displeased at it; and as he thought it an instance of impiety either to slay or imprison them, but still thought it a hazardous thing for to let them have their liberty, with the remembrance of the injuries that had been offered them, he sent some of them and their children for hostages to Rome, to Claudius Caesar, and sent the others to Artabanus, the king of Parthia, with the like intentions.

4. And when he perceived that his mother was highly pleased with the Jewish customs, he made haste to change, and to embrace them entirely; and as he supposed that he could not be thoroughly a Jew unless he were circumcised, he was ready to have it done. But when his mother understood what he was about, she endeavored to hinder him from doing it, and said to him that this thing would bring him into danger; and that, as he was a king, he would thereby bring himself into great odium among his subjects, when they should understand that he was so fond of rites that were to them strange and foreign; and that they would never bear to be ruled over by a Jew. This it was that she said to him, and for the present persuaded him to forbear. And when he had related what she had said to Ananias, he confirmed what his mother had said; and when he had also threatened to leave him, unless he complied with him, he went away from him, and said that he was afraid lest such an action being once become public to all, he should himself be in danger of punishment for having been the occasion of it, and having been the king's instructor in actions that were of ill reputation; and he said that he might worship God without being circumcised, even though he did resolve to follow the Jewish law entirely, which worship of God was of a superior nature to circumcision. He added, that God would forgive him, though he did not perform the operation, while it was omitted out of necessity, and for fear of his subjects. So the king at that time complied with these persuasions of Ananias. But afterwards, as he had not quite left off his desire of doing this thing, a certain other Jew that came out of Galilee, whose name was Eleazar, and who was esteemed very skillful in the learning of his country, persuaded him to do the thing; for as he entered into his palace to salute him, and found him reading the law of Moses, he said to him, "Thou dost not consider, O king! that thou

unjustly breakest the principal of those laws, and art injurious to God himself, [by omitting to be circumcised]; for thou oughtest not only to read them, but chiefly to practice what they enjoin thee. How long wilt thou continue uncircumcised? But if thou hast not yet read the law about circumcision, and dost not know how great impiety thou art guilty of by neglecting it, read it now." When the king had heard what he said, he delayed the thing no longer, but retired to another room, and sent for a surgeon, and did what he was commanded to do. He then sent for his mother, and Ananias his tutor, and informed them that he had done the thing; upon which they were presently struck with astonishment and fear, and that to a great degree, lest the thing should be openly discovered and censured, and the king should hazard the loss of his kingdom, while his subjects would not bear to be governed by a man who was so zealous in another religion; and lest they should themselves run some hazard, because they would be supposed the occasion of his so doing. But it was God himself who hindered what they feared from taking effect; for he preserved both Izates himself and his sons when they fell into many dangers, and procured their deliverance when it seemed to be impossible, and demonstrated thereby that the fruit of piety does not perish as to those that have regard to him, and fix their faith upon him only.[4] But these events we shall relate hereafter.

5. But as to Helena, the king's mother, when she saw that the affairs of Izates's kingdom were in peace, and that her son was a happy man, and admired among all men, and even among foreigners, by the means of God's providence over him, she had a mind to go to the city of Jerusalem, in order to worship at that temple of God which was so very famous among all men, and to offer her thank-offerings there. So she desired her son to give her leave to go thither; upon which he gave his consent to what she desired very willingly, and made great preparations for her dismission, and gave her a great deal of money, and she went down to the city Jerusalem, her son conducting her on her journey a great way. Now her coming was of very great advantage

---

4. Josephus is very full and express in these three chapters, 3., 4., and 5., in observing how carefully Divine Providence preserved this Izates, king of Adiabene, and his sons, while he did what he thought was his bounden duty, notwithstanding the strongest political motives to the contrary.

to the people of Jerusalem; for whereas a famine did oppress them at that time, and many people died for want of what was necessary to procure food withal, queen Helena sent some of her servants to Alexandria with money to buy a great quantity of corn, and others of them to Cyprus, to bring a cargo of dried figs. And as soon as they were come back, and had brought those provisions, which was done very quickly, she distributed food to those that were in want of it, and left a most excellent memorial behind her of this benefaction, which she bestowed on our whole nation. And when her son Izates was informed of this famine,[5] he sent great sums of money to the principal men in Jerusalem. However, what favors this queen and king conferred upon our city Jerusalem shall be further related hereafter.

3 *How Artabanus, the King of Parthia Out of Fear of the Secret Contrivances of His Subjects Against Him, Went to Izates, and Was by Him Reinstated in His Government; as Also How Bardanes His Son Denounced War Against Izates*

1. BUT now Artabanus, king of the Parthians perceiving that the governors of the provinces had framed a plot against him, did not think it safe for him to continue among them; but resolved to go to Izates, in hopes of finding some way for his preservation by his means, and, if possible, for his return to his own dominions. So he came to

5. This further account of the benefactions of Izates and Helena to the Jerusalem Jews which Josephus here promises is, I think, no where performed by him in his present works. But of this terrible famine itself in Judea, take Dr. Hudson's note here:— "This (says he) is that famine foretold by Agabus, Acts 11:28, which happened when Claudius was consul the fourth time; and not that other which happened when Claudius was consul the second time, and Cesina was his colleague, as Scaliger says upon Eusebius, p. 174." Now when Josephus had said a little afterward, ch. 5. sect. 2, that "Tiberius Alexander succeeded Cuspius Fadus as procurator," he immediately subjoins, that" under these procurators there happened a great famine in Judea." Whence it is plain that this famine continued for many years, on account of its duration under these two procurators. Now Fadus was not sent into Judea till after the death of king Agrippa, i.e. towards the latter end of the 4th year of Claudius; so that this famine foretold by Agabus happened upon the 5th, 6th, and 7th years of Claudius, as says Valesius on Euseb. II. 12. Of this famine also, and queen Helena's supplies, and her monument, see Moses Churenensis, p. 144, 145, where it is observed in the notes that Pausanias mentions that her monument also.

Izates, and brought a thousand of his kindred and servants with him, and met him upon the road, while he well knew Izates, but Izates did not know him. When Artabanus stood near him, and, in the first place, worshipped him, according to the custom, he then said to him, "O king! do not thou overlook me thy servant, nor do thou proudly reject the suit I make thee; for as I am reduced to a low estate, by the change of fortune, and of a king am become a private man, I stand in need of thy assistance. Have regard, therefore, unto the uncertainty of fortune, and esteem the care thou shalt take of me to be taken of thyself also; for if I be neglected, and my subjects go off unpunished, many other subjects will become the more insolent towards other kings also." And this speech Artabanus made with tears in his eyes, and with a dejected countenance. Now as soon as Izates heard Artabanus's name, and saw him stand as a supplicant before him, he leaped down from his horse immediately, and said to him, "Take courage, O king! nor be disturbed at thy present calamity, as if it were incurable; for the change of thy sad condition shall be sudden; for thou shalt find me to be more thy friend and thy assistant than thy hopes can promise thee; for I will either re-establish thee in the kingdom of Parthia, or lose my own."

2. When he had said this, he set Artabanus upon his horse, and followed him on foot, in honor of a king whom he owned as greater than himself; which, when Artabanus saw, he was very uneasy at it, and sware by his present fortune and honor that he would get down from his horse, unless Izates would get upon his horse again, and go before him. So he complied with his desire, and leaped upon his horse; and when he had brought him to his royal palace, he showed him all sorts of respect when they sat together, and he gave him the upper place at festivals also, as regarding not his present fortune, but his former dignity, and that upon this consideration also, that the changes of fortune are common to all men. He also wrote to the Parthians, to persuade them to receive Artabanus again; and gave them his right hand and his faith, that he should forget what was past and done, and that he would undertake for this as a mediator between them. Now the Parthians did not themselves refuse to receive him again, but pleaded that it was not now in their power so to do, because they had committed the government to another person, who had accepted of it, and whose name was Cinnamus; and that they were afraid lest a civil war should arise on this account. When Cinnamus understood their

intentions, he wrote to Artabanus himself, for he had been brought up by him, and was of a nature good and gentle also, and desired him to put confidence in him, and to come and take his own dominions again. Accordingly, Artabanus trusted him, and returned home; when Cinnamus met him, worshipped him, and saluted him as a king, and took the diadem off his own head, and put it on the head of Artabanus.

3. And thus was Artahanus restored to his kingdom again by the means of Izates, when he had lost it by the means of the grandees of the kingdom. Nor was he unmindful of the benefits he had conferred upon him, but rewarded him with such honors as were of the greatest esteem among them; for he gave him leave to wear his tiara upright,[6] and to sleep upon a golden bed, which are privileges and marks of honor peculiar to the kings of Parthia. He also cut off a large and fruitful country from the king of Armenia, and bestowed it upon him. The name of the country is Nisibis, wherein the Macedonians had formerly built that city which they called Antioch of Mygodonla. And these were the honors that were paid Izates by the king of the Parthians.

4. But in no long time Artabanus died, and left his kingdom to his son Bardanes. Now this Bardanes came to Izates, and would have persuaded him to join him with his army, and to assist him in the war he was preparing to make with the Romans; but he could not prevail with him. For Izates so well knew the strength and good fortune of the Romans, that he took Bardanes to attempt what was impossible to be done; and having besides sent his sons, five in number, and they but young also, to learn accurately the language of our nation, together with our learning, as well as he had sent his mother to worship at our temple, as I have said already, was the more backward to a compliance; and restrained Bardanes, telling him perpetually of the great armies and famous actions of the Romans, and thought thereby to terrify him, and desired thereby to hinder him from that expedition. But the Parthian king was provoked at this his behavior, and denounced war immediately against Izates. Yet did he gain no advantage by this war, because God cut off all his hopes therein; for the Parthians perceiving

---

6. This privilege of wearing the tiara upright, or with the tip of the cone erect, is known to have been of old peculiar to great kings, from Xenophon and others, as Dr. Hudson observes here.

Bardanes's intentions, and how he had determined to make war with the Romans, slew him, and gave his kingdom to his brother Gotarzes. He also, in no long time, perished by a plot made against him, and Vologases, his brother, succeeded him, who committed two of his provinces to two of his brothers by the same father; that of the Medes to the elder, Pacorus; and Armenia to the younger, Tiridates.

4 *How Izates Was Betrayed by His Own Subjects, and Fought Against by the Arabians and How Izates, by the Providence of God, Was Delivered Out of Their Hands*

1. NOW when the king's brother, Monobazus, and his other kindred, saw how Izates, by his piety to God, was become greatly esteemed by all men, they also had a desire to leave the religion of their country, and to embrace the customs of the Jews; but that act of theirs was discovered by Izates's subjects. Whereupon the grandees were much displeased, and could not contain their anger at them; but had an intention, when they should find a proper opportunity, to inflict a punishment upon them. Accordingly, they wrote to Abia, king of the Arabians, and promised him great sums of money, if he would make an expedition against their king; and they further promised him, that, on the first onset, they would desert their king, because they were desirous to punish him, by reason of the hatred he had to their religious worship; then they obliged themselves, by oaths, to be faithful to each other, and desired that he would make haste in this design. The king of Arabia complied with their desires, and brought a great army into the field, and marched against Izates; and, in the beginning of the first onset, and before they came to a close fight, those Handees, as if they had a panic terror upon them, all deserted Izates, as they had agreed to do, and, turning their backs upon their enemies, ran away. Yet was not Izates dismayed at this; but when he understood that the grandees had betrayed him, he also retired into his camp, and made inquiry into the matter; and as soon as he knew who they were that made this conspiracy with the king of Arabia, he cut off those that were found guilty; and renewing the fight on the next day, he slew the greatest part of his enemies, and forced all the rest to betake themselves to flight. He also pursued their king, and drove him into

a fortress called Arsamus, and following on the siege vigorously, he took that fortress. And when he had plundered it of all the prey that was in it, which was not small, he returned to Adiabene; yet did not he take Abia alive, because, when he found himself encompassed on every side, he slew himself.

2. But although the grandees of Adiabene had failed in their first attempt, as being delivered up by God into their king's hands, yet would they not even then be quiet, but wrote again to Vologases, who was then king of Parthia, and desired that he would kill Izates, and set over them some other potentate, who should be of a Parthian family; for they said that they hated their own king for abrogating the laws of their forefathers, and embracing foreign customs. When the king of Parthia heard this, he boldly made war upon Izates; and as he had no just pretense for this war, he sent to him, and demanded back those honorable privileges which had been bestowed on him by his father, and threatened, on his refusal, to make war upon him. Upon hearing of this, Izates was under no small trouble of mind, as thinking it would be a reproach upon him to appear to resign those privileges that had been bestowed upon him out of cowardice; yet because he knew, that though the king of Parthia should receive back those honors, yet would he not be quiet, he resolved to commit himself to God, his Protector, in the present danger he was in of his life; and as he esteemed him to be his principal assistant, he intrusted his children and his wives to a very strong fortress, and laid up his corn in his citadels, and set the hay and the grass on fire. And when he had thus put things in order, as well as he could, he awaited the coming of the enemy. And when the king of Parthia was come, with a great army of footmen and horsemen, which he did sooner than was expected, (for he marched in great haste,) and had cast up a bank at the river that parted Adiabene from Media,—Izates also pitched his camp not far off, having with him six thousand horsemen. But there came a messenger to Izates, sent by the king of Parthia, who told him how large his dominions were, as reaching from the river Euphrates to Bactria, and enumerated that king's subjects; he also threatened him that he should be punished, as a person ungrateful to his lords; and said that the God whom he worshipped could not deliver him out of the king's hands. When the messenger had delivered this his message, Izates replied that he knew the king of Parthia's power was much greater than his

own; but that he knew also that God was much more powerful than all men. And when he had returned him this answer, he betook himself to make supplication to God, and threw himself upon the ground, and put ashes upon his head, in testimony of his confusion, and fasted, together with his wives and children.[7] Then he called upon God, and said, "O Lord and Governor, if I have not in vain committed myself to thy goodness, but have justly determined that thou only art the Lord and principal of all beings, come now to my assistance, and defend me from my enemies, not only on my own account, but on account of their insolent behavior with regard to thy power, while they have not feared to lift up their proud and arrogant tongue against thee." Thus did he lament and bemoan himself, with tears in his eyes; whereupon God heard his prayer. And immediately that very night Vologases received letters, the contents of which were these, that a great band of Dahe and Sacse, despising him, now he was gone so long a journey from home, had made an expedition, and laid Parthis waste; so that he [was forced to] retire back, without doing any thing. And thus it was that Izates escaped the threatenings of the Parthians, by the providence of God.

3. It was not long ere Izates died, when he had completed fifty-five years of his life, and had ruled his kingdom twenty-four years. He left behind him twenty-four sons and twenty-four daughters. However, he gave order that his brother Monobazus should succeed in the government, thereby requiting him, because, while he was himself absent after their father's death, he had faithfully preserved the government for him. But when Helena, his mother, heard of her son's death, she was in great heaviness, as was but natural, upon her loss of such a most dutiful son; yet was it a comfort to her that she heard the succession came to her eldest son. Accordingly, she went to him in haste; and when she was come into Adiabene, she did not long outlive her son Izates. But Monobazus sent her bones, as well as those of Izates, his brother, to Jerusalem, and gave order that they should

7. This conduct of Izates is a sign that he was become either a Jew, or an Ebionite Christian, who indeed differed not much from proper Jews. See ch. 6. sect. 1. However, his supplications were heard, and he was providentially delivered from that imminent danger he was in.

be buried at the pyramids[8] which their mother had erected; they were three in number, and distant no more than three furlongs from the city Jerusalem. But for the actions of Monobazus the king, which he did during the rest of his life. we will relate them hereafter.

5 *Concerning Theudas and the Sons of Judas the Galilean; as Also What Calamity Fell Upon the Jews on the Day of the Passover*

1. NOW it came to pass, while Fadus was procurator of Judea, that a certain magician, whose name was Theudas,[9] persuaded a great part of the people to take their effects with them, and follow him to the river Jordan; for he told them he was a prophet, and that he would, by his own command, divide the river, and afford them an easy passage over it; and many were deluded by his words. However, Fadus did not permit them to make any advantage of his wild attempt, but sent a troop of horsemen out against them; who, falling upon them unexpectedly, slew many of them, and took many of them alive. They also took Theudas alive, and cut off his head, and carried it to Jerusalem. This was what befell the Jews in the time of Cuspius Fadus's government.

2. Then came Tiberius Alexander as successor to Fadus; he was the son of Alexander the alabarch of Alexandria, which Alexander was a principal person among all his contemporaries, both for his family and wealth: he was also more eminent for his piety than this his son Alexander, for he did not continue in the religion of his country. Under these procurators that great famine happened in Judea, in which queen Helena bought corn in Egypt at a great expense, and distributed it to those that were in want, as I have related already. And besides this, the sons of Judas of Galilee were now slain; I mean of that Judas who

---

8. These pyramids or pillars, erected by Helena, queen of Adiabene, near Jerusalem, three in number, are mentioned by Eusebius, in his Eccles. Hist. B. II. ch. 12, for which Dr. Hudson refers us to Valesius's notes upon that place.—They are also mentioned by Pausanias, as hath been already noted, ch. 2. sect. 6. Reland guesses that that now called Absalom's Pillar may be one of them.

9. This Theudas, who arose under Fadus the procurator, about A.D. 45 or 46, could not be that Thendas who arose in the days of the taxing, under Cyrenius, or about A.D. 7, Acts v. 36, 37. Who that earlier Theudas was, see the note on B. XVII. ch. 10. sect. 5.

caused the people to revolt, when Cyrenius came to take an account of the estates of the Jews, as we have showed in a foregoing book. The names of those sons were James and Simon, whom Alexander commanded to be crucified. But now Herod, king of Chalcis, removed Joseph, the son of Camydus, from the high priesthood, and made Ananias, the son of Nebedeu, his successor. And now it was that Cumanus came as successor to Tiberius Alexander; as also that Herod, brother of Agrippa the great king, departed this life, in the eighth year of the reign of Claudius Caesar. He left behind him three sons; Aristobulus, whom he had by his first wife, with Bernicianus, and Hyrcanus, both whom he had by Bernice his brother's daughter. But Claudius Caesar bestowed his dominions on Agrippa, junior.

3. Now while the Jewish affairs were under the administration of Cureanus, there happened a great tumult at the city of Jerusalem, and many of the Jews perished therein. But I shall first explain the occasion whence it was derived. When that feast which is called the passover was at hand, at which time our custom is to use unleavened bread, and a great multitude was gathered together from all parts to that feast, Cumanus was afraid lest some attempt of innovation should then be made by them; so he ordered that one regiment of the army should take their arms, and stand in the temple cloisters, to repress any attempts of innovation, if perchance any such should begin; and this was no more than what the former procurators of Judea did at such festivals. But on the fourth day of the feast, a certain soldier let down his breeches, and exposed his privy members to the multitude, which put those that saw him into a furious rage, and made them cry out that this impious action was not done to approach them, but God himself; nay, some of them reproached Cumanus, and pretended that the soldier was set on by him, which, when Cumanus heard, he was also himself not a little provoked at such reproaches laid upon him; yet did he exhort them to leave off such seditious attempts, and not to raise a tumult at the festival. But when he could not induce them to be quiet for they still went on in their reproaches to him, he gave order that the whole army should take their entire armor, and come to Antonia, which was a fortress, as we have said already, which overlooked the temple; but when the multitude saw the soldiers there, they were affrighted at them, and ran away hastily; but as the passages out were but narrow, and as they thought their enemies followed

them, they were crowded together in their flight, and a great number were pressed to death in those narrow passages; nor indeed was the number fewer than twenty thousand that perished in this tumult. So instead of a festival, they had at last a mournful day of it; and they all of them forgot their prayers and sacrifices, and betook themselves to lamentation and weeping; so great an affliction did the impudent obsceneness of a single soldier bring upon them.[10]

4. Now before this their first mourning was over, another mischief befell them also; for some of those that raised the foregoing tumult, when they were traveling along the public road, about a hundred furlongs from the city, robbed Stephanus, a servant of Caesar, as he was journeying, and plundered him of all that he had with him; which things when Cureanus heard of, he sent soldiers immediately, and ordered them to plunder the neighboring villages, and to bring the most eminent persons among them in bonds to him. Now as this devastation was making, one of the soldiers seized the laws of Moses that lay in one of those villages, and brought them out before the eyes of all present, and tore them to pieces; and this was done with reproachful language, and much scurrility; which things when the Jews heard of, they ran together, and that in great numbers, and came down to Cesarea, where Cumanus then was, and besought him that he would avenge, not themselves, but God himself, whose laws had been affronted; for that they could not bear to live any longer, if the laws of their forefathers must be affronted after this manner. Accordingly Cumanus, out of fear lest the multitude should go into a sedition, and by the advice of his friends also, took care that the soldier who had offered the affront to the laws should be beheaded, and thereby put a stop to the sedition which was ready to be kindled a second time.

---

10. This and. many more tumults and seditions which arose at the Jewish festivals, in Josephus, illustrate the cautious procedure of the Jewish governors, when they said, Matthew 26:5, "Let us not take Jesus on the feast-day, lest there be an up roar among the people;" as Reland well observes on tins place. Josephus also takes notice of the same thing, Of the War, B. I. ch. 4. sect. 3.

Chapter 6

6 How There Happened a Quarrel Between the Jews and the Samaritans; and How Claudius Put an End to Their Differences

1. NOW there arose a quarrel between the Samaritans and the Jews on the occasion following: It was the custom of the Galileans, when they came to the holy city at the festivals, to take their journeys through the country of the Samaritans;[11] and at this time there lay, in the road they took, a village that was called Ginea, which was situated in the limits of Samaria and the great plain, where certain persons thereto belonging fought with the Galileans, and killed a great many of them. But when the principal of the Galileans were informed of what had been done, they came to Cumanus, and desired him to avenge the murder of those that were killed; but he was induced by the Samaritans, with money, to do nothing in the matter; upon which the Galileans were much displeased, and persuaded the multitude of the Jews to betake themselves to arms, and to regain their liberty, saying that slavery was in itself a bitter thing, but that when it was joined with direct injuries, it was perfectly intolerable, And when their principal men endeavored to pacify them, and promised to endeavor to persuade Cureanus to avenge those that were killed, they would not hearken to them, but took their weapons, and entreated the assistance of Eleazar, the son of Dineus, a robber, who had many years made his abode in the mountains, with which assistance they plundered many villages of the Samaritans. When Cumanus heard of this action of theirs, he took the band of Sebaste, with four regiments of footmen, and armed the Samaritans, and marched out against the Jews, and caught them, and slew many of them, and took a great number of them alive; whereupon those that were the most eminent persons at Jerusalem, and that both in regard to the respect that was paid them, and the families they were of, as soon as they saw to what a height things were gone, put on sackcloth, and heaped ashes upon their heads, and by all possible means besought the seditious, and persuaded them that they would set before their eyes the utter

11. This constant passage of the Galileans through the country of Samaria, as they went to Judea and Jerusalem, illustrates several passages in the Gospels to the same purpose, as Dr. Hudson rightly observes. See Luke 17:11; John 4:4. See also Josephus in his own Life, sect. 52, where that journey is determined to three days.

subversion of their country, the conflagration of their temple, and the slavery of themselves, their wives, and children,[12] which would be the consequences of what they were doing; and would alter their minds, would cast away their weapons, and for the future be quiet, and return to their own homes. These persuasions of theirs prevailed upon them. So the people dispersed themselves, and the robbers went away again to their places of strength; and after this time all Judea was overrun with robberies.

2. But the principal of the Samaritans went to Ummidius Quadratus, the president of Syria, who at that time was at Tyre, and accused the Jews of setting their villages on fire, and plundering them; and said withal, that they were not so much displeased at what they had suffered, as they were at the contempt thereby showed the Romans; while if they had received any injury, they ought to have made them the judges of what had been done, and not presently to make such devastation, as if they had not the Romans for their governors; on which account they came to him, in order to obtain that vengeance they wanted. This was the accusation which the Samaritans brought against the Jews. But the Jews affirmed that the Samaritans were the authors of this tumult and fighting, and that, in the first place, Cumanus had been corrupted by their gifts, and passed over the murder of those that were slain in silence;—which allegations when Quadratus heard, he put off the hearing of the cause, and promised that he would give sentence when he should come into Judea, and should have a more exact knowledge of the truth of that matter. So these men went away without success. Yet was it not long ere Quadratus came to Samaria, where, upon hearing the cause, he supposed that the Samaritans were the authors of that disturbance. But when he was informed that certain of the Jews were making innovations, he ordered those to be crucified whom Cumanus had taken captives. From whence he came to a certain village called Lydda, which was not less than a city in largeness, and there heard the Samaritan cause a second time before his tribunal, and

12. Our Savior had foretold that the Jews' rejection of his gospel would bring upon them, among other miseries, these three, which they themselves here show they expected would be the consequences of their present tumults and seditions: the utter subversion of their country, the conflagration of their temple, and the slavery of themselves, their wives, and children See Luke 21:6–24.

there learned from a certain Samaritan that one of the chief of the Jews, whose name was Dortus, and some other innovators with him, four in number, persuaded the multitude to a revolt from the Romans; whom Quadratus ordered to be put to death: but still he sent away Ananias the high priest, and Ananus the commander [of the temple], in bonds to Rome, to give an account of what they had done to Claudius Caesar. He also ordered the principal men, both of the Samaritans and of the Jews, as also Cumanus the procurator, and Ceier the tribune, to go to Italy to the emperor, that he might hear their cause, and determine their differences one with another. But he came again to the city of Jerusalem, out of his fear that the multitude of the Jews should attempt some innovations; but he found the city in a peaceable state, and celebrating one of the usual festivals of their country to God. So he believed that they would not attempt any innovations, and left them at the celebration of the festival, and returned to Antioch.

3. Now Cumanus, and the principal of the Samaritans, who were sent to Rome, had a day appointed them by the emperor whereon they were to have pleaded their cause about the quarrels they had one with another. But now Caesar's freed-men and his friends were very zealous on the behalf of Cumanus and the Samaritans; and they had prevailed over the Jews, unless Agrippa, junior, who was then at Rome, had seen the principal of the Jews hard set, and had earnestly entreated Agrippina, the emperor's wife, to persuade her husband to hear the cause, so as was agreeable to his justice, and to condemn those to be punished who were really the authors of this revolt from the Roman government:—whereupon Claudius was so well disposed beforehand, that when he had heard the cause, and found that the Samaritans had been the ringleaders in those mischievous doings, he gave order that those who came up to him should be slain, and that Cureanus should be banished. He also gave order that Celer the tribune should be carried back to Jerusalem, and should be drawn through the city in the sight of all the people, and then should be slain.

7 *Felix Is Made Procurator of Judea; as Also Concerning Agrippa, Junior and His Sisters*

1. SO Claudius sent Felix, the brother of Pallas, to take care of the affairs of Judea; and when he had already completed the twelfth

year of his reign, he bestowed upon Agrippa the tetrarchy of Philip and Batanea, and added thereto Trachonites, with Abila; which last had been the tetrarchy of Lysanias; but he took from him Chalcis, when he had been governor thereof four years. And when Agrippa had received these countries as the gift of Caesar, he gave his sister Drusilla in marriage to Azizus, king of Emesa, upon his consent to be circumcised; for Epiphanes, the son of king Antiochus, had refused to marry her, because, after he had promised her father formerly to come over to the Jewish religion, he would not now perform that promise. He also gave Mariamne in marriage to Archelaus, the son of Helcias, to whom she had formerly been betrothed by Agrippa her father; from which marriage was derived a daughter, whose name was Bernice.

2. But for the marriage of Drusilla with Azizus, it was in no long time afterward dissolved upon the following occasion: While Felix was procurator of Judea, he saw this Drusilla, and fell in love with her; for she did indeed exceed all other women in beauty; and he sent to her a person whose name was Simon[13] one of his friends; a Jew he was, and by birth a Cypriot, and one who pretended to be

13. This Simon, a friend of Felix, a Jew, born in Cyprus, though he pretended to be a magician, and seems to have been wicked enough, could hardly be that famous Simon the magician, in the Acts of the Apostles, 8:9, etc., as some are ready to suppose. This Simon mentioned in the Acts was not properly a Jew, but a Samaritan, of the town of Gittae, in the country of Samaria, as the Apostolical Constitutions, VI. 7, the Recognitions of Clement, II. 6, and Justin Martyr, himself born in the country of Samaria, Apology, I. 34, inform us. He was also the author, not of any ancient Jewish, but of the first Gentile heresies, as the forementioned authors assure us. So I suppose him a different person from the other. I mean this only upon the hypothesis that Josephus was not misinformed as to his being a Cypriot Jew; for otherwise the time, the name, the profession, and the wickedness of them both would strongly incline one to believe them the very same. As to that Drusilla, the sister of Agrippa, junior, as Josephus informs us here, and a Jewess, as St. Luke informs us, Acts 24:24, whom this Simon mentioned by Josephus persuaded to leave her former husband, Azizus, king of Emesa, a proselyte of justice, and to marry Felix, the heathen procurator of Judea, Tacitus, Hist. V. 9, supposes her to be a heathen; and the grand-daughter of Antonius and Cleopatra, contrary both to St. Luke and Josephus. Now Tacitus lived somewhat too remote, both as to time and place, to be compared with either of those Jewish writers, in a matter concerning the Jews in Judea in their own days, and concerning a sister of Agrippa, junior, with which Agrippa Josephus was himself so well acquainted. It is probable that Tacitus may say true, when he informs us that this Felix (who had in all three wives, or queens, as Suetonius in Claudius, sect. 28, assures us) did once marry such a grandchild of Antonius and Cleopatra; and finding

a magician, and endeavored to persuade her to forsake her present husband, and marry him; and promised, that if she would not refuse him, he would make her a happy woman. Accordingly she acted ill, and because she was desirous to avoid her sister Bernice's envy, for she was very ill treated by her on account of her beauty, was prevailed upon to transgress the laws of her forefathers, and to marry Felix; and when he had had a son by her, he named him Agrippa. But after what manner that young man, with his wife, perished at the conflagration of the mountain Vesuvius,[14] in the days of Titus Caesar, shall be related hereafter.[15]

3. But as for Bernice, she lived a widow a long while after the death of Herod [king of Chalcis], who was both her husband and her uncle; but when the report went that she had criminal conversation with her brother, [Agrippa, junior,] she persuaded Poleme, who was king of Cilicia, to be circumcised, and to marry her, as supposing that by this means she should prove those calumnies upon her to be false; and Poleme was prevailed upon, and that chiefly on account of her riches. Yet did not this matrimony endure long; but Bernice left Poleme, and, as was said, with impure intentions. So he forsook at once this matrimony, and the Jewish religion; and, at the same time, Mariamne put away Archclaus, and was married to Demetrius, the principal man among the Alexandrian Jews, both for his family and his wealth; and indeed he was then their alabarch. So she named her son whom she had by him Agrippinus. But of all these particulars we shall hereafter treat more exactly.[16]

---

the name of one of them to have been Drusilla, he mistook her for that other wife, whose name he did not know.

14. This eruption of Vesuvius was one of the greatest we have in history. See Bianchini's curious and important observations on this Vesuvius, and its seven several great eruptions, with their remains vitrified, and still existing, in so many different strata under ground, till the diggers came to the antediluvian waters, with their proportionable interstices, implying the deluge to have been above two thousand five hundred years before the Christian era, according to our exactest chronology.

15. This is now wanting.

16. This also is now wanting.

8 *After What Manner Upon the Death of Claudius, Nero Succeeded in the Government; as Also What Barbarous Things He Did. Concerning the Robbers, Murderers and Impostors, That Arose While Felix and Festus Were Procurators of Judea*

1. NOW Claudius Caesar died when he had reigned thirteen years, eight months, and twenty days;[17] and a report went about that he was poisoned by his wife Agrippina. Her father was Germanicus, the brother of Caesar. Her husband was Domitius Aenobarbus, one of the most illustrious persons that was in the city of Rome; after whose death, and her long continuance in widowhood, Claudius took her to wife. She brought along with her a son, Domtitus, of the same name with his father. He had before this slain his wife Messalina, out of jealousy, by whom he had his children Britannicus and Octavia; their eldest sister was Antonia, whom he had by Pelina his first wife. He also married Octavia to Nero; for that was the name that Caesar gave him afterward, upon his adopting him for his son.

2. But now Agrippina was afraid, lest, when Britannicus should come to man's estate, he should succeed his father in the government, and desired to seize upon the principality beforehand for her own son [Nero]; upon which the report went that she thence compassed the death of Claudius. Accordingly, she sent Burrhus, the general of the army, immediately, and with him the tribunes, and such also of the freed-men as were of the greatest authority, to bring Nero away into the camp, and to salute him emperor. And when Nero had thus obtained the government, he got Britannicus to be so poisoned, that the multitude should not perceive it; although he publicly put his own mother to death not long afterward, making her this requital, not only for being born of her, but for bringing it so about by her contrivances that he obtained the Roman empire. He also slew Octavia his own wife, and many other illustrious persons, under this pretense, that they plotted against him.

---

17. This duration of the reign of Claudius agrees with Dio, as Dr. Hudson here remarks; as he also remarks that Nero's name, which was at first L. Domitius Aenobarbus, after Claudius had adopted him was Nero Claudius Caesar Drusus Germanicus. This Soleus as [own Life, sect. 11, as also] by Dio Cassius andTaeims, as Dr. Hudson informs us.

3. But I omit any further discourse about these affairs; for there have been a great many who have composed the history of Nero; some of which have departed from the truth of facts out of favor, as having received benefits from him; while others, out of hatred to him, and the great ill-will which they bare him, have so impudently raved against him with their lies, that they justly deserve to be condemned. Nor do I wonder at such as have told lies of Nero, since they have not in their writings preserved the truth of history as to those facts that were earlier than his time, even when the actors could have no way incurred their hatred, since those writers lived a long time after them. But as to those that have no regard to truth, they may write as they please; for in that they take delight: but as to ourselves, who have made truth our direct aim, we shall briefly touch upon what only belongs remotely to this undertaking, but shall relate what hath happened to us Jews with great accuracy, and shall not grudge our pains in giving an account both of the calamities we have suffered, and of the crimes we have been guilty of. I will now therefore return to the relation of our own affairs.

4. For in the first year of the reign of Nero, upon the death of Azizus, king of Emesa, Soemus, his brother, succeeded in his kingdom, and Aristobulus, the son of Herod, king of Chalcis, was intrusted by Nero with the government of the Lesser Armenia. Caesar also bestowed on Agrippa a certain part of Galilee, Tiberias, and Tarichae,[18] and ordered them to submit to his jurisdiction. He gave him also Julias, a city of Perea, with fourteen villages that lay about it.

5. Now as for the affairs of the Jews, they grew worse and worse continually, for the country was again filled with robbers and impostors, who deluded the multitude. Yet did Felix catch and put to death many of those impostors every day, together with the robbers. He also caught Eleazar, the son of Dineas, who had gotten together a company of robbers; and this he did by treachery; for he gave him assurance that he should suffer no harm, and thereby persuaded him to come to him; but when he came, he bound him, and sent him to Rome. Felix also bore an ill-will to Jonathan, the high priest, because he

---

18. This agrees with Josephus's frequent accounts elsewhere in his own Life, that Tibetans, and Taricheae, and Gamala were under this Agrippa, junior, till Justus, the son of Pistus, seized for the Jews, upon the breaking out of the war.

frequently gave him admonitions about governing the Jewish affairs better than he did, lest he should himself have complaints made of him by the multitude, since he it was who had desired Caesar to send him as procurator of Judea. So Felix contrived a method whereby he might get rid of him, now he was become so continually troublesome to him; for such continual admonitions are grievous to those who are disposed to act unjustly. Wherefore Felix persuaded one of Jonathan's most faithful friends, a citizen of Jerusalem, whose name was Doras, to bring the robbers upon Jonathan, in order to kill him; and this he did by promising to give him a great deal of money for so doing. Doras complied with the proposal, and contrived matters so, that the robbers might murder him after the following manner: Certain of those robbers went up to the city, as if they were going to worship God, while they had daggers under their garments, and by thus mingling themselves among the multitude they slew Jonathan[19] and as this murder was never avenged, the robbers went up with the greatest security at the festivals after this time; and having

---

19. This treacherous and barbarous murder of the good high priest Jonathan, by the contrivance of this wicked procurator, Felix, was the immediate occasion of the ensuing murders by the Sicarii or ruffians, and one great cause of the following horrid cruelties and miseries of the Jewish nation, as Josephus here supposes; whose excellent reflection on the gross wickedness of that nation, as the direct cause of their terrible destruction, is well worthy the attention of every Jewish and of every Christian reader. And since we are soon coming to the catalogue of the Jewish high priests, it may not be amiss, with Reland, to insert this Jonathan among them, and to transcribe his particular catalogue of the last twenty-eight high priests, taken out of Josephus, and begin with Ananelus, who was made by Herod the Great. See Antiq. B. XV. ch. 2. sect. 4, and the note there.

Ananelus.
Aristobulus.
Jesus, the son of Fabus.
Simon, the son of Boethus.
Marthias, the son of Theophiltu.
Joazar, the son of Boethus.
Eleazar, the son of Boethus.
Jesus, the son of Sic.
[Annas, or] Ananus, the son of Seth.
Ismael, the son of Fabus.
Eleazar, the son of **Ananus.**
Simon, the son of Camithus.
Josephus Caiaphas, *the son-in-law to* **Ananus.**

weapons concealed in like manner as before, and mingling themselves among the multitude, they slew certain of their own enemies, and were subservient to other men for money; and slew others, not only in remote parts of the city, but in the temple itself also; for they had the boldness to murder men there, without thinking of the impiety of which they were guilty. And this seems to me to have been the reason why God, out of his hatred of these men's wickedness, rejected our city; and as for the temple, he no longer esteemed it sufficiently pure for him to inhabit therein, but brought the Romans upon us, and threw a fire upon the city to purge it; and brought upon us, our wives, and children, slavery, as desirous to make us wiser by our calamities.

6. These works, that were done by the robbers, filled the city with all sorts of impiety. And now these impostors and deceivers persuaded the multitude to follow them into the wilderness, and pretended that they would exhibit manifest wonders and signs, that should be performed by the providence of God. And many that were prevailed on by them suffered the punishments of their folly; for Felix brought them back, and then punished them. Moreover, there came out of Egypt[20] about this time to Jerusalem one that said he was a prophet,

---

Jonathan, the son of **Ananus.**
Theophilus, his brother, and son of **Ananus.**
Simon, the son of Boethus.
Matthias, the brother of Jonathan, and son of **Ananus.**
Aljoneus.
Josephus, the son of Camydus.
Ananias, the son of Nebedeus.
Jonathas.
Ismael, the son of Fabi.
Joseph Cabi, the son of Simon.
Ananus, the son of Artanus.
Jesus, the son of Damnetas.
Jesus, the son of Gamaliel.
Matthias, the son of Theophilus.
Phannias, the son of Samuel.

As for Ananus and Joseph Caiaphas, here mentioned about the middle of this catalogue, they are no other than those Annas and Caiaphas so often mentioned in the four Gospels; and that Ananias, the son of Nebedeus, was that high priest before whom St. Paul pleaded his own cause, Acts 24.

20. Of these Jewish impostors and false prophets, with many other circumstances and miseries of the Jews, till their utter destruction, foretold by our Savior, see Lit.

and advised the multitude of the common people to go along with him to the Mount of Olives, as it was called, which lay over against the city, and at the distance of five furlongs. He said further, that he would show them from hence how, at his command, the walls of Jerusalem would fall down; and he promised them that he would procure them an entrance into the city through those walls, when they were fallen down. Now when Felix was informed of these things, he ordered his soldiers to take their weapons, and came against them with a great number of horsemen and footmen from Jerusalem, and attacked the Egyptian and the people that were with him. He also slew four hundred of them, and took two hundred alive. But the Egyptian himself escaped out of the fight, but did not appear any more. And again the robbers stirred up the people to make war with the Romans, and said they ought not to obey them at all; and when any persons would not comply with them, they set fire to their villages, and plundered them.

7. And now it was that a great sedition arose between the Jews that inhabited Cesarea, and the Syrians who dwelt there also, concerning their equal right to the privileges belonging to citizens; for the Jews claimed the pre-eminence, because Herod their king was the builder of Cesarea, and because he was by birth a Jew. Now the Syrians did not deny what was alleged about Herod; but they said that Cesarea was formerly called Strato's Tower, and that then there was not one Jewish inhabitant. When the presidents of that country heard of these disorders, they caught the authors of them on both sides, and tormented them with stripes, and by that means put a stop to the disturbance for a time. But the Jewish citizens depending on their wealth, and on that account despising the Syrians, reproached them again, and hoped to provoke them by such reproaches. However, the Syrians, though they were inferior in wealth, yet valuing themselves highly on this account, that the greatest part of the Roman soldiers that were there were either of Cesarea or Sebaste, they also for some time used reproachful language to the Jews also; and thus it was, till at length they came to throwing stones at one another, and several were wounded, and fell on both sides, though still the Jews were the

---

Accompl. of Proph. p. 58–75. Of this Egyptian impostor, and the number of his followers, in Josephus, see Acts 21:38.

conquerors. But when Felix saw that this quarrel was become a kind of war, he came upon them on the sudden, and desired the Jews to desist; and when they refused so to do, he armed his soldiers, and sent them out upon them, and slew many of them, and took more of them alive, and permitted his soldiers to plunder some of the houses of the citizens, which were full of riches. Now those Jews that were more moderate, and of principal dignity among them, were afraid of themselves, and desired of Felix that he would sound a retreat to his soldiers, and spare them for the future, and afford them room for repentance for what they had done; and Felix was prevailed upon to do so.

8. About this time king Agrippa gave the high priesthood to Ismael, who was the son of Fabi. And now arose a sedition between the high priests and the principal men of the multitude of Jerusalem; each of which got them a company of the boldest sort of men, and of those that loved innovations about them, and became leaders to them; and when they struggled together, they did it by casting reproachful words against one another, and by throwing stones also. And there was nobody to reprove them; but these disorders were done after a licentious manner in the city, as if it had no government over it. And such was the impudence[21] and boldness that had seized on the high priests, that they had the hardiness to send their servants into the threshing-floors, to take away those tithes that were due to the priests, insomuch that it so fell out that the poorest sort of the priests died for want. To this degree did the violence of the seditious prevail over all right and justice.

9. Now when Porcius Festus was sent as successor to Felix by Nero, the principal of the Jewish inhabitants of Cesarea went up to Rome to accuse Felix; and he had certainly been brought to punishment, unless Nero had yielded to the importunate solicitations of his brother Pallas, who was at that time had in the greatest honor by him. Two of the principal Syrians in Cesarea persuaded Burrhus, who was Nero's tutor, and secretary for his Greek epistles, by giving him a great sum

21. The wickedness here was very peculiar and extraordinary, that the high priests should so oppress their brethren the priests, as to starve the poorest of them to death. See the like presently, ch. 9. sect. 2. Such fatal crimes are covetousness and tyranny in the clergy, as well as in the laity, in all ages.

of money, to disannul that equality of the Jewish privileges of citizens which they hitherto enjoyed. So Burrhus, by his solicitations, obtained leave of the emperor that an epistle should be written to that purpose. This epistle became the occasion of the following miseries that befell our nation; for when the Jews of Cesarea were informed of the contents of this epistle to the Syrians, they were more disorderly than before, till a war was kindled.

10. Upon Festus's coming into Judea, it happened that Judea was afflicted by the robbers, while all the villages were set on fire, and plundered by them. And then it was that the *sicarii,* as they were called, who were robbers, grew numerous. They made use of small swords, not much different in length from the Persian *acinacae,* but somewhat crooked, and like the Roman *sicae,* [or sickles,] as they were called; and from these weapons these robbers got their denomination; and with these weapons they slew a great many; for they mingled themselves among the multitude at their festivals, when they were come up in crowds from all parts to the city to worship God, as we said before, and easily slew those that they had a mind to slay. They also came frequently upon the villages belonging to their enemies, with their weapons, and plundered them, and set them on fire. So Festus sent forces, both horsemen and footmen, to fall upon those that had been seduced by a certain impostor, who promised them deliverance and freedom from the miseries they were under, if they would but follow him as far as the wilderness. Accordingly, those forces that were sent destroyed both him that had deluded them, and those that were his followers also.

11. About the same time king Agrippa built himself a very large dining-room in the royal palace at Jerusalem, near to the portico. Now this palace had been erected of old by the children of Asamoneus. and was situate upon an elevation, and afforded a most delightful prospect to those that had a mind to take a view of the city, which prospect was desired by the king; and there he could lie down, and eat, and thence observe what was done in the temple; which thing, when the chief men of Jerusalem saw they were very much displeased at it; for it was not agreeable to the institutions of our country or law that what was done in the temple should be viewed by others, especially what belonged to the sacrifices. They therefore erected a wall upon the uppermost building which belonged to the inner court of the temple towards the

west, which wall when it was built, did not only intercept the prospect of the dining-room in the palace, but also of the western cloisters that belonged to the outer court of the temple also, where it was that the Romans kept guards for the temple at the festivals. At these doings both king Agrippa, and principally Festus the procurator, were much displeased; and Festus ordered them to pull the wall down again: but the Jews petitioned him to give them leave to send an embassage about this matter to Nero; for they said they could not endure to live if any part of the temple should be demolished; and when Festus had given them leave so to do, they sent ten of their principal men to Nero, as also Ismael the high priest, and Helcias, the keeper of the sacred treasure. And when Nero had heard what they had to say, he not only forgave[22] them what they had already done, but also gave them leave to let the wall they had built stand. This was granted them in order to gratify Poppea, Nero's wife, who was a religious woman, and had requested these favors of Nero, and who gave order to the ten ambassadors to go their way home; but retained Helcias and Ismael as hostages with herself. As soon as the king heard this news, he gave the high priesthood to Joseph, who was called Cabi, the son of Simon, formerly high priest.

9 Concerning Albinus under Whose Procuratorship James Was Slain; as Also What Edifices Were Built by Agrippa

1. AND now Caesar, upon hearing the death of Festus, sent Albinus into Judea, as procurator. But the king deprived Joseph of the high priesthood, and bestowed the succession to that dignity on the son of Ananus, who was also himself called Ananus. Now the report goes that this eldest Ananus proved a most fortunate man; for he had five sons who had all performed the office of a high priest to God, and

---

22. We have here one eminent example of Nero's mildness and goodness in his government towards the Jews, during the first five years of his reign, so famous in antiquity; we have perhaps another in Josephus's own Life, sect. 3; and a third, though of a very different nature here, in sect. 9, just before. However, both the generous acts of kindness were obtained of Nero by his queen Poppea, who was a religious lady, and perhaps privately a Jewish proselyte, and so were not owing entirely to Nero's own goodness.

who had himself enjoyed that dignity a long time formerly, which had never happened to any other of our high priests. But this younger Ananus, who, as we have told you already, took the high priesthood, was a bold man in his temper, and very insolent; he was also of the sect of the Sadducees,[23] who are very rigid in judging offenders, above all the rest of the Jews, as we have already observed; when, therefore, Ananus was of this disposition, he thought he had now a proper opportunity [to exercise his authority]. Festus was now dead, and Albinus was but upon the road; so he assembled the sanhedrim of judges, and brought before them the brother of Jesus, who was called Christ, whose name was James, and some others, [or, some of his companions]; and when he had formed an accusation against them as breakers of the law, he delivered them to be stoned: but as for those who seemed the most equitable of the citizens, and such as were the most uneasy at the breach of the laws, they disliked what was done; they also sent to the king [Agrippa], desiring him to send to Ananus that he should act so no more, for that what he had already done was not to be justified; nay, some of them went also to meet Albinus, as he was upon his journey from Alexandria, and informed him that it was not lawful for Ananus to assemble a sanhedrim without his consent.[24] Whereupon Albinus complied with what they said, and wrote in anger to Ananus, and threatened that he would bring him to punishment for what he had done; on which king Agrippa took the high priesthood from him, when he had ruled but three months, and made Jesus, the son of Damneus, high priest.

2. Now as soon as Albinus was come to the city of Jerusalem, he used all his endeavors and care that the country might be kept in

---

23. It hence evidently appears that Sadducees might be high priests in the days of Josephus, and that these Sadducees were usually very severe and inexorable judges, while the Pharisees were much milder, and more merciful, as appears by Reland's instances in his note on this place, and on Josephus's Life, sect. 31, and those taken from the New Testament, from Josephus himself, and from the Rabbins; nor do we meet with any Sadducees later than this high priest in all Josephus.

24. Of this condemnation of James the Just, and its causes, as also that he did not die till long afterwards, see Prim. Christ. Revived, vol. III. ch. 43–46. The sanhedrim condemned our Savior, but could not put him to death without the approbation of the Roman procurator; nor could therefore Ananias and his sanhedrim do more here, since they never had Albinus's approbation for the putting this James to death.

peace, and this by destroying many of the *Sicarii.* But as for the high priest, Ananias[25] he increased in glory every day, and this to a great degree, and had obtained the favor and esteem of the citizens in a signal manner; for he was a great hoarder up of money: he therefore cultivated the friendship of Albinus, and of the high priest [Jesus], by making them presents; he also had servants who were very wicked, who joined themselves to the boldest sort of the people, and went to the thrashing-floors, and took away the tithes that belonged to the priests by violence, and did not refrain from beating such as would not give these tithes to them. So the other high priests acted in the like manner, as did those his servants, without any one being able to prohibit them; so that [some of the] priests, that of old were wont to be supported with those tithes, died for want of food.

3. But now the *Sicarii* went into the city by night, just before the festival, which was now at hand, and took the scribe belonging to the governor of the temple, whose name was Eleazar, who was the son of Ananus [Ananias] the high priest, and bound him, and carried him away with them; after which they sent to Ananias, and said that they would send the scribe to him, if he would persuade Albinus to release ten of those prisoners which he had caught of their party; so Ananias was plainly forced to persuade Albinus, and gained his request of him. This was the beginning of greater calamities; for the robbers perpetually contrived to catch some of Ananias's servants; and when they had taken them alive, they would not let them go, till they thereby recovered some of their own *Sicarii.* And as they were again become no small number, they grew bold, and were a great affliction to the whole country.

---

25. This Ananias was not the son of Nebedeus, as I take it, but he who was called Annas or Ananus the elder, the ninth in the catalogue, and who had been esteemed high priest for a long time; and, besides Caiaphas, his son-in-law, had five of his own sons high priests after him, which were those of numbers 11, 14, 15, 17, 24, in the foregoing catalogue. Nor ought we to pass slightly over what Josephus here says of Annas, or Ananias, that he was high priest a long time before his children were so; he was the son of Seth, and is set down first for high priest in the foregoing catalogue, under number 9. He was made by Quirinus, and continued till Ismael, the 10th in number, for about twenty-three years, which long duration of his high priesthood, joined to the successions of his son-in-law, and five children of his own, made him a sort of perpetual high priest, and was perhaps the occasion that former high priests kept their titles ever afterwards; for I believe it is hardly met with be fore him.

4. About this time it was that king Agrippa built Cesarea Philippi larger than it was before, and, in honor of Nero, named it Neronlas. And when he had built a theater at Berytus, with vast expenses, he bestowed on them shows, to be exhibited every year, and spent therein many ten thousand [drachmae]; he also gave the people a largess of corn, and distributed oil among them, and adorned the entire city with statues of his own donation, and with original images made by ancient hands; nay, he almost transferred all that was most ornamental in his own kingdom thither. This made him more than ordinarily hated by his subjects, because he took those things away that belonged to them to adorn a foreign city. And now Jesus, the son of Gamaliel, became the successor of Jesus, the son of Damneus, in the high priesthood, which the king had taken from the other; on which account a sedition arose between the high priests, with regard to one another; for they got together bodies of the boldest sort of the people, and frequently came, from reproaches, to throwing of stones at each other. But Ananias was too hard for the rest, by his riches, which enabled him to gain those that were most ready to receive. Costobarus also, and Saulus, did themselves get together a multitude of wicked wretches, and this because they were of the royal family; and so they obtained favor among them, because of their kindred to Agrippa; but still they used violence with the people, and were very ready to plunder those that were weaker than themselves. And from that time it principally came to pass that our city was greatly disordered, and that all things grew worse and worse among us.

5. But when Albinus heard that Gessius Florus was coming to succeed him, he was desirous to appear to do somewhat that might be grateful to the people of Jerusalem; so he brought out all those prisoners who seemed to him to be most plainly worthy of death, and ordered them to be put to death accordingly. But as to those who had been put into prison on some trifling occasions, he took money of them, and dismissed them; by which means the prisons were indeed emptied, but the country was filled with robbers.

6. Now as many of the Levites,[26] which is a tribe of ours, as were

---

26. This insolent petition of some of the Levites, to wear the sacerdotal garments when they sung hymns to God in the temple, was very probably owing to the great depression and contempt the haughty high priests had now brought their brethren the priests into; of which see ch. 8. sect. 8, and ch. 9, sect. 2.

singers of hymns, persuaded the king to assemble a sanhedrim, and to give them leave to wear linen garments, as well as the priests for they said that this would be a work worthy the times of his government, that he might have a memorial of such a novelty, as being his doing. Nor did they fail of obtaining their desire; for the king, with the suffrages of those that came into the sanhedrim, granted the singers of hymns this privilege, that they might lay aside their former garments, and wear such a linen one as they desired; and as a part of this tribe ministered in the temple, he also permitted them to learn those hymns as they had besought him for. Now all this was contrary to the laws of our country, which, whenever they have been transgressed, we have never been able to avoid the punishment of such transgressions.

7. And now it was that the temple was finished. So when the people saw that the workmen were unemployed, who were above eighteen thousand and that they, receiving no wages, were in want because they had earned their bread by their labors about the temple; and while they were unwilling to keep by them the treasures that were there deposited, out of fear of [their being carried away by] the Romans; and while they had a regard to the making provision for the workmen; they had a mind to expend these treasures upon them; for if any one of them did but labor for a single hour, he received his pay immediately; so they persuaded him to rebuild the eastern cloisters. These cloisters belonged to the outer court, and were situated in a deep valley, and had walls that reached four hundred cubits [in length], and were built of square and very white stones, the length of each of which stones was twenty cubits, and their height six cubits. This was the work of king Solomon,[27] who first of all built the entire temple. But king Agrippa, who had the care of the temple committed to him by Claudius Caesar, considering that it is easy to demolish any building, but hard to build it up again, and that it was particularly hard to do it to these cloisters, which would require a considerable time, and great sums of money, he denied the petitioners their request about that matter; but he did not obstruct them when they desired the city might be paved with white stone. He also deprived Jesus, the son of Gamaliel, of the high priesthood, and gave it to Matthias, the son of Theophilus, under whom the Jews' war with the Romans took its beginning.

---

27. Of these cloisters of Solomon, see the description of the temple, ch. 13. They seem, by Josephus's words, to have been built from the bottom of the valley.

10 An Enumeration of the High Priests

1. AND now I think it proper and agreeable to this history to give an account of our high priests; how they began, who those are which are capable of that dignity, and how many of them there had been at the end of the war. In the first place, therefore, history informs us that Aaron, the brother of Moses, officiated to God as a high priest, and that, after his death, his sons succeeded him immediately; and that this dignity hath been continued down from them all to their posterity. Whence it is a custom of our country, that no one should take the high priesthood of God but he who is of the blood of Aaron, while every one that is of another stock, though he were a king, can never obtain that high priesthood. Accordingly, the number of all the high priests from Aaron, of whom we have spoken already, as of the first of them, until Phanas, who was made high priest during the war by the seditious, was eighty-three; of whom thirteen officiated as high priests in the wilderness, from the days of Moses, while the tabernacle was standing, until the people came into Judea, when king Solomon erected the temple to God; for at the first they held the high priesthood till the end of their life, although afterward they had successors while they were alive. Now these thirteen, who were the descendants of two of the sons of Aaron, received this dignity by succession, one after another; for their form of government was an aristocracy, and after that a monarchy, and in the third place the government was regal Now the number of years during the rule of these thirteen, from the day when our fathers departed out of Egypt, under Moses their leader, until the building of that temple which king Solomon erected at Jerusalem, were six hundred and twelve. After those thirteen high priests, eighteen took the high priesthood at Jerusalem, one m succession to another, from the days of king Solomon, until Nebuchadnezzar, king of Babylon, made an expedition against that city, and burnt the temple, and removed our nation into Babylon, and then took Josadek, the high priest, captive; the times of these high priests were four hundred and sixty-six years, six months, and ten days, while the Jews were still under the regal government. But after the term of seventy years' captivity under the Babylonians, Cyrus, king of Persia, sent the Jews from Babylon to their own land again, and gave them leave to rebuild their temple; at which time Jesus, the son of Josadek, took the high

priesthood over the captives when they were returned home. Now he and his posterity, who were in all fifteen, until king Antiochus Eupator, were under a democratical government for four hundred and fourteen years; and then the forementioned Antiochus, and Lysias the general of his army, deprived Onias, who was also called Menelaus, of the high priesthood, and slew him at Berea; and driving away the son [of Onias the third], put Jaeimus into the place of the high priest, one that was indeed of the stock of Aaron, but not of that family of Onias. On which account Onias, who was the nephew of Onias that was dead, and bore the same name with his father, came into Egypt, and got into the friendship of Ptolemy Philometor, and Cleopatra his wife, and persuaded them to make him the high priest of that temple which he built to God in the prefecture of Heliopolis, and this in imitation of that at Jerusalem; but as for that temple which was built in Egypt, we have spoken of it frequently already. Now when Jacimus had retained the priesthood three years, he died, and there was no one that succeeded him, but the city continued seven years without a high priest. But then the posterity of the sons of Asamoneus, who had the government of the nation conferred upon them, when they had beaten the Macedonians in war, appointed Jonathan to be their high priest, who ruled over them seven years. And when he had been slain by the treacherous contrivance of Trypho, as we have related some where, Simon his brother took the high priesthood; and when he was destroyed at a feast by the treachery of his son-in-law, his own son, whose name was Hyrcanus, succeeded him, after he had held the high priesthood one year longer than his brother. This Hyrcanus enjoyed that dignity thirty years, and died an old man, leaving the succession to Judas, who was also called Aristobulus, whose brother Alexander was his heir; which Judas died of a sore distemper, after he had kept the priesthood, together with the royal authority; for this Judas was the first that put on his head a diadem for one year. And when Alexander had been both king and high priest twenty-seven years, he departed this life, and permitted his wife Alexandra to appoint him that should he high priest; so she gave the high priesthood to Hyrcanus, but retained the kingdom herself nine years, and then departed this life. The like duration [and no longer] did her son Hyrcanus enjoy the high priesthood; for after her death his brother Aristobulus fought against him, and beat him, and deprived him of his principality; and he did himself both reign, and perform the office of high priest to God. But when he had reigned three years, and as many months, Pompey came upon him, and not only took the city of Jerusalem by force, but put him and his children in bonds, and sent them to Rome. He also restored the high priesthood to Hyrcanus, and made him governor of the nation, but forbade him to wear a diadem. This Hyrcanus ruled, besides his first nine years, twenty-four years more, when Barzapharnes and Pacorus, the generals of the Parthians, passed over Euphrates, and fought with Hyrcanus, and took him alive, and made Antigonus, the son of Aristobulus, king; and when he had reigned three years and three months, Sosius and Herod besieged him, and took him, when Antony had him brought to Antioch, and slain there. Herod was then made king by the Romans, but did no longer appoint high priests out of the family of Asamoneus; but made certain men to be so that were of no eminent families, but barely of those that were priests, excepting that he gave that dignity to Aristobulus; for when he had made this Aristobulus, the grandson of that Hyrcanus who was then taken by the Parthians, and had taken his sister Mariarmne to wife, he thereby aimed to win the good-will of the people, who had a kind remembrance of Hyrcanus [his grandfather]. Yet did he afterward, out of his fear lest they should all bend their inclinations to Aristobulus, put him to death, and that by contriving how to have him suffocated as he was swimming at Jericho, as we have already related that matter; but after this man he never intrusted the priesthood to the posterity of the sons of Asamoneus. Archelaus also, Herod's son, did like his father in the appointment of the high priests, as did the Romans also, who took the government over the Jews into their hands afterward. Accordingly, the number of the high priests, from the days of Herod until the day when Titus took the temple and the City, and burnt them, were in all twenty-eight; the time also that belonged to them was a hundred and seven years. Some of these were the political governors of the people under the reign of Herod, and under the reign of Archelaus his son, although, after their death, the government became an aristocracy, and the high priests were intrusted with a dominion over the nation. And thus much may suffice to be said concerning our high priests.

Chapter 11

11 Concerning Florus the Procurator, Who Necessitated the Jews to Take Up Arms Against the Romans. the Conclusion

1. NOW Gessius Florus, who was sent as successor to Albinus by Nero, filled Judea with abundance of miseries. He was by birth of the city of Clazomene, and brought along with him his wife Cleopatra, (by whose friendship with Poppea, Nero's wife, he obtained this government,) who was no way different from him in wickedness. This Florus was so wicked, and so violent in the use of his authority, that the Jews took Albinus to have been [comparatively] their benefactor; so excessive were the mischiefs that he brought upon them. For Albinus concealed his wickedness, and was careful that it might not be discovered to all men; but Gessius Florus, as though he bad been sent on purpose to show his crimes to every body, made a pompous ostentation of them to our nation, as never omitting any sort of violence, nor any unjust sort of punishment; for he was not to be moved by pity, and never was satisfied with any degree of gain that came in his way; nor had he any more regard to great than to small acquisitions, but became a partner with the robbers themselves. For a great many fell then into that practice without fear, as having him for their security, and depending on him, that he would save them harmless in their particular robberies; so that there were no bounds set to the nation's miseries; but the unhappy Jews, when they were not able to bear the devastations which the robbers made among them, were all under a necessity of leaving their own habitations, and of flying away, as hoping to dwell more easily any where else in the world among foreigners [than in their own country]. And what need I say any more upon this head? since it was this Florus who necessitated us to take up arms against the Romans, while we thought it better to be destroyed at once, than by little and little. Now this war began in the second year of the government of Florus, and the twelfth year of the reign of Nero. But then what actions we were forced to do, or what miseries we were enabled to suffer, may be accurately known by such as will peruse those books which I have written about the Jewish war.

2. I shall now, therefore, make an end here of my Antiquities; after the conclusion of which events, I began to write that account of the war; and these Antiquities contain what hath been delivered down to us from the original creation of man, until the twelfth year of the reign

of Nero, as to what hath befallen the Jews, as well in Egypt as in Syria and in Palestine, and what we have suffered from the Assyrians and Babylonians, and what afflictions the Persians and Macedonians, and after them the Romans, have brought upon us; for I think I may say that I have composed this history with sufficient accuracy in all things. I have attempted to enumerate those high priests that we have had during the interval of two thousand years; I have also carried down the succession of our kings, and related their actions, and political administration, without [considerable] errors, as also the power of our monarchs; and all according to what is written in our sacred books; for this it was that I promised to do in the beginning of this history. And I am so bold as to say, now I have so completely perfected the work I proposed to myself to do, that no other person, whether he were a Jew or foreigner, had he ever so great an inclination to it, could so accurately deliver these accounts to the Greeks as is done in these books. For those of my own nation freely acknowledge that I far exceed them in the learning belonging to Jews; I have also taken a great deal of pains to obtain the learning of the Greeks, and understand the elements of the Greek language, although I have so long accustomed myself to speak our own tongue, that I cannot pronounce Greek with sufficient exactness; for our nation does not encourage those that learn the languages of many nations, and so adorn their discourses with the smoothness of their periods; because they look upon this sort of accomplishment as common, not only to all sorts of free-men, but to as many of the servants as please to learn them. But they give him the testimony of being a wise man who is fully acquainted with our laws, and is able to interpret their meaning; on which account, as there have been many who have done their endeavors with great patience to obtain this learning, there have yet hardly been so many as two or three that have succeeded therein, who were immediately well rewarded for their pains.

3. And now it will not be perhaps an invidious thing, if I treat briefly of my own family, and of the actions of my own life[28] while there are still living such as can either prove what I say to be false, or can attest that it is true; with which accounts I shall put an end to these Antiquities, which are contained in twenty books, and sixty thousand

28. See the Life of Josephus.

verses. And if God permit me, I will briefly run over this war[29], and to add what befell them further to that very day, the 13th of Domitian, or A.D. 03, is not, that I have observed, taken distinct notice of by any one; nor do we ever again, with what befell us therein to this very day, which is the thirteenth year of the reign of Caesar Domitian, and the fifty-sixth year of my own life. I have also an intention to write three books concerning our Jewish opinions about God and his essence, and about our laws; why, according to them, some things are permitted us to do, and others are prohibited.

---

29. What Josephus here declares his intention to do, if God permitted, to give the public again an abridgement of the Jewish War hear of it elsewhere, whether he performed what he now intended or not. Some of the reasons of this design of his might possibly be, his observation of the many errors he had been guilty of in the two first of those seven books of the War, which were written when he was comparatively young, and less acquainted with the Jewish antiquities than he now was, and in which abridgement we might have hoped to find those many passages which himself, as well as those several passages which others refer to, as written by him, but which are not extant in his present works. However, since many of his own references to what he had written elsewhere, as well as most of his own errors, belong to such early times as could not well come into this abridgement of the Jewish War; and since none of those that quote things not now extant in his works, including himself as well as others, ever cite any such abridgement; I am forced rather to suppose that he never did publish any such work at all; I mean, as distinct from his own Life, written by himself, for an appendix to these Antiquities, and this at least seven years after these Antiquities were finished. Nor indeed does it appear to me that Josephus ever published that other work here mentioned, as intended by him for the public also: I mean the three or four books concerning God and his essence, and concerning the Jewish laws; why, according to them, some things were permitted the Jews, and others prohibited; which last seems to be the same work which Josephus had also promised, if God permitted, at the conclusion of his preface to these Antiquities; nor do I suppose that he ever published any of them. The death of all his friends at court, Vespasian, Titus, and Domitian, and the coming of those he had no acquaintance with to the crown, I mean Nerva and Trajan, together with his removal from Rome to Judea, with what followed it, might easily interrupt such his intentions, and prevent his publication of those works.

www.ingramcontent.com/pod-product-compliance
Lightning Source LLC
Chambersburg PA
CBHW030533100426
42813CB00001B/235
9781434115072